'Sets a new standard for accessibility and engagement in introductory comparative texts. As a lecturer in Comparative Politics, I think John McCormick's book should be the go-to guide for every student hoping to gain a better understanding of the political world in which we live.'

— **Zachary Taylor**, *University of Wyoming, USA*

'This text offers an excellent introduction to the diversity and breadth of today's comparative politics. Up to date, clearly written and engagingly presented, the country case studies all closely follow the same clear structure, helping students to think comparatively.'

— **Nicolas van de Walle**, *Cornell University, USA*

'*Cases in Comparative Government and Politics* provides a great balance between highlighting important conceptual themes central to comparative study, and introducing students to the wide empirical variety of political systems around the world. The accessible, systematic case studies provide a great basis for an introductory comparative politics course.'

— **Lucy Barnes**, *University College London (UCL), UK*

'One of the most effective and brilliant case-based texts, it explores the political landscape behind twelve diverse countries, shining a light upon the political dynamics that are so crucial to understanding comparative politics.'

— **Daniel Zirker**, *University of Waikato, New Zealand*

'This textbook emphasizes the parts of the course that students always find the most exciting: the cases! Conceptual elements are introduced in the opening chapters and then illustrated by reality, demonstrating that comparative politics is best understood through the actual art of comparison.'

— **Tracy Slagter**, *University of Wisconsin Oshkosh, USA*

'The author brings the discipline to life, writing with clarity, precision and authority.'

— **Elizabeth Monaghan**, *University of Hull, UK*

D0998905

COMPARATIVE GOVERNMENT AND POLITICS SERIES

Published

CASES IN COMPARATIVE GOVERNMENT AND POLITICS

JOHN McCORMICK

 macmillan international HIGHER EDUCATION

 RED GLOBE PRESS

First published 2020 by
RED GLOBE PRESS

Red Globe Press in the UK is an imprint of Springer Nature Limited, registered in England, company number 785998, of 4 Crinan Street, London, N1 9XW.

Red Globe Press® is a registered trademark in the United States, the United Kingdom, Europe and other countries.

ISBN 978–1–352–00741–1 hardback
ISBN 978–1–352–00735–0 paperback

This book is printed on paper suitable for recycling and made from fully managed and sustained forest sources. Logging, pulping and manufacturing processes are expected to conform to the environmental regulations of the country of origin.

A catalogue record for this book is available from the British Library.

A catalog record for this book is available from the Library of Congress.

BRIEF CONTENTS

DETAILED CONTENTS

ILLUSTRATIONS AND FEATURES

COUNTRY PROFILES

COMPARING POLITICAL CULTURE

COMPARING GOVERNMENT

COMPARING POLITICS

FIGURES

TABLES

MAPS

PREFACE

Without comparisons to make, the mind does not know how to proceed.

Alexis de Tocqueville, French author, 1830s

In late 2018, Brazil held presidential elections. More than a dozen candidates competed, all hoping to win the more than 50 per cent of the vote needed to avoid a runoff. One of the leading contenders should have been Luiz Inácio Lula da Silva of the left-wing Worker's Party, who had served two earlier terms as Brazil's leader. But Lula, as he is popularly known, was in jail on charges of corruption, so his place was taken by Fernando Haddad, representing a three-party alliance optimistically known as 'The People Happy Again'. The bulk of international headlines, though, were drawn by the major candidate of the political right, a one-time Army general named Jair Bolsonaro. Heading an alliance known as 'Brazil Above Everything, God Above Everyone', he was routinely described as the Brazilian Donald Trump, and was infamous for defending military rule in Brazil, and for his inflammatory comments about women, gays, foreigners, and indigenous communities.

Bolsonaro won the first round, but not by enough to win outright, so a second round was held three weeks later in which he and Haddad ran off against each other. Bolsonaro prevailed by more than ten percentage points, an outcome that was interpreted by many as a comment by voters on Brazil's problems with corruption and crime, and as a reflection of their low levels of trust in government. Clearly, the result had to be understood in terms of the circumstances in Brazil, but it could also be compared with events in several other countries:

◆ The ongoing popularity of Vladimir Putin in Russia.
◆ The election victory of Rodrigo Duterte in the Philippines.
◆ The British decision to leave the European Union.
◆ The election victory of Donald Trump in the United States.
◆ The resurgence or successes of right-wing anti-establishment parties and leaders in several other parts of the world.

What they all had in common was a surge of populism and nationalism in the wake of declining trust in government and political elites, and a widening sense among many voters of being marginalized and of feeling threatened by the forces of globalization. Each event or trend could be analysed on its own terms, but it was only through comparison that their wider significance could be understood.

These examples illustrate the value and importance of comparative politics. To be sure, we can study individual countries in isolation and learn a great deal about their government and politics, but we can never fully understand them without the context that comparison provides. We can never really know if a country's politics is typical or unusual, we can never fully understand its place in the global system, we cannot draw up universal rules about government and politics, and we would find it harder to make political predictions.

In a neat and tidy world, every country would govern itself in approximately the same way: each would have a set of rules about how government works, there would be leaders in place to provide direction, each would have similar sets of governing institutions with approximately similar powers and functions, and there would be similar systems of law and of courts to support the law. There would be elections and other channels through which citizens could express themselves and be politically active, and there would be rules by which citizens were protected from government and from each other. The world, though, is not a neat and tidy place, and while government everywhere has the same basic role of governing, it comes in many different shades and varieties. Superficially, many of the institutions and processes might look the same, but closer study soon reveals that power and authority are defined, established, distributed, and limited in different ways.

Consider these examples:

◆ Presidents are far from equal: they might be political leaders with substantial powers, they might have a wide range of constitutional or political limits on their powers, or they might be little more than figureheads. They might be elected for one term, two terms, or for as many terms as they can earn for themselves by manipulating elections.

◆ Many countries do not have presidents, but instead have prime ministers, whose routes to power and job descriptions are quite different from those of presidents.

◆ Political parties come in a variety of forms: some countries have none, others have a single legal party, others have a single dominant party, and yet others may have as many as a dozen or more parties with seats in national and local legislatures.

◆ Elections come in many different structural forms: some are run on the basis of winner take all, others are based on dividing seats among parties on the basis of their share of the vote, some require that voters choose only one candidate from their district, others require voters to rank multiple candidates, and yet others are so blatantly manipulated as to make them largely meaningless.

◆ While some countries have political systems that are both transparent and responsive, and have leaders who try to consider the desires and hopes of a wide range of their citizens, others are closed and authoritarian, ruled by an elite that cares little about the wider public interest.

Most of the explanations for these differences lie in history: political systems have evolved differently according to different local circumstances and the influence of key leaders, revolutions, or unique needs. There has been much cross-fertilization along the way as countries have learned from one another, or exported political ideals, or have adopted political ideas from others. Even so, the result has been enormous variety, and we would be mistaken to think that all political systems are approximately the same, even if some are more or less democratic than others. Not only are the rules of government often quite different, but the way ordinary people see government is different, the degree to which they can influence government and political decisions varies from one case to another, and the problems they face are often different.

By comparing political systems, we give ourselves the frame of reference that can help us better understand each other. Once we compare presidents and prime ministers, for example, and how authority is divided in presidential and parliamentary systems, we can better understand the roles of executives and legislatures in different countries. Once we compare the structure of elections, we can better understand how political leaders come to power in the first place, and the limitations placed (or not) on those powers. And once we compare political events around the world, such as the election victories of leaders such as Rodrigo Duterte, Donald Trump, and Jair Bolsonaro, we can better understand whether or not those victories are part of wider trends, and what those trends might mean.

In the chapters that follow, we will be looking comparatively at government and politics by taking twelve cases of political systems chosen to provide a taste of the variety in which government can be found around the world. We will be focusing on history, institutions, and processes, asking several core questions along the way:

◆ Who governs?
◆ How do they govern?
◆ How do political systems evolve?
◆ What are the prevailing norms and values of those systems?
◆ How is power and authority defined, distributed, and limited?
◆ How do people participate in government, and with what results?
◆ What effect do the differences have on the way different countries are governed?

The twelve cases are carefully chosen to illustrate a variety of political types, to illustrate different levels of political development, and to ensure geographical and cultural diversity. The choice of the cases is based on a combination of two well-known political ranking systems: the Democracy Index maintained by the Economist Intelligence Unit in Britain (related to the news weekly *The Economist*), and the Freedom in the World index maintained by the New York-based think tank Freedom House. Both use a variety of political criteria to rank the countries of the world, and our twelve cases are chosen from a range of positions within those rankings – see Table 0.1. The order of the chapters is based on the order of the ranking, so we will begin with three of the most democratic cases (Britain, Germany, and the United States) and end with three of the most authoritarian (Russia, China, and Iran).

We will not be stopping with government and politics, but will also be looking at the economic and social differences among countries – see Table 0.2. These can tell us much about the efficiency (or inefficiency) of governments, and also about the successes or failures of political systems in responding to the economic needs of citizens, and of responding to (and being shaped by) social pressures, values, and divisions. As a rule, democracy and free markets go hand in hand, as do democracy and high levels of social development. But we will also find that

Table 0.1 The cases – Political rankings

	Democracy Index		Freedom in the World		System type
	Score	**Category**	**Score**	**Freedom rating**	
Norway	9.87	Full democracy	100	Free	Parliamentary
Germany	8.68	Full democracy	94	Free	Parliamentary
UK	8.53	Full democracy	94	Free	Parliamentary
Japan	7.99	Flawed democracy	96	Free	Parliamentary
USA	7.96	Flawed democracy	86	Free	Limited presidential
France	7.80	Flawed democracy	90	Free	Semi-presidential
India	7.23	Flawed democracy	77	Free	Parliamentary
Mexico	6.19	Flawed democracy	62	Partly Free	Limited presidential
Nigeria	4.44	Hybrid regime	50	Partly Free	Limited presidential
Turkey	4.37	Hybrid regime	32	Not Free	Limited presidential
Russia	2.94	Authoritarian	20	Not Free	Semi-presidential
Iran	2.45	Authoritarian	18	Not Free	Unlimited presidential
China	3.32	Authoritarian	14	Not Free	Unlimited presidential
North Korea	1.08	Authoritarian	3	Not Free	Unlimited presidential

Sources: Economist Intelligence Unit (2019) and Freedom House (2018b).
Note: Norway and North Korea do not appear as cases in this book, but are included in this table for context, as the highest and lowest ranking countries in the world.

Table 0.2 The cases – Economic and social rankings

	Population (millions)	Gross domestic product ($ billion)	Per capita GDP ($)	Human Development Index	
				Score	**Ranking**
UK	66	2,622	39,720	0.909	Very High
Germany	83	3,677	44,469	0.926	Very High
USA	326	19,391	59,531	0.920	Very High
Japan	127	4,872	38,428	0.903	Very High
France	67	2,582	38,476	0.897	Very High
India	1,339	2,597	1,939	0.624	Medium
Mexico	129	1,150	8,902	0.762	High
Nigeria	191	376	1,968	0.527	Low
Turkey	81	851	10,540	0.767	High
Russia	144	1,577	10,743	0.804	Very High
China	1,386	12,238	8,827	0.738	High
Iran	81	440	5,415	0.774	High

Sources: World Bank (2019) and United Nations Development Programme (2018).

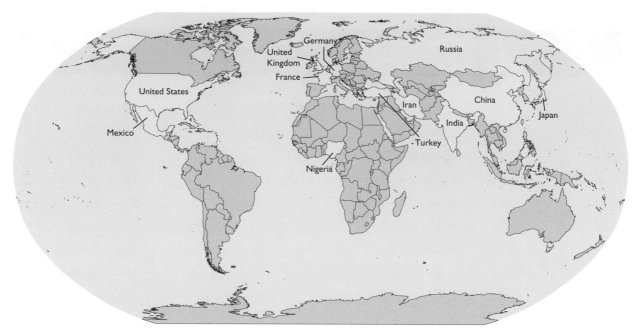

Map 0.1 The cases used in this book

countries with poor records on democracy (Russia being a notable example) occasionally perform well on human development, while several democracies (Britain and the United States being notable examples) continue to struggle with deep economic, social, and cultural divisions.

The book opens with two survey chapters designed to set the scene for the cases:

◆ Chapter 1 offers a review of the field of comparative politics, outlining its purposes, goals, and methods, and explaining the typology used in this book.
◆ Chapter 2 focuses on the structure of political systems, providing a survey of the different aspects of government and politics discussed in the cases, including political development, political culture, key institutions, and political processes.

The remainder of the book is taken up with the case studies, each of them structured around four central topics:

◆ **Political development**. We cannot fully understand a political system without understanding where it came from and how it evolved. Much of what we find in the structure of governments, the traditions of politics, the sources and distribution of wealth, and the divisions within societies is based on historical circumstances, such that the present would be hard to understand without at least a brief review of the past. (And as we will see in Chapter 1, the historical method is one of the approaches we can use in making political comparisons.)
◆ **Political culture**. The personality of political systems is a key part of comparison, as captured in the values and norms that define different systems, and in patterns of political behaviour that are considered either normal or abnormal. Hence it is important that we look at the political personality and expectations of each of our cases.
◆ **Political system**. Understanding how political institutions work is essential to comparison. We need to know how they function, how they relate to each other, from where they derive their authority, the limits that are placed on their powers, and the impact that citizens have on their work. To these ends, this section in each case will describe the institutional 'rules' of the political system, and assess the relationships among its elements.
◆ **Political processes**. Government consists of a network of systems and processes, with leaders and citizens relating to each other in a large and complex series of games. This section focuses on the inputs into those systems, or the ways in which people take part (or are prevented from taking part) in politics. They may do this through voting, lobbying, demonstrating, or supporting political parties and interest groups, but they may also do it through bribery, intimidation, violence, and murder.

Clearly there is a limit to how much we can address in short chapters, but each will provide a taste of the character of government and politics in contrasting situations, and comparisons are made throughout the cases, tying them to one another and to the two opening chapters. You might think of this book as akin to the experience of visiting a restaurant that serves a cuisine with which you are not familiar, so instead of opting for a single dish, you try a sampler dish that gives you a taste of the different options available further down the menu. The sampler provides context, and on later visits you can try the different main dishes and compare among them.

ACKNOWLEDGEMENTS

This has been an unusual project for me in the sense that this book is based on an earlier book for a different publisher: *Comparative Politics in Transition*, published by Cengage in the United States. The first edition of the earlier book came out in 1995, with new editions following until the seventh in 2013. It underwent the normal process of evolution experienced by all textbooks in the constantly changing field of political science, and underwent yet more change with the move to Red Globe Press: the system of classification changed, two new survey chapters were written, three new cases were added (Germany, France, and Turkey), and all other cases were thoroughly revised and updated.

In making the transition to this new book, I want to thank the team at Red Globe Press for their usual professionalism, efficiency, and good humour: Steven Kennedy (before his retirement) and Lloyd Langman oversaw the early development of the project, Lauren Zimmerman was in charge during the review process and completion of the manuscript, Georgia Park managed production of the book, and Ann Edmondson did her usual excellent job with copy-editing. I thank them all for continuing to uphold the best of what I have come to expect from Red Globe Press.

I would also like to thank the nearly two dozen anonymous reviewers who read through different parts of the book, either sharing specialist knowledge on particular countries or taking the broad view of the whole manuscript. They came from Australia, China, France, the Netherlands, New Zealand, South Africa, the UK, and the United States, providing a diverse and helpful set of perspectives on the book as it developed. I also thank my colleague Tijen Demirel-Pegg for her helpful comments on the Turkey chapter. Finally, and most importantly, my love to Leanne, Ian, and Stuart for everything they bring to my life.

ABOUT THE AUTHOR

John McCormick is Professor of Political Science at the Indianapolis campus of Indiana University in the United States. His academic interests focus on comparative politics, environmental policy, global studies, and the politics of the European Union. He is the author of more than a dozen books, including *Comparative Government and Politics, Environmental Politics and Policy*, and *Understanding the European Union* (all from Red Globe Press). He has taught courses at multiple universities in North America and Europe, has visited nine of the twelve countries used as cases in this book, and has lived for extended periods in the United States, Britain, Kenya, South Africa, and Zimbabwe.

GUIDE TO LEARNING FEATURES

Previews, Key Arguments, Overviews
Each chapter begins with a brief preview of what the chapter is about and how it is structured, a set of six key arguments made in that chapter, and a general overview, including – in the twelve case chapters – a brief summary of the key political, economic, and social features of each country.

PREVIEW
Japan has most of the typical features of a parliamentary system, including a symbolic head of state, and a prime minister and cabinet that come out of the legislature. As a case, though, it has many

KEY ARGUMENTS
- Japan is one of the leading examples of the idea that democracy can take root in societies that are modern but not Western.
- Liberal democracy has taken root in Japan only relatively recently, its current political system being based on a constitution adopted only in 1947.
- There has long been a mismatch between Japan's remarkable economic development and the relatively staid nature of its political system.

OVERVIEW
Most of the world's democracies are either European or come out of the European political and social tradition (mainly through the heritage of colonialism). Among the few exceptions are Japan and South Korea, where fundamentally Western ideas of democracy have been grafted onto societies that remain distinctly non-Western. It is clear that Japan is modern but not Western, in the sense that it has become modern without losing sight of its cultural and social identity. Its modernity is most clearly on show in Japan's economic and technological prowess, which has become the stuff of legend. Meanwhile, traditional values are most obvious in its political culture,

TIMELINE

1192	Beginning of the shogun era
1639	Japan cuts its links with the Western world
1853	US fleet forces Japan to open links with outside world
1868	End of shogun rule, Meiji Restoration
1889	New constitution established, followed by legislative elections in 1890
1923	Great Kanto earthquake kills nearly 143,000 people

Timelines
The historical survey of each country includes a brief timeline listing major events in its political development.

Profiles
Each case includes a profile that summarizes the features of its political system, including key economic data, ratings information (political, economic, and social), and a map.

 ## PROFILE JAPAN

Name	Japan (Nihon-koku)	
Capital	Tokyo	
Administration	Unitary, with 47 prefectures and several thousand municipalities.	
Constitution	State formed 5th century (approximately), and most recent constitution adopted 1947.	

COMPARING POLITICAL CULTURE 6
Politics and faction

It is not unusual in democracies for voters and elected officials to lean towards particular leaders within political parties, even while they support the party as a whole. We can see this at work, for example, when candidates from the same party in the United States compete to win the presidential nomination of that party every four years, or when political parties in Germany or India go through their periodic leadership elections; different leaders will attract different blocs of supporters from within the same party. It has even been suggested (see Cohen et al., 2016) that factional politics could become more normal in the American context

Comparing Political Culture
Each of the case study chapters includes a special feature that compares some aspect of political culture in that country with the same phenomenon in other countries, showing how comparison works in more depth.

Comparing Government
Each of the case study chapters also includes a feature comparing some aspect of government across the cases, allowing for more in-depth assessment of their differences and similarities.

 ## COMPARING GOVERNMENT 6
The political role of bureaucrats

Bureaucrats are public servants whose job is to execute government policy while remaining outside the fray of politics. They are not elected, nor – except at the highest levels, as in the case of departmental ministers or secretaries and their deputies – are they appointed by government. Such formalities, though, say little about the political impact of bureaucrats, which is shaped by a combination of tradition and informal preferences. Japan offers an unusual case because of the extent to which bureaucrats

COMPARING POLITICS 6
Politics, society, and happiness

As we saw in Chapter 1, there is an intimate relationship between politics and society. The way political systems function, policy agendas are shaped, and political decisions are taken depends heavily on the structure and preferences of society: the extent to which social divisions exist, for example, as well as attitudes towards minorities, and the relative place of men and women, and of the poor and the wealthy. We have seen the importance in Japan of faction, obligation, and group identity. It is also an unusually homogeneous society, in which almost anything foreign is kept at a distance, including ideas and practices that might help it solve its political and economic problems. The success or failure of democracy depends to a large extent on openness and transparency, commodities that are undersupplied in Japan.

Comparing Politics
Each of the case study chapters also includes a feature focusing on some aspect of the political process across the cases, such as the fairness of elections, the dynamics of coalition governments, and the effects of political corruption.

Table 6.1 Recent prime ministers of Japan

Start of term	Name	Party
August 1989 February 1990*	Toshiki Kaifu	Liberal Democrat
November 1991 July 1993*	Kiichi Miyazawa	Liberal Democrat
August 1993	Morihiro Hosokawa	Eight-party coalition
April 1994	Tsutomu Hata	Eight-party coalition
June 1994	Tomiichi Murayama	Socialist-led coalition
January 1996	Ryutaro Hashimoto	LDP-led coalition

Tables and Figures
The text is dotted with tables and figures that present key data, list the names of modern leaders, give recent election results, summarize electoral trends, or express some of the more complex ideas in visual form. Most are based on the latest data available from the websites of key national and international organizations.

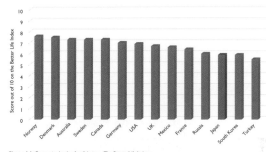

Figure 6.1 Comparing levels of well-being – The Better Life Index
Source: Organization for Economic Cooperation and Development (2017).

DISCUSSION QUESTIONS

1. What is the difference (if any) between modernization and Westernization?
2. It is often said that Japanese prime ministers are caretakers or functionaries, rather than leaders. To what extent could the same be said of the leaders of the other countries assessed in this book?
3. To what extent does exceptionalism in the United States, Japan, and France come from common sources and have common effects?
4. To what extent is factionalism a part of politics in other liberal democracies?
5. What are the costs and benefits of a single-party-dominant system such as that of Japan?

Discussion Questions
Each chapter ends with a set of six open-ended questions designed to help you think about some of the critical issues raised in the chapter.

Chapter Concepts and Key Terms
Each chapter also ends with a list of Chapter Concepts related to the chapter (important terms, events, and people, for example), and a list of Key Terms that apply more generally to government and politics, and which are defined in the margins of the text as well as the Glossary.

CHAPTER CONCEPTS

◆ 1955 system
◆ Diet
◆ Emperor
◆ House of Councillors
◆ House of Representatives
◆ Japan Self-Defence Forces
◆ *Koenkai*
◆ Komeito
◆ Liberal Democratic Party
◆ Meiji Restoration
◆ Recruit scandal
◆ Revolving door
◆ Shinto
◆ Shoguns

KEY TERMS

◆ Factionalism
◆ Iron triangle
◆ Patron-client democracy
◆ Personalism

JAPAN ONLINE

The Japanese Government: www.mofa.go.jp/index.html
Prime minister and cabinet: http://japan.kantei.go.jp/index.html
House of Representatives: www.shugiin.go.jp/internet/index.nsf/html/index_e.htm
Supreme Court: www.courts.go.jp/english
Liberal Democratic Party: www.jimin.jp/english

Online Sources
Each chapter ends with a list of websites containing additional information, with an emphasis on government institutions, political parties, and media outlets.

Further reading
Each chapter ends with a list of several books chosen to provide more detailed and current information and to act as resources for research assignments. The focus is on the most recent books dealing with topics covered in the chapter.

FURTHER READING

Hayes, Louis D. (2017) *Introduction to Japanese Politics*, 6th edn (Routledge). One of the standard texts on Japanese government and politics, including chapters on the political system, political parties, and political participation.
McCargo, Duncan (2012) *Contemporary Japan*, 3rd edn (Red Globe Press). The Japanese volume in the Red Globe series, offering an overview of history, society, culture, government, and the economy.
Pekkanen, Robert J., Steven R. Reed, Ethan Scheiner, and Daniel M. Smith (eds) (2017) *Japan Decides 2017: The Japanese General Election* (Palgrave Macmillan). An edited collection of assessments of the outcome of the 2017 general election and its implications for Japanese government and politics.
Stockwin, Arthur, and Kweku Ampiah (2017) *Rethinking Japan: The Politics of Contested Nationalism* (Lexington Books). An assessment of the implications of the return to power of the LDP in 2012, suggesting that Japan may now be in a new and distinctive political phase.
Sugimoto, Yoshio (2015) *An Introduction to Japanese Society*, 4th edn (Cambridge University Press). A survey of the complexities of Japanese society, arguing that it is more diverse than it is often portrayed.
Walker, Brett L. (2015) *A Concise History of Japan* (Cambridge University Press). As the title implies, a relatively brief outline of Japanese history, with short chapters on each of its key epochs.

GUIDE TO THE WEBSITE

This book is accompanied by a freely accessible website – located at **www.macmillanihe.com/McCormick-Cases** – which provides a range of resources for students and instructors.

FOR STUDENTS

Interactive Map
This feature provides key information and statistics about a range of countries from around the world, allowing students to make quick comparisons.

Guide to Researching Comparative Politics on the Internet
This guide helps students navigate their way through the multitude of resources available on the internet related to the comparative study of politics.

Quizzes and Flashcards
These interactive quizzes and flashcards help students to test their knowledge of the key terms highlighted and defined in each chapter.

Useful Websites
This collection of curated links has been put together to enhance understanding of the key topics in each chapter.

https://www.macmillanihe.com/page/politics-and-international-relations/ >   Lecturer Logout >

Cases in Comparative Government and Politics
by John McCormick

> HOME

+ TEACHING RESOURCES

+ LEARNING RESOURCES

+ ABOUT THIS BOOK

Using twelve pivotal cases, this book brings comparative politics to life by highlighting the key differences in political systems around the world.

This website contains an array of innovative resources to support teaching and learning.

CASES IN COMPARATIVE GOVERNMENT AND POLITICS
JOHN McCORMICK

For students

- *Interactive map* providing key information and statistics about a range of countries from around the world.

- *Guide to Researching Comparative Politics on the Internet,* which helps you to navigate the multitude of resources available on the internet related to comparative politics.

- *Quizzes and Flashcards* to test your knowledge of the key terms highlighted and defined in each chapter.

- *Author Video,* in which John McCormick discusses the discipline of comparative politics, with particular attention to why it is a fascinating, and increasingly relevant, subject.

- *Useful websites:* a collection of curated links designed to enhance your understanding of the key topics in each chapter.

FOR INSTRUCTORS

Testbank
The Testbank comprises a series of pre-prepared multiple choice questions related to the coverage of each of the book's chapters.

Figures and Tables
All the figures and tables from the text are available for download.

PowerPoint Slides
A corresponding set of PowerPoint slides has been prepared for each individual chapter, ready for instructors to adapt and customize to suit their weekly lectures.

LIST OF ABBREVIATIONS

AKP   Justice and Development Party (Turkey)
BCE   Before the Common (or Current) Era
BJP   Bharatiya Janata Party (India)
CCP   Chinese Communist Party
CDU   Christian Democratic Union (Germany)
CE   Common or Current Era
CHP   Republican People's Party (Turkey)
CSU   Christian Social Union (Germany)
DPJ   Democratic Party of Japan
EU   European Union
GDP   Gross domestic product
LDP   Liberal Democratic Party (Japan)
MdB   Member of the Bundestag (Germany)
MP   Member of Parliament
NATO   North Atlantic Treaty Organization
NPC   National People's Congress (China)
PAN   National Action Party (Mexico)
PR   Proportional representation
PRD   Party of the Democratic Revolution (Mexico)
PRI   Institutional Revolutionary Party (Mexico)
SMP   Single-member plurality
SPD   Social Democratic Party (Germany)
UK   United Kingdom
UN   United Nations
USSR   Union of Soviet Socialist Republics

COMPARING GOVERNMENT AND POLITICS

Source: iStock.com/123ArtistImages

1

CONTENTS

- ◆ Overview
- ◆ What is comparative politics?
- ◆ Why do we compare?
- ◆ What do we compare?
- ◆ How do we compare?
- ◆ Classifying political systems
- ◆ Comparing economies
- ◆ Comparing societies
- ◆ The future of comparative government and politics

PREVIEW

This opening chapter introduces comparative politics. It begins with a survey of the personality of this key sub-field of political science, and then discusses the many benefits of comparison. It goes on to look at the topics of comparison, contrasting different levels and units of analysis and discussing the differences between states and nations, and between government and politics. It then outlines the key methodological approaches, explaining the comparative method and the options available in choosing the subjects of comparison, and the distinction between the qualitative, quantitative, and historical methods. The chapter ends with a discussion about the means of classifying different political systems, explains the two key typologies used in this book (the Democracy Index and Freedom in the World), and ends with an assessment of the means and rankings used to compare economies and societies, and the links between political, economic, and social measures.

KEY ARGUMENTS

- ◆ Comparative politics is one of the main (and arguably the most important) sub-fields of political science.
- ◆ We compare for many reasons, including describing political systems, providing context, drawing up rules, and better understanding ourselves and others.
- ◆ There are multiple options regarding how we approach comparison, but the state is the core unit of analysis.
- ◆ The key approaches to comparison include the qualitative, quantitative, and historical methods.
- ◆ There is little agreement on how best to classify different political systems, and yet forming a typology is critical to the process of comparison.
- ◆ Comparing government and politics also benefits from the making of economic and social comparisons among states.

OVERVIEW

Comparative politics is one of the main sub-fields of the discipline of political science. Its goal is to better understand how government and politics work in different societies by comparing among them. There are many benefits to the process of comparison: among other things, it helps us better describe the features of individual systems, it provides us with the context that helps us better understand our own political system, and it helps us better understand others. It is easy and tempting to define government and politics by the qualities of our home political system, but we can never really know how it works, or how it performs, unless we compare it with other systems.

In comparing, we quickly find that government and politics come in a remarkable variety of forms. The most fundamental difference is between democracies and authoritarian systems, but the line between the two types is not clear, and within each type there are multiple variations, ranging from the Scandinavian countries that consistently top most of the comparative ranking charts to the often unstable, corrupt and despotic systems that we find in parts of sub-Saharan Africa and Asia. How is it that countries such as Norway, Sweden, and Finland have been (relatively) so politically successful, and how is it that countries such as North Korea, Syria, and Somalia find themselves in such dire situations? Comparison can help us find the answers.

A second set of differences lies in the structure of political systems. As we will see in Chapter 2, all governments have institutions that carry out either executive, legislative, or judicial functions, but within each of these functions there are multiple varieties. Executives, for example, might be limited presidencies, parliamentary executives, semi-presidential systems, or unlimited presidencies. They each work differently, they each have different sets of powers and responsibilities, and they each relate differently to the other parts of their respective political systems.

A third set of differences can be found in the way that citizens participate in the political process. Consider the fundamental activity of participating in elections. While it might be reasonable to think that the mechanics of elections are the same everywhere, this is not the case. Not only are there multiple ways in which elections can be structured, but there are multiple elective offices, different electoral calendars, and different rules on how election campaigns can be run and how long elected officials can stay in office. And at the heart of the debate about elections is one troubling problem: humans have yet to invent an electoral system in which it is guaranteed that everyone's voice is equally heard, and which results in a fair distribution of power.

Although democracy has long been the blue-ribbon standard of government, it is remarkable how much difficulty many countries have had in achieving the goal of a truly democratic system; the flaws in most political systems are numerous, as reflected in the number of people – even in Scandinavia – who remain politically marginalized. (Winston Churchill had a point when he once quipped that democracy was the worst form of government, except for all the others.) Global history has been characterized by efforts on the part of citizens to govern themselves in a fair and efficient fashion, and for centuries the progress of government has been marked by the spread of democracy. Yet even today, according to Freedom House (2019), only 4 in 10 humans live in countries that could be defined as free. Meanwhile, levels of trust in government continue to fall all over the world, and even countries that were once defined as democratic are experiencing reversals as the inefficiency of their governments seems to grow, as civil liberties are challenged, as voter turnout falls, as political elitism deepens, and as government transparency declines. It is only through comparison that we can explain and develop answers to these quandaries.

WHAT IS COMPARATIVE POLITICS?

Comparison is one of the most basic of all human activities, lying at the heart of almost every choice we make in our lives. Whether we are trying to decide what to have for dinner, which candidate to vote for in an election, or what career to pursue, we will almost always have alternatives, and the most efficient way of deciding is to compare among them. In most cases, comparison is instinctive and subconscious, and not always very scientific. But given that we are already familiar with most of the options available to us, and the potential outcomes (and have hopefully learned by our mistakes), we do not usually need to think too hard or to study too carefully the qualities of the alternatives. Occasionally, though, we are faced with difficult decisions involving complex options, and in order to make good decisions we need to research the alternatives in more depth.

When it comes to making comparisons in the social sciences, the process is less about making choices than about providing explanations, based (ideally) on seeking the context that helps us better understand what we observe. For example, what do authoritarian states have in common, why did the Arab Spring emerge in 2010 and then fade away, why has there been a recent drift away from democracy in countries such as Poland and Turkey, what effect do different electoral systems have on voter turnout and the make-up of governments, and what explains the recent rise of populism in the United States, Italy, and the Philippines?

To better answer such questions, and to better understand and predict human behaviour, we need to examine different situations and cases in order to draw broader inferences about what drives people to act the way they do. In the particular instance of political science, we can learn much by studying government and politics in one country, but we can never really hope to achieve a full understanding, or be sure that we have considered all the explanatory options, unless we make comparisons. Only by looking at institutions and processes across time or across different societies can we build the context that we need in order to gain a deeper understanding of the way in which government functions and politics works.

Comparative politics is one of the major sub-fields of political science (see Figure 1.1), and it is arguably the most important because it goes to the heart of political research. Some have even argued that the comparative method (see later in this chapter) is indistinguishable from the scientific method, and that the scientific study of politics is unavoidably comparative (Almond, 1966, and Lasswell, 1968). The comparative method is certainly one of the oldest tools of political science, used as long ago as the 4th century BCE. by the Greek philosopher Aristotle.

Despite its age and importance, the study of comparative politics – in a methodical and organized social scientific sense – is relatively new. Most studies date back no further than the late 19th century, since when there have been so many changes that it has been hard to keep up; most of today's states, for example, have only been in existence since World War II. For decades, the focus of comparison was on single-country studies, with an emphasis on the 'foreign' rather than on a truly inclusive comparison using a wide variety of cases. (Many of

Comparative politics
The systematic study of the institutions, processes, personality, and performance of government and politics in different societies so as to better understand each of them.

Sub-field	Subject matter
Comparative politics	The comparative study of politics and government in different settings.
International relations	The study of relations between and among states, including diplomacy, foreign policy, international organizations, war and peace.
National politics	The study of politics and government in the setting of individual states.
Political philosophy	The study of political philosophy, addressing issues such as authority, ethics, and freedom.
Political theory	The study of abstract or generalized approaches to understanding political phenomena.
Public policy	The study of the positions taken or avoided by governments in response to public needs.

Figure 1.1 The sub-fields of political science
Note: Political science is sub-divided differently in different countries and by different academic traditions. Other sub-fields include law, methodology, political economy, and public administration.

the earliest scholars of comparative politics were American, who did little to compare the United States with other political systems, instead focusing almost entirely on those others.) Even today, remarkably little attention has been paid to the study of authoritarian political systems, leaving many gaps to be filled. Meanwhile, changes in the nature of government and in public attitudes towards politics have raised many new and intriguing questions for comparativists to address.

WHY DO WE COMPARE?

There is a natural inclination among students of comparative government and politics to use the results of research and study to make judgements, and to declare that one political system or institution is better than another, that one electoral system is fairer than another, or that one country has developed a more effective set of answers to public issues such as poverty, economic decline, or national security. This, indeed, is one of the core values of comparison, and there is much more to the purpose of comparison, which brings with it a wide range of benefits (summarized in Figure 1.2).

Describing political systems

At its simplest, comparison helps us describe the features of political systems, and of the institutions, processes, and principles which make up those systems. In its early years, comparative politics tended to stop here, and 'comparison' was mainly an effort to better describe foreign political systems. It has only been with more recent generations of researchers that there has been more interest in explanation. Meaningful explanation, though, is difficult unless we

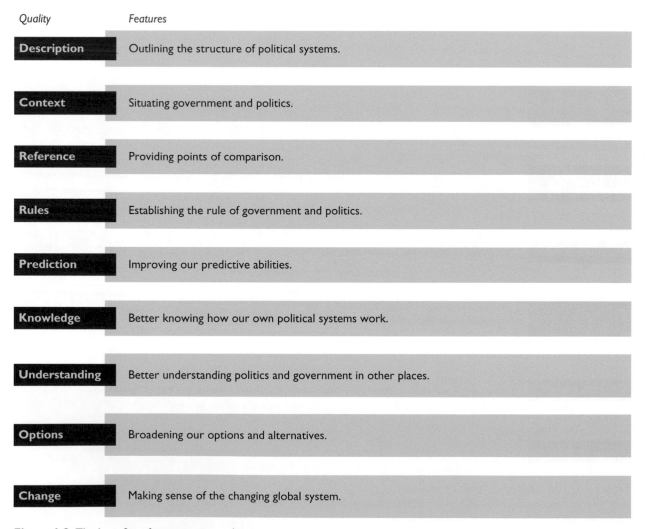

Quality   *Features*

Description   Outlining the structure of political systems.

Context   Situating government and politics.

Reference   Providing points of comparison.

Rules   Establishing the rule of government and politics.

Prediction   Improving our predictive abilities.

Knowledge   Better knowing how our own political systems work.

Understanding Better understanding politics and government in other places.

Options   Broadening our options and alternatives.

Change   Making sense of the changing global system.

Figure 1.2 The benefits of comparative politics

first tie down the 'facts' about politics and government. Comparison contributes by helping us decide which of these facts are the most and least important, which are most and least helpful in offering us deeper insights, and which are most and least worthy of further study.

Providing context

Comparison gives us the context within which to understand how government and politics work. Studying the political system of France, for example, will help us learn how it works and how the relationship between people and government plays out, but the final layer of understanding will always be missing unless we compare our findings with studies of other political systems. Taking the particular case of voter turnout, we know that it is fairly low in France, but we cannot contextualize the figures unless we compare them with other countries. As we will see in Chapter 7, turnout at recent French elections has been about 40 per cent, compared to about 70 per cent in Germany and about 90 per cent in Australia. Why the differences? Comparisons among the cases will help us better understand their individual experiences, and give us deeper insight into the causes and effects of voter turnout patterns. As Lees (2006) puts it, comparison allows single-country scholars to break out of 'the empirical and intellectual silo' in which they find themselves so as to make their work more relevant to the wider discipline of political science.

Providing points of reference

The foreign and unusual will often make little sense unless we can refer it back to something with which we are familiar. So, for example, Americans and Brazilians have presidents who are elected separately from their national legislatures, and the two sets of institutions have a series of checks and balances that are supposed to offset one another and encourage cooperation. But the executives of Britain, Russia, and China have bases of power that are quite different, giving them a quite different relationship with their respective legislatures. By comparing among these cases, we are better able to place them within their different political systems and to better understand their respective roles.

Drawing up rules

Comparison helps us draw up rules about government, develop theories of government and politics, and test hypotheses. This is where we see the *science* in *political science*. Studying a single case helps us draw up rules only about that case, but once we have described and contextualized two or more cases, we will be better able to develop and test explanations of the trends and underlying principles of politics and thus better explain and understand what we have learned (Landman and Carvalho, 2017). For example, there is a famous adage in politics (credited to the 18th-century British politician Lord Acton) that power corrupts, and absolute power corrupts absolutely. A comparative study of democracies and authoritarian systems might help us determine whether or not this is always true.

Improving predictive abilities

Growing out of the advantages offered by better rules and theories, comparison helps us better predict the likely outcome of different courses of political action. Or, at least, it should. Political science has generally had a less than a stellar record in this respect in recent decades, having failed to predict the collapse of communism in the late 1980s, the rise of international terrorism in the 1990s, the Arab Spring in 2010, the British decision in 2016 to leave the European Union, and the election later that year of Donald Trump as president of the United States. An extensive twenty-year study undertaken by Philip Tetlock (2006) in the United States into nearly 300 experts on political and economic matters led him to the conclusion that the average expert did only slightly better in predicting outcomes than a random guesser, prompting ribald comparisons between experts and dart-throwing monkeys.

A core problem, Tetlock argued, is that experts are 'led astray not by what they believe, but by how they think', thus suggesting that there is room for improvement. In a subsequent study, Tetlock and Gardner (2015) argued that predictions could be improved by avoiding many of the standard mistakes of analysis, and instead striking a balance between questions that were either too easy or too difficult to answer, breaking seemingly intractable problems into tractable sub-problems, being careful not to under- or over-react to evidence, being wary of under-confidence and over-confidence, and watching out for hindsight biases (the temptation after an event to claim that you saw it coming). They could also have pointed out that comparison can help us move away from individual cases and look at broader trends. For example, the thinking that led to the Brexit decision in Britain in 2016 was similar to that behind the election of Donald Trump as president of the United States five months later.

Better knowing ourselves

'Knowledge of the self', suggested Dogan and Pelassy (1990), 'is gained through knowledge of others.' By studying the ways in which other societies govern themselves, we can better understand the character, origins, strengths, and weaknesses of our own system of government, as well as our own political patterns and norms. Comparison can give us insight into how power is distributed and limited, can give us a broader perspective of our place in the world, can help us better understand our responses to different kinds of problems, and can help us identify problems that we might not otherwise have known existed. Why is it, for example, that guns are so much a part of American culture? This has not always been the case, and it has only been in the last few decades that gun ownership has become such a contested political issue in the United States. Studying the absence of gun cultures in comparable countries – such as neighbouring Canada – might help us better understand the American situation.

Better understanding others

We live in a global community made up of nearly 200 different states as well as many more political sub-systems (regional, city, and local governments, for example), whose people have often different values and priorities; see Comparing Political Culture 1. Many people forget this, and see the world from the narrow perspective of their own immediate interests. This problem of **ethnocentrism** leads them to project their own values and expectations on to others, instead of trying to understand the world from different perspectives. By studying the way other countries govern themselves and by trying to understand their problems, perceptions, and priorities, we can build

COMPARING POLITICAL CULTURE 1
Sorting myth from reality

Comparative politics is interested not just in how presidents differ from prime ministers, or in how legislatures are structured, or in the effects of different electoral systems. It is also interested in attitudes, norms, and values, or the **political culture** of different societies. For example, what is considered acceptable and unacceptable in the way that government is conducted, what is the political personality of a society, and what is considered usual or unusual in the way that elected leaders conduct themselves or in the way that citizens relate to government and politics?

> **Political culture**
> The sum of a society's values, beliefs, customs, and norms regarding government and politics.

The term *culture* is more troubling than most concepts in the social sciences, because its meaning is contested, and a definition is hard to pin down. It is typically used in an anthropological or sociological sense to describe a community of people with a shared history and common values, beliefs, and customs. But it can also be used to describe a set of assumptions associated with an institution or a society: how it works, how it is structured, and what is considered normal or abnormal (see Gannon and Pillai, 2016). It is as much a matter of how a given society sees itself as of how it sees others, and of how it is seen by others. Care must be taken, though, not to make too many generalizations, because there are differences between elite and mass culture, between urban and rural culture, between the cultures of the young and the elderly, and between the cultures of states that have influential internal divisions, including those along class, ethnic, or religious lines. As we will see, the political culture of a relatively homogeneous society such as Japan, for example, has more internal consistencies than that of diverse societies such as India and Nigeria.

Care must also be taken to distinguish myth and reality. Societies will often have a view about their own political culture that might not square with reality. Many Americans, for example, like to think of their country as exceptional, and as the acme of democracy; its political leaders will often claim that it is the greatest country in the world, and a beacon for democracy (see Chapter 5). Yet the United States has had a poor record of extending equal rights to women and ethnic minorities, has an electoral system that is manipulated to benefit one political party over another, and was recently downgraded in the Democracy Index (see later in this chapter) from a full democracy to a flawed democracy. Similarly, the British like to think of themselves as sensible, moderate, and pragmatic, yet they have undergone more revolutionary changes and more political turmoil than many of them realize (see Edgerton, 2018).

a more balanced view of the rest of the world, avoiding prejudice, and better appreciating the variety and complexity of human society.

Broadening our options

Studying other political systems can show us how similar problems are approached by different societies, can help us identify problems and solutions, and can offer us ideas that might help us improve the way we do things at home or avoid the mistakes made by others. Take, for example, the problem of how to manage municipal waste: the garbage thrown away every day by homes and workplaces in cities and towns, including packaging, food, clothing, containers, plastics, glass, tins and drink cans, paper, and street sweepings. Countries such as New Zealand, Turkey, and Mexico place almost all their waste into landfill, while Germany and Japan place almost none of their waste into landfill, instead relying on incineration and recycling (Organisation for Economic Co-operation and Development, 2015). How have they managed to do that, and to what extent can the German and Japanese models be exported to other countries?

Globalization
The process by which the political, economic, social, and cultural links between and among states become integrated through cooperation, trade, travel, communications, media, investment, market forces, and technology.

Making sense of the changing global system

Keeping up with political change in one country is hard enough, but keeping up with political developments around the world creates additional layers of complexity, and obliges us to study multiple moving targets whose relationships with one another are always evolving. There is no question that the global system is changing rapidly, thanks to a combination of the rise of international cooperation, the expansion of trade, growing volumes of migration and international travel, the digital revolution, and the effects of **globalization**. Comparison can help us sort through the changes in the international system by helping us better understand the causes and effects of change, and better understand its impact on our lives.

At the same time, comparison has its faults and limitations. There is, for example, the technical problem of drawing false or faulty generalizations from the research. This means jumping to conclusions based on weak premises, a problem that can arise from using too few cases, or a non-representative selection of cases, or of assuming that the features of a single case can be extrapolated to all the others. This is all too easy to do for those people who see politics and government in other countries according to what they consider to be normal in their own countries or communities. Another problem arises from the Western-centric nature (or the big-country bias) of much of the research in comparative politics, a sub-discipline that – like many others – tends to be dominated by scholars from the West or from English-speaking countries. The imbalances are reflected in the sheer volume of research (there is far more available on the United States and western Europe, for example, and much less on Central American, sub-Saharan African, and island states), in the bias towards democracies over authoritarian systems, and in the Western lenses through which politics and government around the world is often viewed.

WHAT DO WE COMPARE?

The results of research in any field of study depend on a variety of factors, ranging from the object of study to the level at which we undertake that study, and the methods we use. Almost every field of research in the social sciences has multiple different approaches, with differences of opinion about which works best. Comparative politics is no exception, posing multiple options for researchers.

The first set of options relates to the **level of analysis**, meaning the location, size, or scale of the object of our research interest. The five standard levels are the individual, the community, the institution, the state, and the global system. Of these, the state is the standard point of reference in comparative politics, so this book revolves around whole political systems. But we will also be comparing the institutions and processes within those systems, and the place of individuals within their respective systems. And while there might be five standard levels of analysis, there are many more additional options, including communities, regions, towns, and cities.

The second set of options concerns the **unit of analysis**, or the object or subject of our research. This is the 'who' or the 'what' of research, the possibilities for which are almost limitless. As we will see in Chapter 2, the major options include executives, legislatures, courts, political parties, and elections, but scholars of comparative politics come at them from many different angles; some specialize in a single state using comparative techniques, others opt to be area specialists (studying states in a particular part of the world, like Europe or Asia), others choose

State
A legal and political entity based on the administration of a sovereign territory.

to be institutional or process specialists (studying legislatures or voting, for example), and yet others prefer to be thematic specialists (studying a particular problem or phenomenon affecting a select group of states, such as welfare in wealthy states, the causes of civil war, or the reasons behind the collapse of weak or failing states).

Given its importance to comparison, it is critical to grasp the meaning of the **state**. Whether we are studying the global system or the place of individuals in their local political environment, almost everything is tied back to the personality and behaviour of the state. It is all the more ironic, then, that few concepts in political science have been more thoroughly studied without producing a definition on which there is broad agreement. This is not unusual: there are numerous terms and concepts used in the social sciences without general agreement on exactly what they mean (see Comparing Politics 1 later in this chapter). In the case of 'the state', further confusion is added by the way the term is used in several countries (Australia, Nigeria, and the United States among them) to describe both the legal and political basis of the entire country as well as the sub-national units into which they are divided.

Nation
A mainly cultural and historical concept describing a group of people who identify with one another based on a shared history, culture, language, and myths.

The usual benchmark for understanding the state is the classic definition offered by the German sociologist Max Weber (1864–1920), who described it as an entity with a 'monopoly on the legitimate use of violence'. But while this might have had some resonance when it was proposed in 1919, it now has an anachronistic tone, and we should instead be taking a broader view. The modern state is best defined as a legal and political entity with five features: territory, population, legitimacy, sovereignty, and government (see Figure 1.3). Confusingly, states are often described as countries, but the term *country* has a specific geographical meaning, and usually refers only to a territory and not to the mechanisms of government and power. Adding more confusion, states are also sometimes referred to as nations, but the term *nation* has an entirely different and specific meaning; where a state is a legal and political reality, a **nation** is defined more by history and culture. So while Spain, for example, is a state, it consists of multiple national groups that speak different languages and hold to different cultures; these include Basques, Catalans, and Galicians.

The world has not always been divided into states, and there is no agreement even on when the state system emerged. Its outlines began to appear in Europe in the Middle Ages, and because of the confirmation it gave to several important territorial lines, the 1648 Peace of Westphalia (which brought an end to two long European wars) is often taken as a handy point of reference, such that the modern state system is also known as the **Westphalian system**. But today's global network of states is a relatively new development: when the United Nations (UN) was created in 1945, it had just 51 founder members, with nine more joining by 1950; see Figure 1.4. Today, the UN has 193 member states, the world's newest being South Sudan, created in 2011 with the division of the troubled state of Sudan.

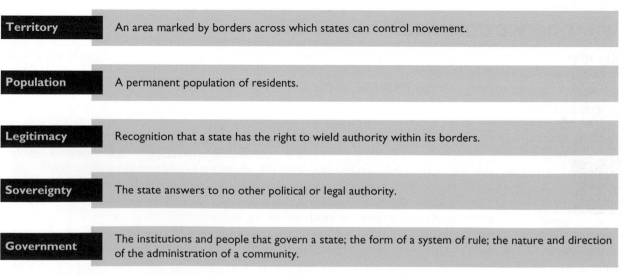

Territory	An area marked by borders across which states can control movement.
Population	A permanent population of residents.
Legitimacy	Recognition that a state has the right to wield authority within its borders.
Sovereignty	The state answers to no other political or legal authority.
Government	The institutions and people that govern a state; the form of a system of rule; the nature and direction of the administration of a community.

Figure 1.3 Five features of the state

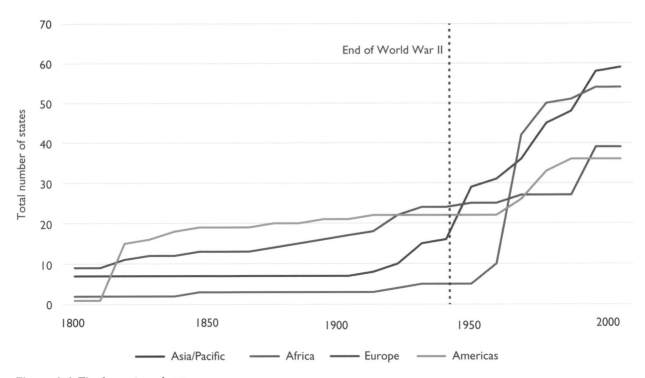

Figure 1.4 The formation of states

Source: Based on (and extrapolated from) appendix in Crawford (2007).

Children in a 'protected civilian' camp run by the United Nations in South Sudan, one of the world's newest states. It became independent in 2011 following a long and bitter civil war with Sudan. It has since suffered ethnic violence and a civil war of its own.

Source: Giles Clarke/Getty Images News.

Not all territories are states, because some of them lack one or more of the required features of a state. For example, Kurdistan, Palestine, and Western Sahara all have populations, territories, and governments, but they lack legitimacy (because they are not recognized under international law), and Western Sahara lacks full sovereignty because it is claimed by neighbouring Morocco. Adding additional complications, all is not equal within the world of states. They vary most obviously in terms of their size, population, and economic wealth, but they also vary in terms of their internal stability or the extent to which they are functionally independent.

◆ Quasi-states are defined by Jackson (1990) as states that won independence from a colonial power but have since lost control over much of their territory. So while they are recognized by the international community as having sovereignty, they barely exist as functioning states. Somalia is an example.

◆ *De facto* states are the opposite in that they control territory and provide governance, but are mainly unrecognized by the international community, and thus have no legal or *de jure* existence (see Pegg, 1998). Examples include Abkhazia, Nagorno-Karabakh, Transnistria, Somaliland, and the Turkish Republic of Northern Cyprus.

◆ Many states have so many internal problems that they hover on the brink of collapse, challenged by ineffective governments, insurgencies or civil wars, dire economic problems, and/or domestic insecurity (see Rotberg, 2004). The problems – and their sources and effects – vary by time and place, and such states are variously known as weak, failing, or failed states. Examples include Afghanistan, Yemen, and the Democratic Republic of Congo.

Within states, we usually focus on three objects of comparison: government, politics, and power. When it comes to **government**, we might be interested in the institutions and people that govern a state, the form of a given political system, or the style and direction taken by the process of administration. In almost all governments there are institutions that carry out executive, legislative, judicial, and bureaucratic functions, and it is the character and nature of these institutions that we are trying to understand when we compare different systems of government. For its part, **politics** is a process focused on the establishment of influence and the sharing of resources. Those resources may be money, opportunity, land, minerals, education, health care, consumer goods, or any of the services that organized societies need in order to function. The study of politics focuses on the way in which decisions are made, which includes the study of all the actors and processes involved (including political parties, elections, interest groups, and public policy), which in turn involves the study of **power**: see Comparing Government 1.

When we compare governments, we ask questions such as these:

◆ How is government structured?
◆ How transparent and responsive is government?
◆ How clear are the rules of government?
◆ Who has power, and how is it divided, limited, and distributed?
◆ Who are the major actors in the political system?
◆ What are the major influences on government and politics?
◆ What is the most representative electoral system?
◆ Are political parties a help or a hindrance?

At the core of comparative studies, though, is an even more fundamental question: what is the purpose of government? At a minimum, governments are expected to govern, meaning that they should provide a system of administration that allows societies to function as efficiently and as equitably as possible, so that problems are resolved and everyone has equal access to opportunities, resources, and protection under the law. Just how this is best done, however, is a matter of opinion, with some favouring a limited role for government in the lives of citizens, but others preferring to see it do more, and being willing to pay the cost in the form of higher taxes. Broadly, the core responsibility of government – and thus the essence of what we study in comparative politics – is the delivery of **political goods**. These were defined by Pennock (1966) as those needs whose fulfilment makes government valuable

Government
The institutions and structures through which societies are governed.

Politics
The process by which people decide – or have others decide for them – how to manage and share the resources of the society in which they live.

Power
The ability to act, or to exert authority and control over others.

Political goods
The commodities or services whose provision is widely considered the primary purpose of government.

COMPARING GOVERNMENT I
Understanding power

If there is a single commodity that lies at the heart of politics and government everywhere, it is power. Theoretically, government (in democracies at least) is supposed to be the servant of the people, meaning that power is in the hands of the people: the job of government is to administer, to make decisions, to promote and protect individual freedoms, to guide markets, and to provide security, all in the name of the people. In reality, government has long functioned and existed in a sphere that is separate from that of the ordinary citizen, with power owned and manipulated by a variety of actors. The study of politics, then, becomes a series of questions relating to power: who has it, who does not have it, how is it given, how is it limited, how is it shared, and why is it given, limited and shared in the particular way that it is? Understanding power involves identifying and tracing the patterns that define government.

The word *power* comes from the colloquial Latin *potere*, meaning 'to be able', which is why it is usually defined as the ability to act and to shape the decisions of others. It is a quality enjoyed most obviously by certain kinds of institutions, such as executives and legislatures, and by states that are either big and/or wealthy and/or stable. Conversely, to lack power – as do many poor or unstable countries – is to fall victim to circumstance and to fall into a reactive mode. Lukes (2005) writes of three dimensions of power, which can be expressed in three questions:

◆ Who prevails when preferences conflict?
◆ Who controls whether preferences are expressed?
◆ Who shapes preferences?

Comparative politics involves looking for – and comparing – the expression and limitation of power in several major spaces, of which three stand out:

◆ The space within which governments act. This is why the study of institutions is so important, because we need to understand what they can and cannot do, and how they relate to one another. We need to look not just at the formal rules but also at the informal relationships among them.
◆ The space within which governments and citizens interact. This is why the study of processes is so important, and why it is important to understand the mechanics of elections, patterns of voting, and the means by which public opinion is shaped and controlled.
◆ The space within which states interact. Even if comparative politics is ultimately interested in domestic political arrangements, patterns, and habits, we are also interested in how these impact the relationships between and among states.

These are all points to bear in mind as we consider the differences and similarities in the distribution of power in and among the cases that follow.

and useful, and more recently by Rotberg (2004) as the functions and purposes for which governments exist. A selection of political goods is listed in Table 1.1.

Different states and leaders have different ideas about how best to deliver political goods. So while democracies claim to believe in an open, competitive, and responsive system of delivery, authoritarian states are less interested in freedom of choice or the general welfare of the population, and determine the delivery of political goods according to the extent to which they will keep governments and elites in power. In the case of failing or failed states, the delivery of political goods has sometimes almost completely collapsed.

Table 1.1 Political goods

Quality	Features
National and personal security	Protecting borders from external threats, and citizens from crimes and threats to personal property; allowing differences to be resolved in a peaceful, equitable, and consistent manner, through an enforceable and effective system of rules and laws.
Political freedom	Upholding and protecting individual rights, promoting equality for all (regardless of race, gender, age, religion, or any other differences), and protecting those least able to protect themselves (such as children, the elderly, and the disabled).
Political participation	Ensuring that all citizens can participate in the political process on a basis of freedom and equality, guaranteeing their freedom of expression and choice.
Economic freedom	Allowing citizens to pursue a livelihood, to prosper by selling their labour and skills for wages, to enjoy the fruits of their labour, to enjoy property rights, and to have equitable access to wealth and other resources.
Infrastructure	Ensuring that all citizens have access to health care, education, energy supplies, transportation, communication systems, consumer protection, a secure banking system, and a clean environment.

HOW DO WE COMPARE?

Having looked at the *why* and the *what* of political comparison, we now need to look at the *how*: the means of making our comparisons, or the critical question of **methodology**. There are many options available, the choice of approach depending on a combination of the number and the kinds of **cases** we want to study, the amount of information available, the preferred method of the researcher, and how a researcher believes that understanding is best acquired.

Case
An instance or example of a phenomenon that is used to illustrate a broader set of arguments or principles, or to narrow a broad field of research into more manageable quantities.

Comparative method
The process by which different cases are compared in order to better understand their qualities, and to develop hypotheses, theories, and concepts.

Variable
A changeable feature, factor, quantity, or element.

At the heart of comparative government and politics – and of research more broadly – is the **comparative method**, a process by which different cases are systematically studied in order to test hypotheses, build theories, and make inferences. The 'method' is usually taken to mean the study of a few carefully selected cases, as distinct from the more abstract analysis necessary with many cases. The method can take different forms (and have different results) according to the number and the type of cases being studied, but we have ambitious goals in mind, as expressed so eloquently by Gabriel Almond, one of the leading names in the study of political science in the United States:

> We … are concerned with sampling the total universe of man's experiments with politics, contemporary and historical, national, sub-national, and international. Increasingly, we select our cases for study in order to test hypotheses about the relations between **variables** – environmental influences on politics, political influences on the environment, and the interaction of political variables with each other (Almond, 1966).

While we can study the broad ideas of comparative government and politics, we can gain more detailed insight by using individual cases to explore or illustrate those ideas. For example, we can study democracy in general terms and perhaps agree on its features and implications, but we can understand it more deeply if we look at cases of democracy in practice, and compare among them. We will find that while democracy has many features in common, including freedom of expression and the rule of law, the balance among those features varies from one case to another.

If all political systems were exactly the same, we would have less need of cases to illustrate their features. But political systems come in many varieties, and in order to really grasp the broad principles by which governments are structured and politics is practised, we need a representative range of cases. Achieving such a range, however, is easier said than done, and researchers face numerous potential pitfalls, of which three are particularly common: the biases that can arise in selection, values, and confirmation (see Table 1.2).

The number, variety, and range of cases used in comparative studies of government and politics are all important, for a variety of reasons. It is not unusual for 'comparative' studies to be based on undertaking an in-depth study of a single case of an institution or phenomenon, using the conclusions to illustrate a wider point. But the conclusions will remain mainly speculative unless additional cases are brought in to the study, adding new information and different perspectives. By definition, after all, comparison means having at least two units of analysis, and using their differences and similarities to shed light on one another. The fewer the cases, the more intensive will be the analysis, but the less chance there will be of the cases representing a sufficient variety of system types, or of being useful for illustrating wider points. The more cases used, the less intensive will be the analysis, and the better the chance of generating more widely applicable conclusions, but the more danger there will be of not being able to assess each of them in enough depth.

At the same time, the kind of cases used is also important, because it will impact the results of the study:

◆ Some cases might be both similar and typical of a kind; for example, coalition governments on the European continent, or authoritarian governments in sub-Saharan Africa.
◆ Others might be the exemplars of a type in the sense that they created a particular category or phenomenon, as in the example of parliamentary systems, which are almost all based on the British founding model.
◆ Yet others may be deviant cases or outliers, and have unusual features, as we will find with the example of the United States in Chapter 5.

One of the core strategic decisions to be made by researchers in comparative politics concerns the extent of the differences and the similarities between the cases, with two broad options being available:

◆ The **most similar system** approach is based on using cases that are as similar as possible except in regard to the topic being studied. The logic here is that the more similarities there are between the cases, the better the chance of identifying what causes the differences in the topic of study. For example, we could try to explain military governments in sub-Saharan Africa by choosing a group of states with similar histories, economies, and social structures, and then work to identify the reasons why some states (such as Nigeria) have had many military governments while others (such as Kenya or Botswana) have had none.
◆ The **most different system** approach is based on using cases that are as different as possible except in regard to the topic being studied. The logic here is to sift through all the differences in order to identify the focused points of commonality. For example, there are many political differences among Argentina, Indonesia, Nigeria, Turkey, and the United States, but they all have presidential executives. Why is that, and what do they have in common that helps explain why they have all opted for presidential systems over parliamentary systems?

The final methodological choice concerns the relative merits of qualitative, quantitative, and historical approaches to research. The first two differ most obviously in that quantitative research is based on the use of data and statistics,

Table 1.2 Potential pitfalls in choosing cases

Problem	Features
Selection bias	Arises when the chosen cases and variables are unrepresentative of the wider class from which they are drawn. Stems partly from the greater volume and availability of information on democracies compared to authoritarian states, for example. Also driven by the language of researchers: more scholarship is available in English than in other languages.
Value bias	Allowing assessments, the choice of facts, and conclusions to be impacted by the values and past experiences of the researcher. Most researchers will remain within their orbits of familiarity, raising the danger of seeing others through the lenses of their own experiences, values, and learning, and even their race, gender, religion, age, or socio-economic status.
Confirmation bias	The tendency to seek out or interpret information that confirms pre-existing beliefs and attitudes, and to ignore information that does not. Arises when researchers have a view in mind before they undertake their research, and pay attention only to the facts and analyses that support that view, ignoring or downplaying any contrary evidence.

Qualitative method
An approach to research that seeks to understand underlying reasons, motivations and trends, often using direct observation of a limited number of cases.

Quantitative method
An approach to research based on the generation and use of numerical data, with an emphasis on quantifying patterns and trends in behaviour, often using many cases.

Historical method
An approach to research based on studying cases from the past, an approach that increases the number of possible cases and can help improve predictions.

Typology
A system of classification based on groupings or types with common sets of attributes, often ranking them within each type.

while qualitative research is not, but the differences go much further. The **qualitative method** seeks to understand the underlying reasons and motivations behind a phenomenon by taking a wide angle approach, and to generate open-ended narratives about that phenomenon. It tends to be descriptive rather than predictive, it typically involves an in-depth comparison of a limited number of cases (otherwise known as small-N), it is based mainly on observation, and it tries to understand the interaction of multiple variables.

By contrast, the **quantitative method** tends to be more abstract, involves more cases (that is, large-N studies), and relies on data from which an effort is made to generalize results. It is based on a narrow angle approach in an effort to be as objective as possible, using experiments and survey research rather than observation. It is heavily reliant on the quality and availability of data, which are not always equally available from cases around the world; there are much more such data available from democracies than from authoritarian regimes, for example. Quantitative research tends to be stronger on breadth than on depth.

Finally, the **historical method** looks at political developments over time, seeking cases from the past to help better understand the present and to better predict the future. Each of the cases in this book offers a brief historical summary, without which many of the present-day features of government and politics in those cases would be harder to understand. Why does Britain have a monarchy, for example, why does the United States still use an Electoral College to determine who wins the presidency, and why has Nigeria had so many military governments? Projecting the past to the future, how is the British monarchy likely to evolve, does the Electoral College any longer serve a useful purpose, and how likely is Nigeria to see a return to military government?

CLASSIFYING POLITICAL SYSTEMS

As we saw earlier, there are 193 states that are recognized under international law and have become members of the UN, along with a small cluster of additional territories – such as Palestine and Western Sahara – that lack either quality. Clearly, making detailed comparisons among so many cases is impractical, and a better way to proceed is by using a **typology**. This allows us to develop political types into which states can be clustered, reducing the sample size to more manageable proportions, allowing us to make assumptions about the states in each type, as well as using case studies to focus more closely on the common features of the different types, helping us develop explanations, establish rules, draw inferences, and test theories.

The ideal typology is one that is simple, neat, consistent, logical, neutral, and as real and useful to the casual observer as to journalists, political leaders, or political scientists. Unfortunately, scholars of comparative politics have been unable to find the Holy Grail of a universal typology, and perhaps never will; they disagree about the value of typologies, and even those who use them cannot agree on the criteria that should be considered. They are also frustrated by the political nature of the ranking process, and by the ever-changing nature of government and politics: typologies change with the times, as does the ranking of states within their different classes or types.

Consider the following examples of typologies, each of which was a product of the era in which it was developed:

◆ The Greek philosopher Aristotle (384–322 BCE) distinguished between states ruled by one person, by a few people, and by many people, and sub-divided each group into good and corrupt forms of rule.
◆ The 18th-century French philosopher Baron de Montesquieu distinguished between republics, monarchies, and despotic systems.
◆ In his work on sources of authority, Max Weber (1947) wrote of traditional (or hereditary) authority, charismatic authority, and legal authority.
◆ In the 1960s, the American political scientist Barrington Moore (1967) distinguished between democratic/parliamentary systems (such as the United States or Britain), fascist/authoritarian systems (such as Nazi Germany), and communist systems (such as the old Soviet Union).

COMPARING POLITICS I
Translating the language of political science

Already in this chapter it has become clear that political science has its own specialized language, with terms such as *political culture*, *state*, *nation*, *government*, and *power*. There will be plenty more such terms in the chapters that follow, and it will also become clear not just that a focused definition of these terms is important, but that there is often much disagreement on what they mean. Unlike the natural sciences (such as physics, biology, and chemistry) where terms have precise and usually unchangeable meanings, the vocabulary of the social sciences is softer and more unstable; the same term can often have different meanings, or be defined differently, according to the time and place in which it is used, or the interpretation of the user.

It can sometimes seem as though social scientists have adopted the claim made by Humpty Dumpty in Lewis Carroll's *Through the Looking Glass*: 'When I use a word ... it means just what I choose it to mean – neither more nor less'. Ironically, terms such as *state* and *democracy* are among the most difficult to pin down precisely because they have been the most thoroughly studied and have been finely parsed and dissected, allowing numerous refinements to be added to our understanding of what they mean (or what different political scientists believe they mean).

Perhaps the best way of approaching the meaning of words in the social sciences is to take the advice offered by the philosopher Ludwig Wittgenstein (1889–1951). He argued that when a term had more than one usage (the term *liberal* being a particularly notorious example), it was best to understand those usages in the way we understand relationships within a family. In other words, the members of the family have common origins and share common characteristics, but if we focus too much on what they all have in common then we will miss the features that make them distinctive (Birch, 2007).

Developing the analogy with families, it is unlikely that we will ever be able to entirely agree on the meaning of most terms in the social sciences. Everyone brings their own perceptions, biases, and priorities to the understanding of key concepts, and even a seemingly simple term such as *democracy* has been subject to at least two millennia of study without final agreement on what it actually means, the debate complicated by the way in which the term is often politically contested. But the details of the definitions we use may not matter so long as they all accurately convey the same general features of the concept we are studying.

◆ The structural-functional model proposed by Almond and Powell (1966) portrayed government as a system made up of structures (institutions) that perform certain functions, and compared how they performed.
◆ Finer (1997) divided states into one of four types: a palace polity (rule by one), a church polity (in which religion played a key role), a nobility polity (where a pre-eminent group or sector had influence), or a forum polity (where authority was conferred on rulers from below).

Comparative politics through much of the Cold War (late 1940s–early 1990s) was dominated by the **Three Worlds system**. This had the benefit of being neat and simple, but it was based less on common political and economic realities than on Cold War assumptions about the structure of the international system, with states classified according to their place in the war:

Three Worlds system
The typology that prevailed during the Cold War, dividing states into three groups based on their place in the conflict.

◆ The First World consisted of wealthy, democratic industrialized states, most of which were partners in the Western alliance against communism.
◆ The Second World consisted of communist regimes, including most of those states ranged against the Western alliance.
◆ The Third World consisted of poorer, less democratic, and less developed states, some of which took sides in the Cold War, but some of which did not.

The typology had a curious history. It came out of the *tiers monde*, or the 'third force' of French political parties in the 1940s that supported neither the government of the day nor the alternative policies of Charles de Gaulle

(Safire, 1978). In 1952, the French demographer Alfred Sauvy borrowed the concept to describe a 'third world' of states that were choosing not to align themselves either with the West or with the Soviet bloc during the Cold War (Wolf–Phillips, 1979). The label stuck, and by the late 1960s the emerging states of Africa, Asia, and Latin America were routinely being described as the Third World. Counting backward, communist states were described as the Second World and industrialized democracies as the First World.

The system provided evocative labels that could be slipped with ease into media headlines and everyday conversation: even today the term *Third World* conjures up powerful images of poverty, underdevelopment, corruption, and political instability, while the complaints of citizens of wealthy countries are often ironically dismissed as 'First World problems'. But it was always too simplistic, and often misleading. The First World had the most internal logic because its members had (and still have) the most in common. The Second World was more problematic because communism was interpreted differently by its members, and was never applied as anticipated by its most influential theorist, Karl Marx. As for the Third World, it never had much internal consistency because its 135 members had many differences: some were democratic while others were authoritarian; some had civilian governments while others had military governments; some were wealthy while others were poor; and some were industrialized while others were agrarian. All that they ultimately had in common was that they were not core protagonists in the Cold War.

In this book, we opt for a political typology based on a combination of two rating systems that divide states broadly into democracies and authoritarian systems, and distinguish among their different levels of political freedom. The first of these systems is the **Democracy Index**

Democracy Index
A political ranking system maintained by the Economist Intelligence Unit, dividing states into full democracies, flawed democracies, hybrid regimes, and authoritarian regimes.

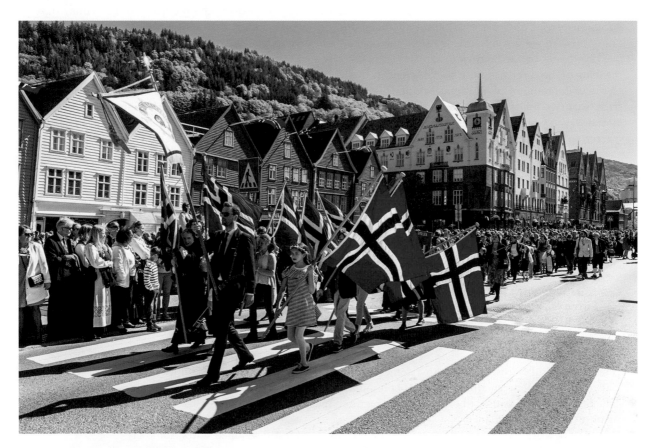

Residents of the town of Bergen in Norway celebrate their country's national day. Norway routinely ranks at the top of most comparative political, economic, and social leagues, suggesting that it has done better than much of the rest of the world in finding the formula for success.

Source: iStock.com/MariusLtu.

maintained by the Economist Intelligence Unit, a research body related to *The Economist*, a British weekly news magazine. It is based on 60 different indicators that are grouped into five categories:

◆ Electoral processes and pluralism.
◆ Protection for civil liberties.
◆ The functioning of government.
◆ Patterns of political participation.
◆ The strength and depth of political culture.

These indicators are then applied to almost every state in the world, giving each a score out of 10. In the 2018 index, about half the world's states were considered democracies, but only 20 were rated as 'full democracies', while 55 were rated as 'flawed democracies'. The balance was divided into hybrid regimes and authoritarian states (see Table 1.3). Norway ranked highest in the list with a score of 9.87 and North Korea ranked lowest with a score of 1.08. The list excluded almost all the island states of the Pacific and the Caribbean, many of which Freedom House (see below) rates as Free.

Freedom in the World
A political ranking system maintained by Freedom House, based on political rights and civil liberties.

The second (and older) rating system is the **Freedom in the World** index published by Freedom House, an international non-governmental organization founded in 1941 and headquartered in New York. The index is based on giving states scores of 1 to 7 according to their records in two broad categories:

◆ Political rights (the ability of people to participate in the political process).
◆ Civil liberties (including freedom of expression, the independence of the judiciary, personal autonomy, and economic rights).

States are then divided into three groups: Free, Partly Free, and Not Free. In a recent index (see Table 1.4), most European countries did well, along with Australia, Canada, Japan, South Korea, and the United States (a rating of Free and a 1 on each scale) while Mexico and Nigeria were rated as Partly Free, and Russia did not do well (having been demoted in recent years from Partly Free to Not Free, with scores of 6 and 5). Freedom House

Table 1.3 The Democracy Index

Type	Number	Features	Examples
Full democracies	20	Scores of 8–10. Respect for civil liberties, political culture conducive to democracy, governmental checks and balances, independent media.	Germany and UK (cases used in this book), along with Australia, Canada, the Scandinavian countries, Mauritius, Uruguay.
Flawed democracies	55	Scores of 6–7.99. Problems that interfere with democracy, such as underdeveloped political culture, low levels of participation, infringements on media freedom.	United States, Japan, France, India, and Mexico, along with South Korea, South Africa, Brazil.
Hybrid regimes	39	Scores of 4–5.99. Deeper faults than flawed democracies, including limits on civil liberties, electoral irregularities, limits on political opposition, widespread corruption.	Turkey and Nigeria, along with Kenya, Ukraine, Pakistan, Iraq, Thailand, Bolivia.
Authoritarian	53	Scores below 3.99. Severe limits on civil liberties, free expression, and political opposition, including manipulated elections and government institutions, and often absolute dictatorship.	China, Russia, and Iran, along with Saudi Arabia, North Korea, Cuba, Zimbabwe.
Unclassified	26*		

Source: Economist Intelligence Unit (2019).
* Based on the total of 193 members states of the UN.

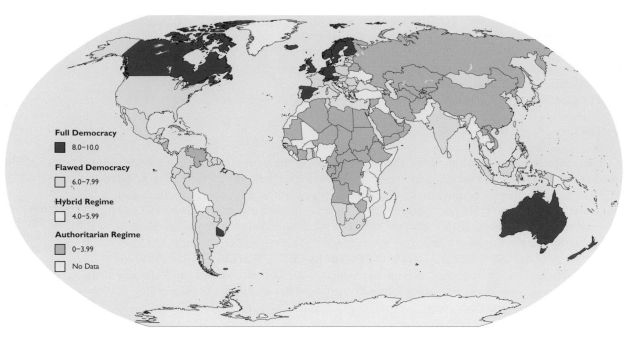

Map 1.1 The Democracy Index

Source: Based on Economist Intelligence Unit (2019).

Table 1.4 Freedom in the World

Type	Number	Cases in this book	Other examples
Free	88	France, Germany, India, Japan, UK, USA.	Australia, Brazil, Canada, Ghana, Senegal, South Africa, South Korea.
Partly Free	58	Mexico, Nigeria.	Indonesia, Kenya, Pakistan, Sri Lanka, Tanzania, Ukraine.
Not Free	49	China, Iran, Russia, Turkey.	Cuba, Egypt, Thailand, and Vietnam, along with 12 countries described as the 'Worst of the Worst', which include North Korea, Saudi Arabia, Somalia, and Syria.

Source: Freedom House (2019).

also publishes an informal category titled 'Worst of the Worst', among which – in 2016 – were Syria, North Korea, Sudan and Saudi Arabia. Historical data are also available on its website, allowing researchers to see how different countries have fared since 1972. In its 2017 report, Freedom House noted with alarm that there had been 11 consecutive years during which there had been a decline in levels of freedom around the world, with setbacks in political rights and civil liberties in multiple countries, including the United States, Brazil, France, South Africa, and South Korea. Populists and autocrats, it declared, had become 'the dual threat to global democracy' (Freedom House, 2018b).

COMPARING ECONOMIES

Political economy
A branch of the social sciences that studies the relationships between markets and the state.

Although we are mainly interested here with comparing government and politics, it is rare that they are assessed in isolation from economic factors. There is such an intimate relationship between politics and economics that there is a field of study known as **political economy**. This looks at topics such as output, trade, debt, the budget, infrastructure, labour, investment, and prices, and is interested in understanding the impact of economics on politics, and vice versa. To a large extent, democracy goes hand in hand with open markets and the generation of wealth; political freedoms generate economic freedoms (and vice versa), and even though many democracies have come under growing criticism for their failure to ensure the equitable spread of wealth and opportunity, the problem of inequality is usually much worse in authoritarian states.

The main comparative economic measure is productivity, which is expressed using **gross domestic product** (GDP) (or gross national product, or gross national income). This is a figure calculated by giving a US dollar value to all the goods and services produced by a state in a year. The numbers generated give us a good idea about the relative size of economies, the data for 2017 revealing that the United States is the wealthiest national economy in the world, with a GDP of nearly $19 trillion (out of a global total of about $80 trillion). China is second, having moved rapidly up the rankings in recent years and overtaken Japan, while the four biggest European economies (German, Britain, France, and Italy) have GDPs between $2 trillion and $4 trillion. By contrast, the smallest economies in the world – many of which are island states in the Pacific or the Caribbean – count their GDPs not in the trillions or the billions, but in the millions (see Table 1.5). It is important to emphasize here that GDP is not a measure of wealth or poverty, nor of the income of the citizens of a given country, so big numbers do not indicate personal or national wealth, and small numbers do not indicate poverty. Changes in GDP, however, can be indicative of changes in economic health.

Gross domestic product
The total value of all goods and services produced by a state in a given year.

GDP provides a measure of the absolute size of national economies but tells us little about relative productivity, because it does not take account of population size. For a more helpful comparative measure, we use per capita GDP, which tells us how much countries are producing per person. If we divide GDP by population (see Table 1.6), we find that Luxembourg headed the table in 2017 with an annual per capita GDP of just under $104,000 (thanks mainly to its large financial services sector), the United States is in the top ten (but some way behind) with just over $57,000, China sinks to the middle of the rankings at $8,100, and states such as Burundi, Malawi, and Niger sit at the bottom of the league with a per capita GDP of less than $400, far below the global figure of $10,000. Put another way, it takes almost 400 Burundians to produce goods and services with the same value as a single Luxembourger. This is not because Burundians work less hard but because what they produce has less value, and the economy of Burundi is still based heavily on agriculture and basic industries.

GDP is a useful means of measurement, but it presents several problems. First, economic production may not be the best measure of human welfare, because material wealth is not the only indicator of the relative ability of societies to meet the needs of their members. Second, the data are subject to all the usual problems with accuracy,

Table 1.5 The five biggest and smallest economies in the world

Country	GDP	Country	GDP
United States	$19.4 trillion	Palau	$289 million
China	$12.2 trillion	Marshall Islands	$204 million
Japan	$4.9 trillion	Kiribati	$186 million
Germany	$3.7 trillion	Nauru	$114 million
UK	$2.6 trillion	Tuvalu	$40 million

Source: World Bank (2019). Data are for 2017.

Table 1.6 The five most and least productive economies in the world

Country	Per capita GDP	Country	Per capita GDP
Luxembourg	$104,000	Mozambique	$426
Switzerland	$80,000	Central African Republic	$418
Norway	$75,000	Niger	$378
Iceland	$70,000	Malawi	$338
Ireland	$69,000	Burundi	$292

Source: World Bank (2019). Data are for 2017.

Purchasing power parity
A method of calculating economic productivity by accounting for differences in the purchasing power of national currencies.

which diminishes in states whose economies are less stable and transparent. Third, GDP is based on placing a monetary value on economic activity, but it does not account for the value of intellectual wealth or voluntary work, nor for the size of the black market (which is biggest in poorer states with unstable economies) and nor for untapped assets, failing to factor in the potential value of minerals, land, water, forests, or ecological variety.

Finally, there is a problem with the way that GDP is calculated. It is usually expressed on the basis of a conversion from local currencies into US dollars at the official exchange rate. But China has been criticized for keeping its currency at artificially deflated prices (so that it can maximize its profits from exports), currencies in many poorer states have unrealistic official values, and costs of living vary from one state to another, and even within states. To give us a more accurate idea of the relative productivity of states, some economists prefer using **purchasing power parity** (PPP), which is based on calculating the value of production using the purchasing power of each national currency. The result can be a dramatic reassessment of the relative size of poorer national economies. For example, China's per capita GDP almost doubles from about $8,000 to about $15,000, while India's almost quadruples from $1,700 to $6,500.

Relative size is not the end of the story when it comes to comparing economies; we also need to look at differences in economic structure. All economic activity falls into one of three categories: industry (which produces tangible, manufactured goods), services (which are intangibles such as insurance, financial services, health care, and retail), and agriculture. Generally speaking, the wealthier and more economically advanced a state, the more it earns from services; the poorer and less developed a state, the more it earns from agriculture. Services are more profitable and are usually a sign of a sophisticated economy and an educated workforce. Agriculture is often less profitable, relies on government subsidies in wealthy states, and is often low scale in poorer states. So, in advanced economies, services account for as much as two-thirds of GDP and agriculture accounts for barely two to three per cent. By contrast, the poorest states in the world have relatively little industry and most of their people still rely on agriculture for a living (see Figure 1.5 for examples).

Another way of using economics to understand political performance is to look at the distribution of wealth, and at the size of the gap between the rich and the poor. Many countries (rich and poor alike) have faced growing criticism for failing to address economic disparities; income inequality has been rising since the 1980s, to the point where the wealthiest one per cent of the population today earns nearly a quarter of national income (Credit Suisse

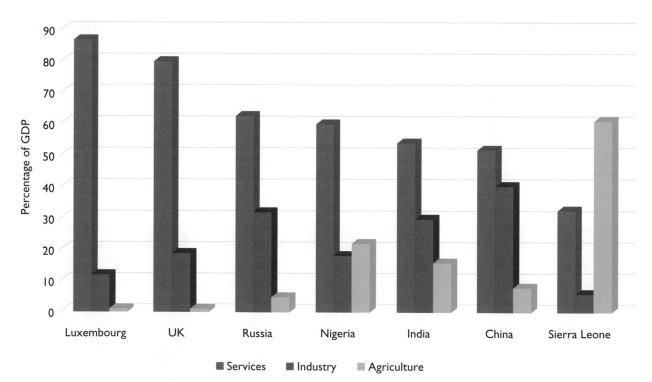

Figure 1.5 Comparing the structure of economies
Source: World Bank (2019). Data are for 2017.

Table 1.7 The five most and least free economies in the world

Country	Ranking	Score	Country	Ranking	Score
Hong Kong	1	9.03	Central African Republic	155	5.01
Singapore	2	8.71	Argentina	156	4.81
New Zealand	3	8.35	Republic of Congo	157	4.80
Switzerland	4	8.25	Libya	158	4.58
United Arab Emirates	5	7.98	Venezuela	159	3.29

Source: Gwartney et al. (2017).

Research Institute, 2018). If a core political good is economic freedom, including equitable access to wealth and opportunity, then these countries are not doing well. One comparative measure in this regard is the **Gini coefficient**, named for the Italian statistician Corrado Gini, who published his ideas in 1912. The measure is based on the simple premise of giving a value of 0 to a state where everyone has equal income and a value of 100 to a state where one person owns all the wealth.

> **Gini coefficient**
> A measure of income inequality, used to show the distribution of wealth in a given population.

On that basis, the global figure has been worsening as countries have become wealthier, reaching its current level of about 65 (Bourguignon, 2015). National figures calculated by the US Central Intelligence Agency (2019) range from a low of 24–25 (Slovakia, Sweden, Ukraine, and Belgium) to a high of 60–63 (Haiti, South Africa and Lesotho), with Germany rated at 27, the European Union at 31, Japan at 38, Russia at 41, the United States at 45, and Nigeria at 49. This measure has the advantage of being simple and easy to use for comparison, but it has been criticized for being a measure of income rather than of opportunity, for having to rely on sometimes unreliable GDP and income data, for failing to take into account the black market (a key source of income in poorer countries), and for measuring current income rather than lifetime income.

Finally, we need to look at economic policies, because governments approach economic management in different ways. Free-market systems such as the United States, Britain, and Japan have less government control over the economy and less public ownership of industries and services, but centrally planned systems such as China have more government regulation and ownership. Meanwhile, emerging Asian and Latin American states have adopted increasingly free-market policies, and less-developed states have failed to develop economic stability and are often handicapped by such problems as an overvalued national currency, high inflation, an inability to raise taxes efficiently, corruption, inefficiency, and a large black market. The poorest states, such as many in sub-Saharan Africa, tend to have less well-developed economic policies, and the question for them is not so much the role that government plays in the marketplace as what they can do to promote economic development.

One useful comparative measure of economic policies is the Economic Freedom Index maintained by the Fraser Institute, a politically conservative Canadian research body that studies markets and the way they work. Starting from the premise that the key ingredients of economic freedom are personal choice, voluntary exchange, freedom to compete, and protection of individuals and property, the index ranks nearly 160 states according to such factors as the size of government income and spending, how the law protects people and property, monetary policies, and trade policies. It then gives those states a ranking on a scale of 10 to 1, with 10 being the freest. It gives Hong Kong and Singapore the highest ratings, places most democracies in the range of 7.5 or better, and ranks India and China at 112 and 113 respectively, among a cluster of Asian, African, and Latin American states (see Table 1.7).

COMPARING SOCIETIES

Just as there is an intimate relationship between politics and economics, so there is also one between government and the society within which it functions. Much of the performance of government is based on the extent to which it reflects (or fails to reflect) the society of which it is a part, and governments are judged and assessed as much as anything on the extent to which they succeed or fail in addressing problems with a strong social dimension, such as crime, substance abuse, educational under-achievement, discrimination, homelessness, and poverty (all of which also have political and economic dimensions). The core question relates to how governments are performing comparatively in terms of meeting the basic needs of their people. There are different ways of understanding 'basic needs', but at a minimum they would include adequate nutrition, education, and health care, and in this regard there are three standard measures of the quality of life:

◆ **Life expectancy**, or the age to which the average resident of a state can expect to live. This is used as an indicator of the quality of health care, but it can also say something about nutrition, environmental quality, and levels of public safety; life expectancy in states torn by crime or civil war can be relatively low. Around the world, figures range from a high of about 75–82 years in democracies, to about 55–65 in states with medium levels of development, and a low of 38–50 in the poorest and most troubled states.

◆ **Infant mortality**, or the number of new-born babies that die within 30 days of birth, expressed as a figure per 1,000 live births. This is another indicator of the quality of health care and nutrition. Unfortunately, infant mortality is a fact of life, and even in the most medically advanced societies there will be some babies born with severe medical problems or dangerously premature. Mortality figures range from a low of about 2–10 per 1,000 in most advanced democracies to a high of as many as 140–170 per 1,000 in states with the least advanced health care systems.

◆ **Adult literacy**, or the percentage of the population that can read and write. The definition of literacy varies from one state to another, and even in those that claim 100 per cent literacy, there are many people who can do no more than read road signs and make only the simplest arithmetical calculations. Most democracies claim literacy rates of 100 per cent, while the rates in poorer states can be as low as 50 per cent.

Human Development Index
A social ranking system maintained by the UN Development Programme, dividing states into those with very high, high, medium, or low levels of development.

One comparative measure of social conditions is offered by the **Human Development Index** (HDI), a rating developed by the United Nations. Using a combination of life expectancy, adult literacy, educational enrolment, and per capita GDP, it rates human development for most of the states in the world as either very high, high, medium, or low. On the 2018 index, European countries did best (along with Australia, Canada, and the United States, and Japan), Russia ranked 49th, Iran was 69th, Mexico was 77th, and China was 90th. The countries with the lowest levels of human development were mainly in Africa and the Middle East (see Table 1.8).

Corruption Perceptions Index
A ranking system maintained by Transparency International, based on perceptions of levels of corruption, and scoring states out of 100.

A final revealing comparative ranking is the **Corruption Perceptions Index** (CPI) maintained by the Berlin-based research body Transparency International. Published annually since 1995, it uses information gathered from business, banks, foundations, and other independent institutions. As the title suggests, it is as much about perception as about objective reality (to the extent that there is such a thing), and yet it gives us a good sense of the relative levels of political effectiveness around the world; the more corrupt a society is, the less effective it is at governing itself. Democracies perform relatively well and authoritarian states less well (see Table 1.9), but corruption is a universal problem, and no society escapes unscathed. Wealth is not always an indicator of performance, since Rwanda (one of the poorer countries in the world, with a per capita GDP of $700) ranked 50th on the CPI in 2016, while Italy (per capita GDP $31,000) ranked 60th.

These are just two of the many social ranking systems that are available, which cover a wide range of topics from educational attainment to gender equality and environmental

Table 1.8 The five most and least developed countries in the world

Country	Rank	Score	Country	Rank	Score
Norway	1	0.953	Burundi	185	0.404
Switzerland	2	0.944	Chad	186	0.396
Australia	3	0.939	South Sudan	187	0.388
Ireland	4	0.938	Central African Republic	188	0.367
Germany	5	0.936	Niger	189	0.354

Source: UN Development Programme (2018). Based on data for 2017.

Table 1.9 The five least and most corrupt countries in the world

Country	Rank	Score	Country	Rank	Score
New Zealand	1	89	Yemen/Sudan	176=	16
Denmark	2	88	Afghanistan	177	15
Finland	3=	85	Syria	178	14
Norway	3=	85	South Sudan	179	12
Switzerland	3=	85	Somalia	180	9

Source: Transparency International (2017).

performance. Questions can be asked (with these, as with political and economic rankings) about the methodology and about underlying biases, care must be taken to look not just at rankings but at scores (Mexico, for example, may rank 74th on the Human Development Index, but its score of 0.774 is not far below the 0.798 achieved by 60th ranked Iran), and raw numbers will only tell us so much. How we interpret such numbers is a separate matter altogether.

THE FUTURE OF COMPARATIVE GOVERNMENT AND POLITICS

Politics is as old as human society, organized government dates back thousands of years, and even the idea of the state dates back several hundred years. All of which makes it surprising that comparative politics as we define it today is a relatively young field of study. In an organized social scientific sense, we have only been studying government and politics comparatively since the late 19th century. However, the focus for decades was more on single-country studies with an emphasis on the 'foreign', rather than truly comparative studies. Also, most of today's states are relatively new creations, having been created only since the end of World War II. Finally, while democracy is deeply studied (and yet, even so, surprisingly poorly understood), authoritarian systems have been much less thoroughly studied.

All of which is by way of emphasizing that the study of comparative government and politics remains full of intriguing and as-yet untapped possibilities. There is no doubting its importance, but we have yet to even agree how to categorize or rank states in a way that helps us find our way through the maze of government in its many contrasting forms: there is broad agreement between the findings of the Democracy Index and Freedom in the World (and the findings of many other ranking systems that have been developed), and yet there are also contradictions. There is also much theoretical and methodological disagreement on the best way of approaching comparison, which is complicated by the uneven depth and quality of the information we have gathered about different political systems. In short, the future of comparative government and politics is wide open: many key questions remain unanswered, and – as we will see in Chapter 2 – political systems continue to change, posing fascinating new questions.

DISCUSSION QUESTIONS

1. What is the main purpose of the comparative study of politics?
2. Is the state still the most useful level of analysis in comparative politics?
3. How many cases, and what kinds of cases, are needed to allow for meaningful comparison?
4. Studying most similar systems or most different systems: is one approach better than the other, and – if so – how?
5. What are the relative strengths and weaknesses of the comparative indices described in this chapter?
6. What questions would you like comparative politics to answer?

CHAPTER CONCEPTS

- Adult literacy
- Ethnocentrism
- Infant mortality
- Level of analysis
- Life expectancy
- Most different system
- Methodology
- Most similar system
- Unit of analysis
- Westphalian system

KEY TERMS

- Case
- Comparative method
- Comparative politics
- Corruption Perceptions Index
- Democracy Index
- Freedom in the World
- Gini coefficient
- Globalization
- Government
- Gross domestic product
- Historical method
- Human Development Index
- Nation
- Political culture
- Political economy
- Political goods
- Politics
- Power
- Purchasing power parity
- Qualitative method
- Quantitative method
- State
- Three Worlds system
- Typology
- Variable

COMPARATIVE GOVERNMENT AND POLITICS ONLINE

Political Resources on the Net: www.politicalresources.net
United Nations: www.un.org
Democracy Index: www.eiu.com/home.aspx
Freedom in the World: https://freedomhouse.org
Fraser Institute: www.fraserinstitute.org
UN Development Programme: http://hdr.undp.org
World Bank World Development Indicators: https://datacatalog.worldbank.org/dataset/world–development–indicators
BBC News: www.bbc.com/news

FURTHER READING

Diamond, Larry, and Marc F. Plattner (eds) (2016) *Democracy in Decline?* (2016) (Johns Hopkins University Press). One of the growing number of assessments about the worrying reversal faced by democracy worldwide.

Dogan, Mattei, and Dominique Pelassy (1990) *How to Compare Nations: Strategies in Comparative Politics,* 2nd edn (Chatham House Publishers). A survey of the methods and approaches of comparative politics, still widely cited despite its age.

Landman, Todd, and Edzia Carvalho (2017) *Issues and Methods in Comparative Politics*, 4th edn (Rout-ledge). A concise survey of the methods and approaches to comparison, including chapters on particular themes in comparative politics.

Lim, Timothy C. (2016) *Doing Comparative Politics: An Introduction to Approaches and Issues*, 3rd edn (Lynne Rienner). A useful survey of comparative methods, with chapters addressing such questions as why states are poor and how transitions to democracy occur.

Lowndes, Vivien, David Marsh and Gerry Stoker (2018) *Theory and Methods in Political Science*, 4th edn (Red Globe Press). A survey of the different theoretical and methodological approaches to the study of political science.

Munck, Gerardo L., and Richard Snyder (2007) *Passion, Craft, and Method in Comparative Politics* (Johns Hopkins University Press). For students who want to take their study of comparative politics to a deeper level, this is an informative series of interviews with some of the leading names in the field, and includes a survey chapter on the past and present of comparative politics.

Visit **www.macmillanihe.com/McCormick-Cases** to access additional materials to support teaching and learning.

POLITICAL SYSTEMS

2

CONTENTS

- Overview
- Political development
- Political culture
- Constitutions
- Executives
- Legislatures
- Judiciaries
- Sub-national government
- Elections
- Political parties
- The future of political systems

PREVIEW

This chapter provides the foundation for the comparisons we will be making among our twelve cases, offering an overview of the major constituent parts of the world's national political systems. In each case, we will be looking at political development and political culture, at constitutions, at the key institutions of government (executives, legislatures, judiciaries, and sub-national government), and at elections and political parties. Before going to that level of analysis, this chapter offers a comparative survey of each of these topics, showing the variety of options available and the many different forms in which the key elements of political systems exist, whether in democracies or in authoritarian states. It soon becomes clear that there is nothing approaching a common template for government and politics, and that the rules adopted for the design of political systems have a variety of origins and effects, and continue to evolve ceaselessly.

KEY ARGUMENTS

- There are many levels of analysis available in comparative government and politics, but the usual point of reference is the state, meaning that we first need to understand whole political systems.

- History and culture are both key to understanding how government and politics works; we need to know both how political systems evolved, and their underlying values.

- Constitutions offer a guide to the structure of political systems, although care must be taken to distinguish constitutional claims from political realities.

- Executives, legislatures, and judiciaries lie at the heart of all political systems, their absolute and relative powers driving our understanding of the dynamics of those systems.

- Almost all political systems are either unitary or federal in nature, with federalism mainly limited to states that are large and/or heterogeneous.

- Elections and parties lie at the heart of the relationship between governments and the governed, but they come in many different forms, with differing results.

OVERVIEW

As we saw in Chapter 1, there are multiple levels of analysis available to us when we compare government and politics, ranging from individual voters through local and regional communities to the global system. The standard point of reference, though, is the state, and this book contains chapters on a representative selection of twelve such states, chosen for their political and geographical variety. They have similarities and differences, but one quality they all have in common is a **political system**. Whether they are democratic or authoritarian, large or small, young or old, each has a set of institutions, rules, and procedures through which they are governed, and which fulfil the same three core functions:

Political system
The institutions, rules, and procedures that shape how people interact in their effort to make and implement collective decisions.

◆ The executive is responsible mainly for executing laws and policies, providing leadership and direction, and setting the tone and character of government.
◆ The legislature is responsible mainly for making, shaping, and confirming the laws that are the basis for government, representing the interests of citizens (in democracies, at least), and deliberating on issues of national importance.
◆ The judiciary is responsible mainly for making sure that governments and citizens adhere to the rules of the system, as outlined in the constitution.

Political systems come in many and varied forms, all of them reflecting the histories, needs, habits, tolerances, norms, and expectations of the societies in which they are found. They all have some kind of executive, for example, they might be led by absolute monarchs, constitutional monarchs, authoritarian presidents, presidents who share powers with legislatures, presidents who share powers with prime ministers, or prime ministers who come out of the legislature. Executives will come to office differently, and will have different terms of office, different sets of responsibilities, and different relationships with the other institutions. A similar range of differences can be found in legislatures, judiciaries, electoral systems, and political parties; the core qualities of each are the same, but they fulfil their functions differently, the balance among them is different, and they reflect the different forms in which democratic and authoritarian systems exist and function.

In each of our twelve cases, we will be looking closely at how political institutions work, and at how people relate to them through different forms of participation. It is in these details that we find the personality and character of different political systems. The details reveal and reflect not just the rules of government, but the political culture of societies, the power of governments, the rights of citizens, and the nature of the relationship between governments and the governed. Before we do that, however, we need to look more broadly at the institutions and processes that lie at the heart of government around the world, and at the different types and forms in which they come. Think of this chapter as offering a horizontal view across all political systems, and as a preview to the more detailed vertical views offered by the twelve cases.

POLITICAL DEVELOPMENT

Each of the cases in this book begins with a summary history of its political development, focusing on the key events and personalities that help explain how its modern political system emerged and was shaped. Just as we can never really know someone else without knowing where they come from and the experiences they have undergone, so it is difficult to fully appreciate the contemporary political arrangements of a country without knowing something about its past. Consider these examples:

◆ To understand Germany and Japan, we need to know how their new political systems were designed after World War II, and to grasp the steps taken in order to make sure that neither country would once again fall victim to political extremism.
◆ The political systems of six of our cases – the United States, France, Mexico, Russia, China, and Iran – were born out of revolution, so it is important to understand the background to those revolutions and the extent to which revolutionary ideals are currently reflected (or not) in their political systems.
◆ Britain is unique among the cases in having a long history of evolutionary political development. Since the last successful invasion of the island of Great Britain in 1066, it has experienced two civil wars and sometimes

considerable violence, but it has seen none of the defining moments at which important changes or departures were made from which we can date the beginning of its modern political system.

◆ We cannot fully understand Turkey today without understanding its emergence from the Ottoman Empire, the way in which its efforts to build democracy were three times interrupted by military coups, and the explanations for its recent drift to authoritarianism.

◆ We cannot fully understand India or Nigeria without looking at their colonial past and taking into consideration the impact of colonialism on the challenges they have faced in building a sustainable political system; India has had more success to date than Nigeria.

Political systems are never static, and constantly evolve according to a mix of domestic and external pressures and needs. Different countries vary particularly in terms of their experiences with democracy and authoritarianism, of their changing needs and circumstances, of the effects of international pressures, and of the levels of stability they have experienced – or failed to achieve – in building their political systems. In looking at political development, it is important to understand how governing institutions were shaped, how the balance of power among political parties has changed, and how electoral systems evolved to become what they are today.

POLITICAL CULTURE

As we saw in Chapter 1, the term *culture* is contested. In spite of this, it is used in a political sense to describe the underlying set of attitudes, norms and beliefs that colour and shape the way in which a political community functions. It asks what is considered usual or unusual, what is considered normal or abnormal, and even what kinds of myths surround the way in which government is thought to work, or citizens are thought to view politics and government. Are they engaged or disengaged, hopeful or cynical, trustful or distrustful, combative or cooperative, and so on.

Each of the cases in this book considers the political culture of the state, the logic being that it is harder to understand political institutions, and the ways in which people relate to government, without first understanding the character of the political environment. Although the features of political culture are typically founded in the history of a state, it is important to note the following points:

◆ All states contain different sets of political values depending on the degree of their stability and diversity: political culture will differ by region, age, social class, political ideology, or ethnicity, and will change with time, influenced by new circumstances and expectations.

◆ A relatively homogeneous country such as Germany, Iran, Japan, or Mexico will have a more settled political culture than a country that is more diverse, such as Britain, India, Nigeria, or Turkey. A distinction must be made between elite political culture, which describes the view of those who are closest to the centres of power, and the views about political culture of those who live more on the margins of national politics; see Comparing Political Culture 2.

◆ In the cases of countries such as India and Nigeria that have emerged from long spells of domination or influence by foreign powers, a distinction must be made between domestic and foreign political values.

Pinning down the political culture of a state is not always easy, because much of what we know about its features come from survey research, and while we have a deep body of results from such research in democracies, the same is not always true of authoritarian states; it is often harder and more dangerous to carry out surveys in countries where governments are closed and where citizens are suspicious of pollsters. As we proceed through the cases in this book, then, the certainties about the features of their political cultures decline.

Constitution
A document or set of documents that outlines the powers, institutions, and structure of government, the responsibilities of the government, and the rights of citizens.

CONSTITUTIONS

At the heart of all political systems lies a **constitution**. This is a document (or a set of documents) that stands as the manual of government, or a 'power map' that can be used to identify the powers of government and the limits on those powers. Every state has one, and they are typically paired with courts whose job is to protect the constitution, and to offer interpretations of its meaning in the event of disputes or uncertainty. There is no universal

COMPARING POLITICAL CULTURE 2
Elitism vs. populism

In democracies, at least, government officials are supposed to be the servants and the representatives of citizens. They are elected by citizens and their job is to consider the needs of society, to identify and solve problems, and to keep the administrative process running. But the reality of being elected to an office that comes with much more power than is available to the average person immediately creates a distance between the governed and the government. Elected officials are in demand, they are approached and influenced by multiple other people with power, and the most powerful among them – notably presidents and prime ministers – can become celebrities, and perhaps the best known and most instantly recognizable members of their communities or states. Little surprise, then, that we often witness the creation of a governing class or elite with an elevated sense of its importance and abilities.

Elitism is not something that most people welcome, and in this sense it is not an element of political culture that grows from below (as do most features of political culture). Instead, it is imposed from above as those in power seek to protect the interests of those who elected them, or who funded their election campaigns, or who belong to their group; such groups may be defined by social class, ethnicity, religion, education, or wealth. In authoritarian states, the problem of elitism is both a cause and an effect of the divisions within society and of the centralization of power: the leader sits at the peak of a pyramid of supporters who must be kept content and engaged, preferably to the exclusion of the members of all other competing groups in that society. Ethnic elites are prominent in Nigeria, for example, while party elites are prominent in China, and religious elites in Iran.

In many democracies – including Britain and the United States – concerns about the power of elites (usually vaguely defined as those with more wealth, more political power, more privileges, and more opportunities) has fed in to the recent revival of populism. This claims to focus on the needs of ordinary people, in contrast to the authority of elites, with several parties and leaders having won new support on the foundation of promising to take on the elite (a view famously encapsulated in Donald Trump's comment as a presidential candidate that he would 'drain the swamp' in Washington DC). It is interesting, though, to see how often populist leaders and parties present themselves as morally superior to the existing political class, and how often the outsiders and populists themselves become insiders and members of a new political elite.

Elitism
The belief or philosophy that a particular group of people in a society have positions or qualities that give them advantages and powers over others.

Populism
The belief or philosophy that ordinary people are at a disadvantage in political decisions, and that they have been marginalized at the expense of the growing wealth and authority of elites.

---

template for a constitution (see Table 2.1), one of the core differences being between those that are codified (existing in a single, structured document, as with most of the cases in this book) and those that are uncodified (found in a cluster of different documents, most famously in the case of the British constitution).

Despite their differences in structure and form, most constitutions fulfil the same four functions:

◆ They outline the broad goals of a state, often using inspirational language and stirring declarations. Hence the US constitution opens with goals that include forming 'a more perfect union' and ensuring 'domestic tranquility', while the Japanese constitution describes government as 'a sacred trust of the people', and the Nigerian constitution notes the dedication of the people to 'the promotion of inter-African solidarity, world peace, international co-operation and understanding'.

◆ They outline the organization and the institutions of government, explaining what each is expected to do, how officeholders come to power, their tasks once in office, and the limitations (if any) on their terms in office.

◆ They describe the limits on the powers of government, and the rights of citizens as they relate to government, typically including freedom of religion, speech, and the press.

◆ They outline the process by which the constitution can be formally amended.

Table 2.1 Comparing constitutions

Country	Date of modern state formation	Date of current constitution	Number of constitutions since formation of state	System type
UK	Debatable. Perhaps 1066	No clear date	1	Unitary parliamentary system with constitutional monarchy.
Germany	1871	1949	3	Federal parliamentary republic.
USA	1776	1789	2	Federal presidential republic.
Japan	1868	1947	2	Unitary parliamentary system with constitutional monarchy.
France	1789	1958	17	Unitary semi-presidential republic. Constitution of the Fifth Republic.
India	1947	1950	1	Federal parliamentary republic.
Mexico	1821	1917	5	Federal presidential republic.
Nigeria	1960	1999	4	Federal presidential republic. Constitution of the Fourth Republic.
Turkey	1923	1982	6	Unitary presidential republic.
Russia	1991	1993	1	Federal semi-presidential republic.
China	1949	1982	4	Unitary communist republic.
Iran	Debatable	1979	2	Unitary Islamic republic.

Note: Many of the dates listed are debatable, depending on how we define the birth of a modern state, and how we define a constitution.

Constitutions do not contain all the rules of government and in fact usually contain many generalities and ambiguities, allowing them to be adapted to meet the changing needs of the societies to which they apply. They also rarely cover every detail of the way in which political systems work: they are supplemented by laws and judicial interpretations, and much of what governments do comes down to a combination of unwritten understandings, customs, and traditions, few (if any) of which are committed to paper. For example, political parties and interest groups were not anticipated by older European constitutions, and yet they have become key parts of most political systems without their work being committed to constitutions (although they will be held accountable for unconstitutional behaviour).

There are many ways of assessing the performance of constitutions, but three stand out: their age, the number of times they have been amended, and the size of the gap between the principles they espouse and the way government functions in practice. The first of these – longevity – is not by itself a measure of performance, particularly since there has been a recent rash of constitution-making: 105 countries adopted new constitutions between 1990 and 2014 (Comparative Constitutions Project, 2018). The age of a constitution must therefore be placed within its wider context, as the following examples show:

◆ Germany and Japan adopted new constitutions in the wake of their defeat in World War II, and France developed an entirely new political system in 1958, adopting its 17th constitution since the 1789 revolution. However, there is nothing to suggest that the current German or French political systems are in danger of collapsing in the same way as some of their predecessors, and in fact their current constitutions may well be the most efficient and effective that either country has ever had.

◆ Mexico – a flawed democracy – has a constitution that is now more than a century old, which might be interpreted as a good sign. However, it has been amended so often as to raise questions about the extent to which the original constitution really applies any more, and Mexicans often have worried conversations about their unfinished revolution.

◆ In the cases of several Latin American states with a long history of political instability, the problems are reflected in large numbers of constitutions: the Dominican Republic has had 32, Venezuela 26, Haiti 23, and Ecuador 20. At the same time, there are authoritarian regimes in other parts of the world which appear to have constitutional stability but where governments often interfere with the work of courts, intimidate their members, and try to force through amendments that would strengthen their powers relative to their citizens (see Ginsburg and Simpser, 2014).

Regarding the number of times a constitution has been amended, there are different ways of interpreting this. Stability and consistency are both desirable, but a long-standing constitution with few amendments might have that record either because it is difficult to change (which can be a problem) or because the constitution may have been allowed to fall behind the times. Conversely, a constitution that has been amended many times might seem to be keeping up with changing demands, but it may also suffer from being too easy to change (also potentially a problem) or may have been meddled with too much for political ends.

The most important performance indicator of a constitution is the gap between theory and practice. Many constitutions include noble principles and objectives, but they mean little unless they are respected and applied. The US Constitution, for example, opens with a reference to the need to 'promote the general Welfare, and secure the Blessings of Liberty', but it was written by a group of white men, many of them slave-owners, and most black men were denied the right to vote in the United States for nearly 90 years after its ratification, and women for more than 120 years. Despite the claims made about liberty, freedom, and democracy in the United States, the American model of democracy has many imperfections; these include a manipulated electoral system, the problems inherent in having only two major national political parties, and the persistence of discrimination against women, ethnic minorities, and the LGBTQ community.

In comparing the political effect of constitutions, there are many additional questions that we can ask. Where does the focus of political power lie? How clearly are the lines of accountability drawn? Is government sufficiently transparent and responsive? Are the variety of a society's needs adequately and fairly reflected in the structure and workings of government? These are all important questions, and constitutions – while rarely providing complete or final answers – are the prime point of reference in trying to develop answers. At the same time, though, we need to be clear about the extent to which constitutions are respected and applied.

EXECUTIVES

The task of a political **executive** is to oversee the execution of laws and policies. However, executives do much more than this functional description suggests: they also lead, inspire (positively or negatively), set the tone of government, and stand as the individuals who are seen to represent the entire government, as well as the country in its dealings with other countries (see Rhodes and Hart, 2014). Although executives are most visibly the people who hold the post of president or prime minister, or the king or queen in absolute monarchies, the executive is much more than one person; most leaders govern with a supporting council of ministers or advisory council, and oversee bureaucracies responsible for the day-to-day operations of government.

Every state has an executive, and each of them carries out the same core function, but they differ in the way they are structured, in how officeholders come to power, and in how the executive relates to the other parts of government and to citizens. There are five different models (summarized in Table 2.2), the key distinction among them being the nature of the relationship between the executive and the legislature.

Parliamentary executive

In this model, found in Britain and all those countries that have adopted the British parliamentary system, the executive consists of a prime minister (or the chancellor in Germany and Austria) and a **cabinet** of ministers, is drawn from the legislature, cannot hold office without majority support (or, at least, strong minority support) in the legislature, and coexists

Executive
The part of government responsible for providing leadership and executing laws and policies, typically with a single leader at the head of a pyramid of government ministers and bureaucrats.

Cabinet
The group of heads of government departments and senior administrators who act collectively as the government or the administration. Also sometimes known as a council of ministers.

Table 2.2 Comparing executives

Type	Features	Cases
Parliamentary	Executive emerges from the legislature and remains accountable to it, and must maintain a legislative majority in order to remain in office.	Australia, UK, Canada, Germany, India, Italy, Japan.
Limited presidential	Executive elected separately from the legislature, with powers limited by the constitution and by the legislature.	Brazil, Mexico, Nigeria, Turkey, USA.
Semi-presidential	Executive elected separately from the legislature, and coexists with an appointed prime minister.	Austria, Egypt, Finland, France, Portugal, Russia, and some Eastern European states.
Unlimited presidential	Executive elected separately from the legislature, but faces few constitutional or political limits.	China, Democratic Republic of Congo, North Korea, Zimbabwe.
Absolute monarchy	A ruling sovereign exerts control, with other members of the royal family in key political and military positions.	None of the cases in this book, but examples include Brunei, Oman, Saudi Arabia, Swaziland.

with a symbolic head of state (see Comparing Government 2). There is no constitutional limit to how long a prime minister stays in office, provided elections are held on the required schedule, and the prime minister keeps the support of enough members of the legislature to form and lead a government.

Under this arrangement, the executive and the legislature are fused, because prime ministers and cabinets are tied to the legislature, and most have seats in the legislature. If members of the governing party or coalition vote against the government or leave the governing coalition, the prime minister's position is weakened, and the executive could even fall if there is a rebellion among members of the governing party or coalition or if the prime minister loses a vote of confidence.

Limited presidential executive

In this model, found in the United States, most of Latin America, and several African and Asian states (see Mezey, 2013), the executive is limited in the sense that it shares powers with other institutions. There is a president elected separately from the legislature for a limited number of fixed-length terms, and who has most of the powers that are divided in the parliamentary system between the head of state and the head of government. Ministers (or secretaries) are usually nominated by the president and confirmed by one of the chambers of the legislature. Presidents are not formally leaders of their parties, and their holding office does not depend on them having the support of a majority of members of the legislature.

Under this arrangement, the executive and the legislature are separate, because neither the president nor members of the cabinet can be members of the legislature, and there is a system of checks and balances between the two. Presidents have constitutional limits placed on their powers, but they also have independent responsibilities (particularly over foreign policy); it helps if they have a sympathetic legislature, but they can outwit a hostile legislature if they are able strategists, and they usually have the power to veto proposals from the legislature. In contrast to the parliamentary executive, they do not lose office if there is a rebellion among members of their party in the legislature, and they do not usually face votes of confidence; they can usually only be removed by successful impeachment.

Semi-presidential executive

In this model, found most famously in France and Russia (see Elgie, 2011) and also known as a dual executive, executive powers are divided between an elected executive president serving fixed (but not always limited) terms and a prime minister and cabinet who head the largest party or coalition in the legislature. The president is head of state but also has considerable powers over policymaking, sharing these with the prime minister in his or her role as head of government. The president and the prime minister do not need to come from the same party; if they do, the prime minister tends to be a functionary of the president, but if they do not, the prime minister can develop more independence.

Under this arrangement, the executive and the legislature are separate, but the president depends on having the cooperation of the prime minister – and preferably the support of a majority of members of the legislature – in order to govern effectively. There is no clear separation of powers, and shrewd presidents can take the credit for successful policies while blaming their prime ministers for failed policies. Presidents do not lose office if there is a rebellion among members of their party in the legislature, and they do not face votes of confidence. If voters return the opposition to power in a legislative election, presidents can find their hands tied. However, if no one party has a majority a president can also exploit divisions in the legislature to make policy.

COMPARING GOVERNMENT 2
Heads of state and government

Executives do more than oversee the execution of policy and law; they also provide leadership and set the national agenda, and are expected not just to be administrators but to inspire as well. This distinction between the symbolic and the political is found most clearly in the two different functions of an executive: to represent the interests of the state and to run the government.

A **head of state** is someone who may or may not be popularly elected but who uses his or her office to represent – theoretically, at least – the interests, goals, and values of the entire population. The head of state is expected to be politically neutral, to look beyond the immediate interests of the incumbent government, to be a symbol of the state and its people, and to be the primary non-political representative of the state in dealings with other states. Heads of state may have a few political powers, but only enough to support their roles as arbiters (for example, stepping in to nominate a head of government if no one party or coalition wins a majority of seats in the legislature). They will have few, if any, powers of appointment to political office.

In terms of how they go about allocating the responsibilities of the head of state, most countries have opted for one of three models:

◆ Some – including Britain, Spain, Belgium, Denmark, Norway, and Japan – still have a **constitutional monarchy**, a position that was once powerful but that has lost most of its formal political powers.
◆ Some – such as those European states that no longer have a monarch, including Italy and Germany – have opted for non-executive presidents. These may be former politicians, but as presidents are expected to be neutral and symbolic figureheads.
◆ Others have opted to combine the functions of head of state and head of government in a single office. This is true of presidential executives such as those found in the United States, most of Latin America, and much of sub-Saharan Africa.

A **head of government** is an elected leader with a set of values and goals that appeals to the people who voted him or her into office. Heads of government have agendas driven by ideological, economic, religious, regional, or nationalistic preferences. They usually rely heavily on the support of their parties, and they tend to be concerned mainly with the interests of those who paid their campaign expenses or voted them into office. Once in office, they appoint all or most of the other senior members of government, who then become part of their administration.

Head of state
The figurehead leader of a state, who may be elected or appointed, or – in the case of monarchs – may inherit the position.

Constitutional monarchy
A hereditary monarchy whose powers (typically reduced from what they once were) are limited by the constitution.

Head of government
The elected leader of a government, who comes to office because of the support of voters who identify with his/her party and platform.

Two of the world's most prominent authoritarian leaders – President Xi Jinping of China (left) and Russia's President Vladimir Putin (right) – review a military honour guard during a welcoming ceremony in Beijing at the start of a state visit to China by Putin.
Source: Greg Baker/AFP/Getty Images.

Unlimited presidential executive

Personal rule
A phenomenon in which a leader accumulates so much power, and such a key role in the political system, that government is shaped and operated on the basis of a single person rather than the office of the executive.

This model at first looks much like the presidential executive, but it is structured in such a way that presidents have greater powers and serve longer terms in office; even lifetime terms if they can keep the support of the elite that is usually the foundation of their power (see Ezrow and Frantz, 2011). They are not, to be sure, literally unlimited in what they can do, but they have much more freedom to govern than is the case with limited presidential executives. This model is found in China and widely through sub-Saharan Africa, where leaders can sometimes accumulate so much power that the executive evolves into a system of **personal rule** focused on a person rather than the office they hold. The president coexists with a legislature, but the president's party is usually the dominant party and the president has so many powers that the legislature is little more than a rubber-stamp institution. There may be limits on the length of presidential terms, but there are no limits on the number of terms, and the president is usually assured of re-election. The focus of power lies with the executive, opening the door to authoritarian leadership.

Absolute monarchy

Historically, many societies were governed by hereditary monarchs who had almost complete control over government, answering only – if to anyone – to a deity, and in some cases being themselves considered living deities. Those days are long gone, but there are still a few countries that have absolute monarchs who come to the office through heredity, hold their offices for life, and are not subject to much in the way of accountability to voters or to other government institutions. (Absolute monarchies should not be confused with constitutional monarchies; see Comparing Government 2.)

As these different examples show, the role of an executive is dependent both upon the powers of the office and the relationship with the legislature. Their relative powers depend on a complex combination of the terms of the office, the leadership qualities of the officeholder, their relationship with the legislature, and their standing in public opinion. While the parliamentary executive and the semi-presidential executive seem to put too much power in the hands of one person, it is not unqualified power; leaders in these systems rely heavily on the base of their support in the legislature.

LEGISLATURES

Although the core task of a **legislature** is to make laws, the story does not end there. The legislative process normally involves the introduction of proposals (or bills), discussion and amendment, and the acceptance or rejection of those proposals. The effect of these duties is to give legislatures several different roles in the political system, ranging from representation to oversight; see Figure 2.1 (see Arter, 2013). In democracies, at least, they are the institutions in which the interests of citizens are most clearly represented. They are usually elected directly by voters, and their major tasks are to protect and promote the interests of society, and to review and approve new laws.

> **Legislature**
> A multi-member representative body which debates public issues and considers and decides upon proposals for new laws and policies.

Although the meaning of the term *representation* might seem obvious, there are many ways in which it can be defined and understood, and it is ironic that in spite of their closeness to voters, legislatures and their members are often not well regarded; they are widely criticized for the slowness and the often-partisan nature of their decision-making. In authoritarian regimes, meanwhile, they are often seen as weak, and as doing little more than providing a fig leaf of legitimacy. The latter have not been as thoroughly studied as their democratic counterparts, though, and recent research suggests that their functions may be more nuanced. Allmark (2012), for example, finds that in some cases they can be a platform for dissent, can help strengthen the domestic opposition, and can promote the political education of citizens.

Function	Features
Representation	Members represent and promote the interests of those who elected them, usually under a party label.
Legislation	Whatever the source of bills, legislatures are responsible for reviewing, amending, and approving new laws.
Spending	Legislatures approve or reject the annual budget prepared by the government.
Making governments	In most parliamentary systems, the government emerges from the legislature and must retain its confidence.
Deliberation	Legislatures debate and provide a public airing for matters of public importance.
Oversight	Legislatures are responsible for overseeing or scrutinizing the executive, keeping it accountable.

Figure 2.1 The functions of legislatures
In authoritarian systems, legislatures play quite different roles: providing an impression of legitimacy, being used to incorporate opponents into the regime, representing local interests, providing a pool of potential recruits to the elite, and acting as a safety valve through which leaders can make concessions without giving up control.

Relationship with the executive

Most of the world's democratic legislatures are deliberative bodies that tend to follow the lead of the executive rather than having any real independence or the ability to set the policy agenda. Particularly in parliamentary systems such as Britain, Japan, and Canada, where the prime minister and most members of the cabinet are also members of the legislature, and where their ability to lead depends on party discipline within the legislature, the powers of legislatures relative to the executive have tended to decline. Hence they have become more a source of votes and support for the goals of the executive than a source of key policy initiatives or places where important decisions are taken. This is particularly true in more authoritarian systems, such as China or Egypt, where the legislature is little more than a rubber stamp for the policies of the leadership, which uses it to legitimize power.

The only exceptions to these deliberative legislatures can be found in the United States and in political systems that have adopted the US model. Where there is a formal separation of powers and a system of checks and balances, legislatures in these examples become important sources of policy initiatives, and executives must often work hard to win the support of legislators to see their pet programmes voted into law. While a failure to win an important vote in a parliamentary system could result in the fall of the government and the resignation of the prime minister, it is not unusual to see votes in the US Congress go against the plans of the president.

Unicameral or bicameral?

Legislatures are structured in different ways, depending on how they are elected and what kind of representation they are expected to provide; see Table 2.3. The most fundamental question about structure concerns whether they have one chamber or two. Even though nine of our twelve cases have bicameral legislatures, these are relatively rare: about 60 per cent of the world's national legislatures are unicameral. Two chambers are normally found in large or diverse countries and are designed to give two different kinds of representation. In federal systems such as

Table 2.3 Comparing legislatures

Country	Name	Number of chambers	Number of representatives	Legislative terms (years)
UK	Parliament	2	790 upper 650 lower	Upper unelected 5 lower
Germany	Bundestag	1*	Variable, with base of 598	4
USA	Congress	2	100 upper 435 lower	6 upper 2 lower
Japan	Diet	2	242 upper 465 lower	6 upper 4 lower
France	National Assembly	2	348 upper 577 lower	6 upper 5 lower
India	Parliament	2	250 upper 545 lower	6 upper 5 lower
Mexico	National Congress	2	128 upper 500 lower	6 upper 3 lower
Nigeria	National Assembly	2	109 upper 360 lower	4 upper 4 lower
Turkey	Grand National Assembly	1	600	4
Russia	Federal Assembly	2	170 upper 450 lower	5 upper 5 lower
China	National People's Congress	1	Nearly 3,000	5
Iran	Majlis	1	290	4

* See Chapter 4 for discussion on whether the Bundesrat in Germany constitutes a second chamber.

in Australia, Germany, India, and the United States, the upper chambers normally provide equal representation for states, regardless of how big or small they are, while lower chambers give equal representation to the people. Legislation will normally have to go through the same stages in both chambers, but – at least in unitary systems – upper chambers will often be weaker than lower chambers and may only have the power of delay. For their part, lower chambers tend to be designed to represent the people in the sense that members come from districts of equal size. In most parliamentary systems, the executive – the prime minister and cabinet – comes from the lower chamber, giving it more political significance.

The nature of representation

Legislatures are the embodiment of representative democracy, meaning that voters elect into office legislators who are then expected to represent their views when policies are debated and bills are voted upon. In authoritarian systems, where elections are manipulated and executives wield most of the power, this process is usually a sham, and most people know it. Nowhere is this more obvious than in China, where the Chinese Communist Party dominates the fielding of candidates at elections, where the National People's Congress meets once annually for sessions of two or three weeks, and where 'representatives' do little more than discuss and endorse decisions already taken by the party.

Even in democracies, there are questions about how legislators represent the views of voters (see Loewenberg, 2016). Much of the debate revolves around the four different ways of understanding representation outlined by Hanna Pitkin (1967):

◆ *Formalistic* representation is concerned with rules, asking how representatives come to office, how they enforce their decisions, how they respond to their constituents, and how they are held accountable by voters.
◆ *Descriptive* representation asks about the extent to which representatives resemble their constituents, the underlying logic that a legislature should be a model of society in the sense that it should be proportional by gender, ethnicity, income, employment, religion, and so on.
◆ *Symbolic* representation is concerned with performance, asking how representatives are seen by their constituents: are they competent, are they partisan, are they approachable, and so on.
◆ *Substantive* representation is concerned with responsiveness, asking how far representatives go in serving the best interests of their voters.

The nature of representation does not stop here, but should also take account of the behaviour of legislators, in the sense of how they relate to the voters. Here, there are at least three options:

◆ The *delegate* model suggests that they should be the mouthpieces of voters, having no autonomy, and acting as delegates for the interests of those who elected them, no matter what the broader national interest.
◆ The *trustee* model suggests that voters give representatives the autonomy to use their best judgement and to act in favour of the greater good, even if it sometimes goes against the short-term interests of their voters or their district.
◆ The *partisan* model is based on the idea of representatives as members of a party, and the expectation that they will make decisions in line with party policy.

None of these models of representation or behaviour fully captures the character of legislatures in all places and at all times, but they offer useful points of reference, providing insight into the work of legislatures. In parliamentary systems, for example, where party discipline is usually tight and members of the same party are expected to vote as a group, legislators will tend to be led from above rather than from below. This means that they will regularly vote as their party leaders instruct rather than being influenced by the views of their constituents or of special interests. In presidential systems, by contrast, legislators are elected separately from the president, and while there is still pressure and expectations from both the executive and parties, there is more chance of legislators voting independently.

JUDICIARIES

Constitutions are neither self-made nor self-implementing, and they need the support of institutions that can enforce their provisions by striking down offending laws and practices. This role has fallen to the **judiciary**; courts are collectively the third branch or element of

Judiciary
A collective term for the judges within the system of courts that interpret and apply the law in keeping with the constitution.

Judicial review
The process by which a judiciary rules on the laws or actions of government on the basis of its interpretation of the constitution.

government, using their powers of **judicial review** to adjudicate legal disputes and to interpret the meaning and the constitutionality of laws and of the actions of government (see Lee, 2011). Members of a judiciary are not expected to make law but only to issue judgements on laws in relation to the constitution. They are also expected to follow rather than lead, in the sense that they are not expected to significantly change the meaning of the law. Finally, they are expected to be independent, and to be protected from any kind of external pressures or influences. But the ideal of being objective and independent is difficult to achieve – judges will come to the job with their own sets of values and their own ideologies, and these will colour how they see the world and how they interpret the law.

As with executives and legislatures, every state has a judicial system, but they differ in how they are structured, in the relationship between the courts and the other parts of government, and in how judges come to office and how long they can serve; see Table 2.4.

Types of courts

Structurally, there are two main options:

Concrete review
Judgements made on the constitutional validity of law in the context of a specific case. Sometimes known as the American model.

◆ *Supreme court.* As the name implies, a supreme court is the highest court within a jurisdiction, whose decisions are not subject to review by any other court. Supreme courts are usually the final court of appeal, listening – if they choose – to cases appealed from a lower level. They also mainly use **concrete review**, meaning that they ask whether, given the facts of the particular case, the decision reached at lower level was compatible with the constitution.

Table 2.4 Comparing judiciaries

Country	Type of court	Number of members	Tenure	Appointment process
UK	Supreme	12	Lifetime.	Appointed by monarch on advice of prime minister, based on recommendations of selection commission.
Germany	Constitutional	16	12-year terms, age limit 68.	Half each elected by Bundestag and Bundesrat.
USA	Supreme	9	Lifetime.	Nominated by president, confirmed by Senate.
Japan	Supreme	15	Age limit of 70.	Appointed by cabinet based on list submitted by court.
France	Constitutional	Up to 12	Single 9 years.	Three each appointed by president and both chambers of legislature.
India	Supreme	31	No fixed terms; age limit 65.	Appointed by president on recommendation of Chief Justice and four senior judges.
Mexico	Supreme	11	Single 15 years.	Nominated by president, confirmed by Senate.
Nigeria	Supreme	14	Age limit of 70.	Nominated by president, confirmed by Senate or judicial commission.
Turkey	Constitutional	17	Single 12 years.	Three elected by legislature, balance appointed by president from nominations by lower courts.
Russia	Constitutional	19	Age limit of 70.	Nominated by president, confirmed by Federation Council.
China	Supreme	13	5-year terms, limit of two.	Appointed by legislature.
Iran	Constitutional	19	5-year terms, age limit of 70.	Appointed by Supreme Leader.

Members of the Federal Constitutional Court of Germany stand at the opening of a hearing. The court is famous for its independence and for having helped build the constitutional strength of the modern German political system.
Source: Uli Deck/AFP/Getty Images.

♦ *Constitutional court.* Where a supreme court is a judicial body making the final ruling on all appeals (not all of which involve the constitution), a constitutional court is more akin to an additional legislative chamber. In this system, ordinary courts are not empowered to engage in judicial review, with appeals to the supreme court; instead, the review function is exclusive to a separate constitutional authority (see Vanberg, 2015). They mainly practise **abstract review**, judging the intrinsic constitutional validity of a law without limiting themselves to the particular case. In addition, constitutional courts can issue advisory judgements on a bill at the request of the government or legislature, often without the stimulus of a specific case. These latter judgements are often short and are usually unsigned, lacking the legal argument used by supreme courts.

One of the defining features of a successful and stable political system is a belief in the **rule of law**. An effective legal system, in turn, has at least four requirements:

♦ A workable and respected constitution that can form the basis of the system of laws.
♦ Law-making institutions that can develop laws that respond to the needs of the majority while protecting the minority (and allow both groups adequate input into the law-making process).
♦ The effective implementation of those laws by an efficient bureaucracy and police force.
♦ Judiciaries that can be arbiters over the law-making process, ensuring that the actions of government and of individuals, corporations, and other bodies, meet the letter of the law, as well as the terms and spirit of the constitution.

Abstract review
Advice (not usually binding) given by a court on the constitutionality of a law or public policy. Sometimes known as the European model.

Rule of law
The idea that the distribution of power is determined and limited by a system of laws to which all citizens are equally subject.

Restraint vs. activism

Judicial restraint
The view that judges should apply the letter of the law, leaving politics to elected bodies.

Judicial activism
The willingness of judges to venture beyond narrow legal reasoning so as to influence public policy.

A critical question about courts is whether or not they can be independent, and make judgements that are not impacted by political considerations. The trend in recent decades has been away from **judicial restraint** to **judicial activism**, with judges becoming more willing to enter political arenas that would have once been left to elected politicians and national parliaments (see Coutinho et al., 2015). This is explained in part by the increasing reliance on regulation as a tool of government (regulations tend to be more open to judicial challenge than many other kinds of government action), in part by the prestige of the judiciary in the wake of the reduced public standing of executives and legislatures, and in part by the willingness of citizens, corporations, and interest groups to become more active in the judicial arena. The varied levels of judicial independence and activism are, in turn, a function of the terms of appointment of judges.

Nature of appointment

Courts vary in terms of the number of their members, the manner in which judges come to office (whether it is by election or by appointment), the limits on their tenure, and which institutions are involved in appointments and monitoring. For example, Mexican, Russian, and US judges are nominated by the president and confirmed by the upper chamber of the legislature. Meanwhile, France and Poland turn this around by giving the president the power of confirmation, choosing from a list nominated by a judicial council.

As regards terms in office, a few countries – including Britain, the United States, Belgium, the Netherlands, and Denmark – give their justices lifetime appointments, and they can only be removed for serious dereliction of duty. Life terms help give them independence (they do not face the problem of being threatened with non-renewal for not agreeing with the incumbent administration), provide continuity and stability, and ensure that the accumulated abilities and knowledge of judges can be brought to bear on the judicial system. However, life terms also run the danger of creating courts that might lose touch with political opinion, provide fewer opportunities to inject new thinking and values into the work of courts, and can raise the political stakes involved in new appointments. Little surprise, then, that recent appointments to the US Supreme Court have been so politically charged.

By contrast, most courts place term limits on judges; hence those in the European Court of Justice (one of the institutions of the European Union) serve six-year renewable terms, while Indian judges must retire at 65, and Japanese judges at 70. This creates advantages and disadvantages that are opposite to those of lifetime appointments. Term limits open the door to greater political manipulation, raise the danger of too many changes in the direction of judicial thinking, and can result in experienced judges being replaced too quickly by new judges. At the same time, such limits also ensure that fresh thinking is regularly injected into the work of courts, helping them to better keep up with the needs of society.

SUB-NATIONAL GOVERNMENT

Comparative politics tends to focus mostly on government and politics at the national level, but it can just as easily make comparisons at the regional and local levels (local government is the lowest tier, closest to the daily lives of most citizens, while regional government functions somewhere between the local and the national level). The functional equivalents of national constitutions, executives, legislatures, and courts can all be found at some or all these levels.

Unitary system
One in which all significant power rests with the national government, and in which local units of government have little or no independent power.

Many countries have political parties and interest groups that function only at the regional or local level, and local elections are sometimes a key part of the electoral calendar. Also not to be ignored are the ways in which the administration of states are structured, and the balance between the parts and the whole. We might think of states as units, but some of those units are more internally cohesive than others, and a large part of the success or failure of a political system can be measured by the way in which powers and responsibilities are vertically dispersed. The key distinguishing factor in systems of administration is the relative balance of power between national and sub-national levels of government. There are two main options for organizing this.

Unitary system

The most common arrangement for administration is the kind of **unitary system** found in about 90 per cent of the states in the world: most power rests with the national government, while sub-national units of government have relatively little independence. National government is responsible for almost all key policy areas, the primary taxes are national taxes, national elections are more significant than local elections in determining the distribution of power, and local government units can be redesigned and abolished by national government. Of the twelve cases in this book, half are unitary: Britain, Japan, France, Turkey, China, and Iran. With the notable exception of China (and perhaps Britain), these are all either small and/or relatively homogeneous societies where there are too few political and social divisions to make minorities fearful of the hegemony of the majority. This is where unitary systems work best.

Federal system

Much rarer than unitary systems, but being home to about 37 per cent of the world's population, **federal systems** work best in states that are either large, heterogeneous, or based on the voluntary union of previously independent groups of people. There are about two dozen federations in the world (see Map 2.1), including the other half of our cases (Germany, India, Mexico, Nigeria, Russia, and the United States) as well as Australia, Canada, and several smaller states such as Austria, Belgium, and Switzerland. The one country most obviously missing from this list is China, the biggest by population, where the efforts made by the Communist Party to wield control have discouraged it from devolving power in a federal system.

> **Federal system**
> One in which two or more levels of government coexist, each with independent powers and responsibilities.

In a federal system, power is divided between two or more layers of government, each of which has independent powers, with the lower levels having more power than is the case in unitary systems. National (or federal) government is typically responsible for broad economic policy issues, foreign policy, and defence, while local government is usually responsible for policing, education, and other issues, and both levels have their own taxing and law-making powers. The relationship between the parts, and the views about which level should be responsible for what, vary by time and place:

◆ In the United States, federalism was originally seen as the only arrangement that could unite 13 mutually suspicious colonies that had tried several years of confederalism before they agreed to a closer union. At first, states operated with a high degree of independence, but the federal government accumulated more powers (either real or implied), such that the balance has changed in favour of the centre.
◆ In Russia, by contrast, so much power has been accumulated at the centre that much of the Russian form of federalism exists in name only. It is revealing that where members of the upper chamber of the Russian Federal

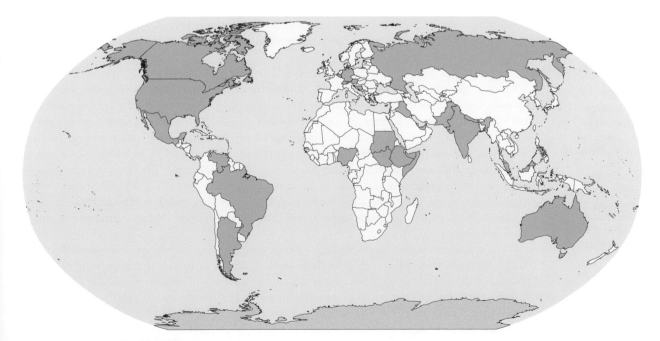

Map 2.1 The world's federations

Assembly – the Federation Council – were once elected or appointed by local government, their appointment is now subject to the approval of the president of Russia.

◆ In Nigeria, the only attempt to create a unitary state led to the overthrow of the government in 1966. The number of states has tripled since 1975 in an effort to ensure the unity of Nigeria by breaking up the major ethnic groups and by addressing the fears of minority ethnic groups that one of the larger groups would dominate national government. Ironically, Nigerian national identity remains weak, but poorer regions of Nigeria are disinclined to see the country break up because they would then lose access to their share of the profits from the oil-rich states in the south.

The way the different communities and elements of a state agree to jointly govern and rule themselves says much about the quality and durability of the political system in which they coexist.

Regional and local government

Although the emphasis in the cases in this book is on government and politics at the national level, it is important to remember that regional and local government within countries can be an important part of the wider political picture. This is certainly true in federal systems, but is true everywhere because sub-national government is closer and usually more approachable, often represents natural communities and reinforces localized identities, and often deals with matters that are of the most immediate interest to citizens: these include education, policing, land use, local economic development, social services, and the provision of basic services. In particular, urban government is important to those parts of the world with the majority of their people living in towns and cities; globally, just over half the population now lives in an urban area. In authoritarian regimes, regional or local leaders can often be important because they have long histories in the community, and national leaders rely on them to maintain control.

ELECTIONS

One of the hallmarks of a democracy is an electoral system in which every citizen can take part in regular, free, and fair elections. Conversely, one of the hallmarks of an authoritarian state is an arrangement in which elections are manipulated so as to ensure the ongoing rule of the elite and to sideline the opposition. Even in the most democratic and egalitarian of situations, however, elections are only fair if every citizen has the same voting power, if every vote cast is counted, and if seats are divided among candidates competing for office in a way that reflects the balance of opinion in the electorate. Unfortunately, this simple formula has proved hard to achieve, because the arithmetic of most electoral systems means that some votes count more than others: no system has yet been worked out that is simple and that accurately reflects voter preferences. We can see the difficulties involved by considering the four different categories into which most electoral systems fall (see Farrell, 2011, and Herron et al., 2018).

Plurality systems

Single-member plurality
An electoral system based on districts that each have one representative, and in which the winner is the candidate with the most votes.

The most common option here is the **single-member plurality** system (also known as winner take all or first-past-the-post), in which all competing candidates for a given office run off against each other, and the one with the most votes is the winner. The system is used to elect presidents as well as legislatures; in the case of the latter, a country is divided into districts with roughly equal population size, and each district is contested by as many candidates as meet the qualifications needed to run (such as age and citizenship). Every voter casts a single vote, and the candidate who wins the most votes wins the district. They only need to win more than anyone else (a plurality), and a majority is not required. For presidential elections, meanwhile, the same principle applies with the entire country being considered a single electoral district.

The system is simple, does not require much thought from voters, and gives each district a single representative. However, it tends to work in favour of parties that have solid blocks of support around the country and against parties whose support is more widely and thinly spread (the latter often come second or third), and it often leads to victorious parties winning a bigger percentage of seats than votes. It also provides no representation for voters who did not support the winner, an outcome that can be particularly problematic in executive elections. The more rarely used single non-transferable vote (SNTV) is discussed in more detail in Chapter 6: Japan.

Table 2.5 Comparing executive elections

Country	Features
Britain	Parliamentary, with prime minister determined by party leadership and balance of party seats in legislature.
Germany	As Britain.
USA	President elected separately from legislature, via an Electoral College, and limited to two four-year terms.
Japan	As Britain, with additional influence of factions within major parties.
France	President elected separately from legislature, requiring majority (possibility of two rounds) and limited to two five-year terms.
India	As Britain.
Mexico	As US, but president limited to single six-year term.
Nigeria	As US, but president required to win majority of all votes cast and at least 25 per cent of the vote in at least two-thirds of states. Possibility of two runoffs.
Turkey	As France, but no prime minister.
Russia	As France, but president limited to no more than two consecutive six-year terms.
China	Elected by lower levels of communist party to lifetime term.
Iran	President elected separately from legislature, requiring majority (possibility of two rounds) and limited to no more than two consecutive four-year terms.

Majority

This system – which can also be used for executive and legislative elections – requires that winning candidates earn a majority of the votes cast, which usually means the use of a two-round election. Under this system, multiple candidates compete against one another in the first ballot, and a winner is declared if he or she wins more than half the vote. Failing that, a second ballot is held that usually involves just the two highest-placed candidates from the first round. The second round is usually preceded by bargaining among parties as the two final candidates try to encourage voters from other parties to support them.

A much rarer option is the alternative vote system, otherwise known as instant runoff or ranked voting. This requires that voters must rank the candidates running for office, and if one of them wins a majority, that candidate wins. If no one wins a majority, candidates with the fewest number of votes are eliminated and vote totals are reassigned until one has a majority. Only Australia and Papua New Guinea use this system for national legislative elections.

The logic behind the majority system is that no candidate should be elected to office without proving themselves acceptable to most voters. The major advantage, then, is that candidates must make an effort to reach out to voters who might not otherwise have supported them. The major disadvantages are that majority systems extend the election season and that – as we will see in the case of France in Chapter 7 – voters might be tempted to blow off steam by supporting more extreme candidates in the first round.

Proportional representation (PR)

Widely used in legislative elections in Europe, **proportional representation** gives political parties seats in proportion to the number of votes they receive. It comes in several different forms, the most basic of which is the party list system. This divides a country into districts with roughly equal population size that are bigger than the districts used in the SMP system and that are represented not by a single member but by multiple members. Each of the competing parties publishes a ranked list of candidates, voters choose among the parties, and seats are divided up among the parties in proportion to the share of the vote they receive.

Proportional representation
An electoral system in which the number of seats won by each of the competing parties is proportional to the number of votes they each win.

Table 2.6 Comparing legislative elections

	Features	Cases
PLURALITY		
Single-member plurality (SMP)	Districts are represented by single members, the candidate winning the most votes (a plurality) prevailing.	UK, India, Iran, Nigeria, USA, and many others.
Single non-transferable vote	Voters are given multiple candidates from which to choose in a multi-member district, the candidates winning the most votes prevailing.	Afghanistan, Kuwait.
MAJORITY		
Two-round system	If no candidate wins a majority on the first ballot, the leading candidates (usually the top two) face a second, runoff election. Used more often for presidential elections.	France, Russia, and Turkey (from cases in this book), and many others, including Argentina, Brazil, Egypt, Indonesia, Poland.
Alternative vote	A rare system in which voters must rank candidates, who must win a majority of votes in order to win.	Australia and Papua New Guinea.
PROPORTIONAL		
Party list system	Votes are cast for a party's list of candidates, and the seats in a district divided up among parties in proportion to their respective shares of the votes.	Much of Europe and Latin America, Indonesia, South Africa, Turkey.
Single transferable vote	Voters rank candidates in a district, with those winning a minimum quota being elected, and remaining votes reallocated until all seats are filled.	Ireland and Malta.
MIXED		
Majoritarian	Some seats are determined by PR and others by SMP or two-round elections. Effectively two separate elections.	Japan, Mexico, Russia, South Korea, Venezuela.
Proportional	Voters choose a local representative using SMP, and vote for a party using PR. Share of seats under PR can be topped up according to share of votes under SMP.	Germany and New Zealand.

A threshold is also usually used so that no party wins seats unless it wins a minimum proportion of the vote, usually somewhere between 2 and 7 per cent. A rarer and more complex version of PR is the single transferable vote system, which – like the alternative vote – requires voters to rank candidates and involves some redistribution of votes until all available seats have been filled. It is discussed in more detail in Chapter 8: India.

Mixed systems

The fourth option is a hybrid of SMP and PR, designed to capitalize on the advantages of both and to minimize the disadvantages. In the majoritarian version, voters are given two votes, one to choose their local representative using SMP, and one to vote for a party using PR. Variations on this system are used in Germany (see Chapter 4 for more details), Japan, and Mexico, and for elections to the Scottish and Welsh regional assemblies in Britain. For example, Scotland has 129 seats in its assembly, 73 of which are decided by SMP, and the remaining 56 of which are divided among eight parliamentary regions, each represented by seven members. Constituency winners are determined by a plurality, and the regional seats are divided among the parties according to the proportion of the

COMPARING POLITICS 2
Terms of office

While there is agreement that democracy demands the placing of limits on the powers of elected officials, there is no agreement concerning either the number or the length of their terms in office. As we will see in Chapter 9: Mexico, term limits are typically imposed on executives in democratic presidential systems, and in some supreme or constitutional courts, but there are no such limits on prime ministers in parliamentary systems, or on legislatures anywhere. In authoritarian systems, meanwhile, executives will typically keep their grip on power for as long as possible.

Limits on the number of terms served by elected officials, though, present a different set of questions from those raised by the length of a term. How long does it take for a newly elected president or representative to grow into their job, and how often after that should they be required to stand for re-election? The numbers run the gamut from a low of two years for members of the US House of Representatives to a high of nine years for members of the upper house of the national legislature in Liberia, and eight years for members of the upper house in Brazil and Chile. Stretching a point, members of the upper house of the British Parliament have lifetime appointments, but they also have significantly fewer powers than the lower house. The vast majority of terms for both executives and legislatures are in the range of four to six years.

The main advantages of shorter terms are that they ensure that voters have regular opportunities to comment through the ballot box on the performance of elected officials, and they discourage those officials from taking voters for granted. The main disadvantages are that frequent elections court the danger of promoting voter apathy, they force parties and candidates to spend less time on government business and more time fund-raising and campaigning, they interfere with the development of long-term views on public policy, and they heighten the danger of high turnover in public office.

seats they win. The plurality system usually works in favour of bigger parties, whereas the regional system works in favour of smaller parties, which tend to win no seats under the plurality system.

Looking at these options, it is clear that the single-member plurality system is the simplest and quickest, but it is also potentially the least fair; see Chapter 3: UK. The other options may take more thought and effort, but they have the benefit of more accurately reflecting voter preferences. Even assuming we can agree on the best electoral system, though, the discussion about representation goes on to include more technical questions such as the number and the terms of office of elected officials. At one end of the scale, we find the indirect and lifetime appointment of the Supreme Leader of Iran or the president of China, or the lengthy hold on power (based in part on rigged elections) of several central Asian and sub-Saharan African leaders. At the other end of the scale, we see the kind of rapid turnover of leadership found in Japan or in European states with unstable coalition governments. In Comparative Politics 2 we look in more detail at some of the implications of different terms.

POLITICAL PARTIES

Political parties are the lifeblood of government and politics. They are a key mobilizing and organizing device, bringing together people with similar views about how to govern, and working to pursue their goals by supporting the efforts of their members to win election and to hold political office. This is true even in those democracies where party membership and identification is on the decline, and in those authoritarian systems that go to great lengths to control the activities of parties, or even to ban them altogether; limits and bans reflect the extent to which authoritarian elites fear the opposition that would come from a competitive party system. Even though disillusionment with parties has grown, as they are criticized for promoting narrow political agendas, it is hard to imagine democratic political systems functioning without them.

Political party
A group identified by name and ideology that fields candidates at elections in order to win public office and control government.

Political cleavage
The tendency for voters to divide into like-minded voting groups based on political, economic, or social differences.

The earliest parties formed either around elite groups within legislatures, or were mass movements formed outside legislatures to promote the interests of large segments of society, such as the working class. They initially worked outside the institutions of government, but increasingly became a formal part of government, promoting a wide range of interests, and being based on a wide variety of **political cleavages**, ranging from social class to economic status, religion, and even regional differences. They use varied methods to win and keep power, they often relate in different ways to voters and to the institutions of government, and although some still work outside the political system, others sit at the heart of that system.

Political parties perform six main functions:

◆ Providing a foundation for the exercise of power by governments.
◆ Providing guidance by giving voters and candidates ideological labels and other reference points that help them better understand the policy options before them.
◆ Aggregating the interests of voters with a common set of values and goals.
◆ Mobilizing voters to take part in elections.
◆ Recruiting members and candidates for elected office.
◆ In authoritarian regimes, they focus less on providing alternatives than on controlling and limiting those alternatives.

If there was a 'natural' arrangement for party systems (one in which all potential parties could form and re-form without political or legal limits), it would probably be one in which multiple parties formed around a wide range of ideological alternatives. In reality, though, a combination of legal limits placed on parties and of political advantages exploited and missed has produced five main kinds of party systems (summarized in Table 2.7).

No-party systems

In a small number of authoritarian states, mainly in the Middle East, political parties are not allowed to form or to operate. Groups and movements often function that, if given the opportunity, would almost certainly evolve into parties with competing platforms. However, authoritarian government is almost by definition opposed to tolerating alternatives, and thus parties are illegal. The one case of a no-party system in this book is Iran, where – as we will see in Chapter 14 – there is little history of political party activity, and not much more today than a cluster of ideological groups into which candidates and elected officials organize themselves.

Single-party systems

These were once common, being found throughout the communist world and in many African and Arab states, but they are today limited to the world's few remaining communist states: China, Cuba, Laos, North Korea, and Vietnam. Here, monopoly parties claim to be able to reflect the broad interests of voters, and to offer democracy

Table 2.7 Comparing party systems

Type	Features	Cases
No-party	No formal parties allowed to compete.	Iran, Oman, Saudi Arabia.
Single-party	Only one significant party legally allowed.	China, Cuba, North Korea.
Dominant party	One party almost always in government, whether alone or in coalition.	Japan, Russia, Singapore, South Africa.
Two-party	Two major parties compete to form single-party governments.	Australia, UK, United States.
Multi-party	Three or more major parties win legislative seats in elections, and multi-party coalitions are usual.	Most of Europe, along with India, Mexico, Nigeria, Turkey.

within a single party, while in reality working to tighten the grip of government and to ensure uniformity of purpose among voters. They often try to give the impression of democracy without actually giving voters the opportunity to have much impact on policy, which is instead made by the party leadership, using elections as a means of giving its decisions an aura of legitimacy. Clearly, choice lies at the heart of democratic systems, and hence an absence of choice precludes the possibility of democracy.

Dominant party systems

These are found in countries where there is a choice of multiple parties, but one dominates the others and becomes the perpetual party of government. In some cases, as with the close association between United Russia and Vladimir Putin (see Chapter 12), such dominance is a reflection of authoritarianism at work. Dominant parties, though, can also be found in democracies. In India until the 1990s, for example, the Congress Party was consistently either the governing party or the biggest party, its power underpinned by a combination of the charisma of the Nehru-Gandhi dynasty and a divided opposition. In Japan, meanwhile, except for breaks in 1993–96 and 2009–12, the Liberal Democratic Party has governed since 1955, thanks to a combination of fair means (it has an impressive network of grassroots supporter groups, for example) and more questionable means, such as the distribution of patronage.

Two-party systems

These are increasingly unusual, and are mainly the product of the single-member plurality electoral system, which helps parties with large blocks of support turn votes into seats; smaller parties with more thinly spread support more often come in second or third. It is not unusual for one or other of the two parties to lose support and be supplanted by another party, but the two-party dominance is maintained by the electoral system. Britain is an example, having long been dominated by the Labour and Conservative parties, with smaller parties rarely being able to enter government. The United States is an even more certain example: thanks to a combination of legal and political advantages, there is little likelihood of the Republicans or the Democrats facing any serious challenges to their dominance, and few third parties make a showing. They are both parties that contain many shades of opinion, party discipline tends to be loose (members of Congress from one party often cross over to vote with the other), and they run elections in most states, even manipulating electoral districts to increase their chances of winning seats; see Chapter 5.

Multi-party systems

In democracies, multi-party systems are the norm, as often as not because elections are based on proportional representation, which contributes to multi-party systems by making it easier for small parties to win seats and harder for large parties to win clear majorities. In several European countries (notably Germany, France, and Italy), there are enough parties to prevent the creation of governing majorities, resulting in **coalition governments** formed by two or more parties. The coalition partners usually must make more effort to reach compromises, and governments can be fragile. This has not affected political stability in Germany, but Italian coalitions often have to depend on parties with fewer than a dozen members who can hold all the others to ransom and exert an influence out of all proportion to their size and following. Coalitions collapse so often that in the period 1945–2018, for example, Italy had more than 60 governments.

Coalition government
An arrangement in which a government is formed through an alliance involving two or more political parties.

The manner in which parties are structured and the role they play in their respective political systems will fundamentally change the nature of those systems, and influence how citizens relate to government. In China, for example, the dominance of the Chinese Communist Party ensures that politics takes place almost entirely within a single party, offering citizens few choices and encouraging a sense of either towing the party line or being excluded from decision-making. In the United States, the dominance of the Democrats and Republicans constitutes a political duopoly, and while it offers a limited choice to voters, many of them like neither of the two alternatives, and are left cut off from mainstream decision-making. Having too many parties, by contrast, can create confusion in the minds of voters, can encourage political instability, and can create damaging political division and marginalization. Comparativists can determine which option works best, and where, by studying different party systems and drawing conclusions about which has resulted in the most responsive and transparent form of government.

THE FUTURE OF POLITICAL SYSTEMS

Neither government, politics, nor the structure or character of political systems is static. Each constantly changes according to new needs and circumstances, to the ebb and flow of public preferences and political opportunism, to internal and external influences, to the changing balance of political power, and to the public agenda. Occasionally, entire political systems will be swept aside in the wake of war or revolution.

As a result, the portrait that is painted in this chapter of political systems can only be a record of the present. Political systems are based in history, to be sure, so there are many similarities between the way that institutions in many of our cases work and are structured today and the way they worked and were structured years, decades, or – in a few instances – centuries ago. But as the chapters that follow will show, change is one of the few consistencies in government and politics, and years or decades from now there will be differences in the way that every government works.

We are only beginning to scratch the surface of the impact of the digital revolution on government, and that impact will continue to evolve, in both positive and negative ways. Change will also come as human needs evolve, as new challenges demand to be met, and as the relationships among countries and communities change. Where once it was imperialism and religion and war that drove the work of governments, today there is a greater sense of a need to work on shared problems, such as terrorism, financial problems, trade, and climate change. This will inevitably change the way that governments set their agendas, and require new political structures and approaches. In short, the future of government and politics is full of remarkable possibilities.

DISCUSSION QUESTIONS

1. Is there such a thing as a perfect political system, or does the definition of perfection vary from one political situation to another based on different cultural values, economic need, and social reality?
2. Is elitism an inevitable part of government and politics?
3. Are non-executive heads of state helpful or not?
4. Is democracy and efficiency better served by a strong executive or a strong legislature?
5. Should courts be guided more by concrete review or by abstract review?
6. Which of the electoral systems outlined in this chapter is the most efficient in terms of reflecting the wishes of voters?

KEY TERMS

- Abstract review
- Cabinet
- Coalition government
- Concrete review
- Constitution
- Constitutional monarchy
- Elitism
- Executive
- Federal system
- Head of government
- Head of state
- Judicial activism
- Judicial restraint
- Judicial review
- Judiciary
- Legislature
- Personal rule
- Political cleavage
- Political party
- Political system
- Populism
- Proportional representation
- Rule of law
- Single-member plurality
- Unitary system

POLITICAL SYSTEMS ONLINE

Comparative Constitutions Project: http://comparativeconstitutionsproject.org
Inter-Parliamentary Union: www.ipu.org
Global Judicial Integrity Network: www.unodc.org/ji
Election Guide: www.electionguide.org

FURTHER READING

Arter, David (ed.) (2013) *Comparing and Classifying Legislatures* (Routledge). A survey of the state of knowledge about legislatures, with chapters on European, Latin American and African cases.

Boix, Carles, and Susan C. Stokes (eds) (2007) *The Oxford Handbook of Comparative Politics* (Oxford University Press). Although more than 1,000 pages in length, this is a rich survey of the many different dimensions of comparative politics.

Herron, Erik S., Robert J. Pekkanen and Matthew S. Shugart (2018) *The Oxford Handbook of Electoral Systems* (Oxford University Press). An edited collection on the structure and effects of different electoral systems, including individual chapters on elections in 18 countries.

Lawson, Kay, and Jorge Lanzaro (eds) (2010) *Political Parties and Democracy* (Praeger). A five-volume edited collection looking at political parties in the Americas, Europe, Asia, Africa, and the Arab World.

Lee, H. P. (2011) *Judiciaries in Comparative Perspective* (Cambridge University Press). An edited collection of studies of judiciaries in Australia, Britain, Canada, New Zealand, South Africa, and the United States.

Rhodes, R. A. W., and Paul 't Hart (eds) (2014) *The Oxford Handbook of Political Leadership* (Oxford University Press). A general survey of political leadership, including chapters on different kinds of executives.

Visit **www.macmillanihe.com/McCormick-Cases** to access additional materials to support teaching and learning.

UNITED KINGDOM

Source: Getty Images

CONTENTS

- Overview
- Political development
- Political culture
- Political system
- Political processes
- The future of British government and politics

PREVIEW

The value of the United Kingdom as a case lies in the age and continuity of its political system, and its significance as the birthplace of the parliamentary system and of many of the philosophies underlying democratic government. Britain – as it is usually known – has also undergone many changes since 1945 that add to its value as a case: the end of empire, the creation and decay of a welfare state, Britain's changing global role, and deep internal divisions that have shaken the foundations of the British state, even raising questions along the way about what it means to be British. A divisive and controversial decision in a 2016 national referendum to leave the European Union broke open many of the fault lines in British politics and society. A country with a long history now faces many troubling challenges, and a deeply uncertain future.

KEY ARGUMENTS

- Britain is one of the oldest continually functioning political systems in the world, but is currently undergoing dramatic and often worrying political change.

- Much of the change and uncertainty stems from Brexit: the decision by Britain to leave the European Union, an event whose consequences are hard to predict.

- Although Britain has one of the world's best-known and oldest monarchies, political leadership is focused in the office of the prime minister.

- Suggestions that the office of prime minister has been 'presidentialized' at the expense of the sovereignty of Parliament remain open to debate.

- The unitary nature of Britain has changed as power has been devolved to elected assemblies in Scotland, Wales, Northern Ireland, and London.

- The party system has changed as party identification has weakened, and the issues that divide Britain have become more diverse.

OVERVIEW

Britain (formally the United Kingdom, or UK) is one of the exemplary cases in comparative politics by virtue of being the birthplace of the parliamentary system, which is at the heart of government in almost every democracy. It was also the birthplace of the industrial revolution and of modern ideas about capitalism, many of which were outlined in *The Wealth of Nations*, an influential 1776 treatise by the Scottish political economist Adam Smith. As creator of the world's largest empire, its political and economic influence was felt globally, and while its global reach is today much reduced, it remains the world's fifth biggest economy, and is a leading member of all the key international organizations, notably the North Atlantic Treaty Organization (NATO), the UN Security Council (on which it has veto power), and the G7 and G20 groups of major economic powers. But it currently finds itself in a state of crisis, with deep underlying political and social divisions that were implicated in the result of a 2016 national referendum on continued membership of the European Union (EU). By a small majority, the British opted to leave the EU – a phenomenon dubbed '**Brexit**' – and thereby raised many questions about the future direction of their country.

In political terms, Britain is the benchmark example of a parliamentary democracy. It has the world's most famous monarchy, but the monarch has little remaining political power, most of which rests with the prime minister and Parliament. Both these institutions have undergone fundamental change in recent decades, with the executive exerting new powers over the legislature (until the squabble over Brexit muddied the waters of the relationship). Britain is also distinct from most other countries in its record of relatively evolutionary political development; it has suffered civil wars and political conflict, but the root of the modern British political system can be traced back through changes and developments dating back centuries. The results have been by no means perfect, and questions are regularly raised about government secrecy, social inequalities, a flawed electoral system, and recent trends that have placed more power in the hands of the prime minister. It continues – for now, at least – to be ranked as a full democracy in the Democracy Index, but it is hard not to wonder how much longer this will last.

In economic terms, Britain has the typical features of a post-industrial free-market society. It exports a variety of manufactured goods and has plenty of prime agricultural land, but most of its jobs and wealth are generated by services, particularly banking and other financial services. It was once the world's biggest economy, and the pound sterling was the world's most powerful currency, but since World War II Britain has had to adjust to reduced economic influence in the world, and to being integrated into the broader European economy. It joined the European Economic Community (precursor to today's European Union) in 1973, but was long resistant to the goals of European integration, refusing – for example – to adopt the European single currency, the euro. It suffered substantially in the wake of the global financial crisis, and now faces an uncertain future as it addresses the fallout from Brexit.

In social terms, Britain continues to wrestle with several important divisions. Prime among these is regional identity, marked by cultural and political differences among the English, the Scots, the Welsh, and the Northern Irish. Social class was once the defining quality of British society, and while class divisions have declined, they still play a role in the way many Britons think about each other, and have spilled over into growing gaps in wealth and opportunity. Finally, Britain since the 1950s has become a society of new racial and religious diversity, multiculturalism playing an ever more important role in national life as Britain continues to be a magnet for immigration from many parts of the world, and increasingly in recent decades from other parts of Europe.

POLITICAL DEVELOPMENT

Most liberal democracies have at some point experienced a war or a revolution leading to the introduction of a new or altered system of government: Germany had a new system imposed on it after World War II, France adopted a new constitution in 1958, and Spain began a transition to democracy following the end of the Franco dictatorship in 1975. By contrast, Britain has never replaced one system of government with another, but has instead made changes that have built on the foundations of existing arrangements. The changes have not always come easily, and Britain today continues to face significant problems for which there are few easy solutions, but it is telling that Britain is one of the few countries in the world that has no national holiday marking the date of independence or a revolutionary event.

Formation of the British state

Britain's early political and cultural form was dictated by invasion. The native people of the British Isles were the Celts, the ancestors of the Irish, Scots, and Welsh of today. When the Romans invaded in 55 BCE and occupied what is now England and Wales, the Celts were pushed west and north and England developed a distinctive political and economic character. The Roman exit at the beginning of the 5th century CE left behind a political vacuum into which moved several waves of invaders, notably Germanic tribes such as the Angles and the Saxons (from which come the names *England* and *Anglo-Saxon*). Then came Viking invasions in the eighth and ninth centuries, followed by the last successful invasion of the British Isles, by the Normans in 1066. This brought political stability and centralization to England, but the Celts remained separated ethnically, culturally, and linguistically. Religious differences were added in 1534, when King Henry VIII dissolved England's ties with the Catholic Church and created the Church of England.

Divine right
The pre-modern idea that monarchs ruled with a direct mandate from God.

Until about 800 years ago, Britain – like all of Europe – was a feudal society. Sovereign power lay in the hands of monarchs, who ruled by **divine right** and governed the peasant majority through a land-owning aristocracy. The powers of monarchs and aristocrats began their long and sometimes violent decline in 1215 when King John agreed to **Magna Carta**, a document that obliged him to consult with his aristocrats before levying taxes, and prevented him from arbitrarily arresting or seizing property from his subjects. This heralded the beginning of a long process of democratization in Britain.

More change came in 1265 with the convening of the first Parliament. It was unelected, met only sporadically, and was dominated by the aristocracy, but monarchs came to rely on it for political support. Tensions between crown and Parliament remained, however, finally boiling over in 1642 with the outbreak of a civil war between monarchists and parliamentarians. This led to the declaration of a brief republic (1649–60) under the military dictatorship of Oliver Cromwell. When King James II (reigned 1685–88) tried to win back the divine right of monarchs, a Bill of Rights was drawn up which confirmed the supremacy of Parliament over the monarch. Meanwhile, war and attrition led to the dominance of England over its Celtic neighbours; a union with Wales was formalized in 1536–42, and with Scotland in 1707, while Ireland by the late 18th century had to all intents and purposes become part of the British state.

Economic and political change (17th–19th centuries)

Industrial revolution
The era (roughly 1750s–1840s) during which Britain, followed by other countries, switched from an agricultural to an industrial economy.

Beginning in the late 17th century, Britain underwent wide-ranging economic change, which led in turn to political and social change. New and more efficient processes for smelting iron and making steel were developed, the steam engine was invented, industry was mechanized, and large-scale business enterprises emerged (see Osborne, 2013). This in turn brought about improvements in transport, which led to the growth of commerce and markets. As the birthplace of the **industrial revolution**, Britain was forged into the world's first and most powerful industrial state and by the mid-19th century was producing two-thirds of the world's coal, half its steel, half its cotton goods, and almost all its machine tools.

Parliament was still dominated by aristocrats representing mainly rural areas, many of which had only a handful of voters and in some of which a seat in Parliament could be bought. The new middle class of industrialists and entrepreneurs found this unacceptable, and pressure for change led to a series of changes that began with the Great Reform Act of 1832, designed to eliminate corrupt electoral districts; to extend the vote to the wealthy, the upper middle class, and women; to introduce secret voting; create single-member parliamentary districts with roughly equal populations; and to take most remaining significant political powers away from the aristocratic House of Lords. One of the effects was to spark the growth of mass-membership political parties.

From empire to the welfare state (18th century to early 1960s)

With its industry growing, Britain's priority was to find new markets and sources of raw materials, and to build on its competitive advantage over its European rivals, particularly France. Thus began an expansive programme of colonization. After losing its 13 American colonies in 1781, Britain turned its interests to Australia, Canada, New Zealand, parts of West Africa, most of southern and eastern Africa, many Caribbean and Pacific islands, the Asian subcontinent, and parts of Southeast Asia. At its height during the late Victorian era, the **British Empire** included about a quarter of the world's population.

The beginning of the end of the imperial era came with World War I, after which the United States and the Soviet Union began to emerge as economic and military giants, a transition finally confirmed by World War II. Britain entered the latter in 1939 as the world's biggest creditor nation, and although it played a leading role in fighting and winning the war, it emerged six years later as one of the world's biggest debtor nations. It suffered widespread physical damage, its economy was devastated, its political influence diminished, its export earnings were halved, food was still being rationed as late as 1954, and most of its colonies were agitating for independence.

The post-war period saw the completion of a **welfare state** and the shift to a managed economy. Pensions had been introduced in 1908 and national health and unemployment insurance in 1911, but the welfare system was completed only after 1945, when voters wanting a new start swept a socialist Labour government into power. A National Health Service was created that provided free care for almost everyone; there was an expansion of welfare for the unemployed, the ill, and families with children; and basic services such as railways and the steel industry were nationalized.

> **Welfare state**
> A state that provides through law for people in need, such as the poor, the elderly, the handicapped, or anyone otherwise economically or physically disadvantaged.

TIMELINE

1066	Norman invasion
1215	Magna Carta agreed
1536–42	Union with Wales
1642–49	Civil war leads to deposition of the monarchy until 1660
1707	Union with Scotland
1750s–1840s	Industrial revolution
1832	Great Reform Act
1914–18	World War I
1939–45	World War II
1947	Independence of India and Pakistan
1957–68	Independence of most of Britain's African colonies
1973	Britain joins the European Economic Community
1979	Margaret Thatcher wins first of three elections
1994	Opening of English Channel tunnel connecting Britain and France
1997	Election of Tony Blair as Labour prime minister ends nearly 18 years of Conservative government
2000	Elections held for first-ever elected mayor of London
2001–03	UK supports US-led invasions of Afghanistan and Iraq
2014	Scottish voters turn down independence in a referendum
2016	British voters opt to leave the European Union in the Brexit referendum

But while its economy prospered in the 1950s and 1960s, Britain saw its global influence beginning to decline thanks to a combination of the end of its empire (which had been almost entirely dismantled by the end of the 1960s), the handicaps posed to industrial success by class divisions, an education system that was prejudiced against business as a career, low levels of mobility within the labour force, inadequate investments in industry and in research and development, and high levels of government involvement in production and employment (Marr, 2017). A new low was reached during the 'winter of discontent' in 1978–79 when public-sector workers went on strike across Britain, almost shutting the country down.

> **European Union**
> A regional integration association through which most European states have built closer economic and political ties, notably a single European market.

Europe and Thatcherism (1970s–2000s)

A landmark event took place in 1973, when Britain joined the European Economic Community (EEC) (now the **European Union**). A free-trade agreement among selected Western

Euroscepti-cism
Opposition to the process of European integration, or to the direction being taken by that process.

European states, the Community – created in 1958 – was aimed at bringing down the barriers to trade and the movement of people, with the goal of creating a unified European market. Dreamers even talked about the possibility of the eventual creation of a United States of Europe. Britain was slow to warm to the Community, arguing that its main interests lay outside Europe, and soon became notable for its **euroscepticism** (Geddes, 2013).

Reflecting growing public concern about the state of the economy and new international competition, a Conservative government under Margaret Thatcher was elected in 1979 and launched a programme of wide-ranging change. She argued that government was too big and that special interests (especially labour unions) had too much influence on government. **Thatcherism** became the watchword in politics and economics, its key elements being the creation of a new 'enterprise culture' aimed at making British industry more competitive, and the privatization of state-owned services and industries. Thatcher was criticized for failing to meet the needs of the underclass and for widening the income gap, but Britain by the late 1990s was a more dynamic society, the changes reflected in the renewal of cities, in the rise of a new entrepreneurial spirit, and in the growth of the middle class and the consumer society. But economic, social, and regional divisions worsened, and Thatcher's long-term legacy remains hotly disputed to this day.

Thatcherism was reflected in the policies pursued between 1997 and 2007 by the Labour government of Tony Blair. Astonishing political analysts with the scale of its victory, the rejuvenated Labour Party swept the internally divided Conservative Party out of office after 18 years in power, winning a large majority. Under Tony Blair, 'New' Labour abandoned many of its traditionally socialist ideas, underlining the importance of the free market but also emphasizing the need to improve education, rebuild the National Health Service, and take a tough stance on crime. However, Blair will be best remembered for just one, highly controversial policy decision: his support of the US-led invasion of Iraq in 2003, which was deeply unpopular, lost him considerable political support, and played the key role in his decision to step down in June 2007.

Blair was replaced as party leader and prime minister by his finance minister Gordon Brown, who inherited a political agenda full of troubling problems, including the mixed progress that Britain was making in living up to its new multicultural identity: the number of Britons belonging to ethnic and religious minorities had grown since the 1950s, feeding into the same kind of social tensions that have been felt in France, and more recently in Germany (see Chapters 4 and 7). Britain has also had to deal with the ongoing challenges posed by regionalism (see Comparing Political Culture 3), the stresses over its troubled relationship with the rest of the European Union, and the fallout from the global financial crisis that began in 2007. The May 2010 general election resulted in a drubbing for Labour, which lost more than a quarter of its seats in Parliament, but the Conservatives did not win enough seats to form a government in their own right. This resulted in a 'hung Parliament', or one in which no one party had a majority. Britain briefly had to live with a political arrangement common in continental Europe: a coalition government made up of the Conservative and Liberal Democratic parties. (For more details on coalition governments, see Chapter 4: Germany.)

Britain today

Two sets of developments have led to concerns that the decline of Britain – so much a part of public and political conversations in the 1960s and 1970s, but about which less had been said in the 1990s – has moved back into the headlines. The first of these was the problem of terrorism. Britain is not a newcomer to terrorism, having been the site of numerous attacks tied to the political conflict in Northern Ireland, with groups supporting continued union with Britain ranged against those supporting the reunification of Ireland. An attempt was even made on the life of Margaret Thatcher in 1984, and a mortar attack launched on the office of the prime minister in London in 1991. With the Northern Irish peace agreement reached in 1998, the threat of terrorism from that quarter subsided, but was replaced by attacks carried out by Islamic extremists. Bombs in London in 2005 killed 52 and injured more than 770, and another bomb at a concert in Manchester in 2017 left 22 dead and 120 injured. As with the United States and in its European neighbours, Britain found itself obliged to tighten public security, leading to charges that the government was impinging on civil liberties.

The second problem stems from a set of social and economic divisions with many and complex roots. There has been a widening and visible gap between the rich and the poor, leaving social exclusion in its wake. There have been charges that globalization and immigration have taken jobs away, leaving many Britons languishing on the margins of the economy. There have also been concerns about the decline of the family and of the kind of social support and stability offered by parents. These and other problems were seen to be behind the break out of riots in several major English cities in August 2011, marked by arson, violence, and vandalism, and leading to several deaths, numerous injuries, and several thousand arrests (Lammy, 2011).

The United Kingdom has been deeply divided in recent years over the question of leaving the European Union. Here, demonstrators in London protest government policy for providing no clarity about Britain's future relationship with the EU. *Source: SOPA Images/LightRocket/Getty Images.*

Britain's regional divisions came to the fore again in 2014 when a referendum was held in Scotland on the question of independence. Although the outcome was a decision – by a vote of 55 per cent in favour and 45 per cent against – to remain part of the United Kingdom, the undercurrent of Scottish nationalism has not gone away. A political earthquake was then sparked in 2016 by a national referendum on the question of Britain's continued membership of the European Union. It was widely expected that Britons would vote to remain within the EU, but they opted – by 52 per cent to 48 per cent – in favour of Brexit, initiating a political and economic crisis. The vote was seen not only as a rejection of the EU but as criticism of globalization, the power of the British political class, and the economic divisions of the country. The decision can justifiably be described with terms such as *momentous*, *transformative*, *pivotal*, and *revolutionary*. As this book went to press, the terms of Brexit were still being negotiated, the petulant nature of the debate emphasizing the many divisions within British politics and society.

POLITICAL CULTURE

Tying down the political values of a society is never easy, especially one with as long a history as Britain. Much has changed in recent decades as many of the qualities that once characterized British politics – including **pragmatism** – have been challenged. The British were always modest in terms of their expectations of government and their aspirations for their own lives, but their expectations have recently declined. Hart (1978) once suggested that while Americans emphasized 'what democracy is and should be', Britain had been 'characterized by a more pragmatic and less urgent emphasis on what democracy is and can be'. The level of urgency has changed in recent years with rising concerns about elitism, the growing gap between rich and poor, and the future of a viable Britain outside the EU. Faith in the tried and tested has been replaced by new uncertainties about where the country is heading.

Pragmatism
A practical view of politics, emphasizing what is possible over what is desirable.

Another quality of British political culture that has changed has been the level of faith in government. While political alienation is often obvious in Italy and France and among disadvantaged Americans who feel cut off from government, Britain was once marked by strong feelings of allegiance towards the political system (but not to politicians). Such feelings were tied closely to Britain's long history of relative political stability, contrasting with

COMPARING POLITICAL CULTURE 3
Politics and national identity

There are few states in the world that are homogeneous in cultural, racial, ethnic, or national terms; as we saw in Chapter 1, there is often a mismatch between state borders and the identities of the people who live within them. The stability of states can be threatened by the tensions created by these divisions, and how states respond to the divisions says much about their history and their political personality. **National identity** is particularly troubled in the post-colonial states of sub-Saharan Africa, whose borders were imposed on them by European powers, obliging people of different ethnicities to live together in often troubled relationships. The resulting tensions have often spilled over into violence and even civil war, as when Biafra seceded from Nigeria in 1967, or when Eritrea won back its independence from Ethiopia in 1993, and South Sudan split from Sudan in 2011.

In Britain, too, questions are posed about national identity, and about what it means to be British. It may be one of the world's older states, with a political system whose origins date back centuries, and it may also be a democracy, but this has not always guaranteed a strong sense of unity. This is because the United Kingdom of Great Britain and Northern Ireland (its official title) is actually four countries in one: Great Britain – made up of England, Scotland, and Wales – and Northern Ireland. Despite the existence of a 'United' Kingdom, **regionalism** is a factor in national politics and some in Scotland and Wales even support the idea of independence from England.

Pressure for **devolution** led the Blair government to agree to the creation of regional assemblies for Scotland, Wales, and Northern Ireland in 1998–99. Supporters of devolution hoped that this would reduce demands for independence, particularly in Scotland. But those demands continued, prompting a 2014 referendum on independence, and while a majority voted against the idea, there are still many Scots who support independence, particularly since Scotland voted against Britain leaving the EU, in contrast to majority support for Brexit in England. Regionalism raises questions about what it means to be British, and about how British politics differs from politics in the four individual countries.

Several other cases in this book face their own difficulties with regionalism and national identity. Russia, for example, contains between 60 and 90 national minorities, many of whom live on the margins of the country and several of whom want greater self-determination and even full independence. Consider the case of Chechnya, home to a Muslim minority conquered by Russia in 1858, which has repeatedly seen times of instability as an opportunity to break free. The break-up of the USSR sparked a war between Russia and Chechnya in 1994–96 that claimed the lives of as many as 100,000 Chechens – about one-tenth of the population. Hostilities broke out again in 1999, when Russia (ignoring international criticism but backed by domestic public opinion) launched an air and land attack on Chechnya, razing the capital of Grozny and generating a flood of refugees to neighbouring republics. Direct control from Moscow was instituted in May 2000.

What is it that drives governments to work so hard to keep their states together even in the face of violent efforts to secede? What does the difficulty of building a strong sense of national identity say about the wisdom and future viability of divided states? Should such states not simply concede their problems and arrange for a divorce (as did Czechoslovakia in 1993 when it split into the Czech Republic and Slovakia)?

National identity
Identification with a state or nation, as determined by a combination of language, place of birth, and citizenship.

Regionalism
An ideology or philosophy favouring the interests of regions and localities within states over the interests of those states as a whole, including autonomy and in some cases independence.

Devolution
The transfer of powers from the centre to the parts, as in the case of powers being transferred from national government in London to regional governments. Differs from federalism in that such powers can be withdrawn by central government.

the often revolutionary and violent change experienced by political systems in other European states. However, the sense of allegiance is on the decline due to a growing sense of political and economic division, and a declining faith in the capacity of the political system to respond to Britain's problems. Recent studies suggest that the British are more willing to use unconventional forms of political participation than the citizens of any other democracy, such as signing petitions, attending lawful demonstrations, joining a boycott or wildcat strike, and even refusing to pay taxes (for example, see Whiteley, 2011).

The British tend to be a private people, hence the often-quoted phrase that an Englishman's home is his castle. This sense of privacy has combined with the sense of the exclusivity of government to create a gap between the governed and the governors. Issues of national security are subject to secrecy in every democracy, but government critics charge that state secrets are too narrowly defined in Britain. Those critics say that this has helped increase the power and reduce the accountability of the police, weakened the power of Parliament at the expense of central government, promoted the use of surveillance, reduced the right to personal privacy, and allowed the government to interfere with media freedom. Such secrecy has become increasingly unacceptable and there has been a movement in recent years for greater freedom of information and improved accountability. Successive governments have promised more open administration, and information has become more freely available, but the most significant changes came during the Blair administration, which opened up the bureaucracy and made government departments subject to performance reviews based on their services to the public.

POLITICAL SYSTEM

There are five key principles that give the British political system its personality:

◆ It is a constitutional monarchy in which government is carried out in the name of the monarch, but the prime minister is the true political leader.
◆ It is a unitary state, meaning that most significant authority is concentrated in national government, leaving the Scottish, Welsh, and Northern Irish regional assemblies, and London city government, as junior members in the governing structure.
◆ There is a fusion of the executive and the legislature, with all members of the executive (the prime minister and senior government ministers) also being serving members of Parliament.
◆ There is a belief in responsible government, meaning that government ministers are held responsible to Parliament for the management of their departments.
◆ Britain's membership of the European Union has meant that it has been subject to the common laws and policies of the EU.

None of these principles is static, the changes among them having accelerated in recent years as the balance of power between the centre and the parts has changed, as the executive and the legislature have jockeyed for influence, as faith in government and the political class has declined, and as Britain's relationship with the European Union has changed.

The constitution

Most democracies have written constitutions in which the powers of government and the rights of the governed are outlined. However, not all of them have a **codified constitution**, or one in which all the elements are contained within a single document; in rare cases, they can be more abstract, consisting of laws and customs that have the same function as a single written document. Britain is one of the constitutional rarities in that it lacks a codified document, its constitution instead being found in five key sources – see Table 3.1 (Leach et al., 2018).

While codified constitutions typically spell out how government works and are supported by constitutional courts that have the power to interpret and build upon the written rules, government in Britain – suggests Norton (2016) – is determined 'on the basis of what has proved to work rather than on abstract first principles'. Supporters of this approach argue that the absence of a codified constitution allows for greater flexibility, but critics contend that there is too much potential for the abuse of powers by a strong prime minister, or – as Brexit and other recent referendums have indicated – the replacement of parliamentary sovereignty with the concept of the 'the will of the people' (Barnett, 2016). The result has been growing support for a codified constitution.

Name	United Kingdom of Great Britain and Northern Ireland
Capital	London
Administration	Unitary, with regional assemblies in Scotland, Wales, Northern Ireland.
Constitution	Date of state formation arguably 1066; uncodified constitution.
Executive	Parliamentary. The head of government is the prime minister, who is head of the largest party or coalition, and governs in conjunction with a cabinet. The head of state is the monarch.
Legislature	Bicameral Parliament: lower House of Commons (650 members) elected for renewable five-year terms, and upper House of Lords (about 800 members) consisting of a mix of hereditary and life peers, and senior members of the Church of England.
Judiciary	Supreme Court created 2009 with 11 members appointed for life, with mandatory retirement at 70 or 75, depending on date of appointment.
Electoral system	The House of Commons is elected using single-member plurality. Different systems used for elections to regional assemblies.
Party system	Two-party dominant, with Conservatives on the right and Labour on the left. Smaller parties and regional parties significant, but rarely enter government.

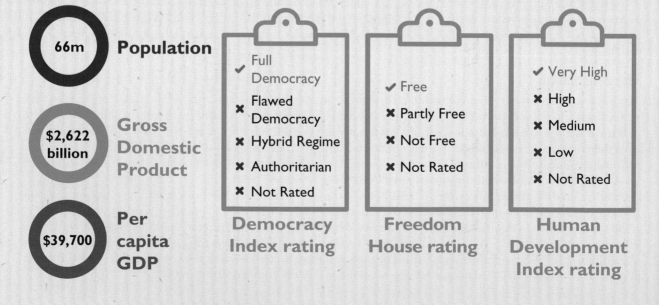

Population	66m
Gross Domestic Product	$2,622 billion
Per capita GDP	$39,700

Democracy Index rating
- ✓ Full Democracy
- ✗ Flawed Democracy
- ✗ Hybrid Regime
- ✗ Authoritarian
- ✗ Not Rated

Freedom House rating
- ✓ Free
- ✗ Partly Free
- ✗ Not Free
- ✗ Not Rated

Human Development Index rating
- ✓ Very High
- ✗ High
- ✗ Medium
- ✗ Low
- ✗ Not Rated

Table 3.1 Five sources of the British constitution

Source	Features
Statute law	Acts of Parliament that override common law and have the effect of constitutional law. They include laws that outline the relative powers of the two houses of Parliament.
Common law	Judgements handed down over time by British courts. Among the more significant are those dealing with freedom of expression and the sovereignty of Parliament.
European law	British membership of the EU has left it subject to laws adopted by the EU, which have overridden British laws where the two have conflicted, in those policy areas where the EU has primary authority. These include trade, agriculture, social issues, and the environment.
Customs and conventions	These do not have the force of law but have been followed for so long that they are regarded as binding. For example, there are no laws stating that the prime minister and cabinet should come out of the majority party in Parliament; this is simply a convention.
Commentaries	These are written by constitutional experts such as Walter Bagehot and Albert Venn Dicey (author in 1885 of *The Law of the Constitution*).

Head of state: the monarch

Except for a brief spell between 1649 and 1660, when a republic was proclaimed, Britain since the 10th century has been a **monarchy**. This literally means 'rule by one', but more specifically it means a system governed by someone who usually comes to that position by birth or heredity. British kings and queens once had a near-monopoly on political power but began giving it up with Magna Carta, and the monarch is now little more than a ceremonial head of state, expected to be a neutral symbol of history, stability, tradition, and national identity. It is often said that the monarch reigns but does not rule. The present monarch – Queen Elizabeth II, who has been on the throne since 1952 – is limited to the following so-called reserve powers (Norton, 2014):

Monarchy
A political system in which the head of state is determined by heredity, and holds power for life or until voluntarily renouncing that power. The role of monarchs in democracies is constitutionally limited.

◆ Calling new elections. She has the right to dissolve Parliament and call new elections, but she does this only at the request of the prime minister.
◆ The power of veto. Just as presidents of the United States must sign all new congressional bills before they become law, the Queen gives the Royal Assent to all new legislation. Theoretically, this gives her the right of veto, but it is no more than a symbolic power; the last time a monarch vetoed a law was in 1707.
◆ Conferring with the prime minister. She meets with the prime minister at confidential weekly meetings, during which she has the right (according to the 19th-century constitutional authority Walter Bagehot (2017)) 'to be consulted, the right to encourage, and the right to warn'.
◆ Forming a government. Once an election has been held, the prime minister must formally meet with the Queen to request her permission to form a government. If the prime minister has a solid majority, this is a formality. But if no one party has an absolute majority, the Queen steps in as an arbitrator, and can name the person she thinks is in the best position to be able to form a government.
◆ Address to Parliament. At the annual State Opening of Parliament (usually held in November), the Queen gives an address in which she outlines the government's programme. However, the address is written by the government, and the Queen simply reads it aloud.
◆ Symbol of the state. Above all, the Queen is a visible symbol of unity and executive authority. She is head of the Church of England and commander-in-chief of the armed forces. Many public duties are carried out in her name, and British postage stamps, coins, and banknotes bear the Queen's image instead of the name of the country.

As an individual, Queen Elizabeth is popular, but opinion polls show that public support for the monarchy has slipped since the mid-1980s to about 70 to 75 per cent. The death of Princess Diana, former wife of Prince Charles (heir to the throne), in August 1997, sparked a re-appraisal aimed at making the monarchy more relevant to public life in Britain. The once unthinkable – that a divorced heir to the throne could become king – has been accepted; Prince Charles married his long-time friend Camilla Parker-Bowles (herself divorced) in April 2005, although the public has been divided over whether or not they want to see Prince Charles succeed to the throne (if he did not, then the job would go to his eldest son Prince William). The national celebrations that surrounded the Queen's Diamond Jubilee in 2012 were an opportunity to celebrate the monarchy, but also to question its place in British political life. One of the strengths of the British monarchy – and the major reason it has lasted so long – is that it has been more adaptable than many of its continental European counterparts.

> **Prime minister**
> The head of government in a parliamentary system, typically the person who heads the party or coalition with the most seats in the national legislature.

The executive: prime minister and cabinet

The British head of government is the **prime minister**, who provides policy leadership and oversees the implementation of the law through a cabinet of senior ministers. By definition, the prime minister is the leader of the political party or coalition with the most seats in the lower chamber of Parliament, the House of Commons. As long as they can keep the support of their party in Parliament, prime ministers have more power over deciding which laws will

COMPARING GOVERNMENT 3
Monarchs and presidents

As we saw in Chapter 2, a distinction must be made between heads of state and heads of government; the former have mainly symbolic powers while the latter have substantive political powers. In parliamentary systems, the two functions are divided between two people, with a prime minister (or chancellor in Germany and Austria) typically heading the government, and the head of state taking the form of a constitutional monarch or a non-executive president. What are the differences between the latter, and what are the effects of having a monarch as opposed to a non-executive president?

Monarchs were once common, being found in most of Europe, the Middle East, Asia, and Africa, but they are relatively rare today. There are seven in Europe (Belgium, Britain, Denmark, the Netherlands, Norway, Spain, and Sweden), eight in the Middle East and North Africa (Bahrain, Jordan, Kuwait, Morocco, Oman, Qatar, Saudi Arabia, and the United Arab Emirates), six in Asia (Bhutan, Brunei, Cambodia, Japan, Malaysia, and Thailand), two in southern Africa (Lesotho and eSwatini), and one in the Pacific (Tonga). More than a dozen former British colonies and dominions still recognize the authority of the British monarch (including Australia, Canada, and several Caribbean states), but the constitutional links have weakened.

Monarchies are typically based on heredity, with the title passing down through the family, usually via the eldest son. In the case of constitutional monarchies, the work of the ruler is limited to symbolic functions, while the world's few remaining cases of an **absolute monarch** (including Brunei and Saudi Arabia) see far more power focused in the hands of the royal family. For their supporters, monarchs play the useful role of providing a living symbol of the state, its history, and its culture, and providing a figure in government who (at least in the case of constitutional monarchies) is non-partisan and rises above the fray of politics, encouraging a sense of national unity. For their critics, monarchs are undemocratic, and represent the kinds of class divisions and sense of entitlement that run counter to the idea of democratic equality.

> **Absolute monarch**
> One who typically has a large measure of control and power, standing in contrast to the kind of constitutional monarchies found in democracies.

In most parliamentary systems, the monarch has been replaced by a non-executive president, who carries out many of the same symbolic functions as a monarch without being part of a hereditary succession. There is no consistency to the way in which such presidents come to office, which could be via popular vote (as in Finland, Ireland, and Portugal), via election by members of the national legislature (as in Greece, Iraq, and Israel), or election through a special electoral college, often comprising the national legislature along with representatives from regional or local government (as in Germany, India, and Italy). Even though there is a political element to the manner in which they come to office, non-executive presidents are still mainly expected to limit themselves to ceremonial and non-political duties.

be passed and which policies adopted than presidents of the United States, whose decisions are routinely checked and balanced. At the same time, prime ministers can be removed relatively easily from power: they might lose the support of their own party and be removed as party leader, or they might lose a vote on a major piece of legislation and feel obliged to step down, or they might lose a formal **vote of confidence** and be required to resign. The latter last happened in Britain in 1979, bringing down the government of James Callaghan and leading to new elections. An effort to bring down the May government in early 2019 during the disruptions over Brexit failed when the government survived a vote of confidence by the narrow margin of 325 votes to 306. May's credibility as prime minister, however, suffered a significant blow, and she resigned in June.

As head of government, the prime minister sets the national political agenda, oversees the military, appoints ambassadors, manages crises, leads his or her party, and represents Britain overseas (see Leach et al., 2018). Two powers in particular define the office:

◆ The power to call a general election. Elections must be held at least once every five years, and prime ministers could once call them early, if – for example – the polls indicated that their party had the best chance of winning. More rarely, they may be obliged to call an election because they have lost a parliamentary vote or the support of their party. A law was adopted by Parliament in 2011 by which fixed terms of five years were established, but early elections can still be called with parliamentary approval, as happened in 2017 when Prime Minister Theresa May – hoping to strengthen the position of her government – called a **snap election** three years ahead of schedule.

◆ The power of appointment. As well as being party leader, the prime minister decides the size of the cabinet, calls and chairs cabinet meetings, appoints and removes members of the cabinet and other senior government officials (about 100 people in all), regularly reshuffles the cabinet (bringing in new members and either removing existing members or moving them to new posts), and can even reorganize government departments.

British prime ministers are normally seasoned national politicians who have worked their way up through the ranks of their party and Parliament. They must be members of the House of Commons and usually serve a long apprenticeship before winning the leadership of their parties; it took Gordon Brown 25 years of sometimes impatient waiting between the time he was elected to Parliament and the time he became prime minister in 2007, but Tony Blair, David Cameron, and Theresa May rose to the top relatively quickly, serving as members of Parliament for 14 years, nine years, and ten years respectively, before becoming prime minister.

Prime ministers govern with the help of a **cabinet**, which consists of all the heads of senior government departments (such as the foreign secretary and the defence secretary), numbering about two dozen in all. The cabinet is always appointed from within Parliament, senior cabinet members become national figures, and reputations can be made and broken according to their performance in the cabinet.

The British cabinet meets frequently and is an important part of the policymaking structure of government: between them, the prime minister and cabinet constitute Her Majesty's Government. Although prime ministers are technically no more than 'first among equals' (*primus inter pares*) in the cabinet, their powers of appointment and agenda setting mean that loyalty to the leader is an essential prerequisite for cabinet members. The cabinet functions on the basis of **collective responsibility**, meaning that once it has made a policy decision, all members are expected to support that decision in public regardless of their personal feelings and to take responsibility for its success or failure.

The manner in which prime ministers govern depends on their different management styles. Margaret Thatcher led from the front, reduced the number of cabinet meetings, and was famous for her forcefulness and for stretching the powers of her office almost to their limit. John Major made more use of his cabinet, allowed a greater variety of opinions, emphasized collegiality and consensus, and intervened less in the affairs of departments. Tony Blair developed a reputation for imposing strong discipline on his party and his cabinet, delegated discretion to strong ministers prepared to follow the government line, but was also accused of micromanaging business to an extent never seen before. David Cameron launched a strong series of policies in office, driven mainly by the perceived need to cut government spending in the wake of the economic downturn, but had limits placed on him because he governed in a coalition.

Vote of confidence
A formal vote in Parliament on the performance of the government, which – if lost – would trigger the resignation of the prime minister.

Snap election
One called unexpectedly before the end of the full term of a legislature.

Collective responsibility
The idea that decisions taken by a group (as in parliamentary government) are taken collectively and that all members must stand or fall by those decisions.

Table 3.2 Modern prime ministers of Britain

Start of term	Name	Party
July 1945	Clement Attlee	Labour
February 1950	Clement Attlee	Labour
October 1951	Winston Churchill	Conservative
May 1955	Anthony Eden	Conservative
January 1957*	Harold Macmillan	Conservative
October 1959	Harold Macmillan	Conservative
October 1963*	Alec Douglas-Home	Conservative
October 1964	Harold Wilson	Labour
March 1966	Harold Wilson	Labour
June 1970	Edward Heath	Conservative
February 1974	Harold Wilson	Labour
October 1974	Harold Wilson	Labour
April 1976*	James Callaghan	Labour
May 1979	Margaret Thatcher	Conservative
June 1983	Margaret Thatcher	Conservative
June 1987	Margaret Thatcher	Conservative
November 1990*	John Major	Conservative
April 1992	John Major	Conservative
May 1997	Tony Blair	Labour
June 2001	Tony Blair	Labour
May 2005	Tony Blair	Labour
June 2007*	Gordon Brown	Labour
May 2010	David Cameron	Conservative/Liberal Democratic coalition
May 2015	David Cameron	Conservative
July 2016*	Theresa May	Conservative
June 2017	Theresa May	Conservative
July 2019*	Boris Johnson	Conservative

In these years, leadership of the governing party changed – through health, resignation, or loss of political support – without a general election being held.

There have been suggestions that the office of prime minister has become increasingly 'presidentialized', for several reasons:

◆ More power has been accumulated by officeholders.
◆ Prime ministers have become more detached from other parts of government.
◆ The executive has become more visible than the legislature.
◆ There has been more media manipulation and spinning of the messages sent out by prime ministers, who have increasingly bypassed their parties and appealed directly to voters, often using social media.
◆ Personalities and public images have come to play an increasingly important role in the work of the prime minister. (The rather stilted personality of Theresa May, for example, earned her the nickname 'Maybot'.)

Such assertions have been directed not just at the British prime ministers, but also at the prime ministers of Australia and Canada (see Heffernan and Webb, 2007). The thesis is rejected by Dowding (2013), who argues that British prime ministers are much more powerful within their office than is the case with – for example – US presidents. He contends that the offices of prime minister and president serve different functions, that the roles of the two positions relative to their political parties are different, that popular representation of prime ministers as presidential tends to be superficial, and that 'the institutions of presidential and parliamentary systems are so different that any global force acting upon them are as likely to drive them further apart as lead them to converge'. That personality has come to play a more important role in the way that prime ministers are perceived is also true of presidents, and the role of personality relates not so much to the powers of the office as to the characteristics of individual leaders.

The legislature: Parliament

The parliamentary model is one of Britain's most successful exports; in whole or in part it has been copied by every other Western democracy, including Australia, Canada, Japan, and most other European states. Also known as the **Westminster model** – because the Houses of Parliament are situated in the district of Westminster in central London – it dates back more than 750 years to the convening of the first English Parliament in 1265. Parliament – whose name derives from the French word *parler*, meaning 'to talk' – has three main functions:

> **Westminster model**
> The system of government based on the British parliamentary model, with a prime minister, a cabinet, and a bicameral legislature.

◆ It is where laws are introduced, discussed, and either rejected or accepted.
◆ It is where existing laws are amended or abolished.
◆ It is responsible for checking on government policy and debating major issues.

It may seem powerful, but because a prime minister with a strong majority can usually rely on the loyalty of party members, Parliament usually spends most of its time debating or confirming the programme of the government and has less power to block the executive than the US Congress. For example, it was only in November 2005 – more than eight years after coming to office – that Tony Blair lost his first legislative vote in Parliament (over the question of how long suspected terrorists could be held without charge). But – as noted earlier – new questions have recently been asked about the sovereignty of Parliament relative to the people; national referendums, for example, are intended only to be advisory, raising the question of whether Parliament should have gone along with the outcome of the Brexit vote, particularly given that most members of Parliament were in favour of the UK remaining within the EU.

Parliament has two chambers with different structures and powers.

House of Lords

The so-called upper house, the Lords recalls the days when Britain was ruled by aristocrats. Members must be **peers**, which meant – until 1999 – that they were either hereditary or were appointed to the House for a life term as a reward for public service or political loyalty. The House of Lords may be both unrepresentative and undemocratic, but it has little power: it can introduce its own legislation, and all bills going through Parliament must be approved by the Lords, but its decisions can be overruled by the Commons and bills on taxation or spending do not need the approval of the Lords. However, it has more time to debate issues than the Commons, it often debates controversial issues, it can force concessions from the Commons, its committees often make valuable contributions to policy debates, and it is a useful point of access for lobbyists.

After removing the rights of most hereditary peers to sit in the House in 1999, the Blair government appointed a commission to decide what form the new chamber should take. Proposals ranged from an all-appointed chamber to a fully elected chamber, but there was no political agreement on how to proceed, as a result of which the House of Lords today sits in a state of limbo with an uncertain future. For now, at least, it has three kinds of members:

◆ Life peers, or Lords Temporal. Numbering just under 700, these are mainly people who have been in public service and are rewarded with a life peerage by the Queen on the recommendation of the prime minister. Many life peerages are political rewards, where favours are returned, or where peerages are given in order to build party numbers in the Lords.
◆ Religious leaders, or Lords Spiritual. These consist of the 26 bishops of the Church of England, an interesting concept given the Western democratic belief in a separation of church and state.
◆ Hereditary peers. A group of 90 has been allowed to stay on pending the next stage in the process of reform.

Except for the bishops, most members of the House of Lords are affiliated with one of the major political parties (in mid-2018 there were 249 Conservative peers, 186 Labour peers, and 98 Liberal Democrats), but a large number – known as crossbenchers – declare themselves independents.

House of Commons

The House of Commons is the more powerful chamber of Parliament, with five major roles: to represent, to make laws, to keep the prime minister accountable, to be a forum for national debate, and to act as a recruitment pool for members of government (Leach et al., 2018). It consists of 650 **Members of Parliament** (MPs) elected by direct universal vote from single-member districts. Debates are presided over by a Speaker, who is elected by the House from among its members, usually comes from the majority party, and has several administrative powers, but is expected to be non-partisan in dealings with the House.

To encourage debate, the chamber of the House has been kept small, with benches rather than seats (Figure 3.1). The governing party sits on one side, with the prime minister and senior ministers on the front bench. MPs without government office, or with only junior office, sit behind the front bench and are known collectively as **backbenchers**. The next biggest party in Parliament sits across from the governing party and acts as the official opposition. The **leader of the opposition** sits directly opposite the prime minister, beside a **shadow cabinet** of opposition MPs responsible for keeping up with – and challenging – their counterparts on the government front bench. If the opposition were to win a majority in an election and become the government, the leader of the opposition would normally become prime minister and many members of the shadow cabinet would become the real cabinet. In other words, the shadow cabinet keeps the government accountable while acting as a government in waiting.

Anyone who has seen the Commons in action will wonder how it ever achieves anything. As the news weekly *The Economist* once colourfully put it, MPs 'snigger and smirk. They sneer and jeer. They murmur and yawn. They gossip salaciously in the bars. They honk and cackle when the Prime Minister or his opposite number is trying to talk. They are like unruly schoolchildren, egged on by the frisson of a chance of being spanked by [the] Speaker but knowing they will usually get away with naughtiness' (quoted by Darnton, 1993). In fact, most of the real work of Parliament is done in committees, where specialists go over the details of bills and invite outside experts to give testimony. The chamber of the Commons is normally quiet, except during controversial debates or Prime Minister's Questions, a half-hour session that is held every Wednesday afternoon during which MPs can ask the prime minister for information on government policy.

Queen Elizabeth II and her husband Prince Philip oversee the annual State Opening of Parliament. Held in the chamber of the House of Lords in the British Parliament, this event illustrates the symbolic role of the monarch in British government – she reads an address that is written for her by the government of the day.
Source: WPA Pool/Getty Images News.

HOUSE OF COMMONS

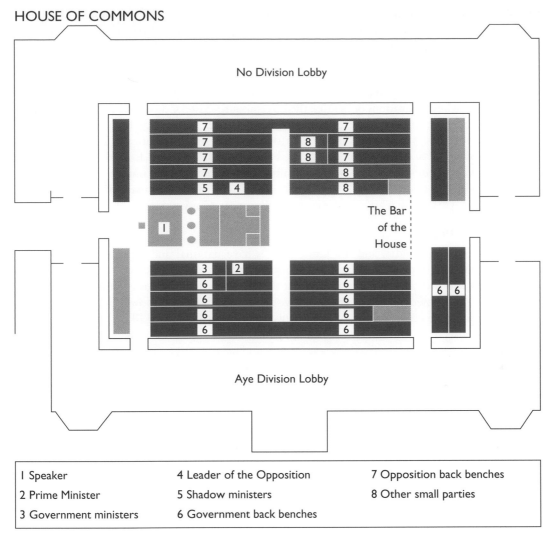

Figure 3.1 Floor plan of the House of Commons

1 Speaker	4 Leader of the Opposition	7 Opposition back benches
2 Prime Minister	5 Shadow ministers	8 Other small parties
3 Government ministers	6 Government back benches	

Party discipline is tight in the British system, because MPs are expected to vote with their parties, a process overseen by parliamentary **whips**: members of the house responsible for organizing party members to take part in debates and votes. Rumbles of discontent are normal, however, and party revolts or a loss of party support have led to eight of the twelve Conservative leaders since 1900 stepping down mid-term. One recent example was that of David Cameron, who resigned as prime minister and party leader in 2016 after losing the Brexit referendum that he was expected to win. He was replaced by Theresa May, who initially built a 20-point lead in opinion polls, but then took a number of actions and made a number of statements that undermined her popularity. When she tried to strengthen her position by calling an early election in June 2017, her party lost seats and its parliamentary majority, and rumours were rife that opponents within the party were placing themselves to replace her as party leader and prime minister. A breakdown of party cohesion – usually dubbed a 'backbench rebellion' if it is big enough – is normally interpreted as a sign of weakness and can lead to the resignation of a prime minister, or even the calling of a new general election.

Social contract An actual or philosophical agreement between the rulers and members of a community regarding their respective rights and duties.

The judiciary: Supreme Court

It is ironic that Britain – home to John Locke (1632–1704), a political theorist associated with ideas such as a **social contract** and the separation of powers (see Chapter 5: United States) – has no codified constitution, and until 2009 lacked even a constitutional court. Instead, judicial review was carried out in a complex system of courts topped by a Court of Appeal and the House of Lords, where law lords heard final appeals in five-person benches.

This changed with the creation in 2009 of an independent Supreme Court of the United Kingdom, with 11 members appointed by a commission. It is the highest court of appeal in the country, hearing civil cases impacting the whole of the UK, criminal cases impacting everywhere but Scotland, and also ruling on disputes about the authority of Parliament and of the Scottish and Welsh regional assemblies. Its creation was an important step in separating the legislative and judicial functions in British government.

The role of judicial review in the British system has also been impacted by the work of the European Court of Justice (ECJ). One of the key institutions of the EU, the Luxembourg-based Court does not have a formal European constitution to interpret, but instead has a series of European treaties and a large body of European law, whose primacy over national law is established. The place of the court in British political life is now uncertain given questions about the outcome of the Brexit negotiations, but even outside the EU Britain will be impacted by ECJ decisions because it will continue to trade with EU member states. Britain is also impacted by the European Court of Human Rights, which is based in Strasbourg, France, and issues rulings on matters dealing with breaches of individual rights in the 47 states that are signatories to the European Convention on Human Rights.

Sub-national government

Federations such as Germany, India, and the United States have national and local levels of government with independent powers and distinct rights and responsibilities. Britain, by contrast, is a unitary state, where local government units have so little independent power that they can be reformed, restructured, or even abolished by the national government. However, recent changes have altered the balance of power between national and local government, devolving more power to local government and creating something like a quasi-federal system.

Scotland and Wales were given their own elected regional assemblies in 1998, with the first elections held in 1999. Members of both are elected for fixed four-year terms and have a variety of powers over local matters such as education, health services, housing, transport, and policing. The 129-member Scottish Parliament also has limited tax-raising powers, but the 60-member National Assembly for Wales does not. The 108-member Northern Ireland Assembly has powers over local issues and also has two councils that address joint policymaking with Ireland and with the British Parliament.

England has no regional assembly of its own but instead has a complex patchwork of unitary and two-tier local authorities, responsible for matters such as education, transport, housing, highways, local services, refuse disposal, and the police. Interestingly, London – which, with its surrounding suburbs, is home to about one-third of the British population – had its elected city government abolished in 1986 by the Thatcher government, but the Blair administration decided that a city the size of London needed its own government, so a law was passed creating in 2000 a new elected government consisting of a mayor and a 25-member Greater London Assembly. In 2016, Labour candidate Sadiq Khan was elected mayor of London, becoming the first Muslim to become mayor of a major European city.

POLITICAL PROCESSES

As with all democracies, Britain has many channels through which its citizens can take part in politics, express their opinions, and have their views reflected in government policy. These include regular elections, political parties representing multiple sets of positions across much of the ideological spectrum (although two – Labour and the Conservatives – dominate the system), a broad and active interest group community, and a diverse media establishment. The options have increased in recent years as the number of elections and parties has grown, the electoral system has diversified, and the number of sources of political news has increased. Only about 1 in 10 Britons has a deep interest in politics, but most take some periodic interest, usually in the lead-up to elections. However, thanks to a combination of social divisions, declining faith in politicians and the political system, and the heated disagreements over Brexit, politics in Britain has become more divided and political debates have become less civil.

The electoral system

Because it is a small country with a unitary system of administration, Britain has relatively few elective offices. Hence the election process is generally simple and quick. Parties choose who will run in their name, elections for the executive and the legislature are combined, and no one can become prime minister without leading a political party. And because party leaders are normally established public figures, they do not need the expensive and lengthy process of public familiarization demanded of candidates in American elections. But the dynamics of British elections have undergone significant change in recent decades: party identification has declined, voters make their choices less on long-term party loyalty than on short-term factors such as the image of party leaders, and election campaigns have become more centralized, with a focus on key target seats that parties hope to wrest from one another (Denver and Garnett, 2014).

British voters are faced with three sets of elections, and periodic referendums.

General elections

Members of the House of Commons are chosen in the general election, the major event on the national political calendar. The UK is divided into 650 constituencies (electoral districts) of roughly equal population size, each represented in the house by a single Member of Parliament (MP). At least once every five years, every seat must be contested in a general election, on a date chosen by the prime minister and approved by Parliament with at least 18 days' notice. Election campaigns typically last a matter of weeks, the choice for voters being made easier by the fact that most parties have distinctive platforms, and voters will tend to vote more for parties than for individuals. Almost everyone older than age 18 can vote, and turnout is normally about 65 to 70 per cent, a little below the average for Western Europe.

The British general election uses the single-member plurality system, under which the winning candidate does not need a majority, but simply needs to win more votes than any other candidate. This system has been criticized in recent years because, although it may be simple and quick, it is not always fair. It tends to favour parties that have large blocks of concentrated support around the country (like Labour and the Conservatives) but works against the interests of parties whose support is more thinly spread (like the Liberal Democrats). The former are better placed to win seats, while the latter more often come in second or third; see Comparing Politics 3.

European elections

As a member of the EU, Britain has the right every five years to elect 72 representatives to the 751-member European Parliament (EP) in Strasbourg, France. In contrast to the single-member plurality system used for general elections, Britain – like all other EU countries – uses proportional representation for EP elections, with the country divided into several multi-member Euro-constituencies. Direct elections to the EP have been held only since 1979, and many British voters have never fully taken to the EU, so turnout at European elections in Britain is among the lowest in the EU: after running at about 36 per cent (far below even the modest EU average of about 55 per cent), it fell to an all-time low of 24 per cent in 1999, before climbing back up to 35–40 per cent in 2004–14. These figures are also a reflection of the limited powers of the EP, which cannot introduce new laws and has only a share in final decisions on adoption. If the UK leaves the EU as anticipated, then it will lose the right to elect representatives to the European Parliament.

Local elections

Because Britain is a unitary state and local authorities have limited power, most voters do not have much interest in local elections. District, county, city, and town councils are all elected on a fixed four-year cycle, but voters usually make their choices on the basis of national issues and the performance of the national government. They vote along party lines, and turnout is rarely higher than 40 per cent. There was hope that the creation of regional and London assemblies might improve turnout, because the assemblies have powers over a variety of local government issues, and so the stakes in the elections have been raised. But over the course of five sets of elections held between 1999 and 2016, turnout in Scotland dropped from 58 per cent to 50 per cent before rising slightly in 2016, and in Wales hovered around 40–45 per cent. Scottish and Welsh assembly elections are based on a combination of winner take all and PR, while regional and European elections in Northern Ireland use a variation of PR known as the single transferable vote (STV).

Referendums

The referendum has become an increasingly common option for British voters in recent decades, with mixed results for the health of democracy. The first ever national referendum was held in 1975, on the question of continued membership of the European Economic Community, but rather than being an exercise in democracy, it was more an effort by the governing party to put to rest an internal dispute over Europe.

The same motivation was behind the 2016 Brexit vote, which was intended to end squabbles over the EU within the Conservative Party. Most experts and political leaders expected a strong vote in favour of remaining, but it was clear that many dubious claims were made during the referendum campaign, and that many voters did not understand either the EU or the impact of EU membership on Britain. Many used the vote to express their

COMPARING POLITICS 3
Can elections ever be fair?

Because legislatures are supposed to reflect and represent the wishes of the electorate, elections should ideally reflect the balance of voter preferences. As we saw in Chapter 2, though, we have mainly failed in our efforts to develop electoral systems that are fair in terms of reflecting voter support. In few places is this more clear than in the single-member plurality (SMP) system used for elections to the British House of Commons. SMP has the advantage of being simple, and tends to produce stable and accountable one-party governments, but it rarely produces results where the percentage of votes cast for a given party translate into an equal percentage of seats in Parliament.

An example is offered by the 2015 general election, when the Conservative party won only 37 per cent of the national vote, but nearly 51 per cent of the seats in Parliament, giving it a majority and enough seats to form a government. The result for Labour was slightly more balanced: it won 30 per cent of the votes cast and 36 per cent of the seats in Parliament. Among smaller parties, the results were more patently unbalanced: the UK Independence Party won 13 per cent of the votes but only one seat (0.15 per cent of the total), the Liberal Democrats won 8 per cent of the votes but just 1 per cent of the seats, while the Scottish National Party was able to convert a 4.7 per cent share of the vote into 56 seats, or nearly 9 per cent of the total (see Figure 3.2) (Cowley and Kavanagh, 2016). In purely numerical terms, then, supporters of the Conservatives and the Scottish Nationalists were significantly over-represented, while supporters of UKIP and the Liberal Democrats were significantly under-represented.

The problem has not gone unnoticed, and efforts have been made to change the British electoral system, including a 2011 referendum on switching to the complex and unusual alternative vote system described in Chapter 2. It was rejected by more than two-thirds of voters. Britain is not alone in experiencing this mismatch between voter preference and seats won by competing parties. Canadian elections produce similar results, while India – see Chapter 8 – has similar problems: at the 2014 general election, the Hindu nationalist Bharatiya Janata Party won 51 per cent of the seats in the Indian parliament with just 31 per cent of the national vote. Germany has made heroic efforts to address the problem of electoral imbalance, using a mix of SMP and proportional representation, and awarding parties additional balancing seats if they win fewer SMP seats than their levels of voter support suggest they deserve – see Chapter 4. In the United States, the problem goes beyond the arithmetic of electoral systems; there, the problem of gerrymandering results in a deliberate manipulation of electoral districts to skew results. In authoritarian systems, meanwhile, many other methods are used to fix results; see Chapter 12: Russia.

dismay with the effects of globalization and immigration, and there was a marked difference of opinion by age and level of education: younger and better educated voters preferred by large margins that the UK remain within the EU.

Several important referendum votes have also been held at the regional level, most focused on the question of devolving powers from London or setting up regional assemblies. The most significant was the 2014 vote on independence for Scotland, which was defeated by 55 per cent to 45 per cent. Following the huge gains made at the 2015 general election by the Scottish National Party, and Scotland's rejection of Brexit in 2016, there was speculation that it was only a matter of time before a second vote on Scottish independence would be held. (For an assessment of referendums globally, see Qvortrup, 2014.)

Political parties

Britain has a wide range of political parties, covering many different ideological positions. Most have strong internal organization, and voters historically tended to be loyal to parties, using them to provide the reference points for their political opinions and for the choices they made at elections. Although several dozen parties have contested recent general elections, Britain since World War II has been commonly portrayed as a two-party system dominated by the Labour Party on the left and the Conservative Party on the right. Between them, these two parties usually win about 70 to 75 per cent of the vote and about 85 to 90 per cent of the seats in Parliament. However, the party

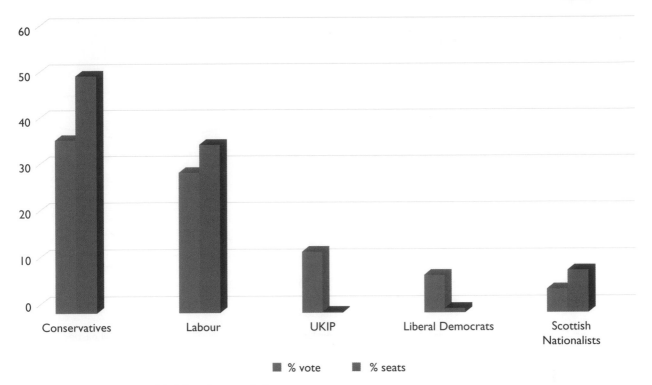

Figure 3.2 Results of the 2015 British general election

system has become less stable in recent years (Clark, 2012), as reflected in the rise of support for smaller parties, and the failure of either of the two major parties to win majorities in 2010 or 2017. Party identification among voters has declined, and smaller parties have increased their national presence as the use of proportional representation in local and European elections has allowed them to win seats and build experience.

Labour Party

The **Labour Party** was founded as a socialist party in 1900 and first came to prominence in the 1920s but only won outright majority power for the first time in 1945. It immediately set about building an expanded welfare state, but spent most of the 1950s in opposition, returning to power in 1964 and again in 1974 before going into opposition in 1979, losing four straight general elections and undergoing a crisis of confidence before electing Tony Blair as its leader in 1994. Blair moved quickly to 'modernize' the party by adopting what he called a new 'left-of-centre agenda' of the kind associated with the so-called **third way** in politics: a philosophy that lay somewhere between mainstream right-wing conservatism/capitalism and traditional socialism, and that distanced the party from its traditional ties with labour unions.

The changes had the desired effect, and the so-called 'New Labour' stormed to victory in 1997, while the Conservatives lost half their seats, including all their seats in Scotland and Wales. The turnaround seemed to symbolize a desire among Britons for change and a concern that Conservatives had paid too little attention to social problems. Blair was given a second term in office in 2001 with his majority barely changed, but voter turnout was down, an outcome interpreted as criticism of the government for the continuing problems in Britain's public services, and as a lack of enthusiasm for the opposition Conservative Party. In 2005 Labour – for the first time in its history – won a third successive victory, although Blair's majority fell and his margin of victory was the lowest for a party in the modern era. Enthusiasm for Blair had clearly lost its lustre, thanks in large part to his controversial decision to support the 2003 invasion of Iraq. He resigned in 2007, making way for Gordon Brown, but when the global financial crisis began to make itself felt, questions were raised about Brown's economic acumen, and he seemed unable to make a connection with the British public. Labour lost the 2010 and 2015 elections.

The more traditionally socialist Jeremy Corbyn was elected party leader following the 2015 defeat, and proved divisive thanks to his lacklustre leadership style and more uncompromisingly left-wing policies (such as

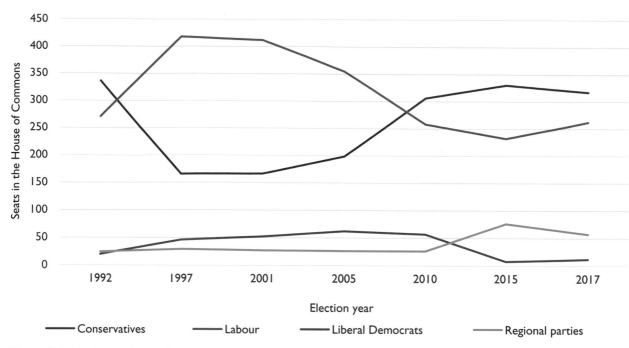

Figure 3.3 Legislative electoral trends in Britain

nuclear disarmament and his plans to renationalize public utilities and the railways). He surprised many by a more dynamic showing at the 2017 election, in which he drew the support of many younger voters upset by Brexit and the policies of the Conservatives. Labour still fell short of the number of seats needed to form a government, however, and Corbyn was widely criticized for his unwillingness to take a firm position in the debate over Brexit.

Conservative Party

The **Conservative Party** (also known as the Tories, the word *Tory* being a term of abuse – meaning a Catholic outlaw – introduced during a debate over the royal succession) dates back to the late 17th century, and has alternated in power with Labour since 1945, winning office again in 2010 after 13 years in opposition. The Conservatives are a pro-business, anti-regulation political party, with many shades of opinion: right-wingers in the party emphasize social discipline, authority, continuity, and morals, while moderates emphasize the creation of wealth and efficient economic organization. Margaret Thatcher broke with many of the party traditions upon becoming party leader in 1975, and for more than a decade the party reflected her support for monetarist economic ideas such as controls on government spending, reducing the role of government in the marketplace, low taxation, and a free market. She also promoted private enterprise and private ownership, believed in a strong global role for Britain and close Anglo-American relations, and was hostile to many aspects of European integration.

Following its defeat at the hands of Tony Blair in 1997, the party was troubled by disunity and by the lack of a leader who could take on and undermine Labour. In 2005, the party elected its fourth leader in less than ten years: David Cameron was seen by some as young, fresh, and a strong challenger to the Labour government, but he seemed to others to be too much an old-style Conservative leader (born into wealth and educated at a private school and at Oxford University), was criticized for being more interested in style than in substance, and the lead held by the Conservatives in opinion polls was ascribed less to the strengths of the party than to Labour's internal problems.

The Conservatives were unable to win a clear majority in the 2010 election, forcing them into an uncomfortable coalition with the Liberal Democrats. Cameron then won an outright majority in 2015, and proceeded with his plans to hold the Brexit referendum in 2016. When the vote went against him (he had campaigned for Britain to remain within the EU), he resigned and was replaced by Theresa May. While she started in a strong position, she rapidly lost support and popularity, calling the snap election in 2017 in which the Conservatives fared poorly; she remained in power only thanks to an agreement with a small Northern Irish party. Her government immediately became bogged down in arguments over the terms of Brexit. She stepped down in mid-2019, and was replaced by former foreign minister and Brexit supporter Boris Johnson.

Liberal Democrats

A small, moderate centre party, the Liberal Democratic Party was created in 1988 when members of a Labour splinter group joined forces with the Liberal Party, one of the oldest parties in Britain and for many years the major opposition to the Conservatives. For a while in the 1980s the new alliance seemed poised to take over from Labour as the major opposition party, and when it contested its first general election in April 1992 as the renamed Liberal Democrats, it won nearly 18 per cent of the vote but only 20 seats. In the 1997 election the Liberal Democrats more than doubled their representation in Parliament, winning 46 seats, the best result for a third party since the 1920s. They added more seats in 2001 and 2005, but then entered an uncomfortable coalition with the Conservatives in 2010 for which they were heavily criticized, and lost almost all their seats in 2015. The party has recently seen a revival based on its strong opposition to Brexit.

Other parties

There are many other smaller parties in Britain, most of which represent either regional or narrower interests. The centre-left Scottish National Party campaigns for independence for Scotland and made a strong showing at Scottish Parliament elections in 1999 and 2003 before winning a plurality in 2007. Meanwhile, its Welsh counterpart, Plaid Cymru, has never won more than about a quarter of the vote in Welsh assembly elections. There are also nearly a dozen parties that are active only in Northern Ireland; the biggest are the Ulster Unionists, who represent continued union for Northern Ireland with Britain, while the smaller Sinn Fein has campaigned in the past for the reunification of Ireland. Parties with a narrower agenda include the anti-European UK Independence Party, which, as already noted, won 13 per cent of the vote in 2015 but only one seat in Parliament, and then ceased to have much purpose following the Brexit referendum. It was superseded in 2019 by the Brexit Party.

THE FUTURE OF BRITISH GOVERNMENT AND POLITICS

Britain is distinguished from almost every other country in the world by its long and relatively evolutionary history of political development. The rarity of domestic conflict and revolutionary change allowed it to build enduring political institutions and to be home to many influential political and economic thinkers. Stability also provided the foundations for an industrial revolution and for the creation of an extensive empire, thereby promoting the spread of British political and economic ideas.

However, much has since changed for Britain and its people. It went through two costly world wars, its empire is no longer, and the rise of American, Japanese, and German power forced Britain to undergo a process of political and economic change that has not yet ended. It began by restructuring its economy, building a welfare system, and rethinking both its military role in the world and its attitude toward its European neighbours. After a long period of pessimism, Britain's political and economic readjustment had by the 1990s begun to develop long-term stability. This was replaced by confusion and uncertainty in the wake of the global financial crisis and the Brexit vote.

Troubling questions now hang over Britain's future. Its regional divisions are deeper than ever, the relative poverty and marginalization of the northern parts of England contrasting with the wealth of the south and the global view of most Londoners. Nationalism persists, and the pressures for Scottish independence have not gone away. The fight over Brexit has divided ordinary people from one another and from their political leaders, while political parties are divided over their positions on Brexit. The terms of Britain's departure from the EU had still not been resolved as this book went to press, but whatever the outcome, worrying doubts now cast long shadows over Britain's economic future and its place in the world.

DISCUSSION QUESTIONS

1. Brexit: Good idea or bad?
2. Scottish independence: Good idea or bad?
3. Should Britain codify its constitution?
4. What are the advantages and disadvantages of having a monarchy?
5. What could Britain learn from other countries in regard to the weaknesses in its electoral system?
6. Can Britain survive its current political, economic, and social difficulties?

CHAPTER CONCEPTS

◆ Backbenchers
◆ Brexit
◆ British Empire
◆ Cabinet
◆ Codified constitution
◆ Conservative Party
◆ House of Commons
◆ House of Lords
◆ Labour Party

◆ Leader of the opposition
◆ Magna Carta
◆ Member of Parliament
◆ Parliament
◆ Peers
◆ Shadow cabinet
◆ Thatcherism
◆ Third way
◆ Whips

KEY TERMS

◆ Absolute monarch
◆ Collective responsibility
◆ Devolution
◆ Divine right
◆ European Union
◆ Euroscepticism
◆ Industrial revolution
◆ Monarchy
◆ National identity

◆ Pragmatism
◆ Prime minister
◆ Regionalism
◆ Snap election
◆ Social contract
◆ Vote of confidence
◆ Welfare state
◆ Westminster model

UNITED KINGDOM ONLINE

Office of the Prime Minister: www.gov.uk/government/organisations/prime-ministers-office-10-downing-street
UK Parliament: www.parliament.uk
Royal Family: www.royal.uk/royal-family
Conservative Party: www.conservatives.com
Labour Party: www.labour.org.uk
BBC News: www.bbc.com/news
The Guardian: www.theguardian.com
The Independent: www.independent.co.uk
The Times: www.thetimes.co.uk

FURTHER READING

Evans, Geoffrey, and Anand Menon (2017) *Brexit and British Politics* (Polity). One of many assessments of the causes and effects of the British decision to leave the European Union.

Griffiths, Simon, and Robert Leach (2018) *British Politics*, 3rd edn (Red Globe Press); Bill Jones and Philip Norton (2014) *Politics UK*, 8th edn (Routledge); and Robert Leach, Bill Coxall, and Lynton Robins, *British Politics*, 2nd edn (Red Globe Press, 2011). Three examples of the many general surveys of British politics.

Heffernan, Richard, Colin Hay, Meg Russell, and Philip Cowley (eds) (2016) *Developments in British Politics 10* (Red Globe Press). The latest in a series of edited studies of the British political system, including chapters on Parliament, elections, parties, and regional developments.

Marr, Andrew (2017) *A History of Modern Britain* (Pan Macmillan). A best-selling history of Britain from the end of World War II to Brexit.

McCormick, John (2017) *Contemporary Britain*, 4th edn (Red Globe Press). A general introduction to the history, politics, society, and economy of Britain.

Rogers, Robert, and Rhodri Walters (2015) *How Parliament Works*, 7th edn (Routledge), and Cristina Leston-Bandeira and Louise Thompson (2018) *Exploring Parliament* (Oxford University Press). Two studies of the structure, procedures, and political role of the British Parliament.

Visit **www.macmillanihe.com/McCormick-Cases** to access additional materials to support teaching and learning.

GERMANY

4

CONTENTS

◆ Overview
◆ Political development
◆ Political culture
◆ Political system
◆ Political processes
◆ The future of German government and politics

PREVIEW

Germany's value as a case lies in its remarkable transformation since 1949. It was long politically divided into eastern and western territories that straddled the fault lines of the Cold War, and was finally reunited only in 1990. Despite this, it developed a new and workable political form, with an efficient parliamentary system of government based on a federal republic. This has helped Germany to achieve stability, and to become Europe's leading political and economic actor: it is the fourth biggest economy in the world, as well as a leading actor in the European Union. It has yet to close the political, economic, and social gaps between east and west, and today faces new pressures from waves of immigration that have alarmed many of its citizens. Nonetheless, the German case can tell us a great deal about the qualities necessary for political and economic success.

KEY ARGUMENTS

◆ After centuries of political change, Germany has found a workable political form since 1949, although it is still working through the implications of reunification in 1990.

◆ Germany finds itself continuing to ask questions about its political identity, as well as its place within the European Union.

◆ The German political system is a parliamentary democracy based on a federal republic, with some distinctive features based on avoiding the mistakes of its political past.

◆ Although Germany has two national legislative chambers, the 'lower' Bundestag has more visibility and political influence than the 'upper' Bundesrat.

◆ Germany is unusual in using a mixed member proportional representation electoral system, which is complex but arguably fairer than the systems used by many of its neighbours.

◆ From a time when two major parties dominated German politics, there has been new fluidity as party identification has weakened and voter turnout has fallen.

OVERVIEW

Germany has long been one of the most powerful and influential countries in Europe, the trend continuing with the way that it has reinvented itself in recent decades as the leading actor in the European Union, and a key player in the global economy. It remains something of a reluctant power, however, with many Germans unwilling to see their country assert itself too obviously, preferring instead to focus on domestic matters. It has been successful in building a stable and workable political system whose achievements stand in contrast to the tumult of its earlier experience with democracy under the Weimar Republic. At the same time, it has seen troubling changes in recent years with the combined effects of falling voter turnout at elections, a move away from the once predictable dominance of two major political parties, widespread dismay arising from the arrival of new waves of immigrants, and concerns about falling population numbers.

In political terms, Germany over the last century has evolved from an authoritarian monarchy to a democracy to a totalitarian regime and back to a democracy. Its current political system − one of the few ranked as a full democracy in the Democracy Index − is a federal parliamentary republic, with a figurehead president and a chancellor elected out of the lower of two legislative chambers (the Bundestag). Federalism has meant the decentralization of power to 16 Länder (or states), with politicians from the Länder often playing an influential role in national politics. Berlin may be the seat of the federal government and the biggest German city by population (about 3.5 million people), but there is no one obvious centre of power; Germany has no equivalent of London, Rome, or Madrid. The financial capital is Frankfurt, and the biggest industrial centres are in the west along the Rhine and Ruhr valleys.

In economic terms, Germany is clearly the powerhouse of Europe: it is the fourth largest economy in the world (after the United States, China, and Japan), as well as the largest in Europe, accounting for more than a fifth of the combined gross domestic product of the European Union . It is the largest manufacturing economy in Europe, and is also a major exporter, ranking second only to China and well ahead of the United States and Japan; in recent years it has had the highest export surplus of any country in the world. It has become famous for the quality of its engineering, the efficiency of its vehicle industry (notwithstanding the scandal that broke in 2015 involving efforts by Volkswagen to cheat its way past US emission standards), and is a major producer of wind and solar power technology.

In social terms, Germany has many of the same divisions as its neighbours (particularly obvious in the persistent income differences between western and eastern Germans), and is experiencing the same growth of ethnic diversity. Since inviting Turks to Germany as guest workers in the 1960s, the number of Germans with Turkish heritage has grown to about 2–4 million (the estimates vary), to which has recently been added new waves of immigrants and refugees from Syria, Afghanistan, and Iraq. Germany's population stands at 83 million, but in spite of the arrival of new immigrants, falling birth rates mean that it is projected to fall to about 79 million by 2050. As its domestic social structure changes, it is also important to remember that Germans make up the largest national group in Europe; as well as their obvious concentration in Germany, German-speakers are found also in Austria, Belgium, Italy, Luxembourg, Poland, and Switzerland.

POLITICAL DEVELOPMENT

Germany is a newer state than most people think: it only came together as a united political entity for the first time in 1871. It then underwent traumatic change related to its involvement in two world wars, and spent more than 40 years divided into two separate states before being reunited in 1990. Although Lemke and Welsh (2018) use adjectives such as *fractured* and *tortuous* to describe Germany's modern political development, the political system developed by West Germany after World War II has proved successful and resilient, offering a foundation for Germany's growth as the economic engine of Europe. Germans remain hesitant about their country playing a leading role in international affairs, though, and resistant to investing heavily in the building of a large military, Hence German influence in Europe and the world tends to be subtle rather than obvious.

The origins of Germany

Unlike Britain and France, most of what is now Germany was not conquered by the Romans, who found the Rhine and the Danube to be useful and natural defensive barriers. The area was not immune to later invasions, though, notably from the Franks of what is now France, and the Magyars of eastern Europe. In 800 CE, the Holy Roman Empire was declared by the emperor Charlemagne, covering almost all of what is now Germany (as well as Austria and parts of Poland, the Czech Republic, and Italy). While it lasted until its final destruction in 1806 by Napoleon, it was never a unified entity, consisting of a patchwork of numerous kingdoms and principalities, coexisting with the rising power of Prussia. After the defeat of Napoleon, European powers meeting at the 1815 Congress of Vienna established the German confederation, a loose association of 39 independent states.

The key figure in the creation of the German state was Otto von Bismarck (1815–98), minister president of Prussia from 1862. With his negotiating skills and appeals to German patriotism, Bismarck was able to pull the states of the confederation together into what some call the Second German Empire, formed in January 1871. Germany now underwent a period of rapid industrialization, but no efforts were made to democratize the new state, which was ruled in an authoritarian fashion by a Kaiser (emperor) and a supporting aristocracy. Nationalism also played a key role in shaping the new Germany, its leaders looking with interest at the way in which Britain and France had established strong centralized states and stable political systems, and noting how even small countries such as the Netherlands had been able to forge themselves into world powers.

The Germans responded by building a strong bureaucratic system, which Bismarck used to justify his argument that the Prussian model was the one that other German states should adopt if Germany was to become a world power. Bismarck succeeded so well that Germany developed a sense of superiority over neighbouring states, built a large military, and established an empire in eastern and south-western Africa. This chapter ended with the outbreak in August 1914 of what was then known as the Great War.

From the Weimar Republic to the Third Reich (1919–45)

Following Germany's defeat in the war, and the abdication of Kaiser Wilhelm II in November 1918, a new political arrangement was created in the form of the Deutsches Reich (German Realm, or Empire), known more commonly as the **Weimar Republic** after the city in which its constitution was adopted in 1919. Based on a democratic parliamentary system, with a president as head of state and a chancellor as head of government, it might have worked but for the burden of economic reparations foisted on Germany by the terms of the 1919 Treaty of Versailles. There was also political unrest as numerous political parties were created that reflected divisions in the German electorate, with none having enough seats to form a workable majority or coalition government.

The end of the Weimar Republic began in 1929 with the fallout from the Great Depression, and the rise of **Nazism**. The National Socialist German Worker's Party (the Nazis) exploited the fears of many Germans by making appeals to nationalism, while blaming Jews and ethnic minorities for the country's problems. The party's leader – Adolf Hitler from 1921 – was able to exploit nationalist sentiment to eliminate his opposition, and claimed that he could deliver Germany from its political chaos and rebuild its confident past; the Nazis named their new regime the Third Reich, based on retroactively labelling the Holy Roman Empire and the Second German Empire as its predecessors. Between 1928 and 1932, the Nazis were able to increase their support from two per cent of the electorate to 33 per cent, leaving President Paul von Hindenburg with little choice but to appoint Hitler as chancellor in 1933. With Hindenburg's death in August 1934, Hitler took over the powers of the president and declared himself Führer (Leader).

Hitler created a **totalitarian** system, and argued the need for 'living space' for Germans, by which he forced a union with Austria and the occupation of parts of Czechoslovakia. The Nazi invasion of Poland in September 1939 set off World War II, pitting Germany and Italy first against Britain and France, and eventually against the USSR and the United States. At the height of Nazi power, Germany occupied most of central and Eastern Europe, the western USSR, and all of France. Hitler, however, was unable to launch his planned invasion of Britain, found himself overextended on the Soviet front, and from 1941 had to cope also with the military power of the United States. The Third Reich ended with Hitler's suicide in April 1945.

Nazism
A form of extreme nationalism based on theories of racial superiority, hostility to welfare and communism, and hostility to democracy, with a single all-powerful leader.

Totalitarianism
An absolutist form of authoritarian rule, based either on a guiding ideology or the goal of major social change, with total control exercised by a leader, state, or party over all aspects of public and private life.

⚭ TIMELINE

800–1806	Holy Roman Empire
1815–71	German confederation
1871	Unification of Germany under Prussian leadership
1871–1918	Second German Empire
1919	Treaty of Versailles imposes reparations on Germany
1919–33	Weimar Republic
1933	Hitler becomes chancellor
1934–45	Third Reich
1949	Foundation of West Germany (May) and East Germany (October)
1957	West Germany is co-founder of European Economic Community
1961	(August) Construction of Berlin Wall
1973	West and East Germany join the United Nations
1989	Fall of the Berlin Wall
1990	(October) Reunification of Germany
2001	Military deployment to Afghanistan is Germany's biggest outside Europe since 1945
2002	Euro replaces Deutsche Mark
2005	Angela Merkel elected first female German chancellor
2010–11	Germany plays leading role in bailout of debt-ridden Greece
2013–18	Germany witnesses surge in immigration
2018	Merkel steps down as leader of Christian Democrats

Post-war division (1945–90)

The closing months of World War II had degenerated into a race between the Western Allies and the Soviets for control of post-war Europe, resulting in the division of Germany into four zones of occupation administered separately by the Soviets, the Americans, the British, and the French. Berlin, while surrounded by the Soviet zone, was similarly divided four ways. In short order, work was begun on establishing two Germanies (see Map 4.1):

◆ In the west, the allied zones came together in May 1949 as the new Federal Republic of Germany (**West Germany**), based on a new democratic constitution, with a capital in the provincial city of Bonn. The first elections to the new state were held in August 1949, a pattern soon emerging of dominance by two major political parties (the Christian Democratic Union (CDU) and the Social Democrats (SPD)), with the balance held by smaller parties.

◆ In the east, the Soviet zone was shaped into the new German Democratic Republic (**East Germany**), created in October 1949 with a separate constitution, a one-party communist government, and a capital in East Berlin. Although it supposedly became a sovereign state in 1955, it was tied closely into the Soviet sphere of influence.

For its first 14 years, West Germany was led by Konrad Adenauer, the moderate and pragmatic leader of the CDU. His priorities were to rebuild the German economy and to establish a new and stable political system. After some initial uncertainties, the economy began to grow in the 1950s on the back of injections of foreign assistance. Building political stability was more challenging, however, mainly because of the uncertain national identity of West Germany. Adenauer concentrated on making it firmly part of the Western alliance against the Soviets, but the new country was approached with caution even by its allies. German military rearmament was carried out within the context of the new North Atlantic Treaty Organization (NATO), which West Germany joined in 1955. Efforts

Map 4.1 The Cold War division of Germany

were made to channel economic development through Western European cooperation, leading in 1958 to the launch of the six-member European Economic Community (precursor to today's European Union).

The construction in 1961 of the **Berlin Wall**, cutting off West Berlin from East Germany, physically symbolized the ideological divisions between the two parts of Germany, and seemed to end any real possibility of reunification. The idea never went away, however, and was exemplified by the **Ostpolitik** (Eastern Policy) pursued by the West German Social Democrats, and aimed at encouraging cooperation with East Germany. Peace treaties were signed with the Soviet Union and Poland, and the divisions of Berlin were loosened, but enthusiasm for the policy had waned by the late 1970s; many West Germans felt that they were paying too much for minimal concessions from the East.

Although West German economic growth was impressive, it served to reveal the country's social divisions. The failure of either of the major political parties to move quickly enough generated demands for more radical change, as a result of which a variety of new alternative social, political, and student organizations became active. Most notably, the Greens were formed in the 1970s around environmental and anti-nuclear sentiment, while there was emerging support for parties on the far right of the political spectrum.

Reunification (1990)

The post-war division of Germany had long been seen by most Germans as a temporary arrangement. With a thawing of the Cold War in the mid-1980s, the path seemed to be open for greater east–west accommodation and for East Germany to pull away from the Soviet sphere. Events now moved quickly, even in the face of concerns among its allies about the implications for new German power in Europe, and concerns within Germany about the economic and social costs of the wealthy and democratic west absorbing the relatively poor and undemocratic east.

The challenges of reunification included the following:

◆ Integrating the individualism, ambitions, and global view of West Germans with the more passive introversion of East Germans.
◆ Confronting the prospect of high unemployment in the east as inefficient state-run businesses and industries were transformed to meet the needs of the market economy.
◆ Meeting the enormous costs of reunification, including modernizing the transport and communications system in the east, building new housing stock, creating new jobs, covering new social security and unemployment benefits, cleaning the polluted East German environment, harmonizing the education and health care system, and paying for the repatriation of Soviet troops.

The administration of Christian Democratic chancellor Helmut Kohl proceeded regardless, announcing a ten-point programme for reunification in November 1989. A monetary, economic, and social union came into effect in July 1990, a reunification treaty was signed in August, and the two Germanies were formally reunited – with Berlin as their capital – on 3 October. In June 1991, the seat of government was moved from Bonn to Berlin. Following reconstruction of the old Reichstag building, the German legislature met in the new building in 1999, for the first time since 1942.

Germany today

Given Germany's chequered history, it is remarkable how much success it has achieved in building a new, prosperous, and reunited country. To be sure, the divisions between its eastern and western regions remain, and as a global economic leader, Germany was deeply impacted by the fallout from the global financial crisis beginning in 2007, the effects of a crisis within the eurozone sparked by problems in Greece in 2009, and the challenges posed by increased immigration in the wake of the civil war in Syria beginning in 2011. Many in Germany have felt the strains of expectations and pressures to help bail out troubled members of the eurozone, and more recently of the arrival of large numbers of refugees and asylum-seekers.

Regardless, Germany's political system has withstood the pressures, and Germans themselves have moved in new political directions. The Social Democrats held power from 1998 to 2005, after which the Christian Democrats under Angela Merkel won four straight general elections, and the once-reliable two-party alignment has weakened. The Left has emerged out of the Party of Democratic Socialism that replaced the West German communists, while Alliance 90/The Greens is an association between non-communist eastern German parties and the Greens, sitting on the moderate left of the political spectrum. On the right, meanwhile, the Alternative for Germany (AfD) was founded in 2013, and today promotes a combination of nationalist, populist, and eurosceptic policies. Reflecting concerns about immigration, AfD derives most of its support from eastern Germany and was able to win 13 per cent of the seats in the German Bundestag at the 2017 elections.

Pedestrians walk through Potsdamer Platz in Berlin, whose resurgence as the capital of a new Germany reflects the remarkable success of the country in transforming itself into Europe's leading political and economic power.
Source: iStock.com/querbeet.

The changing balance of party support has made it difficult for either of the major parties to form governments in association with smaller parties, with the result that Angela Merkel has had to preside over three grand coalitions between the CDU and the SPD. Also, and in spite of perceptions that she is the strongest leader in Europe (and perhaps, given mixed opinion about Donald Trump, the strongest leader in the Atlantic Alliance), Merkel has been widely criticized for being too reactive and cautious as a leader (see Introduction to Padgett et al., 2014), and her days in office are now clearly numbered. Germany also remains less than certain about its place in global affairs: while most Germans remain deeply committed to the European Union, their country is not the global power that its economic reach and military potential might suggest.

POLITICAL CULTURE

At first glance, Germany might appear to be one of the most successful, confident, and affluent countries in Europe, which has travelled a long way beyond its past difficulties. In reality, Germans have long suffered from self-doubt and from concerns about the direction in which their country is headed, and it should come as little surprise that one of the German words borrowed by English is *angst* (or anxiety). At the same time, the **German Question** has long loomed large in the way its neighbours have regarded the size, power, and changing borders of Germany. Even with reunification, questions remain about the impact of Germany on the European Union and its place in international affairs (Lemke and Welsh, 2018). Some expect German leadership, but others fear the prospects of that leadership.

COMPARING POLITICAL CULTURE 4
Politics, patriotism, and nationalism

Government and politics – as we saw in Chapter 3 – has a close relationship with national identity, which – in turn – has a close relationship with **patriotism** and **nationalism**. Without a strong sense of what a state represents, and of the political values of the state, it is not easy for government and citizens to move in the same direction. There will inevitably be ideological divisions that spark competing political parties and movements, and that push government in different directions. The ideal, though, is that citizens still feel as though they are part of a shared endeavour in which they can feel a sense of pride, or patriotism. There is often a fine line, though, between feeling proud and feeling exclusive or superior, and the tensions can lead to secession, division, or – in the most extreme cases – to war.

Germany has a troubled relationship with all three concepts. While Germans have a strong sense of national identity, it has not been attached to a strong and stable state or – at least until recently – to a consistent political system. They are far from unique in this regard, and almost all of the countries used as cases in this book (with the possible exceptions of the United States, Japan, and France) have an uncertain definition of their national identity. Even where they have strong symbols, such as flags and anthems, it is not always clear what they stand for, and this is certainly a problem in Germany with its troubled past. Pride in the political system has grown in Germany, but Germans have conflicting views about patriotism because of its problematic association with nationalism during the Second Reich and the Nazi era.

A strong sense of national identity and patriotism does not necessarily equate with trust in government (see Chapter 7), but effective government is hard to achieve in the face of weak identity. The United States has a strong sense of national identity, for example, but trust in government has recently reached an all-time low and the country is deeply divided. Britain, meanwhile, has seen a growth of nationalism as Scotland pulls away from England, as English nationalism has become increasingly equated with racism and intolerance, and as Britain pulls away from the European Union. For its part, Nigeria has faced the consistent problem of trying to build a workable political system and a strong sense of national unity in a society marked by deep ethnic and religious divisions.

Patriotism
Pride in country, identification with country, or devotion to country, as reflected in an association with the history, symbols, and myths of that country.

Nationalism
The belief that a group of people with a common national identity has the right to form an independent state and to govern itself free of external intervention. Can also indicate a sense of exclusivity and superiority over others.

Part of the explanation for these uncertainties lies in the relative newness of Germany as a state. Germans may be one of Europe's oldest linguistic, ethnic, and cultural units (Langenbacher and Conradt, 2017), but modern Germany has a shorter history than – for example – Britain or France. Its borders have often changed, the effects of world wars and of Cold War divisions ensuring that they reached their final shape only in 1990. Although reunification might seem to have resolved many doubts and uncertainties, the eastern and western parts of Germany still have differences of opinion about their political, economic, and social directions, and questions continue to be asked about what it means to be German: see Comparing Political Culture 4. To such questions have more recently been added concerns about the impact of immigration: first came the mainly Turkish guest workers of the 1950s and 1960s, and Germany's relatively generous laws on asylum have combined more recently with its economic pull to draw refugees, asylum-seekers, and unauthorized immigrants from the former Yugoslavia and the Middle East.

As regards attitudes towards politics, Roberts (2016) identifies three phases in the shaping of German political culture. The first, covering about the first twenty years of West Germany, was marked by a toleration of democratic politics but an unwillingness to be politically active. Politics was not held in high esteem, and many Germans felt that participation was not worth the effort (although, as we will see later in the chapter, turnout at elections was high). The second phase, running until reunification, involved a normalization of attitudes about politics, and a sense that participation was both necessary and useful. West Germany, in this sense, became more like its democratic neighbours. In the third phase, since 1990, there has been a division of attitudes sparked by the contrasting values and expectations of eastern and western Germans. The new Germany was created nearly thirty years ago, but attitudes take longer than this to change, and although Roberts considers German political culture to be more homogeneous than ever before, declining voter turnout and the growing fragmentation of the party landscape might seem to indicate otherwise.

POLITICAL SYSTEM

Germany is a parliamentary democracy with a figurehead president, an elected chancellor (equivalent to a prime minister), a bicameral legislature, a federal system of administration, and multiple political parties. It is also – unlike Britain or Japan, but like the United States, India, and Nigeria – a **republic**. As with all political systems, though, the brief description says little about the nuances of German government and politics, which have evolved according to the unique circumstances of the country and the values of its people. The German system particularly contrasts with those of many of its neighbours in that while their governmental structures have evolved over a long period of time in response to a combination of domestic and foreign pressures, the modern German system is mainly the result of demands made on western Germany after World War II by its British, French, and American occupiers, who were determined to make sure that Germany would never again become a threat to peace in Europe.

The constitution

The German constitution is known as the **Basic Law** (*Grundgesetz*, which can also be translated as Fundamental Law). The choice of this term reflected the way in which much about the post-war West German political system was seen as temporary. Hoping for reunification between east and west, and wanting to avoid the permanence that would be indicated by a constitution, the framers instead agreed a Basic Law that was seen as provisional, pending the eventual agreement of a constitution of a reunified Germany. In the event, the Basic Law became permanent, with East Germany acceding to most of its provisions after reunification.

The Basic Law went into force in May 1949, and amounted to a revolutionary change in the direction of German politics, both in terms of the institutions it created and in terms of the new emphasis it placed on **civil liberties**. There were strong doubts that it would succeed. After all, this was only the second time in German history that it had established a democratic political system, the first – the Weimar Republic – having clearly been a failure. Weimar was associated with an unstable executive, too many political parties, and the eventual rise of Nazism, and it was with these memories in mind that the framers of the Basic Law began their

Republic
A political system in which all members of the government are either elected or appointed by elected officials, and there are no hereditary positions, as there are in monarchies.

Civil liberties
The rights that citizens have relative to government, and that should not – in democracies, at least – be restricted by government. They include freedom of expression and association.

Name	Federal Republic of Germany (Bundesrepublik Deutschland)
Capital	Berlin
Administration	Federal republic, with 16 Länder (states).
Constitution	Date of state formation 1871, and most recent constitution (the Basic Law) adopted 1949.
Executive	Parliamentary. The chancellor leads a cabinet of between 14 and 20 ministers, while a president (elected to five-year terms – renewable once – by a special convention of the Bundestag and Länder) serves as a mainly ceremonial head of state.
Legislature	Bicameral: a Bundestag of at least 598 members elected for renewable four-year terms. Although it functions like an elected upper house, the 69-member Bundesrat consists of delegates drawn from the Länder.
Judiciary	The Federal Constitutional Court has proved to be highly influential as an arbiter of the constitution. It has 16 members, with eight each elected by the Bundestag and the Bundesrat, serving single 12-year terms with mandatory retirement at age 68.
Electoral system	The Bundestag is elected through a mixed member system, with half elected using single-member plurality and half using party list proportional representation. Members of the Bundesrat are nominated by the Länder.
Party system	Multi-party. The leading parties are the Christian Democratic Union (CDU), with its Bavarian partner the Christian Social Union (CSU), and the Social Democratic Party (SPD). Other significant players are the Alternative for Germany, the Left Party, and the Green Party.

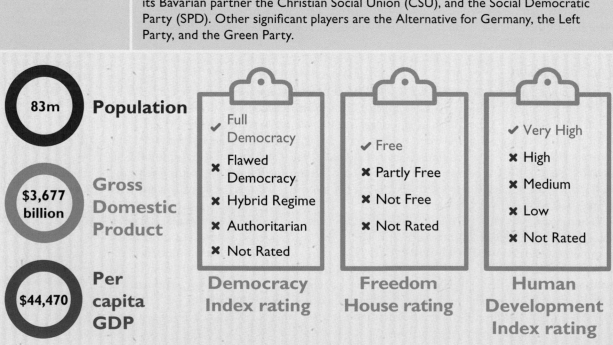

Population 83m

Gross Domestic Product $3,677 billion

Per capita GDP $44,470

Democracy Index rating
- ✓ Full Democracy
- ✗ Flawed Democracy
- ✗ Hybrid Regime
- ✗ Authoritarian
- ✗ Not Rated

Freedom House rating
- ✓ Free
- ✗ Partly Free
- ✗ Not Free
- ✗ Not Rated

Human Development Index rating
- ✓ Very High
- ✗ High
- ✗ Medium
- ✗ Low
- ✗ Not Rated

work. The model they chose was a parliamentary system within a federal republic, retaining some of the features of Weimar but abandoning others:

◆ Under Weimar, and much like the contemporary French system, there was a powerful president and a functionary prime minister (known in Germany as a chancellor). The latter could be fired by either the president or the legislature, as a partial result of which there were 14 chancellors during the 15 years of Weimar. Under the Basic Law, the presidency has been stripped of almost all its political powers, and the chancellor can only be removed by the legislature based on a constructive vote of no confidence by which a replacement must first be agreed.

◆ Under Weimar, the legislature could select some government ministers, a job which falls exclusively to the chancellor under the Basic Law.

◆ Under Weimar, no threshold was set for winning seats in the Reichstag (the legislature), meaning that it was possible for even small parties to win seats, creating a divided and often unstable legislature. Under the Basic Law, parties must win at least five per cent of the vote in order to win any seats.

Significantly, the first 19 articles of the Basic Law focus on civil liberties, meaning that they are given a prominence designed to contrast with the weaknesses of political rights during the Weimar years. Partly as a result, Germany since 1949 has built a responsive and transparent system of government that leaves it squarely within the select group of countries defined by the Democracy Index as full democracies; it scores particularly well on the protection of civil liberties. The Basic Law is protected by a Constitutional Court that is famously independent of the political fray (see later in this section), and amendments are made by changes to the law, needing the support of two-thirds of the members of the Bundesrat and of the Bundestag. No changes are allowed to the articles dealing with civil liberties.

Head of state: the president

The president is the German head of state, with a mainly symbolic role in German government. The officeholder is elected for a maximum of two five-year terms by a Federal Convention (that is, an electoral college) made up of the full membership of the Bundestag and an equal number of delegates from state parliaments. The winner needs the support of an absolute majority of the electoral college, failing which the election can go to as many as three rounds, with a plurality (or simple majority) being enough in the third round. Three presidential elections since 1949 have gone to a third round, most recently for Christian Wulff in 2010. Few presidents have served more than one term, and all – so far – have been men.

The president is usually a well-respected senior politician who is acceptable to all political parties. The job comes with an array of mainly technical and ceremonial responsibilities: the president signs new laws into effect (but has little or no say on their content), appoints ministers nominated by the chancellor, and appoints or removes chancellors (but this is usually only a formality, since it will almost always be clear which candidate for chancellor has enough

Table 4.1 Modern presidents of Germany

Name	Beginning of term	Political party
Theodor Heuss	1949, 1954	Free Democrats (FDP)
Heinrich Lübke	1959, 1964 (resigned)	Christian Democrats (CDU)
Gustav Heinemann	1969	Social Democrats (SPD)
Walter Scheel	1974	FDP
Karl Carstens	1979	CDU
Richard von Weizsäcker	1984, 1989	CDU
Roman Herzog	1994	CDU
Johannes Rau	1999	SPD
Horst Köhler	2004, 2009 (resigned)	CDU
Christian Wulff	2010 (resigned)	CDU
Joachim Gauck	2012	Independent
Frank-Walter Steinmeier	2017	SPD

support in the Bundestag to form a government). Theoretically, the president could refuse to sign a new law or turn down a candidate for a ministerial position, but this rarely happens; there is a difference, in this regard, between what the president can do and what the president is expected to do. The president also appoints judges and senior members of the military, and can declare a national emergency if the Bundestag cannot be convened.

Presidents are expected to be non-partisan and to refrain from making political statements, but their backgrounds as politicians mean that politics occasionally spills over into their elections, and into their actions while in office (Roberts, 2016). This happened, for example, with Horst Köhler, one of Germany's most popular presidents. Just under a year into his second term in office, in May 2010, he resigned following criticism of comments he made in a radio interview suggesting that German troops could be deployed, if necessary, to protect German trade interests. While the comment was controversial, Köhler's decision to resign was widely seen as an over-reaction. In 2017, Frank-Walter Steinmeier was elected as the 12th president of Germany after a long career in national politics. A Social Democrat, he had twice served as minister of foreign affairs under Chancellor Angela Merkel, and briefly as Germany's deputy chancellor.

The executive: chancellor and Council of Ministers

The **chancellor** of Germany is the functional equivalent of the prime minister in a parliamentary system, although the position is sufficiently powerful that Germany is sometimes described as a 'chancellor democracy'. One key difference with Britain is that where the British prime minister is typically head of the political party that wins the most seats after a general election, it is not enough for a German chancellor to be head of their party: they must also be elected by the Bundestag in a secret ballot on the basis of a nomination by the president, whose decision is in turn a reflection of the outcome of federal elections. Parties typically enter those elections with clearly identifiable 'chancellor-candidates' in place, and the candidate who is able to form a government after the election wins the office. The chancellor's terms in office coincide with the terms of the Bundestag, and the chancellor can serve an unlimited number of terms. West Germany's first post-war leader was Konrad Adenauer, who served five terms in office (two of them less than a year each) for a total of more than 14 years, while Helmut Kohl served five terms for a total of more than 16 years.

Other than through death, resignation, or loss of support within their own party, chancellors lose office only if their party loses an election or if the chancellor is removed through a **constructive vote of no confidence** in the Bundestag. It is 'constructive' in the sense that a vote can only be held on removing an incumbent if there is already agreement on a successor, thereby preventing the kind of situation that prevailed during the Weimar Republic when opposition parties were able to work together to remove chancellors but usually did not have enough votes to appoint a successor. A few other countries – including Belgium, Hungary, Israel, and Spain – have adopted the same model. In Germany, the constructive vote has only succeeded once, when the SPD-FDP coalition government of Chancellor Helmut Schmidt fell apart in 1982 over disagreements on spending policy, and the Bundestag elected CDU chair Helmut Kohl to succeed Schmidt. In 2001, Chancellor Gerhard Schröder survived a similar vote over the decision of his government to deploy several thousand German troops in support of the US-led military campaign in Afghanistan.

While most parliamentary systems allow prime ministers to call a snap election, only in exceptional circumstances can this happen in Germany: following a successful constructive vote of no confidence, following the loss of a government's majority by members changing party affiliation, or following a decision by a chancellor to seek a new mandate for policy change. Only four times have elections been called early: in 1972, 1983, 1990, and 2005.

While chancellors can be removed by losing a constructive vote of no confidence, they can also potentially shore up their position by calling for a vote of confidence, naturally hoping that they win, ideally by a convincing margin. Should a chancellor lose such a vote, they can either resign, stay on at the head of a minority government, ask the president to call an early election, or be removed through a constructive vote of no confidence. Social Democrat Gerhard Schröder was the last chancellor to use a vote of confidence, which he did twice. He won in 2001, when he linked his decision to deploy German troops to Afghanistan to confidence in his government, but he 'lost' in 2005. Following a major defeat for his party (the Social Democrats) in state elections in North Rhine-Westphalia, Schröder called a vote of confidence that he deliberately set out to lose (he asked members of his own party in the Bundestag to abstain) so that new elections would automatically be triggered, which he hoped to win and thus to earn a mandate for his policies. In the event, both the Social Democrats and the opposition Christian Democrats lost seats, and subsequent negotiations led to the creation of a grand coalition with Angela Merkel as the new chancellor.

The chancellor appoints a Council of Ministers mainly from within the membership of the Bundestag, and has a similar working relationship with those ministers as do British prime ministers with their ministers. There is less

Table 4.2 Modern chancellors of Germany

Name	Beginning of term	Party
Konrad Adenauer	1949, 1953, 1957, 1961, 1962	CDU/CSU, in coalition with the Free Democrats and/or the German Party
Ludwig Erhard	1963, 1965	CDU/CSU-FDP
Kurt Kiesinger	1966	CDU/CSU-SPD grand coalition
Willy Brandt	1969, 1972	SPD-FDP
Helmut Schmidt	1974, 1976, 1980	SPD-FDP
Helmut Kohl	1982, 1983, 1987, 1991, 1994	CDU/CSU-FDP
Gerhard Schröder	1998, 2002	SPD-Green
Angela Merkel	2005, 2009, 2013, 2017	CDU/CSU-SPD grand coalition (2005–09 and 2013–present) or coalition with FDP

of a tradition of collective responsibility in Germany, however, with ministers tending to be advisors to the chancellor rather than heads of government departments with their own distinct sets of government responsibilities. The tradition of coalition governments also means that chancellors will need to appoint members of their partner parties to the council, and the negotiations on the formation of new governments can often take weeks as a result.

Most national leaders have large staffs of advisors, but countries such as Germany and the United States are distinctive for the prominent role that those staffs play in government. Just as senior White House staff such as the president's chief of staff often become closely associated in the public mind with US administrations, so they do in Germany, where the Chancellery is the functional equivalent of the White House. With a staff of several hundred, it has considerable powers over the agenda of the Bundestag, being one of the major sources – along with the federal bureaucracy – of proposals for new laws and policies. The most powerful post is the head of Chancellery, effectively chief of staff to the chancellor, who is usually a member of the federal cabinet, sets up cabinet meetings, oversees the German intelligence service, and acts as an intermediary between the chancellor and ministers.

As well as the need to retain public and party support, there are three main sets of constraints on the power and authority of a chancellor (Roberts, 2016):

◆ It is rare that a chancellor heads a one-party government (it has so far happened only once, in 1957–61), meaning that chancellors are always heads of coalition governments, and are obliged to keep the members of the coalition happy. This is particularly challenging during periods of grand coalitions between the major parties (see later in this chapter).
◆ Chancellors must work not just with the Bundestag but also with the governments of the Länder, which means that they must often negotiate with regional leaders in order to make sure that their policies are implemented.
◆ Chancellors must also work within the limits posed by the autonomy of other institutions, including the Constitutional Court and the famously independent Bundesbank, the central bank of Germany. Until Germany adopted the euro in 2002, the Bundesbank wielded considerable influence over German monetary policy, and even now remains a major actor within the European Central Bank.

Germany also has a deputy chancellor, appointed by the chancellor from among senior government ministers (usually the foreign minister), and usually – in the case of coalition governments – from the junior party in the coalition. The deputy fills in for the chancellor when the latter is absent, running cabinet meetings for example, but does not automatically succeed to the chancellorship – except in an interim role – if the position becomes vacant due to death, resignation, or loss of political support. Only two deputy chancellors – Ludwig Erhard and Willy Brandt – have gone on to become chancellor.

The legislature: Bundesrat and Bundestag

Just under 60 per cent of the world's legislatures are limited to a single chamber (Inter-Parliamentary Union, 2019). The rest have two chambers, each of them typically given different sets of powers designed to allow different kinds

Weak bicameralism
An arrangement in which one chamber of a bicameral legislature clearly has more power than the other, in contrast to the more balanced arrangement found in a system with **strong bicameralism**.

of representation, to offer a system of checks and balances, to allow for a sharing of the workload, or to provide for more considered deliberation over new laws and policies. Like every other federation in the world, Germany has a bicameral legislature: one chamber (the **Bundesrat**) is designed mainly to represent the interests of the Länder, while the second chamber (the **Bundestag**) is designed to represent the people more generally. Unlike almost every other federation, however, Germany has no collective name for the two chambers, and it is debatable whether it has opted for a habit of **weak bicameralism** or **strong bicameralism**.

The Bundestag has the moral and strategic advantage of being elected (the Bundesrat is appointed) and can thus claim to be more directly representative of the interests of German voters. The result, for Langenbacher and Conradt (2017), is that the Bundestag is Germany's 'main political battleground' while the Bundesrat is the 'quiet' and often underrated second chamber. Not everyone agrees on the relative modesty of the Bundesrat, though; for Roberts (2016), it 'is the most powerful second chamber in western Europe', possessing 'considerable positive and negative rights in relation to the legislative process' as well as several powers that are shared equally with the Bundestag.

Bundesrat (Federal Council)

Like the second chambers of most of the other federations in this book – notably the United States, India, Mexico, and Nigeria – the Bundesrat represents the interests of the self-governing provinces of the country. Unlike the US, Mexican or Nigerian senates, though, but in the same spirit as the Rajya Sabha in India, the Bundesrat is not directly elected. Instead, it has 69 seats (or, more accurately, votes) distributed among the governments of Germany's 16 Länder, approximately in proportion to the size of their populations: for example, Bavaria and North Rhine-Westphalia each have six seats, and Bremen and Hamburg each have three. The political make-up of the chamber is determined by the results of elections in the Länder, with each multi-member delegation coming from the majority party or coalition in each state, and being expected to vote together as a bloc. Because state elections happen on their own schedule, changes in the membership of the Bundesrat happen often.

The Bundesrat's powers range from the substantial to the modest:

◆ It must approve all bills proposed by the Bundestag that relate to the responsibilities of the Länder (that is, in the areas of education, policing, regional planning, and local transport). If the two chambers disagree on a draft bill, a mediation committee must be formed with equal numbers from both chambers to shape a compromise. Failing that, the Bundesrat can veto bills from the Bundestag, although it rarely does. A veto can be overturned by a simple majority in the Bundestag, but if the Bundesrat rejects a bill with a two-thirds majority, the Bundestag must respond with its own two-thirds majority, a much harder target to meet.
◆ It can initiate proposals for new laws (a power it has used more often in recent years).
◆ It can require federal ministers to address its members, which might act as a deterrent concerning controversial policies or proposals for new laws.
◆ It has equal powers with the Bundestag over constitutional amendments (which need two-thirds support in both chambers), over the election of the president and members of the Constitutional Court, and over the impeachment of the president.

The Bundesrat also has an important role as a potential opposition: because its membership reflects party support in the Länder and not the outcome of national elections, it can sometimes be under the control of parties opposed to the government.

Bundestag (sometimes translated as Federal Diet)

In spite of the powers of the Bundesrat, the Bundestag is the more politically powerful of the two chambers, because it is directly elected, because the balance of party numbers among its members determines the make-up of the government, and because it elects the German chancellor. It is also the major institution for the consideration and passage of new laws, and it has key powers over running the federal bureaucracy and the German military.

Situated in the old Reichstag building in Berlin, the Bundestag has a minimum of 598 members (Members of the Bundestag, or MdBs). The actual number depends on the outcome of Germany's complex mixed member electoral system in which parties might win surplus seats or be awarded levelling seats to make sure that they are represented in proportion to their shares of the vote. After the 2013 election, for example, the Bundestag had 631 members, while it had 709 members after the 2017 election. Each MdB serves a four-year term with the possibility of an unlimited number of terms. The Bundestag will normally see out its full four-year terms, but elections may be called earlier in the event of a loss of political support or a majority by the governing party. This has so far happened four times, in 1972, 1983, 1990, and 2005.

Much like the British House of Commons (but, as we will see in Chapter 5, unlike the US House of Representatives), the Bundestag has only limited control over the introduction of proposals for new laws, which come mainly from the government in power. There also tends to be tight party discipline, meaning that members of the different party groups (or *Fraktionen*) are expected to work closely together, whether in support of or opposition to the legislative programme of the government. Even though the powers of the Bundestag relative to those of the chancellor have grown, it still tends to be a supporter rather than a driver of government.

The judiciary: Federal Constitutional Court

Judicial power in Germany is vested in a system of Länder and federal courts, topped by the Federal Constitutional Court. The latter was the first body of its kind in Germany, making it unusual among modern German political institutions in that it did not build off a similar court supporting the Weimar constitution. Its design was influenced by the US occupation authorities after 1945 and their long experience with constitutional courts. Similar to the US Supreme Court, but unlike the British Supreme Court, the German court has powers of judicial review (interpreting the Basic Law in the event of disputes or disagreement about the meaning or reach of federal law), of adjudicating disputes between the federal government and Land governments, and of protecting civil liberties.

Based in Karlsruhe in south-western Germany, the Court has 16 members, half elected by the Bundestag and half by the Bundesrat, and each serving single 12-year terms, and being at least 40 years old and no older than 68. The Court is sub-divided into two eight-member senates, each with its own president and area of specialization: one is responsible for protecting civil liberties while the other is responsible mainly for cases involving federal–state or state–state disputes over federal law. One of the justices is appointed president of the whole court, the position alternating between the two senates.

The independence of the Constitutional Court is underlined by its powers to recruit and supervise its employees, by its financial autonomy, and by its monopoly over the impeachment of its members: only the German president, on a motion from the court, can remove a justice of the court. Successful elections of justices require two-thirds majorities in either the Bundestag or the Bundesrat, meaning that there must be much greater multi-party support for nominees than is the case in the increasingly partisan US Supreme Court, and the participation of the Bundesrat gives the Länder a greater role in shaping the court than is the case in the United States, where judges in the court system are nominated by the president and confirmed by the US Senate.

Sub-national government

Germany is a rare example of a European federal state. Only four other European countries – Austria, Belgium, Bosnia and Herzegovina, and Switzerland – operate as federations, an option that is usually adopted only for large or divided states; see Comparing Government 4. In the German case, there has been a history of the kind of division of powers found in federal systems, dating back to the Holy Roman Empire and running through to the German confederation (1815–66). Even during the more centralized systems of government that existed in Germany between unification in 1871 and the end of the Nazi era, many of the states or provinces of Germany continued to have separate identities. As a result, when the occupying allied powers pressed for the creation of a federal West Germany after World War II, Germans had little difficulty complying, and the map of reunified Germany even today has some similarities with medieval maps of the region.

Germany today is divided into 16 Länder (singular: Land), including the three city-states of Berlin, Bremen, and Hamburg. They vary in geographical area from Bavaria in the south (just over 70,000 square kilometres) to Saarland in the south-west (2,600 sq. km), and in population size from North Rhine-Westphalia in the west (nearly 18 million people) to Bremen (with 660,000 people). They also vary by economic wealth, the five Länder that once made up East Germany still lagging some way behind their western counterparts. Several efforts have been made to reorganize the states more equitably in terms of area and population, but this has always come against the opposition of political leaders, bureaucrats, and public opinion in the states.

Each Land has its own government that mirrors that of the federal government: there is a minister president (or mayor in the cases of the city states), a cabinet of ministers, and a unicameral Landtag elected for terms of four or five years, depending on the state. Much like the chancellor, the minister president of each Land is elected by the legislature and then appoints ministers, sometimes subject to the approval of the Landtag. Minister presidents and ministers also represent their states as members of the Bundesrat, and the leadership of states can sometimes be used as a launch pad for higher office; Kurt Kiesinger, Helmut Kohl, and Gerhard Schröder were all minister presidents before becoming chancellors of Germany, while Willy Brandt was mayor of Berlin. Bavaria has a unique position in national government through the activities of the Christian Social Union (CSU), a party that is active only in Bavaria and that is routinely a partner of the Christian Democrats in national government.

COMPARING GOVERNMENT 4
The impact of federalism

Political systems are defined in part by the relationship between the whole (the national government) and the parts (regional and/or local units of government). As we saw in Chapter 2, that relationship usually takes one of two main forms: a federal system in which two or more levels of government coexist with independent powers, or a unitary system in which there may also be different levels of government, but power is focused at the national level. The vast majority of the world's states are unitary, mainly because they are small enough to have a single system of administration. In about two dozen other cases, meanwhile, states are either big enough or diverse enough to merit having a federal system. Of the cases used in this book, half are federal and half are unitary.

Of the federal states, a combination of size and historical circumstances accounts for this option in five: India, Mexico, Nigeria, Russia, and the United States. Germany is one of the outliers, since it is neither particularly big nor particularly diverse. It ranks 62nd in the world by area (it is slightly smaller than Japan, and just over half the size of France, both unitary states), and by population it is about the same size as Turkey and Iran, both also unitary states. This begs the question of why Germany is federal. The simple answer is that federalism reflects the historical divisions within what is now Germany, and federalism was imposed on it by the occupying allied powers after World War II as a way of helping offset the possibility of the kind of concentration of power in the centre that played into the hands of Hitler and the Nazis. German federalism is also driven more by administrative needs than a division of power; most policy is made at the federal level, with Länder given wide latitude to implement laws and policies as they wish.

Federalism in bigger and/or more diverse countries is usually a reflection of historical circumstances in which several political units became part of something bigger, but it was decided that a large measure of political authority should be retained by those units. The United States, for example, became independent as a cluster of previously separate colonies that initially formed a confederation, which was soon replaced by a federation in which states kept a large measure of control over regional affairs and had their own separate constitutions and political institutions. Australia and Canada had similar origins, their separate states and provinces continuing today to maintain sub-national control within federal systems. The effect of federalism in all three countries is to bring everyone under common jurisdiction on matters of foreign, defence, and monetary policy – for example – while giving them their separate powers and identities within sub-national states and provinces.

POLITICAL PROCESSES

Germany does not have a long history of parliamentary democracy, a fact that makes its relative stability since 1949 all that more remarkable. It has experienced many of the same occasional changes in direction and habits that all democratic systems have gone through, and will continue to go through, but there has been a clear evolutionary quality to Germany's post-war political development, even given the disappointment of the Cold War split and the challenges of reunification in 1990.

At least initially, most west Germans passively accepted their new system of government, and avoided much discussion about the nature of their new democracy. From the 1960s, however, there was a notable change of attitude, with Germans becoming more accepting of the new system while also becoming more politically active. Once they had become used to the post-war settlement, they began to participate more actively, preferring conventional forms of participation (such as voting) while also occasionally being willing to explore more radical and unconventional options of a kind not always found in Britain or France, for example.

The electoral system

As citizens of a federal system, German voters take part in three main sets of elections: the federal elections that determine control of the Bundestag and the chancellorship, elections within the Länder, and – ranking a distant third in importance – elections to the European Parliament.

Federal legislative elections

The major election in Germany is the one for the Bundestag, held every four years unless an election is called early as a result of a political crisis or impasse of some kind. Germany uses a system known as **mixed member proportional representation** (MMP) (or the additional member system) in which every voter casts two votes on the same ballot:

◆ With their first vote, or *erststimme*, they make a choice among competing candidates listed by name in their home districts based on a single-member plurality (SMP) system. Germany is divided into 299 districts, and the candidate winning the most votes in each district is elected to the Bundestag. This vote is also sometimes known as a direct mandate, or as a constituency or 'personal' vote.

◆ With their second vote, or *zweitstimme*, based on proportional representation (PR), voters choose among competing parties running in each of Germany's Länder. Each Land is given a different number of seats in proportion to the size of its population, and those seats are then distributed among the competing parties in proportion to the number of votes that each of them receives, provided that they win at least five per cent of the vote, or at least three direct mandate seats. Each party enters the election with a list of candidates ranked by the party, whose allotment of seats is then filled from the list. This is sometimes known as a party list vote, and is arguably the more important of the two.

If all voters were to choose the same party in both votes, then the share of seats won by each party would be the same in the first and second votes. However, split-ticket voting (using the first vote to support a candidate from one party, and the second vote to support a different party) became more common, being an option now used by more than 25 per cent of voters. The result was that the share of seats won by different parties in the two votes was not the same, and some parties won more seats (known as surplus or overhang seats) in the first vote than was merited by their share of the second vote. Also, the bigger parties had an advantage because they could afford to field candidates in all the single-member districts. This was deemed unfair in a 2009 decision by the Constitutional Court, so a new third element was added to the voting calculations:

◆ If a party wins more seats in the first vote than in the second vote, then all other parties are compensated by being given extra seats (known variously as balancing, levelling, or adjustment seats) so that the total number of seats they win is more reflective of their share of the vote. No party will have seats taken away, but parties whose share of the second vote is significantly larger than its share of the first vote will make sometimes large gains. Also, the total number of seats in the Bundestag is likely to increase, as it did between the 2013 and the 2017 elections, from 631 to a record 709.

The system combines the advantages of two other electoral systems (SMP and PR) while offsetting their relative disadvantages. An example of the effect is offered by the results of the 2017 elections (see Table 4.3). The Christian Democrats did exceedingly well in the first vote, winning more than twice as many seats as their share of the vote would seem to indicate. However, their share of first and second votes was similar, so they were given only a modest 15 balancing seats. By contrast, and emphasizing the importance of the second vote, the Free Democrats won no seats under the direct mandate, but nearly 11 per cent in the party list vote. They were thus compensated with 80 balancing seats in the Bundestag that they would not otherwise have had.

Few Germans are concerned that the eventual number of seats in the Bundestag, and their distribution among parties is not known until after all the results are in. It requires workers to move in to the Bundestag chamber after an election and to either add new seats or take away unwanted seats, while Bundestag staff must reassign offices to MdBs based on election results. These are small sacrifices to make, however, in the interests of maintaining one of the fairest of all electoral systems, and one that comes closest to ensuring that the distribution of seats among parties reflects voter preferences. Even so, few countries use it: Germany, Bolivia, Lesotho, New Zealand, and the regional legislatures of Scotland and Wales in the UK.

Although turnout at German elections has traditionally been higher than has been the case in most other democracies, there have been worried discussions in recent years as the numbers have fallen – from a high of 91.1

Table 4.3 Results of the 2017 German federal election

Party	First vote – Direct mandate			Second vote – Party list		Final outcome	
	% share votes	Seats	% share seats	% share votes	Seats	Seats	% share seats
Christian Democrats	30.2	185	62.9	26.8	15	200	28
Social Democrats	24.6	59	19.7	20.5	94	153	22
Alternative for Germany	11.5	3	1.0	12.6	91	94	13
Free Democrats	7.0	0	0	10.7	80	80	11
The Left	8.6	5	1.7	9.2	64	69	10
Alliance 90/The Greens	8.0	1	0.3	8.9	66	67	9
Christian Social Union	7.0	46	15.4	6.2	0	46	6
Other parties	3.1	0	0	5.1	0	0	0
TOTAL	100%	299	100%	100%	410	709	

per cent in 1972 to a low of 70.8 per cent in 2009. Turnout has been helped by an electoral system in which almost every vote counts and by the legal requirement that elections be held on a Sunday. In recent elections, the numbers have been deflated by lower turnout levels in eastern Germany, and by a growing sense among voters in Germany – as elsewhere – that parties work less to represent the will of voters than to perpetuate their own hold on power. Even so, Germany has traditionally performed better with turnout than either the UK or France – see Figure 4.1.

European elections

Like all other members of the EU, Germany is represented in the European Parliament (EP), and German voters take part every five years in elections to the EP. The whole country is considered a single electoral district, with Germany's 96 seats in the EP divided up among parties on the basis of proportional representation. At the 2014 elections, 14 German parties won seats in the EP, although the CDU, the SPD, and the Greens among them won two-thirds of the total. Germans tend to have the same mixed opinions as other EU voters about the European Parliament elections, and turnout has fallen from a high of 66 per cent in 1979 to about 43–48 per cent.

Local (regional) elections

All countries have sub-national units of government, but they typically play a more significant role in federations such as Germany or the United States than in unitary systems such as Britain or Japan. The vesting of powers in the governments of the Länder means that there is much at stake in the outcome of elections, the winners going on not just to provide regional government but also to influence national government through their work in the Bundesrat.

Land elections in Germany, like Land political systems, are a smaller version of national elections. They are mainly held on a four-year cycle, using either the same MMP method as federal elections or a simplified version, and – except for the usually short-lived activities of local protest parties, and the unique place of the Christian Social Union Bavaria – they are contested by the same political parties. As with many sub-national elections in other countries, the results are often seen as an indicator less of local political trends than of the mood of the electorate towards national government and policy; in this sense they can often play an important role in national politics.

Political parties

The German political party system has gone through four distinct phases in the modern era, taking it from feast to famine and back again:

◆ During the Weimar era, there were numerous parties represented in the Reichstag – ranging from a low of 12 to a high of 25 – creating instability.
◆ During the Nazi era, all parties but the National Socialists were banned, creating stability at the cost of democracy.

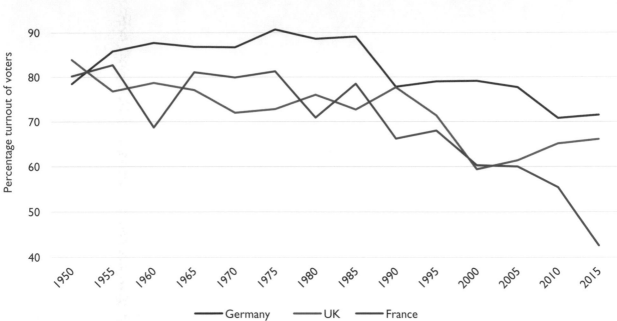

Figure 4.1 Comparing voter turnout trends

◆ After 1949, the multi-party system was rebuilt, but with care taken not to repeat the chaos of the Weimar era (hence the use of the threshold by which no party could win seats in the Bundestag unless it won at least five per cent of all votes cast). The result was a stable system in which two parties dominated, with three other significant supporting parties.

◆ In the fourth and current phase, there has been new fluidity as party identification has weakened, resulting in a weakening of the two-party dominance.

In summary, the two major parties have been the Christian Democrats on the moderate right (working in conjunction with their Bavarian partner, the Christian Social Union) and the Social Democrats on the moderate left. Meanwhile, the Free Democrats have acted as a swing party in the centre, the Greens have represented environmental and social justice issues, and smaller parties on the right have gathered the support of protest voters concerned mainly about immigration and asylum.

The most notable trend of recent years has been a process of **partisan dealignment**, which has been seen also in several other European countries, including Britain and Sweden. The explanations behind this vary from one situation to another, but they include reduced voter trust in parties and a decline in the ideological differences among parties in the middle of the political spectrum. In the case of Germany (see Dalton, 2014), the weakening of class and religious differences has softened the association with parties, and voters increasingly enter elections prepared to vote on the basis of issues and candidates rather than identification with a given party. This change, combined with the arithmetic of the mixed member electoral system, has produced a more complex party landscape and a habit of coalition governments; see Comparing Politics 4.

Christian Democratic Union (CDU)

Sitting on the moderate right of the political spectrum, the Christian Democrats have been the biggest and most consistently popular of Germany's parties, winning – during their peak years – almost half the vote at general elections, and prospering even against the background of an increasingly diverse and secular Germany (Green and Turner, 2015). In order to understand its place in German politics, it is important to understand **Christian Democracy**,

Partisan dealignment
The weakening of links between voters and parties, as voters identify less with parties, and membership of parties falls.

Christian Democracy
A political philosophy associated mainly with continental Europe that applies Christian principles to public policy without being overtly religious. Christian Democratic parties are moderately conservative on social and moral issues, and progressive on economic issues.

COMPARING POLITICS 4
Coalition governments

At least as far as the members and supporters of a given political party are concerned, the ideal outcome of an election is one in which their party wins an outright majority, controlling both the executive and the legislature. In this scenario, the party controls all the major institutions, controls the flow of new laws and policies, and – provided it can address any internal divisions that might arise – will be firmly in the driving seat of government. Unhappily for most parties, this kind of outcome is found only in authoritarian states where elections are manipulated in order to ensure strong majorities, or in parliamentary democracies dominated by two major parties (Britain being a rare example). In presidential systems such as the United States, Mexico, and Nigeria, it is often the case that one party wins the executive but fails to win a majority in the legislature, leading to divided government. The same is often true in semi-presidential systems such as France or Poland.

The more common (and even usual) outcome in parliamentary democracies is that no one party wins enough votes and/or seats to govern alone, leaving two or more parties obliged to form a coalition government. The parties together will then have enough seats to control the legislature, the dominant party controls the executive, and the secondary party or parties are usually given a few senior positions in government in return for their support. The result is political compromise: none of the parties involved have entirely their own way, being obliged to make concessions in return for the support of the others. The more parties involved in the coalition, the more concessions need to be made, the more unstable the agreement, and the more influence wielded by the smaller parties involved. Israel and Italy are the epitome of unstable coalitions, their electoral systems allowing many parties to win seats in their national legislatures, the small parties often being able to make demands representing the sometimes unpopular views of their relatively small voting bloc.

Germany has seen perpetual coalitions since 1949, with no one party having enough seats to govern alone. In most cases the coalitions have been politically logical, as with the Social Democrats and the Greens governing together in 1998–2005. The centrist Free Democrats, meanwhile, have been sufficiently flexible as to form coalitions sometimes with the Christian Democrats and at other times with the Social Democrats. The acme of coalitions, though, is achieved when the two major parties – the Christian Democrats and the Social Democrats – have not been able to reach agreement with any of the smaller parties, and have instead opted to form a joint **grand coalition**. This has happened four times so far: once in 1966 with the relatively short-lived government of Kurt Kiesinger, and three times during the administration of Angela Merkel. While there are clearly challenges to be faced by the conservative CDU/CSU and the relatively liberal SPD achieving accommodations, it could also be argued that grand coalitions of this kind are the best form of democracy, because they involve compromises among parties supported by a large majority of German voters.

> **Grand coalition**
> An arrangement in which the major political parties in a country form a coalition, rather than one major party forming a coalition with smaller parties.

continental Europe's most successful and popular political movement after 1945, being particularly prominent in Germany, Italy, Austria, and the Benelux countries (Belgium, the Netherlands, and Luxembourg).

It emerged from a late-19th-century split among parties of the right, some of which felt that the relationship between church and state should remain close, while others did not. The first Christian democratic party was founded in Italy in 1919 by the Catholic priest Luigi Sturzo, who hoped to reconcile the goals of Catholicism and democracy. This meant respecting the division between church and state while promoting the kinds of social reforms of which the church would approve. Driven into exile in 1924 by the rise of the fascists in Italy, Sturzo set up an international movement in Paris, among whose earliest members was a young Konrad Adenauer. Among other philosophies, Christian democracy supported the idea of European integration as a means for discouraging war in the region.

After 1945, Christian democracy was revived on the basis of its appeal in those countries that had suffered most from Nazism and now saw the new threat posed by communism. It had three key principles:

◆ Personalism, meaning that individuals should develop through their responsibility to others, notably to the family and the community. Christian democrats, for example, tended to be supportive of labour unions.
◆ Subsidiarity, meaning that political power should be decentralized as far as possible.
◆ Free-market economics, supporting the view that governments should intervene in the marketplace as little as possible.

The German Christian Democrats came together after World War II when opponents of parties on the left formed a coalition (see Mitchell, 2012). They succeeded everywhere except in the southern state of Bavaria, which had a history of regional party politics, revived in 1945 with the creation of the Christian Social Union (CSU). More socially conservative than the CDU, it has long dominated Bavarian state politics while being in a permanent coalition with the CDU at the national level.

The CDU/CSU won a slim plurality in the first national elections held in West Germany in 1949, and its leader Konrad Adenauer won enough support to be elected the first chancellor of the new West Germany. The CDU went on to hold the position of chancellor for 28 of the 41 years that West Germany existed, and for all but seven years since. Among its dominating personalities was Helmut Kohl, West German chancellor from 1983 to 1990, and first chancellor of a reunified Germany between 1990 and 1998. Angela Merkel was head of the party from 2000 to 2018 (when she was succeeded by Annegret Kramp-Karrenbauer) and was the dominant figure in both German and European politics. While the CDU could once be sure of a 45–50 per cent share of the national vote, however, that share has slipped since reunification, reaching a new low in 2017 when it was able to win only 28 per cent of the

The political torch is passed in 2018 as Annegret Kramp-Karrenbauer (right) is elected general secretary of the German Christian Democrats. This was widely interpreted as a step towards the end of the long and influential role of Angela Merkel (left) as chancellor of Germany and a dominating figure in European politics.
Source: Sean Gallup/Getty Images News.

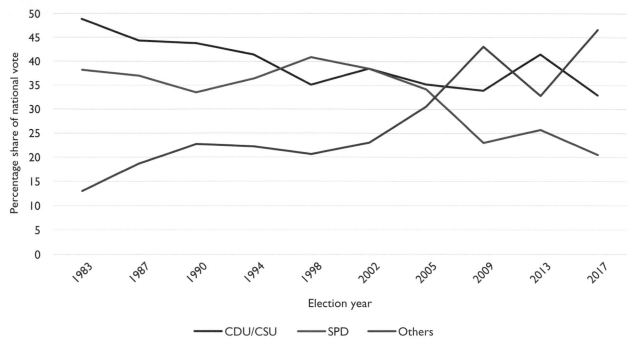

Figure 4.2 Legislative electoral trends in Germany

seats in the Bundestag, leaving Merkel with no choice but to continue in her grand coalition with the Social Democrats. The CDU has particularly felt the effects of most eastern Germans not having the same kind of middle-class interests and religious affiliations that were once the foundation of CDU support.

Social Democratic Party (SPD)

The major alternative to the CDU for many years, and the only other party to hold the chancellorship of Germany (1969–82 and 1998–2005), the SPD sits on the moderate left of the political spectrum and is the oldest still-functioning party in Germany. It dates back to the 1860s and was the only major Weimar-era party to re-emerge after 1945. It seemed doomed to be limited to about 30 per cent of voter share in the 1950s, mainly because it emphasized its Marxist roots at a time when West Germany was on the frontlines of the Cold War and the free-market policies of the CDU were more popular. Under the guidance of Willy Brandt, its first major leader (and mayor of West Berlin), it moderated its positions and built on the distinctions between the young and dynamic Brandt and the ageing Konrad Adenauer.

The SPD finally entered government for the first time in 1966 in a grand coalition with the CDU/CSU, arguing that it needed experience in government to show voters that it had the potential to govern alone. Brandt held the chancellorship in 1969 in a coalition with the Free Democrats, and remained in power for the next 13 years. By the early 1980s it had come to be criticized for its lack of clear policies towards the Soviet Union and for cutting social programmes and increasing defence spending, and it began to lose support to the emerging Greens. The CDU/CSU regained control under Helmut Kohl in 1983, and the SPD has since held the chancellorship only once (with Gerhard Schröder in 1998–2005), against a background of sliding support; its share of the vote has been cut in half since the heady days of the Brandt government, reaching a new low of 20 per cent in 2017.

Other parties

Outside the arenas of the CDU/CSU and the SPD, German party politics has become increasingly fractured and changeable in recent decades, the result of party dealignment, a move to issues-based voting, the impact of reunification, concerns on the left about social issues, and concerns on the right about immigration. The effects are reflected in vote shares: until 2005, the CDU/CSU and the SPD among them had always held a solid 80–90 per cent majority share of the vote. In 2009, for the first time, minority parties together won more than either the CDU/CSU or the SPD, and in 2017 they won nearly half the vote. To be sure, the minority parties were pulling German voters in opposite directions, so this was hardly a united voter bloc, but the decline of the major parties was notable.

Initially, the grip of the two major parties was potentially impacted most directly by support for the Free Democrats, a centre-left party that won seats only in the proportional representation segment of elections and yet often held the balance of power. They spent many years in coalition with the CDU/CSU and then with the SPD, and then again with the CDU/CSU. In return, they held good positions in the governing cabinet, most famously in the 18-year tenure of FDP leader Hans-Dietrich Genscher as German foreign minister. Its role in politics has declined, though, with developments elsewhere in party politics, and while it won a record 14.6 per cent share of the vote in 2009, its share was cut by more than two-thirds in 2013.

Also on the left, the German **Greens** (*Die Grünen*) quickly established themselves as the most successful of Europe's Green parties after emerging in the 1970s, first winning seats in the Bundestag in 1983. They took positions that were pro-environment and anti-nuclear, attracting disillusioned social democrats and younger voters attracted by their rejection of conventional politics. They formed a coalition in 1993 with the eastern German Alliance 90, and were able to win enough votes in 1998 and 2002 to enter a 'red-green' coalition government with the SPD. Since then they have typically won an 8–10 per cent share of the vote in national party list elections.

Green politics
A political philosophy based on ecological wisdom, sustainability, social justice, grassroots democracy, and non-violence.

Further on the left, the Party of Democratic Socialism emerged after reunification as a successor to the East German Communist Party. It won few votes nationally, however, and tended to be seen as a protest party for eastern Germans concerned about their place in the new Germany. The party merged with another on the left in 2007 to form The Left (*Die Linke*), winning nearly 12 per cent of the vote and 76 seats in the Bundestag in 2009.

On the right, meanwhile, several parties have been active, united by their concerns about immigration. The National Democrats were founded in 1964 and the Republicans in 1983, initially complaining about immigration from East Germany, of ethnic Germans from Eastern Europe, and about people seeking political asylum. The right had its biggest impact in major cities such as Berlin and Frankfurt, where jobs and housing were in particularly short supply, but neither the National Democrats nor the Republicans have ever won any seats in the Bundestag. A new party, the Alternative for Germany (AfD) was founded in 2013, narrowly missing the threshold for Bundestag seats in the federal election that year. It ran more strongly in 2017, winning 94 seats in the Bundestag, and – with the CDU/CSU and FDP entering another grand coalition – being able to claim to be the largest opposition party in the Bundestag. Its positions lie in a combination of German nationalism, populism, and Euroscepticism, with racist and Islamophobic currents.

THE FUTURE OF GERMAN GOVERNMENT AND POLITICS

For Langenbacher and Conradt (2017), Germany has much to offer the student of comparative politics: it is a prime example of the complexities and difficulties of political development and political change, it is a case study of the effects of international developments on domestic politics, it is a case study of the relationship between government and the economy in one of the world's leading capitalist economies, and it plays an important role in the international community. It may not have veto power in the United Nations, as do five other countries in this book (Britain, the United States, France, Russia, and China, that is, the winners of World War II), but it more than makes up for this with its dominating role in the European Union.

Its past has undoubtedly been troubled, and even since the end of World War II it has gone through two key phases: Cold War division followed by reunification. The first of those phases did not stop it from building an effective political system and a world-leading economy, and even if it currently faces many questions arising from greater social diversity and declining faith in politics, Germany's future is given new importance by the dual threats posed by a more belligerent Russia and a more nationalist United States. Germany continues to sit between the two, in much of the same way as it did during the Cold War, and continues – whether willingly or not – to lead the European Union as Britain steps aside and France continues to wrestle with its own internal divisions. This is a time of ongoing change in a country that has seen more changes than most, and much of what happens in the democratic world hinges on the choices that Germans will make.

DISCUSSION QUESTIONS

1. What are the major challenges that face German political leaders today?
2. Is Germany any more or less subject to the influences of its past than is the case with other European democracies?
3. Is the constructive vote of no confidence a governing tool from which other countries might usefully learn?
4. How do the outcomes of the mixed member proportional representation electoral system compare with those of single-member plurality or proportional representation systems?
5. How does partisan dealignment in Germany compare with trends in other European democracies?
6. What difference do party coalitions make to the quality and responsiveness of government and politics?

CHAPTER CONCEPTS

- Basic Law
- Berlin Wall
- Bundesrat
- Bundestag
- Chancellor
- Constructive vote of no confidence
- East Germany

- German Question
- Mixed member proportional representation
- Ostpolitik
- Weimar Republic
- West Germany

KEY TERMS

- Christian Democracy
- Civil liberties
- Grand coalition
- Green politics
- Nationalism
- Nazism

- Partisan dealignment
- Patriotism
- Republic
- Strong bicameralism
- Totalitarianism
- Weak bicameralism

GERMANY ONLINE

Office of the Chancellor: www.bundesregierung.de/breg-en/chancellor
Federal Government: www.bundesregierung.de/breg-en
Bundesrat: www.bundesrat.de/EN/homepage/homepage-node.html
Bundestag: www.bundestag.de/en
Christian Democratic Union: www.cdu.de ★
Social Democratic Party: www.spd.de ★
Deutsche Welle: www.dw.com/en/top-stories/s-9097
Der Spiegel: www.spiegel.de/international
Die Zeit: www.zeit.de/english/index
Frankfurter Allgemeine: www.faz.net/aktuell ★

★ *German only*

FURTHER READING

Caldwell, Peter C., and Karrin Hanshaw (2017) *Germany Since 1945: Politics, Culture, and Society* (Bloomsbury). An assessment of contemporary German history, reviewing its political, cultural, and social evolution since the end of World War II.

Colvin, Sarah (ed.) (2016) *The Routledge Handbook of German Politics and Culture* (Routledge). An edited collection of studies of different facets of German politics, including history, institutions, processes, and chapters on Germany's place in Europe and the world.

Langenbacher, Eric, and David P. Conradt (2017) *The German Polity*, 11th edn (Rowman & Littlefield), and Geoffrey K. Roberts (2016) *German Politics Today*, 3rd edn (Manchester University Press). Two survey textbook of German government and politics, with chapters on history, political culture, institutions, parties, elections, and policies.

Lemke, Christiane, and Helga A. Welsh (2018) *Germany Today: Politics and Policies in a Changing World* (Rowman & Littlefield). Another survey text, with chapters on institutions and processes, as well as assessments of the effects of immigration, and of Germany in the EU and the wider world.

MacGregor, Neil (2016) *Germany: Memories of a Nation* (Penguin). An illustrated history of Germany, published in conjunction with a BBC radio series of the same name.

Padgett, Stephen, William E. Paterson, and Reimut Zohlnhöfer (eds) (2014) *Developments in German Politics 4* (Red Globe Press). The German volume in the Red Globe Press series of developments in contemporary national government and politics.

Visit **www.macmillanihe.com/McCormick-Cases** to access additional materials to support teaching and learning.

UNITED STATES

CONTENTS

- Overview
- Political development
- Political culture
- Political system
- Political processes
- The future of American government and politics

PREVIEW

As the world's biggest economic and military power, the United States is hard to ignore as a case in comparative politics. Its global reach means that its domestic decisions are of interest far outside its borders; the outcome of American elections and the policies of its presidents matter to friends and foes alike. And yet the United States can sometimes puzzle foreign observers, just as it sometimes puzzles its own citizens. Many claims are made for the democratic qualities of the American political model, and for the opportunities inherent in the American Dream, with Americans and their leaders routinely describing their country as the greatest in the world. The American system of government, though, is rife with structural problems, and the faith of citizens in their elected officials (and sometimes in each other) has been tested by deepening political, economic, and social divisions that government seems unwilling or unable to address.

KEY ARGUMENTS

- The United States is a country of political contrasts, its belief in democracy being offset by the persistence of worrying political, economic, and social challenges.

- The rise of the United States to global power was based on the size and reach of its economy and of its military, but it today faces many threats to its global influence.

- The American political system is based on three branches of government whose powers are mutually checked, balanced, and shared within a federal system.

- Many aspects of the American political system are idiosyncratic, including its low rate of legislative turnover, the manipulation of electoral districts for partisan gain, its two-party system, and the influential role of money in politics.

- While the branches of US government should ideally work in concert, growing partisanship has resulted in frequent gridlock.

- Elections in the United States are longer, more numerous, and more expensive than in any other democracy.

OVERVIEW

As the world's biggest military power and one of its four biggest economic powers (the others being the European Union, China, and Japan), the United States has both driven and been deeply affected by the changes that have come to the world in the last few decades. During the Cold War it led the Western alliance against the threats posed by the Soviets and their clients, and was also the world's economic leader, reflected in the sheer size of its economy, the strength of the US dollar, and the reach of US corporations. The United States remains powerful and influential today, but it also faces many challenges, few of which have straightforward solutions. Its political system suffers many structural defects, it must address new economic competition on an unprecedented level, it faces numerous internal divisions that have led to political and social tensions, and it is caught up in a struggle against global terrorism.

In political terms, the United States is the epitome of the presidential system of government: it has three separate branches whose powers are shared, checked, and balanced with one another. This is a structure that has been copied in several Latin American and African countries, with local adaptations. The United States is also notable for the vertical separation of powers between the federal government in Washington DC and the governments of the 50 states, and for the ongoing debate about the sharing of those powers. It is alone among democracies in having a political system dominated by two major political parties, retains a peculiarly anachronistic method of electing presidents through an electoral college, and allows political parties to draw the lines of electoral districts to their benefit. Problems such as these have undermined the quality of American democracy, as a result of which its ranking in the Democracy Index in 2016 fell from a full democracy to a flawed democracy.

In economic terms, the United States has the world's biggest national economy in absolute terms, and is the fourth biggest country by land area after Russia, Canada, and China, and the third biggest by population after China and India. It has a wealth of natural resources, from land and minerals to fuels, forests, and cropland. The US dollar is the world's strongest and most respected currency, the United States is a major trading power and the world's technological leader, and US corporations such as WalMart, Apple, General Motors, ExxonMobil, Boeing, and Microsoft have global reach. But the US economy continues to face the kinds of structural vulnerabilities that sparked the global financial crisis of 2007–10, and enormous wealth coexists with the persistently high levels of poverty, with a growing gap between the rich and the poor.

In social terms, the United States is both a multicultural society and one with critical divisions. The sources and effects of these pose more challenges to policymakers today than they have for many years. Not only do Americans face deepening racial and religious tensions, but there have been concerns about ideological differences and the growing incivility of political discourse, as well as differences of opinion on a wide range of political and social issues, from abortion to gun control, racial discrimination, capital punishment, same-sex marriage, immigration, and the role of government in the lives of citizens.

The United States is a large, wealthy, and complex country that is often hard to understand, for Americans as well as for others who need to deal with and come to grips with what it represents. The success of the American brand of democracy has often been exaggerated in the past, as have the extent of the opportunities provided by its economy; many succeed and do well, but many others do not. There is little question that, for many Americans, the future is rife with uncertainties.

POLITICAL DEVELOPMENT

Most Americans have little sense of the political history of their country beyond a sometimes idealized version of America's relationship with democratic values. Unlike Europeans, for whom history is important (sometimes too important) for an understanding of themselves and of their relations with each other, most Americans live more in the present and think more in terms of what might be, rather than what once was. Most Europeans originally emigrated to North America to find new beginnings, and even today Americans like to reinvent themselves, changing homes and jobs more often than almost anyone else, particularly the relatively immobile Japanese. Political, economic, and social change are accelerating the pace of that reinvention, pushing the United States in new directions whose ultimate destination is not always clear.

The particular circumstances of the United States in the late 18th century drove it to develop what were then unique ideas about government, including a written constitution and a political system in which powers were divided horizontally among the institutions of government and vertically between national government and the states. Since then, politics has been driven by debates over the appropriate role of government and the relations between the federal government and the states. There have been problems and failures along the way, and the international image of the United States has suffered recently in the wake of the war in Iraq, the global financial crisis, and the populism that fed in to the controversial election of Donald Trump in 2016. Regardless, the long-term result of its evolution has been a successful and dynamic society whose influence is felt all over the world.

The colonial era (1607–1776)

Although the Americas were inhabited by native peoples when Columbus arrived in the 'New World' in 1492, the modern political values of the United States are ultimately the product of its European roots. The United States was settled by Europeans, Europeans continued to arrive in large numbers in the 19th and early 20th centuries, and although African-Americans arrived on the back of the slave trade, and immigrants from Latin America and Southeast Asia have changed the social and cultural balance of the United States in the last few generations, it is still ultimately a product of European political and cultural traditions.

The first colonists came from Britain, settlement accelerating with the Puritan migrations of the 1630s. By the early 18th century, Britain had colonized the eastern seaboard, setting up colonies that were administered by appointed governors with substantial powers and by elected legislatures. British monarchs tightened their control over the colonies, but not so much that the colonists were encouraged to think about independence (see Taylor, 2012). The mood began to change in the 1760s, however, when new taxes and duties were imposed in the aftermath of the French and Indian wars, and criticism of British interference in American domestic affairs began to grow. Revolution broke out in April 1775, the colonies declared independence in July 1776, and the creation of the United States was confirmed with the surrender of British forces at Yorktown in October 1781.

State-building (1776–1865)

For its first few years, the United States was a loose association governed by the **Articles of Confederation**, under which Congress had the power to make war and peace, conduct foreign affairs, and borrow and print money, but could collect taxes or enforce laws only through the states. A combination of problems – among them the financial difficulties of fighting the war with the British, local insurrections, the barriers to trade among the states, and the handicaps posed by the lack of a single currency – led to a Constitutional Convention in 1787 designed to address the defects of the Articles of Confederation. The result was a new constitution and a new federal system in which power was divided, checked, and balanced among the states and three major branches of national government: the president, a bicameral Congress, and a judiciary.

There was also territorial expansion, the country doubling in size with the 1803 Louisiana Purchase. Texas was annexed in 1845, the Pacific Northwest was absorbed in 1846, and the Southwest was surrendered by Mexico in 1848; see Map 5.1. These territories were gradually populated through government programmes to promote population expansion into the western frontier, as a revolution in transport connected much of the eastern half of the country with roads, canals, and railroads. The national economy began to diversify, with the emergence of a cotton- and slave-based economy in the south and – in the north – the development of cities and industry and the steady growth of immigration from Europe. Between 1790 and 1860 the population of the United States grew from 4 million to 31 million.

The economic and social divisions between the North and the South spilled over in 1860 with the election as president of Abraham Lincoln, a member of the northern-based, antislavery Republican Party. Secessionist views picked up steam in the south, leading to the declaration in February 1861 of the Confederacy (eventually joined by 11 states) and the outbreak in April of the **Civil War**. The war lasted four years, cost half a million lives, brought an end to slavery, and obliged Americans to make important new choices about their political, economic, and social future.

Reconstruction and growth (1865–1945)

Following the Civil War, the United States was transformed from a society in which half of all workers had been employed in agriculture to one in which industry played the dominating economic role. It was the age of the railroad and the entrepreneur, of technological change, of the growth of monopolies and cities, and of expansion to the West. The influence of political parties began to decline as that of interest groups – representing the new sectors that emerged out of these economic changes – began to rise.

Map 5.1 The territorial expansion of the United States

In spite of a tendency towards **isolationism**, the United States also became increasingly active in world affairs, its main focus being on commerce with eastern Asia and on watching political developments in the Caribbean and Central America. Its new international role was emphasized by its brief war with Spain in 1898, its decision to enter World War I in April 1917, and its involvement in the peace conference at Versailles in early 1919 and in the creation of the League of Nations. The years of prosperity that followed the war ended with the Wall Street crash of October 1929, which ushered in the Great Depression, prompting the federal government to take a new approach to economic and social issues. President Franklin Delano Roosevelt took office in 1933 and announced his New Deal policy aimed at economic recovery. Notable among the changes of the 1930s were the introduction of social security and the creation of public works programmes.

While these developments were taking place at home, problems that had been unresolved – and even created – by the Versailles conference were feeding into the growth of Nazism in Germany, and Hitler's expansionism in Europe sparked the outbreak of World War II in September 1939. The United States initially chose to remain officially neutral, but the Roosevelt administration gave economic and military assistance to Britain and then entered the war following the Japanese attack on Pearl Harbor in December 1941. It quickly took over the leading role in planning and fighting the war, in both the European and Pacific theatres.

From Pax Americana to 9/11 (1945–90)

With the end of the war in 1945, the old regime under which world affairs had been dominated by European powers was replaced by the era of the **Pax Americana** (a general peace with the United States at its core). This revolved around two military **superpowers** – the United States and the Soviet Union – who were now engaged in a new kind of global hostility in which conventional military conflict was replaced by the threat of nuclear weapons and by the **Cold War** between blocs led by the Americans and the Soviets. The conflict occasionally broke out

Isolationism
A line of policy that supports the avoidance of foreign involvement and alliances.

Superpower
A state with the military, economic, and political resources to be active at a global level.

Cold War
A 'war' of words, ideas, ideology and proxy military conflicts between the United States and the Soviet Union between the late 1940s and 1989–90.

⚲⚲⚲ TIMELINE

1492	Christopher Columbus unwittingly reaches the West Indies
1565	St Augustine is first permanent European settlement in North America
1620	Arrival of Pilgrims aboard the *Mayflower*
1776	Declaration of Independence
1846–48	US acquires California, Texas, and other territory in wake of Mexican War
1861–65	Civil War
1917–18	US intervenes in Great War
1929	Wall Street crash ushers in Great Depression
1933	Launch of Roosevelt's New Deal economic recovery programme
1941	US enters World War II
1963	Assassination of President John F. Kennedy
1954–68	Height of the civil rights movement
1965–73	Height of the Vietnam War
1972–74	Watergate scandal
2000	George W. Bush declared winner in contentious presidential election
2001	Terrorist attacks on World Trade Center and Pentagon kill 3,100 people
2003	US-led invasion of Iraq begins
2007	Beginning of global economic crisis, dubbed by some the Great Recession
2008	Barack Obama becomes first black leader of a Western democracy
2016	Donald Trump elected president on back of populist wave

into fighting wars between clients of the two sides, as in Korea in 1950–53, Vietnam in the 1960s and early 1970s, and Afghanistan in 1979–89 (see Gaddis, 2006).

At home, the economy began a period of sustained expansion, with mass production and consumerism feeding off each other and more Americans enjoying an improved quality of life. But behind the façade there was simmering social discontent. Women and ethnic minorities were denied equal opportunity, and women began to be more assertive in their demands for change, while the civil rights movement used the court system successfully to challenge segregation. The **Great Society** programmes of the Johnson administration were aimed at combating poverty and discrimination, but while they expanded the activities of the federal government in social policy, they also emphasized the gaps between aspirations and realities. Americans were deeply split in the late 1960s and early 1970s over the war in Vietnam, and faith in government was undermined by the Watergate scandal, which began when staff from the presidential campaign of Richard Nixon broke into the headquarters of the Democratic Party and Nixon tried to cover up their actions. The optimism of the 1950s began to be replaced by doubts, disillusionment, and declining trust in government.

In 1980 Ronald Reagan was elected president, pulling vital support from a religious right that favoured a redefinition of moral values. He moved the United States into conservative positions on economic and social issues, and worked to revive the American spirit, proclaiming that it was 'morning in America'. **Reaganomics** (a philosophical cousin of Thatcherism in Britain) was based on addressing double-digit inflation, high interest rates, and unemployment by cutting back on the role of the government in the economy and reducing taxes. Reagan also moved to rework the US presence in global affairs by rebuilding the military. While the United States came out of recession, and both inflation and unemployment fell, the combination of reduced taxes and increased military spending produced a burgeoning federal budget deficit and the national debt grew – during the Reagan years alone – from $1 trillion to $3 trillion. (By late 2018, in the wake of a combination of Bush-era tax cuts and defence spending, and financial bailouts organized by Bush and Obama, the debt stood at nearly $22 trillion.) (For a review of the United States since 1945, see Cullen, 2017.)

By the 1990s, Americans were divided over the appropriate role of government and the direction that their country was taking on social, economic, and foreign policies. Despite strong economic growth, including low unemployment, high productivity, and new consumer confidence, polls found declining levels of faith and trust in government and elected officials. There were concerns that politics in the United States was driven less by voting and parties than by special interests, and that elected officials in Washington DC had forgotten the needs and priorities of their constituents. How could the wealthiest country in the world still have so many of its people living in poverty? How could it have infant mortality rates that were higher and a life expectancy that was lower than those in several other democracies? How could a country built on equality and individual rights still witness so much discrimination against women, ethnic minorities, and gays?

George W. Bush was elected president in 2000 in a controversial election, having run on a platform driven heavily by domestic issues, and having lost the popular vote to his opponent Al Gore, while winning the Electoral College vote (see later in this chapter). Then came **9/11**: the shocking terrorist attacks of 11 September 2001, which were to prove a turning point in the direction of US foreign policy. After winning plaudits for his quick decision to invade Afghanistan, Bush took the controversial step in March 2003 of launching an attack on Iraq, which he accused of developing weapons of mass destruction. Questions were raised about the legality of the war, and about the wisdom of ending decades of US policy by launching a pre-emptive attack on another country. Questions were also raised when the Bush administration oversaw the biggest reorganization of US government in 50 years through the creation of a new Department of Homeland Security. More questions were raised with the passage of the USA Patriot Act, which gave the federal government unprecedented powers to investigate the personal affairs of Americans.

Bush was re-elected with a small margin of victory in 2004, but his administration's response to the devastation caused by Hurricane Katrina in August 2005 was ham-fisted, and the Democrats took back control of Congress in mid-term elections in 2006. The breaking of the global financial crisis in 2007 – which began in the United States and then spread abroad – made matters worse, and by October 2008 a Gallup poll found that just nine per cent of Americans were satisfied with the direction the country was taking (tying the 1979 all-time low). With an approval rating of just 23 per cent, Bush was the most unpopular president since Harry S. Truman. (However, Congress had an even lower approval rating of just 18 per cent, tying a record low.)

The United States today

The key theme in the 2008 presidential election was change, support for which was reflected in new levels of voter interest and the record amounts of campaign funding attracted by the two major parties. Just what was meant by 'change' was open to interpretation, but the issues that worried presidential candidates and voters alike included the accelerating global financial crisis, the weakness of the US dollar, the rising national debt, illegal immigration, international terrorism, the persistence of poverty, declining educational standards, environmental degradation (particularly a weak response to climate change), and ongoing social and economic divisions.

Barack Obama won an historic victory in November, becoming the first black leader of a Western democracy, and immediately launched a programme of efforts to contain the financial crisis, to end the war in Iraq, to rebuild the faith of Americans in national government, and to reform the health care system. But many of the economic problems persisted, and Obama was criticized for spending more rather than less. Anti-big government sentiment spawned the Tea Party movement, which was instrumental in the Democrats losing their majority in the House of Representatives in November 2010.

Change was again a key theme in the 2016 presidential election, which saw the Democratic Party divided between Bernie Sanders – a notably liberal candidate who won the support of many young voters by criticizing the gap between the rich and the poor – and Hillary Clinton, who stood to become the first woman elected to the US presidency, but was seen by many as too closely associated with the political establishment. The Republicans, meanwhile, saw numerous candidates contesting the nomination, the eventual winner being Donald Trump, a political outsider whose candidacy was seen as representing a reaction against the political class, globalization, and illegal immigration, and as representing a desire – as he put it – to 'drain the swamp' in Washington DC and to 'make America great again'.

Trump lost the popular vote by more than two percentage points but won the Electoral College vote by a margin of 304 to 227. As president he became embroiled in a crisis over alleged corruption and Russian interference in the US election, became notorious for expressing himself in often provocative and contradictory terms on Twitter, and

Hats for sale outside a rally given by President Donald Trump, among whose most famous campaign promises was to 'make America great again'. Often reduced to the acronym MAGA, the idea was embraced by his supporters but rejected by critics as code for isolationism and nationalism.
Source: iStock.com/JRLPhotographer.

pursued policies (and a style of governing) that helped drive his disapproval rates to record lows. He continued to be supported by his base, however, in which evangelical Christians and rural white voters figured prominently.

POLITICAL CULTURE

Discussions about American political culture often emphasize ideas of liberty, equality, and democracy. It is these values, many Americans argue, that have made the United States a 'beacon of liberty', long drawing immigrants seeking relief from discrimination and authoritarianism, or looking for economic opportunity. But do the claims hold up to objective scrutiny? Most other democracies also have long and strong records of liberty, equality, and democracy, and many rank higher than the United States on the Democracy Index and Freedom in the World. It is not the democratic record of the United States that makes it distinctive so much as some of the interesting variations on the theme of democracy that are found in the American model.

Perhaps the most distinctive quality of American political culture lies in a combination of individualism and limited government. In contrast to most Europeans, most Americans would argue that government should do little more than provide selected public services, uphold the rule of law, and help individuals to achieve their goals. This is part of the reason why the United States is the only advanced democracy without a universal national health care system, and why large government programmes are so often criticized by many Americans. Although most of them would agree with the 18th-century political theorist Thomas Paine when he said: 'That government is best which governs least', large federal government programmes are a core feature of the American political landscape, from social security to Medicare, public education, subsidies to farmers, and bailouts to failing corporations. Americans have an instinctive preference for self-reliance, and yet also have a contradictory willingness to rely on the government.

While Europeans tend to believe in equality of outcome, meaning that they are more willing to see the state intervening to redistribute wealth and opportunity so as to help those who are disadvantaged, Americans tend to believe in equality of opportunity (Prestowitz, 2003). Thus, runs the ideal, there should be economic and political equality of a kind that allows all to succeed provided that they work hard enough and take the initiative. Political debate in the United States is peppered with words such as *dream* and *vision*, with much reflection on progress in achieving the ultimate goal of the **American Dream**. This is a concept first popularized by the historian James Truslow Adams in his 1931 book *The Epic of America*, where he wrote of 'that dream of a land in which life should be better and richer and fuller for every man, with opportunity for each according to his ability or achievement' (Adams, 1931). It has gone on to be associated with ideas of the United States as a land of opportunity, but while the dream is there, many Americans are still denied equal opportunity, and the divisions in American society suggest that the sentiment in the second paragraph of the Declaration of Independence – that all men are born equal – is still more an aspiration than a reality.

Another distinctive quality of American political culture is the widely held view that the United States is an exceptional society, one favoured by circumstances (and perhaps even by God), and which stands as an example for others to follow (see Comparing Political Culture 5). Opinion polls show that Americans are among the most patriotic people in the world, reflected in the ubiquitous flying of the American flag, and repeated claims by

COMPARING POLITICAL CULTURE 5
Are some states exceptional?

One of the ongoing themes in American studies over the years has been **exceptionalism**: the idea that the United States is a unique society, that its people inhabit a unique place in the world, and that its values – political, economic, and social – offer both hope and unusual opportunities for the rest of humanity. The notion dates back to the first settlers, and to the suggestion by John Winthrop – Governor of the Massachusetts Bay Colony – that the Puritans should create 'a city upon a hill' that would mark a clear break from the corrupt society they had left behind. The term *exceptional* was first used by the French political commentator Alexis de Tocqueville in the 1830s in his landmark study *Democracy in America*.

> **Exceptionalism**
> The belief by its people and leaders that their country is a unique and exceptional society.

Particularly during the Cold War, many Americans came to see themselves and their country as charged with saving the world from itself. One historian suggests that exceptionalism 'permeates every period of American history and is the single most powerful agent in a series of arguments that have been fought down the centuries concerning the identity of America and Americans' (Madsen, 1998). Bill Clinton took a slightly different approach, describing the United States as 'the indispensable nation', which alone could make the difference between war and peace, between freedom and repression, and between hope and fear (Clinton, 1996).

There is a religious element to the notion, reflected in the views of some Americans that their country is 'blessed', and in the way that American presidents will habitually end their speeches with the phrase 'God bless America'. George W. Bush described the United States as 'the brightest beacon for freedom and opportunity in the world', and in his 2004 speech to the Republican National Convention argued that it had 'a calling from beyond the stars to stand for freedom'. Barack Obama continued to speak of exceptionalism, although it seemed less convincing against the background of his country's political and economic divisions.

While there is no doubting that the particular story of the creation and evolution of the United States is unusual, most other countries could claim a similar degree of uniqueness of their own. Just looking at the cases in this book, for example, it would be hard to find too many societies that emerged and developed in quite the same way as Britain, China, or Iran, and we will see in Chapters 6 and 7 that the Japanese and the French make claims to exceptionalism that are not that different from those made by Americans. As for the political, economic, and social values of the United States, many other countries could reasonably claim to subscribe to the same ideas about democracy, equality, and free markets. Comparative studies can pay a useful role here by helping us define how different societies see themselves, the extent to which they can justify claims of exceptionalism, and how such claims shape their place in the world.

PROFILE UNITED STATES

Name	United States of America
Capital	Washington DC
Administration	Federal, with 50 states and the District of Columbia.
Constitution	State formed 1776, and most recent constitution came into force 1789.
Executive	Limited presidential. A president elected for a maximum of two four-year terms, supported by a vice president, an Executive Office of the President, a White House Office, and a federal cabinet.
Legislature	Bicameral Congress: lower House of Representatives (435 members) elected for renewable two-year terms, and upper Senate (100 members) containing two senators from each state, elected for renewable six-year terms.
Judiciary	A dual system of federal and state courts headed by the federal Supreme Court with nine members nominated by the president and confirmed by the Senate for lifetime terms.
Electoral system	One of the few large countries still employing the single-member plurality method. Formally, the president is elected indirectly through an Electoral College.
Party system	Multi-party, but dominated by the conservative Republican Party and the liberal Democratic Party.

 326m Population

 $19,390 billion Gross Domestic Product

 $59,530 Per capita GDP

✘ Full Democracy
✔ Flawed Democracy
✘ Hybrid Regime
✘ Authoritarian
✘ Not Rated

Democracy Index rating

✔ Free
✘ Partly Free
✘ Not Free
✘ Not Rated

Freedom House rating

✔ Very High
✘ High
✘ Medium
✘ Low
✘ Not Rated

Human Development Index rating

American political leaders and citizens that their country is the greatest in the world (even if such 'greatness' is almost impossible to objectively measure and substantiate). While patriotism describes love of country, it occasionally spills over into nationalism, which can include an implication of superiority over others. Nationalism was part of the basis for the attractions of Donald Trump, who ran on a platform pledged to 'make America great again' by – in part – making it less beholden to international organizations and foreign governments, resisting globalization, and clamping down on both legal and illegal immigration. The implication here was that the US was no longer exceptional, even if – as Trump claimed in his inaugural speech – it would continue to 'shine as an example … for everyone to follow'.

POLITICAL SYSTEM

In addition to the typical features of a democracy (including representative government and support for the rule of law), four key principles give American government its particular personality:

◆ It is a republic, which – as we saw in Chapter 4 – is a political system in which all members of government are either elected or appointed by elected officials. This is true also of every other case in this book except Britain and Japan, both of which have monarchs.

◆ It is a federation, the appropriate division of powers between the federal government and the states having been a constant theme in American political debate.

◆ There is a **separation of powers** among three branches of government: the presidency, Congress, and the federal court system.

◆ A system of **checks and balances** divides powers and responsibilities and obliges the key institutions – and the different levels of government – to work together to make and implement policy. The deepening and hardening of political divisions in recent decades has had the effect of making such cooperation hard to achieve.

> **Separation of powers**
> An arrangement in which the executive, the legislature, and the judiciary are given distinct but complementary sets of powers, such that neither can govern alone and that all should, ideally, govern together.

This combination makes the United States unusual among liberal democracies. Of the world's 193 states, barely two dozen are federations (including Brazil, Germany, India, and Russia), while the rest are unitary systems in which most political power is vested in national government. The United States is also unusual among democracies in not using a parliamentary system with a fused executive and legislature. Democratic heads of government are often prime ministers who depend for their power on having the support of most members of the national legislature. By contrast, American presidents (like those in Mexico, Nigeria, and Russia) are elected separately from the legislature, and cannot always rely on a friendly Congress, even when the same party dominates both institutions.

The constitution

The constitution of the United States is not just one of the oldest such documents in the world, but it is also perhaps the most influential, containing ideas that have long been at the heart of debates about democracy, and standing as a model for many newer constitutions in other parts of the world. It is the centrepiece of the American political system, the blueprint by which the United States is governed, and the subject of much debate and analysis among lawyers and scholars.

One of the ongoing debates about how to understand the US constitution revolves around **originalism** (Wurman, 2017). This is based on the idea of following the 'original' meaning of the constitution as intended by those who wrote it in 1787, the logic being that such an approach better respects the intentions of the authors and ensures more consistency in the actions of government. Among the criticisms of originalism are that it is not always possible to know what the authors meant by their choice of words, it does not allow flexibility in the approach of government, and it does not allow the constitution to evolve. This is particularly true of gun ownership, which seems to be protected by the Second Amendment to the constitution, which was inserted only in the interests of forming militias.

The constitution is remarkable for its age, but it has been formally amended only 27 times in nearly 230 years. For some, this is a sign of the agelessness of its content, but for others it is a worrying indication that it has fallen behind the times. The amending process appears relatively simple – amendments must be proposed either by two-thirds of both houses of Congress or by two-thirds of state legislatures, and then ratified by three-quarters of state legislatures, usually within ten years – but it has been difficult to win political support for such amendments. This leaves constitutional change to three other options: judicial review by the US Supreme Court, the passage of new laws that outline details of the structure of government (for example, laws have established the size of the House of

Representatives and the Supreme Court and have created all federal courts below the level of the Supreme Court), or the adoption of customs and traditions, out of which have developed – for example – political parties.

The executive: president

The presidency of the United States is often described as one of the strongest government offices in the world, and in terms of the resources that US presidents have at their disposal, this is true: the president is commander-in-chief of the world's most powerful military and makes decisions affecting the world's biggest national economy. There are even complaints that the presidency has become imperial in nature, and that its powers need to be checked more rigorously (see Schlesinger, 2004, and Healy, 2008). However, compared with the leaders of other democracies, the president is often hamstrung: his policy options are limited by Congress and the courts, and many of the most important decisions about government and policy are taken outside the White House. In essence, the power of presidents boils down to their ability to persuade, and to build coalitions of support inside and outside Congress.

The framers of the US constitution feared anarchy (too little government) and tyranny (too much government) in about equal measure and wanted to make sure that the executive and the legislature checked each other. Throughout the 19th century, Congress dominated and few presidents were able to make much of a mark on government (among the notable exceptions being Abraham Lincoln). The situation changed with Franklin D. Roosevelt (1933–45), who exerted the powers of the office rather than simply responding to Congress. Since then, the role of the presidency has been transformed, for five main reasons.

◆ Presidents have won more powers to set the policy agenda, which has motivated them to work harder at winning congressional support. With the growing divisions within the United States, this has become more difficult.
◆ The president is better placed to respond quickly to policy needs than Congress, which is big, cumbersome, and increasingly divided along party lines.
◆ The global power of the United States has led to high expectations on the president to provide leadership on foreign and defence policy.
◆ Presidents are more newsworthy than Congress and have exploited this to manipulate the media and public opinion, even more so in the era of social media.
◆ The presidency itself has grown, making it easier for presidents to respond to a broader set of policy issues. George Washington had just one staff member, Lincoln had four, and Roosevelt had 50; by contrast, today's presidents have more than 2,000 people working directly for them.

The constitution says that anyone who is a natural-born citizen, is older than 35 years of age, and has been a US resident for at least 14 years can be president. In reality, the ability to raise large amounts of campaign funds is critical, and elected political background is important, preferably as a state governor or a US senator. Governors were once prime contenders for the presidency, but this changed in the 1960s and 1970s, when a rash of former senators ran, including the Kennedy brothers and Richard Nixon. Then came Watergate, and the reaction against Washington 'insiders' gave the advantage to state governors: Jimmy Carter from Georgia, Ronald Reagan from California, Bill Clinton from Arkansas, and George W. Bush from Texas. The 2008 election was unusual in that both of the candidates for the major parties (Barack Obama and John McCain) were sitting US senators. The 2016 election was even more unusual, resulting as it did in the election of the ultimate outsider, Donald Trump, a businessman with no experience in elected office.

The enumerated constitutional powers of the president are modest: they include being commander-in-chief and having the powers to grant pardons, to make treaties (with Senate approval), to nominate ambassadors and federal court judges, and to veto congressional bills. Looking beyond the formal limits, the president has multiple different roles. Prime among these are the combined tasks of being head of government and head of state. In the former role, presidents are politicians, representatives of their party, and champions of their particular policy objectives. They need to keep the support of the voters who elected them into office (often described as 'the base'), the members of Congress on whom they depend to vote their programmes into law, the Washington establishment, and the national media.

Presidents are also heads of state, in which role they are expected to carry out many of the symbolic duties reserved in other states to the monarch or to non-executive presidents, such as acting as a national figure at times of crisis. This can be time-consuming but can also be politically important – presidents who associate themselves with popular feelings of patriotism and national unity can elevate themselves above partisan politics. There is no guarantee, however, that this will help them achieve policy change, as Barack Obama found in the case of the many speeches he had to make following mass shootings of the kind that are all too tragically part of the American landscape.

Table 5.1 Modern presidents of the United States

Start of term*	Name	Party
1933 (March)	Franklin D. Roosevelt	Democrat
1945 (April)	Harry S. Truman	Democrat
1953	Dwight Eisenhower	Republican
1961	John F. Kennedy	Democrat
1963 (November)	Lyndon B. Johnson	Democrat
1969	Richard M. Nixon	Republican
1974 (August)	Gerald Ford	Republican
1977	Jimmy Carter	Democrat
1981	Ronald Reagan	Republican
1989	George H. W. Bush	Republican
1993	Bill Clinton	Democrat
2001	George W. Bush	Republican
2009	Barack Obama	Democrat
2017	Donald Trump	Republican

January unless otherwise indicated

The president is also commander-in-chief. Only Congress can declare war, but presidents are in charge of US armed forces and of making decisions on their involvement in military operations, and Congress is unlikely to oppose a president during times of crisis. Presidential powers declined after Vietnam, and the 1974 War Powers Act made it illegal for presidents to commit US troops overseas for more than 60 days without Congressional approval. But George W. Bush reasserted his military powers when he was able to convince Congress in 2002 to give him sweeping authority in preparation for the 2003 invasion of Iraq.

Presidents also take the lead in the making and pursuit of foreign and economic policy. As well as having sole power to negotiate treaties with other countries, and to extend diplomatic recognition to foreign governments, they also tend to lead Congress in shaping the priorities of foreign policy. On the economic front, Congress alone has powers over fiscal policy (taxing and spending), but the White House must develop the federal budget and presidents can influence the direction taken by economic policy. Indeed, the political fortunes of presidents often rise and fall with the state of the economy, and the president is usually closely identified in the public mind with economic issues, such as the rate of economic growth and inflation. As Bill Clinton's advisor James Carville once famously noted in a listing of the most important Clinton campaign messages, 'It's the economy, stupid.'

Finally, presidents have five other more focused sets of obligations:

◆ *Chief executive.* Presidents head the federal cabinet and the federal bureaucracy, using their authority to make sure that congressional laws are executed. In this role they also have the right to issue executive orders, which are targeted at government departments and agencies and are designed to improve or change the work of government.

◆ *Agenda setter.* The president has considerable influence over setting the national political agenda, outlining its key points in the annual State of the Union address. Presidents also need a well-developed media strategy, exploiting the newsworthiness of almost anything they do, from making an important policy speech to buying a new family dog.

◆ *Moral leader.* Unlike the citizens of any other democracy, most Americans long looked to the president to set the moral tone for the country. A president is expected to have an upstanding personal life, and to be honest, compassionate, open-minded, good-humoured, and competent, as well as setting a good overall example. Critics of Donald Trump charge that he has performed poorly on all these fronts, but many of his supporters argue that his character does not matter, and seem to forgive his amorality, misogyny, nepotism, and misrepresentations.

◆ *Crisis manager.* Life is often unpredictable, and crises break to which government must respond, such as war and conflict, natural disasters such as hurricanes and floods, and tragically frequent mass shootings. As one person, the president is in a better position to respond quickly than is Congress, and is expected to provide leadership in such instances (Magleby et al., 2015).

◆ *Party leader.* Although American political parties have their own governing committees and chairs, presidents become *de facto* leaders of their party while in office, and the goals of the party are heavily influenced by presidential programmes.

Despite all these roles – and the constitutional powers of the president – the performance of individual presidents is ultimately tied to other, more informal and often less quantifiable factors. These include the ability of a president to communicate their programme and message, their capabilities as organizers and builders of a governing team, their political skills (how well or how badly they are able to work with others to build support for their programme), their sense of direction (or what President George H. W. Bush once famously described as 'the vision thing'), and their emotional intelligence: how well they manage anger and stress, how secure they feel in themselves, and their sense of moral character (Greenstein, 2009).

To do their jobs, presidents have become dependent on an expanding body of people and institutions that collectively represent 'the presidency'. Most notable among these are the staff within the White House itself, including the president's chief of staff, the press secretary, congressional liaison staff, and a string of advisors on a wide range of policy issues. These positions are all appointed by the president and help keep him informed, and also become associated in the public mind with the administration. The president also governs with the help of the federal cabinet, which consists of the heads of major government departments, including defence, justice, the treasury, and homeland security. The president nominates cabinet heads, who must then be confirmed by the Senate. Cabinets in parliamentary systems (such as the UK or India) are like governing committees, are deeply involved in making political decisions, and meet as often as once per week; by contrast, the US cabinet is more of an advisory body and rarely meets to discuss policy as a group.

The president is also helped by a vice president, whose job is traditionally considered one of the least important in government. Vice presidents may be 'a heartbeat away from the presidency', but most spend their time in relative obscurity, their role dependent almost entirely on the wishes of the president. The significance of the office may be changing, however: several modern vice presidents have used the office as a launch pad for a bid for the presidency, and it was clear that George W. Bush's vice president – Dick Cheney – played a central role in both making the policies of the administration and in conveying them to the media and the public, while Donald Trump's vice president – Mike Pence – developed a reputation for loyalty to his president while also being closely watched given his potential for replacing an unpopular and divisive incumbent.

The legislature: Congress

Like all large, federal states, the United States has a bicameral legislature, the work of each chamber designed to provide different levels of representation. The Senate represents the states in the sense that each of them has the same number of Senators, regardless of the size of each state, while the House of Representatives is designed to more directly represent the people, in the sense that its seats are divided up among states according to their population size.

Congress was designed by the framers of the constitution to be the most powerful branch of government, and so it was for about 150 years; few presidents were able to challenge congressional power, and most of the key political struggles took place within Congress rather than between Congress and the president. During the 20th century, however, presidential powers grew (for reasons explained earlier) and decision-making within Congress was decentralized (Burke, 2016). The result has been more of a balance between the two branches, whose need for each other to govern effectively has grown.

The constitution gives Congress several formal powers, including the authority to levy taxes, borrow money, coin money, declare war, raise armies, determine the nature of the federal judiciary, and regulate commerce with foreign governments and among states. In practice, however, the powers of Congress rest mainly in four areas:

◆ Law-making. Congress is where federal laws are introduced, discussed, and either accepted or rejected.

◆ Oversight. Congress checks on the work of the federal bureaucracy, making sure that it carries out the intent of Congress.

◆ Budgetary matters. Congress has the final say over the federal budget, which is developed by the White House Office of Management and Budget but must be approved by Congress.

◆ Confirming appointments. The Senate has the power to check and confirm all key presidential appointees except those who work directly for the president in the White House.

Legislation can be introduced in either chamber of Congress (with the exception of revenue bills, which can only be introduced in the House of Representatives). All bills are sent to the relevant committee, are then sent for debate by the chamber as a whole before being voted on, and are then sent to the other chamber where they go through the same stages. If a bill passes both chambers, it is sent to the president, who can either sign it into law or exercise a veto. A presidential veto can in turn be overridden in Congress by a vote of more than two-thirds of the members of both chambers.

Despite being the political institution that is closest to the people, polls show that Congress is the least popular of the three branches of government, earning a 69 per cent disapproval rating in 2015 (Pew Research Center, 2015). There are several reasons for this: it does not have the same aura as the other institutions, it is most closely involved in the process of law-making and so is more deeply involved in the struggles of politics, and members of Congress are local representatives who tend to pursue narrow interests at the expense of the greater good.

Senate

The **Senate** is the upper chamber of Congress, with two senators elected from each of the 50 states, for a total of 100. They serve six-year renewable terms, and elections are staggered so that one-third of members stand for re-election every two years. This arrangement of giving every state the same number of senators regardless of size was a result of what was known as the Great Compromise, driven by concerns among smaller states that their voices would be drowned out by larger states. With two members each in the Senate, the effect was to leave smaller states over-represented and larger states under-represented; thus the nearly 600,000 residents of Wyoming have the same degree of representation as the 39 million residents of California.

Sessions of the Senate are overseen by a president, who is – *ex officio* (that is, by virtue of his or her office) – the vice president of the United States. This is a largely symbolic position, and the president of the Senate can cast a vote only in the case of a tie; most of the time, the president is represented by a junior senator acting as president *pro tempore*. Much more significant is the post of Senate majority leader, held by a member of the majority party in the Senate. The majority leader schedules debates, assigns bills to committees, coordinates party policy, appoints members of special committees, and generally oversees the functioning of the Senate to suit the purposes of the majority party.

In terms of its powers over introducing, discussing, and voting on legislation, the Senate has equal powers with the House of Representatives. However, it also has the unique power of approval over presidential nominations for appointments to the cabinet, the Supreme Court, lower federal courts, key government agencies such as the Federal Reserve Board, and ambassadorial posts.

House of Representatives

The **House of Representatives** is the lower chamber of Congress, and has 435 members elected for renewable two-year terms, all of whom come up for re-election at the same time. According to the constitution, all congressional districts must be reapportioned every ten years to reflect changes in the population. Because of these changes, southern and western states such as Florida and California have gained new seats in recent decades at the expense mainly of older industrial states such as New York and Pennsylvania.

The leader is the Speaker of the House, who comes from the majority party. In contrast to the Speaker in parliamentary systems, who is expected to be non-partisan (see Chapter 3), the Speaker of the House is a partisan leader with considerable powers: he or she presides over debates, recognizes members who wish to speak, votes in cases of a tie, interprets questions of procedure, and influences the committee system by assigning bills to committees and deciding who should sit on special and select committees. In 2006 Nancy Pelosi of California became the first woman to hold the post, losing it in 2010 to John Boehner of Ohio. In 2019, she became the first former-Speaker to return to the position since the 1950s.

The judiciary: Supreme Court

A body such as the US **Supreme Court** is central to the success of constitutional government, because of its power of judicial review (ruling on the laws or actions of government on the basis of its interpretation of the constitution; see Chapter 2). Remarkably, judicial review is not a power given to the court by the constitution; the Court won this power for itself in the *Marbury* v. *Madison* decision of 1803 by which the Court announced that it could declare an act of Congress void if it was inconsistent with the constitution. The US constitution also says nothing about

COMPARING GOVERNMENT 5
Legislative turnover

One of the more notable characteristics of the US Congress is its low rate of **legislative turnover** at elections: on average since 1945, about 94 per cent of incumbent members of the House and 84 per cent of members of the Senate have been re-elected (Brookings Institution, 2017), and the absence of term limits means that many members of Congress serve for decades in office, sometimes well past the standard retirement age. Although the research on legislative turnover is patchy (most has focused on Europe), enough is known to indicate that the numbers for the United States are higher than average. This is reflected in Figure 5.1, which combines two sets of data from different countries at different times.

> **Legislative turnover**
> The rate of change in the membership of a legislatu re following an election.

Low turnover has the advantages of bringing experienced legislators back into office, and of ensuring greater confidence and efficiency among legislators in offsetting the executive. But it has the disadvantages of building a class of professional politicians, of preventing the injection of new ideas, and of making it less likely that the make-up of a legislature will keep up with the changing make-up and needs of the voting public. Mexico offers an extreme case of high turnover, which is guaranteed by a ban on consecutive terms in office in the national Congress and in state legislatures (although elected officials reaching their limit in one body can simply run for election to another; see Chapter 9).

The study of eight Western European legislatures by Gouglas et al. (2018) concludes that rates of turnover are impacted by several factors:

◆ The dynamics of politics as a career: the more political positions there are, and the higher the status and wages of being a politician, the higher the turnover.
◆ The structure of legislatures: strong bicameral legislatures and multiple levels of government create more opportunities for political advancement, creating more turnover as legislators move up or down in the system.
◆ Affirmative action policies: gender quotas are a driver of change, and thus of higher turnover.
◆ Political turbulence and volatility: the more routine the election, the lower the turnover. An example of volatility and high turnover comes from the 1958 French general election, held just after the coming into force of the new constitutions of the Fifth Republic (see Chapter 7), when only 24 per cent of incumbents were returned to office.

Turnover is also lower in the United States thanks to its unique system of drawing the lines of electoral constituencies, which gives parties greater control over influencing the outcome of elections. While most democracies give the job to independent electoral commissions, in most states in the US the task is controlled by the biggest political party in that state, which will manipulate the boundaries of electoral districts so as to make sure that its candidates face the fewest challenges from opponents and the greatest prospect of being re-elected. This process is known as **gerrymandering**, and was named for an early 19th-century governor of Massachusetts named Elbridge Gerry, under whose administration a strangely shaped district was likened to a salamander, generating the portmanteau *gerrymander*. Several legal challenges have recently been made to this practice, and in 2018 the state of Pennsylvania was forced by its own state court to redraw the lines of electoral districts just months before the November mid-term elections.

lower federal courts, and yet a complex system of district courts and courts of appeal has been built over time, now hearing about 10 million cases each year.

The Supreme Court has nine members, nominated by the president and confirmed by the Senate for lifetime terms, with one of their number appointed as Chief Justice. Below the Supreme Court there are Courts of Appeal and District Courts with about 750 federal court judges who must also be nominated by the president and approved by the Senate. Plaintiffs who lose their cases in lower courts can appeal to have them heard by the Supreme Court, which receives several thousand petitions every year but usually agrees to review only about 90–120 cases that it believes have important constitutional implications. Since World War II, the Court has paid particular attention to

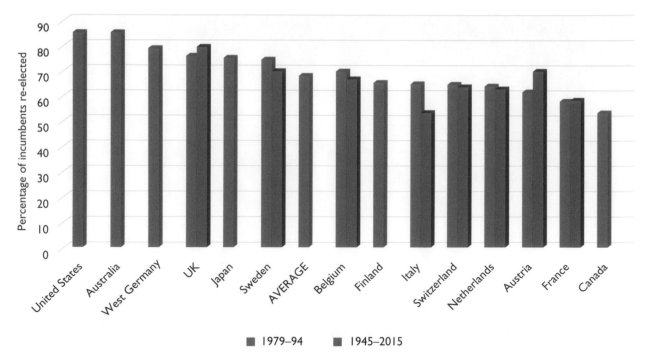

Figure 5.1 Comparing rates of legislative turnover

Sources: Data for 1979–94 are from Matland and Studlar (2004), while those for 1945–2015 are from Gouglas et al. (2018), who look only at Western Europe.

Note: Figures are for elections to the lower or sole chamber of each country's legislature.

cases relating to civil liberties, civil rights, and social equality. Among the most famous of its decisions were *Brown* v. *Board of Education* in 1954, which ended formal racial segregation in schools, and *Miranda* v. *Arizona* in 1966, relating to the rights of criminal defendants, and *Citizens United* v. *FEC*, which ruled that corporations have free speech rights protected by the First Amendment to the US constitution.

Because of the political implications of many Court decisions, and because of the lifetime tenure of justices, appointments can be both contested and controversial. Court appointments have become increasingly politically charged as the role of the courts in the political system has changed. Theoretically, judges are expected to exercise restraint by limiting changes and setting aside personal views, but many have been accused of activism and of being too swayed by ideology. For that reason, the political leanings of judges have become a critical issue in debates over appointments, with both parties in Congress working to block the confirmation of judges who they consider to be too partisan. This is particularly true of the Supreme Court, whose judges can be removed from office only for serious dereliction of duty.

Particular controversy surrounded the political manoeuvring involved in the efforts to replace Antonin Scalia, a famously conservative Supreme Court justice who died in February 2016. With 11 months still left in his term, President Barack Obama had the right and duty to appoint a successor, and nominated a lower court judge named Merrick Garland. But Republicans in the Senate refused even to hold hearings into his nomination, instead holding out in the hope that a Republican would win the November 2016 presidential election and nominate a more conservative candidate.

This was what happened when Donald Trump won the presidency and nominated the conservative Neil Gorsuch to replace Scalia. Nominations to the Supreme Court need a super-majority of 60 votes in the Senate, and when it quickly became clear that Democratic and independent Senators – who held 48 seats in the chamber – would not support Gorsuch, the Senate Republican leadership changed the rules so that a nominee could be confirmed by a simple majority. Gorsuch's nomination was duly confirmed. An even greater political struggle surrounded the 2018 appointment of Brett Kavanaugh, who was charged (late in the confirmation process) with incidents of sexual assault during his teenage years. The stakes were considerably greater, because his confirmation (by 50 votes to 48) promised to ensure that the ideological balance of the Court would remain in favour of conservatives for many years to come.

The US Supreme Court building in Washington DC. The Court has long been seen as a symbol of the strength of constitutional government in the United States, but the politicization of Court appointments and the partisan nature of many of its decisions have come to symbolize the depth of the ideological divisions that plague the United States. *Source: iStock.com/YinYang.*

Sub-national government

The United States is a federation, in which powers are divided between the national government in Washington DC and the governments of the 50 states, each of which has its own constitution, elected governor and elected state legislature, and appointed constitutional court. Within states, power is further sub-divided, with separately elected bodies for city and county government (something not mentioned in the constitution, as a result of which there is enormous variety in local political offices). Although the federal government is responsible for most aspects of economic, foreign, and defence policy, state and local governments are responsible for managing most of the welfare system, maintaining state highways, managing land use, executing many federal laws and regulations, and overseeing education and policing.

The United States is too big and diverse to be governed under the kind of unitary systems of administration used in Britain and Japan, which would anyway fly in the face of American political culture and its emphasis on keeping government as close as possible to the people. Although federalism helps deal with the size and diversity of the country, allows different states to adopt different positions on key issues that are in tune with local opinion, and offers citizens more opportunities for participation in government, it also creates problems. It slows the process of decision-making, it can make people too focused on narrow goals and values rather than looking at the broader national interest, and it can hamstring the ability of national government to address economic and social differences within the country.

The United States began as a loose association under the Articles of Confederation, which lasted only from 1781 to 1789 before being replaced by the current federal system. But the nature of the association between Washington DC and the states has never ceased to be the subject of political debate, particularly as more power has been accumulated over time by the federal government:

◆ The emphasis in the 19th century was on **dual federalism**, an arrangement in which the powers of the federal government and the states were clearly defined.

◆ Between the Civil War and the New Deal policies of Franklin D. Roosevelt in the 1930s there was a steady shift of power towards the federal government. This created a new system of **cooperative federalism**, in which the different layers of government worked together to address problems, rather than making policies separately.

◆ Since the Reagan administration there has been a new assertion of the rights of states, in a phenomenon known as **new federalism**. The trend can be likened to the devolution of powers from central government to the regions in Britain.

The debate over the appropriate role of central and local government remains unresolved in the United States, as it does in many other countries, whether they are federal or not. There has been a particularly active debate about decentralization in developing countries, and about the extent to which it promotes good governance (see Grindle, 2009).

POLITICAL PROCESSES

The American electoral and party system is rife with paradoxes, of which four stand out:

◆ Voters are faced with more elected offices and elections than in any other democracy, yet voter turnout rates are often low.

◆ American political culture emphasizes civic duty, yet as the number of eligible voters has increased, the proportion who vote has fallen.

◆ American political democracy emphasizes democracy and equality, and yet government is dominated by heterosexual white older men.

◆ The United States has some of the oldest political parties in the world, yet Americans are offered fewer choices in the way of parties with a chance of winning office than any other democracy.

All four of these phenomena are related, and reflect the problem of reduced political engagement that has been witnessed in many democracies in recent decades. They also give political processes in the United States several distinctive features:

◆ Party dynamics are binary to an unusual degree. Were a greater variety of parties to have a realistic chance of winning elections, there might – based on the evidence from other countries – be higher turnout. As it is, the Democrats and the Republicans have consistently held almost all seats in Congress, and one or the other has won every modern presidential election, giving vote options an unnaturally black-and-white quality. While differences between the two major parties periodically emerge over social and economic issues, they are adept at reinventing themselves and reaching out to voters with related interests.

◆ Elections are long and lengthy. This has become a particular problem with presidential elections, where early candidates may begin subtle campaigning as much as two years before the event itself. In the year leading up to the election, media coverage is so intense – and often becomes so negative – that it runs the risk of boring many voters.

◆ Elections are remarkably expensive, each election cycle breaking records for spending as the laws on campaign financing have been loosened – see Comparing Politics 5.

While turnout has improved, the overall trends should also be seen in conjunction with the different numbers found among different groups: whites turn out more than ethnic minorities, the wealthy turn out more than the poor, and older voters turn out more than the young. Government tends to look like those Americans who vote most often, and to be more responsive to the needs of those who vote than of those who do not, as a result of which many groups remain relatively marginalized in government.

The electoral system

Elections in the United States are longer, more numerous, and more expensive than in any other democracy. In order to give citizens the opportunity to have as much say as possible in government, elections are held for offices ranging from the president of the United States down through multiple and often relatively minor offices in state and local government. Meanwhile, the importance of candidates over party affiliation means that first-time candidates are obliged to work harder to make themselves known to the electorate, demanding a long process of familiarization that results in election campaigns that can last several months and can be expensive.

COMPARING POLITICS 5
Money and elections

Jesse Unruh, Speaker of the California state legislature in the 1960s, once quipped that 'Money is the mother's milk of politics.' This has always been true of the United States, notably in the 19th century, when political favours were openly bought by many of the owners of the new corporations then being established in the United States. More recently, the role of money in politics has grown in the wake of changes made to campaign finance laws.

The main problem is the high cost of elections: successful candidates in House elections must now expect to spend several hundred thousand dollars each time they run, while successful Senate campaigns run into the millions of dollars. Total spending for Congressional election campaigns grew from $1.6 billion in 1998 to nearly $6 billion in 2018, while the cost of presidential elections grew from $1.4 billion in 2000 to $2.8 billion in 2008, dropping slightly to $2.4 billion in 2016 (Centre for Responsive Politics, 2019). Although American political culture places a premium on equality and access to government, the costs of running for office have become so high that only those with access to large sums of money can now realistically hope to win (see Mutch, 2014). Changes to federal law in 1974 obliged candidates to be less reliant on a few large sources of funding and to raise smaller amounts of money from a broader constituency, but the *Citizens United* decision by the Supreme Court in 2010 ruled that government could not restrict independent political spending by corporations and interest groups, opening the door to large new levels of spending.

There are many other democracies that have few if any limits on campaign spending, including Australia, Denmark, Germany, the Netherlands, Norway, Spain, and Sweden. But most of the spending in the United States goes on television advertising, which is not allowed in these other countries, thus reducing the need and opportunities for spending. Also, there is public funding of campaigns in these countries, and the campaigns are short, again reducing the need and opportunities for spending. Similar factors come to bear in countries that limit contributions and spending (such as Canada, France, and Japan) and in countries that limit spending but not contributions (such as Austria, Hungary, Italy, and the UK). In poorer and/or more authoritarian states, meanwhile, there is more manipulation of elections, and thus less need to spend on advertising (although there may be more need to spend on 'favours' to local leaders and social groups in order to encourage their support for governing parties).

Election season is also made longer by the use of a **primary** system for most key offices. Rather than parties choosing who will run for office in their name, as is the case in parliamentary systems, the choices are made in the United States by voters casting ballots in primaries. Voters choose from among competing potential candidates, and the winner is then adopted by the party to run in the general election. Primaries are democratic in the sense that they place the choice of party candidates in the hands of voters, but they also add time and expense to the electoral process, weaken the grip of political parties, give a few — sometimes unrepresentative — voters considerable impact on the outcome of the nomination process, and occasionally leave parties with candidates they would rather not have (Donald Trump being a case in point, rejected as he was by many supporters of the Republican Party).

Primary
An election in which voters choose the candidate that will run for their party in the general election.

Presidential elections

Without question the dominating event in the American electoral calendar is the race for the presidency, which is the focus of intense national and international media scrutiny and has become the longest and most expensive election in the world. The election is held every four years, and although the formal election season is confined to the months leading up to election day, an informal 'pre-primary' season can emerge as much as three years earlier with media speculation about possible candidates, followed by the formation by anticipative candidates of exploratory committees. As long as 18 months before the election, the main contenders will begin to visit key states, and some may already have picked up enough sense about the balance of public opinion to have withdrawn.

The formal primary season begins in the February before the election with votes in the states of New Hampshire and Iowa, running until the holding of national party conventions in late summer. These once confirmed the choice of candidate for the major parties, but today they are little more than self-indulgent media events designed to crown the candidates. The actual presidential campaign traditionally runs from early September until election day in early November, with all costs at this stage met out of public funds. Media coverage of the candidates intensifies, and televised debates are held, although these are not so much one-on-one debates as carefully designed opportunities for the candidates to outline their programmes.

The final stage is the election itself. Even though the candidates for the Republican and Democratic parties alone have a realistic chance of winning, as many as a dozen candidates have run in recent elections, and since the 1990s there have been occasionally significant third-party challenges (Figure 5.2). The United States uses a unique form of indirect voting for presidents, with voters making their choices in state-level elections, which are then converted into votes in an **Electoral College**. Devised at the time of the writing of the US constitution, this was a compromise between those who wanted Congress to select the president and those who wanted the people to elect the president. Each state is given as many Electoral College votes as it has members of Congress, and in most states the presidential candidate that wins the most popular votes wins all the Electoral College votes for that state. One of the effects of the college is that candidates are encouraged to focus all their efforts and attention on the larger states, often bypassing smaller states or those they are sure to win or lose. As a result, a presidential candidate could theoretically be elected by winning pluralities of the popular vote in just the dozen largest states.

> **Electoral College**
> A body of electors brought together to decide the holder of a higher office.

Federal legislative elections

Every two years, all 435 members of the House of Representatives – and one-third of the members of the US Senate – run for re-election using a single-member plurality system. As with the presidential race, candidates must be selected in primaries, but – as we saw earlier – incumbents are rarely seriously challenged and re-election is usually assured. Legislative primaries attract less media and public interest than their presidential equivalents, but this does not mean that candidates do not spend a proportionate amount of effort and money in running for office. This is particularly true of Senate campaigns, where the competition and public interest can sometimes be more intense than is the case with House campaigns (because there are fewer Senators and they represent entire states rather than local districts).

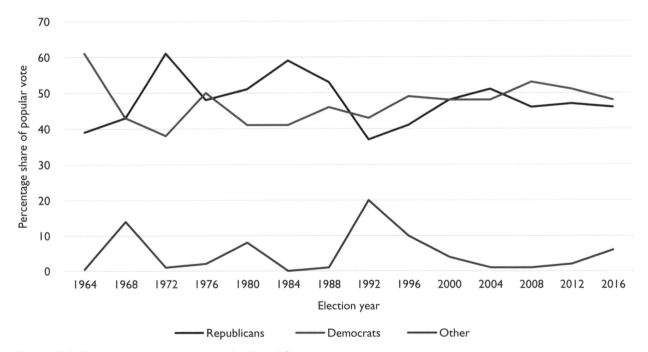

Figure 5.2 Executive electoral trends in the United States

State and local elections

Americans can vote in a wide range of elections at the local level, from those for state governors and legislators to those for mayors, city councillors, sheriffs, district attorneys, state auditors, library trustees, coroners, town clerks, and local school boards. The races for governors and mayors usually draw the most voter interest, with those for local positions being less interesting, if only because most voters know little about the competing candidates. As a result, turnout at local elections may be as low as 20–30 per cent. There has been more awareness in recent years, though, of the importance of state politicians in shaping electoral districts, with the result that more attention is now paid to the outcome of elections for governors and state legislatures.

Political parties

Compared to other democracies, most of which have multiple parties representing a wide range of political ideologies, political parties play a more focused role in American politics, which has largely been reduced to a binary choice between Democrats on the left and Republicans on the right. These two parties have held a duopoly since the 19th century, winning every presidential election in modern history, and between them holding almost all the seats in the US Congress (Figure 5.3). Their grip is based on a variety of factors: the use of the single-member plurality electoral system gives the two major parties a strong institutional incentive to alter their electoral strategies so as to make sure that breakaway parties or minor parties fail to develop much influence or win seats; both the Democrats and the Republicans are automatically included on general election ballots, whereas third parties must meet the requirements set by different states, such as filing petitions. Both major parties are also adept at reaching out for independent voters in the middle of the political spectrum, and their domination is helped by the usually limited support for parties or candidates with stronger left-wing or right-wing ideological positions.

Democratic Party

The **Democratic Party** traces its roots back to the 1820s and long had its most important base of support in the south. After decades spent mainly in political opposition, the party was swept into office in 1932 on the back of demands that government take a more hands-on approach in dealing with economic and social problems in the wake of the Great Depression. Since World War II, it has held the White House during the Truman, Kennedy, Johnson, Carter, Clinton, and Obama administrations, and held a 40-year majority in both houses of Congress before losing it to the Republicans between 1996 and 2006, and again in 2010. From the 1930s, Democrats tended

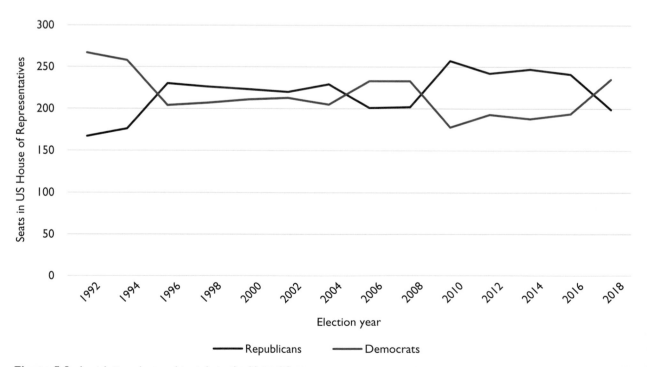

Figure 5.3 Legislative electoral trends in the United States

to be the party of the disadvantaged, sitting mainly on the moderate left-wing, favouring social welfare, regulation of big business, and environmental management. Starting in the 1960s, Democrats became increasingly divided over civil rights, alienating many of their white Southern supporters. Today, they have the advantage among poorer, less educated and working class Americans, dominating most cities, enjoying the support of minorities, and winning a bigger share of the vote of suburban residents and educated women.

Republican Party

The **Republican Party** (also known as the Grand Old Party, or the GOP) traces its roots back to just before the Civil War, when Democrats opposed to slavery broke away to form the new party. When the South lost the war, the primarily northern-dominated Republicans went on to win almost every presidential election for the next 50 years, and then alternated with the Democrats after World War II under the presidencies of Eisenhower, Nixon, Reagan, the two Bushes, and Trump. After 40 years in opposition in Congress, the Republicans won back a majority in 1996. Most members are moderate conservatives, but the party contains many shades of opinion, ranging from traditional conservatives keen on minimizing the role of government in the economy, to neoconservatives driven by a desire to institutionalize their religious and moral values by limiting access to legal abortion, promoting prayer in schools, and opposing LGBT rights. The Republicans have long had the advantage among wealthier and suburban voters, among social conservatives and evangelicals, and among voters living in western states such as Arizona, Utah, and Kansas. They have recently lost their advantage in the suburbs, though, while picking up the support of many poorer and rural voters. The changing demography and political preferences of Americans does not augur well for the future of the party.

Other parties

The United States has a long history of minor parties, but the control exerted by the two major parties over the electoral process has combined with the arithmetic of the single-member plurality system to prevent any of them from doing much more than acting as spoilers. Thus the moderately conservative Reform Party that formed around the presidential bid of Texas billionaire H. Ross Perot in 1992 took away enough votes from Republican George H. W. Bush to help Bill Clinton win the presidency that year, and again in 1996. Similarly, the pro-environmental Green Party ran Ralph Nader as its presidential candidate in 2000 and took enough votes away from the Democrats to help George W. Bush win. The Libertarian Party holds conservative economic positions and liberal social positions but has not yet had much of an impact on the presidential election. None of these parties has yet won seats in Congress, even though they have won 3–4 per cent of the vote at recent House elections.

THE FUTURE OF AMERICAN GOVERNMENT AND POLITICS

The 20th century was often described as the American century, a reflection of the extent to which the new-found military and economic power of the United States made it a global leader, notably after World War II. Its population grew and became more affluent, its corporations became world leaders, its economy became the engine of worldwide economic growth, and it led the Western alliance in its opposition to the Soviet bloc during the Cold War.

At the same time, the United States went through important internal political and social change. The political voice of women and ethnic minorities became more influential, and demographic changes led to a redefinition of the balance of power: the population became older and more ethnically diverse, suburbs expanded at the expense of downtown areas, and southern states grew relative to the old industrial northern states. Cynicism about politics fuelled a reaction against politics-as-usual and contributed to declining support for political parties and falling turnout at elections.

The United States today faces new debates about the nature of politics, notably the increasing diversification and stratification of American society, manipulation of the electoral system, the excessive influence of interest groups, the structural problems with campaign funding, and worrying trends in the civility of political discourse. It also faces many pressing economic challenges (budget deficits, a trade deficit, new competition from abroad, a burgeoning national debt, and the widening gap between rich and poor), as well as domestic social needs (notably the persistence of poverty and racism). Finally, it must redefine its place in a world in which the sources and the nature of international threats have changed. The next few years promise to be an interesting and challenging time in American politics as politicians and voters rethink their priorities.

DISCUSSION QUESTIONS

1. Is the United States exceptional, and – if so – how? If not, why not?
2. What are the effects on government of the differences in the way that executives and legislatures relate to one another in the United States and in parliamentary democracies?
3. What does the United States need to do to regain its ranking on the Democracy Index as a full democracy?
4. Has the US Supreme Court become too political, and – if so – what could it learn from the way that supreme courts in other democracies are structured?
5. Is it time for the Electoral College to be abolished?
6. Are there too few nationally competitive political parties in the United States?

CHAPTER CONCEPTS

- 9/11
- American Dream
- Articles of Confederation
- Checks and balances
- Civil War
- Congress
- Cooperative federalism
- Democratic Party
- Dual federalism
- Gerrymandering
- Great Society
- House of Representatives
- New federalism
- Originalism
- Pax Americana
- Reaganomics
- Republican Party
- Senate
- Supreme Court

KEY TERMS

- Cold War
- Electoral College
- Exceptionalism
- Isolationism
- Legislative turnover
- Primary
- Separation of powers
- Superpower

THE UNITED STATES ONLINE

White House: www.whitehouse.gov
Senate: www.senate.gov
House of Representatives: www.house.gov
Supreme Court: www.supremecourt.gov
Democratic Party: www.democrats.org
Republican Party: www.gop.com
New York Times: www.nytimes.com
Washington Post: www.washingtonpost.com
CNN: www.cnn.com
Fox News: www.foxnews.com

FURTHER READING

Barbour, Christine, and Gerald Wright (2017) *Keeping the Republic: Power and Citizenship in American Politics*, 8th edn (Sage), and Karen O'Connor, Larry J. Sabato, and Alixandra B. Yanus (2014) *Essentials of American Government*, 11th edn (Pearson). Representative examples of the many introductory US politics texts.

Duncan, Russell, and Joe Goddard (2018) *Contemporary United States*, 5th edn (Red Globe Press). A general survey of the United States, with chapters on its history, government, political system, culture, and economy.

Levitsky, Steven, and Daniel Ziblatt (2018) *How Democracies Die* (Crown). One of several studies asking worried questions about the declining health of American democracy.

Pfiffner, James P., and Roger H. Davidson (2012) *Understanding the Presidency*, 7th edn (Longman); Roger H. Davidson, Walter J. Oleszek, Frances E. Lee, and Eric Schickler (2018) *Congress and Its Members*, 16th edn (Sage), and Lawrence Baum (2016) *The Supreme Court*, 12th edn (CQ Press). A representative selection of texts on the three branches of national government in the United States.

Robertson, David Brian (2012) *Federalism and the Making of America* (Routledge). A study of the way federalism works in the United States, and how it affects American politics and economics.

Vallely, Richard M. (2013) *American Politics*; Charles O. Jones (2016) *The American Presidency*, 2nd edn; Donald A. Ritchie (2016) *The US Congress*, 2nd edn; Linda Greenhouse (2012) *The US Supreme Court*; and L. Sandy Maisel (2016) *American Political Parties and Elections*, 2nd edn. Five publications in the long list of Very Short Introduction titles from Oxford University Press.

Visit **www.macmillanihe.com/McCormick-Cases** to access additional materials to support teaching and learning.

JAPAN

6

PREVIEW

Japan has most of the typical features of a parliamentary system, including a symbolic head of state, and a prime minister and cabinet that come out of the legislature. As a case, though, it has many distinctive and unique political features that make it quite different from other parliamentary systems. These include dominance by a single political party (made possible in part by a divided opposition), a relatively weak office of the prime minister, a strong role for political factions over political parties, and an influential political role for the bureaucracy. Recent reforms to the electoral system have brought changes to the distribution of power, and there are indications that the executive may be growing stronger on the back of new stability within the governing Liberal Democratic Party. Even so, Japan still has much to do if its government is to be able to address economic decline and political dissatisfaction.

KEY ARGUMENTS

◆ Japan is one of the leading examples of the idea that democracy can take root in societies that are modern but not Western.

◆ Liberal democracy has taken root in Japan only relatively recently, its current political system being based on a constitution adopted only in 1947.

◆ There has long been a mismatch between Japan's remarkable economic development and the relatively staid nature of its political system.

◆ Politics in Japan is closely associated with often traditional ideas about loyalty, obligation, and hierarchy, with power based on factions and a web of patron-client relationships.

◆ The bureaucracy plays an unusually powerful role in Japanese government, based on iron triangles involving government, bureaucracy, and business.

◆ Elections and the party system in Japan have revolved around a single dominant party (the Liberal Democrats) and a divided and frequently changing cluster of opposition parties.

OVERVIEW

Most of the world's democracies are either European or come out of the European political and social tradition (mainly through the heritage of colonialism). Among the few exceptions are Japan and South Korea, where fundamentally Western ideas of democracy have been grafted onto societies that remain distinctly non-Western. It is clear that Japan is modern but not Western, in the sense that it has become modern without losing sight of its cultural and social identity. Its modernity is most clearly on show in Japan's economic and technological prowess, which has become the stuff of legend. Meanwhile, traditional values are most obvious in its political culture, where Western ideas about democracy have intermingled with Japanese ideas about faction, obligation, and group identity.

In political terms, Japan is a relative newcomer to democracy. It was a feudal society until 1868, when it embarked on a short-lived experiment in parliamentary democracy, followed by a brief foray into imperialism during which it conquered large parts of the neighbouring East Asian mainland and then went to war in 1941 with the United States and its allies. Parliamentary democracy was forced on Japan during the American occupation after World War II and has generally worked well. However, there are – as we will see – several important differences between the Japanese model and the way government works in most other democracies. Problems such as corruption and the long dominance in Japan of a single political party (the **Liberal Democratic Party**) have combined to earn the country a ranking of a flawed democracy in the Democracy Index.

In economic terms, Japan has the world's third biggest national economy after the United States and China, ranking in the top twenty in per capita terms. It has few natural resources, few minerals, and limited farmland and must import most of its iron and energy needs and nearly one-third of its food needs. However, it has turned adversity into opportunity by protecting its domestic market with formal and informal trade barriers, and by developing a manufacturing sector that leads the world in engineering, machinery, road vehicles, and electronic products. This helped make Japan wealthy during the 1960s, 1970s, and 1980s, but a combination of problems – including a troubled banking system, corporate difficulties, bad investment choices, a too-powerful bureaucracy, and a political system that seems to be immune to reform – brought an economic downturn in the 1990s, and another in the 2010s.

In social terms, Japan is notable for its homogeneity. There are no major ethnic minorities or regional languages, most of Japan's people are Shinto or Buddhist, and its social hierarchy is rarely seriously questioned (Sugimoto, 2015). For a city of its size, Tokyo is distinct for its lack of racial diversity, and unlike many other economically successful countries, Japan has kept out immigrants who might have helped fuel economic growth. Minorities make up just two per cent of the population of Japan, and include about 3 million *burakumin* (or 'village people', whose marginal position is much like that of India's untouchables – see Chapter 8) and about 700,000 descendants of Koreans brought to Japan as forced labour before and during World War II. History and geography have combined to create a society that places a premium on consensus, conformity, and compromise and in which people allow the state to intervene in their lives to a substantial degree.

POLITICAL DEVELOPMENT

Japan's physical isolation from the Asian mainland has helped create a strong sense of identity that has allowed the Japanese to adhere to their own political and social values while adopting the best that others have had to offer. Their ancestors came from the Asian mainland, most likely by way of Korea, developing a society based around clans and heredity, and beginning a practice of adopting foreign models in the 6th century when Buddhism, Confucianism, and Chinese script were introduced from China. Traditional beliefs in nature worship were nonetheless preserved and distinguished from Buddhism by the name **Shinto** (or 'way of the gods'), which still remains the major religion of Japan.

Also on the Chinese model, a permanent imperial capital was founded in the 8th century near Kyoto and a centralized administrative structure created. Emperors ruled Japan, but their power declined as they rewarded members of their families with grants of land, thereby reducing their revenues and influence. The power shift was confirmed in 1192, when – following a series of brutal civil wars – Japan was united under a military dictatorship. Yoritomo Minamoto was appointed by the emperor as the first *shogun* (or general) and had enough independent power to found a separate capital at Kamakura (south of Tokyo). The title of shogun became hereditary, and for nearly 700 years the shoguns were the major force in Japanese government.

The era of the shoguns (1192–1868)

The shoguns ruled through a complex hierarchy of territorial lords (*daimyo*) and warriors (*samurai*). The *samurai* lived by a code of conduct based on loyalty, obligation, and self-discipline. By the beginning of the 17th century, power had shifted to the Tokugawa shogunate, which ruled Japan from its new capital at Edo (now Tokyo), and closed Japan off from the outside world, creating *sakoku*, or 'the closed country'. Christianity was forbidden, no one was permitted to leave, and the Dutch were the only Westerners allowed to trade with Japan, from a restricted island enclave in Nagasaki harbour.

Japan now entered a period of 250 years of peace and isolation, during which Edo became the largest city in the world. The country came under centralized and authoritarian bureaucratic rule, with a well-established system of law and order and flourishing free enterprise. Although the shoguns were supposedly in charge, real power was wielded by a small council of advisors, establishing a tradition of collective leadership that persists today. By the 19th century, however, it had become clear that the system was unable to keep pace with social changes or to resist the demands of Western countries impatient to trade with Japan (Gordon, 2013).

The end of Japanese isolationism came in July 1853, when commodore Matthew Perry of the US Navy sailed into Tokyo Bay with a demand from President Millard Fillmore that Japan open its doors to trade. The Tokugawas no longer had the power to resist, and a treaty was signed with the United States in 1854, granting limited trading concessions. Agreements with European powers followed, ironically fulfilling the worst fears of Japanese rulers about destabilizing foreign influences. The last Tokugawa shogun abdicated in 1867, and the emperor Meiji was restored to power in 1868.

Limited democracy and imperialism (1868–1945)

The **Meiji Restoration** of 1868 marked the watershed between the old regime and the new era of modernization. It was decided to create a new system of government that could lead Japan into the international community. Shopping around for what they defined as the best of everything, Japanese leaders copied the British parliamentary system, French local government, the Prussian (German) civil service, the American system of currency, the Belgian banking system, and the Prussian and French military. They also systematically studied European constitutions before drawing up and adopting the 1889 Meiji Constitution, based mainly on the Prussian model.

Japanese industry grew, a powerful new military was built, a new sense of national consciousness emerged, and the population doubled between 1867 and 1913. Japan won wars against China (1894–95) and Russia (1904–05), and occupied Korea and much of Manchuria (in what is now northern China) after the Russo-Japanese war, confirming Japan's emergence as a regional power. Japan's leaders hoped that its democratic and economic progress could be underwritten by peaceful trade with the rest of the world, but several obstacles prevented this from happening: a tendency towards factionalism and political corruption, and the fallout from the Great Depression of the 1930s. The Depression not only brought reduced export earnings and unemployment, but also worsened poverty in the rural areas from which many members of the military came.

Among junior army officers and right-wing intellectuals at the time of the Depression there was a view that Japan's economic ills could be blamed on politicians and capitalism, and the military became a new force in government. Japan now took a more belligerent position in foreign affairs, formalizing its occupation of Manchuria in 1932 by establishing the puppet state of Manchukuo under the heir to the Chinese throne. Its actions broke international law, and Japan withdrew from the League of Nations. In 1937, Japan invaded China, capturing the Chinese capital of Nanjing and slaughtering tens of thousands of civilians. Japan then allied itself with Germany and Italy in 1940, signed a non-aggression pact with the Soviet Union in 1941, and invaded Indo-China. On 7 December 1941, Japan attacked Pearl Harbor in Hawaii, bringing a declaration of war by the United States and Britain.

Occupation and the rise of the new Japan (1945–90s)

Although Japan initially made considerable territorial gains, an Allied counter-attack halted their advance in 1942, and the United States delivered the final blow in August 1945 with the dropping of atomic bombs on Hiroshima and Nagasaki, leading to a Japanese surrender. Japan emerged from the war with its economy in ruins, its social and political systems fragile and confused, and under foreign occupation for the first time in its history. US General Douglas MacArthur was appointed the Supreme Commander for the Allied Powers (SCAP) and was charged with disarming, democratizing, and permanently demilitarizing Japan (Gordon, 2013). He oversaw the creation of a political and social system that combined elements of the pre-war system with elements of Western-style democracy, reformed the Japanese military into a self-defence force, and arranged for the writing of a new constitution, which was adopted in May 1947. The US occupation ended in April 1952.

☶ TIMELINE

1192	Beginning of the shogun era
1639	Japan cuts its links with the Western world
1853	US fleet forces Japan to open links with outside world
1868	End of shogun rule, Meiji Restoration
1889	New constitution established, followed by legislative elections in 1890
1923	Great Kanto earthquake kills nearly 143,000 people
1931	Japanese invasion of Manchuria
1937	War breaks out between China and Japan
1941	Japan attacks Pearl Harbor; declaration of war by the United States
1945	Atom bombs dropped on Hiroshima and Nagasaki
1945–52	US military occupation
1955	Liberal Democratic Party takes power for the first time
1956	Japan joins United Nations
1993	Elections briefly end 38-year monopoly on power by the Liberal Democrats
2009	Landslide election victory for Democratic Party of Japan
2011	China overtakes Japan as world's second largest economy; powerful offshore earthquake sets off tsunami and seriously damages coastal nuclear energy plant. More than 28,000 dead
2012	Liberal Democrats return to power after general election
2019	Emperor Akihito abdicates and is succeeded by his son Naruhito

Japanese politics has since undergone a complex process of evolution, divided by Gaunder (2011) into three periods:

◆ The years after World War II during which there was a process of democratization under the guidance of the US occupation.
◆ A period between 1955 and 1993 (often known as the '**1955 system**') marked by economic growth and the dominance of the Liberal Democratic Party (LDP).
◆ The period since 1993 during which the LDP has been internally divided and there has been more fluidity in party politics and government. (It has since been suggested – see later in this section – that the 2012 general election marked the beginning of a fourth period marked by renewed LDP dominance.)

Under the 1955 system, a pattern of consensus government was re-established, with power exercised by a bureaucracy supported, encouraged, and sometimes influenced by the LDP. Within barely a generation, isolationism and feudalism had given way to a new system of democratic government that helped Japan become one of the world's major economic powers and made household names of corporations such as Canon, Fujitsu, Honda, Mitsubishi, Sony, Toshiba, and Toyota. Japan became the world's biggest creditor nation, its stock market one of the most influential, its currency (the yen) one of the strongest, and its banks among the world's largest. Japan established its place as a world leader in the development of new technology and the application of that technology to efficient and dependable manufactured goods.

Behind the impressive figures, however, there have long been concerns that Japan has not had the kind of stable and transparent political system needed to meet the needs of a major economic power. Bowen and Kassiola (2016) describe the system as dysfunctional, meaning that democracy persists even when it does not work very well. 'Japan's democracy is real', they argue, 'but it suffers from personalism, graft, cronyism, favouritism, bribery, money politics, factionalism, and collusion', with a level of corruption that is pervasive, and also structural in the sense that it is built in to the political system. It persists, they continue, partly because the politicians who engage in corruption are nearly always re-elected, and thus have little reason to change their behaviour.

Among the most infamous examples of corruption was the **Recruit scandal** of the 1980s, when it was revealed that political donations had been given to leading politicians and government officials in the form of shares in the Recruit Corporation, an information and property conglomerate. When Recruit shares were offered publicly in late 1986, the new shareholders reaped instant and large profits. News of the scandal led to the resignation of 42 politicians and bureaucrats, including Prime Minister Noboru Takeshita. Subsequent scandals revealed bureaucratic corruption in the ministry of health that allowed 2,000 haemophiliacs to contract AIDS through transfusions of tainted blood, and incompetence in the government response to a devastating 1995 earthquake in the southern city of Kobe.

Critics of the status quo began calling in the early 1990s for a 'third opening', which, like the trade openings of 1853–54 and the SCAP occupation of 1945–52, would bring the kinds of changes to government, education, and economic and foreign policy Japan needed to become a true superpower. But the first two openings took place under authoritarian governments, and Japan in the 1990s lacked the kind of leaders who could either build a consensus on the need for reform, or who could build the authority to impose it (Gordon, 2013). The prospects for political change were first suggested when the monopoly of the LDP was broken in 1993–94 with the brief formation of an unstable eight-party coalition government. (Its first leader, Tsutomu Hata, holds the unenviable record – at 63 days – of the shortest tenure as prime minister of Japan since 1945.)

On the economic front, Japan witnessed changing fortunes. Japanese industry and technology, once a watchword for cheap and disposable products, had by the 1980s become a watchword for excellence and reliability – but then Japan entered its longest post-war recession, and its GDP fell by a quarter in the late 1990s (a period now known as the lost decade (Kingston, 2011)). It weathered the global financial crisis of 2007–08 well but then saw its GDP contract again by nearly 30 per cent between 2012 and 2015, and witnessed the dual problems of reduced consumer spending and a shrinking and ageing population (its population fell by 0.16 per cent in 2017, and the proportion of its population aged 65 or older – at 27 per cent – is the highest in the world (data from World Bank, 2019). While industrial production has grown, and unemployment in 2018 was running at just two per cent, retail sales and consumer confidence have fallen, the Tokyo stock market (the Nikkei 225) lost a remarkable 75 per cent of its value between 1990 and 2010, and Japan has experienced several recent periods of deflation. China overtook Japan to become the world's second largest economy in 2011 and Japan's GDP in 2017 was still ten per cent lower than it had been in the early 1990s.

Japan today

Politically, Japan remains a difficult country to reform. It needs leadership, but the notion of leadership – or at least of individuals rising above the pack – runs counter to Japan's collectivist political culture. Instead of transparency and accountability, there is obfuscation and a tendency to hide behind the protective barrier of the group. Prime ministers who are appointed to office on a promise of reform typically end up being overly cautious, and business continues as usual. Change is occurring, however, regardless of the policies pursued by Japanese leaders: the electoral system has been reformed, the bureaucracy is not as powerful as it once was, and younger Japanese are rebelling against formality and conformity. The 2009 elections brought a major turnaround when the Liberal Democrats were trounced by the Democratic Party of Japan (DPJ), which campaigned on promises of reversing Japan's economic decline. But it was a false dawn, because the Liberal Democrats were back in control three years later.

A cataclysm of another kind came in March 2011 when Japan was struck by a triple disaster: an earthquake (the most powerful ever recorded in Japan) that set off a tsunami (more than 28,000 people died in the combined events) and caused damage to a nuclear power station at Fukushima (releasing dangerous quantities of radioactivity and raising new questions worldwide about the wisdom of nuclear power). Japan sits on one of the most seismically active areas on earth and is quite used to earthquakes, having suffered seven with a magnitude of 8.0 or greater in the last 120 years. The Great Kanto earthquake of 1923 was the most deadly, killing nearly 143,000 people, but the economic ramifications of the 2011 event – named the Eastern Japan Great Earthquake Disaster – were felt not only throughout Japan but globally as the supply of parts from Japanese manufacturers to vehicle and electronic plants in many parts of the world was disrupted.

The divided and inexperienced DPJ government was unable to survive long and the 2012 election saw the LDP returned to power with a massive new majority. Such was the significance of the election result that Stockwin and Ampiah (2017) believe that Japan is now in a new '2012 system' in which the LDP is in a much stronger electoral position, with factionalism less evident than before, the opposition much weakened, and politics coloured by 'an essentially nationalist agenda never absent from the party's ranks'. The centre of political gravity, they suggest, has moved further to the right, with support for the assertion of Japanese national identity, the removal of restrictions on the freedom of action of the Japanese military, and the establishment of what is sometimes known – in the context of foreign relations – as a 'normal state'. The implication here is that Japan should be allowed to use its military for more than defence, and that it should revise its pacifist constitution (see later section on Japanese constitution).

The famous Shibuya pedestrian crossing in central Tokyo, the largest city in the world by population. Despite the dynamism and wealth this image conveys, Japan's economy and political system have both witnessed changing fortunes in recent years.

Source: Getty Images.

POLITICAL CULTURE

Despite the many and rapid changes that Japan has witnessed in the last century, many traditional aspects of Japanese political culture remain intact, or – at least – play an important residual role in understanding Japan. Increased criticism, however, has been directed at the emphasis placed on group orientation, hierarchy, mutual obligation, and consensus, which are charged with acting as a brake on Japan's political modernization and for contributing to instability in the leadership of the world's third biggest economy. The result has been new questions about the extent to which the standard descriptions of Japanese politics any longer apply, the suggestion being made that Japanese democracy is increasingly lively and dynamic, with politicians and parties increasingly willing to listen to what citizens have to say (Stockwin, 2008; Kabashima and Steel, 2010).

Although almost every country has some kind of social hierarchy, it is particularly obvious in Japan, where people are divided into groups that are not only ranked in relation to each other but also internally. Where politics in most liberal democracies is driven by majoritarian democracy and by winners and losers, decisions in Japan tend to be made by consensus, there is little room for individualism, and emphasis is placed on the group. This is visible, for example, in the value given to teamwork in Japanese corporations.

Japanese politicians occupy their posts not necessarily because they are good leaders but because of their seniority, their acceptability to the group, their paternalistic concerns for the people, and their ability to build a consensus rather than impose their preferences on others. The emphasis on group leadership is one reason few outsiders can name Japanese politicians: few rise above the pack, stay in office long, or threaten the political status quo, and many of the most successful politicians come from families with a tradition in politics. For example, former Prime Minister Junichiro Koizumi's father and grandfather were both members of the Japanese legislature, and Prime Minister Shinzo Abe's maternal grandfather was Nobusuke Kishi, prime minister from 1957 to 1960.

The collective society is also behind the idea of Japanese exceptionalism; many Japanese think of their country as unique, assume that their culture cannot be adopted by foreigners, and have a poor record of assimilating non-Japanese. For example, the descendants of the Koreans who were brought to Japan as labourers in the early 20th century are still treated as foreigners, are denied jobs in the bureaucracy or teaching, cannot vote, and are generally regarded as second-class citizens (McCargo, 2012). Japanese exclusionism, notes Arudou (2015), is both subtle (as when suggestions are rejected for their 'lack of precedent') and overt (as when signs are posted by businesses saying 'No foreigners allowed').

Group identity is also reflected in Japanese ideas about loyalty, obligation, and hierarchy. Political power is based on a web of patron-client relationships: social and financial ties that bind a small political elite and promote nepotism and factionalism; see Comparing Political Culture 6. These values help explain the Japanese support for militarism and imperialism in the 1930s, promoted by military leaders under the guise of loyalty to the emperor. Today, they are reflected in the way workers tend to stay with one company all their lives, in the persistence of factions within political parties, and in the frequency of influence peddling in politics. More even than Britain, and far more than the United States, Japanese society is based on status and rank (see Sugimoto, 2015). Everyone is made aware of their place relative to others, a premium is placed on group harmony, and people feel discouraged from speaking out, rocking the boat, or rising above the pack through their excellence or obvious achievements (McCargo, 2012). As the performance of Japanese business and industry shows, the Japanese are goal-oriented, but their goals are driven less by personal ambition than by collective achievement.

COMPARING POLITICAL CULTURE 6
Politics and faction

It is not unusual in democracies for voters and elected officials to lean towards particular leaders within political parties, even while they support the party as a whole. We can see this at work, for example, when candidates from the same party in the United States compete to win the presidential nomination of that party every four years, or when political parties in Germany or India go through their periodic leadership elections; different leaders will attract different blocs of supporters from within the same party. It has even been suggested (see Cohen et al., 2016) that factional politics could become more normal in the American context thanks to the rise of new political media and changes in campaign finance laws.

These divisions, though, are different in both degree and reach from the kind of institutionalized **factionalism** found in Japanese politics. Factions are usually both permanent and well organized, and go beyond politics, being found also in business, higher education, and even schools of sumo wrestling. Wherever they are found, they serve the same basic purposes of providing group identity and personal connections, and encouraging individual and group advancement.

> **Factionalism**
> The division of society, government, or institutions into groups formed around a leader and competing with one another for authority and influence.

The word *faction* is the nearest English translation of the Japanese word *habatsu*, describing groups of party members who form around a single leader, who is responsible for negotiating on their behalf with the prime minister of the day, for raising campaign funds and running electoral campaigns, for promoting the policy goals of the group, and perhaps even becoming prime minister if the leader wins enough support. Almost every party has factions, few having been able to achieve the kind of discipline needed to prevent the emergence of *habatsu* (McCargo, 2012).

Factions may help prevent too much centralization of power and allow different policies to be discussed within one party, but the problems they cause are legion. They weaken the power and authority of party leaders, encourage elitism and nepotism, and contribute to the prominent role of money in Japanese politics: the factions provide the money and contacts to help with election campaigns, and the bigger factions regularly raise more money for their candidates than the parties raise as a whole. The changed place in government of the LDP, where factionalism seems to be on the wane, may lead to a weakening of the hold of factions on political power, but the traditional nature of factionalism means that it will not easily or quickly die.

PROFILE JAPAN

Name	Japan (Nihon-koku)
Capital	Tokyo
Administration	Unitary, with 47 prefectures and several thousand municipalities.
Constitution	State formed 5th century (approximately), and most recent constitution adopted 1947.
Executive	Parliamentary. The head of government is the prime minister, who is head of the largest party or coalition, and governs in conjunction with a cabinet. The head of state is the emperor.
Legislature	Bicameral Diet: lower House of Representatives (465 members) elected for renewable four-year terms, and upper House of Councillors (242 members) elected for renewable six-year terms.
Judiciary	Supreme Court (15 members; 14 appointed by the cabinet from lists submitted by the court; chief justice appointed by the emperor on recommendation of the cabinet). Must retire at age 70.
Electoral system	Mixed member majoritarian system: 296 members of the House of Representatives are elected using single-member plurality, and 179 through party list proportional representation (PR). In the House of Councillors, 146 are elected using single-member plurality, and 96 through PR.
Party system	Multi-party, but long dominated by the conservative Liberal Democratic Party.

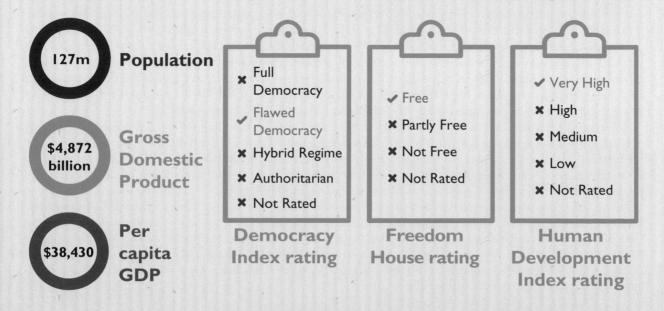

127m Population

$4,872 billion Gross Domestic Product

$38,430 Per capita GDP

Democracy Index rating
- ✗ Full Democracy
- ✓ Flawed Democracy
- ✗ Hybrid Regime
- ✗ Authoritarian
- ✗ Not Rated

Freedom House rating
- ✓ Free
- ✗ Partly Free
- ✗ Not Free
- ✗ Not Rated

Human Development Index rating
- ✓ Very High
- ✗ High
- ✗ Medium
- ✗ Low
- ✗ Not Rated

POLITICAL SYSTEM

Personalism
Political allegiance to a person rather than to a political party or ideology.

Patron-client democracy
An informal relationship between governors and the governed, often involving the trading of favours in return for political support.

Much like Britain, Japan is a constitutional monarchy with a parliamentary government presiding over a unitary state. As a democracy, it has many of the same political institutions, values, and processes as Britain, Germany, and the United States: these include representative government, support for the rule of law, and competition among groups representing different interests. But where Japan parts company with the others is in the extent to which it has institutionalized group politics, and in the emphasis placed on achieving a consensus. The methods used to build that consensus include **personalism**, factionalism, the exchange of political favours, and an almost constant process of bargaining within and among big business, political parties, and the senior levels of the bureaucracy. For these reasons, Japan some time ago earned itself the label '**patron-client democracy**' (Ike, 1972). (Compare this with a similar arrangement in Nigeria – see Chapter 10.)

The pressure and desire to break with these habits has grown in recent years, driven by increased cynicism towards government among voters and by political scandal, which has been a problem for decades but still fails entirely to go away. Changes were made to the structure of the political system in 1994–96, the most important of which was the replacement of the old electoral system – in which members of the same party were obliged to run against each other and which resulted in many small parties winning seats – by a mixed system of single-member plurality and proportional representation (PR). This helped make the party system more stable, but not enough for critics of group politics; calls have continued to be made for additional reforms.

The constitution

Japan was governed for most of its history without a written constitution, relying instead on custom and tradition. This changed in 1889 with the adoption of the Meiji Constitution, designed not just to lay down rules on the distribution of power, but also to convince Western countries that Japan should be taken seriously and treated equally, and to promote social discipline and national unity so that Japan could deal with the economic and security challenges posed by its opening to the West. Although the Meiji Constitution provided a bridge for Japan's transition from a feudal to a modern society, it was authoritarian and was based on the idea that government was omnipotent and benevolent and gave rights and liberties to citizens as gifts. As a result, it gave rise to a tradition of party politics and electoral competition, devolving power to a new generation of leaders.

The current Japanese constitution dates from 1947, and neither came out of Japanese political tradition, nor was it even written by the Japanese themselves. Seeing the disagreement among Japanese leaders about the future course of their country after World War II, General MacArthur instructed his Government Section to write the constitution, which it did in just six days in 1946. Had the Japanese themselves done the job, it might have been less liberal and more paternalistic. The fact that it was written by foreigners – and so quickly – is remarkable. That it was generally accepted by the Japanese, even though it includes many principles alien to Japanese political culture, is even more remarkable. That it is still working more than 70 years later is perhaps most remarkable of all.

The new constitution created a parliamentary system similar to the one that had existed until the late 1920s, and replaced the emperor-based state with the doctrine of popular sovereignty. It guaranteed basic human rights, renounced war and the maintenance of military forces, abolished the aristocracy, severely limited the powers of the emperor (who had to renounce his divinity), and created a new supreme court. Where the pre-war distribution of power and responsibility had been unclear, the new constitution provided more clarity.

It has not been amended once since it was adopted, mainly because amendments are difficult to achieve: they need a two-thirds majority in both houses of the Diet (the Japanese legislature), and must then be put to a national referendum. Many of the rules of government, such as the structure of elections and the number of members of the Diet, have instead been changed by the passage of new laws. With China and North Korea as close neighbours, Japan is located in a region of significant security tensions (see Map 6.1); hence one of the more persistent and controversial suggestions has been to change the provisions relating to the status of Japan's military (the **Japan Self-Defence Forces**, or JSDF) so that it becomes a more conventional defence force, and to do away with the pacifist elements of the constitution, notably Article 9, which reads as follows: 'Aspiring sincerely to an international peace based on justice and order, the Japanese people forever renounce war as a sovereign right of the nation and the threat or use of force as means of settling international disputes.' However, no party has had the necessary two-thirds majority in the Diet to take the first step in the process.

Map 6.1 Japan and its neighbours

Head of state: the emperor

Both Britain and Japan are constitutional monarchies, meaning that their governments are headed by hereditary leaders who have little real direct political power but whose role is to act as the symbolic leader of the state. One technical difference between the two offices is that the British monarch is head of state, but the Japanese **emperor** – according to the constitution – is only the 'symbol of the state'. The distinction stands as a reminder that the emperor continued to play a key role in the political system long after the British monarchy had lost its most substantial powers.

Japan's current emperor is Naruhito (b. 1960), the 126th descendant of the first emperor of Japan and the grandson of Emperor Hirohito (1902–89), who holds a controversial place in Japanese history because of questions about his part in Japan's role in World War II. Naruhito succeeded to the throne in April 2019 after the abdication of his father Akihito, and much like the British monarch he presides over openings of the Diet, his seal is needed for important state documents, and he confirms the person chosen to be prime minister by the Diet. His political role, though, is carefully limited: the constitution notes that 'the advice and approval of the Cabinet shall be required for all acts of the Emperor in matters of state' (Article 3) and that the emperor 'shall perform only such acts in matters of state as are provided for in the Constitution and he shall not have powers related to government' (Article 4).

The emperor is also the head of the Shinto religion, and a living embodiment of the history and culture of Japan, even more so than most other monarchs: although Japan has used the Gregorian calendar since 1873, the numbering of years in Japan is still based on the reign of the emperor (hence 2019 was Reiwa 1, or the first year of the reign of the Reiwa Emperor Naruhito). Naruhito and his wife Masako have only one child, Princess Aiko. Her birth in 2001 sparked a lively debate about whether the law (which allows only male succession) should be changed. The issue was postponed in 2006 when Naruhito's younger brother Prince Akishino and his wife had a son named Hisahito, who is now heir to the throne.

The executive: prime minister and cabinet

Japanese prime ministers are among the weakest heads of government of any democracy, given few opportunities to exert much leadership. Where British prime ministers lead and become dominating figures in politics, often taking a leading role on the international stage as well, Japanese prime ministers tend to be party functionaries, are more like keepers of the helm than captains of the ship, do not stay in office long, and – in spite of Japan's global economic reach – rarely leave a lasting personal stamp on government or become well known outside Japan. Turnover in recent years has been rapid: while the United States had three presidents and Britain had four prime

Table 6.1 Recent prime ministers of Japan

Start of term	Name	Party
August 1989 February 1990*	Toshiki Kaifu	Liberal Democrat
November 1991 July 1993*	Kiichi Miyazawa	Liberal Democrat
August 1993	Morihiro Hosokawa	Eight-party coalition
April 1994	Tsutomu Hata	Eight-party coalition
June 1994	Tomiichi Murayama	Socialist-led coalition
January 1996 October 1996*	Ryutaro Hashimoto	LDP-led coalition
July 1998	Keizo Obuchi	LDP-led coalition
April 2000 June 2000* July 2000	Yoshiro Mori	LDP-led coalition
April 2001 November 2003* September 2005*	Junichiro Koizumi	LDP-led coalition LDP-Komeito coalition
September 2006	Shinzo Abe	LDP-Komeito coalition
September 2007	Yasuo Fukuda	LDP-Komeito coalition
September 2008 August 2009*	Taro Aso	LDP-Komeito coalition
September 2009	Yukio Hatoyama	DPJ-led coalition
June 2010	Naoto Kan	DPJ-led coalition
September 2011	Yoshihiko Noda	DPJ-led coalition
December 2012* December 2014* October 2017*	Shinzo Abe	LDP-Komeito coalition

* General elections

ministers between 1990 and 2018, for example, Japan had 14 prime ministers, serving average terms of 19 months each. The notable exceptions to this rule were Junichiro Koizumi, who held the office for more than five years until 2006, and Shinzo Abe, who was still in office after six years as this book went to press.

Technically, the Japanese legislature – the Diet – chooses the prime minister from among its members, with a vote in both its chambers. However, because the lower House of Representatives has more power than the upper House of Councillors, and because political parties tend to vote together, what happens is that the prime minister comes out of the majority party (or coalition) in the House of Representatives. But the story does not end there: because most parties are broken into factions, prime ministers need the support of enough of those factions to win office. During times when the LDP is in government, the prime minister is not necessarily the leader of the LDP, nor even the leader of the biggest faction within the party, nor even the leader of *any* faction, but rather the person who wins enough support among the competing factions to head a government (thereafter needing only formal confirmation in office by the emperor).

Limits are placed on prime ministerial power by the bureaucracy, factions within political parties, party leaders, the consensus style of Japanese politics, and – within the LDP – a long-standing rule (changed only in 2017) that no prime minister could serve more than six years in office; the limit is now nine years. The standing of prime ministers in the polls is only marginally important to their power base, some may not even have policies of their own, and few have succeeded in making substantial changes to government policy.

To be sure, they have often significant political powers at their disposal, including being head of the cabinet, being able to hire and fire members of the cabinet and all other senior members of the government and their party, and being able to appoint the chairs of key governmental advisory councils. Even so, the goals of prime ministers are usually less important to understanding Japanese politics than the policies of the governments they lead. In the case of LDP prime ministers, they are rarely changed at elections, nor do their positions depend on how popular they are with voters; instead they are usually changed in midstream as a result of several weeks (sometimes even months) of negotiation within the party.

A billboard in Kyoto advertises the Liberal Democratic Party of Prime Minister Shinzo Abe, who has been unusual among modern Japanese leaders in the extent to which he has come to dominate politics in a society marked by a preference for group leadership.
Source: iStock.com/winhorse.

The dictum that power and popularity are not necessarily synonymous in Japanese politics is illustrated by the example of Shinzo Abe. When he first came to office in 2006, Abe was notable for being Japan's youngest post-war prime minister (he was born in 1954) and for being the first born after the war. Born into a political family, Abe was elected to the House of Representatives in 1993 and won national attention for his hard line on North Korea, coming to the office of the prime minister with the advantage of a strong LDP majority in the House of Representatives. However, he was quickly undermined by the involvement of several of his ministers in financial scandals. When the LDP lost elections to the House of Councillors in July 2007 – losing control for the first time in 52 years – he found his approval ratings falling, and resigned. He rebuilt his position within the LDP, and returned as prime minister in 2012 at the head of an LDP coalition government. Abe then won the 2014 general election running mainly on an economic platform, and won yet again in the 2017 general election, establishing his place as Japan's longest-serving prime minister.

Inoguchi and Jain (2011) have used the analogies of *karaoke* and *kabuki* to explain the nature of leadership in Japan, and how it has recently changed. Leadership in Japan could once be likened to *karaoke* (entertainment in which amateurs sing along to recorded background music) in the sense that political leaders were once provided with policy scripts by bureaucrats, and then tried to make those statements their own in order to convince voters that they deserved re-election. Prime ministers and government ministers may have changed frequently, but

COMPARING GOVERNMENT 6
The political role of bureaucrats

Bureaucrats are public servants whose job is to execute government policy while remaining outside the fray of politics. They are not elected, nor – except at the highest levels, as in the case of departmental ministers or secretaries and their deputies – are they appointed by government. Such formalities, though, say little about the political impact of bureaucrats, which is shaped by a combination of tradition and informal preferences. Japan offers an unusual case because of the extent to which bureaucrats are involved in making – rather than simply implementing – law and policy. The relationship is so close that the term '**iron triangle**' is used to describe the links between the government, the bureaucracy, and big business.

The influence of the Japanese bureaucracy is explained by several factors:

> **Iron triangle**
> An arrangement by which political power in countries such as Japan is focused on a relationship between the governing party, bureaucrats, and business.

◆ The bureaucracy is generally efficient and, as such, has contributed to Japan's post-war economic and political success (although it has made more than its fair share of blunders). Japan is one of the few countries (France being another) where being a bureaucrat is a high-status occupation, subject to demanding entrance exams and long working hours. The higher levels are dominated by the top graduates of the best law schools, notably those at the universities of Tokyo and Kyoto.

◆ It is usual in Japan to find a '**revolving door**' at work, by which bureaucrats first run government ministries, then retire to become corporate executives or to sit in the Diet. This is common in the United States and France as well, and is criticized in both countries, but in Japan it is known as *amakudari*, or 'descent from heaven'.

◆ More than in any other liberal democracy, policy decisions are made out of public view and mostly within government ministries. This process has reached the point where there is a standing joke that the Diet passes a law, and the bureaucrats then write it.

One comparative study of bureaucracies (Peters, 2018) makes the point that government leaders often find it harder to control bureaucracies than they had anticipated before coming into office; this is particularly true given that citizens demand more from government, and that the governments of wealthy democracies offer a wide range of services that must be staffed and managed. Bureaucracies everywhere also have a continuity and a level of access to information that is not the case with transitory governments (politicians come and go, but bureaucrats often have long careers), giving them strategic advantages. In the case of Japan, the political power of bureaucrats has gone further than in other democracies, but this is not to suggest that their peers in other countries do not also have a significant role to play in government.

policies changed only slightly – and deep reforms were avoided – because bureaucrats preferred incremental change. More recently, Japanese politics has taken on some of the features of *kabuki* theatre in the sense that it has become more colourful and interesting because leaders have brought their distinctive style to the debate, have tried to achieve an emotional connection with voters, and have more actively pursued their own policies.

As with all parliamentary systems, the Japanese prime minister governs in conjunction with a cabinet of Ministers of State (senior government ministers), all of them appointed by the prime minister, who also has the power to remove them. They must all be members of the Diet, and (a reflection of the circumstances under which the 1947 constitution was written) cannot be from the military. While cabinets in most parliamentary systems have a degree of freedom of action (so long as they toe the line defined by the prime minister), the Japanese cabinet is comparatively weaker, and more of an extension of the authority of the prime minister. Ministers of State also find themselves facing limits imposed by the unusually powerful reach of the bureaucracy – see Comparing Government 6.

The legislature: Diet

The name of the Japanese legislature is usually translated into English with the anachronistic term **Diet**, even though the most accurate translation of the Japanese name (*Kokkai*) is National Assembly. It has all the typical law-making powers of a democratic parliamentary legislature, with standard powers over law-making and over the budget, the ability to unseat the prime minister and cabinet through a vote of confidence, a question time for members of the cabinet, and a range of specialist committees. There is one key difference between the British and Japanese models, though: while the former defers to the power of the prime minister and cabinet, the latter typically defers to the power of the governing party or coalition and to the bureaucracy.

The Diet has two chambers.

House of Councillors (*Sangi-in*)

The House of Councillors is the upper house, consisting of 242 members serving fixed six-year terms, with half the members standing for re-election every three years. The house replaced the pre-war House of Peers, an almost direct copy of the old British House of Lords. Its members included the imperial family, hereditary aristocrats, army representatives, and government appointees. The US occupation authorities after World War II argued that Japan did not need an upper house because it was a unitary state and did not have local government units that needed separate representation at the national level. The Japanese, on the other hand, argued that a second chamber was needed to check the popularly elected lower chamber. In any event, an upper house was created, but with no clear idea about what it should do, beyond giving local districts of government (prefectures) some representation.

Chaired by a president chosen from among its members, the chamber can reject bills from the House of Representatives, but the lower house can override the rejection with a two-thirds majority. Treaties and budgetary matters do not need its agreement, and the most the house can do is to delay the passage of legislation. Its most important role in recent years has been in allowing voters to comment on the record of the government between elections to the House of Representatives.

House of Representatives (*Shugi-in*)

The House of Representatives is the lower – and more powerful – of the two houses of the Diet, consisting of 465 members elected using a combination of single-member plurality and proportional representation. Elections must be held within four years of each other, but the House of Representatives rarely sees out a full term. The lower house is presided over by a speaker, chooses the prime minister, passes laws, passes the budget, makes treaties, and can override an upper house veto with a two-thirds majority.

No legislature can be fully understood without looking at such factors as the origins and diversity of its membership, the rules of the chamber, the number of parties represented, and political traditions. In this regard, the House of Representatives has several notable features:

◆ The Diet meets for only five months per year, two months of which are usually tied up over the annual budget debate. By contrast, the British Parliament meets for seven months, and the US Congress for eight months.
◆ Even though the House of Representatives contains relatively few parties, and is usually dominated by the LDP, its powers are compromised by the factional divisions within the major parties, and by the tradition of consensus politics that makes most legislators disinclined to disagree with the executive.
◆ About a third of legislators come to office with a background in local politics, 16 per cent have a background in the bureaucracy, and nine per cent have experience working for labour unions (Fukumoto, 2011).

One of the most notable features of the Japanese Diet, and of Japanese politics more generally, is the limited role played in government by women (see Dalton, 2015). Several East and Southeast Asian states (including Indonesia, the Philippines, South Korea, Taiwan, and Thailand) have had women who have served as president or prime minister, but few Japanese parties have had female leaders, and Japan – with women making up just ten per cent of the members of the Diet in 2017 – compares poorly to most other countries (see Comparing Politics 14). Even though Yoriko Koike won the governorship of Tokyo in 2016, she did so only as an independent after her party – the LDP – had refused to endorse her, and she campaigned against a background of considerable hostility from male politicians.

The judiciary: Supreme Court

One of the legacies of the US role in designing the post-war Japanese political system is the existence of a separate Supreme Court with the power of judicial review. Separation of the judiciary from the executive was motivated by American plans to decentralize Japanese government so as to prevent a repeat of pre-war authoritarianism. The allied occupation force under SCAP transferred authority over the courts from the Ministry of Justice to a new Supreme Court, giving it powers as the guardian of civil rights and liberties written into the new constitution. In the case of the United States, much of the justification for setting up its Supreme Court came from the need to have an authority that would rule in disputes between the states and the federal government. As a unitary state, Japan does not have such disputes, so the Japanese court has less to do.

The Supreme Court has 15 judges, 14 of whom are chosen by the cabinet from lists submitted by the court. The Chief Judge is appointed by the emperor on the recommendation of the cabinet. New members of the court must be confirmed by a popular vote at the next general election and again at the general election following ten years of service, and they must retire at age 70. Partly because of the turnover and their lack of activism, Japanese Supreme Court judges remain little-known public figures and are routinely reconfirmed.

The Japanese preference for consensus encourages them to attach less importance to formal rules and regulations than they do to custom. Most Japanese assume that disputes can be worked out through informal discussion and compromise, and falling back on laws and rules is often seen as an admission of failure. One consequence of this is that Supreme Court decisions in Japan impact a narrower range of policy issues than is the case with the US Supreme Court, and the power of judicial review is not accepted or understood in the same way as it is in the United States.

Probably the most important difference between the US and Japanese courts is their relative roles in politics. The US Supreme Court is supposed to be a neutral arbiter that simply rules on the constitutionality of government laws and actions. However, it has often been activist and thus has had a key role in influencing public policy. By contrast, the Japanese Supreme Court tends to avoid using its powers of judicial review and becoming involved in controversial public issues. It is also inclined to support the government, rather than acting as a check on the powers of the executive or the legislature.

Sub-national government

With its small geographical size, social homogeneity, and consensual political culture, Japan is a unitary system of government. No surprise, then, that it is highly centralized, and that local government is correspondingly less important. There are two main levels of sub-national government: 47 local districts known as prefectures, which in turn coordinate the activities of municipalities, which may be cities, towns, or villages, depending on the distribution of population. Prefectures are run by elected governors and single-chamber assemblies, but they have relatively few powers or responsibilities; local units of government have no independent powers, and can be created, abolished, or reorganized by central government. In contrast to Britain, which has seen regular disputes between central and local government, Japanese local government generally operates as a willing and efficient channel for the implementation of central government policies. Local governments are allowed to collect only 30 per cent of their own revenue needs, depending for the rest on grants from central government, with only limited freedom on how to spend those grants.

POLITICAL PROCESSES

Japan has most of the typical structural features of a democracy except one: a truly competitive party system. The dominance of the Liberal Democrats – whether in government alone or as part of a coalition – has often tended to reduce most other parties to a token opposition, and factionalism has meant that voters have often had a bigger impact on internal party politics than they have had on competition among parties (Hayes, 2017). The influence of voters has been further reduced by the secrecy that often surrounds government, which has prevented voters from feeling involved in national issues. Most important, however, is that power in government has long been shaped more by the role of the bureaucracy than by that of voters.

It became clear in the late 1980s and early 1990s that Japanese voters – especially younger ones – were becoming tired of political corruption, of the factions that divided the parties, and of the role of special interests. Changes were made to the election laws in 1994, but opinion polls in 1996 revealed that about half of all voters still did not identify with any of the parties on offer. They made their point by voting with their feet: turnout at elections fell from 70 per cent during the 1980s to 60 per cent in the late 1990s, reaching an all-time low of just under 53 per cent in 2014. Reducing the minimum voting age from 20 to 18 in 2016 (against a background of widespread public opposition, particularly – ironically – from younger voters) apparently made little difference, with turnout in 2016 climbing by just one percentage point.

The 1994 election reforms were aimed at making elections less expensive and thus less prone to bribery and corruption, but all they did was to make the party system more fluid and to make clear the need for further reforms. The problem has long been that the political leaders who need to make the necessary changes benefit too much from the status quo, and also face a bureaucracy that has long been hostile to change. The accumulated frustrations of voters was expressed most forcefully in 2009, when turnout briefly went back up to nearly 70 per cent and the LDP was thrown out of office.

The electoral system

As in all parliamentary systems, the critical election in Japan is the general election, which directly determines the membership of the Diet, and indirectly determines the membership of the executive. General elections are as short in Japan as in most parliamentary systems (campaigning is restricted by law to a maximum of 30 days), but they are neither as inexpensive nor as simple.

General elections

Japan uses a mixed voting system for elections to the Diet. In the 242-member House of Councillors, 146 members are elected using the single-member plurality system while 96 members are elected using multi-member districts and proportional representation (PR). Members of the chamber serve fixed six-year renewable terms and elections are staggered, with half the members coming up for re-election every three years. At the election, each party publishes a list of at least ten candidates for each PR district, ranked in order of priority, and voters choose one of the competing lists, the seats being divided among parties in proportion to the votes received by each.

The House of Representatives, meanwhile, has seen significant recent changes. Until 1994, it had 511 members elected on the basis of the rarely used single non-transferable vote (SNTV) system. There were 130 districts, each represented by between two and six members. Every voter in each district voted for one candidate only, and when the votes were totalled, the candidates with the most votes were declared elected, even if they all came from the same party. Although this system provided a more accurate reflection of voter preferences than a single-member plurality, it generated several problems:

◆ Interparty competition was weakened at the expense of intraparty competition because candidates from the same party had to run against one another.
◆ With candidates from the same party obliged to run against each other, and struggling to show voters how they were different from one another, the role of money and patronage was heightened, and corruption was rife.
◆ Smaller parties rarely had enough resources or support to run enough candidates in each district or to win enough votes to challenge the LDP majority, but – particularly in larger districts – they did not need to win many votes in order to win a seat, with the result that many small parties won seats in the Diet (Gaunder, 2011).
◆ While the LDP typically dominated, the opposition was divided as a result of large numbers of parties winning seats in the Diet.

The 1994 revisions to the electoral law have given the House of Representatives the same mixed electoral system used in the House of Councillors: it now has 475 seats, of which 296 are elected by single-member plurality and 179 by PR, for renewable terms of a maximum of four years. Voters cast two ballots: one for a candidate under SMP and one for a party under PR. There are 11 PR districts, which overlap the single-member districts, and candidates can run in both. Thus, if they lose in a single-member district, they might still win enough votes to be elected under PR.

Although election campaigns in Japan are short, and the laws on funding appear to be strong, a combination of political realities, loopholes, and ambiguities has encouraged an unfortunate tradition of law-breaking and law-bending. Changes to the law in 1975, for example, placed limits on political contributions from corporations, but failed to limit the number of political organizations that could receive those contributions. As a result, more such organizations were created to channel funds to parties and candidates. Meanwhile, the laws on election publicity are strong, placing limits on everything from door-to-door canvassing to signature drives, mass meetings, polling, unscheduled speeches, parades, and literature produced by candidates. The effect, though, notes Gaunder (2011) has been to drive much of the campaigning underground or around the law: since they mainly apply only to the official election period, many politicians simply increase their unofficial campaigning before the official period starts, or provide information designed to promote public understanding of political issues without making mention of the election.

Local elections

In addition to the Diet elections, Japanese voters take part in a variety of local elections. Mayors and members of the assemblies of villages, towns, and cities are elected, as are governors and members of the assemblies of Japan's prefectures. As in all unitary systems, however, the significance of local government elections is relatively minor, except as a potential (but not always reliable) indicator of support for political parties.

Political parties

Japan has a relatively short history of party politics, but one that has gone through – and continues to undergo – many changes. Several parties were formed after the Meiji Restoration, but they were not constitutionally recognized, and any potential for the development of a multi-party system was halted in the 1930s with the Great Depression and the rise of Japanese militarism. Party politics only entered its active growth phase after World War II, when – after a wave of new party formations and mergers – the '1955 system' emerged with a single dominant party (the Liberal Democrats) and a much smaller opposition in the form of the Japanese socialists. The LDP solidified its position during the 1960s, while the left was split between socialists and communists.

Every government was formed and led by the Liberal Democrats, who dominated both houses of the Diet until 1989, when the LDP lost its majority in the House of Councillors for the first time. Another dramatic turn came with the 1993 elections to the House of Representatives, when defections from the LDP resulted in big losses, the emergence of three new parties, and formation of the first non-LDP government since 1955. There were predictions that a two-party system might emerge, with the LDP on the right and the New Frontier Party (NFP) on the left, but this idea died in late 1997 with the collapse of the NFP.

Indications that the new Democratic Party of Japan (DPJ) might then emerge as a competitor to the LDP at first came to little, and the LDP staged a comeback in 2005. But then came the remarkable result of the 2009 general election, in which the LDP and the DPJ almost exactly reversed their representation in the House: the LDP went from almost 300 seats to just under 120 while the DPJ went from 113 seats to nearly 310 and was able to form a government for the first time. This lasted only until 2012, when the LDP was able to make a comeback in what seemed to be the beginning of a new era of stable LDP dominance.

Liberal Democratic Party (LDP)

Except for a brief break in 1993–94, and a longer break between 2009 and 2012, the LDP has governed Japan either alone or in coalition since 1955. This remarkable record gives it a plausible claim, argues Reed (2011), to being the world's most successful political party. This is all the more remarkable, he goes on, given that it has never been a particularly popular party, has often suffered from weak leadership and policy incoherence, and has often become embroiled in corruption and political controversy. And yet it has wielded so much influence and control, argue Stockwin and Ampiah (2017), that it could long be regarded 'as a kind of internally competitive political system in its own right'.

The secrets of its success can be found in the way it has managed to avoid deep internal splits (a problem that has afflicted most other Japanese political parties), in its chameleon-like personality, its willingness and ability to accept coalition partners when needed, its capacity to benefit from the ambiguities and opportunities contained within Japanese electoral law, and the extent to which it reflects the peculiarities of Japanese society. On the latter point, for example, the party has long had an impressive network of grassroots supporter groups (**koenkai**), consisting of friends and supporters with personal (rather than political) ties to Diet members. The *koenkai* may be less concerned about party policies than about ensuring the re-election of their representatives, but they have also been a solid source of power for the LDP.

COMPARING POLITICS 6
Politics, society, and happiness

As we saw in Chapter 1, there is an intimate relationship between politics and society. The way political systems function, policy agendas are shaped, and political decisions are taken depends heavily on the structure and preferences of society: the extent to which social divisions exist, for example, as well as attitudes towards minorities, and the relative place of men and women, and of the poor and the wealthy. We have seen the importance in Japan of faction, obligation, and group identity. It is also an unusually homogeneous society, in which almost anything foreign is kept at a distance, including ideas and practices that might help it solve its political and economic problems. The success or failure of democracy depends to a large extent on openness and transparency, commodities that are undersupplied in Japan.

In addition to its exceptionalism, the disadvantaged place of women, and the social and political roles of faction (all discussed elsewhere in this chapter), there are two other notable features about Japanese society that have important political and economic consequences:

◆ The Japanese population has been in decline since 2005, and the number of Japanese in their 20s is falling. This is having an impact on the labour market, placing a greater burden on the young to look after the elderly and to meet the bill for social security and health care, and placing greater pressure on older Japanese to work longer. These are trends that are found in several other liberal democracies (most notably Germany and Italy), but their effects are felt more deeply in Japan.

◆ The Japanese are less happy than the citizens of most democracies, according to surveys such as the Better Life Index, which looks at the quality of housing, education, health care, and the environment (see Figure 6.1). This is despite living in a wealthy country with a deep sense of its own history and culture, with a greater life expectancy than anyone else, and with a bigger middle class and smaller income disparities than in the United States or almost any Western European country. The causes of this apparent unhappiness are unclear, but part of the problem may stem from long working hours, the ageing of the population, and Japan's overbearing bureaucracy (Kingston, 2017).

Of course, contentment and happiness are hard to measure, because everyone has their own definition of what they need in life to make them happy, but the indicators seem to suggest that Japan faces more challenging problems when it comes to keeping its population happy than – for example – the Scandinavian countries.

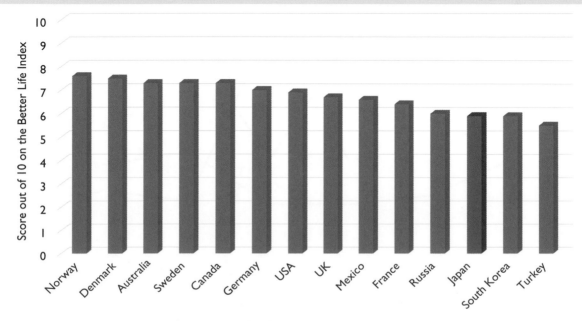

Figure 6.1 Comparing levels of well-being – The Better Life Index
Source: Organisation for Economic Co-operation and Development (2017).

The LDP can trace its roots back to the 1870s, but it was reformed in 1955 when the two main conservative parties (the Liberals and the Democrats) joined forces to prevent the Socialists from winning power. It then became the dominating influence in Japanese politics, regularly winning more than 50 per cent of the vote in general elections. However, a string of scandals and mounting criticism of the electoral system steadily drove away its supporters, leading to the drama of the 1993 elections. It regained some of its lost ground in 1994, forming a minority government with the support of the Socialists and the New Harbinger Party. It stayed in government – but always in coalition with other parties – until 2005, when it won back its majority, losing it again in 2009.

The LDP is a mainstream conservative party that is pro-business and yet has traditionally been stronger in rural Japan than in the urban areas. At least until recent efforts to diminish the role of faction, it was less a party than a coalition of factions; hence the common jibe that the LDP was neither liberal, nor democratic, nor even a party. Each faction was headed by a senior party figure, every LDP member of parliament was associated with one of these factions (of which there have usually been five to seven, but as many as ten) and party leadership was decided by inter-factional bargaining. So strong was the LDP in 1955–93, and so important the role of faction, that the real struggles for political power in Japan took place within the LDP rather than among different parties.

By the 2000s, though, Japanese voters were neither as conservative nor as patient as they had once been, and many were tired of politics as usual. The party particularly suffered from the changing fortunes of prime minister Junichiro Koizumi (in office 2001–06), who was beloved by cartoonists for his distinctive wavy grey-black hair. While popular among voters tired of old-style LDP politics, he was outside the LDP mainstream, and was accused by critics of being arrogant and out of touch. The 2009 electoral victory of the Democratic Party promised to shake up Japanese government and party politics, but proved short-lived, and the LDP victories in 2012, 2014 and 2017 – with Shinzo Abe as prime minister – seemed to be indicative of a new era of stable LDP dominance underpinned, as noted earlier, by a newly-revived strand of Japanese nationalism.

No discussion of the LDP would be complete without reference to the much smaller **Komeito**, or Clean Government Party (CGP). Although it has never won more than about 30–35 seats in the House of Representatives in recent elections, it is one of the oldest parties in a country where parties come and go, and wields influence as a partner to the LDP. It was created in 1964 as the political wing of Soka Gakkai, Japan's largest lay Buddhist organization, its name reflecting its desire to promote less corrupt and more values-based politics. It participated in the 1993–94 anti-LDP coalition government, and in 1998 – following its merger with the New Peace Party – changed its English name to New Komeito (even though its Japanese name remained unchanged), and the adjective

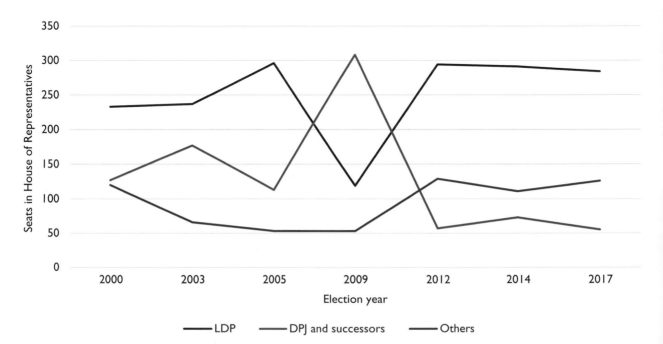

Figure 6.2 Legislative electoral trends in Japan

New was finally dropped in 2014. The party since 1998 has been in a coalition with the LDP, which needed Komeito to maintain its majority after the 2000 and 2003 general elections. Although the LDP had a solid majority after the 2005 election and since 2012, it has remained in coalition with Komeito, which brings to the table the powerful electoral machine offered by Soka Gakkai, and the electoral strengths that Komeito has in urban areas (complementing the LDP's strengths in rural areas) (Itoh, 2015).

Democratic Party of Japan (DPJ)

Although it was short-lived (founded in 1996 and closed down in 2018), the DPJ was notable for coming closer than any party to breaking the LDP stranglehold on Japanese politics. It stormed home in the 2009 general election, winning a clear majority by taking nearly 65 per cent of the seats in the House of Representatives, but then quickly fell apart due its inexperience and internal divisions: during its 39 months in power, it was led by three different prime ministers. For Pekkanen et al. (2018), the DPJ victory was perhaps less than it seemed: the party had been formed in the first place by collecting together as candidates 'anyone who opposed the LDP, without serious reference to their policy preferences', and the party was able to defeat the LDP in 2009 only because the LDP was failing to govern effectively; voters did not vote for the DPJ so much as they voted against the LDP.

The DPJ was a centrist party that traced its origins to a game of musical chairs played by Japanese parties during the 1990s in the wake of changes in electoral laws. The introduction of the mixed SMP/PR electoral system encouraged smaller parties to unite with one another in order to increase their chances of winning seats in the Diet. The Social Democrats (SDP) and the moderately left-wing New Harbinger Party (NHP) were the key actors in the process which resulted in the creation of the DPJ in September 1996. More parties joined the group in 1998, when the DPJ became the major opposition to the LDP-Liberal government, and its potential was confirmed at the June 2000 elections when it won enough seats to become the *de facto* opposition to the LDP. Although the party failed miserably at the 2005 House of Representatives elections, Yukio Hatoyama took it into its 2009 general election landslide, becoming only the fourth non-LDP prime minister of Japan since 1955.

As is often the case with new parties coming to power for the first time, the DPJ found that being in government made quite different demands from those it faced in opposition. The party lacked a majority in the House of Councillors, proposed an unpopular consumption tax designed to offset Japan's national debt, and suffered from internal divisions that resulted in leadership changes. It was comprehensively defeated in the 2012 general election, its share of seats falling from more than 300 to less than 60. The remains of the party imploded, with defections in 2016 and 2017 that spawned new parties, including the Constitutional Democratic Party of Japan (the CDP), created just a few weeks before the October 2017 elections. In May 2018, the remains of the DPJ merged with the one-year-old Party of Hope to form the Democratic Party for the People.

Other parties

Although the LDP has consistently failed to be a widely popular party, and although there have been many attempts to form a stable opposition, party politics outside the LDP has long been unstable. Even in the current era of renewed LDP dominance, note Pekkanen et al. (2018), voters remain unsure about which alternative party will be a credible challenger, and political elites 'cannot seem to coordinate on a single vessel for challenging the LDP'. Several times it has seemed as though habits were about to be broken, but even the 39-month government of the DPJ proved to be transitory. Opposition parties come and go as they are created, as they briefly seem to do well, as they merge with others, and as they fade away, leaving the political landscape littered with dashed hopes and small parties with compelling names; consider, among recent examples, the People's Life Party, the Happiness Realization Party, and the Party for Future Generations.

On the political left, the Japan Socialist Party (JSP) and its successor Social Democratic Party (SDP) have at times appeared to on the verge of a breakthrough, but always fell short. The Socialists, for example, won 33 per cent of the vote in 1958 but subsequently lost support because of their more militant policies, including criticizing the US–Japanese relationship and opposing nuclear power. In 1986, leadership of the party fell to Takako Doi, Japan's first female party leader. She established herself as a popular and outspoken figure, began moderating the policies of the party, and had the party change its name to the SDP. She offended many of the party's supporters, however, by abandoning most of the SDP's traditional policy positions in the interests of forming a coalition with the LDP in 1994. Despite reappointing Takako Doi leader (she stepped down in 2003), the party became a shadow of its former self. In the wake of LDP election victories since 2012, it is hard to identify the seeds of a new and meaningful opposition party (see Pekkanen and Reed, 2018).

THE FUTURE OF JAPANESE GOVERNMENT AND POLITICS

Japan has seen a dramatic transformation in the last 70 years. Defeated in war and economically devastated, it was faced in 1945 with the challenge of adopting a new political system imposed on it by the terms of the peace settlement, becoming more fully a part of the international community, and building economic independence against a background of limited natural resources. Its GDP today is more than 110 times bigger than it was in 1960 (those of the United States and Britain, by contrast, are each only 35 times bigger), its industries and services have grown in leaps and bounds, and Japanese products, sold all over the world, have become synonymous with quality and durability.

However, its economy has not fared well in recent decades, and even if Japan is a wealthy country, many argue that its political system has not modernized sufficiently to keep up with needs. Vested interests, factionalism, and deal-making have dominated the policymaking process, self-interest on the part of party leaders has helped perpetuate a corrupt electoral system, and Japan has been left with a strangely archaic way of governing itself. The political reforms begun in the 1990s have not gone far enough, and even if the '2012 system' leaves the LDP in a stronger and less factionalized position than before, a political arrangement based on one strong party and a deeply divided opposition will always have difficulties engaging all its citizens and generating new ideas. Japan also faces the formidable economic challenge of planning for the combined effects of a declining birth rate, the world's highest life expectancy, and an aversion to immigration. More than any other advanced industrial economy, Japan has too few working people to support its elderly population, a problem with no easy solution.

DISCUSSION QUESTIONS

1. What is the difference (if any) between modernization and Westernization?
2. It is often said that Japanese prime ministers are caretakers or functionaries, rather than leaders. To what extent could the same be said of the leaders of the other countries assessed in this book?
3. To what extent does exceptionalism in the United States, Japan, and France come from common sources and have common effects?
4. To what extent is factionalism a part of politics in other liberal democracies?
5. What are the costs and benefits of a single-party-dominant system such as that of Japan?
6. What reforms are needed to bring greater efficiency to the Japanese political system?

CHAPTER CONCEPTS

◆ 1955 system
◆ Diet
◆ Emperor
◆ House of Councillors
◆ House of Representatives

◆ Japan Self-Defence Forces
◆ *Koenkai*
◆ Komeito
◆ Liberal Democratic Party
◆ Meiji Restoration

◆ Recruit scandal
◆ Revolving door
◆ Shinto
◆ Shoguns

KEY TERMS

◆ Factionalism
◆ Iron triangle

◆ Patron–client democracy
◆ Personalism

JAPAN ONLINE

The Japanese Government: www.mofa.go.jp/index.html
Prime minister and cabinet: http://japan.kantei.go.jp/index.html
House of Representatives: www.shugiin.go.jp/internet/index.nsf/html/index_e.htm
Supreme Court: www.courts.go.jp/english
Liberal Democratic Party: www.jimin.jp/english
Komeito: www.komei.or.jp/en/about
Democratic Party of Japan: www.dpj.or.jp/english/index.html
Asahi Shimbun: www.asahi.com/ajw
Japan Times: www.japantimes.co.jp

FURTHER READING

Hayes, Louis D. (2017) *Introduction to Japanese Politics*, 6th edn (Routledge). One of the standard texts on Japanese government and politics, including chapters on the political system, political parties, and political participation.

McCargo, Duncan (2012) *Contemporary Japan*, 3rd edn (Red Globe Press). The Japanese volume in the Red Globe Press series, offering an overview of history, society, culture, government, and the economy.

Pekkanen, Robert J., Steven R. Reed, Ethan Scheiner, and Daniel M. Smith (eds) (2017) *Japan Decides 2017: The Japanese General Election* (Palgrave Macmillan). An edited collection of assessments of the outcome of the 2017 general election and its implications for Japanese government and politics.

Stockwin, Arthur, and Kweku Ampiah (2017) *Rethinking Japan: The Politics of Contested Nationalism* (Lexington Books). An assessment of the implications of the return to power of the LDP in 2012, suggesting that Japan may now be in a new and distinctive political phase.

Sugimoto, Yoshio (2015) *An Introduction to Japanese Society*, 4th edn (Cambridge University Press). A survey of the complexities of Japanese society, arguing that it is more diverse than it is often portrayed.

Walker, Brett L. (2015) *A Concise History of Japan* (Cambridge University Press). As the title implies, a relatively brief outline of Japanese history, with short chapters on each of its key epochs.

Visit **www.macmillanihe.com/McCormick-Cases** to access additional materials to support teaching and learning.

FRANCE 7

PREVIEW

The value of France as a case stems from its long history of political turbulence, and from its ongoing struggle to find a workable political form based on the principles of freedom, equality, and fraternity that were the rallying cries of the 1789 French Revolution. It also continues to struggle with defining the ways in which its traditions of exceptionalism, republicanism, and secularism must adapt to new circumstances. France is a unitary state that is often touted as the benchmark for the semi-presidential model of government, and which also – unusually – uses majority systems for both presidential and legislative elections. The rules of French government continue to evolve, and its political leaders continue to wrestle with ideas about politics and society that are rooted in local communities. France is also an important European state facing the challenge of adapting its unique traditions to a more globalized and competitive world.

KEY ARGUMENTS

◆ France is a country that has seen much political change, and even today continues to adjust the structure of its political system.

◆ Symbols and history play a key role in defining the French political system, although levels of public trust in government are low.

◆ France has had 16 constitutions since the Revolution, and while that of the Fifth Republic endures, it also continues to be adjusted and questioned.

◆ The semi-presidential system in France creates an ambiguous and sometimes troubling relationship between president and prime minister.

◆ Local government plays an important role in French politics and society, in spite of the emphasis historically given to national identity in France.

◆ French political parties are numerous and changeable, and are often able to achieve power only when they work together with like-minded parties.

OVERVIEW

France may be one of the world's leading liberal democracies, but it lacks some of the stability and continuity that is usually (if not always deservedly) associated with democracies. It has gone through multiple political forms since its 1789 revolution, and even though its most recent constitution – that of the Fifth Republic – is more than sixty years old, it continues to experience change and tumult.

In political terms, France is notable for its use of a **semi-presidential system** (otherwise known as a dual executive) in which power is shared between an elected president and a prime minister appointed out of the legislature, the National Assembly. The division of power depends on party numbers in the legislature; if the president's party is strong, then the president is strong, but if opposition parties are strong, then the prime minister has the advantage. Recent problems in France have led to its downgrading since 2010 in the Democracy Index from a full democracy to a flawed democracy: while it performs well in the fairness of its elections, in its record on political participation, and in the protection of civil liberties, it fares less well in terms of the functioning of its government, the health of its political culture, and levels of trust in government.

> **Semi-presidential system**
> One in which executive powers are shared between a president and a prime minister.

In economic terms, France is a wealthy country with a population and an economy that are about the same size as those of Britain. The French have a high standard of living when measured by the provision of education, health care, and infrastructure, but the economic news in recent years has painted a more complex picture: unemployment has remained stubbornly high at about 9–10 per cent, public spending is high, France fares poorly on league tables of economic freedom, and concerns have been raised about the effects of France's relatively short work week (the French work about 1,500 hours per year, compared to almost 1,700 hours in Britain and almost 1,800 in the United States (Organisation for Economic Co-operation and Development, 2018) and relatively young retirement age (just over 60). At the same time, France has developed a reputation as a global leader in technology, with a nuclear power programme that meets two-thirds of its electricity needs, its leading role in the European Space Agency and the Airbus aircraft consortium, and its construction of one of the world's most advanced high speed rail systems (the TGV, or *Train à Grande Vitesse*).

In social terms, France has a strong sense of national identity but still finds itself dealing with numerous internal divisions, including social class, religion, and ethnicity. It is one of the oldest states in the world, and yet different parts of the country have different histories, customs, and traditions. A history of invasions and internal change has left the French people with ancestors from Italy, Spain, Germany, and the Celtic regions; in the region of Brittany, the Bretons are related to the Welsh, the Irish, and the Scots. Not only do about one-third of French people speak a regional language, but the social and ethnic diversity of the country has grown as a consequence of France's history as a colonial power. Immigrants have arrived from France's former colonies in West and North Africa, as a result of which ethnic minorities now make up about 15 per cent of the population, and Muslims about nine per cent (the largest share of any European country outside the Balkans (Hackett, 2017)).

POLITICAL DEVELOPMENT

Unlike Britain, which has experienced a relatively evolutionary (if not always necessarily peaceful) history of political change, France has been more volatile, like Germany in the depth and frequency of the new directions it has taken. It is one of the oldest countries in the world, and yet its current political system dates back only to 1958. Meanwhile, support for democracy and individual rights may lie at the core of its founding political documents, but it has suffered sometimes remarkable levels of violence as it has tried to find its ideal political form. It was a monarchy until 1792, when a revolution led to the execution of the king and several years of instability before Napoleon took power in 1799. It has since worked its way through multiple different political systems, several revolutions, and more than one political coup. Even though the French political system is quite different today from what it was even as recently as the late 1940s, influences from earlier political systems still make themselves felt in the structure of the French system and in debates about its future.

Origins of the French state

As with many other parts of Europe, the early political, economic, and cultural forms of what is now France were shaped by invasion. Migrations in the 8th century BCE brought the region under the control of Celtic-speaking people known as the Gauls, but internal divisions left them unable to fend off a series of Roman invasions beginning in 121 BCE, ending in complete subjugation by the Romans in 49 BCE. The Gauls adopted the Roman way of life, with Latin as the common language and Lugdunum (now Lyon) as their capital. Christianity arrived in the 1st century CE, and with the decline of Rome from the mid-3rd century, Germanic tribes began to invade what was now known as Gaul. By the end of the 4th century CE, the northern part of the region was ruled by the Franks (from which the name of France derives), with Paris as their capital. Frankish control had expanded to the entire region within 150 years.

An Arab invasion was fended off at the battle of Poitiers in 732, and in 800 the Frankish king Charlemagne was crowned emperor of the Holy Roman Empire, seen as a successor to the Roman empire. With internal divisions and raids by Arabs and Vikings, France became fragmented, a process that continued with royal marriages and land acquisitions involving French and English monarchs that changed political boundaries, but also allowed the economy to grow and the arts to flourish. By the late 15th century, the English had been driven out, and the territorial outlines of today's France had been largely settled.

The French Revolution and its aftermath (1789–99)

By the end of the 17th century, France had become both the major power in Europe and an absolute monarchy, during an era later described as the *ancien regime* (the old order) to distinguish it from the post-revolutionary era. The power of kings was summarized in the words of the King Louis XIV: 'L'etat c'est moi' (I am the state). France was embroiled in several expensive wars, however, and aristocrats railed against the powers of an increasingly corrupt and ineffective monarchy (Cole, 2017). Resistance deepened when France declared war on Britain in support of the American war of independence, and new taxes were proposed as a means of paying for the war. In May 1789, three Estates-General that had not met since 1614 were recalled, representing the nobility, the clergy, and the people. Angered at its relative lack of influence, the third estate declared itself to be the true representative body of the people, and in June proclaimed the creation of a new National Assembly. Although King Louis XVI capitulated and ordered all three estates to work and vote as a single body, he also ordered troops to march on Paris. A popular uprising led to the storming of the Bastille (a fortress and prison in Paris, whose fall on 14 July is still celebrated in France as Bastille Day), marking the outbreak of the tumultuous **French Revolution**.

On the back of a wave of popular discontent, the National Assembly in August adopted the **Declaration of the Rights of Man and Citizen**, which remains even today one of the core documents in the definition of individual rights. Influenced by the idea of **natural rights**, it held that all people were born free and equal, that human rights included 'liberty, property, safety, and resistance against oppression', and that law was the expression of the general will. Discontent continued to brew, however, and France became divided between those who thought the revolution had gone far enough and those who wanted more change.

> **Natural rights**
> Those rights (such as to life, liberty, and property) supposedly given to humans by God or by nature, their existence taken to be independent of government.

A new constitution was adopted in 1791 by which the king had to share power with the National Assembly, but it was too late: against a background of growing panic in the face of war with Austria and Prussia, an uprising led to the abolition of the monarchy and the declaration of the **First Republic** in September 1792. The king was executed in January 1793, and more unrest led to the start of the era known as 'the Terror', marked by arbitrary arrests and executions of anyone considered to be 'enemies of liberty'. This finally ended in November 1799 with a military coup that brought the military leader Napoleon Bonaparte to power.

From Napoleon to the Third Republic (1799–1940)

Napoleon's regime provided France with some much-needed stability, his military genius allowing him to dominate much of central Europe, while he crowned himself emperor of the First French Empire in 1804 and ruled on the basis of a uniform legal system known as the *Code Napoleon*. He also built a professional and elitist bureaucracy whose traditions persist even today. Napoleon overextended his military with an invasion of Russia in 1812, however, and he was forced to abdicate in 1814 and was sent into exile. He returned briefly to power before his final defeat at the Battle of Waterloo in 1815, and the monarchy was restored under King Louis XVIII, brother of the executed king.

Economic and popular discontent continued to simmer, industrialization proceeding more slowly than was the case in several other Western European states. A July 1830 revolution led to the replacement of King Charles X with his cousin Louis Philippe, who was forced to abdicate during another revolution in 1848 that brought a final end to the French monarchy. The constitution of the **Second Republic** was adopted, with a new office of president limited to a single term. The first officeholder, Louis Napoleon (a nephew of Napoleon I), balked at the restriction, led a coup in 1851, dissolved the National Assembly, and organized a referendum at which support was given to change the constitution. In 1852 he made himself Emperor Napoleon III, head of the Second Empire. This came to an end following a series of disastrous wars that culminated with the French defeat at the hands of the Prussians in 1870, and the abdication of Napoleon.

In 1875, the National Assembly adopted the constitution of the **Third Republic**. This remains the longest-lasting of France's different political systems, in which government was shared between an elected president and legislature. For Sowerwine (2018), it 'rebuilt France as a great power while making it one of the world's first and most successful national democracies'. It was undermined, though, by critical weaknesses, not least the weakness of the presidency and the persistence of party divisions: presidents rarely saw out their full seven-year terms, and the legislature could rarely agree. It was, nonetheless, during this era that France built most of its colonial empire, in Indochina (now Cambodia, Laos, and Vietnam), Polynesia, Madagascar, and West Africa.

World War I (the Great War of 1914–18) caused enormous disruption: it was fought in part on French soil, it resulted in the deaths of 1.3 million French soldiers, and it caused extensive damage to infrastructure. France was also left in debt, and in spite of reparations wrested from Germany under the terms of the 1919 Treaty of Versailles, France's economy struggled, its problems exacerbated by the effects of the Great Depression in the early 1930s. The downfall of the Third Republic was ultimately assured by the outbreak of World War II in September 1939.

From World War II to the Fifth Republic (1940–58)

The German invasion of May–June 1940 ended with the surrender of France and the dissolution of the Third Republic. The north of the country was directly occupied by the Germans, while the puppet regime of **Vichy France** was created in the southern half of the country and France's colonies, under the administration of

⚇ TIMELINE

1789	French revolution overthrows monarchy
1792	Creation of First Republic
1804–14	Napoleon emperor of First French Empire
1815	Napoleon defeated at Waterloo; restoration of monarchy
1848	End of monarchy; creation of Second Republic
1852	Creation of Second Empire
1870	Creation of Third Republic
1940–44	Nazi occupation and Vichy France
1946	Creation of Fourth Republic
1950	Schuman Declaration on European cooperation
1954	French defeat in Indochina; start of Algerian war of independence
1958	Creation of Fifth Republic
1962	Independence of Algeria
1968–69	Student uprisings and general strike
1970	Death of Charles de Gaulle
1981	François Mitterrand elected first socialist president
2002	Euro replaces French franc
2005	France rejects EU constitution in national referendum
2015	Terrorist attacks in Paris claim more than 130 lives
2017	Emmanuel Macron sweeps to power on a wave of demands for change

Marshal Philippe Pétain. All of France was eventually fully occupied by German or Italian forces in November 1942. Meanwhile, General Charles de Gaulle (1890–1970) became head of the French government in exile and the Free French Forces, which served with the other allied states in the fight against Nazism, while a resistance movement worked within France to sabotage German operations. With liberation in 1944, de Gaulle became head of a new provisional government, which governed until the creation of the new French **Fourth Republic** in October 1946.

Although France saw rapid rebuilding and economic growth after the war, including the launch of a new welfare system, the wartime division had left it traumatized, and the constitution of the Fourth Republic retained many of the handicaps of the Third Republic, including a weak executive and a strong assembly divided by many political parties. Meanwhile, France – like Britain – found itself struggling to maintain its empire, notably in Indochina where a war for independence broke out in late 1946. A humiliating military defeat in 1954 at Dien Bien Phu (in the north-western region of what is now Vietnam) led to French withdrawal and the beginning of US involvement in the region.

At home, France took the lead in efforts to encourage regional economic integration in western Europe, with the May 1950 Schuman Declaration – named for French foreign minister Robert Schuman – calling for cooperation in the interests of regional peace. It led to the creation in 1952 of the European Coal and Steel Community, and in 1958 of the European Economic Community (precursors to today's European Union). While they were met with an initial lack of enthusiasm (only six countries joined), the idea of integration began to take hold.

New political challenges arose in 1958 with the outbreak of conflict in Algeria, which had been conquered by France in 1839–75 and subsequently administered as a part of mainland France. With threats of civil war and rebellion in the air, de Gaulle was called back to office (he had retired in 1946) and given emergency powers for six months to oversee the creation of a new political system. A commission was convened, and the constitution of the new **Fifth Republic** was approved overwhelmingly in a national referendum, coming into force on 4 October 1958. It ended 80 years of legislative dominance, argues Sowerwine (2018), and provided for a strong presidency working alongside a weaker National Assembly, with a prime minister appointed by the president out of the largest party or coalition. De Gaulle was elected president in December and inaugurated in January 1959. One of his first actions was to resolve the crisis in Algeria, which became independent in July 1962.

The Fifth Republic has proved to be a stable political system, even if it had a rocky start: it faced challenges with the Algerian crisis, several attempts on the life of de Gaulle, and student/worker protests in 1968–69 that were followed by de Gaulle's resignation (he died in 1970). Control of the presidency and the National Assembly was to range between socialists, centrists, and conservatives, while France continued to play a key role at the heart of the European Community, which evolved during the 1990s into the European Union.

France today

In few places does history continue to play so central a role in the politics of the present as in France, which continues even today to wrestle with the meaning of the 1789 revolution, its troubling division during World War II, its colonial heritage, and its place in the international system. It is a wealthy and productive state (although it suffered, like many western European states, from the effects of the global financial crisis of 2007–08), its culture is one of the most sophisticated in Europe (little wonder that it is the biggest tourist destination in the world), and it continues to be a formidable military power with an independent nuclear deterrent.

It has a sensitivity, however, about the political and cultural dominance of the Anglo-Saxon world, and is undecided about its place in the European Union; it has been one of the leaders of the EU, and the bond between France and Germany has been central to the process of European integration, but France sent shockwaves across the EU in 2005 when – in a national referendum – its people rejected a proposed EU constitutional treaty that had been shaped in meetings co-chaired by former French president Valéry Giscard d'Estaing. At home, meanwhile, it made several constitutional changes intended to rework the powers of government and to devolve more powers to its regions and local units of government.

Multiculturalism has proved a problem also for France, where many immigrants have arrived from former colonies, contributing to social and political tensions made more difficult by a debate over the place of Muslims in a secular society. Opposition to immigration and to the soft borders of the European Union have fed into the rise of the far-right National Front (renamed National Rally in 2018), whose candidates have come second in several recent presidential elections. France has also been a target for international terrorists: a January 2015 attack by

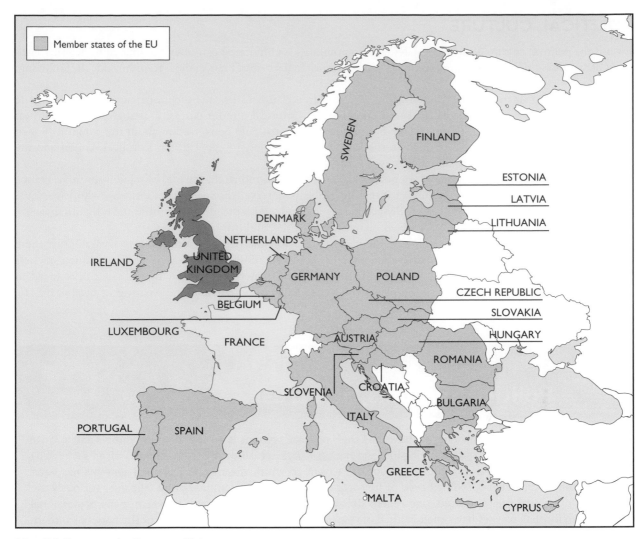

Map 7.1 France in the European Union
Note: At the time that this book went to press, the UK was negotiating an exit from the EU.

al-Qaeda on the office of the satirical weekly newspaper *Charlie Hebdo* in Paris took 14 lives, 130 Parisians died during a series of coordinated shootings and bombings in Paris in November 2015, and 86 more died during a vehicle-ramming attack in the southern city of Nice in July 2016.

The occupancy of the office of the presidency has undergone significant changes in recent terms: the relative flamboyance of the politically conservative Nicolas Sarkozy ended in 2012 with the election of the more subdued François Hollande, the first socialist to hold the office since 1995. Hollande campaigned on the basis of several radical policies, including an increase in the top rate of income tax to 75 per cent, but found his popularity dropping to record lows in the wake of criticism of his indecisive leadership. Barely a year before the 2017 election, a former banker and economics minister named Emmanuel Macron (who had never held elective office) launched an independent bid for the presidency on the foundation of a new movement, *La République En Marche!* (usually shortened to *En Marche!*). Attracting voters from the centre-right and left, and using a wide array of modern campaigning techniques (including grassroots mobilization and social media – see Evans and Ivaldi, 2018), he convincingly won the May election by a large margin (although voter turnout was an all-time low of just under 49 per cent), and *En Marche!* won a majority in the parliamentary elections that followed a month later. His victory seemed to represent the ongoing desire among French voters for renewal and change, but Macron was hardly the first presidential candidate to offer such an option, and he was soon criticized for his imperious style of government.

POLITICAL CULTURE

Even if the political culture of different states (and communities within states) can often be difficult to describe or to assess, it can also sometimes be summarized in a few key terms. In the case of France, those terms include the following:

◆ *Exceptionalism*: Much like the United States, France often claims to be an exceptional society that has gone through distinctive political change based on particular historical circumstances, creating a unique political culture. In both countries, though, there has recently been a national conversation about the extent to which each can still claim to be exceptional. In the French case, pressures to adapt to the European Union and the changes wrought by globalization have raised many questions.

◆ **Republicanism**: Although a republic is a political system without a monarch, the idea of republicanism in France goes further, describing a system in which the indivisible state serves the interests of citizens, who have equal rights and duties. The idea has been challenged in recent decades with the growing ethnic and religious diversity of France, which has challenged the idea of shared values, rules, and institutions.

◆ *Secularism*: As elsewhere, this encapsulates the idea that religion and the state must be kept separate, that there should be no state religion, and that French citizens should be allowed to follow freely the religion of their choice, or even no religion at all. Religious tensions remain, nonetheless, a new factor being introduced in recent decades with a debate over the place of Islam in French society, and the wearing of headscarves by Muslim women (which is also a social issue).

COMPARING POLITICAL CULTURE 7
Politics, symbols, and trust

Much of the identity and meaning of states and their political systems is wrapped up in symbols and in their related traditions. Flags, anthems, slogans, and national days are all part of the picture, often generating strong emotions and sparking debates about the extent to which the meaning of such symbols has been maintained or threatened, remembered or forgotten. Americans, for example, often take very seriously the way their national flag is treated, one recent debate centring around the way in which many professional American football players have knelt instead of remaining standing during the playing of the national anthem at the start of games, in protest at racial injustices. They have been widely criticized for 'dishonouring' the flag and the memories of those who have died in war.

France has its own set of symbols that are seen to represent the state and the values for which France stands: the tricolour flag, the allegorical figure of Marianne (personifying liberty and reason, and found, for example, on French stamps and used for the French design on euro coins), the national anthem (*La Marseillaise*, whose origins lie in events during the revolution), the revolutionary motto of *Liberté, Égalité, Fraternité* (freedom, equality, fraternity), and the Declaration of the Rights of Man and Citizen, which holds a place in the French national psyche much like the Declaration of Independence in the United States.

While symbols may be important, though, their strength may not always be reflected in high levels of faith or trust in government, and – in fact – their active use may be a reflection less of confidence in a political system than of declining confidence in that system. That is, voters who are cynical about government or who feel that their country is threatened by immigration or globalization may be tempted to fall back on their faith in symbols of the state, its history, and its political culture.

Levels of trust in government have been low and/or declining in many democracies in recent decades, even in countries where symbols are still prominent and highly regarded. The belief that governments will generate competent decisions has been challenged by an array of problems, ranging from corruption to elitism, widening political and economic divisions, worries about the effects of globalization, and the ongoing fallout from the global financial crisis of 2007–08. Figure 7.1 shows some of the results of the Trust Barometer maintained by Edelman, a US-based marketing consultancy, which has been researching levels of trust in government, business, media, and non-governmental organizations since 2001. It is interesting that levels of trust are so low in some of the more historically successful democracies, such as France, Britain, and the United States.

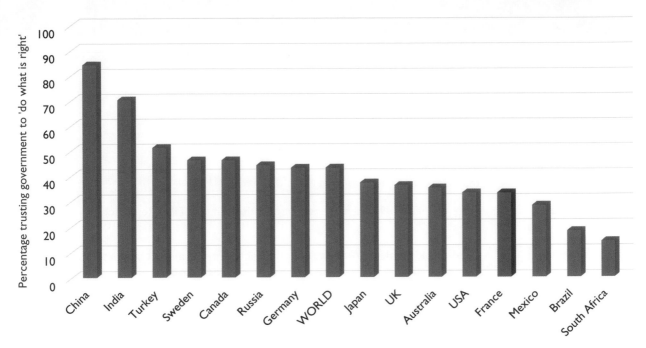

Figure 7.1 Comparing levels of trust in government
Source: Edelman (2018).
Note: Based on fieldwork in 28 countries, excluding Iran and Nigeria.

Much debate has also centred in France on the question of its national identity, the definition of which is based more on myth than reality. Nationalism and patriotism have long been a key theme in French national life and in the politics of France, reflected in factors as varied as the importance of symbols (see Comparing Political Culture 7), de Gaulle's efforts to rebuild France's global role, and the reaction against immigration. Many in France have long been convinced of the universal value and superiority of French culture and civilization, and the word *grandeur* (greatness) often appears in discussions about French political culture. This is an abstract idea, though, and it is notable how much cynicism many in France have towards the state and its institutions. Identity, argues Cole (2017), is rooted less in the nation than in localities or towns, while Sowerwine (2018) notes the irony in the contrast between the importance of towns and villages, on the one hand, and – on the other hand – the fact that many villages are either semi-deserted or are the location of holiday homes for city dwellers and foreigners. He also notes the impact of globalization on France, as reflected in the popularity of fast food chains in a country famous for its distinctive cuisine, and its cheese and wine.

POLITICAL SYSTEM

So far, we have looked at three parliamentary systems (Britain, Germany, and Japan) and a presidential system (the United States). France offers a different approach, combining elements of the parliamentary and presidential models to produce a semi-presidential system in which a directly elected president shares executive powers with an appointed prime minister. Although this arrangement was found in the Weimar Republic in Germany (see Chapter 4), France is widely considered to be the pioneer. The system was designed at the behest of Charles de Gaulle when he considered the disarray of the Fourth Republic and looked for a more stable means of governing. Even though the heritage of the *ancien regime* continued to be felt in a fear of strong leaders, the constitution of the Fifth Republic provided for a strong executive while encouraging parties to work together in order to win power.

The constitution

France has had no fewer than 16 constitutions since the Revolution (Elgie et al., 2016). These have generated several different political systems, including a monarchy, two empires, five republics, and a short period of foreign occupation. Even though it is now clearly based on the principles of the Fifth Republic, there are important threads that connect the current constitution to its predecessors. Consider, for example, the opening words of its Preamble: 'The French

Name	France (République française)
Capital	Paris
Administration	Unitary republic, with three levels of sub-national government: regions, *départements*, and municipalities.
Constitution	State formed 1789, and most recent constitution (the Fifth Republic) adopted 1958.
Executive	Semi-presidential. A president directly elected for no more than two five-year terms, governing with a prime minister who leads a Council of Ministers accountable to the National Assembly. There is no vice president.
Legislature	Bicameral Parliament: lower National Assembly (577 members) elected for renewable five-year terms, and upper Senate (348 members) indirectly elected through local governments for six-year terms.
Judiciary	French law is based on the Napoleonic Codes (1804–11). The Constitutional Council has grown in significance and has had the power of judicial review since 2008. It has up to 12 members serving single nine-year terms. Three each are appointed by the incumbent president, the National Assembly, and the Senate, while the balance are former presidents of France.
Electoral system	A two-round system is used for both presidential and legislative elections, with a majority vote needed for victory on the first round.
Party system	Multi-party, with the Socialists dominating on the left, backed by greens, leftists and radicals, while the Republicans (formerly Union for a Popular Movement) dominate on the right, and a new centrist party (*En Marche!*, or Forward!) was the base for the victory of President Emmanuel Macron in 2017. The far-right National Rally has also been making gains.

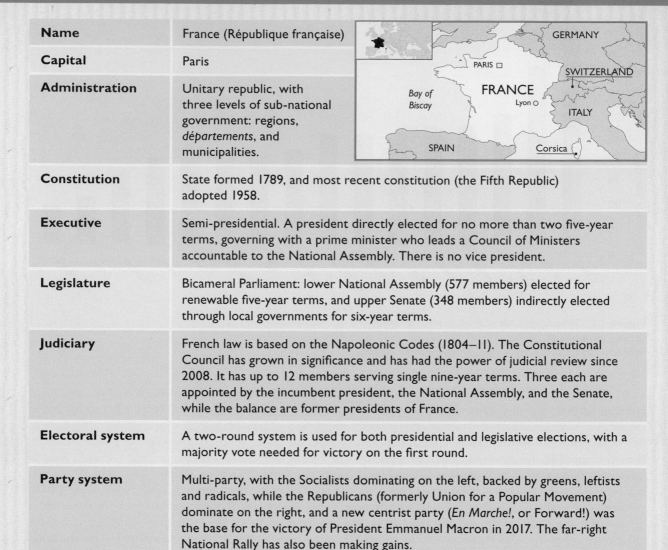

67m Population

$2,582 billion Gross Domestic Product

$38,480 Per capita GDP

Democracy Index rating

- ✖ Full Democracy
- ✔ Flawed Democracy
- ✖ Hybrid Regime
- ✖ Authoritarian
- ✖ Not Rated

Freedom House rating

- ✔ Free
- ✖ Partly Free
- ✖ Not Free
- ✖ Not Rated

Human Development Index rating

- ✔ Very High
- ✖ High
- ✖ Medium
- ✖ Low
- ✖ Not Rated

people solemnly proclaim their attachment to the Rights of Man and the principles of national sovereignty as defined by the Declaration of 1789, confirmed and complemented by the Preamble to the Constitution of 1946'.

Many of the core political principles of the French political system are listed in Article 1 of the constitution (emphasis added):

> France shall be an indivisible, *secular*, democratic and *social* Republic. It shall ensure the *equality* of all citizens before the law, without distinction of origin, race or religion. It shall respect all beliefs. It shall be organised on a *decentralized* basis.

Such ideals are not easily won or sustained, and France has often found itself struggling to live up to its aspirations, challenged by the pressures of globalization, immigration, and internal economic, religious, ethnic, and generational divisions. Nonetheless, the Fifth Republic has proved to be relatively stable, owing much to the difficult times in which it was drafted, and also to the personality of Charles de Gaulle, who wanted a strong executive that would prevent the confusion that had often surrounded governments during the Third and Fourth Republics. In this it has mainly succeeded, although concerns about France's difficulties have raised the occasional debate about the possibility of a Sixth Republic, with term limits on the president, a reformed electoral system, and perhaps even abolition of the Senate (Taylor, 2007).

Meanwhile, changes have come as a result of two dozen amendments (all but five of them since 1992), including the following:

◆ A 1962 amendment replaced election of the president by an electoral college with direct election by voters.
◆ A 2000 amendment reduced the term of a president from seven years to five years.
◆ A 2005 amendment agreed a Charter for the Environment, with reference to its 'rights and duties' added to the Preamble to the constitution.
◆ A 2008 amendment limited the president to two consecutive terms in office.

Amendments can take one of two roads: the most commonly used option is a proposal by majorities in both chambers of Parliament, and ratification by three-fifths of members in a joint meeting of both chambers (known as a Congress), while the second option is for a proposal passed by both chambers to be put to a national referendum.

The executive: president, prime minister, and Council of Ministers

We saw in Chapter 3 that the prime minister of Britain comes out of Parliament (in the sense that he/she is the leader of the biggest party or coalition in the legislature), while we saw in Chapter 4 that the president of the United States is elected by voters (albeit via an electoral college). The French executive is something of a combination of these two models, with a president elected directly by voters and a prime minister appointed by the president on the basis of party numbers in the National Assembly. The president is head of state, and shares the powers of head of government with the prime minister. This is the classic case of a semi-presidential executive, a model that Elgie (2011) argues can be found – to different degrees – in about 50 countries (see Comparing Government 7).

The office of the president was designed by Charles de Gaulle as a reflection of his views about leadership, and came with so many powers that he was immediately accused by his critics of having plans to become a dictator. This did not happen, and nor have any of his successors tended towards dictatorial powers or designs, even if they have occasionally exerted their authority to an extent that generated much criticism (as, for example, when François Mitterrand changed the legislative electoral system in 1985). De Gaulle's hope was that the president could rise above narrow party politics and be an arbitrator (the key adjective used in the constitution to describe the office), a mediator, and a guide, while at the same time having close control over government. In some respects it is a semi-monarchical office, with a combination of symbolic and executive powers.

At first, presidents were elected for renewable seven-year terms by an electoral college consisting of members of Parliament and representatives from local government. This allowed presidents to govern for an unusually long time without having to worry about running for re-election, thereby providing France with a continuity of leadership that it had rarely enjoyed under earlier constitutions. Direct election was instituted with effect from the 1965 election, and the terms of office were reduced in 2000 to five years (with an unlimited number of terms, but only two to be held consecutively). Although the latter change suggested a reduction in the powers of the presidency, the office has actually accumulated more powers over the decades at the expense of Parliament, in a similar fashion to the accumulation of powers of the US president at the expense of the US Congress.

COMPARING GOVERNMENT 7
The semi-presidential system

Even if we might think of Britain as the baseline against which other parliamentary systems can be understood, or the United States as the baseline against which other presidential systems can be understood, every political model varies from one situation to another. This is also true of semi-presidential systems. They all have an elected president who shares executive power with a prime minister responsible to the legislature, but the dynamic is different according to the relative balance of those powers, with important implications (see Elgie, 2011). Consider the following variations, suggested by Shugart and Carey (1992):

◆ In *presidential-parliamentary systems*, the president has the power both to appoint and to dismiss the prime minister, who can also be removed by failing to win a vote of confidence in the legislature. In other words, the prime minister and cabinet are responsible both to the president and to the legislature. Countries that use this system include Austria, Cuba, Mozambique, Namibia, Russia, Senegal, and Turkey.

◆ In *premier-presidential systems*, the president has the power to appoint the prime minister and cabinet, but they can only be formally removed by the legislature, through a loss of a vote of confidence. In other words, the prime minister and the cabinet are responsible only to the legislature. Countries that use this system include Algeria, the Democratic Republic of Congo, Egypt, France, Mongolia, Poland, Portugal, and Ukraine.

A third and more informal variation is found in countries where semi-presidentialism is introduced deliberately (and usually temporarily) as a means of power sharing. Consider the case of Kenya in 2008, when disputed national elections sparked riots that led to several hundred deaths, prompting a constitutional change that created a new post of prime minister to be held by the leader of the opposition. It did not last long (the office of prime minister was abolished in 2013), but it briefly helped keep the peace. The same pattern was repeated in Zimbabwe in 2009–13.

A final question to consider is the extent to which presidential systems such as the United States, Mexico, and Nigeria can sometimes adopt some of the features of semi-presidentialism without formally using that model. If, in these countries, the party of the president holds a majority in the legislature, and the president has a good relationship with the party in the legislature, then this is clearly a presidential system. However, if the same party controls both the executive and the legislature but the president does not see eye to eye with the party leadership, or if the opposition party holds a majority in the legislature, then is this not to all intents and purposes an informal semi-presidential system, with executive powers shared by the president and the leader of the legislature?

As well as being commander-in-chief, making senior appointments to the bureaucracy, signing bills into law, representing France in meetings with other national leaders, being able to negotiate treaties, and having the power to issue pardons, the most substantial power of the president is to appoint (but not dismiss) the prime minister. The relationship between the two positions is at the heart of the French system, presidents typically working to portray themselves as heads of state while treating prime ministers as political managers, but the balance depends on the level of public support enjoyed (or lost) by the president, and party numbers in the National Assembly.

Usually, the president's party has a majority in Parliament, the president can appoint a prime minister from the same party, and the prime minister has few powers compared to the president. The president can also appoint a prime minister from a different party, as did Emmanuel Macron in 2017 when he appointed conservative Édouard Philippe to the job. Occasionally, an opposition party or coalition dominates Parliament, and the president is obliged to appoint an opposition prime minister. This has happened three times in France, most recently when the conservative Jacques Chirac was obliged to appoint the socialist Lionel Jospin as prime minister in 1997, in an arrangement known as **cohabitation**. (Although the term *cohabitation* is rarely used in connection with presidential systems such as the United States, it often happens, when a president from one party is faced with a legislature dominated by another.)

Cohabitation
An arrangement in which a president from one party is obliged – because of party numbers in the legislature – to appoint and work with a prime minister from another party.

The president also has the following powers:

◆ To sign bills into law after they have been adopted by Parliament. Presidents have no power of veto, their disapproval being limited to returning a bill to Parliament for reconsideration. If passed again, the president has no choice but to sign the proposal into law.
◆ To dissolve Parliament (after consultation with the prime minister) and call new elections within 20–40 days. This can be done any time that the president considers it expedient (although at least a year has to pass between each set of elections), but the power is more often used as a bargaining tool than actually implemented. Since the president does not usually have to stand for re-election at the same time (unless their term is up), this can be a significant political power.
◆ To appoint the members of the Council of Ministers (the cabinet) on the recommendation of the prime minister, to preside over weekly meetings of the Council, and – on the recommendation of the prime minister – to appoint and remove its members.
◆ To declare a national emergency should the president see serious and immediate threats to 'the institutions of the Republic, the independence of the Nation, the integrity of its territory or the fulfilment of its international commitments'. Following the November 2015 terrorist attacks in Paris, for example, an emergency was declared, ending – after two extensions – in November 2017.
◆ To call a national referendum on issues that do not involve changes to the constitution, allowing the president to bypass Parliament and take an issue directly to the people. This has only happened once, when de Gaulle was able to change the means of electing the president in 1962.
◆ To wield important symbolic powers as the guide of France, helped by the ability of the president to claim to be the only person in government with a national mandate. There is much pomp and circumstance surrounding the office, based in the sumptuous Elysée Palace in Paris, which stands in contrast to the relatively modest official residences of the British prime minister and the German chancellor.

There is no vice president in France. If the office of the president becomes vacant, or if the president becomes incapacitated, the position is filled temporarily by the president of the Senate, and an election for a new president must be held within 35 days. Presidents can also be removed by Parliament through impeachment for 'a breach of his duties incompatible with his continuing in office', which is initiated by one of the chambers of Parliament and needs a two-thirds majority in favour in order to succeed. In this case, the same rules apply for a replacement.

The presidency is defined not just by the terms of the constitution but also by expectations about the governing style of the officeholder, which is key to distinguishing among the different holders of the office (see Cole, 2017). The contrasting styles of Nicolas Sarkozy and François Hollande provide a good example. Following 12 years of Jacques Chirac and his efforts to project a popular style as president of all of France, Sarkozy opted for a more overtly 'presidential' approach, winning office on the assumption that a change of style would also involve a change of policy (Cole et al., 2013). His personal life soon came under scrutiny, however: there were accusations that his tastes were too expensive, headlines were made by his 2007 divorce from his second wife and his marriage to the French-Italian supermodel Carla Bruni, and suspicions of nepotism surrounded his efforts to arrange political office for one of his sons. His style was widely considered inappropriate or unsuitable to the office, and fed into the election victory in 2012 of the more 'normal' François Hollande, a result described by Cole et al. (2013) as something of 'an anti-Sarkozy referendum'.

Hollande, though, also had a colourful private life: his long-standing partner Ségolène Royal lost the 2007 presidential election to Nicolas Sarkozy, and a month later she and Hollande ended their relationship after the latter's affair with a journalist named Valérie Trierweiler. No president, however, has yet outdone François Mitterrand, who not only successfully concealed that he suffered from prostate cancer throughout his presidency (he died from it eight months after leaving office), but also had a 32-year extramarital affair with a woman 27 years his junior. The two had a daughter whose existence was only made public when she attended Mitterrand's funeral, along with the former president's wife, two sons, and lover.

If the president is both head of state and head of government, the prime minister occupies an often ambiguous position between the presidency and Parliament, with many of the less colourful qualities of a manager and administrator. Prime ministers are appointed by the president, usually but not always from within the membership of the National Assembly, and have the following key functions:

◆ To act as a link between the president and the National Assembly.
◆ To engage in the finer detail of policymaking (allowing the president to take a broader view).

Table 7.1 Modern presidents and prime ministers of France

Beginning of term	President	Ideology	Prime Minister	Party
1959	Charles de Gaulle	Conservative	1959 Michel Debré 1962 Georges Pompidou	Conservative Conservative
1965	Charles de Gaulle	Conservative	1968 Maurice Couve de Murville	Conservative
1969	Georges Pompidou*	Conservative	1969 Jacques Chaban-Delmas 1972 Pierre Messmer	Conservative Conservative
1974	Valéry Giscard d'Estaing	Centre-right	1974 Jacques Chirac 1976 Raymond Barre	Conservative Independent
1981	François Mitterrand	Socialist	1981 Pierre Mauroy 1984 Laurent Fabius 1986 Jacques Chirac	Socialist Socialist Conservative†
1988	François Mitterrand	Socialist	1988 Michel Rocard 1991 Édith Cresson 1992 Pierre Bérégovoy 1993 Édouard Balladur	Socialist Socialist Socialist Conservative†
1995	Jacques Chirac	Conservative	1995 Alain Juppé 1997 Lionel Jospin	Conservative Socialist†
2002	Jacques Chirac	Conservative	2002 Jean-Pierre Raffarin 2005 Dominique de Villepin	Conservative Conservative
2007	Nicolas Sarkozy	Centre-right	2007 François Fillon	Centre-right
2012	François Hollande	Socialist	2012 Jean-Marc Ayrault 2014 Manuel Valls 2016 Bernard Cazeneuve	Socialist Socialist Socialist
2017	Emmanuel Macron	Centre	2017 Édouard Philippe	Centre-left

* *Died in office.*

† *Periods of cohabitation.*

◆ To focus on domestic policy while the president drives foreign and defence policy (a reflection of de Gaulle's interest in foreign policy matters, and his obsession with strengthening the French role in international affairs).

◆ To help promote the president's legislative programme (and to absorb the fallout from unpopular policies).

◆ To help promote the political standing of the president.

Although presidents clearly hold most of the political cards, there is much that they can do only with the support of a prime minister; according to the constitution, the power to 'determine and conduct the policy of the nation' lies with 'the Government' (defined as the prime minister and the Council of Ministers), and the prime minister 'shall direct the operation of the Government'. It is notable that while presidents have the power to appoint the prime minister (depending on party support in the National Assembly), the constitution is unclear about whether or not they can dismiss the prime minister. It was rumoured that de Gaulle required his prime ministers to give him a signed but undated letter of resignation at the start of their term of office. Otherwise, loss of parliamentary support is usually enough to give the president cause to ask a prime minister to resign. Failing that, a prime minister can be forced out through the loss of a vote of confidence in the National Assembly, although this has only happened once during the Fifth Republic, in 1962 (see section on National Assembly).

Prime ministers have the thankless tasks of supporting a presidential programme with which they might not entirely agree, and of ensuring that the president wins all the credit for successful policies while being used by the president as a scapegoat for unsuccessful or unpopular policies. Prime ministers must also do their job while being careful not to appear to be too independent or ambitious, or more popular than the president, and the latter will be watching for efforts by a prime minister to use the office as a springboard for a presidential bid; both Georges Pompidou and Jacques Chirac served terms as prime minister before being elected president.

In contrast to the relative stability of the office of president, there has been considerable turnover in the office of prime minister, driven mainly by the changing political calculations of presidents. Between 1958 and 2018, there were eight presidents but 22 different prime ministers serving a total of more than 40 terms. Bernard Cazeneuve spent the shortest time in office (just over five months in 2016–17), Georges Pompidou the longest (six years and two months), and only one woman – Édith Cresson, in 1991–92 – has ever held the office.

The legislature: Parliament

The French Parliament is bicameral, consisting of a relatively weak Senate and a stronger National Assembly. Both chambers can introduce new bills, and both – along with the government – have the power of amendment. Overall, though, the powers of Parliament have declined under the Fifth Republic, a reflection of concerns about the instabilities it faced under the Fourth Republic. It is today one of the weakest legislatures in Europe, with a limited role in the shaping of legislation, thereby posing a greater risk of the president taking action that goes against public opinion.

Senate (Sénat)

This is the upper house of Parliament, designed to represent the interests of local units of government. It has almost the same powers as the lower National Assembly over the introduction, amendment, and adoption of new laws, but if the two chambers disagree, the National Assembly – where the majority of members are usually on the side of the government – has the final say. The Senate has 348 members, with 328 elected by an electoral college made up of elected representatives from France's 96 local government *départements*, 12 elected by the Assembly of French Citizens Abroad (a body that represents the interests of French citizens living outside France), and eight elected from French overseas territories. Senators served nine-year terms until 2004, when the term was reduced to six years. They are limited to a single term, with half the Senate stepping down every three years.

The Senate is something like the British House of Lords in the sense that it is an anachronism, tracing its origins back to Senates set up as mainly advisory bodies under the First and Second Empires, and to the Chamber of Peers that existed when the monarchy was re-established between 1814 and 1848. The manner by which it is elected gives it a small town and rural bias, which has meant a tilt in its membership towards parties of the right. Although this has occasionally generated protests from French socialists (at least until they won a majority in the Senate in 2011), the relatively strong role played by the National Assembly in making policy and law means that the work of the Senate draws less political and media attention.

National Assembly (Assemblée nationale)

Although it is the lower house of Parliament, the National Assembly – like many so-called lower houses – is the more significant of the two parliamentary chambers in France. Party numbers in the chamber determine the make-up of governments and their ability to pursue their policy programmes; the bigger and more stable the majority, the stronger the government. The National Assembly also draws much more media and public attention than the Senate.

The chamber has 577 deputies elected using a two-round system for five-year terms. Elections can be called early by the president (provided that at least 12 months have passed since the last election), but the reduction in 2000 of the term of the president from seven years to five has made early elections less likely; most recent terms have run their full five years. The last time an election was called early was in 1997, when President Jacques Chirac – suffering reduced approval ratings in the wake of troubled efforts to reform the welfare system – tried to catch the political opposition unprepared by calling an election a year early, and became the first French president since 1877 to lose an election he had called early.

The National Assembly has the power to remove the government either through a vote of censure tied to a specific bill or through a vote of confidence, but while both are often proposed, only one vote of confidence has been lost during the Fifth Republic. This happened in 1962 when de Gaulle bypassed the National Assembly in calling a referendum on changing the means by which the president was elected (replacing an electoral college with a direct vote). A National Assembly vote brought down the government, but de Gaulle won the referendum, called an election a year early, and his party was returned to power with an increased majority.

The judiciary: Constitutional Council

The constitution of the Fifth Republic is supported and protected by the work of the Constitutional Council, the highest constitutional authority in France, which alone has the power of judicial review. Since a 1971 decision, the court has been obliged to refer in its decisions not only to the constitution but also to the Declaration of the Rights of Man and Citizen, and to the preamble to the constitution of the Fourth Republic. Both the latter include rights that are still considered relevant to constitutional issues in France.

Although the Constitutional Council is the functional equivalent of the US Supreme Court, there are several key differences:

◆ Unlike the US Supreme Court, which rules on laws and the actions of government after they have happened (*a posteriori*), the Constitutional Council can either rule on laws after they have been voted on by Parliament but before they reach the president for signature (*a priori*), or can rule on existing laws based on a challenge from the president, the prime minister, or Parliament.

◆ There is no single hierarchy of courts in France as there is in the United States. A Council of State acts in an advisory role, reviewing draft government bills and decrees, while a Court of Cassation hears appeals on criminal and civil cases. This arrangement is a result of long-held resistance in France to the idea of a single supreme court with the power to overturn legislation, a throwback to the pre-revolutionary era when courts often blocked new laws and political reforms.

◆ In the United States, anyone with legal standing (the ability to show harm from a law or action of government) can take a case to the US Supreme Court. In France until 2010, only the president, senior members of Parliament, or a group of at least 60 Senators or deputies could take a case to the Court. Since then, individual citizens who are party to a law suit or trial have been able to ask the Court for a review of the constitutionality of the law applied to the case.

◆ The Council is responsible for overseeing elections in France, including making sure that they are conducted properly, checking to see that campaign spending limits are respected, ensuring the legitimacy of referendums, and issuing official results. The US Supreme Court would only become involved in election decisions if a case was submitted questioning the outcome (as happened with the 2000 US presidential election).

◆ Where the US Supreme Court has issued many rulings dealing with questions of civil liberties and civil rights, the French Constitutional Council has rarely done the same.

◆ The Constitutional Council is much less political than the US Supreme Court, where – despite claims to the contrary – appointments and decisions are often politically fraught.

The Council consists of nine members who serve non-renewable nine-year terms, with three members renewed every three years. Three each are appointed by the president of France and the presidents of the Senate and the National Assembly, and the president of the Council is appointed by the president of France. As many as three former presidents of France (known as *les sages*, or 'the wise') are also given lifetime membership of the Council, but few choose to take part in its work; as of mid-2018, only one of France's living former presidents – the 92-year old Valéry Giscard d'Estaing – was active in the work of the Council.

Sub-national government

Although the constitution emphasizes the decentralization of power in France, and there is a complex system of local governments, France is a unitary system in which the state plays a strong role. Although the meaning of the term *state* is debatable in the French context, it encapsulates not just the usual institutions and processes of government, but also the history and identity of France. While the state is strong, much of French identity – as we saw earlier in this chapter – is wrapped up in an often mythical ideal about life in the rural areas of France, where town and village life play an important role.

Recent rounds of reorganization dating back to 1982 have left France with three levels of sub-national government: 16 regions, 96 *départements*, and nearly 37,000 *communes* (municipalities). The network of *départements* was created by Napoleon early in the 19th century, and each is run by its own **prefect** and elected assembly. Prefects are representatives of the French state, appointed by the president on the recommendation of the prime minister and Minister of the Interior, and act as agents of *départements,* representing interests upwards as much as transmitting commands downwards. Communes, meanwhile, which vary in size from a few dozen people to several tens of thousands, are predominantly rural and are governed by elected mayors and councils based in the local city hall.

While France is a unitary state with a strong centralized government, the rural areas and small towns such as this one –
Rochefort-en-Terre in the western region of Brittany – still play a strong role in the definition of French national identity.
Source: iStock.com/RolfSt.

France's colonial past lives on (in a modest way) with the existence of its overseas territories, known as *départements-régions d'outre-mer*, or D-ROMs. These include Réunion in the Indian Ocean, Guadeloupe and Martinique in the Caribbean, French Guiana, and the approximately 150 islands of French Polynesia, including Tahiti. They collectively have a population of less than 3 million people (less than five per cent of the French population), but are politically integrated into France, have representatives in the Senate and the National Assembly, and are also considered to be part of the European Union.

POLITICAL PROCESSES

France has all the usual channels for political participation associated with democracies, including a regular schedule of elections, a wide range of political parties, and a varied community of interest groups and media. Unlike the relative stability of Britain, Germany, and the United States, however, and in spite of de Gaulle's best efforts, the party system in France is highly unstable. Two clusters – parties of the right and parties of the left – have usually dominated, but there have been regular changes within each cluster, and recent years have seen realignments with the rise of the right-wing National Rally and the remarkable victory in 2017 of *En Marche!*, a new centrist political party.

France has also been notable for the persistence of a revolutionary tradition (or, as Cole (2017) suggests, a revolutionary myth) that is still reflected in the willingness of mass movements to take to the streets in pursuit of their objectives. Demonstrations by students and trade unionists hastened the resignation of Charles de Gaulle in 1969, for example, and French farmers have developed a reputation for their capacity to protest changes in policy that they fear might undermine their incomes or livelihoods. For Bivar (2018), this reflects their hard–nosed business acumen and interests in the implications of global trade and mass production. French farmers have been known to block highways with slow-moving tractors, and to dump straw, vegetables, or manure on city streets to block traffic.

The electoral system

While most of its European neighbours use either proportional representation or mixed electoral systems, France has opted for majority elections for its major offices, with the prospect of two rounds. This is the same system used in Russia (see Chapter 12), as well as Austria, Finland, and Portugal, although it is much more rarely used for legislative elections than for executive elections. France is also unusual for choosing to hold presidential and legislative elections at a different time: except when the National Assembly is dissolved early, the presidential election is held in late April (with a second round in May), and the National Assembly elections are held in June. This means that voters do not make a single set of decisions on who to vote for, but focus first on the presidential election and then – knowing the result – decide their choice for the parliamentary election.

Presidential elections

France uses a two-round system for its presidential elections. Candidates must collect signatures from at least 500 elected officials in national or local government, from at least 40 different *départements*. Within the bigger parties, candidates are chosen through primaries, long restricted to members of each party, but replaced in some cases in recent years with open primaries in which all eligible French voters can take part. Elections are then held within 20–35 days of the end of the incumbent's term in office. All eligible candidates compete, and if anyone wins more than 50 per cent of votes cast, they are declared the winner. Otherwise, the election goes to a second round held two weeks later involving only the two highest-placed candidates from the first round. It is often said that the French vote with their heart in the first round and with their head in the second round.

All ten presidential elections held so far under the Fifth Republic have gone to a second round, the margins of the winners in the first round having shrunk in recent elections. Where once the winner of the first round might have attracted as much as 44 per cent of the vote, a growth in the number of candidates has meant that several recent elections have produced first-round winners with barely a fifth of the vote. Twice, in 1981 and 1995, the second-placed candidate in the first round went on to win the second round and the presidency; there are no guarantees, then, that a strong showing in the first round will carry over. For its part, the 2017 election was remarkable for the absence of a clear winner in the first round, which produced four candidates who won almost equal shares of the vote – see Table 7.2.

Legislative elections

For most of the life of the Fourth Republic, France used proportional representation for elections to the National Assembly. This was part of the reason why so many political parties won seats, leading to the instability of governments. With the Fifth Republic, France opted for the same two-round majority system as used in presidential elections: all districts have a single representative, with any candidate winning more than 50 per cent of the vote in the first round being declared the winner. This rarely happens; only four deputies won in the first round in 2017,

Table 7.2 Results of the 2017 French presidential election

Candidate	Party	First round		Second round	
		Number of votes (millions)	Percentage share	Number of votes (millions)	Percentage share
Emmanuel Macron	*En Marche!*	8.66	24.0	20.74	66.1
Marine Le Pen	National Front	7.68	21.3	10.64	33.9
François Fillon	Republicans	7.21	20.0		
Jean-Luc Mélenchon	*La France Insoumise*	7.06	19.6		
Benoît Hamon	Socialist	2.29	6.4		
Nicolas Dupont-Aignan	*Debout La France*	1.69	4.7		
Five others		1.47	4.0		

for example, and the remaining 573 seats went to a second round. In the absence of a winner, all candidates earning at least 12.5 per cent of the vote in the first round run off in a second round held a week later, with the top-placed candidate winning, whether or not they have a majority.

Although anyone crossing the 12.5 per cent bar has the right to run in the second round, what often happens is that the major parties reach agreements in advance with their ideological cousins not to run against each other and split the vote. One of the effects of two rounds is that many voters will find themselves having to choose in the second round among parties other than their own, obliging them to think more carefully about the remaining options. The two-round system has given France a level of political stability that was missing under the Fourth Republic, and a controversial return to proportional representation in 1985 did not last long, being used just once – in 1986 – before a return to the two-round system in 1988.

European and local elections

Executive and legislative elections attract most of the public and scholarly attention in France, as they do in most countries, for the simple reason that they determine who will control government (or, in authoritarian systems, will ensure the continued control of the ruling elite). Such elections are often described as **first-order elections** because of the stakes involved. There are other sets of elections as well, often described as **second-order elections** because the stakes are lower. In the cases of Germany and France, second-order elections include those to the European Parliament (held on a fixed five-year schedule, using proportional representation with – in France – the whole country treated as a single 74-member district) and a variety of local elections (regional, departmental, and municipal) held on different schedules. Local elections should not be overlooked, though: not only is local government important in France (see Comparing Politics 7), but local elections – like European elections – offer a useful indicator of the state of the different national parties between national elections. Since turnout at both European and local elections is lower than at national elections, though, care has to be taken with the way the results are interpreted.

> **First- and second-order elections**
> Elections ranked according to the stakes in the results, with first-order elections shaping national governments, while local elections are often considered second-order.

COMPARING POLITICS 7
The role of local government

The American politician Tip O'Neill (Speaker of the US House of Representatives in 1977–87) once famously quipped that 'all politics is local', implying that the success of politicians at every level is closely tied to their ability to meet the demands of local voters. With states as the standard unit of analysis, comparative politics ventures relatively rarely into government and politics at the sub-national level. This is unfortunate, because while developments at the national level – including election results, the changing fortunes of parties, and the evolution of public policy – obviously tell us a great deal about the character of government and politics, voters are most immediately impacted by the work of local politics and politicians.

As we have seen, local factors play a key role in French government. Identity is closely associated with local communities, local units of government are represented nationally through the Senate, prefects and mayors play an important role in politics, and there have been growing pressures for more local autonomy. For Cole and Pasquier (2013), the growing power of local and regional authorities in public policy is 'one of the most striking features of the erosion of the … myth of the unity and indivisibility' of the republic in France. We can look at the fortunes of political parties and election results at the national level, but they will often tell a different story from developments at the local level, where parties will often have clearly defined blocks of support and a long history of political success.

The importance of local government in France is all the more surprising given that it is a unitary system. Less surprising is the importance of local government in federal systems such as Germany, the United States, India, Mexico, Nigeria, and Russia. Except in the case of the latter, where – as we will see in Chapter 12 – local units of government are heavily controlled by the federal government in Moscow, the states and provinces into which each of these countries is divided are often smaller versions of the federal government, with their own constitutions, executives, legislatures, and – notably in Germany and India – their own political parties.

Political parties

The party system in France is complex and changeable, a reflection of the manner in which French political parties often exist less to offer alternative policy platforms than to act as a foundation for their presidential candidates. One of de Gaulle's goals in drafting the constitution of the Fifth Republic was to encourage parties to work together, thereby addressing the instabilities of the Third and Fourth Republics that had stemmed in large part from the large number of parties that had won seats in the National Assembly. The Fifth Republic has proved to be a success in the sense that parties have had to form pacts and to occasionally merge with one another in order to win power. However, the party system has been volatile, and is summarized by Gougou and Labouret (2013) as follows:

◆ Until 1981, a 'bipolar quadrille' with the socialists and communists on one side and the conservatives and centre-right on the other.
◆ After 1981, consolidation of their respective positions by the socialists and the conservatives, with the rise of the far right.
◆ After 2007, a collapse of the old order with the rightward shift of conservatives and the opening of new space in the centre of the political spectrum.

Fuelled by these changes, by disagreements over France's place in the European Union, and by declining trust in government, a political earthquake took place in the political centre in 2016–17 with the rapid rise and remarkable victory of Emmanuel Macron and his centrist *En Marche!* coalition in presidential and legislative elections. Its successes broke with the pattern of alternating power between socialists and conservatives, but whether this will prove to be a temporary or a permanent change remains to be seen.

Parties of the left

On the furthest left of the political spectrum, the Communist Party (*Parti communiste français*, or PCF) has long been active, although it has become steadily more marginal; it has never been able to repeat its peak performance of a 28 per cent share of the vote in the November 1948 parliamentary election. In a similar vein to Italian communists, it put forward a philosophy known as Eurocommunism, designed to promote communist ideas within Western European liberal democracy. It then joined a Union of the Left with the socialists in 1972, by which the two parties undertook not to split the vote by running against each other in parliamentary districts, a plan that worked mainly to the benefit of the socialists. The communists steadily lost support, and their percentage share of the vote in the first round of National Assembly elections has recently fallen to single digits, although it continues to be influential in a few local governments. In the 2017 elections, it won barely one per cent of the vote, less even than the new left-wing populist *La France Insoumise* (France Unbowed) created in 2016.

The major political party on the left is the Socialist Party (*Parti socialiste*, or PS). Founded in 1905, it spent the early decades of the Fifth Republic in the political wilderness while government was dominated by leaders and parties from the right and the centre-right. François Mitterrand took charge of the party in 1958, and spent the next 23 years building its ranks and moderating its positions. He first pulled together three smaller socialist parties into a single and bigger grouping, and then formed the Union of the Left with the communists. After two failed attempts to win the presidency, he finally prevailed in May 1981. A month later, the socialists stormed home in legislative elections, becoming only the second party to win an absolute majority in the National Assembly since the French Revolution. Mitterrand portrayed himself as the most moderate and viable choice for the left in France, working to decentralize government to the regions while extending government control over the economy.

Although Mitterrand won a second term in 1988, the party had clearly peaked, and its support began to wane, even if it remained strong in some areas, such as all major cities and rural south-west France. It won back the presidency under François Hollande in 2012, but this was at least as much a function of the unpopularity of President Nicolas Sarkozy as of the popularity of the socialists (Sawicki, 2013). In two of the last four presidential elections, its candidate failed to qualify for the second round, and it had its worst result ever in 2017: just 6.4 per cent of the vote in the presidential election, and just 31 seats in the National Assembly elections.

Parties of the centre

The political centre in France has seen at least as much change as the right and the left, with two parties having the strongest records. The first of these was the Union for French Democracy (UDF), a centre-right party founded in 1978 as a coalition of smaller parties designed to provide a platform for the re-election of President Valéry Giscard d'Estaing in 1981. It failed when Giscard was beaten by François Mitterrand, but it had a strong presence in the

Emmanuel Macron greets supporters during the 2017 French presidential election campaign. Macron shook up the party landscape as the head of his new party *En Marche!*, but the novelty he offered soon wore off amid criticisms of his imperious style and unpopular economic reform policies.
Source: Thierry Chesnot/Getty Images News.

National Assembly until the mid-1990s. Just as the communists and socialists had formed their Union of the Left and agreed not to split votes, so the conservative Rally for the Republic and the UDF copied this formula by forming a Union for France, which won a large majority in the 1993 elections. The party subsequently fell victim to factionalism, and by 2007 had split into two smaller parties.

The political centre was dramatically revived in 2016 with the foundation of *La République en Marche!* (loosely translated as 'The Republic on the move!', but usually shortened to *En Marche!*, which can be translated as 'Forward!' or 'Onward!'). This was created by Emmanuel Macron, a 38-year-old economics minister in the government of François Hollande who was making plans to run for the presidency in 2017. With a pro-business, pro-European Union platform, Macron won an impressive 24 per cent of the vote in the first round of the presidential election, and an even more impressive 66 per cent in the second round. This victory was followed a month later when *En Marche!* won 308 seats in the National Assembly, clearly giving Macron – the youngest president in French history – a mandate for change. As with so many political candidates who have promised change, though, and particularly those who come to office without much political experience, Macron found his promises hard to keep, and his standing in opinion polls fell quickly.

Parties of the right

The political right in France has undergone similar changes to those on the left, if not always for the same reasons. Its initial foundations lay with the philosophy of **Gaullism**, based on Charles de Gaulle's ideas about a new role for France in the world (related to patriotism, republicanism, and exceptionalism) and his skills in holding the right together, but it has been challenged by inroads from the left, and more recently from the far right and the political centre.

The right came out of World War II discredited by charges that many of its supporters had collaborated with the Nazis. In an effort to revive its base, de Gaulle founded the Rally of the French People (RPF) in 1947, which went into decline when he retired, and then – following his re-entry into politics as president in 1958 – was

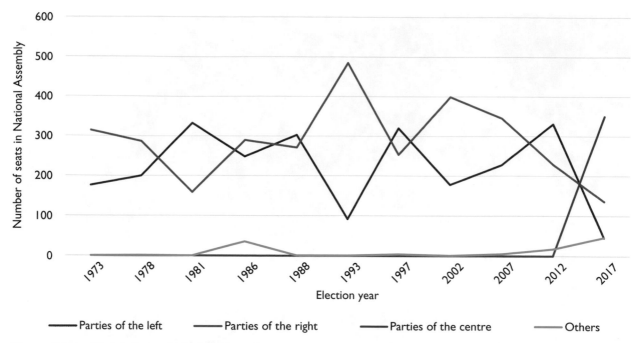

Figure 7.2 Legislative electoral trends in France

revived as the Union for the Defence of the Republic (UDR). This won majorities in several National Assembly elections and was the foundation for George Pompidou's presidential victory in 1969. The party was socially conservative and pro-business, supporting a strong French military and the idea of European integration with France at its core.

By 1974, the party was all but comatose, but then came under the leadership of Jacques Chirac, who changed its name in 1976 to Rally for the Republic (RPR). Still identified as Gaullist, it was difficult to situate precisely on the political spectrum, and just as the PS became a vehicle for the political aspirations of Mitterrand, so the RPR became one for Chirac, who was elected mayor of Paris in 1977. After being defeated twice by Mitterrand (for whom he briefly served as prime minister), Chirac finally won the presidency in 1995 and again in 2002, portraying himself as the younger and more dynamic alternative to his opponents while also being the modern embodiment of Gaullism.

In 2002, following Chirac's success in the presidential election, the Union for a Popular Movement (UMP) was formed as a successor to the RPR, designed to pull together parties of the right and to fend off the rising challenge of the National Front (Haegel, 2013). Despite its newness, it went on to win an absolute majority in that year's National Assembly elections. Its candidate Nicolas Sarkozy won the presidency in 2007, and the party retained its National Assembly majority. Under Sarkozy, the party took strong positions on law and order and tried to impose stronger controls on immigration, but was also criticized for what some saw as too many concessions to the National Front (see below). In 2012, Sarkozy became only the second incumbent president to lose re-election (the other being Giscard in 1981), and the UMP saw a significant drop in its share of seats in the National Assembly.

In 2015, there was another change of name as the UMP became The Republicans, a controversial decision given that many would argue that almost everyone in France is a republican, and thus the term should be above party politics. The change did little for the political right, however, because – in 2017 – François Fillon became the first presidential candidate for the party of the right during the Fifth Republic to fail to survive to the second round in the presidential election. Its ill fortunes continued a month later when it won just 82 seats in the National Assembly elections, a far cry from the heady days when its predecessors won more than 350 seats.

The politics of the right became more complicated during the 1980s with the rise of the National Front (FN), a populist/nationalist right-wing party whose support grew from less than one per cent in the 1974 presidential election to nearly 17 per cent in 2002, when its long-time leader Jean-Marie Le Pen edged out the socialist candidate Lionel Jospin to make it through to the second round (where he was comprehensively defeated by Jacques Chirac). A veteran of the Indochina and Algerian wars, and an admirer of Vichy leader Marshal Pétain, Le Pen's policies were anti-immigrant and openly racist, among his assertions being that the Nazi gas chambers during World War II were 'an historical detail' and that France was in danger of becoming an Islamic republic. The FN benefitted from attracting much of the protest vote that had previously gone to the communists, and continued to do well in local elections. Its new leader – Le Pen's daughter Marine – survived to the second round of the 2017 presidential election, in which she won more than a third of the vote. However, the party has never fared well in National Assembly elections. In 2018, it changed its name to the National Rally.

THE FUTURE OF FRENCH GOVERNMENT AND POLITICS

The government and politics of France has little of the stability and predictability that might normally be expected from a liberal democracy, and least of all from a state with such a long history. While most of its European neighbours have a political system and a body of political parties that date back many decades, France continues to see much change in the way it governs itself, a tradition that dates back more than 200 years.

The constitution of the Fifth Republic was intended to provide the executive with greater powers and to reduce the multi-party confusion that often reigned in the National Assembly, but while it resulted in important steps in that direction, the rules continue to change. As recently as 2000, a critical redirection was taken when the term of the president was reduced from seven years to five years, to be followed eight years later by the imposition of a two-term limit on the presidency. Meanwhile, the once predictable party system – dominated by conservatives on the right and socialists on the left – has been shaken up with emergence of an entirely new centrist party that swept elections for the presidency and the National Assembly, the collapse of the socialists, and the fracturing of the political right with the rise of the National Rally. Along the way, France's efforts to maintain its principles of exceptionalism, republicanism, and secularism have proved challenging.

Where this leaves France is unclear, particularly given how little trust most French citizens have in their government. France should have a strong sense of national identity, and the French should be proud of a culture with deep roots and a strong sense of itself, and yet many in France seem to remain uncertain about what it means to be French and how to define their preferred system of government.

DISCUSSION QUESTIONS

1. Compare and contrast the role of national identity in understanding politics and government in the different cases used in this book.
2. Can France's ideas about republicanism continue to survive in an increasingly diverse and globalized world?
3. Have the adjustments made to the structure of the French political system improved the efficiency and responsiveness of that system, or should yet more changes be made?
4. In what kind of political, economic, and social circumstances is the semi-presidential system likely to work best?
5. Should the president of France be given clear powers to dismiss and replace the prime minister, if needed?
6. Does the changeability of the French party system help or hinder efforts to achieve an efficient and responsive political system?

CHAPTER CONCEPTS

- Declaration of the Rights of Man and Citizen
- *Département*
- Fifth Republic
- First Republic
- Fourth Republic
- French Revolution
- Gaullism

- National Assembly
- Parliament
- Prefect
- Republicanism
- Second Republic
- Senate
- Third Republic
- Vichy France

KEY TERMS

- Cohabitation
- First-order elections
- Natural rights

- Second-order elections
- Semi-presidential system

FRANCE ONLINE

President of France: www.elysee.fr ★
Government of France: www.gouvernement.fr/en/composition-of-the-government
National Assembly: www2.assemblee-nationale.fr/langues/welcome-to-the-english-website-of-the-french-national-assembly
La Republique en Marche! https://en-marche.fr ★
Socialist Party: www.parti-socialiste.fr ★
The Republicans: www.republicains.fr ★
National Rally: www.rassemblementnational.fr ★
Le Monde: www.lemonde.fr ★
Le Figaro: www.lefigaro.fr ★
Libération: www.liberation.fr ★
France 24: www.france24.com/en

★ *French only*

FURTHER READING

Cole, Alistair (2017) *French Politics and Society*, 3rd edn (Routledge). A survey of the French political system, with chapters on history, political culture, institutions, parties, and society.

Cole, Alistair, Sophie Meunier, and Vincent Tiberj (eds) (2013) *Developments in French Politics 5* (Red Globe Press). An edited collection on the state of French politics and government in the years leading up to the Hollande presidency.

Elgie, Robert (2011) *Semi-Presidentialism: Sub-types and Democratic Performance* (Oxford University Press). An assessment of the semi-presidential model, outlining its key features and variations.

Elgie, Robert, Emiliano Grossman, and Amy G. Mazur (eds) (2016) *The Oxford Handbook of French Politics* (Oxford University Press). An edited collection of studies of different facets of French politics, including governance, institutions, processes, civil society, and public policy.

Evans, Jocelyn, and Gilles Ivaldi (2018) *The 2017 French Presidential Elections: A Political Reformation?* (Palgrave Macmillan). An analysis of the outcome and significance of the 2017 elections in France.

Sowerwine, Charles (2018) *France since 1870: Culture, Politics and Society*, 3rd edn (Red Globe Press). A history of France from the beginning of the Third Republic to the Macron presidency.

Visit **www.macmillanihe.com/McCormick-Cases** to access additional materials to support teaching and learning.

INDIA

8

PREVIEW

India's value as a case lies in its status as the world's largest and most diverse democracy. Independent only since 1947, it has adapted the British parliamentary model to an environment with enormous cultural, social, and religious variety, with mixed results. After many years in which politics was dominated by a single political party – and a single political family – recent decades have seen more splintering of an already complex system of national and regional political parties, and the rise of a new wave of Hindu nationalism. India is an emerging global power with nuclear weapons, and is on the brink of overtaking China as the largest country in the world by population, and yet its economy remains notably staid, while poverty is widespread. The potential for growth is compromised by extensive state intervention, endemic corruption, an inefficient bureaucracy, and numerous social divisions that have sparked repeated communal strife.

KEY ARGUMENTS

◆ India is an emerging global power, and yet it continues to face numerous political, economic, and social challenges.

◆ Long dominated by the Congress party and by the Nehru-Gandhi dynasty, India has seen a recent shift towards the Hindu nationalist policies pursued by the Bharatiya Janata Party.

◆ Corruption has been a persistent problem in Indian politics, bringing down several governments and undermining the work of the bureaucracy.

◆ India's model of democracy is marred by fragile multi-party government coalitions, troubling social divisions, and occasional political violence.

◆ The once dominating role of the prime minister may be on the decline as political parties (of which there are many) become the new centres of power.

◆ More than is true of most other countries, regional political parties play a key role in Indian politics, at both the regional and the national levels.

OVERVIEW

India is a land of dramatic contrasts. It has one of the world's oldest cultures, yet it has been an independent state only since 1947. It is the world's largest democracy, yet it has so many social divisions that it seems constantly to hover on the brink of disintegration. It is poor (with a per capita GDP of just under $2,000 and many of its people living in abject poverty) and crowded (with more than 1.3 billion people living in an area one-third the size of the United States), and yet it is a nuclear power with a bigger consumer market than that of any European country. It has a large and growing middle class, it not only feeds itself but is a net food exporter, and economic liberalization has led to accelerating industrial growth. Like China, India has the potential to become one of the economic superpowers of the 21st century.

In political terms, India rightly describes itself as the world's largest democracy (by population). It has a written constitution that is generally respected, has had multiple free elections and more than a dozen prime ministers since 1947, and has several national political parties as well as many more regional and local parties. Party competition is keen, voter turnout is high, and there is an extensive free media. Unfortunately, it perhaps has too *much* democracy: the number of political parties has prevented any one from winning a clear majority in recent years, which has undermined India's prospects for the kind of stable and consistent leadership that it needs in order to ensure sustained growth. Its problems have caused it to be ranked in the Democracy Index as a flawed democracy.

In economic terms, India has one of the world's biggest and fastest growing economies, but it has suffered from many years of unmet potential, and the benefits of its economic development have failed to reach down to the poorest of its citizens. India's economy is about the same size as those of Britain and France, whose populations are one-twentieth the size. The root problems are the large role still played by the state in the economy, and the challenge of dealing with India's rapid population growth: it is projected to overtake China in 2022 to become the world's largest country. Recent governments have increased the pace of liberalization, but there is a broad consensus that India has only recently begun to achieve its economic potential.

In social terms, India is home to almost every division known to humanity. There is a notable urban–rural divide, with most Indians still living in villages and rural areas, while India also has some of the biggest and most crowded cities in the world, such as Mumbai (formerly Bombay), Kolkata (formerly Calcutta), Delhi, Chennai (formerly Madras), and Bangalore. There is dramatic cultural and linguistic diversity, with three racial strains (Aryan, Dravidian, and proto-Australoid), 16 major languages (English and Hindi are the two official national languages), 30 additional languages, each with 1 million speakers or more, and many different scripts. Disputes over state and religious boundaries have been common since independence, leading to secessionist movements and insurrections.

India also has remarkable religious diversity: more than 80 per cent of its people are Hindu, but they live alongside a large Muslim community (11 per cent of the population) and a vocal Sikh minority (two per cent). Religious conflict regularly leads to communal violence and spills over into politics, most notably with the rise of support for the Hindu nationalist Bharatiya Janata Party. India is also divided by a complex caste system that has failed to go away despite modernization and economic development. We are studying it here as a case in comparative politics, but it is so large and diverse that it offers many possibilities for comparisons within its own borders.

POLITICAL DEVELOPMENT

India has been an independent state only since 1947, but its culture is one of the oldest, most complex, and most sophisticated on Earth, with a history that dates back more than 5,000 years. Unlike many other former colonies, where pre-colonial political values were largely subsumed to those of the new imperial power, many of the links between the traditional and the modern can still be found in Indian politics today.

The Hindu heritage

Before the arrival of Europeans, the Indian subcontinent was made up of numerous principalities, kingdoms, and empires. A civilization that paralleled that of Egypt in importance emerged in the Indus River Valley between 4000 and 2500 BCE. Beginning in about 1500 BCE, waves of nomadic Indo-Aryans began arriving in the northern and central plains from the Caucasus, pushing the native Dravidians further south. The fusion of Aryan and Dravidian culture played a role in providing the foundations for **Hinduism**, now the world's third largest religion after Christianity and Islam.

A second religious and social influence came in the 5th century BCE with the teachings of Siddhartha Gautama (c. 563–483 BCE), better known as Buddha. By about 250 BCE, what is now India was mainly Buddhist, but Hindu priests argued that Buddhism was subservient to – and part of – Hindu belief. A third influence was introduced in about 1000 CE, when Muslims invaded the area. By the early 16th century, most of the northern half of India was under the control of the Mughals, a dynasty created by descendants of Genghis Khan (see Fisher, 2016). Through all of this upheaval, India remained a village society, divided into competing kingdoms and principalities but with central authority barely affecting the life of the average villager.

By the beginning of the 18th century, Mughal power in India had all but disintegrated, undermined by internal rebellion and creating a power vacuum into which Europeans moved relatively easily. Attracted by the prospects of trade, Britain, Portugal, France, and Holland competed for influence in the region, but it was the British who emerged as the dominant power; from their base in Bengal in the east, they eventually moved into most of what are now India, Pakistan, Bangladesh, Sri Lanka, and Burma. In some cases they used direct control, and in others they allowed existing leaders to keep power. By setting rulers and religious groups against one another and establishing military dominance, Britain had brought the entire subcontinent under its direct or indirect control by the early 1850s.

The British heritage (18th century to 1947)

The creation of the **British Raj** (*raj* is Hindi for *reign*) was achieved with a remarkably small number of people: at no time in the 19th century were there more than 65,000 British troops or 500 administrators in India, and less than 60 per cent of India came under direct British control (see Judd, 2005). Until 1857, India was not even directly ruled by the British government but was administered (and in a sense 'owned') by the 1,700 shareholders of the East India Company, founded in 1600. India was united for the first time and social reforms were made, leading to the abolition of traditions such as *suttee* (the burning of widows on the funeral pyres of their husbands). Western education, science, and technology were introduced; English was introduced as the lingua franca; a railroad and communications network was developed; and investments were made in industry and agriculture.

British imperialism, though, was not universally welcomed. In 1857 came the Indian Mutiny, when Indian soldiers (or sepoys) – who were already concerned about the spread of Christian influence – rebelled as rumours spread that the cartridges issued for their new rifles were greased with a mixture of cow fat (which offended Hindus) and pig fat (which offended Muslims). Although Britain now took over direct administration of India from the East India Company and Queen Victoria was declared empress of India in 1877, the cracks in the edifice of the Raj had begun to show. The emerging Indian middle class was unwilling to accept foreign domination, and in 1885 the Indian National Congress (INC, known more usually as **Congress**) was founded to campaign for greater self-determination. Initially moderate, it became more militant as Britain rejected its demands for equality. When nearly 380 people were killed and 1,200 wounded while defying a ban on public meetings in the city of Amritsar in April 1919, the INC – inspired by its leader **Mahatma Gandhi** – began campaigning for independence.

Gandhi opted for a strategy of non-violent civil disobedience, or non-cooperation that he described as *satyagraha* (roughly translated as 'soul force' or 'truth force'). This cut to the heart of the British administrative system, which was based on ruling India mainly through Indians themselves. Through resistance, non-cooperation, hunger strikes, and other symbolic acts for which he was repeatedly imprisoned, Gandhi drew attention to the injustices of British rule and focused the attention of a mass movement on achieving independence. Gandhi also advocated social change among Indians themselves, but found himself having to walk a careful line between campaigning for independence and trying to encourage Hindus and Muslims to live together.

A large measure of self-government was introduced in 1935, and elections were held and a new constitution published in 1937, but it was too late, and the independence movement intensified in 1942 when the 'Quit India' campaign was launched by Gandhi. Calls for full independence were complicated by divisions between Hindus and Muslims. Gandhi hoped for a united, independent India, but Muslims were doubtful about living in a Hindu-dominated state. Britain was now faced with two conflicting demands: the Muslim League, led by Muhammed Ali Jinnah (1876–1948), wanted India partitioned into Hindu and Muslim states and then given independence, while Gandhi wanted India to be given independence and to be allowed to settle the religious problem itself.

Against a background of mounting violence, Britain opted for partition, and in August 1947 the separate states of India and Pakistan became independent (Khan, 2017). Partition gave rise to one of the biggest human migrations in history, with Muslims moving to Pakistan and Hindus to India; more than 12 million people migrated (as many as 1 million dying in the process), but 20 million Hindus remained in Pakistan and 40 million Muslims in India, which still has the third-biggest Muslim population in the world (after Indonesia and Pakistan). In January 1948, Gandhi was assassinated by a Hindu nationalist angry at his efforts to accommodate India's Muslims.

TIMELINE

1526	Foundation of the Mughal Empire
1600	Establishment of the British East India Company
1858	Britain assumes direct control over India from the East India Company
1885	Foundation of Indian National Congress
1947	Independence and partition of India and Pakistan
1948	Mahatma Gandhi assassinated
1950	New constitution comes into force; India becomes a republic
1971	Pakistan civil war, India–Pakistan war, creation of Bangladesh
1974	India explodes underground nuclear device
1984	Indira Gandhi assassinated
1991	Rajiv Gandhi assassinated
1996	Bharatiya Janata Party (BJP) emerges as single largest party after elections
1998	BJP-led coalition forms government; India and Pakistan carry out multiple nuclear tests
2000	Indian population reaches one billion
2002	More than 1,000 people killed in Hindu–Muslim violence
2004	Congress returns to power in coalition government
2007	Launch of India's first commercial space rocket, carrying Italian satellite
2008	Nearly 170 people killed in terrorist attacks in Mumbai
2014	BJP wins general election; Narendra Modi becomes prime minister

The emergence of independent India (1947–90s)

India entered independence torn by religious strife and facing the challenge of forging a nation out of many hundreds of princely states (semi-sovereign principalities that had been only indirectly ruled by the British). A new constitution was written, and with its adoption in 1950 the last ties with the British crown were cut and India became a republic. The princes were made to give up their political powers, the old British provinces were abolished, and a federal system was introduced.

The administration of Prime Minister Jawaharlal Nehru followed a moderately socialist economic line, with a limited land reform programme and a series of five-year plans that emphasized the growth of heavy industry. A new agricultural initiative was also launched, which eventually made India self-sufficient in food. These achievements, though, were offset by India's population growth, its religious and social divisions, and conflicts with its neighbours, including Pakistan, China, and Sri Lanka. The province of **Kashmir** has been a particular source of tensions between India and Pakistan, leading them to war with each other in 1947 and 1965. The significance of the dispute has escalated with the development by both countries of nuclear weapons programmes; India carried out its first underground tests in 1974, and Pakistan in 1998.

India's government was dominated for more than 40 years by Congress, which has itself long been dominated by the **Nehru-Gandhi family dynasty**: Jawaharlal Nehru was prime minister for nearly 17 years (1947–64), and his daughter Indira Gandhi (no relation to the Mahatma) was the major figure in national politics for the next 20 years (nearly ten of which she spent as prime minister, often pushing the powers of the office to new extremes). She was grooming her son Sanjay to replace her, but when he was killed in a 1980 plane crash, she recruited her son Rajiv to replace her. Following her 1984 assassination by her Sikh bodyguards (in the wake of her attempts to put down an insurrection by Sikh extremists), Rajiv took over as prime minister. With his assassination in May 1991 by a sympathizer of Sri Lanka's Tamil Tiger guerrilla movement, the influence of the family briefly declined, but Congress eventually recruited as its leader Rajiv's Italian-born widow, Sonia. She turned down the opportunity to become prime minister in 2004, and her son Rahul led the party to its worst-ever election defeat in 2014.

Hindu nationalism on the rise (1990s–present)

The most notable recent developments in Indian politics have been the rise of the right-leaning Hindu nationalist **Bharatiya Janata Party** (BJP) – founded in 1980 – and the fragmentation of the party system. Where the INC (usually just known as Congress) was once dominant and there were several smaller parties in opposition, party politics has since evolved into a competition between the BJP and its allies, Congress and its allies, and a medley of smaller regional and ideological parties. The BJP first came to power in 1996 under its leader Atal Behari Vajpayee in 1996, but he lasted only a matter of days in office, and did not return to sustained power until 1998. By then, the BJP had moderated its policy positions, the talk of militant Hindu nationalism that had circulated in the early 1990s having all but disappeared.

This is not to say that India did not take an assertive role in foreign policy, however – an invasion of Kashmir in May 1999 by Pakistani and Afghan irregulars led to a two-month conflict, with a death toll estimated to be in the thousands. Added to the tensions between India and Pakistan caused by Kashmir were worries over the development of nuclear weapons by both countries. When India carried out five nuclear tests in May 1998, Pakistan responded with six, and both countries were heavily criticized by world leaders.

India's political divisions have been emphasized by the convoluted structure of recent governments. The BJP-led Vajpayee government (1998–2004) was a multi-party coalition whose work was routinely interrupted by internal squabbles, a problem exploited by the opposition Congress Party, which returned to power in 2004 at the head of a 12-party alliance, with former finance minister Manmohan Singh as prime minister. Much was expected of the new government, but it proved cautious, and critics charged that it failed to produce the economic changes needed to help India catch up with a rapidly growing China.

Congress and Singh were returned to a second term in 2009 with an increased majority, but – on a wave of public anger at corruption and weak economic growth – the BJP won the 2014 elections, becoming the first party to win a majority in the Indian Parliament since 1984. Narendra Modi became prime minister, and while setting out to expand India's global presence, to increase foreign investment, to increase spending on infrastructure, and to improve bureaucratic efficiency, also drew controversy for his association with right-wing politics and the concept of **Hindutva**. While this originally meant 'Hinduness' and the following of Hinduism, it has come to be seen by its critics as a means of establishing the hegemony of Hindus and the Hindu way of life (see discussion in Sharma, 2011). It also disadvantages women and the one-fifth of Indians who are not Hindu.

India today

In recent decades, India has experienced changes in domestic political realities and economic policies, as well as the pressures and opportunities of globalization. However, while there is no question about India's achievements, it continues to face many problems:

◆ Religious, class, and social inequalities persist, making it more difficult to encourage Indians to work together on their country's political challenges.

◆ Corruption also persists, leaving India in 79th place out of 176 on the 2016 Corruption Perceptions Index. For Kumar (2011), it is a pervasive problem that undermines the social fabric and the political structure of India. The causes of corruption lie in a combination of excessive regulation, complicated tax and licensing systems, a bureaucracy with too many discretionary powers, and too little transparency in government activities.

◆ Despite recent economic growth and liberalization, the vast majority of Indians live a pre-modern lifestyle, many live in crushing poverty, and India – in spite of its economic growth and technological achievements – is still a poor country. Its per capita GDP of just under $2,000 places it on a par with Djibouti, Nicaragua, and Nigeria. In terms of human development, and the provision of education, health care, and other public services, India does barely better than neighbouring Bangladesh, long a global watchword for poverty; the two countries have similar rankings in the Human Development Index.

◆ Terrorism has long been a problem in India, stemming mainly from the activities of separatist groups, religious organizations, and left-wing politics. Thanks in part to its role as the financial, commercial, and entertainment capital of India, Mumbai has been a particular target: seven bomb blasts on trains in 2006, thought to have been linked to Pakistan-based Islamic extremism, took 209 lives, while attacks linked to Islamic extremism in 2008 took another 164 lives.

Addressing such problems is complicated by the deep divisions in Indian government and politics: at the 2014 elections, 38 political parties – many of them active only at the local rather than the national level – won seats in the lower chamber of the Indian Parliament. While the BJP won a slight majority, its philosophy of Hindu nationalism remains controversial and divisive.

POLITICAL CULTURE

Political culture is easiest to define when a political system has settled features and values. Even after more than 70 years of independence, however, politics in India remains unpredictable. Not only do social divisions continue to threaten the viability of the state, but the party system has seen constant change, a modern urban society coexists with a traditional village society, and the competing roles of secularism and Hinduism in politics remain unresolved. Despite these uncertainties, there are several distinct facets to Indian political culture.

The most prominent has been the emergence of a dominant state, which has come to affect every sphere of Indian life and has promoted a new but divided pan-Indian middle class. One of the consequences has been a tendency towards homogenization and away from recognizing the variety of Indian society. This has led to a political system based increasingly around popularity contests and elections that have become quasi-presidential in character. Nowhere was personality more obviously on show than in the role played for several decades by the Nehru–Gandhi dynasty, whose persistence suggested that personality was more important than ideology or administrative ability. At the same time, the dominance of the state has not been enough to prevent social, economic, and religious fragmentation.

India is also notable for being a village society. All societies have their traditional elements, which have varying degrees of influence on politics. Despite the power of the modern Indian state and central government, most Indians still live a simple village life that is largely bypassed by national politics, except during elections, when candidates fleetingly become interested in the village vote. Television, satellite dishes, cell phones, and the internet may have reached many villages, but life for the average villager still extends no more than a few miles from their home. The **caste** system also has a strong hold, limiting opportunities for villagers, and traditional local community values still play an important role in Indian politics; see Comparing Political Culture 8.

Caste
A system of social and economic divisions that pervades Indian society and politics.

India is one of the most dynamic and fastest-growing countries in the world, yet most of its people still live a simple village life often bypassed by urban politics and the influences of globalization. Here social workers meet with women and children in a village to help improve their standard of living.
Source: iStock.com/AnantAgarwal.

COMPARING POLITICAL CULTURE 8
Politics and class

Class divisions are a key part of understanding political divisions in many countries. They were, for example, the spark that led to the creation of many of the earliest mass political parties in Europe: working class socialist parties played an important role in education and political socialization, overseeing activities designed to tie their members closer to their party. Even though most have since evolved into catch-all parties that work to draw support from as many quarters as possible, social class remains an important part of understanding and assessing political values and preferences.

In India, political and social divisions are tied most closely to caste, an idea related to class but which has worked its way more deeply into India's social structure. A complex Hindu hierarchy, caste was originally based on family and occupation and went on to encourage social segregation, with the behaviour of castes restricted and controlled, no intermarriage allowed across castes, and different jobs carried out by particular castes. The more than 3,000 castes and sub castes can be generally aggregated into four broad types or *varna*: the Brahmins (priests), Kshatriyas (warriors), and Vaisyas (merchants) (collectively the 'forward castes'), and the Sudras (menial labourers).

Just how much caste matters is disputed. On the one hand, Jodkha (2018) suggests that it is more 'active and agile' today than ever before. On the other hand, Corbridge et al. (2013) argue that caste differences have weakened as they have intersected with other social divisions, such as those based on wealth and gender. One notable part of the debate about caste is the place of India's 150 million **Dalits** (formerly called untouchables), who were once regarded as almost subhuman and who performed service jobs such as laundry, scavenging, sewage disposal, and removal of the dead. The status of 'untouchable' was formally abolished with the 1950 constitution, and a controversial affirmative action policy reserved jobs, scholarships, government positions, and even seats in Parliament for historically disadvantaged peoples (known formally as Scheduled Castes and Scheduled Tribes). Recent suggestions that the number of reserved positions be increased led to large-scale rioting by the so-called forward castes and remains a bone of contention, which in turn sharpens caste identities.

Although the idea of class is often defined differently, and might be seen as the antithesis of the kind of social equalizing that should be part of the growth of democracy, it continues to be part of political conversations in many different environments. In Britain, for example, the government's Office for National Statistics still recognizes several different occupation-related categories, ranging from higher professional and managerial to 'semi-routine occupations', while many people continue to classify each other based on a combination of occupation, education, and social background. In the United States, meanwhile, politicians often bemoan threats to the American middle class, a term which is rarely defined and can sometimes seem to apply to almost everyone.

Adding further complications to Indian politics has been the physical violence growing out of political, social, and religious division. Violence against women has been a particular problem, as exemplified by a string of recent and horrifying gang rapes. These have long been a problem for poorer women, but drew wider attention only with the fatal rape of a medical student in Delhi in 2012 (Drèze and Sen, 2013). More pervasive and intrusive, however, is the more generalized problem of **structural violence**. Examples include the oppression of women (a form of structural violence perpetrated by male-dominated political systems), and the kind of extreme poverty perpetrated by one part of society on another. In its Indian context, structural violence refers to the invisible effects of poverty, inequality, and caste oppression, which have a psychological impact on the way Indians relate to their political system.

Structural violence
The intangible forms of oppression built into social and political systems.

As urban India has modernized and as the middle-class consumer society has grown, so have the expectations and frustrations of Indians (especially urban Indians). India may be a nuclear power and an aspiring space power (it has launched numerous satellites, many of them on its own Polar Satellite Launch Vehicle), but gaps have grown between aspiration and achievement, and the government has been unable to keep up with the demands of new groups entering politics. In particular, the middle classes have become impatient with India's poverty and with what they see as the limits placed on social change by the traditional sector.

Name	Republic of India (Bhāratīya Ganarājya)
Capital	New Delhi
Administration	Federal republic consisting of 29 states, with seven union territories governed directly from New Delhi.
Constitution	State formed 1947, and most recent constitution adopted 1950.
Executive	Parliamentary. The prime minister selects and leads the Council of Ministers (cabinet). The president, elected for a five-year term by an electoral college, is head of state, and formally asks a party leader to form the government.
Legislature	Bicameral Parliament: upper Rajya Sabha (Council of States) with most of its 250 members elected for fixed six-year terms by state legislatures, and lower Lok Sabha (House of the People) with 545 members elected for renewable five-year terms.
Judiciary	Independent Supreme Court consisting of 31 judges appointed by the president following consultation with the courts. Judges must retire at age 65.
Electoral system	Elections to the Lok Sabha are by single-member plurality. The Election Commission of India, established by the constitution, oversees national and state elections.
Party system	Multi-party, with a recent tradition of coalitions. The two major parties are the Bharatiya Janata Party and the once-dominant Congress Party. Regional parties are also important.

1,339m Population

$2,600 billion Gross Domestic Product

$1,940 Per capita GDP

✗ Full Democracy
✓ Flawed Democracy
✗ Hybrid Regime
✗ Authoritarian
✗ Not Rated

Democracy Index rating

✓ Free
✗ Partly Free
✗ Not Free
✗ Not Rated

Freedom House rating

✗ Very High
✗ High
✓ Medium
✗ Low
✗ Not Rated

Human Development Index rating

POLITICAL SYSTEM

Formally, India is a federal republic with a parliamentary system of government. It is also a democracy, if democracy is measured by the existence of free political parties, competitive elections, different forms of participation and representation, the stability and continuity of political institutions, and the protection of individual rights and freedoms. But the Indian form of democracy is flawed, undermined by several problems that have long stood in the way of equality and transparency:

◆ There may be regular elections, but they are often accompanied by unrest and fraud, and in some cases have been suspended because of violence.
◆ Indian prime ministers once had more potentially dictatorial powers than their liberal democratic counterparts, although this has changed as leaders have had to rely on fragile multi-party coalitions as the base of their support.
◆ India may be federal in theory, but in practice the central government wields so much power over the states that state governments have little real independence. Again, though, this has been changing with the rise of regional political parties.
◆ The rights of individuals may be constitutionally protected, but many minorities still rail against the authority of central government and the caste system.

For now, India is best seen as an emerging democracy in the sense that it is still working to develop the political and economic form best suited to the needs of its people. It has the potential to become a stable, influential, and wealthy state, but many handicaps must first be removed.

The constitution

The constitution of India is one of the longest in the world, with 395 articles, 8 schedules, and more than 100 amendments. The wording occasionally sounds like parts of the US Declaration of Independence, but the principles come out of the British system of government. The constitution was drawn up by a Constituent Assembly indirectly elected in 1946 by India's provincial assemblies. The Assembly became the provisional government following independence and oversaw the drafting of the constitution in 1948–50. Among its priorities were the following: to establish a democratic, sovereign, and independent republic; to ensure the unity of India; to offset the potential for violence and disorder; and to establish economic independence and self-sufficiency (Thiruvengadam, 2017). Despite the discussions that followed, the dominance of the Assembly by the Congress Party meant that a handful of Congress leaders – including Jawarhalal Nehru – set the course for the debate and influenced the final form of the constitution, which went into effect on 26 January 1950.

One of the more controversial elements of the constitution was the power it gave to the president (on the advice of the prime minister) to suspend or abrogate freedoms during a 'grave emergency', that is, when the security of India or its territory were threatened by 'external aggression or internal disturbance'. Emergencies were declared in 1962 and 1971 during conflicts with China and Pakistan, but emergency powers were given their loosest interpretation by Prime Minister Indira Gandhi in June 1975, when she 'advised' the president to declare an emergency in response to an alleged threat to internal security from her political opposition. After she lost the 1977 election, the constitution was quickly changed so that emergency powers could be declared only in the event of external aggression or armed rebellion.

Head of state: the president

India's decision to keep the parliamentary system of government after independence was unusual; almost all other former European colonies (except Australia, Canada, and New Zealand) opted for a presidential system with American undertones. Some Indians have since called for the creation of a semi-presidential system along French or Russian lines, but the parliamentary system persists and includes a president with similar (mainly symbolic) powers as those of the German president.

The president of India is elected for a renewable five-year term by an electoral college made up of members of both houses of Parliament and of the state legislatures. A vice president is also elected in the same way, and several have gone on to become president. Given the long dominance of the Congress Party in Indian politics, presidents were often the handpicked choices of the party, and had similar qualities and backgrounds. President K. R. Narayanan, elected in 1997, was notable for being the first Dalit to become president. He was succeeded by A. J. P. Abdul Kalam, a retired scientist who was architect of India's missile programme (for which he earned the nickname

Table 8.1 Presidents and vice presidents of India

Start of term	President	Vice president
1950	Rajendra Prasad	–
1952	Rajendra Prasad	Sarvapalli Radhakrishnan
1957	Rajendra Prasad	Sarvapalli Radhakrishnan
1962	Sarvapalli Radhakrishnan	Zakir Hussain
1967	Zakir Hussain*	V. V. Giri
1969	V. V. Giri	G. S. Pathak
1974	Fakhruddin Ali Ahmed*	B. D. Jatti
1977	Neelam Sanjiva Reddy	Mohammed Hidayatullah (from 1979)
1982	Gaini Zail Singh	Ramaswamy Venkataraman (from 1987)
1987	Ramaswamy Venkataraman	Shankar Dayal Sharma
1992	Shankar Dayal Sharma	K. R. Narayanan
1997	K. R. Narayanan	Krishan Kant
2002	A. P. J. Abdul Kalam	Bhairon Singh Sekhawat
2007	Pratibha Devisingh Patil	Mohammad Hamid Ansari
2012	Pranab Mukherjee	Mohammad Hamid Ansari
2017	Ram Nath Kovind	Venkaiah Naidu

* Died in office.

'Missile Man'), and was India's third Muslim president. Pratibha Patil, elected in 2007, was notable for being the first woman ever to hold the position, while Ram Nath Kovind came to office in 2017 as India's first president from the BJP.

The president technically 'appoints' the prime minister and members of the Council of Ministers, although – like the British monarch and the Japanese emperor – all he or she really does is confirm as prime minister the leader of the largest party or coalition. The president also has several other constitutional powers, but these are exercised on the advice of the Council of Ministers, which is dominated by the prime minister. These powers include the ability to dissolve Parliament, declare a state of emergency, declare an emergency in a state and rule that state by decree, veto parliamentary bills, and promulgate ordinances that have the same power and effect as acts of Parliament. The president is also the commander-in-chief and appoints state governors and Supreme Court justices. The vice president takes over temporarily if the president dies, resigns, or cannot carry out the duties of office, and (paralleling the job of the US vice president in the US Senate) is *ex officio* chairman of the Rajya Sabha (the upper house of Parliament).

Despite having to make almost all their decisions on the advice of the prime minister, presidents have several times had to step in to arbitrate following indecisive elections. For example, after the collapse of the Janata government in 1979, President Sanjiva Reddy asked Charan Singh (leader of a Janata splinter party) to be prime minister, but Singh was unable to form a workable government and resigned. Reddy then asked Singh to oversee a caretaker government, which held power until the January 1980 elections returned Indira Gandhi to power. Similarly, President Shankar Dayal Sharma had to step in several times during 1996–97 to identify the politicians in the best position to form a government during the confusion that followed the 1996 national elections, and in 2004, President Abdul Kalam was involved in the naming of Manmohan Singh as prime minister, after Congress leader Sonia Gandhi had turned down the job.

The executive: prime minister and Council of Ministers

In theory, Indian prime ministers – like their counterparts in other parliamentary systems – are the leaders of the majority party or coalition in Parliament. However, the reality has never been quite that simple, because the fluidity of party politics has meant that – in the interests of building a stable coalition – parties may bypass the party leader and look elsewhere. For example, Deve Gowda, who was appointed prime minister in May 1996, was not the leader of any of the parties in the governing coalition but was chief minister of the southern state of Karnataka. He was recruited by other chief ministers who wanted someone sympathetic to the cause of local government. Meanwhile, Prime Minister Manmohan Singh was never elected to Parliament – he was instead an appointed member of the upper house of Parliament.

Prime ministers appoint and oversee the Council of Ministers (although the appointments are technically made by the president on the recommendation of the prime minister). Like the British and Japanese cabinets, this council consists of the heads and deputy heads of government departments. Ministers must either be members of Parliament (either house) or within six months of their appointment must become members by nomination or by winning a by-election. Unlike the British cabinet, which has about two dozen members, the council is too big (about 45 members) to work effectively as a body and never meets collectively. A tradition has instead evolved of convening a smaller cabinet of the 15 to 20 most important government ministers, which meets weekly, takes collective responsibility, and generally works more like the British cabinet.

Table 8.2 Prime ministers of India

Start of term	Name	Party or coalition
September 1947 May 1952* March 1957* January 1962*	Jawaharlal Nehru[†]	Congress
June 1964	Lal Bahadur Shastri[†]	Congress
January 1966 March 1967* March 1971*	Indira Gandhi	Congress and Congress (R)
March 1977*	Morarji Desai	Janata Front
July 1979	Charan Singh	Janata (S)
January 1980*	Indira Gandhi[†]	Congress (I)
October 1984 December 1984*	Rajiv Gandhi	Congress (I)
December 1989*	V. P. Singh	Janata Dal-led coalition
November 1990	Chandra Shekar	Janata Dal (S)
June 1991*	P. V. Narasimha Rao	Congress (I)
May 1996*	Atal Behari Vajpayee	BJP-led coalition
May 1996	Deve Gowda	United Front coalition
April 1997	Inder Kumar Gujral	United Front coalition
March 1998* October 1999*	Atal Behari Vajpayee	BJP-led coalition
May 2004* May 2009*	Manmohan Singh	Congress-led coalition
May 2014 May 2019	Narendra Modi	BJP-led coalition

* *General elections*
† *Died in office*

Note: R, S, and I denote factions of their respective parties; see later section on political parties.

COMPARING GOVERNMENT 8
Political families

There has been much worried debate in several countries in recent years about the emergence of a **political class** of politicians who spend sometimes long years in office, removed from the daily realities of the constituents they represent. While they can bring expertise and commitment to their jobs, they can also pose a threat to representative democracy, particularly when they have different backgrounds and interests from those of the general population (see Allen, 2018). The rise of political classes has been one of the explanations behind the rising unpopularity of government in several countries, including the United States, Britain, France, and Italy.

> **Political class**
> A group of professional politicians with similar backgrounds, interests, and values.

Another level of political exclusivity is offered by political families, with multiple members winning office and sometimes taking on the features of dynasties. In the United States, for example, several members of the Kennedy and Bush families have won office, while – as we saw in Chapter 6 – multiple recent political leaders in Japan have come out of a family tradition in government. India may not necessarily have a tradition of political families, but it instead has a single family – the Nehru-Gandhis – that has played a central role in Indian politics since independence, giving new prominence to the role of personality politics.

This has worried many Indians, for several reasons:

◆ Personal leadership is fragile, as emphasized by the assassinations of Indira and Rajiv Gandhi, the traumatic effects of which showed just how far India had come to depend on individuals rather than institutions.

◆ Leaders who come to power through inheritance need to show little in the way of character or past performance, which means that they may not be battle hardened by the time they come to power. Rajiv Gandhi, for example, had no plans to enter politics until the death of his younger brother Sanjay in 1980. In just four years, Rajiv was transformed from a commercial airline pilot into a prime minister.

◆ Dynasties can tend toward authoritarianism, as exemplified by the performance of Indira Gandhi, with her 1975 declaration of an emergency designed to offset her political opposition, and her efforts to manipulate the Indian Supreme Court.

Although no Gandhi has been prime minister of India since 1989, the Italian-born and Catholic Sonia Gandhi (Rajiv's widow) led Congress into the 1999, 2004, and 2009 general elections, and had the option of becoming prime minister in 2004, while her son Rahul led Congress into both the 2014 and 2019 general elections.

Recent events suggest that the power of the office of the prime minister may be on the wane and that parties have instead become the new centres of power. Much of the early power of the office had been tied to the personalities of the Nehru-Gandhi dynasty; see Comparing Government 8. When Narasimha Rao became the first non-member of the family to hold office for a full term (1991–96), he not only made popular policy decisions but also reduced the influence of personality. However, 27 parties won seats in Parliament after the 1996 elections, the traditional power of Congress was gone (although the party remained a key power broker), and power was dissipated as India was ruled by a series of multi–party coalitions. Deals were vigorously pursued behind the scenes, bringing three prime ministers to office in the space of a year, including one (Atal Behari Vajpayee, leader of the BJP) who was in office for just 12 days, while his two successors held office for 10 months and 11 months, respectively. Since 1998 there has been more consistency in the office, but the two major parties – the BJP and Congress – have had to rely on the support of party coalitions.

The legislature: Parliament

As in Britain, the prime minister and the cabinet in India are collectively responsible to Parliament and must keep its confidence to stay in power. When Congress was dominant, Parliament took a subsidiary role in the relationship between executive and legislature, with members of Parliament tying their political careers to the fortunes of the prime minister. On several occasions, however, the support of Members of Parliament (MPs) has been critical to the continued power of the government. This has become clear in recent years as governments have been based on coalitions of multiple parties.

Parliament consists of two chambers, which have the same powers over legislation but are elected differently.

Council of States (*Rajya Sabha*)

The **Rajya Sabha** is the upper house, indirectly elected to represent the states and territories of India. It has 245 members, of which 12 are appointed by the president to represent the professions, the sciences, and the arts. The remaining 233 members are elected for non-renewable six-year terms by the members of the state legislatures. The number of members from each state is decided on the basis of population, with the nine smallest states and territories having one member each and the largest (Uttar Pradesh) having 31. Unlike the lower house, the Rajya Sabha has fixed terms, so it cannot be dissolved by the president. Like the US Senate and the Japanese House of Councillors, elections are staggered, with one-third of its members retiring every two years. No less than 28 parties had seats in the chamber in 2018, helping to leave the governing BJP-led coalition government – with just 89 seats – far short of a majority.

House of the People (*Lok Sabha*)

Like many lower houses in bicameral legislatures, the **Lok Sabha** is the more powerful of the two chambers. It has 545 members, elected using the single-member plurality system for maximum five-year terms: 523 are elected by voters in the states, 20 are elected by voters in the union territories (see later in this chapter), and two seats are reserved for Anglo-Indians (people of mixed British and Indian descent), the holders being nominated by the president of India. Seats in the Lok Sabha are allocated among the states and territories on the basis of population, with each district roughly the same size in terms of population. Meanwhile, 131 seats are set aside for Scheduled Castes and Tribes.

A notable feature of Indian politics is the relative under-representation of citizens at the national level: where the average British MP represents 101,000 people and the average member of the US House represents 740,000 people, the average Indian MP comes from a district of more 2.4 million people; see Figure 8.1. For Indians to have

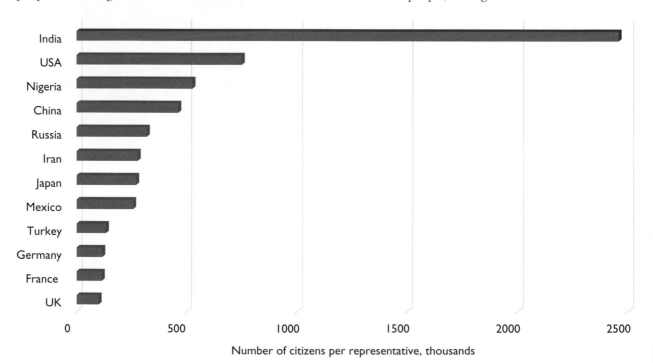

Figure 8.1 Comparing levels of political representation

Note: Based on lower or sole chamber of legislature.

the same level of per capita representation as Americans, the Lok Sabha would need nearly 1,800 members. Of course, quality and quantity are not the same, and in comparing countries, we need to allow for the differences between federal systems such as India, where citizens have representation in state as well as federal legislatures, and unitary systems such as Britain and Japan, where local legislatures – even if elected – have less legislative power than national legislatures. Even so, it is hard for one person to represent the interests of more than 2 million.

The Lok Sabha must meet at least twice per year, with no more than six months between sessions. Like the British House of Commons, it is essentially a debating chamber that provides support and opposition to the government. It has most of the trappings of the Westminster model, such as a neutral speaker elected from among the members of the house, parliamentary committees, and government question time, but – thanks to the forcefulness of many Indian prime ministers and to the high turnover among members after elections – it was for a long time less powerful in real terms than the House of Commons. With the advent of the multi-party coalitions since the 1990s, it has taken on a more significant role.

The judiciary: Supreme Court

India has a Supreme Court responsible for interpreting the constitution and arbitrating in the case of disputes between the states or between the Union (federal) government and the states. The Court originally had eight members, but the number has been steadily increased to deal with a growing workload, reaching its current total of 31 in 2008. Judges normally sit in benches of two to three members, or five members for more important cases. They are appointed by the president after consultation with members of the Court and the state courts, with steady turnover guaranteed by the requirement that members can hold office only until age 65. Normally, the most senior judge automatically becomes Chief Justice when the incumbent retires, although Indira Gandhi broke this precedent by promoting her own candidates over senior judges, leading to protests from the legal profession about political interference.

The Court has the power of judicial review (see Chapter 2), but the Indian constitution is so detailed that the Court has less latitude to interpret its meaning than its US counterpart. Just as the US Supreme Court spent its early years defining its powers in relation to Congress and the presidency (finally winning the power of judicial review with *Marbury* v. *Madison* in 1803), so the Indian court had a running battle for many years with Parliament, particularly over the issue of the fundamental rights of Indians contained in Articles 12–35 of the constitution. Several amendments have been passed redefining the relative powers of the Court and Parliament. The 24th Amendment, passed in 1971, gave Parliament the power to amend any part of the constitution, but the Court decision *Keshavananda Bharati* v. *State of Kerala* in 1973 declared that any amendments that attacked the 'basic structure' of the constitution would be invalid.

The Supreme Court played a critical role in uncovering and pursuing the scandal that proved to be one of the final straws that broke public support for Congress in 1996. In 1991, police discovered evidence that a business family, the Jains, had been bribing senior members of the government. When four citizens filed a public interest suit with the Supreme Court, its judges took the opportunity to order an investigation. It was finally revealed in January 1996 that 65 politicians and bureaucrats – including perhaps Prime Minister Narasimha Rao himself – had received more than $18 million in bribes.

Sub-national government

India is a federal republic, with the Union government at the centre and powers over many local issues devolved to the governments of the 29 states (with their own governments) and seven union territories (ruled directly by the Union government). However, it is a relatively centralized federal system, and the tensions arising from demands for greater decentralization have been a constant theme in Indian politics. Several of the states are big enough to be countries in their own right: in terms of population, Uttar Pradesh (200 million people) is nearly as big as Brazil, West Bengal (91 million) is bigger than Germany or Iran, and Rajasthan (68 million) is bigger than Britain or France. (A proposal to create a new state named Telangana out of portions of the existing state of Andhra Pradesh led to violent protests in 2008.)

The issue of who has the real power in the relationship between the centre and the states is debatable. In many respects, the balance lies with the Union government:

◆ It has control over defence policy, foreign affairs, and income tax.
◆ In a conflict between the Union and the states, Union law prevails.
◆ The Union government has the power to change the boundaries of states, create new states, and even abolish existing states.

◆ Most controversially (see Padmanabhan, 2016), the president of India, on the 'advice' of a state governor, can declare an emergency and transfer powers over the state to the Indian Parliament. An emergency can be declared if a state fails to comply with a law passed by Parliament, thereby effectively forcing that state to comply. Central control was exerted, for example, in 1983 in Punjab after several months of religious and political violence, and in 2018 in Kashmir after the BJP government ended its alliance with a local political party.

◆ The Union government has the power of the purse and can decide how to share national revenues out among the states.

Despite their relative weakness, though, the states cannot be ignored. The Union government relies on state governments to implement policy in several key areas, the performance of national parties at the state level affects the overall strength of those parties, opposition to national parties running in state elections can be turned into opposition at the national level, and recent coalitions at the national level have depended on key regional parties for their support.

Every state has a government that mirrors the structure of the Union government. Each has a figurehead governor appointed by the president of India for five-year terms. To discourage parochialism and encourage objectivity, the governor is usually from another state and is someone who is both politically neutral and acceptable to the state government. Governors appoint the chief ministers, although all they actually do is confirm the leader of the biggest party or coalition in the state assembly. Chief ministers are members of the state assembly, are directly elected in a state-wide vote, and govern with the help of a Council of Ministers. Most states have a unicameral Legislative Assembly (Vidhan Sabha), but five of the larger states also have an upper Legislative Council (Vidhan Parishad). The assemblies consist of anything between 60 and 500 members (depending on the size of the state) who serve five-year terms. For their part, union territories are governed directly by the Indian federal government, represented by lieutenant governors or administrators appointed by the president of India.

In the years after independence, the Union government had so many powers that India was once described (Wheare, 1951) as only 'quasi-federal'. By the 1960s some observers were denying that India was federal at all (Chanda, 1965), and others spoke instead of a kind of 'cooperative federalism'. There was more centralization during the era of Indira and Rajiv Gandhi, but the balance has changed back to the states in recent years with the rise of regional political parties, some of which have become big enough to be nationally important. Although there were only about 15 to 20 recognized state parties active until the early 1990s, that number has more than doubled in recent years.

The southern state of Tamil Nadu has been a particularly colourful hotbed of regional politics, with numerous parties, some of them promoting Tamil self-determination. The biggest are the Dravida Munnetra Kazhagam (DMK) and a splinter party, the AIADMK, led in its early years by a popular movie star named M. G. Ramachandran. After his death in 1987, the party split into factions, one led by his widow and the other by his former leading actress, Jayaram Jayalalithaa (1948–2016). The latter swept to victory in the 1991 state elections and Jayalalithaa became chief minister of Tamil Nadu. Her party also won 18 seats in the Lok Sabha, became part of the BJP-led government in 1998, then brought the government down by withdrawing its support in April 1999. The AIADMK has also become active in several other states, and after the 2014 elections had almost as many seats in the Lok Sabha as the much-diminished Congress Party.

Government is also important at the local level, its structure saying much about the nature of politics in India. During the debates over the writing of the constitution, some argued that India should be set up as a decentralized state based on village *panchayat* (councils of elders). Others argued that India had long colonial-era experience with representative parliamentary government and that the unity of India could be ensured only through a strong, centralized authority. The need to recognize India's cultural diversity and to keep the princely states happy led to the decision to create a federal system, while – below the states – there are three levels of *panchayat*: those based in individual villages (of which there are nearly 600,000), those bringing together clusters of villages, and those covering districts within India's states. Although their financial resources remain limited, *panchayats* are protected by the constitution and remain embedded in India's cultural attachment to the ideal of village self-governance.

POLITICAL PROCESSES

The claim that India is the world's biggest democracy is true enough if we go by numbers alone: nearly 825 million Indians were eligible to vote at the 2019 general election, or about as many people as the United States and the European Union combined. But while elections are generally free and fair, and India has a free press and a variety of interest groups, political corruption is a problem, with bribery, voter intimidation, and vote rigging all too common. Politics is also occasionally marred by violence: nearly 300 people died during the troubled 1991 elections, for example, and nearly 40 people were killed in fighting between rival political parties in West Bengal in May 2008, with some shot to death as they waited to vote, and others set on fire in their homes (*The Economist*, 2008). While recent elections have been more peaceful, occasional bomb explosions and clashes between supporters of competing parties are not unknown. At the heart of many incidents are Maoist rebels known as Naxalites, whose primary goal has been to bring attention to social injustice in India's rural areas (Corbridge et al., 2013).

Despite the challenges, national election results generally reflect the preferences of voters, whose political awareness makes them increasingly difficult to manipulate. Political activity and literacy is particularly high among the urban middle classes, and turnout at elections is generally high, even in rural districts.

The electoral system

Indian voters take part in two sets of elections, to the Lok Sabha and to state assemblies, each of which must be held at least once every five years. They were once held at the same time, but since 1971 it has been common to hold them separately. The voting age is 18, and voter turnout grew from nearly 47 per cent in 1952 to an average of about 60–65 per cent. By every measure, the scale of Indian elections is astonishing: at the 2019 general election (the largest election ever held in the world), more than 600 million voters turned out to vote at more than 1 million polling stations, choosing among more than 8,000 candidates. The election was so enormous that it was held in nine phases over a period of five weeks – a big improvement over the 1950s, when elections took four months to complete.

General elections

India uses a simple single-member plurality (SMP) system for elections to the lower house (the Lok Sabha). The country is divided up into 543 constituencies, each of which is contested by multiple candidates at the election. The sheer size

The sheer scale of election campaigns in India is reflected in this image of a 'mega rally' convened in Kolkata (formerly Calcutta) during the 2019 election season. Organized by the state government of West Bengal, it was open to all parties opposed to the ruling BJP government.
Source: NurPhoto/Getty Images.

of India, however, combined with its large variety of political parties, gives Indian elections the kind of scale not found in most other parliamentary systems: on average, 15 candidates compete in every district, and the spread of voter support means that winners often attract a small share of the overall vote, and have small winning margins. Adding more colour to the contests, many candidates run as independents, and many districts offer voters a 'none of the above' option (which occasionally attracts as much as two per cent of the vote, even in a crowded field of candidates). India is one of the few countries to offer this option, the others including Colombia, Greece, Spain, and Ukraine.

Each state in India is allotted seats in proportion to the size of its population, leaving Uttar Pradesh in the north with 80 and the eight smallest states with less than ten seats each. The union territories each have one MP, except for the National Capital Territory of Delhi, which has seven. As in all parliamentary systems using SMP, the holder of the office of the prime minister in India is determined by a combination of the balance of seats held by different parties, the leadership of those parties, and the coalitions they form among themselves. Elections are normally held every five years, but they can be called earlier if demanded by political circumstances; this has so far happened five times. The 2019 elections were the 17th held in India since independence.

The low level of literacy in rural India means that ballots must be printed with the name of the party and an easily recognizable symbol (see Figure 8.1). Election campaigns are short (three weeks), meaning that rural candidates must undertake a gruelling campaign, visiting several hundred villages in a single district, often travelling nearly impassable roads. Although most villages now have televisions and there is increased access to the internet, most candidates still try to reach people through leaflets, speeches, and personal influence. Appeals will often be made based on class, community, caste, faction loyalty, and charisma, but issues are not forgotten. Campaigns have been known to become 'waves' or landslides, such as the wave of sympathy that led to the election of Rajiv Gandhi in 1984 in the wake of his mother's assassination. The label *wave* should not be taken too literally, however, because no one party has ever won a majority of votes (even if some have won a majority of seats in the Lok Sabha).

Elections to the Rajya Sabha – in which the voters are not ordinary citizens, but the members of state legislatures – are held on a fixed cycle, with one-third of its 233 elected members retiring and being replaced every two years. Given that every state is on a different electoral cycle, however, there have been elections to the Rajya Sabha held somewhere in India every year since 1952. As with the Lok Sabha, the distribution of seats among India's states is based on population, with Uttar Pradesh having 31 seats and the nine smallest states each having one seat. As for the election process, the Rajya Sabha is one of the few political institutions in the world to use the single transferable vote (STV) system, which is neither easy to explain nor to understand.

It can be illustrated using the example of the southern state of Tamil Nadu, which – with its 18 members of the upper house – replaces 6 of them every two years. In order to determine the outcome of the election, a quotient must first be established to determine how many votes are needed to win a seat, using this formula:

Quota = Number of votes divided by (number of open seats + 1)

In the case of Tamil Nadu, its voters are the 235 members of its state legislature, so the formula works out as $235/(6+1) = 33$. This means that anyone running as a candidate needs at least 33 votes to succeed. Each party obviously knows how many members it has in the state legislature, which means that it knows how many members it can successfully elect to the Rajya Sabha based on the quota of 33, and hence those members effectively run unopposed. But if there are parties with fewer than 33 members in the state legislature, then a vote must be held for the remaining

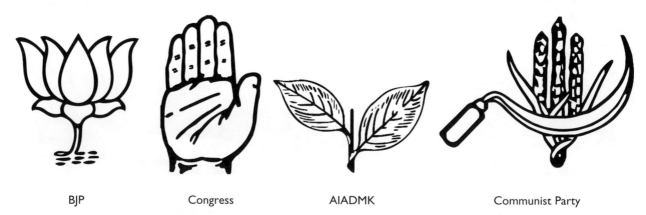

BJP   Congress   AIADMK   Communist Party

Figure 8.2 Examples of Indian political party symbols

open seats. Every member of the state legislature ranks the competing candidates by preference, and if – in the example of Tamil Nadu – any of them win at least 33 first-preference votes, they are declared elected. If there are candidates left over who have not achieved 33 votes, then the one with the lowest number of votes is eliminated, and his/her votes are transferred to the voter's next preferred candidate. The process is continued until every seat is filled.

STV has the benefit of ensuring approximately proportional representation for different parties, including assurance that smaller parties are not overlooked, and it also reduces the occurrence of 'wasted' votes (those cast for losing candidates). At the same time, though, it demands thought on the part of voters, because they need to rank candidates by preference, and it also takes time to calculate the results. Perhaps little wonder, then, that it is not widely used. Apart from India, which is unusual in combining it with indirect election, it is used for national legislatures only in Ireland and Malta, for upper house elections in Nepal and Pakistan, and for regional elections in Australia and New Zealand.

State and local elections

In addition to national elections, Indian voters also take part in regular state assembly elections. These are held at five-year intervals and contested by both national and regional parties. Given the strength of some of the bigger regional parties, and the role of state legislatures in electing the Rajya Sabha, the outcome of state elections often has important national implications.

Political parties

The Indian party system has developed extraordinary complexity. From a time when it was a relatively stable arrangement with Congress at its core, it has become more unstable and fragmented, with new parties coming and going, while national parties lose ground to an increasingly busy community of regional parties. The effects of the atomization of the party system are illustrated by comparing the results of two elections:

◆ In 1957, 13 parties won seats in the Lok Sabha, with Congress taking 371 (or 75 per cent of the total, even though it won only 48 per cent of the vote), the Communist Party coming a distant second with just 27 seats, and independents holding 41 seats.

◆ In 2014, 35 parties won seats in the Lok Sabha, with the BJP taking 282 (or 51 per cent of the total, even though it won only 31 per cent of the vote), and Congress coming a distant second with just 44 seats, while the 19 smallest parties each won between one and three seats, and three members sat as independents.

The number of parties has never been constant, nor does the number matter as much as the nature of the coalitions they form. Hence, the best way of trying to understand the Indian party system is not to look at each party in turn, but to follow the different phases in the relationship among the major national parties and the many competing smaller parties.

Congress dominant (1947–67)

The first phase of Indian party politics revolved around the Indian National Congress, which was the major force in the independence movement, and – until 1967 – routinely won four times as many votes as any other party. Like the Japanese Liberal Democrats, it consisted of several factions bound by a consensus, was flexible enough to absorb policies from other parties, and ran a political machine based on patronage and political favours. Virtually all significant Indian politics took place within Congress, which – thanks to the charisma and ability of Jawaharlal Nehru – had a cohesion and sense of direction that the weak and fragmented opposition lacked. The centralization of Congress had already begun to break down when Nehru suffered a stroke and died in 1964, by which time factional differences had emerged based on personality rather than ideology. The end of the unified Congress system was confirmed in the 1967 state and national elections, which left the party with a reduced majority in the Lok Sabha.

Congress divided (1967–77)

Newly installed as prime minister, Indira Gandhi moved to assert her control of Congress, which immediately split into two factions. To win a mandate for her wing, she called a general election in 1971, which resulted in a landslide for her newly named Congress (R) (for Requisitioned, and then for Ruling). State elections in 1972 resulted in another landslide for Congress (R), which now became all but Gandhi's personal fiefdom; she centralized decision-making power by making senior appointments on the basis of personal loyalty and by regularly reshuffling the cabinet to make sure no one could build a strong opposing base. She even renamed her party Congress (I) (for Indira).

As criticism of her autocratic methods grew, she 'advised' the president to declare a national emergency and went on nationwide radio to warn that 'a widespread conspiracy' had been growing against her and that the armed forces had been incited to mutiny and the police to rebel. Gandhi tried to paint herself as the saviour of Indian democracy and called a snap election in March 1977, but the opposition was able to quickly form a new coalition, the Janata Front, and campaigned on a manifesto that argued that voters were faced with a choice between 'freedom and slavery; between democracy and dictatorship'. Janata and its allies won a majority, Gandhi lost her own Lok Sabha seat, and Congress (I) was reduced to 154 seats. The result was, to many, vindication that Indian democracy was strong enough to withstand abuses of power.

The Janata Coalition (1977–80)

Despite its mandate, Janata rapidly fell apart, largely because of a lack of direction, personality clashes, and a series of unpopular policy decisions. Janata leaders also made the mistake of launching personal attacks on Gandhi and even occasionally placing her under house arrest, making her a martyr in the eyes of many. Gandhi rebuilt both her political reputation and her faction of Congress, and won re-election to the Lok Sabha. But she faced criminal prosecution on charges of misconduct and abuse of authority, and after refusing to testify before a parliamentary inquiry into the activities of an automobile company founded by her son Sanjay, she was held in contempt and jailed for a week. Before the government could prosecute Gandhi, the Janata government had fallen and new elections were held in January 1980. Gandhi portrayed herself as the only person capable of forming a strong government, campaigned tirelessly, and was returned with a strong majority. Party politics was still, it seemed, personality politics.

The Gandhis Return (1980–89)

Gandhi's moment of triumph was short-lived. Sanjay was killed in a plane crash in June 1980, so Indira persuaded her elder son, Rajiv, to enter politics. When Indira was assassinated in October 1984, Rajiv was drafted to replace his mother, automatically becoming prime minister. Two months later, seeking his own mandate, he called a new general election and was returned with a landslide. Rajiv Gandhi was young and charming, portrayed himself as spokesman for a new generation, and vowed to end corruption and prepare India for the 21st century. His lack of a political past helped him portray himself as a figure of renewal and change, and of stability and continuity, but he won the prime ministership partly because of sympathy over the assassination of his mother and partly because of the inability of the opposition to offer a credible alternative. Once in power, he became increasingly arrogant, centralizing power in his office and in the hands of a small group of advisors, and launching an anti-corruption campaign that upset many powerful business leaders. A united opposition was eventually able to grow around a new centrist National Front coalition created by former finance minister V. P. Singh. In November 1989, with Rajiv's five-year term up, new elections were held.

Congress in Opposition (1989–91)

India's ninth free election was significant in that – unlike all eight previous elections – the outcome was not a foregone conclusion. For the first time, Indian voters were offered a straight choice between two leaders who were truly being compared as alternatives: Rajiv Gandhi and V. P. Singh. There was no particular crisis, there were plenty of strong political issues, and Singh and his coalition partners ran a coordinated campaign against Congress, agreeing not to run against each other in most constituencies. The result was huge losses for Congress and the rise of the Hindu nationalist Bharatiya Janata Party (BJP), which increased its support from 1 per cent to 16 per cent. V. P. Singh formed a government with the help of the BJP and communist parties, but when his coalition fell apart after barely 11 months in office, Rajiv Gandhi was invited by India's president to form a new government. He instead opted to support the socialist Chandra Shekar, and India witnessed the peculiar sight of a government run by Shekar and his 54 MPs, backed by the 213 Congress MPs and their allies.

When Rajiv Gandhi withdrew his support in March 1991, Chandra Shekar's 117-day government fell, and a new election was called for May – the second in 18 months. On 21 May, while campaigning in the southern state of Tamil Nadu and apparently headed for victory, Rajiv Gandhi was killed when a suicide bomber blew herself up only feet away from him. Rajiv's Italian-born wife, Sonia, was asked to take over Congress and to run for prime minister but she refused, and Congress went into the remainder of the election with a new leader – the 70-year-old P. V. Narasimha Rao – and several contenders for the post of prime minister. When Congress won, Rao became prime minister at the head of a minority government, but the Lok Sabha remained divided among numerous political parties. Congress had the most seats, with 244 (45 per cent of the total), with the BJP a distant second, and 25 parties represented in all, 11 of them with just one seat each.

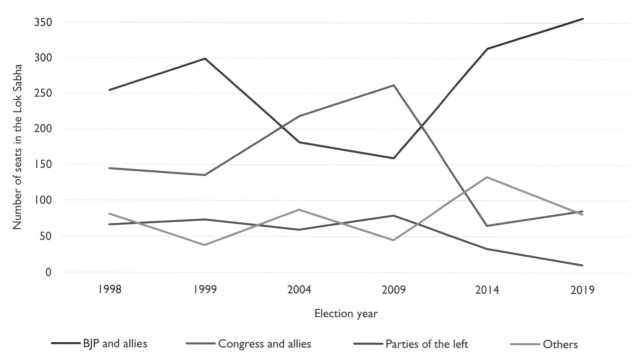

Figure 8.3 Legislative electoral trends in India

COMPARING POLITICS 8
Regional political parties

Most major political parties have a national base; they may have strengths in different parts of a given state, with some doing better in urban areas than rural areas (or vice versa), but they still ultimately deal with national issues, run on a national platform, and claim to represent the interests of a national electorate. At the same time, regional political parties should not be forgotten. They have played an increasingly critical role in Indian politics, dividing seats in the Lok Sabha to the extent that the BJP and Congress have often relied on them for control of the government. The Election Commission of India (2019) recognized 49 state parties in 2019 (along with seven national parties).

Regional parties often play a key role in other countries as well. As a political movement, regionalism has a variety of goals, including decentralization, a recalculation of the distribution of national resources, greater recognition for cultural minorities, greater autonomy, self-government, and even – in some cases – independence. Examples of regional political parties include the following:

◆ The Northern League in Italy, which wants a federal Italy and greater autonomy for the northern regions of the country.
◆ The Parti Québécois, which wants independence for Quebec from Canada.
◆ The Scottish National Party, which wants independence for Scotland from the United Kingdom.
◆ Several parties campaigning for the independence of Sardinia from Italy.
◆ Others – such as the Christian Social Union of Bavaria and political parties operating in Northern Ireland – that are not necessarily interested in autonomy or independence, but simply have strong local roots.

Regionalism can be beneficial in giving representation to the interests of minorities within a state, occasionally having the effect of bringing more people into politics and taking the head of steam off pressures for secession. But it can also be costly in the sense of encouraging voters and politicians to place narrow local interests above broader national interests. The case of India shows how it can lead to a splintering effect, where national government comes to rely on the support of multiple regional political parties.

Congress and the BJP take turns (1991–)

Following Rajiv's death, India (or Congress at least) seemed obsessed with identifying someone who could take up the Gandhi mantle. No one was found, however, and Narasimha Rao surprised many observers with his abilities as a political tactician and with his popularity, helped in large part by his economic liberalization policies. He quickly ran into problems, however, beginning in December 1992 with the destruction of a mosque in the city of Ayodhya, on the site of which Hindu extremists wanted to build a temple; some 2,000 Indians died in the ensuing violence. Rao moved too slowly to control the violence, defections weakened his coalition, and in 1996 news broke of yet another corruption scandal involving senior politicians and bureaucrats, including Rao himself and seven cabinet ministers.

In the May 1996 elections, Congress was routed, the Hindu-nationalist BJP increased its representation by one-third to become the biggest party in the Lok Sabha for the first time, and parties representing regional interests and the lower castes made notable gains. No one party won more than 30 per cent of the seats, however, leaving a leadership vacuum. A BJP-led government collapsed after just 12 days and was replaced by a left-leaning 13-party coalition that lasted just 10 months before collapsing. Its successor fell apart after 11 months, and the March 1998 election resulted in a new government headed again by the BJP and its leader, Atal Behari Vajpayee. Meanwhile, Sonia Gandhi had broken a long silence and taken over the leadership of Congress.

The Vajpayee government lost a vote of confidence in mid-1999, obliging it to call a new general election (the third in three years). The economic record of the Vajpayee government was poor, but it faced a divided opposition, it had a popular leader, and it profited from a wave of patriotic sentiment with its handling of tensions in the Kashmir in May–July. The BJP picked up only three more seats in the Lok Sabha, but Congress fell to a new low of 112 seats and Vajpayee was able to form a new government, becoming the first prime minister since 1971 to win consecutive elections. The continued rise of the BJP now left India with a party system in which the old dominance of Congress had gone, and the membership of the Lok Sabha had become highly fragmented.

The 2004 elections saw the return of Congress in a minority, multi-party coalition. There had been much speculation about whether Sonia Gandhi would become prime minister, followed by the suggestion that her 33-year-old son Rahul – newly elected to Parliament to his father's district of Amethi – be recruited in her place. Instead, leadership of India fell surprisingly to Manmohan Singh, former leader of the opposition in the Rajya Sabha. Singh governed at the head of a 12-party alliance, which relied on the support of smaller and mainly left-wing parties to give it the majority it needed. In all, 40 parties now held seats in the Lok Sabha, of which 25 each had five seats or fewer.

Congress did well at the 2009 elections, picking up 61 new seats and giving Singh's governing coalition a near-majority, with the BJP coming second. Singh became the first Indian prime minister since Jawaharlal Nehru to be returned to office after a full five-year first term, suggesting some new potential stability in the office of the prime minister. But there was poor economic news (including low economic growth and high inflation), new corruption scandals, and ongoing religious and social tensions. Congress went into the 2014 elections under the leadership of Rahul Gandhi, while the BJP was led by Narendra Modi, Chief Minister of the western Indian state of Gujarat.

Although the BJP won only 31 per cent of the vote, this was enough to give it a small majority in the Lok Sabha, while Congress saw the worst defeat in its history, losing 162 seats and ending up with just 44. Even though it had enough seats to form a government by itself, the BJP now headed a 23-party coalition that gave it nearly 62 per cent of the seats in the Lok Sabha. The result, concluded Wallace (2015), reflected a combination of a strong leader, a strong party, and Indian regionalism. It was also a reflection of the extent to which the fight against corruption has moved to the higher reaches of the agenda of Indian elections (Gould, 2016).

In preparation for the 2019 elections, Rahul Gandhi replaced his mother as president of Congress.

THE FUTURE OF INDIAN GOVERNMENT AND POLITICS

Questions have been raised regularly since India's independence in 1947 about the country's governability and political stability. Several times the country has seemed to be on the brink of breaking down in religious, social, and economic chaos, and yet it has survived. It has come through territorial wars with its neighbours, internal secessionist struggles, frequent communal violence, a dangerous reliance for leadership on a single family, and attempts by some of its leaders to subvert the democratic process. It still has many social tensions, its population growth poses a constant set of new challenges, and its economy still suffers from the burden of a long history of state intervention. That intervention helped India feed itself and develop an extensive industrial base, but it now needs to accelerate the process of economic liberalization and allow its entrepreneurs to create the same opportunities at home as those who have left India have created abroad.

India is now increasingly spoken of in the same breath as China as having the potential to become one of the wealthiest and most prosperous countries in the world, but it must first balance its political, economic, and social reforms. China has opted to guide its development through authoritarianism and a refusal to offer much in the way of political choice. India has opted for the harder path of democracy, but – given the number of parties that now win election in its national parliament – it may be suffering from too much democracy. It faces the ongoing challenges of struggling with political and social divisions, with the handicap of endemic corruption, with divisions between the rich and the poor, with bridging the needs of its urban and rural populations, and with fulfilling its economic potential in a way that equitably spreads the benefits.

DISCUSSION QUESTIONS

1. How do India and Nigeria compare when it comes to the role in their current political and social challenges of the British colonial heritage?
2. How do the effects of caste on Indian politics compare with the effects of class in countries such as Britain and the United States?
3. How does the role of religion in politics compare in the cases on India, the United States, and Iran?
4. Which is best for a divided society such as India: multi-party coalition governments or strong leaders with legislative majorities?
5. Compare and contrast the relationship between union and state government in India with the federal systems in the United States and Germany.
6. Looking at the data presented in Figure 8.1, is there an optimum ratio for the number of constituents per elected national legislator?

CHAPTER CONCEPTS

- Bharatiya Janata Party
- British Raj
- Congress (Indian National Congress)
- Dalits
- Hinduism
- Hindutva
- Kashmir
- Lok Sabha
- Mahatma Gandhi
- Nehru-Gandhi family dynasty
- Rajya Sabha

KEY TERMS

- Caste
- Political class
- Structural violence

INDIA ONLINE

Government of India Portal: www.india.gov.in
GOI Directory: http://goidirectory.nic.in
Prime Minister's Office: www.pmindia.gov.in
Indian Parliament: http://parliamentofindia.nic.in
Supreme Court of India: www.sci.gov.in
Bharatiya Janata Party: http://bjp.org
Indian National Congress: www.inc.in/en
The Hindu: www.thehindu.com
The Times of India: http://timesofindia.indiatimes.com

FURTHER READING

Charlton, Sue Ellen M. (2015) *Comparing Asian Politics: India, China, and Japan*, 4th edn (Routledge). A comparative textbook survey of the three Asian case study countries in this book.

Datta, Rekha (2018) *Contemporary India: The Basics* (Abingdon: Routledge). A brief survey of the political, economic, cultural, and social landscape of India.

Drèze, Jean, and Amartya Sen (2013) *An Uncertain Glory: India and its Contradictions* (Princeton University Press). A critical analysis of the problems facing India today, arguing that public debate too often overlooks social and economic deprivation.

Jacobsen, Knut A. (ed.) (2016) *Routledge Handbook of Contemporary India* (Routledge), and Atul Kohli and Prerna Singh (2013) *Routledge Handbook of Indian Politics* (Routledge). Edited collections providing – respectively – a general survey of India and a more focused survey of its government and politics.

Mitra, Subrata K. (2017) *Politics in India: Structure, Process and Policy*, 2nd edn (Routledge). An introductory survey of Indian politics, including chapters on leadership, the federal structure, and parties and elections.

Sullivan, Kate (2015) *Competing Visions of India in World Politics: India's Rise Beyond the West* (Palgrave Macmillan). An edited collection of chapters assessing India's changing place in the world.

Visit **www.macmillanihe.com/McCormick-Cases** to access additional materials to support teaching and learning.

MEXICO

9

PREVIEW

Mexico's value as a case lies in what it can tell us about the circumstances of politics and government in Latin America, where many countries have experienced stops and starts in their recent experiments with democracy. After a long history of political instability, followed by decades of dominance by a single political party, Mexico has evolved since the 1990s into a multi-party system, but one in which some of the traditions of the past – including corruption – continue to cause problems. Mexico has also long continued to struggle with the influence of the neighbouring United States, and has been shaken since 2006 by a violent drug war that has interfered with its ability to reform itself. It offers a good example of a flawed democracy, giving us insight into the problems that a country can face as its tries to build a more democratic and transparent system of government.

KEY ARGUMENTS

◆ Mexico has recently undergone a political transition towards multi-party democracy, but finds itself handicapped by its inability to throw off many old habits.

◆ Oil, drugs, and the proximity of the United States have proved a troubling combination in Mexico's efforts to build political and economic stability.

◆ Formally, Mexico is a federal republic with a presidential executive. In reality, it has many nuances that give it a distinctive political personality.

◆ The power of the Mexican president has declined in recent decades as party competition has grown and Congress has won new influence.

◆ Elections have become more competitive, and the landscape of political parties has become more diverse, and yet there are still indications of electoral malpractice.

◆ Corruption is an ongoing problem in Mexico, made worse by the effects of its drug war and by party factionalism.

OVERVIEW

Mexico should be one of the success stories of Latin America: it has a large population with a growing middle class, it is one of the world's leading oil producers, and a programme of democratization in the 1990s had the effect of turning it from a one-party dominant system to a diverse multi-party system (something which even the neighbouring United States cannot claim). Unfortunately, it remains handicapped by a host of problems. As well as endemic corruption, a weak record on human rights, and widespread poverty, it has also been shaken since 2006 by a turf war among Mexican drug cartels that has taken tens of thousands of lives. The effects of the political reforms have been less than hoped for, and Freedom House – after upgrading Mexico in 2001 from Partly Free to Free – downgraded it in 2011 to Partly Free, with a ranking of Not Free on matters of press freedom. Meanwhile, it is ranked in the Democracy Index as a flawed democracy.

In political terms, Mexico is a federal republic with a limited presidential executive and a separately elected bicameral legislature. It also has several distinctive political features: Mexican presidents, for example, have more power than their US counterparts and the political system is one of the more heavily centralized examples of federalism. This has left political scientists undecided about how best to describe Mexico. Some call it authoritarian, while others pepper their analyses with terms such as *bureaucratic*, *elitist*, and *patrimonial*. Reforms have weakened the grip of such traditions, but some worry that the process of change has become stalled (see Tuckman, 2012). It is telling that the subtitle of a well-known textbook on Mexican politics (Camp, 2013) has changed over the course of recent editions from *Decline of Authoritarianism* (1999) to *The Democratic Transformation* (2002), *The Democratic Consolidation* (2006), and *Democratic Consolidation or Decline?* (2013).

In economic terms, Mexico is one of the 15 biggest economies in the world, with export-led growth, a service-based economy, and a rapidly developing industrial base, but it has often-startling economic and social paradoxes. It is common to hear talk of two Mexicos: one wealthy, urban, and modern and the other poor, rural, and traditional. One in ten Mexicans is illiterate, yet one in six goes on to higher education (a figure comparable to that of many wealthy democracies). Mexico City is a nightmare of congestion, yet it has an extensive subway that carries as many passengers every day as the New York City subway. Within sight of urban slums with open sewers you might see smartly dressed investment brokers driving to work in bullet-proof air-conditioned luxury cars, using mobile phones to close a deal or make a restaurant reservation.

In social terms, Mexico has few serious religious or ethnic problems. More than 90 per cent of Mexicans are Catholic and **mestizo** (of mixed Spanish and native American blood), and only about five per cent of the population is pure native American (descendants of Mayans, Zapotecs, and Tarascans). They may be few, but they have had a greater impact on Mexican society and politics than their northern cousins have had on US society. Because native identity in Mexico has cultural rather than racial connotations, it is possible to move across cultures, and there is less direct racism or discrimination in Mexico than in the United States (although racism certainly exists). But, also like their US cousins, native and African-descended Mexicans are poorer and more politically marginalized than *mestizos* and European-descended people. Their problems have been deepest in several poorer southern states, where poverty has occasionally spilled over into violence, emphasizing the economic gaps between rich and poor in Mexico.

POLITICAL DEVELOPMENT

Unlike either the United States or Canada – which come mainly out of the European tradition and where early colonists did not try to integrate with natives but destroyed them or pushed them aside and seized their land – Mexico is a product both of its European and of its native American heritage. It is, as the Mexican Nobel laureate Octavio Paz (1979) once put it, a 'land of superimposed pasts' and continues today to be a melding of European and native American ideas about law, government, and society. From the 12th to the early 16th century the region was dominated by the Aztecs, who ruled from their capital at Tenochtitlán (now Mexico City) with castes of religious and military leaders and a centralized tax and court system. Despite its past, modern Mexican government is mainly a product of changes that have taken place since the arrival of the Europeans.

Spanish occupation (16th century to 1821)

The Spanish arrived in 1519 under the command of Hernán Cortés, subjugating the ruling Aztecs relatively easily. Not only did the Spaniards have better weapons but they also had horses (which the Aztecs had never seen before), and were helped by fragmentation within the Aztec empire and by the resentment of tribes under Aztec rule, who took the opportunity to rebel. By the middle of the 16th century, all of what is now Mexico and the south-western United States had been conquered and occupied. Unlike North America, where British settlers rarely intermarried with native Americans, the mixing of Spaniards and native Americans was encouraged, creating a new *mestizo* culture-overlaid Catholicism, whose principles became embedded in political culture (Camp, 2013). The Spanish also brought diseases to which the natives had no immunity, such as measles and smallpox, as a result of which the native population was almost halved.

Independence and war (1810–48)

Partly inspired by their US neighbours, Mexican revolutionaries began agitating for independence in the early 19th century. The struggle became one between Spanish administrators (the *peninsulares*) on the one hand and *mestizos* and African- and Spanish-descended Mexicans on the other. But the Mexican independence movement was aimed not so much at promoting liberalism and equality as at preserving privilege and elitism. Independence was declared on 16 September 1810, sparking a long and bitter war with Spain (1810–21). Mexico then tried to build its own empire in Central America, but its economy was weak, and there was a power struggle between liberals calling for a democratic, federal system of government and conservatives favouring a more centralized system. Politics broke down in revolution, foreign encroachment, rigged elections, and frequent changes in leadership; in the first 50 years of independence alone, there were 30 presidents.

Mexico also suffered as a result of conflicts with the United States. In 1825 it invited Americans to settle in and develop Texas, which was then part of Mexico. By 1830, about 20,000 settlers had arrived, alarming Mexico into banning further immigration and trying to tighten its control over the new arrivals in 1835. The immigrants responded in 1836 by declaring their independence and requesting US annexation. Although General Antonio López de Santa Anna defeated the defenders of the Alamo mission in San Antonio in March, he soon afterwards

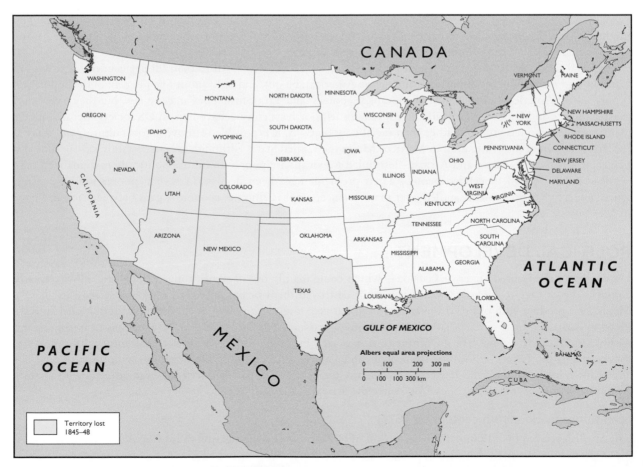

Map 9.1 Mexico's loss of territory to the United States

TIMELINE

250–900	Mayan city states flourish in far south of modern Mexico
1428–1521	Aztecs establish control over central modern Mexico
1519	Spanish occupation begins
1810	Declaration of independence
1810–21	War of independence
1836	Secession of Texas
1846–48	War with the United States leads to loss of California and other territories
1876–1911	Era of the *Porfiriato*
1913–17	Revolution and civil war
1953	Women given the right to vote
1982	Debt crisis
1994	Mexico joins North American Free Trade Agreement; suppression of guerrilla rebellion in southern state of Chiapas
1996	Political reform package unanimously passed by both houses of Congress
2000	PRI loses presidency for first time in 71 years, loses majority in Senate
2006	Government crack-down on drug cartels sparks drug war
2010	200th anniversary of Mexican independence
2012	PRI regains presidency
2017	Death toll from start of Mexican drug war reaches 240,000
2018	Morena party alliance wins presidency of Mexico, office of mayor of Mexico City, and majority in Congress

lost the battle of San Jacinto and was forced to agree to Texan independence. In 1845 the United States annexed Texas over Mexican protests, precipitating what Mexicans know as the War of the American Invasion of 1846–48, which ended with Mexico ceding half its land area (including what are now California, Arizona, and New Mexico) to the United States; see Map 9.1.

Mexico saw further threats to its independence when France, Britain, and Spain demanded reparations for losses suffered during the war. Napoleon III of France took advantage of Mexico's internal weaknesses in 1864 by declaring a French-dependent Mexican empire with Archduke Maximilian of Austria as emperor. A resistance movement overthrew and executed Maximilian in 1867, and Benito Juárez became president. Many political changes were introduced, including stronger civil liberties, regular elections, reductions in the powers of the church, and expanded public education. While Juárez remains the country's most beloved president, these changes did not amount to a new liberal order, and in 1877 the military government of José de la Cruz Porfirio Díaz came to power.

The *Porfiriato* (1877–1910)

Porfirio Díaz dominated Mexican politics for 35 years, serving as president for all but one four-year term (1880–84). During the era that came to be known as the ***porfiriato*** (see Edmonds-Poli and Shirk, 2015), Mexico enjoyed political stability and economic expansion. National income, foreign investment, and trade all grew; the railways were expanded; and new tracts of land were opened to settlers. But economic gains came at the cost of political freedom: Díaz ended free elections, curtailed freedom of speech and the press, put down dissent in the rural areas, ignored the separation of powers and states' rights, and tried to suppress native American culture. Elections were held, but the results were rigged. Large landholders became wealthy, but the middle classes were excluded from power, peasants lost their land, and most Mexicans remained illiterate. When Díaz announced that he would step down in 1910 and then changed his mind, a rebellion broke out, and Díaz resigned and went into exile in 1911.

Revolution and civil war (1910–17)

The **Mexican Revolution** is often described as one of the first great social revolutions of the 20th century, predating both its Russian and Chinese equivalents. But while Russian revolutionaries claimed that they wanted to end inequalities and spread political and social justice, those in Mexico proved to be mainly interested in creating opportunities for themselves and reducing the power and influence of foreign capitalists. The first revolutionary leader of Mexico was Francisco Madero, a member of a wealthy landowning family. Although he restored freedom of the press and individual property rights, he allowed many officials from the Díaz era to stay in office and ultimately failed to win over the peasants. In 1913 he was murdered in a US-sponsored coup led by the brutal and corrupt Victoriano Huerta. A violent civil war broke out, with three competing groups ranged against Huerta: a peasant army led by Emiliano Zapata, an army of workers and cattlemen led by Francisco 'Pancho' Villa, and a group of ranchers and businessmen led by Venustiano Carranza. More than a million people died during the course of the war, Carranza emerged victorious by 1915, and Villa and Zapata were both later assassinated.

In 1917 a new constitution was drawn up that has been the basis of Mexican government ever since. Radical and progressive, it included many core democratic ideals, such as religious freedom, and freedom of the press, of speech, and of peaceful assembly. It went further, though, in outlining a right to universal public education, rights for workers, state control over natural resources, and the power of the federal government to redistribute land. Many Mexicans have long argued that the goals of the revolution have not yet been met, pointing to the remaining authoritarian qualities of Mexican politics, the number of people still living in poverty, the political and economic disadvantages faced by women, the unequal distribution of land, and concerns about Mexico's economic independence.

Stabilizing the revolution (1924–40)

Of the early post-revolutionary presidents, two in particular made key contributions to Mexico's political development. The first was Plutarco Elías Calles (1924–28), who in 1929 created the National Revolutionary Party as a way of quelling opposition, preventing armed insurgencies, and perpetuating his political influence. Its name was changed in 1945 to the Institutional Revolutionary Party (producing, in Spanish, the acronym PRI, pronounced 'pree'), and it went on to govern Mexico for the rest of the century. Even more influential was Lázaro Cárdenas (1934–40), the most left-wing of Mexico's presidents. He redistributed more land than his seven predecessors combined, supported labour unions, and – most important – launched a programme of economic nationalization. Concerned at the extent to which Mexican companies were controlled by foreigners, particularly British and US investors, he brought several industries under state control (compensating the affected corporations) and in 1938 created the state oil corporation, today called Petróleos Mexicanos (or **Pemex**). For all these changes – aimed at economic and political equality and stability, and at asserting Mexican independence – Cárdenas remains the most revered of Mexico's post-revolutionary presidents.

The oil crisis and its implications (1976–94)

Mexico's political development paved the way for economic growth in the 1960s and 1970s, but underlying structural problems began to make themselves felt. Falling agricultural exports indicated a loss of competitiveness, leading in turn to middle class discontent. The government clamped down, killing and torturing dissidents, and when students used the media spotlight provided by the 1968 Mexico City summer Olympics to demand political liberalization, as many as 500 were killed by the army, sparking political crisis.

To make matters worse, Mexico's economy was in trouble. The discovery of vast new oil reserves in the 1960s and 1970s encouraged the government to make heavy investments in transport, industry, communications, health care, and education. However, high spending brought inflation and when the price of oil began to fall, Mexico borrowed to cover its spending, building a large national debt. Chastened, the government began a shift away from centralized economic management to a more open and competitive free-market system. The fragility of Mexico's economic situation was emphasized by the collapse of the peso in 1994, prompting an international rescue package of loan guarantees to again help Mexico avoid defaulting on its debt. In that same year, Mexico joined in the North American Free Trade Agreement (NAFTA) with the United States and Canada.

The fragility of Mexico's political situation, meanwhile, was emphasized by unrest in the poor southern states of **Chiapas**, Oaxaca, and Guerrero. Complaining about being cheated out of their land and being denied basic services, and feeling the effects of falling coffee prices, peasants in Chiapas rebelled in January 1994 (see

Oppenheimer, 1998, and Preston and Dillon, 2004). Troops were despatched to put down the rebellion, resulting in more than 150 deaths, and while a peace agreement was eventually signed, the military presence continued. Even more worryingly, drug trafficking was growing in response to demand in the United States, and made more difficult to control by police and political corruption, which in turn harmed US–Mexican relations.

Democratization takes hold (1990s–early 2000s)

The changing character of Mexican society and the rise of an urban middle class made it more difficult for PRI administrations to resist demands for greater democracy. A series of electoral reforms was made, which encouraged the rise of opposition parties and gave them more seats in the national Congress. The share of the PRI vote fell steadily as the governing party lost the support of unions and of a middle class hurt by Mexico's worsening economic problems. In 1997, PRI lost its majority in the lower chamber of Congress (the Chamber of Deputies) for the first time since 1929, and in 2000 lost its majority in the Senate and – most remarkable of all – lost the presidency of Mexico. The new president, Vicente Fox, came from the opposition National Action Party (PAN), and promised fiscal reform, sustainable economic growth, more social spending, political decentralization, and a more assertive foreign policy. He found, though, that reforming the system was more difficult than he had anticipated, thanks to the persistence of entrenched political and economic interests.

Questions remained about the extent to which Mexico had changed. In 2006, the candidate of PAN, Felipe Calderón, won a bitterly contested presidential election over his liberal opponent Andrés Manuel López Obrador of the Party of the Democratic Revolution (PRD). The margin of victory was barely 250,000 votes, leading to charges by the opposition of vote rigging. It took a court decision to confirm Calderón in office, and his agenda reflected the many problems that Mexico continued to face: he launched a programme to create new jobs so as to stem the flow of migration to the United States; launched an anti-poverty drive aimed at Mexico's poorest urban areas; and promised to address the problems of corruption, violent crime, and tax evasion. He also made the fight against Mexico's drug gangs a priority, as a result of which a bitter and violent **drug war** broke out that caused a dramatic increase in homicides. From 2006 to the end of 2017 there were more than 240,000 murders, raising troubling questions about the underlying stability of Mexico's political reforms.

Mexico today

Mexico has undergone a major political and economic transformation in the last three decades. On the political front, it launched a series of changes that moved it in the direction of a multi-party democracy, taking powers away from the executive. However, one of the results has been occasional gridlock, with much-needed tax, energy, and labour reforms falling prey to partisan bickering. On the economic front, the state has retreated from the marketplace in the wake of an extensive programme of privatization, under which inefficient state-owned monopolies have been replaced by more competitive privately owned businesses better placed to take on international competition. The Mexican marketplace, however, remains far from open, and continues to fail to create as many well-paying jobs as it needs.

Mexico is not yet a full democracy. Its political institutions have not developed the necessary consistency and predictability, there is still much to be done to improve the quality of life for its people (especially those living in rural areas), corruption is still a problem in government and public services, public safety is not all it should be, and Mexico's record on human rights and media freedom needs improvement.

Finally, no assessment of Mexico can ignore the way it is influenced by – and influences – the United States, with which it shares a 3,000km land border. Few pairs of neighbouring countries anywhere in the world have such a closely intertwined relationship, summarized in the famous quip by Mexican dictator Porfirio Diaz: 'Poor Mexico. So far from God and so close to the United States.' The two have a long and troubled history, and the relationship today is political, economic, cultural, and personal in nature, leading Selee (2018) to describe it as more like a seam than a barrier. Americans worry about migration and drug imports from Mexico and other countries in Latin America, prompting Donald Trump to promise the building of a border wall. At the same time, the United States relies heavily on seasonal labour from Mexico, from which it also imports much of its oil and many agricultural products. Hispanics make up the largest ethnic minority in the United States, which is also home to an estimated 13 million undocumented migrants from south of the border. What one country does has long mattered to – and affected – the other.

A stretch of the border wall separating Mexico from the United States. The relationship between the two countries has long been both important and troubled, with significant political, economic, and social implications for them both.

Source: iStock.com/Rex_Wholster.

POLITICAL CULTURE

It was once said that while North American political culture is driven by the values of John Locke and liberalism (see Chapter 3), Latin American political culture is 'elitist, hierarchical, authoritarian, corporatist, and patrimonialist' (Wiarda and Kline, 1990). Thanks to the rising demand for political modernization in the wake of economic modernization, Mexican political culture has become a mix of the old and the new. At its heart is the idea of the unfinished revolution: while Americans tend to focus on the future, Mexicans hark back to the past, to missed opportunities and unfulfilled dreams. Revolutionary principles and national aspirations are perpetuated by the myths built around heroes as varied as Cuauhtémoc (nephew of the Aztec emperor Moctezuma and leader of the opposition to the Spanish conquistadors) and Miguel Hidalgo y Costilla, the priest who declared Mexico's independence, and was executed for treason.

The contradictions are reflected in the hierarchical and elitist nature of Mexican society, based in part on the influence of the Catholic Church. Spanish Catholicism was based on the idea that political authority emanated from God, and all lower levels of society had progressively less power and status. Mexican society is still class-based, with real power held by an elite whose attitudes remain paternalistic and authoritarian. The elite was once made up almost exclusively of the military; today it consists mainly of technocrats and of the entrepreneurs who have benefited most from privatization. The new wealth of Mexico's elite was illustrated in 2007 when the *Forbes* list of the world's wealthiest people declared that Carlos Slim – a businessman with extensive holdings in telecommunications – had overtaken Bill Gates to become the world's wealthiest person. (He had slipped to number 7 on the list by 2018.)

One explanation for the failure of democracy fully to take hold in Mexico can be found in the persistence of corporatism – see Comparing Political Culture 9. Another and related explanation can be found in the phenomenon of the *camarilla*: a group of people who have political interests in common and rely on one another for political advancement. Each has a single leader or mentor at its core, as a result of which personalities become more important than ideology or policies in determining political behaviour, and power revolves around patron–client relationships, with followers providing support in return for political favours. Political careers often depend heavily on 'old-boy networks', which contribute to the corruption that is a common feature of Mexican politics. (Compare this with similar networks in Japan and Nigeria.)

The foundation of that corruption lies in the tradition of elitism and political centralization that provides tempting opportunities for the misuse of power for personal gain. The complexity of regulations and laws combines with the inefficiency of the bureaucracy to make many people conclude that it is cheaper to bribe than to be honest; less scrupulous police and junior officials make matters worse by sometimes demanding *una mordida* (a bite) to take care of business. The extent of the problem is difficult to measure because it usually involves influence peddling and the trading of favours rather than open bribery or embezzlement, but it persists in government, the bureaucracy, labour unions, and the police, hampering Mexico's efforts to become a successful democracy. As a result, Mexico has fallen steadily down the ranking of countries in the Corruption Perceptions Index: from 72nd in 2007, to 98th in 2010, to 135th in 2017.

Yet another explanation for the problems of democracy in Mexico lies in the persistence of **machismo** (assertive masculinity). It expresses itself most obviously in the political marginalization of women, who won the right to vote only in 1953 and still rarely move into positions of authority within government. In 2006 a new federal post of special prosecutor was created to address the problem of violent crime against women, which had been highlighted by the unsolved murders over a period of 12 years of more than 300 women in the city of Ciudad Juarez. *Machismo* can also be seen more broadly in political violence, such as demonstrations, riots, kidnappings, political assassinations, and the drug war.

The stakes in the drug trade are substantial, involving billions of dollars in profits from exports to the United States, and the extent of the violence involved has been remarkable. In some small towns in northern Mexico, entire police departments have resigned and drug gangs rule the streets. Gun battles have broken out between gangs

COMPARING POLITICAL CULTURE 9
Corporatism

Mexico offers an example of a phenomenon often found in several Latin American and European societies: **corporatism**. A corporatist state is one in which groups representing major social and economic interests are incorporated by government, and are given privileged official positions, access to government, and permission to bargain with the government on public policies, in return for which their members must respect and support the policies agreed on. It traces its origins to the Catholic Church in Europe, the term deriving from the Latin word *corpus* (meaning 'the body'), and describing efforts made by the church to coordinate civic groups and unions that were not formally part of the church (Edmonds-Poli and Shirk, 2015).

> **Corporatism**
> An arrangement by which groups in society are incorporated into the system of government.

The effect is to create a system that is based on patronage and that works against political or economic liberalism. In the Mexican case, the most important groups are workers, peasants, and the 'popular' sector (mainly the middle classes, small businesspeople, government employees, and the professions). But the signs of corporatism in Mexico are fading: economic changes have opened up the Mexican marketplace, and democratic changes have coupled with improved education to make Mexicans more difficult to manipulate. The result has been a move toward the pluralist ideas associated with liberal democracy.

Corporatism is also found in other parts of the world, with similar effects. In several continental European countries, for example, including Austria, the Netherlands, and the Scandinavian states, there has been a tradition of business and labour working closely with government to negotiate wage increases, tax rates, and social security benefits. Industrial associations and labour unions have been particularly active in this, reaching agreements with government and undertaking to ensure the compliance of their members. The effects have weakened in recent years as union membership has fallen and free-market thinking has strengthened, but corporatist thinking has not entirely gone away.

Name	United Mexican States (Estados Unidos Mexicanos)
Capital	Mexico City
Administration	Federal republic, with 31 states and the Federal District of Mexico City.
Constitution	State formed 1821, and most recent constitution adopted 1917.
Executive	Limited presidential. A president is elected for a single six-year term, and there is no vice president.
Legislature	Bicameral Congress of the Union: lower Chamber of Deputies (500 members) elected for three-year terms, and upper Senate (128 members) elected for six-year terms. Members may not serve consecutive terms.
Judiciary	Supreme Court of 11 members nominated for single 15-year terms by the president and confirmed by the Senate.
Electoral system	A simple plurality vote determines the presidency, while a mixed-member system is used for the Chamber of Deputies and the Senate: 300 single-member plurality (SMP) seats and 200 proportional representation seats in the Chamber, and a combination of SMP, first minority, and at-large seats in the Senate.
Party system	Multi-party. Mexico was long a one-party system, but democratic reforms since the 1990s have broadened the field such that three major parties now compete at the national and state level, with a cluster of smaller parties.

129m Population

$1,150 billion Gross Domestic Product

$8,900 Per capita GDP

Democracy Index rating
- ✗ Full Democracy
- ✓ Flawed Democracy
- ✗ Hybrid Regime
- ✗ Authoritarian
- ✗ Not Rated

Freedom House rating
- ✗ Free
- ✓ Partly Free
- ✗ Not Free
- ✗ Not Rated

Human Development Index rating
- ✗ Very High
- ✓ High
- ✗ Medium
- ✗ Low
- ✗ Not Rated

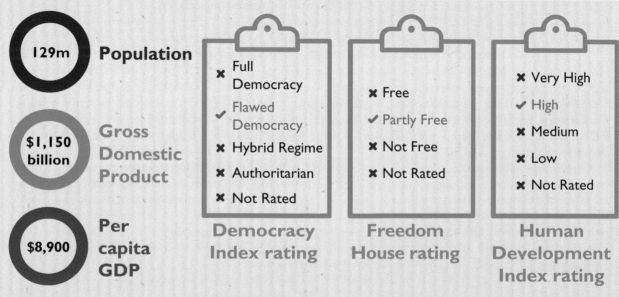

fighting over turf, and the gangs have taken on the police and the army, occasionally using grenade launchers and automatic weapons, and typically ignoring any members of the public (including children) who become caught in the crossfire.

POLITICAL SYSTEM

Superficially, the Mexican political system looks much like that of many other federal republics with presidential executives: it has an elected president, a bicameral legislature, an independent judiciary, a system of checks and balances, competing political parties, and states with their own powers and elected local governments. Like most political systems, though, the Mexican system has several features that make it distinctive:

◆ The presidency is a powerful office, with Congress and the judiciary playing mainly supporting roles. As well as serving a single six-year term, which removes the need to worry about re-election and changes the way that incumbents think about public opinion, the president also has wide-ranging control over appointments to key positions in government, can – like Russian presidents – issue decrees and declare states of emergency, and has substantial powers of patronage.

◆ The Mexican federal model involves a high degree of centralization of power. This is partly due to the constitution, which gives the federal government opportunities to intervene in the affairs of Mexico's 31 states, and partly due to economic and political realities: Mexico City is so big and dominant that its influence over national affairs far outstrips that of most other federal capitals in the world, with the exception of Moscow.

To be sure, the degree of centralization has declined in recent decades. The end of PRI's monopoly meant that presidents could no longer appoint their successors as they once did, and can no longer control government as actively as they once did through patronage and through managing the electoral process. There is now multi-party competition in Mexico, elections are more honest and competitive, the checks and balances between president and legislature are more meaningful, and power has been redistributed to a broader base.

Not all, however, is at it seems, and Tuckman (2012) takes a particularly bleak view of the opportunities that Mexico has missed. If defined in the narrow sense of having free and fair elections, she argues, Mexican democracy is solid. However, if defined in the broader sense of there being systematic means by which citizens can hold elected representatives accountable, then democracy has not yet been achieved. The sense that something has gone 'terribly wrong', she observes, reflects the problem of 'weak and malleable state institutions at all levels – institutions that cannot cope with the tasks at hand'. Politics, she continues, is rarely about the promotion of a vision or the search for solutions to problems, and instead continues to be bogged down in 'corruption, nepotism, clientelism, ineptitude, authoritarianism, cynicism, and impunity'. Mexico's democratic transition is, at best, partial and interrupted.

The constitution

Adopted in 1917, the Mexican constitution is one of the oldest in Latin America. Its adoption marked a radical change in direction; where its predecessors had drawn heavily on the US constitution and were seen less as blueprints for government than as outlines of goals to which Mexico aspired, the 1917 constitution was grounded more firmly in the realities of Mexico. One of its core principles is **economic nationalism**, prompted by worries about the looming economic power of the United States. To protect Mexican interests, the authors of the constitution included limits on foreign investment and foreign ownership of land and other natural resources, denied anyone but Mexicans the right to own land or water resources, and – in the controversial Article 27 – vested ownership of all minerals and other underground resources in the state. Ideas like these have become difficult to defend as Mexico has had to open up its market under the pressures of globalization and free trade.

> **Economic nationalism**
> Attempts made by a country to protect its economy from foreign control by limiting access.

Another distinctive principle is the effort to make clear the gap between church and state. The constitution's effort to limit the influence of the Church and military represents a major difference between Mexico and other Latin American countries, large and small alike. Until reforms to the constitution in 1992, the church had no legal standing in Mexico, which meant that priests could not vote (although many did anyway), and it was barred from owning property or taking part in politics. This did not stop church leaders from campaigning for social justice, however; priests have long been active in defending the rights of native Mexicans, in criticizing electoral fraud, and in speaking out about the problems of poverty. During the PRI era, Mexicans frustrated with the weakness of opposition parties often turned to the church as a vehicle to express their political demands (Camp, 2013).

The Mexican constitution is not difficult to change: amendments need the support of only two-thirds of members of Congress and a majority of state legislatures. The result is that Mexican leaders will sometimes propose packages of constitutional amendments. For example, long-held criticisms of Mexico's judicial system prompted overwhelming support in 2008 for an amendment designed to provide for a more open system of trials, including a presumption of innocence until guilt is proven and a guarantee that suspects would be represented by qualified public defenders. The change followed years of criticism that Mexico had a criminal justice system marked by arbitrary detention, fabrication of evidence, unfair trials, and abuse of human rights.

The executive: president

Presidents dominate the Mexican political system, but not to the extent that they once did. During what Weldon (1997) describes as the era of hyperpresidentialism, a combination of unified government, strong party discipline, and presidential control of the ruling party meant that presidents could lead forcefully, and none ever had their legislation turned down by Congress. The powers of the office have since declined, but it is still described with the term *presidencialismo* (presidentialism) (Camp, 2013). The formal powers of the Mexican presidency in several areas go beyond those of most other presidents:

◆ Presidents can appoint and dismiss cabinet members, control party nominations for Congress and state governors, appoint the leadership of Congress, and appoint the heads of state-owned banks and industrial enterprises.
◆ They can introduce bills to Congress, and through the power of decree (the *reglamento*) can decide how a law passed by Congress is enforced.
◆ They command the military and have the power to declare war and to use the armed forces both for external defence and for internal security, to declare a 'state of siege', and to assume emergency powers.
◆ They have the power to direct foreign policy, to control and regulate foreign investment in Mexico, to control the supply of newsprint to the press and to give concessions for radio and TV channels, and even to oversee the writing and updating of primary school textbooks.

Informally, the power of appointment allows presidents to build a powerful *camarilla*, dispensing offices and influence in return for loyalty. Presidents can also exploit the aura of their office for political ends, attracting the kind of attention reserved in parliamentary systems for monarchs or non-executive presidents. This was long carried to the extreme in Mexico, where care was taken to immunize the president from criticism and to hold cabinet ministers or others in government responsible for policy failures. Now that the one-party monopoly is over, presidents are more open to criticism and to challenges from the opposition, and more often need to make use of the presidential veto.

The terms of eligibility for Mexican presidents are demanding: a candidate must be Mexican by birth, have a mother or father who is Mexican by birth, must be at least 35 years old, must have been resident in the country for at least a year prior to the election, cannot be an official in a church or religious organization, and cannot have been on active military service in the six months prior to the election. Once elected, they are limited to a single six-year term, or *sexenio*, and govern with a cabinet consisting of nearly two dozen secretaries and the Attorney General. Secretaries usually have past political experience as governors or senators, and only the Attorney General is subject to confirmation by the Senate. The cabinet meets rarely and plays only a marginal role in national politics.

All Mexican presidents so far have been men, they have come mainly from politically prominent, urban, upper-middle-class families, and – particularly in recent years – they have served apprenticeships not as *políticos* (elected officials) but as *técnicos* (government bureaucrats). For many years, they were typically graduates of the National Autonomous University (UNAM) in Mexico City, and several also attended graduate school in the United States. Vicente Fox broke the mould in several ways, having been raised in a rural part of Mexico and coming to the presidency with experience as a state governor. Calderón continued the trend, having served in the Chamber of Deputies and coming to the presidency with a background in law, while Enrique Peña Nieto was a state deputy and a state governor. Meanwhile, the current president – Andrés Manuel López Obrador (known by his initials as AMLO) – was active in state politics before rising to prominence as mayor of Mexico City. He won the presidency in 2018 at the head of Morena, a new party created in 2012.

The process by which presidents are chosen has undergone a radical overhaul in recent years. Until 2000, the PRI candidate always won, and was chosen as candidate through a secret selection process within PRI known as *dedazo*, or pointing the finger. As incumbents approached the end of their term, they would look for someone who had the qualifications needed to deal with Mexico's most pressing problems (which were usually economic) and who had the support of key political leaders, notably former presidents, party leaders, and leaders of the military,

Table 9.1 Modern presidents of Mexico

Start of term	Name	Party
1946	Miguel Alemán Valdés	PRI
1952	Adolfo Ruiz Cortines	PRI
1958	Adolfo López Mateos	PRI
1964	Gustavo Díaz Ordaz	PRI
1970	Luis Echeverría	PRI
1976	José López Portillo	PRI
1982	Miguel de la Madrid	PRI
1988	Carlos Salinas de Gortari	PRI
1994	Ernesto Zedillo	PRI
2000	Vicente Fox	PAN
2006	Felipe Calderón	PAN
2012	Enrique Peña Nieto	PRI
2018	Andrés Manuel López Obrador	Morena

Andrés Manuel López Obrador – popularly known as AMLO – waves after being sworn in as Mexico's new president in December 2018. His victory at the head of a new political party represented a widely felt desire by Mexicans to bring an end to the country's drug war and to address the persistent problem of corruption.

Source: Alfredo Estrella/AFP/Getty Images.

the labour movement, and the business community. The name of the successor was then made public, a party convention ratified the choice, and a national campaign was launched to build public recognition.

An attempt was made in 1988 to make the nomination process more democratic, a dissident group within PRI demanding greater openness in selecting a successor for Miguel de la Madrid. When it failed, one of its leaders – Cuauhtémoc Cárdenas – broke away from PRI and ran against Carlos Salinas, the anointed PRI candidate. Heading a coalition of parties on the left, Cárdenas officially won 31 per cent of the vote, while the right-wing National Action Party (PAN) candidate (Manuel Clouthier) won nearly 17 per cent. Although most independent estimates suggest that Cárdenas probably won, Salinas was declared the winner, but with the slimmest margin of any PRI candidate for president (50.7 per cent) and only after a lengthy delay in announcing the results, blamed on a 'breakdown' in the computers counting the votes (Preston and Dillon, 2004). Fulfilling a promise made soon after coming to office in 1994, President Ernesto Zedillo ordered a review of the selection process, which resulted in the replacement in 1999 of the *dedazo* system with open party primaries.

The process by which presidents are replaced, if needed, is unusual. Most presidential executives include a deputy or vice president who can take over the office in the event of the death, resignation, or impeachment of the incumbent. In Mexico, there is no vice president. Instead, if a president leaves office during the first two years of their term, Congress is transformed into an electoral college that appoints an interim president by majority vote, and elections are then organized to decide a new president to see out the remainder of the six-year term. If the president leaves office during the last four years of their term, Congress elects a substitute president to see out the remainder of the term. Neither has ever so far happened.

The legislature: Congress

Mexico's national legislature – formally the Congress of the Union – has traditionally had little power, prestige, or influence over the president and, until recently, did little more than legitimize the actions of the president and confirm the policies of PRI. This began to change in the late 1970s as PRI altered the electoral system to give opposition parties more seats in Congress. As opposition numbers grew, and as PRI's share of the vote fell, Congress became more openly critical of the president and won more power.

It became a major political actor as a result of the 1997 elections, when PRI lost its majority in the Chamber of Deputies for the first time. Although opposition parties were divided among themselves, PRI could no longer rely on Congress to support the programme of the president, whose grip on power began to loosen. With Vicente Fox's victory in 2000, the role of Congress changed again; instead of rubber-stamping the president's policies, it became the chief source of opposition. With no one party any longer winning a majority of seats in the Chamber of Deputies, presidents must now work harder to build a consensus in support of their programme and their policies.

The new dynamic was on show with the victory of the Morena party in the 2018 elections. AMLO – having brokered deals with his coalition parties and with the Green Party – won the presidency, while Morena also took the mayorship of Mexico City, the second most important position in Mexican politics. It failed to win majorities in either chamber of the Mexican Congress, however, meaning that the initial excitement about López Obrador's victory was likely to wear off as he found himself having to work with a divided legislature: Morena held only 43 per cent of the seats in the Senate and only 38 per cent of the seats in the Chamber of Deputies, with the remainder in both cases divided among eight other parties.

Among the structural features of Congress, one in particular stands out: consecutive terms in either chamber are forbidden. This means that a new crop of legislators enters both chambers after each election, and senators and deputies must skip a term before being eligible for re-election. Members of Congress who cannot get enough of politics move alternately from one chamber to the other, and even have spells in state or local government. The ban on consecutive terms, note Edmonds-Poli and Shirk (2015), is of great historical significance to Mexicans, given the abuse of elective office during the *porfiriato*, but it creates at least two problems:

◆ Members of Congress have few opportunities to build extended political experience. True, this means that Mexico does not face the same problem as many other political systems of the emergence of a political class (see Chapter 8). However, a more effective balance between building experience and ensuring turnover might better be sought in limiting the number of terms legislators can serve.
◆ Political parties are strengthened at the expense of voters, who have little opportunity to reward or punish legislators for their job performance. Legislators instead see themselves as more responsible to parties, which control their political futures, and are more likely to reward legislators who respect party discipline.

The Mexican Congress has two chambers.

Senate (*Cámara de Senadores*)

The Senate represents the 31 states and the Federal District of Mexico City. Each is represented directly by three Senators elected using a mixed-member electoral system, and an additional 32 at-large Senators are elected from Mexico as a whole, for a total of 128. Senators serve six-year terms, but cannot serve more than one term consecutively; this means that every election produces a new line-up of Senators. Elections are held at the same time as the presidential election (a system of staggered elections was introduced in 1991 but suspended in 1993).

PRI had a monopoly of Senate seats until 1976, when the Popular Socialist Party was given a seat in return for keeping quiet about fraud in a state election. In 1988 the opposition Cárdenas Front won four Senate seats, and in 1993, electoral reforms not only increased the number of seats in the Senate from 64 to 128 but also changed the electoral process to the system used today. As a result, the 1994 elections saw 32 opposition senators elected, a number that grew to 51 in 1997, and to 68 in 2000, when PRI lost its Senate majority for the first time. By 2018, nine parties were represented in the Senate, with none holding a majority.

Chamber of Deputies (*Cámara de Diputados*)

Much like the US House of Representatives, the Chamber of Deputies represents the people rather than the states, and has many of the standard features of a law-making body, along with the sole ability to approve the federal budget. Its 500 members are elected for three-year terms using a mixed-member system. As with the Senate, PRI once had a lock on the chamber, winning as many as 85 per cent of the seats in the Chamber in the 1970s. The number of seats in the Chamber was increased in two stages to its current total of 500, and a breakthrough came in 1988 when opposition parties won enough seats to at least temporarily meet their long-held demands for a meaningful role in government, and to deny PRI the two-thirds majority needed to amend the constitution. Opposition parties went on to win majorities in 1997, 2000, and 2003, and by 2006 PRI had been reduced to the third-biggest party in the Chamber. Like the Senate, the Chamber by 2018 had members from nine parties, with none holding a majority.

The judiciary: Supreme Court

The Mexican judiciary long played only a supporting role in government and was more apolitical than its US counterpart. Its 25 members were hand-picked by the president, and could be removed only by the president, which had the effect of keeping the court firmly under executive control. It occasionally – and usually reluctantly – passed down decisions against the executive, but it did little to limit executive power or to control electoral fraud, and generally protected the interests of political and economic elites. However, President Zedillo launched efforts to change its role by replacing all its members in 1995, bringing the Senate into the appointment process, introducing the power of judicial review, and appointing a member of the opposition party PAN as attorney general.

The Supreme Court of Justice of the Nation has 11 members, including a president, each appointed for single 15-year terms. Members are nominated by the president and confirmed by two-thirds of the Senate, and can be removed by the Mexican president only with the approval of the Senate. The president of the court is elected by the membership of the court, and is limited to a four-year term that can be repeated, but not consecutively. Below the Supreme Court there is a system of circuit courts of appeal and district courts. The Supreme Court appoints circuit and district judges for renewable four-year terms.

While most English-speaking countries base their legal systems on English common law, Mexico uses the Roman civil law tradition. The former tends to be adversarial or accusatorial rather than inquisitorial, and relies heavily on precedent (the principle of *stare decisis*, or standing by previous decisions) while the latter is based on written codes and the written opinions of legal scholars (Avalos, 2013). One of the most important types of cases heard by Mexican federal courts is an *amparo* suit, a concept invented in Mexico and for which there is no direct equivalent elsewhere. *Amparo*, which literally means favour or protection, is designed to protect individual rights other than physical liberty (protected by the principle of *habeas corpus*), and can be used in several ways: as a defence of rights, as protection against unconstitutional laws, or to force examination of the legality of judicial decisions (Avalos, 2013).

Sub-national government

Mexico has a federal system of administration, with the country divided into 31 states and the government of Mexico City. Each state has its own constitution and judiciary, along with a governor elected for a non-renewable six-year term, a small unicameral Chamber of Deputies whose members are elected using a mixed-member plurality and PR system for non-consecutive three-year terms, and nearly 2,500 municipalities (*municipios*), which may be towns, counties, or consolidated city-county governments.

The Mexican constitution somewhat grandly declares that the states are 'free and sovereign' (Article 40), but this claim is much less than it seems, because the Mexican federal model is more centralized than is the case with many other federal systems. For example, although Mexican state governments have independent powers, it has been unusual for a state government to contradict or defy a federal government decision or ruling. Also, the federal Senate has the power to remove an elected governor, whose successor may be nominated by the president and confirmed by the Senate. Because each state has its own electoral cycle, and because the *sexenios* of governors do not necessarily coincide with those of presidents, incoming presidents always inherit incumbent governors, over whom they may not have as much control as they would like. Despite this, governors are dismissed much more rarely today than they were during the turbulent 1920s and 1930s, and state governments generally have a larger measure of autonomy over their routine functions, the federal government usually intervening only in cases of extreme corruption or abuse of power.

Municipal government in Mexico is defined under the Constitution (Article 115) and has most of the standard duties associated with administration at the local level, including the provision of public services. At the same time, the growing power of local administrators has combined with their immediate exposure to the drug war and the shortage of police in Mexico to make their lives unusually dangerous. Whether it is because they have decided to take on the drug gangs, or are seen to be threatening the power of local drug lords, or because they have chosen to side with one gang over another, mayors – as well as mayoral candidates and former mayors – find themselves being the target of the gangs. Between 2010 and 2017, a total of 42 mayors were killed in Mexico, along with 61 former mayors (*The Economist*, 2018).

The other notable point about Mexican local politics is the size and influence of Mexico City. The capital is home to 9 million people, and the surrounding state of Mexico to a further 16 million, meaning that just over one in five Mexicans lives in or near the capital. One of the effects of its size has been to create inequalities in the distribution of public investment and in access to public services: the Mexico City area is the source of more than half of all federal government revenues and receives more than half of all spending on education, health, and public housing. Mexico City is also home to many in the political elite; about 40 per cent of all federal government officials are born in Mexico City.

Little surprise, then, that the position of mayor of Mexico City (strictly speaking, head of government or *Jefe de Gobierno*) is considered the second most important political office in Mexico. The position was created in 1997 after decades of resentment that the city was governed by a Head of the Federal District Department (popularly known as the 'regent') appointed by the president of Mexico. This had the effect of making it an extension of the federal government. Since the creation of the elected mayor, who – once again – serves a single six-year term, PRD has had a lock on the office, with both its most recent presidential candidates – Cuauhtémoc Cárdenas and Andrés Manuel López Obrador – holding the position. In 2018, Claudia Sheinbaum of Morena became the first woman elected mayor of Mexico City. Only nine women have ever been elected to state governorships, including Claudia Pavolovich Arellano, elected governor of the north-western state of Sonora in 2015.

POLITICAL PROCESSES

The way in which Mexicans are represented in national politics has changed out of all recognition in recent years. PRI once manipulated the system to ensure continued control, meddled with the results of elections, adjusted the electoral system to give opposition parties enough seats in Congress to keep them cooperative but to deny them power, and was careful to incorporate any groups that might pose a threat to the status quo. In short, key political decisions were made more as a result of competition within PRI than of competition among different parties and interest groups. Elections were used less to determine who would govern than to mobilize support for those who already governed; that is, they were used to legitimize power rather than to distribute power (Camp, 2013).

Reforms to the electoral system have since allowed opposition parties to win more power. With majorities in both chambers of Congress, and their victory in the 2000, 2006, and 2018 presidential elections, those parties have now become a more important force in government, and politics has moved outside PRI to a broader public constituency. The result has been a vibrant three-party system, the centrist PRI competing for influence with the more conservative National Action Party (PAN) and the more liberal Party of the Democratic Revolution (PRD), the latter recently superseded by the National Regeneration Movement (Morena).

The electoral system

The process of electoral reform first moved into high gear in 1977–78, when the number of legal political parties grew from four to seven, a mixed-member plurality and PR electoral system was introduced, and a quarter of the seats in the Chamber of Deputies were effectively reserved for opposition parties (provided that they ran candidates

COMPARING GOVERNMENT 9
The government of cities

With more than half of all humans now living in towns or cities (a tipping point that was reached in 2007, according to the United Nations), urban government has taken on a new significance in our definition and understanding of what is politically important. Compared to those who live in rural areas, city-dwellers tend to be wealthier, better educated, and more active in politics, while having easier access to the resources and networks needed to be politically influential, having a wider variety of priorities and values, and acting as a major source of government revenues. (Urban life, though, comes with more than its share of transience, exposure to crime, and weakened connections to traditional networks, such as family.)

Most of the world's largest cities by population also tend to be in the world's most populous countries, notably China, India, Bangladesh, Pakistan, and Nigeria. As a result, they exert less influence, proportionally, over the countries in which they are situated. In other cases, such as Moscow in Russia, London in the UK, Cairo in Egypt, and Tehran in Iran – a combination of history, geography, and sheer size combines to increase the reach and influence of urban government, sometimes creating an 'us and them' mentality in which those outside the capital city come to resent its dominance. This applies to some extent to Mexico City, which is further to the political left than most other parts of Mexico, and is big enough to have acted as a base for the presidential campaigns of candidates from the PRD and Morena.

Another kind of influence is brought to bear by the rise of the global city, or one whose wealth or role in trade and communications has grown in reach and significance such that it transcends national borders. Such cities are more likely to take a global outlook than other parts of the countries in which they are situated, perhaps leaving them with different perspectives not just from their rural neighbours but also from the residents of other cities in the country. Recent examples of this phenomenon at work include the way in which London has become a multicultural city that voted heavily in favour of Britain remaining part of the European Union in the 2016 Brexit referendum, and the way in which New York City has taken positions on immigration and climate change in direct contrast to those of the Trump administration.

> **Global city**
> A city that holds a key place within the global system via its financial, trade, communications, or manufacturing status. Examples include Dubai, London, Moscow, New York, Paris, Shanghai, and Tokyo.

in at least one-third of electoral districts). Subsequent changes included adding another 180 PR seats in the Chamber of Deputies, doubling the number of Senate seats (from 64 to 128), creating an independent Federal Electoral Institute, introducing tamperproof photo ID cards for voters, and broaching the idea of allowing expatriate Mexicans (as many as 10–15 million in all) to vote in presidential elections. Elections are now subject to such close domestic and foreign scrutiny that it has become difficult for parties to manipulate the outcome.

Political scientists initially theorized that the motive behind all these changes was to build a bipartisan system in which PRI and its main conservative opposition, PAN, became the permanent parties of government, leaving the left-wing Party of the Democratic Revolution (PRD) marginalized (Alcocer, 1995). PAN proved less willing to cooperate than PRI had hoped, however, and the PRD did better than expected in elections, creating a fluid situation. The PRI hegemony is clearly long gone, Mexican elections are fairer than they have ever been, and voter interest has been piqued.

Mexicans take part in three main sets of elections.

Presidential elections

The presidential election is held every six years. Each of the major parties fields a single candidate, and there is a straight winner-take-all contest among those candidates. Although PRI once routinely won with an 85 to 95 per cent share of the vote (peaking in 1976 with a remarkable but barely believable 98.7 per cent share), its dominance has steadily diminished, and in 1994 Ernesto Zedillo became the first PRI candidate to win with less than 50 per cent of the vote (see Figure 9.1). In the landmark 2000 election, the PRI share of the vote fell to 36.7 per cent as Vicente Fox of PAN won the presidency, and in 2006 it fell to just over 22 per cent. Turnout at recent presidential elections, meanwhile, has been in the range of 58–80 per cent.

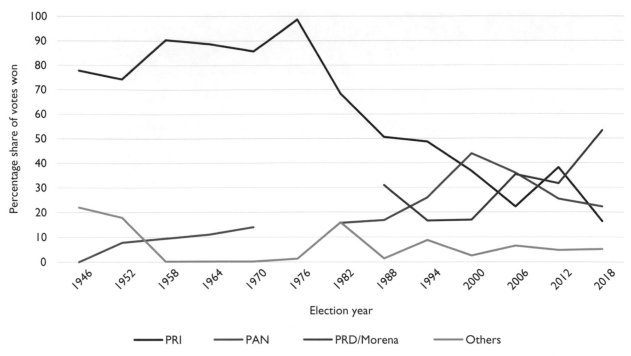

Figure 9.1 Executive electoral trends in Mexico

The election itself is held in July, but the president does not formally take office until the following December. This gives Mexican presidents one of the longest **lame duck** periods in the world. In parliamentary systems, new prime ministers typically take office within hours of winning an election; in the United States there is a period of two months between the election and the presidential inauguration. Five months may have suited Mexican presidents during the PRI era, giving incumbents plenty of time to work with successors on ensuring policy continuity and giving PRI officials plenty of time to learn about their new leader. It is doubtful, however, whether such a long period of transition is any longer useful.

Lame duck
A term describing elected officials or institutions whose successors have already been elected or appointed, and that are seeing out the closing days of their term.

Legislative elections

Elections to the Mexican Senate are held every six years, at the same time as the presidential election, and all Senate seats are contested at the same time. Changes introduced in 1993 produced the current unusual variation on a mixed-member electoral system: the party that wins the most votes in each of the 31 states and in the Federal District of Mexico City wins two of the three seats from each electoral district, the second-placed party (the 'first minority') wins the third seat, and a separate group of 32 Senators is elected on an at-large national basis, with seats distributed among political parties using a system of proportional representation. This arrangement is unique, its design coming as a result of early efforts to change the electoral system so as to give minority parties a better chance of winning seats.

For their part, elections to the Chamber of Deputies are held every three years. All 500 seats are contested at the same time, using a mixed-member electoral system similar to that used in Germany (see Chapter 4): 300 seats are decided on the basis of single-member plurality, and 200 are decided by proportional representation (PR). Voters cast two votes: one for the so-called 'uninominal' member for their district and one for a party list of so-called 'plurinominal' candidates running at large in the local electoral region. Mexico is divided into five such regions, and the formula is designed so that no party can win more than two-thirds of the seats altogether. Voter turnout at congressional elections has ranged as high as 78 per cent (in the presidential election year of 1994), but has fallen to about 60–63 per cent in recent presidential election years and as low as 41 per cent in non-presidential election years. While there was once barely a difference between turnout in presidential election years and mid-term elections years, turnout in the latter is now consistently lower than in the former.

Table 9.2 Results of recent presidential elections in Mexico

Year	Candidate	Party	Number of votes (millions)	% share
2000	Vicente Fox Quesada	PAN	16.0	43.8
	Francisco Labastida Ochoa	PRI	13.6	36.7
	Cuauhtémoc Cárdenas Solórzano	PRD	6.2	16.9
	Gilberto Rincón Gallardo	PDS	0.6	1.7
	Others		1.1	1.0
2006	Felipe Calderón	PAN	15.0	35.9
	Andrés Manuel López Obrador	PRD	14.7	35.3
	Roberto Madrazo	PRI	9.3	22.3
	Patricia Mercado	Social Democrat	1.1	2.7
	Others		1.2	3.8
2012	Enrique Peña Nieto	PRI	19.2	38.2
	Andrés Manuel López Obrador	PRD	15.8	31.6
	Josefina Vázquez Mota	PAN	12.7	25.4
	Gabriel Quadri de la Torre	New Alliance	1.1	2.3
	Others		1.3	2.5
2018	Andrés Manuel López Obrador	Morena	30.1	53.2
	Ricardo Anaya	PAN	12.6	22.3
	José Antonio Meade	PRI	9.3	16.4
	Jaime Rodríguez Calderón	Independent	3.0	5.2

Note: Morena   National Regeneration Movement
      PAN   National Action Party
      PDS   Social Democratic Party
      PRI   Institutional Revolutionary Party
      PRD   Party of the Democratic Revolution

State and local elections

Mexican states operate on their own electoral cycles, which rarely coincide with national cycles. Elections are held for the governors of states and for single-chamber state assemblies, and for municipal governments headed by presidents (the equivalent of mayors) and councils. During the PRI era, states had minimal impact on national politics because almost all governors were from the party, which also held large majorities in state assemblies. With opposition parties winning more state elections in recent years, however, results have come to matter more. PRI has continued to play a dominating role in state politics, although the number of governorships it held fell from 19 in 2011 to 14 in 2018.

Political parties

As discussed earlier in the chapter, Mexico has been a multi-party system since 1929, but PRI held a majority in both houses of Congress until 1997, won every presidential election until 2000, and until recently controlled almost every state government. Five parties then won seats in Congress in 1997, and with the PRI stranglehold weakening, the significance of parties has changed. In recent years, three major parties have dominated Mexican politics, with smaller parties gaining ground.

Institutional Revolutionary Party (*Partido Revolucionario Institucional*) (PRI)

For decades the only party that mattered in Mexico, PRI has recently fallen on hard times. During its heyday, it was not a political party in the liberal democratic sense because it was created less to compete for power than to

COMPARING POLITICS 9
Term limits

One of the recurring themes in this book has been declining faith and trust in government, a problem addressed in more detail in Chapter 7. One of the causes of this decline has been the rise in many countries of a political class of politicians who often spend many years in office, becoming professional politicians whose lives and interests might be removed from the daily realities of their constituents (see Chapter 8). One solution to this problem, assuming we define it as a problem, is to institute **term limits**. This would prevent the development of a political class or a political elite, encourage more frequent turnover in the membership of government institutions, encourage the injection of new ideas into government, and help address the problem of low turnover discussed in Chapter 5. Ultimately, it might also help address the problem of declining trust.

> **Term limits**
> The placing of limits on the number of terms that can be served by elected officials, either consecutively or in total.

We have seen in our cases that term limits are imposed on judiciaries in many countries, including a restriction on the number of terms judges can serve or limits on their maximum age. Most presidential executives are also limited in the number of terms they can serve, whether it is two terms in total (as in the United States) or a maximum of two consecutive terms (as in France, Iran, and Russia). There are also countries that have imposed term limits at the sub-national level, as in the case of 15 of the states in the United States (Caress and Kunioka, 2012). When it comes to national legislatures, though, it is rare to find limits imposed on the number of terms that can be served. Mexico is one of the exceptions, with its limit of a single six-year term on the president and state governors, and a long-time ban on consecutive terms for members of Congress and state legislatures lifted in 2015 by the Peña Nieto administration.

Although term limits may have advantages, they also have disadvantages:

◆ They might discourage people from running for office.
◆ They would prevent good leaders and legislators from staying in office.
◆ They would limit the abilities of elected officials to develop the experience and contacts needed to do the best job for their constituents.
◆ They would weaken the institutional memory of legislatures, because there would be regular injections of novice representatives who would have to learn on the job.
◆ They would create lame duck legislators whose terms have a defined end point.
◆ They would weaken the powers of elected officials relative to lobbyists and bureaucrats, who can build many years of experience in government and so can be at an advantage over elected officials.

Surprisingly little research has been done on the topic, though, and comparative politics has much to offer by taking – for example – the large body of research on term limits in US states, or in national executives and judiciaries, or the more modest research on the Mexican case, and extrapolating to see what might happen if limits were imposed more widely.

decide how power would be shared; it served as a political machine designed to mobilize voters and to give the impression of overwhelming support for the regime (Edmonds-Poli and Shirk, 2015). It kept its grip on power by being a source of patronage, incorporating the major social and economic sectors in Mexico, co-opting rival elites, and overseeing the electoral process. It had no obvious ideology, but instead shifted with the political breeze and with the changing priorities of its leaders. Politics in Mexico was not so much about competition among different parties as it was about competition among different factions within PRI – in this sense it was much like Japan's Liberal Democratic Party (see Chapter 6).

The signs of PRI's decline date back to the 1970s, when turnout at elections fell and the party could no longer argue that people had faith in the system. In order to encourage greater turnout, PRI increased the number of seats in Congress and the balance between those chosen using SMP and those using PR, but while turnout increased, more people started voting for opposition parties. At the same time, Mexicans were becoming better educated, more affluent, and more worried about Mexico's economic problems, and because PRI had governed for so long, it had no one else to blame. Meanwhile, as workers saw their real incomes falling, they became less pliant and more demanding, and PRI lost its once-strong base among labour unions.

A political earthquake struck in 1997 when PRI lost its majority in the Chamber of Deputies for the first time in its history. It was now obliged to negotiate, bargain, and compromise, something that it had never really had to do before. At the 2000 congressional elections its share of seats in the Chamber of Deputies fell yet further, it lost its majority in the Senate for the first time, and it lost the jewel in the crown of Mexican politics, the presidency. PRI initially had a crisis of confidence, but then found a new role for itself as the party of opposition. In the run-up to the 2003 congressional elections, PRI decided that at least 30 per cent of its candidates would be younger than 30 years old and at least half would be women. This tactic seemed to work, because PRI increased its share of congressional seats. But then it chose a party traditionalist named Robert Madrazo for its candidate in the 2006 presidential race, and he won just over 22 per cent of the vote, while the party lost more than half its seats in the Chamber of Deputies.

PRI scrambled to respond, with Beatriz Paredes in 2006 becoming only the third woman ever to be chair of the party. It recovered some ground in the 2009 mid-term and state elections, and then recaptured the presidency in 2012 with the victory of Enrique Peña Nieto. At first, matters went well for Peña Nieto, with efforts to break up Mexico's monopolies, to liberalize the energy sector, and to reform public education. But the drug war sparked in 2006 by PAN president Felipe Calderón continued, pushing public safety to the top of the list of concerns in opinion polls; Mexico's murder rate rose to 16 per 100,000 people, which was lower than several other countries but still placed it in an unenviable position – see Figure 9.2. Combined with persistent corruption, the violence pushed Peña Nieto's approval rating down to just 12 per cent in 2017, the lowest for any Mexican president since polling began in 1995, and the party reached a new all-time low in 2018: its presidential candidate won just over 16 per cent of the vote, and the party lost more than 75 per cent of its seats in the Chamber of Deputies.

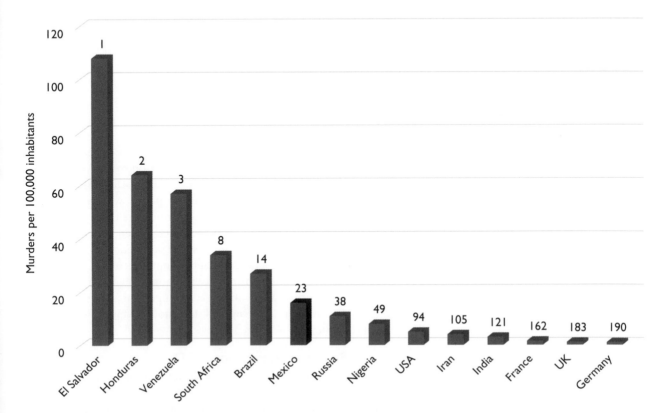

Figure 9.2 Comparing murder rates

Source: UN Office on Drugs and Crime at https://data.unodc.org (retrieved May 2018).

Note: Data are for 2015. Numbers on columns indicate global ranking out of 219 states and territories.

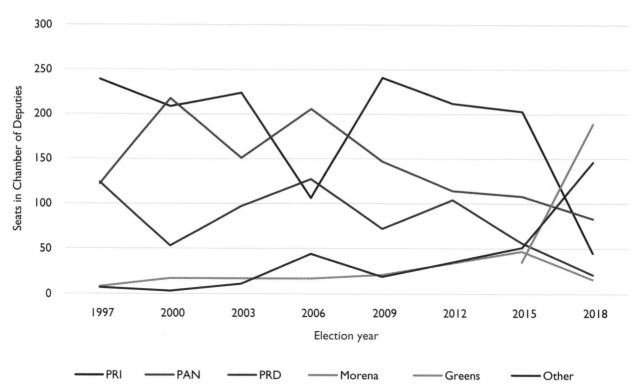

Figure 9.3 Legislative electoral trends in Mexico

National Action Party (*Partido de Acción Nacional*) (PAN)

A conservative party, PAN was founded in 1939 and until the early 1990s played the role of loyal opposition. It was pro-clerical, pro-American, and pro-business, favouring a limited government role in the economy and the promotion of private land ownership rather than communal ownership. It was strongest in the urban areas of the wealthier northern and central states but was seen as the party of money and drew little support from rural or working-class voters. This began to change in the late 1980s when a new and younger generation of pro-business members joined the party, promoting new policies and irking the old-style party members known as *panistas* who had dominated its leadership until then.

In 1989, PAN took control of the government of the northern state of Baja California, becoming the first opposition party officially to win a state election in Mexico since the Revolution. It went on to take three more state governments, and in 1994 its candidate Diego Fernandez came second in the presidential election, and PAN won the second biggest block of seats in the Chamber of Deputies. Its steady rise to power was capped by its victories in the 2000 and 2006 presidential elections and its gains in Congress, where it became the biggest party. In 2006 it won enough seats in Congress to take back the plurality that it had lost in 2003. It then lost this in 2009, a comment by voters on the worsening public security situation in Mexico, and lost the presidency in 2012.

It continues to be the major conservative party in Mexico, being opposed to abortion, for example, and having a strong religious tilt to its positions on education and morality. It also continues to promote free-market economic policies, favouring private property and opposing state intervention, and enjoying its strongest support from socially conservative and wealthier middle- and upper-class urban Mexicans. Having said this, though, it is undermined by factionalism and often finds itself internally divided on policy.

Party of the Democratic Revolution (*Partido de la Revolución Democrática*) (PRD)

Founded in 1988, PRD soon became the major opposition party on the left of Mexican politics. It grew out of mergers involving small left-wing parties and defectors from PRI. In 1988 the PRD joined with three smaller parties and a group of PRI dissidents to form an electoral alliance that provided a platform for the presidential candidacy of Cuauhtémoc Cárdenas and contested that year's congressional elections. Cárdenas had high name recognition, being the son of President Lazaro Cárdenas, the hero of the oil nationalization of the 1930s. Officially, Cárdenas won 31 per cent of the vote (the best result ever for an opposition candidate), but he may in fact have won the election, losing only because of fraud. His alliance also won four Senate seats and more than tripled its representation in the Chamber of Deputies.

The 1997 electoral season saw PRD's numbers in the Chamber of Deputies nearly double, but Cárdenas came a disappointing third in the 2000 presidential election, and the party lost more than half its seats in the Chamber of Deputies. It subsequently broke down in factional fighting, its major bright spot being that it has held the office of mayor of Mexico City since its creation in 1997: Cuauhtémoc Cárdenas was followed by Andrés Manuel López Obrador (AMLO), who stepped down as mayor in July 2005 for his presidential run. Although he fell just 244,000 votes short of Felipe Calderón, he won more than twice as many votes as any previous PRD candidate. He refused to recognize Calderón's victory, launched legal challenges to the outcome, and even had himself sworn in as the 'legitimate' president of Mexico in a symbolic alternative inauguration.

In preparing for the 2012 presidential election, AMLO set up a cross-party National Regeneration Movement (Morena). Following his defeat, he left PRD and registered Morena as a political party, raising concerns that he would split the left-wing vote. Morena made modest gains in local elections, and then won 35 seats in the 2015 mid-term Congressional elections. AMLO became its presidential candidate for 2018, the PRD combining in a marriage of convenience with PAN to support the candidacy of Ricardo Anaya Cortés. The strategy worked for AMLO, who also benefitted from the unpopularity of Peña Nieto and his failure to resolve the drug war or to address corruption, and he romped home with more than 53 per cent of the vote. Morena also made major gains in the Senate and the Chamber of Deputies.

Other parties

Mexico has long had a cluster of smaller political parties, some of which have hovered on the brink of extinction. They include the Worker's Party – whose candidate Cecilia Soto Gonzalez in 1994 became the first woman ever to make a showing in a Mexican presidential election – and the Popular Socialist Party, which was for many years the main opposition party on the left. The Ecological Green Party of Mexico (founded in 1986) surprised almost everyone by winning nine congressional seats in 1997 and finally establishing a national presence. Its representation in the Chamber of Deputies reached a new peak of 47 seats in 2015, but it then fared poorly in 2018. This was an election that not only saw the emergence of Morena as the newly dominant party in Mexico, but also saw the re-emergence of the Worker's Party and a strong result for a new conservative party, the Social Encounter Party. The days of a system dominated by PRI, with smaller parties winning a few token seats, were long gone.

THE FUTURE OF MEXICAN GOVERNMENT AND POLITICS

Mexico's political development has been driven in recent years by the tensions arising out of two competing sets of forces: the need for political liberalization against a background of the changing expectations of Mexican consumers and voters, and the need for economic liberalization against a background of fragile economic growth. Democratic reform and economic modernization have come, but while the clock cannot be turned back, the changes are far from complete, and there is growing impatience within the Mexican middle class with the slowness of recent reforms. To some extent Mexico has become the victim of its own success, because opposition parties have used their new powers and influence to block much-needed economic change, fearing that the wealthy will benefit and the poor will suffer. Mexico also faces critical structural problems, ranging from corruption to over-centralization, and challenges to public order posed by the activities of drug cartels and the desperation of Mexico's poorest citizens.

Although Mexico's democratic credentials are stronger today than they were even two decades ago, many questions hang over its future. More than many other countries in the world, Mexico is influenced by the presence of a powerful neighbour: the overwhelming impact of the United States has had mixed results for Mexico in the past, and continues to make itself felt today as Mexico's major trade partner, major source of foreign investment, and major target for drugs and undocumented migrants. The United States also continues to rely on Mexico as a source of cheap labour and a market with large unmet potential. Mexico's future depends on how well it continues to adapt to the evolution of its democracy, and how soon it can make sure that the benefits of its economic development can be more widely and equitably spread.

DISCUSSION QUESTIONS

1. To what extent, and with what effects, is Mexico still influenced by its proximity to the United States?
2. Using the United States, France, Mexico, and Iran as cases, what evidence is there to suggest that revolutions never fully achieve their goals?
3. How does corporatism in Mexico compare with that in Scandinavia, and does it present any unique problems or opportunities?
4. Is the one-term limit on Mexican presidents a model that could be usefully exported? If so, why? If not, why not?
5. What are the political implications of the rule that for many years Mexican legislators could not serve consecutive terms?
6. What have been the costs and benefits of Mexico's shift from a one-party-dominant to a multi-party system, and what lessons could be learned more broadly from this?

CHAPTER CONCEPTS

- *Camarilla*
- Chamber of Deputies
- Chiapas
- Congress
- *Dedazo*
- Drug war
- *Machismo*
- *Mestizo*

- Mexican Revolution
- Pemex
- *Políticos*
- *Porfiriato*
- *Presidencialismo*
- Senate
- *Sexenio*
- *Técnicos*

KEY TERMS

- Corporatism
- Economic nationalism
- Global city

- Lame duck
- Term limits

MEXICO ONLINE

Office of the President: www.gob.mx/presidencia
Senate: www.senado.gob.mx ★
Chamber of Deputies: www.diputados.gob.mx
National Action Party: www.pan.org.mx ★
Institutional Revolutionary Party: www.pri.org.mx ★
Party of the Democratic Revolution: www.prd.org.mx ★
Mexico Daily: www.mexicodaily.com

★ *Spanish only*

FURTHER READING

Camp, Roderic Ai (2013) *Politics in Mexico: Democratic Consolidation or Decline?* 6th edn (Oxford University Press) and Roderic Ai Camp (2017) *Mexico: What Everyone Needs to Know*, 2nd edn (Oxford University Press). The standard introduction to the history and politics of Mexico, and a more recent assessment by the same author.

De la Calle, Luis, and Luis Rubio (2012) *Mexico: A Middle Class Society* (Washington DC: Mexico Institute). Argues that Mexico is becoming a middle class society, in which increasing numbers of people behave and perceive themselves as middle class.

Edmonds-Poli, Emily, and David A. Shirk (2015) *Contemporary Mexican Politics*, 3rd edn (Rowman & Littlefield). Another overview of Mexican politics, looking at its history, institutions, and policies.

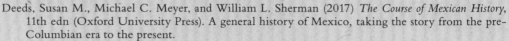

Deeds, Susan M., Michael C. Meyer, and William L. Sherman (2017) *The Course of Mexican History*, 11th edn (Oxford University Press). A general history of Mexico, taking the story from the pre-Columbian era to the present.

Tuckman, Jo (2012) *Mexico: Democracy Interrupted* (Yale University Press). An assessment by an American journalist with long experience in Mexico of the possibilities and problems following in the wake of recent political developments.

Selee, Andrew, and Jacqueline Peschard (2010) *Mexico's Democratic Challenges: Politics, Government, and Society* (Stanford CA: Stanford University Press). An edited collection looking at the effects of Mexico's democratic reforms, with a focus on institutions and parties.

 Visit **www.macmillanihe.com/McCormick-Cases** to access additional materials to support teaching and learning.

NIGERIA

10

PREVIEW

With a population of nearly 190 million and considerable oil wealth, Nigeria should also be a key actor in the international system. However, it has failed to overcome major ethnic and religious divisions, or to eliminate the role of the military in government. As a case, its main value lies in what it can tell us about the struggles that sub-Saharan African countries have faced in building united and workable political systems out of a heritage of colonialism. Nigeria is currently enjoying its longest spell of civilian government since independence in 1960, offering hope for its long-term political stability. However, its economy remains dominated by oil, corruption is rife at every level of society, security concerns and poor infrastructure discourage foreign investment, and Nigeria has failed to build the kind of political system needed to bring its large and diverse population together on a strong foundation of national unity.

KEY ARGUMENTS

◆ Nigeria offers many useful insights into hybrid political regimes, and into the dynamics of sub-Saharan African states plagued by military interventions in government.

◆ One of Nigeria's major challenges has been to overcome its substantial ethnic, regional, religious, and economic divisions.

◆ While structurally the same as most other presidential executives, the Nigerian political system has many unique qualities driven by local needs and conditions.

◆ Nigeria is well into its longest sustained experience with civilian and multi-party politics, but it has not yet been able to fully address the disruptive effects of corruption and electoral fraud.

◆ It has been many years since Nigeria was last under the rule of the military, but the political influence of the military has not entirely disappeared.

◆ Developing a stable party system is challenging in a society such as Nigeria, where ethnic differences tend to crowd out ideological differences.

OVERVIEW

Nigeria is a useful laboratory in which to study both African politics and the government of hybrid regimes, for several reasons. It is a relatively young country that is still struggling to develop a stable political system and a national identity in the face of troubling ethnic and religious divisions. Its political problems have produced both civilian and military governments, which have covered the spectrum from authoritarian to progressive. And it is interesting to observe the impact of its oil wealth, which makes it a major regional power while also posing political challenges by encouraging internal divisions and pervasive corruption tied to the dominance of its oil industry.

In political terms, understanding Nigeria is complicated by the lack of durable political patterns. Since independence in 1960, there have been three civilian governments, five successful and several attempted military coups, a civil war, and nearly 30 years of military government. The first civilian government (1960–66) was based on the parliamentary system, but the second and third (1979–83, and 1999–present) were based around a presidential executive. The first and second civilian governments broke down in ethnic conflict, and the current civilian government faces the continued challenge of encouraging Nigerians to pull together. Nigeria in 2007 made the transition from one civilian government to another for the first time in its history, and saw an incumbent president defeated in open elections in 2015 for the first time. It was upgraded from an authoritarian regime to a hybrid in the Democracy Index in 2015, but the long-term prognosis for the Nigerian model of democracy remains uncertain.

In economic terms, Nigeria is both large and poor. It is the biggest country in Africa, with an estimated population of nearly 190 million. Growing annually at 2.6 per cent, the sheer size of the population strains infrastructure that is already inadequate. Nigerians have a per capita GDP of $1,970, but this figure overlooks the country's large informal sector, and is based on the unrealistically low exchange rate of the Nigerian currency, the naira; the economy is probably bigger than the official numbers suggest. Nigeria's core economic problem is its heavy reliance on oil, which accounts for almost all its exports. Not only does this mean that the size and health of the entire economy is driven by the international market price of oil, but so are government revenues. To make matters worse, much of the oil wealth has been squandered or stolen (mainly by politicians, government officials, and criminals), and there have been bitter political arguments over how to spend and distribute the balance.

In social terms, Nigeria has several critical divisions. The most important is ethnicity (Nigeria has somewhere between 250 and 400 different ethnic groups, depending on how they are defined), and efforts to encourage these groups to think of themselves as Nigerians have had mixed results. Nigeria is also divided by religion, with a mainly Muslim north, a non-Muslim south, and controversial pressures from the north to expand the reach of *sharia*, or Islamic law. Tensions have grown since 2002 with the activities of the militant Islamist group Boko Haram, which has been engaged in bombings, assassinations, and abductions aimed at the creation of an Islamic state. Finally, Nigeria is divided by geography, with a north that is dry and poor and a south that is better endowed in resources and basic services. Most of the best agricultural land is in the heavily populated south, while most of the northern half of the country is savanna or semi-desert, with varying potential for agriculture. Regional tensions have been made worse by oil, most of which lies either in the south-east or off the coast of Nigeria, but many of the profits from which have gone to political elites in other parts of the country.

POLITICAL DEVELOPMENT

The difficulties of building a stable and united state out of a deeply divided society might once have been blamed on the legacy of colonialism, but Nigeria has now been independent for nearly 60 years, and Nigerians must take more of the share of the blame for their problems. Their leaders have failed to build a sense of national unity, to ensure the equitable spread and careful investment of the country's oil wealth, or to build successful civilian political institutions, and have allowed inefficiency and corruption to become hallmarks of the national bureaucracy. The result has been a story of unfulfilled dreams and missed opportunities, where narrow agendas have undermined the larger goals of building a stable and successful society. For Diamond (2008), democracy and governance in Africa are in a constant state of transition or suspension, and the region cannot realistically 'suddenly reverse course and institutionalise stable democratic government by simply changing leaders'. Working towards the vision of a democratic government, he continues, is 'likely to be gradual, messy, fitful and slow'. For Adejumobi (2010), meanwhile, there is a large mismatch in supply and demand for democracy and good governance in the region. Both arguments are well illustrated by the case of Nigeria.

The precolonial era (900 BCE–1861)

The early history of Nigeria – like that of Europe – was one of cultures and kingdoms that rose, fell, and combined with one another. From 900 BCE to 200 CE, what is now central Nigeria was dominated by the Nok, who discovered how to smelt iron and built a rich and advanced culture. Muslim traders began arriving in about 700 CE, and by the 14th century the region was dominated by the kingdoms of Mali, Ghana, and Kanem-Bornu, connected by trade routes that stretched to Europe and the Middle East. By the 16th century the key influence in the north was the Songhai Empire, while the rich and influential Benin culture dominated in the south.

The Portuguese were the first Europeans to explore the area, setting up coastal trading stations in the late 15th century, and founding Lagos as their main base. When they began shipping slaves to the Americas to work in mines and on sugar plantations, the **slave trade** became the biggest influence on the development of West Africa. While the creation of states in the area preceded the start of the slave trade, note Falola and Heaton (2008), it provided important sources of revenue that contributed to the consolidation of their wealth and power. The French, British, and Dutch followed in the 17th century, Britain becoming the biggest trader before banning the slave trade in 1807 (it was universally banned in 1833). European interests turned instead to ivory, palm oil, and the expansion of Christianity.

Slave trade
The organized shipment of slaves from West Africa to the Americas, beginning in the 15th century and ending with abolition in 1833.

The colonial era (1861–1960)

Britain annexed Lagos in 1861 and then conquered the rest of what was to become Nigeria, encouraged by concerns about French colonial expansion across the Sahel and North Africa. Separate protectorates were declared over Northern and Southern Nigeria in 1900, which were combined in 1914 into the colony and protectorate of Nigeria. Creating some of the divisions that persist today, Britain used indirect rule in the north through traditional Muslim leaders, and direct rule in the south through an advisory Legislative Council. The divisions were deepened in 1939 when Britain split Nigeria into three provinces, based on peanuts in the North, cocoa in the West, and palm oil in the East. Demands were meanwhile growing for greater self-determination for Nigerians, and after World War II, Britain began planning for Nigerian independence. A new constitution was published in 1954 that created a Nigerian federation, regional elections were contested by several political parties and movements (almost all of them regionally based), and Nigeria became independent on 1 October 1960.

Independence and the First Republic (1960–66)

Independent Nigeria was a federal parliamentary democracy with the British monarch as head of state, legislative power vested in a bicameral parliament, executive power in a prime minister and cabinet, and judicial authority in a Federal Supreme Court. In 1963, Nigeria cut its remaining ties to the British Crown and became a republic with a new non-executive president, a post filled by the veteran politician **Nnamdi Azikiwe** (1904–96). The new republic almost immediately became tangled in a web of ethnic and religious tensions (see Comparing Political Culture 10), as a result of which squabbling broke out among political parties that had broken down on regional lines, there were strikes by workers complaining about low pay, and charges of political corruption flew. National elections were held in 1964 amid concerns about fraud, and regional elections in the west in 1965 were marred by civil unrest and riots. Meanwhile, the military had been attracting some of the best and brightest Nigerians, who watched the chaos of civilian politics with growing dismay.

Military government I (1966–79)

On 15 January 1966, Nigeria experienced its first military coup, staged by a group of officers from the Igbo ethnic group in south-east Nigeria, headed by Major Johnson Aguiyi Ironsi. The civilian prime minister and other senior national and regional political leaders were murdered, and the federal system was abolished. Northerners now feared that Igbos planned to establish control over Nigeria, and within days hundreds of northern Igbos had been beaten and killed in outbreaks of civil unrest. Within months, northern army officers had staged a second coup, murdering Ironsi and replacing him with Lieutenant Colonel Yakubu Gowon, a Christian from Nigeria's central region (sometimes known as the Middle Belt).

Gowon restored the federal structure and promised a return to civilian rule following agreement of a new constitution, but Igbos remained nervous and tensions boiled over in 1967 when the Igbo-dominated eastern region declared its independence as the state of **Biafra**. Nigeria was now torn by a civil war between the Nigerian federal government and the secessionist Biafrans led by Lieutenant Colonel Odemegwu Ojukwu. The war dragged on for 27 months, the Biafrans fighting tenaciously out of fear that northern Muslims were bent on their

TIMELINE

11th century	Beginning of formation of city-states in area of what is now Nigeria
1485	First Portuguese trading post established
1809	Foundation of Islamic caliphate of Sokoto
1833	Abolition of the slave trade
1914	Creation of the British colony and protectorate of Nigeria
1960	Independence of Nigeria
1963	Nigeria becomes a republic
1966	Coup leads to first period of military government
1967–70	Nigerian civil war
1979–83	Second Republic
1983	Coup leads to second period of military government
1991	Abuja becomes Nigeria's new capital
1999	Civilian rule returns with creation of Fourth Republic
2000	Adoption of Islamic *sharia* law by several northern Nigerian states
2006	Helped by high oil prices, Nigeria pays off almost all its national debt
2009	Outbreak of Boko Haram insurgency
2011	First transition from one civilian Nigerian president to another
2014	Boko Haram kidnap nearly 300 girls from school in northern Nigeria
2015	First electoral defeat of one civilian Nigerian president by another; Nigeria upgraded in Democracy Index from authoritarian to hybrid regime

extermination. Cut off by a naval blockade, Biafra was finally all but starved into submission, with the loss of as many as 2 million lives. (See Achebe, 2013, for a personal memoir of the war and its implications.) The war ended in January 1970, and Nigeria was 'reunited'.

Gowon did much to patch up the wounds caused by the civil war, but he was slow to return Nigeria to civilian government and did too little to curb inflation, economic mismanagement, and the squandering of Nigeria's oil profits. In July 1975, reform-minded senior officers seized power in a bloodless coup. The new leader was Murtala Muhammed, a member of the Hausa-Fulani ethnic group from northern Nigeria, who won praise by purging the army, announcing a four-year timetable for the return to civilian rule, and dismissing government officials and military officers on charges of corruption. But he also upset those who had gained illicitly from the Gowon years, and within seven months of coming to office was assassinated during a failed coup attempt by followers of Gowon. Muhammed was succeeded by Lieutenant Colonel Olusegun Obasanjo, who was notable for being Nigeria's first leader from the Yoruba ethnic group of south-western Nigeria, and who promised to respect the goal of a return to civilian rule.

The Second Republic (1979–83)

For its new civilian system of government (the **Second Republic**), Nigeria opted for the US model, with a directly elected president, a bicameral National Assembly, and a separate Supreme Court. National elections in 1979 resulted in a clean sweep of the presidency and the legislature by Shehu Shagari and his National Party of Nigeria. In order to help promote national unity, he announced plans to move Nigeria's capital from Lagos to Abuja, 540km (300 miles) to the north in the geographical centre of the country. However, he was unable to curb corruption, and when the international oil price fell in the early 1980s, the Nigerian economy hovered on the brink of collapse. New elections were held in 1983 as planned, but although they were contested by five parties, and Shagari won a second term, the parties again broke down along ethnic and regional lines, and the elections were marred by violence and ballot-rigging.

Military government II (1983–99)

Three months into his second term, Shagari was ousted in Nigeria's fourth successful military coup. His successor – Muhammadu Buhari, a veteran of at least two earlier coups – showed too many signs of authoritarianism, and was ousted 18 months later in yet another coup. He was replaced by Major General Ibrahim Babangida, a Middle Belt Muslim who won praise both inside and outside Nigeria for paving the way to a new civilian government, named the **Third Republic**: political parties were legalized, state governments and a new National Assembly were elected, and a presidential election was held in 1993. This was apparently won by Moshood Abiola of the new Social Democratic Party, but Babangida claimed that the election had been rigged and refused to release the results. The outcry that followed persuaded him to step down and to hand over power to a transitional civilian government, which was itself ousted within three months by Brigadier Sani Abacha, the Nigerian defence minister. When Abiola defiantly proclaimed himself president, he was jailed and his wife was later murdered, allegedly by common criminals but more likely for political reasons.

Abacha announced plans to return Nigeria to civilian rule, but was openly contemptuous of human rights. He sentenced Obasanjo and others to life imprisonment in July 1995 on charges of helping plot a coup, and allowed the execution in November of activists from the Ogoni tribe of south-eastern Nigeria led by the nationally famous novelist and TV scriptwriter Ken Saro-Wiwa. The Ogoni live among the oil fields of the Niger delta, and had seen few of the profits from that oil, as well as suffering the effects of severe environmental problems. When four pro-government Ogoni chiefs were murdered in 1994, Saro-Wiwa was accused of organizing the murders, and was tried by a military tribunal and executed. Abacha would probably have engineered his own victory in a 'civilian' presidential election had he not died of a heart attack in June 1998 (an event popularly described by Nigerians as the 'coup from heaven').

The Fourth Republic (since 1999)

Plans for the Third Republic having been abandoned, the **Fourth Republic** came into being following elections in 1998–99. The presidential election was won by former military leader Olusegun Obasanjo, who promised to alter the style of Nigerian politics by building strong political institutions that could withstand the threats posed by social and economic divisions, breaking the power of elites, dealing with Nigeria's systemic corruption, and moving quickly to renegotiate a national debt repayment schedule and to repair Nigeria's relations with its trading partners and sources of lending.

Despite his efforts, Nigeria continued to suffer economic problems, corruption, religious and ethnic violence, crime in its major cities, and a dispute over the place of Islamic *sharia* courts in Northern Nigeria. Obasanjo was able to win a second term in 2003, but Nigeria's prospects barely improved, and the president undermined his credibility by lobbying for an amendment to the constitution that would have allowed him a third term. Offering some modest but welcome signs of democracy, the amendment was defeated by the Nigerian Senate in May 2006.

The 2007 presidential election was historic in the sense that, for the first time in its history, Nigeria saw a transfer of power from one civilian leader to another. It became clear, however, that Obasanjo had worked to manipulate the outcome: the winner was the all-but-unknown Umaru Yar'Adua, governor of the northern state of Katsina. The day before the primary election, all other major candidates mysteriously withdrew, and the election itself was marred by what international monitors described as multiple 'irregularities' (including the murder of voters and candidates), prompting calls for it to be cancelled. When Yar'Adua took office, the ongoing influence of Obasanjo was reflected in the appointment of four of his ministers to senior positions in the new government.

Nigeria also faced a new threat in the form of attacks by the Islamic militant group **Boko Haram** (see Smith, 2015). With origins dating back to the 1990s in the north-eastern Nigerian state of Borno, it supports the establishment of an Islamic state and the implementation of *sharia* law, and launched an armed insurgency in July 2009. This has resulted in numerous deaths, skirmishes with the Nigerian military, and – most infamously – the 2014 kidnap of nearly 300 Nigerian schoolgirls, sparking international attention and condemnation.

Nigeria today

The new tradition of civilian government in Nigeria continued in 2010 when Umaru Yar'Adua died in office after a long illness and was replaced, as the constitution dictated, by his incumbent vice president, Goodluck Jonathan. He won his own mandate when new elections were held in April 2011, but while he had a clear base of support in the south, he had little in the north, and many northern Nigerian voters felt that it was still the turn of a northerner to hold the presidency. The outcome of the election was greeted by riots and civil disturbances in the north, illustrating once again the deep religious, ethnic, and regional divisions that have troubled Nigeria since independence.

Even though the military was no longer running Nigeria, its continued role in politics was reflected in the way that a former military leader – Olusegun Obasanjo – had engineered a victory for himself in 1999 as a civilian president, a pattern that was now repeated with the revival of Muhammadu Buhari, a military leader from the 1980s. After having been defeated in the 2003, 2007, and 2011 elections, Buhari ran again in 2015, and this time won office. The result was notable for being the first time in Nigerian history that an incumbent had been defeated in a presidential election. Despite the hope this offered for Nigerian democracy, the military remains a force that cannot be ignored, and Nigeria once again experienced the almost unique problem of illness removing the president from the political scene; Jonathan had been Nigeria's youngest president, aged 53 when he came to office, but Buhari was more than 20 years older, and several times disappeared from public view, making visits to London for undisclosed health problems, leaving the government temporarily in the hands of vice president Yemi Osinbajo. (This did not prevent him from winning a second term in 2019.)

In spite of some positive political developments, not least being that Nigeria has now been under civilian rule for nearly 20 years, the political future for the country continues to remain uncertain: it promises much, but has long had an unfortunate record of failing to deliver. Nigeria could be a democratic leader for sub-Saharan Africa, but it has been unable to rid itself of the influence of the military, or to fully address its problems with corruption, leaving many to doubt the quality and durability of Nigerian democracy. It could also be the economic powerhouse of sub-Saharan Africa, but has so far failed to use its oil wealth effectively or to build an economic system that spreads opportunity. Poverty is widespread and persistent, with two-thirds of Nigerians living on less than a dollar per day, and investment in infrastructure has been far from adequate. Under the circumstances, it is difficult to be optimistic about the longer-term prospects for Africa's largest state.

Traffic and pedestrians at a downtown market in Lagos, the former capital of Nigeria. With a population of about 200 million, Nigeria is by far the biggest country in sub-Saharan Africa, and one of the biggest in the world.
Source: iStock.com/peeterv.

COMPARING POLITICAL CULTURE 10
Politics and ethnicity

In few states in the world do the boundaries of states coincide with those of nations or ethnicities (two terms with approximately the same meaning, and related etymologies in Greek and Latin). This has left most of them as multi-national or multi-ethnic states. For centuries, national differences have been a problem – and a cause of war – in Europe, while ethnic differences have had a similar effect in much of Africa. As much as national differences have caused tensions in states such as Britain, Spain, and Belgium (see Chapter 3), interfering with the effort to build a sense of unity, ethnic differences have done the same in Nigeria, Kenya, and the Democratic Republic of Congo, among many other African states.

Group identity is a natural inclination for many people and can help give them a sense of who they are, but problems arise when groups become exclusive and compete with others for access to power and resources, while worrying about loss of status or opportunity. This is certainly true of ethnic tensions in Nigeria, where members of one ethnic group – no matter how much they deny it – will always have a sneaking suspicion that other groups will gain the upper hand unless their group is well represented in the power structure.

Ethnicity is the feature that most clearly distinguishes one African from another. When outsiders look at Nigeria, they see Nigerians, but when Nigerians look at one another, they are more likely to see members of different ethnic groups; there are at least 250, of which the biggest are the **Hausa-Fulani** in the north, the **Yoruba** in the south-west, and the **Igbo** in the south-east. The greatest barrier to the creation of a stable state, a workable system of government, and a strong economy in Nigeria is the failure of so many of its people to put the national interest above narrow regional interests.

Nigeria's ethnic divisions are so persistent that they once led a frustrated Wole Soyinka – the Nigerian novelist and Nobel laureate for literature – to dismiss the idea of a Nigerian nation as a 'farcical illusion' (Soyinka, 1996). In pre-colonial times, ethnic groups had worked out a balance among themselves that protected them from too much external interference. But the creation of Nigeria forced these groups to live and work together and to build shared systems of government and administration. It also set them on a path of mutual hostility as they competed for power and resources and struggled to preserve their identity. It will take time and considerable moral courage for them to put aside their hostility and to learn to trust each other.

POLITICAL CULTURE

In a society as diverse and unstable as Nigeria, it is difficult to distinguish indigenous political values from those created by the mix of African and European political traditions. One Nigerian political scientist (Ekeh, 1989) once argued that the political culture of most states can be traced back to 'some epochal beach-head in its history', such as the American Revolution in the United States or the Bolshevik Revolution in Russia, but that the epochal events in Nigeria were the slave trade and colonialism, which left negative legacies such as corruption, violence, and mistrust. Through all the problems that have been created, however, it is still possible to identify several themes in the country's political culture.

The most notable is that despite all the problems they have witnessed (or perhaps *because* of those problems), Nigerians believe in democracy. Every military government has been seen as temporary, and military leaders who were slow in delivering on promises of a return to civilian government quickly found themselves in trouble. For their part, civilian governments may have numerous problems, but Nigerians believe that democratic civilian rule is better than unelected military government, and they support political parties, a free press, interest groups, and social organizations. The First and Second Republics may have failed, but work continues today on the building of a durable democratic system.

The biggest barrier to success lies in another of the core realities of Nigerian political culture: the multi-ethnic state. Nigerians differentiate themselves less by class or occupation than by **ethnicity**, and hence ethnic divisions are more important to understanding Nigerian society than social or labour divisions. Whether we call it ethnicity or tribalism, it involves

Ethnicity
The identification of a group of people with one another, based on a shared language, history, and culture, and encouraging adherence or loyalty to the group.

Name	Republic of Nigeria
Capital	Abuja
Administration	Federal republic, with 36 states and a Federal Capital Territory.
Constitution	State formed 1960, and most recent constitution adopted 1999.
Executive	Limited presidential. A president elected for a maximum of two four-year terms, supported by a vice president and cabinet of ministers, with one from each of Nigeria's states.
Legislature	Bicameral National Assembly: lower House of Representatives (360 members) and upper Senate (109 members), both elected for fixed and renewable four-year terms.
Judiciary	Federal Supreme Court, with up to 21 members nominated by the president, and either confirmed by the Senate or approved by a judicial commission. Age limit is 70.
Electoral system	National Assembly elected using single-member plurality. President elected in national contest, and must win a majority of all votes cast and at least 25 per cent of the vote in at least two-thirds of Nigeria's states. Possibility of two runoffs.
Party system	Multi-party, led by the centrist People's Democratic Party and the conservative All Nigeria People's Party.

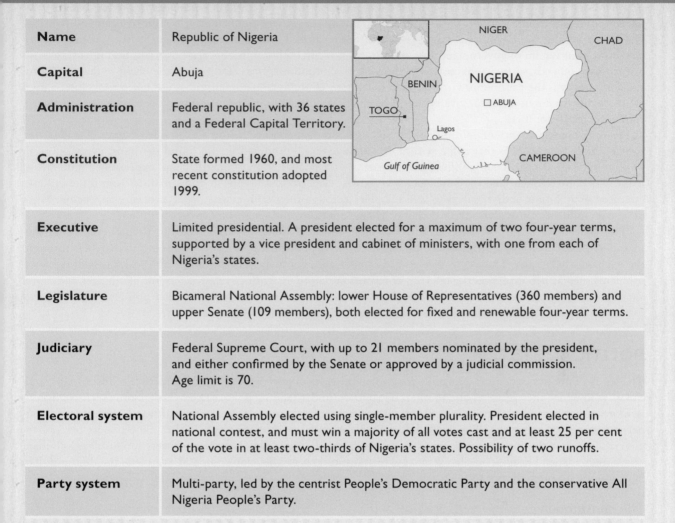

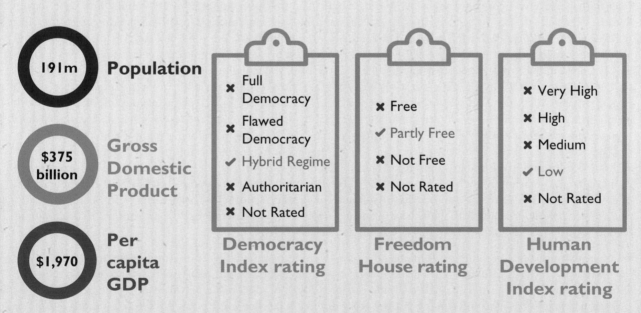

191m Population

$375 billion Gross Domestic Product

$1,970 Per capita GDP

Democracy Index rating
- ✘ Full Democracy
- ✘ Flawed Democracy
- ✔ Hybrid Regime
- ✘ Authoritarian
- ✘ Not Rated

Freedom House rating
- ✘ Free
- ✔ Partly Free
- ✘ Not Free
- ✘ Not Rated

Human Development Index rating
- ✘ Very High
- ✘ High
- ✘ Medium
- ✔ Low
- ✘ Not Rated

adherence or loyalty to a region or tribe, a sense of exclusivity, and discrimination against people from other ethnicities or tribes (see Comparing Political Culture 10). Ethnicity was less of a problem in the pre-colonial era because different groups had worked out a balance among themselves and had their own territories and political systems. It became a problem only when colonial frontiers forced different ethnic groups to live together and to develop a joint system of government. Because there is no state tradition in Nigeria, Nigerians find it hard to trust government officials, so they look instead to their ethnic communities for stability, and they believe that loyalty to the community is the paramount virtue. So far, a tradition of Nigerian nationalism has not taken root, and politics routinely breaks down in ethnic rivalry. For Adediji (2015), ethnicity has been and will continue to be a primary cause of African conflicts.

Another notable quality of political culture in Nigeria is the pervasive role of elitism (see Chapter 2), and of the patron–client relationships that come with it. To some extent, both qualities are found in almost every political system, but they are particularly influential in systems with smaller pools of qualified and experienced individuals from which government and the bureaucracy can draw. Nigeria's elite tends to come mainly from three groups: educated or ambitious individuals who win influence through their own efforts (legal or otherwise), people who have won influence through traditional clan or village positions, and senior officers in the military.

The concentration of power in the hands of these elites has limited citizen access to the policy process, the members of the elites setting up relationships with networks of political supporters who are obligated to them through the exchange of favours. This is a feature also of democracies, but their leaders must build a wider base of support, problems such as nepotism and the offering of favours are more easily discovered as a result of a bigger and more varied media establishment, and there are many independent channels through which political views can be expressed and opposition exerted that counterbalance the accumulation of power by elites.

POLITICAL SYSTEM

The study of politics in democracies often focuses on the rules of government and the structure of institutions, and the ways in which they relate to one another. By contrast, understanding politics in a hybrid regime such as Nigeria is more a question of understanding the problems experienced in building those institutions and giving them permanence and legitimacy. The Fourth Republic has outlasted Nigeria's two earlier experiments in civilian government, but the military still exerts influence in the background, and the prospects for sustained civilian government depend heavily on the extent to which institutions can develop roots and overcome the divisions that have so long plagued Nigerian society.

The constitution

Nigeria has had seven constitutions since World War II. The first two (adopted in 1947 and 1951) were flawed because they were drafted by the British with little input from Nigerians, and because they encouraged regionalism without giving the regions much power. The third was drawn up with the input and support of Nigerians and paved the way to self-government in 1956. It was then replaced by the independence constitution of 1960, which was amended in 1963 to declare Nigeria a republic and to replace the British monarch with a Nigerian head of state. It was replaced in 1979 by the new constitution of the Second Republic, based on a presidential rather than a parliamentary executive. This was in turn suspended with the return to military government in 1983, and work began on the constitution of the Third Republic. Before it could be put into force it was suspended by the Abacha regime and was replaced in 1999 by the constitution of the Fourth Republic, which remains in effect today.

The current constitution borrows heavily from its predecessors, and is notable for its length and detail: its authors went to great pains to be as thorough as possible in order to minimize the chances of misinterpretation. As a result, it has 320 articles, several schedules, lengthy lists outlining the policy responsibilities of the different branches of government, and – just in case anyone has any doubts – a glossary defining the meaning of terms such as *authority*, *decision*, *government*, and *law*. Although there are many similarities with democratic constitutions, it also contains several features that reflect the particular problems and needs of Nigeria:

◆ National unity is a key theme, emphasized in the opening paragraphs with the argument that Nigeria is an 'indivisible and indissoluble' state. The duties of the state include fostering a feeling of belonging and involvement so that 'loyalty to the nation shall override sectional loyalties'. Remarkably, the state is also responsible for encouraging 'inter-marriage among persons from different places of origin, or of different religions, ethnic or linguistic associations or ties'.

◆ Like its predecessors, it includes measures designed to make sure that the national government is not dominated by any one region or ethnic group. For example, the winning candidate in a presidential election requires at least 25 per cent of the vote in two-thirds of Nigeria's 36 states, and the federal government must include ministers drawn equally from all 36 of those states.

◆ Seven articles discuss citizenship, and thirteen articles outline the fundamental rights of citizens. For example, torture, slavery, forced labour, 'corrupt practices', and abuse of power are all outlawed; privacy of homes and phone conversations is guaranteed; and – going well beyond most democratic constitutions – discrimination on the grounds of 'place of origin, sex, religion, status, ethnic, or linguistic association or ties' is prohibited.

Nigeria's approach to constitutions is an example of **constitutional engineering**. Where most democratic constitutions have grown out of political and social realities, Nigeria's most recent constitutions have sometimes not only ignored those realities, but have set out to change political behaviour. For example, the committee appointed to write the 1979 constitution was told by the military government to draw up a document that would eliminate 'cut-throat political competition', develop consensus politics, promote national interests over regional interests, and eliminate the excessive centralization of power (Graf, 1988). The constitution of the Fourth Republic is clearly based on attempts to encourage Nigeria to move beyond its ethnic and religious divisions. A laudable goal, perhaps, but one that poses considerable challenges.

> **Constitutional engineering**
> A deliberate attempt to change political and social behaviour through the rules and goals included in a constitution.

The executive: president

Like almost all Britain's former African colonies, Nigeria entered independence with a Westminster-style parliamentary system: the legislature and the executive were fused, the government was headed by a prime minister and Council of Ministers, and the British monarch was head of state. Former British colonies with predominantly white populations such as Australia, Canada, and New Zealand took much the same approach, still recognize the British monarch as head of state today, and still use the parliamentary system. By contrast, most of Britain's former African and Asian colonies and possessions – notably India and Pakistan – rejected the monarchy as a symbol of colonialism. In 1963, Nigeria followed suit by becoming a republic (see Chapter 4) and replacing the monarch with a non-executive presidency elected by parliament for a five-year term.

With its return to civilian rule in 1979 and again in 1999, Nigeria opted for a presidential executive, which shares powers with a separately elected legislature. Many other African states have done the same, and in many cases have seen their presidencies turn into powerful offices with often authoritarian qualities. Why is Nigeria more attracted to the presidential executive than to the parliamentary executive? The main problem with the latter is that it fuses the executive and the legislature, and is based on the relative size of political parties in the legislature. So in a state such as Nigeria, where parties often break down on regional or ethnic grounds, there is the danger that the executive and the legislature could fall into the hands of a single ethnic group. By contrast, the presidential executive divides power between the executive and the legislature, and the president must win support from across the country in order to win office.

The executive under the Fourth Republic is elected by direct universal vote to a four-year term in office, renewable once, and there is a separation of powers among the executive, legislative, and judicial arms. For example, the president has the power of appointment, but all senior nominations must be approved by the Senate. Presidents cannot declare war without the approval of the National Assembly, and while they can veto new legislation, the veto can be overturned by the National Assembly with a two-thirds majority.

The president governs in conjunction with a cabinet of ministers, formally known as the Government of the Federation. The number of ministers – and their portfolios – can be changed by the president without Senate approval, and there must be at least one minister from each of Nigeria's 36 states. This latter requirement – which makes Nigeria notably different from other federal systems – has stretched the possibilities for the number of meaningful policy portfolios. Along with important jobs, such as commerce, foreign affairs, defence, and justice, there are less important ones, such as the ministries of aviation, power and steel, solid minerals, and sport.

Nigeria also has a vice president, who would step into the presidency in the event of the death, resignation, or removal of the incumbent. Again with an eye to ensuring that no one ethnic group dominates government, the constitution requires that vice presidents come from a different part of the country than the president. Umaru Yar'Adua chose as his vice president Goodluck Jonathan, a Christian Ijaw who was the incumbent governor of Bayelsa State in southern Nigeria. (Jonathan's wife's name is Patience, the two of them together offering a nice

Table 10.1 Leaders of Nigeria

Start of term	Name	Ethnicity/region	Religion	Reason for leaving office
1960	Sir Alhaji Abubakar Tafawa Balewa	Hausa-Fulani	Muslim	Killed in coup
1966 (Jan)	Johnson Aguyi-Ironsi	Igbo	Christian	Killed in coup
1966 (July)	Yakubu Gowon	Middle Belt	Christian	Coup
1975	Murtala Muhammed	Hausa-Fulani	Muslim	Killed in coup
1976	Olusegun Obasanjo	Yoruba	Christian	Retired
1979 1983	Shehu Shagari	Hausa-Fulani	Muslim	Coup
1984	Muhammadu Buhari	Hausa-Fulani	Muslim	Coup
1985	Ibrahim Babangida	Middle Belt	Muslim	'Retired'
1993 (Aug)	Ernest Shonekan	Yoruba	Christian	'Resigned'
1993 (Nov)	Sani Abacha	Northerner	Muslim	Died in office
1998	Abdulsalam Abubakar	Northerner	Muslim	Retired
1999 2003	Olusegun Obasanjo	Yoruba	Christian	End of term
2007	Umaru Yar'Adua	Fulani	Muslim	Died in office
2010 2011	Goodluck Jonathan	Ijaw	Christian	Electoral defeat
2015 2019	Muhammadu Buhari	Hausa-Fulani	Muslim	–

summary of the qualities needed by Nigeria's leaders.) When Yar'Adua became ill and disappeared from public life in November 2009, Jonathan began taking over the reins of government, becoming acting president in February 2010, and president upon Yar'Adua's death in May 2010. When Jonathan was defeated in the 2015 election by the Muslim northerner Muhammadu Buhari, the new vice president was Yemi Osinbajo, a Lagos-born lawyer.

As in most other countries, the formal rules of the office of the presidency in Nigeria say nothing about the role of personality: the true nature of the job is determined by the ability (or inability) of incumbents to orchestrate public opinion and the legislative and judicial branches to achieve their goals. Nigeria's leaders are faced with the added challenge of having to use the force of their personalities to promote national unity. Nigerian military leaders have been helped by their ability to suspend the constitution, rule by decree, and use the military as a means of control, while civilian leaders have been helped by being the only politicians elected from a national constituency. But the Second Republic ultimately failed less because it was structurally flawed than because President Shehu Shagari was unable to provide the leadership needed to address corruption and ethnic conflict. In turn, the survival of the Fourth Republic into a second administration depended in large part on the ability of Olusegun Obasanjo to lead and to avoid repeating the mistakes of the Shagari administration.

The legislature: National Assembly

In some ways like Russia, Nigeria has had more experience with executive politics than with legislative politics. During periods of military government, leadership has been focused in the hands of the officers in charge, and during periods of civilian government, legislatures have been trampled in the rush to win control of the executive.

Under the Fourth Republic, Nigeria has a bicameral National Assembly with powers to check and balance those of the executive.

COMPARING GOVERNMENT 10
The line of executive succession

Political leaders are only human, and there are many reasons why they might not be able to see out their full term in office: they might die in office, or have to step down as a result of illness, or they might be removed as a result of impeachment or a loss of political support. For this reason, it is important to have arrangements agreed for the line of succession, so that a position of leadership can be filled quickly and predictably. Nigeria has had to make use of such arrangements more often than most countries, having had five of its leaders die in office, albeit three of them as a result of military coups.

In parliamentary systems such as Britain or Japan, the line of succession tends towards the informal. There are often hopeful future leaders circling the incumbent, many or all of them already serving in a senior position in government. If a leadership position becomes unexpectedly available, replacement is usually a matter of the contenders sniffing the political breezes, sounding out colleagues, and – if the signs are good – competing in an internal election for leadership of the governing party or the major party in a coalition. In Japan, leaders are usually replaced through the less predictable process of the leader of a faction within the governing Liberal Democrats winning enough support to be confirmed as prime minister. Whatever the system, it is rare that an outgoing leader is replaced by someone who is completely unknown to voters or has no political experience, even if the new office-holder is one of several potential successors.

In limited presidential executives such as the United States, or dual executives such as France or Russia, there is typically a more formal process involved in succession. In those countries with a vice president, it is normally a matter of that person being sworn in to see out the remainder of the term of their predecessor. Voters know not just who their president is, but who is second in line, and often third, fourth, and beyond. In the United States, the Speaker of the House of Representatives is third in line, followed by the president *pro tempore* of the Senate, followed by all 15 members of the federal cabinet, in an order established by a law passed in 1947. In countries that have no vice president, such as Mexico (see Chapter 9), other arrangements are made to ensure completion of the term of the outgoing president.

In unlimited presidential executives, such as those found in many sub-Saharan African countries, there may be formal arrangements for a succession to a vice president, but it typically has less meaning or constitutional significance given that presidents try to stay in office as long as they can, and might only be removed through natural or violent death that sets off political upheavals in which the successor is the survivor or winner of the struggle that ensues, rather than someone who was being prepared to succeed.

Senate

Representing the states, the Senate has 109 members: three each from Nigeria's 36 states and one from the Federal Capital Territory of Abuja. Unlike the United States, where federal senators represent their entire state, Nigeria has opted for a system in which each state is divided into three senatorial districts, and the successful candidate must win only a plurality of votes in their district. Senators serve fixed and renewable terms of four years, and all stand for re-election at the same time. The Senate is presided over by a president elected from among its members and who is third in line to the presidency of Nigeria after the vice president.

House of Representatives

Representing the people (rather than the states), the lower chamber of the National Assembly has 360 members elected on the basis of a single-member plurality from districts of roughly equal population size, and is presided over by a Speaker elected by the House. As with the Senate, members are elected for fixed four-year and renewable terms, and elections to both chambers are held at the same time. In line with the principle of separation of powers, any member of the National Assembly who is appointed to a position in government or wins a seat in state or local government must vacate their National Assembly seat.

Both chambers must meet for at least six months each calendar year. They have the same powers to initiate, change, and approve legislation, and normally conduct all their business in English. Reflecting concerns about Nigeria's problems with corruption, the constitution requires that before taking up their seats, all National Assembly members must declare their assets and liabilities and must also declare any pecuniary interests they might have in any matters coming up for discussion. The constitution also bars anyone from becoming a member of the Assembly who is a member of a 'secret society', who is 'adjudged to be a lunatic', or who is 'declared to be of unsound mind'. How these latter conditions are measured or established is not explained.

The judiciary: Supreme Court

Through all the changes in Nigerian politics since 1960, only one institution has remained relatively stable: the judiciary. Military governments typically suspend political parties, abolish civilian political institutions, and sometimes use military tribunals, but they typically allow the courts to continue functioning, and even use them to underpin the return to civilian rule. Although the judiciary ideally acts as guardian and interpreter of the constitution, this is not easy when the constitution is suspended or rewritten. For every new constitution there must be a new set of interpretations, and the establishment of a new set of precedents, a difficult task when dealing with documents that are often only a few years old.

The Supreme Court has as many as 21 members overseen by a chief justice, nominated by the president, and either confirmed by the Senate or approved by a judicial commission. The Chief Justice is nominated by the president of Nigeria, and must be confirmed by the Senate, and there is an age limit of 70 for all members of the court. Below the Supreme Court is a system of federal and state courts of appeal and high courts, and a separate system of *sharia* courts to deal with issues of Islamic law (for more details, see Chapter 14 on Iran). Since they were created in 2000, *sharia* courts have been controversial. Restricted to 12 northern Nigerian states, they deal only with matters of family law and petty crime, but southern Nigerians worry that their work poses a threat to civil rights across the country. They captured international headlines in 2002 when a woman named Amina Lawal was convicted in a *sharia* court of committing adultery and giving birth to an illegitimate daughter. In line with Islamic law, she was sentenced to be buried up to her waist and stoned to death (by men). She initially accepted the sentence but then appealed her case to a higher court after lawyers took up the case. The court ruled in her favour.

Sub-national government

In its attempts to achieve a balance between state and federal government, Nigeria has much in common with other federal systems built on significant historical internal divisions, such as the United States and India. Nigeria's federal–state tensions have the added complication of ethnic hostilities and jealousies, the roots of which lie in the creation of a British colony whose boundaries took no heed of cultural realities. As noted earlier, Britain ruled Nigeria first as two separate territories, and then as three regions, a problem reflected in concerns among southerners since independence about the power of the predominantly Muslim north (which has produced more than half of Nigeria's political leaders).

In their attempts to reduce regionalism, Nigerian governments have changed internal boundaries so often that the map of Nigeria has frequently had to be redrawn: a fourth region was created in 1963, the four regions were replaced by 12 states in 1967, and the number of states has since been increased in increments to its present total of 36 (see Map 10.1). In spite of all these efforts, the government of the Fourth Republic has had to work hard to continue to prevent regionalism interfering with attempts to build a unified Nigerian state.

Each state is governed by an elected governor serving renewable four-year terms and a unicameral House of Assembly. The latter has between three and four times as many seats as the state has in the national House of Representatives – at least 24 and no more than 40. Governors have the power of veto, but this can be overruled by a two-thirds majority in the House of Assembly. While these are the rules of the formal institutions, local politics is also often given another dimension by the role of traditional leaders. As a colonial power, Britain strengthened their position by often ruling through them, and they continue to have influence today. Nowhere is this more clear than in the **caliphate of Sokoto**, which dates back to the early 19th century when it replaced the many city-states that had existed for centuries in what is now northern Nigeria, bringing together emirates from the different ethnic groups. The caliphate still has its own administrative structure, which coexists with that of federal Nigeria. The leader is the sultan, responsible for the administration of Islamic law, enforcing orthodox Islamic practice, and supervising local taxes.

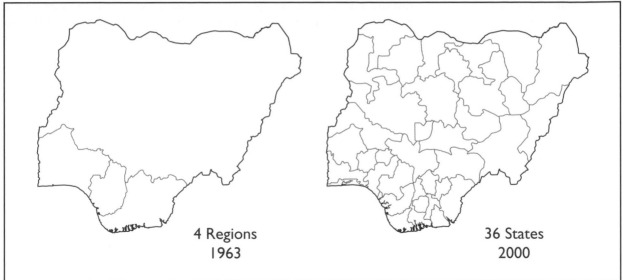

Map 10.1 Internal boundary changes in Nigeria

Although their power has been reduced, traditional political units have the advantages over modern units of longevity, legitimacy, and deep roots in local culture. They may be unelected, argues Baldwin (2015), but their longer time horizons give them an ability to organize responses to rural problems that elected officials might lack. By contrast, elected legislatures and competing political parties are alien and so have had trouble developing a firm foundation. Nigerian federal governments face a dilemma: should the special place of traditional leaders in the community be exploited to extend the reach of federal government and to support programmes of modernization and democratization, which might then weaken the power of traditional leaders? Or should traditional leaders be bypassed and their powers reduced, thereby risking the anger of local communities and reducing the credibility and popularity of the federal government?

The military

In few of the cases used in this book does the military play so critical a role in politics as in Nigeria. To be sure, it has been nearly 20 years since Nigeria was governed by the military, but this does not mean that it has disappeared as a political actor. Thanks to weaknesses in the conduct of civilian politics and the zest for power of some of Nigeria's military leaders, the country has spent 27 years under military rule since independence in 1960, and it was not until 2007 that Nigeria saw its first transition from one civilian administration to another, and not until 2015 that a civilian president was removed from office through loss of a popular vote. With each year that passes, the military role in politics recedes, in Nigeria as in many other sub-Saharan African states that once lived under military dictatorships: there were coup attempts between 2010 and 2016 in several African countries, including Benin, Burkina Faso, Burundi, Chad, Gambia, Lesotho, Mali, and Niger, but they rarely succeeded, suggesting – in the view of commentators such as Ntomba (2015) – that African politics may have turned a critical corner.

Historically, the problem has often been seen to have stemmed from the divisions in African society, which have left the military as the only institution with strength and continuity. In Nigeria, only one coup (in 1976) was an attempt by a deposed regime to win back power; most of the others were responses to political crises, and most were initially welcomed by Nigerians. In every case, the military stepped in supposedly to restore order, and although Nigeria's military governments routinely suspended the constitution and abolished most civilian political institutions, they allowed the judiciary, the courts, the bureaucracy, the police, and public and private businesses to carry on as usual (although 'business as usual' typically meant continued corruption and incompetence).

Just like the military itself, Nigeria's military governments were centralized and hierarchical and allowed few significant alternative sources of power. Although most Nigerian military leaders could not be described as full-fledged autocrats, they never pretended to be democratic, and used their terms in office to institute policies that varied from the peculiar to the openly authoritarian:

◆ The Buhari regime (1983–85) decided that military-style discipline was needed to correct Nigeria's problems, so required Nigerians to stay at home one day per month to help clean up their neighbourhoods, and forced bureaucrats who arrived late for work to do the 'frog-jump' (jumping up and down in a squatting position with their hands on their ears).

◆ Concerned about the possibilities of a counter-coup, the Babangida regime (1985–93) in 1990 ordered the execution of 69 army officers, each tried before a military tribunal.

◆ The Abacha regime (1993–98) forced confessions by beating, starving, or hanging dissidents upside down; refused public trials for political prisoners; and had convicted criminals shot to death without the right of appeal. Abacha's record was so extreme that, ironically, it did some good: he gave military government such a bad name as to undermine the prospects of its return.

In order to rule, Nigeria's military governments created their own sub-culture of administrative institutions, which paralleled civilian institutions but were based on rule by decree. During the first period of military government (1966–79), a Supreme Military Council (SMC) made up of selected senior officers was the principal policymaking forum, while a Federal Executive Council made up of senior federal bureaucrats was responsible for implementing the decisions of the SMC. More bodies were later added, including a Council of States that oversaw federal–state relations, and a National Security Organization (NSO), charged ominously with controlling 'opponents of the state'.

During the second military era (1983–99), all five institutions were initially revived. Ibrahim Babangida changed the name of the SMC to the Armed Forces Ruling Council (AFRC), and Sani Abacha symbolically renamed it the Provisional Ruling Council. Like all military leaders, Abacha was careful to watch out for opposition and to prevent anyone building too much power or offering too much opposition to his policies.

Nigerian soldiers take part in a parade marking their country's 58th anniversary of independence, in October 2018. The military has not governed the country for many years, but its place in Nigerian politics remains important, even from behind the scenes.

Source: Sodiq Adelakun/AFP/Getty Images.

However, it was soon clear that he was one of the exceptions to the general rule of military leaders who claimed that they had no long-term plans to hold onto power. He used the governing institutions to make sure that when Nigeria returned to civilian rule, it would do so under his control. It was only his death in 1998 that prevented this from happening.

While military governments may now be a rarity, in Nigeria and in other sub-Saharan African states, the political influence of the military has not gone away. There are often suspicions that the Nigerian military is keeping a close eye on the performance of civilian government, and stands ready to step in if problems become serious. Former military leaders such as Obasanjo and Buhari have also reinvented themselves as civilian leaders, a pattern found in several other African countries, but which is likely to diminish as the number of military officers with political experience declines.

For Ntomba (2015), military governments have gone out of fashion for several reasons: coups are more quickly condemned by regional and continental bodies such as the African Union, there is less public tolerance for military governments (which are quick to make themselves more palatable by labelling themselves provisional, and promising a return to elected civilian government), and both public and political opinion is opposed to any kind of intervention that might interfere with the kind of increased investment and economic development that is more likely to come to states with stable, democratic, and credible government. It was telling that when Robert Mugabe was finally removed from power in Zimbabwe in 2017 (after 37 years as president), the move was not formally described as a coup, in spite of the role of the army in his ouster.

POLITICAL PROCESSES

Nigerians take politics seriously, sometimes so seriously that their disagreements lead to ethnic and religious conflict. Urban Nigerians tend to be more politically active than those in rural areas, partly because they are closer to the centres of power, partly because of their higher levels of education and standards of living, and partly because the more unscrupulous among them have the most to gain from abusing power. Rural Nigerians have neither the personal mobility nor the same levels of access to the channels of participation or communication available to urban Nigerians. Many also value local and community politics over national politics and come under the influence of traditional ethnic and clan leaders.

The electoral system

The Nigerian electoral system is fairly straightforward. From local councils to the National Assembly, all elected officials win office through a single-member plurality system, and all officials serve the same unlimited four-year terms. Presidents and state governors alone are subject to term limits and to the possibility of two- and even three-round ballots. Elections are overseen by government commissions, which have come under a variety of different names, the body currently responsible being the Independent National Electoral Commission (INEC). Like its predecessors, its job is to oversee the electoral process and make sure that vote rigging and intimidation are minimized, and – on the basis of the census – to redraw electoral districts every ten years as necessary.

Presidential elections

Presidential elections are normally held every four years. There are no national primaries, the candidates for the presidency from each of the major parties instead being chosen by a vote within the party. The successful candidate must win at least half the party vote; otherwise a second round is called between the two top-placed candidates from the first round. Although Obasanjo claimed to have won the nomination for his party in 2003 relatively fairly, the story in the opposition All Nigeria People's Party was different: 12 candidates ran for the nomination, but 11 either withdrew or failed to attend the nominating convention, and former military dictator Muhammadu Buhari won with 4,328 votes in his favour and just 30 against. History was repeated in December 2006 in the ruling People's Democratic Party, when Obasanjo allegedly had all the main contenders stand down so that Umaru Yar'Adua could win the nomination.

More concerns about the credibility of the Nigerian presidential election were raised in the 2015 cycle, when presidential and legislative elections were scheduled to be held on 14 February. Following problems with an election for a governor in a southern state, questions were raised about the preparedness of the country to proceed with elections, and polls found that few Nigerians had any confidence that they would be conducted honestly.

COMPARING POLITICS 10
Politics and corruption

Corruption is a problem in every society. No matter how stringent the law, or how deeply bad behaviour is frowned upon, there will always be those who will try to use their offices for private gain. They may engage in fraud, bribery, patronage, nepotism, or embezzlement, or conspire with others to manipulate the outcome of elections. Such actions are illegal, and — like all law-breaking — may not always be seen or revealed, the attraction being increased by the possibility of large pay-offs, whether financial or political.

> **Corruption**
> The abuse of public office for private gain.

In Chapter 9, we saw some of the problems that Mexico must face because of its culture of corruption, a record that earned it 135th place out of 180 in the 2017 Corruption Perceptions Index (see Chapter 1). Russia tied with Mexico, and Iran was 130th, while Nigeria was ranked 148th (although this was an improvement on 2000, when it was ranked in last place). Its unenviable reputation of being one of the more corrupt societies in the world (Okoosi-Simbine, 2011) stems mainly from a combination of its oil wealth, its centralization of political power, and an irresistible desire on the part of many Nigerians to make sure that their community or ethnic group does not suffer to the benefit of another.

Nigerians in positions of authority are offered many temptations to profit themselves and their friends and networks at the expense of others, and nepotism and corruption have become so normal that many locals call it 'the Nigerian factor'. And it is not just Nigerians who feel the effects; many outside Nigeria are familiar with receiving emails from Nigerian sources notifying them of winning a lottery, or offering millions of dollars to help settle the affairs of someone who has purportedly died and left no successors. Named '419 scams' after the section of the Nigerian penal code dealing with fraud, these so-called 'advance-fee' scams actually date back many decades, but Nigerians have exploited the internet to make them a global phenomenon (Ellis, 2016).

More worryingly for the interests of democracy and economic development, corruption can undermine the quality of governance by leading to the manipulation of elections, and can discourage foreign investment and the equitable distribution of resources. The temptations to abuse the system are greatest for those with the most power, which is why military leaders and authoritarian presidents often have the worst records; it would be hard to surpass that of Sani Abacha, who was alleged to have stolen $4.3 billion while in office, and whose wife Maryam was caught trying to leave the country after his death with 38 suitcases full of cash (Mark, 2012).

Citing problems with the distribution of voter cards and concerns about the threat to security posed by Boko Haram, the INEC postponed the elections until the end of April. This led to charges of political manipulation, given that polls showed diminishing support for the incumbent president, Goodluck Jonathan, and the move met with domestic and international criticism. There were no further delays, and apart from attacks launched by Boko Haram, the elections went ahead peacefully and were acclaimed by international election observers as being fair and transparent.

The desire to make sure that Nigerian presidents win office with a broad national base of support is reflected in the unusual requirements set by the constitution of the Fourth Republic. In order to win the presidential election, the successful candidate must earn a majority of all votes cast and at least 25 per cent of the vote in at least two-thirds of Nigeria's 36 states. (Similarly, state governors must win at least 25 per cent of the vote in at least two-thirds of the local government districts within their state.) In the event that no candidates meet the terms of this formula, runoff elections are held between the two top finishers, and if neither of them meets these terms, a third runoff is held that requires a simple majority. So far, every presidential candidate has met the requirements in the first round.

Legislative and local elections

In addition to their presidents, Nigerians also elect members of the Senate and the House of Representatives, the governors and assemblies of 36 states, mayors of major cities, and the councils of nearly 800 local government areas.

Table 10.2 Results of recent presidential elections in Nigeria

Year	Candidate	Party	Number of votes (millions)	Percentage share
2007	Umaru Yar'Adua	People's Democratic Party	24.6	69.8
	Muhammadu Buhari	All Nigeria People's Party	6.6	18.7
	Atiku Abubakar	Action Congress	2.6	7.5
	Other (15 candidates)		1.4	4.0
2011	Goodluck Jonathan	People's Democratic Party	22.5	58.9
	Muhammadu Buhari	Congress for Progressive	12.2	32.0
	Nuhu Ribadu	Change	2.0	5.4
	Other (17 candidates)	Action Congress	1.5	3.7
2015	Muhammadu Buhari	All Progressives Congress*	15.4	54.0
	Goodluck Jonathan	People's Democratic Party	12.8	45.0
	Other (12 candidates)		1.1	1.0
2019	Muhammadu Buhari	All Progressives Congress	15.2	55.6
	Atiku Abubukar	People's Democratic Party	11.3	41.2

Alliance of Action Congress, Congress for Progressive Change, and ANPP.

With an estimated voting-age population of about 110 million people, Nigeria's elections are the biggest in sub-Saharan Africa, creating substantial organizational demands. While recent rounds have been declared fair and transparent by international election observers, the association of elections with fraud and violence has not entirely gone away.

Nigeria is also representative of Africa in the sense of having voters that are younger than those in older established democracies, the median age of its population being just under 18 years, far below the oldest country in the world (Japan, with a median age of more than 45), and only just above the youngest country in the world (neighbouring Niger, with a median age of just over 15) (see Figure 10.1). This means that Nigerian political parties and candidates must be sure to appeal to a younger demographic, and efforts were made during 2016–17 to reduce the minimum age required of presidential candidates from 40 to 35, and of gubernatorial candidates from 35 to 30. The relative youth of voters in Nigeria and other parts of Africa also poses the question of whether the voting age should be reduced so as to engage voters earlier than is currently the case.

Political parties

Nigerian party politics has had a chequered history. The evolution of the party system has three times been interrupted by the intervention of the military, which in each case banned existing parties and insisted on the creation of new parties free of allegiances to regions and ethnic groups. In spite of efforts such as these, few parties have been able to develop a truly national platform, mainly because Nigeria lacks the same kinds of economic and ideological divisions that have spawned political parties in democracies, of the kind that we saw in Britain (Chapter 3) and Germany (Chapter 4). Instead, parties have tended to be built on regional and ethnic differences, thereby accentuating the country's domestic divisions and undermining efforts to build a national political system. It has only been in the last few years that the party system has been able to build stability and regularity, evolving into a system with two dominant parties and a cluster of smaller parties.

The First, Second, and Third Republics

The roots of the Nigerian party system can be traced to the early 20th-century nationalist movement and the foundation of the National Congress of British West Africa, whose first meeting in 1920 was attended by delegates from Nigeria, Gold Coast (now Ghana), Sierra Leone, and Gambia. The most celebrated of Nigeria's early political leaders was Dr. Nnamdi 'Zik' Azikiwe (1904–96), an Igbo who in 1944 co-founded the first Nigerian party with a national platform, the National Council of Nigeria and the Cameroons (NCNC). 'Zikism' became synonymous for many with Nigerian nationalism, even though the NCNC drew most of its support from eastern Nigeria.

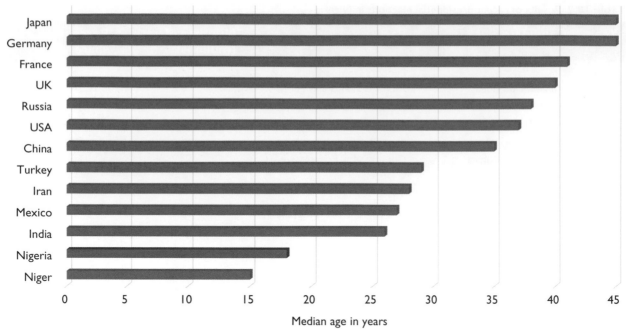

Figure 10.1 Comparing the median age of populations
Source: United Nations Statistics Division (2018).
Note: Data are for 2012.

In 1948 the Yoruba-based Action Group (AG) was founded, while northern interests were represented by the Northern People's Congress (NPC), founded in 1949.

All three parties claimed to reject tribalism, but they all swept their respective states in the 1951 regional elections, beginning a tradition of close identification between party, region, and ethnic group. They also contested the 1959 federal elections, and when none won a clear majority, the NPC and NCNC agreed to form a coalition government. It was with this tripartite NCNC-AG-NPC system that Nigeria became independent, but hopes for the perpetuation of a multi-party democracy disappeared as a crisis developed over the 1962 census and the 1964 federal elections, when northern and southern parties accused each other of rigging the results and the NPC refused even to take part. The chaos that followed led to the January 1966 military coup and the banning of parties.

During preparations for the return to civilian government under the Second Republic in the late 1970s, new efforts were made to avoid ethnic politics by agreeing detailed rules on party formation: membership had to be open to all Nigerians, party names and emblems could not reflect regional or ethnic interests, and party headquarters could be situated only in Lagos, the federal capital. A Federal Election Commission was created to screen all parties, to make sure they met the terms of the new rules, and to oversee the elections. Despite this, the 1979 elections revolved around a tripartite contest strongly reminiscent of the First Republic: the victorious National Party of Nigeria (NPN) was seen by many as the successor to the NPC, the Unity Party of Nigeria looked remarkably like the old Action Group, and the spirit of the NCNC was revived in the Nigerian People's Party, which ran Nnamdi Azikiwe as its presidential candidate.

In the lead-up to the 1983 elections, there were more accusations of fraud, with the NPN accused of manipulating the election, changing the timetable to its own advantage, and refusing to register new parties. The new electoral register drawn up for the election showed a hard-to-believe 34 per cent increase in the number of voters, and the elections themselves were marred by charges of abuse and cheating. When Shehu Shagari won re-election with an increased share of the vote (up from 34 per cent in 1979 to nearly 48 per cent in 1983), the credibility of the new administration suffered a fatal blow. Three months later, it was ousted by a military coup.

In preparing for the return to civilian rule under the Third Republic, the Babangida regime prevented anyone with experience in politics from running for election, hoping (as he put it) to replace 'old brigade' politicians with a 'new breed' of leaders driven by ideology and unencumbered by the regional ties that had caused so many problems for earlier civilian governments. Announcing his transition plans in 1987, Babangida – who described political parties as 'natural grounds for the idle and illiterate who over the years have failed to qualify for any reputable profession' – said he would allow only two parties to contest the new elections.

Thirteen political groups applied for registration as parties, but amid suspicions that most were being manipulated behind the scenes by former politicians, Babangida rejected all their applications and arranged for the creation of two new parties, the Social Democratic Party (SDP) and the National Republican Convention (NRC), 'one a little to the left, and the other a little to the right of centre', as he described them. Babangida even provided them with offices, official colours, and election symbols. In spite of his efforts, the NRC developed a northern tilt while the SDP had a southern tilt.

In an effort to prevent ballot rigging in the elections that followed, secret votes were not allowed; instead, voters at each polling station had to line up behind photographs of their preferred candidates. They were then counted and the results announced immediately. The elections passed off peaceably, both parties winning a spread of governorships and state assemblies, but presidential primaries had to be re-run after the NEC accused all 23 candidates of cheating, and Babangida annulled the result in 1993 amid suspicions that his favoured candidate had lost. With the crisis that followed, Babangida resigned and the party system was once again suspended.

The Fourth Republic (since 1999)

The Abacha regime set up a new national electoral commission, and municipal elections were held in March 1996 without parties, which were then allowed to form in preparation for new federal elections. When most were quickly disqualified by Abacha, it became clear that he planned to manipulate the electoral system so as to win office as president in a civilian election. Following his death, it was decided to wipe the slate clean and start all over again. The new system – overseen by a new Independent National Electoral Commission – resulted in the development of three major new parties, with which Nigeria went into the elections for the government of the new Fourth Republic:

◆ *People's Democratic Party (PDP).* Describing itself as a centrist party, the PDP takes a neoliberal view on economic issues (favouring a free market and limited government regulation), and conservative social positions, being opposed – for example – to homosexuality and same-sex marriage. It was initially led mainly by veteran politicians, including several former military officers brought together by their mutual opposition to the Abacha regime. It did well in local elections in 1998 and in elections to the National Assembly in 1999, and its candidate Olusegun Obasanjo rounded off the results by winning the presidency with a solid 62.8 per cent share of the vote. Its successes were repeated in 2003, 2007, and 2011, but it lost the presidency in 2015.

◆ *All Nigeria People's Party (ANPP).* The second largest party and therefore the major opposition, the ANPP took moderately conservative positions and was initially backed by wealthy businesspeople brought together by their support of Sani Abacha. It formed a pact with the Alliance for Democracy, which was mainly of convenience, given that the latter is a moderately liberal party. The ANPP was dissolved in 2013 when it merged with other parties to form the All Progressives Congress (APC). The latter won the presidency and majorities in the House of Representatives in 2015 and 2019.

◆ *Alliance for Democracy (AD).* The AD was a regional party with a firm base of support among the Yoruba in south-western Nigeria, where it won local and state elections in six states in 1999. It quickly became embroiled in controversy, however, when members of the party in the Lagos state legislature broke into two factions supporting different leaders. When members began throwing chairs and tables at each other during a meeting, the police had to be called in to restore order. The party was dissolved in 2006.

The 2003 elections were significant because there was no certainty that Obasanjo (who was running for a second term) would be nominated once again as the candidate for the PDP, and – unlike the military – no Nigerian civilian government had ever organized successful elections. Voters were given a choice of 22 registered political parties, but all three of the major party candidates were former Army generals: Obasanjo himself, Muhammadu Buhari (military leader in 1984–85) and the former Biafran rebel leader Odemegwu Ojukwu. Meanwhile, rumours were rife that another former military leader – Ibrahim Babangida – was using his money and influence behind the scenes to influence the outcome. Despite the usual charges of fraud and the usual violence that accompanies Nigerian elections, Obasanjo was elected to a second term as the PDP candidate.

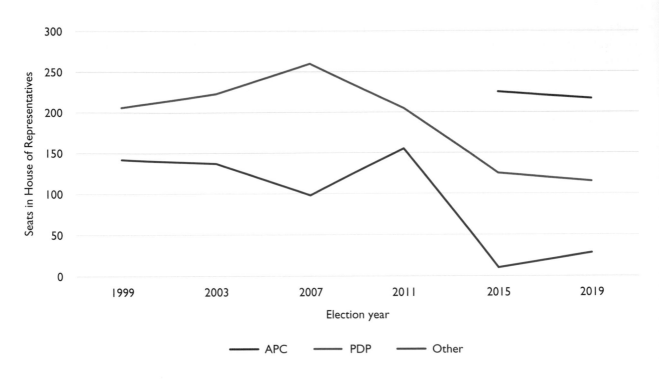

APC   All Progressives Congress (an alliance of Action Congress, Congress for Progressive Change, and ANPP).

PDP   People's Democratic Party

Figure 10.2 Legislative electoral trends in Nigeria

The 2007 elections saw the People's Democratic Party and the All Nigeria People's Party running again, against the new Action Congress formed out of the Alliance for Democracy and several smaller parties. The PDP increased its share of the vote in the presidential race from 62 per cent to nearly 70 per cent, and won strong majorities in legislative elections, winning 77 per cent of the seats in the Senate, and 72 per cent of those in the House of Representatives. While the results of the 2007 legislative elections were widely questioned, more care was taken to improve organization of the 2011 elections, which were twice delayed because of concerns about logistical problems. The outcome was a reduced majority for the PDP, whose representation fell from 260 to 205, and small gains for a wider selection of opposition parties.

The reshaping of the party system continued with the 2015 election cycle (see Odukoya, 2013). The PDP remained the dominant party, fielding incumbent Goodluck Jonathan as it presidential candidate, while four smaller parties merged to form an electoral alliance known as the All Progressives Congress (APC), fielding Muhammadu Buhari as its presidential candidate. While the APC takes a more liberal position than the PDP on economic issues, it takes a more conservative position on social issues, a reflection of its large base of support in the Muslim north of Nigeria. The APC swept to power in 2015, winning the presidency along with majorities in both the House of Representatives and the Senate. When Jonathan conceded defeat to Buhari, the event was notable for being the first time in Nigerian history that a candidate from an opposition party won a presidential election against an incumbent. This continued to augur well for the development of civilian and party politics in Nigeria.

THE FUTURE OF NIGERIAN GOVERNMENT AND POLITICS

'The trouble with Nigeria' wrote the novelist Chinua Achebe in 1983, 'is simply and squarely a failure of leadership. There is nothing basically wrong with the Nigerian character. There is nothing wrong with the Nigerian land or climate or water or air or anything else. The Nigerian problem is the unwillingness or the inability of its leaders to rise to the responsibility, to the challenge of personal example which are the hallmarks of true leadership.'

Achebe did not live to see the relatively peaceful presidential transition of 2015, and it is interesting to speculate what he would have thought, and whether he would have had reason to issue a more optimistic assessment. Nigeria's political record has improved, and so has its economic outlook, thanks mainly to the rise in the international price of oil and strengthened investor confidence. But for Nigeria to 'work' there will need to be a more sustained transformation in the way Nigerians relate to one another, setting aside ethnic and religious differences and trying to think of themselves more actively as Nigerians. It will also take a fundamental transformation of the economy, with Nigeria moving away from its dependence on oil and broadening the sources of its income, and moving away from the tradition of monopoly and incompetence that characterizes its state-owned businesses, which are in urgent need of privatization.

Nigeria's future remains frustratingly uncertain. It is one of the two biggest and most powerful countries in sub-Saharan Africa (along with South Africa), it has a large and energetic population that favours democracy over military government, it has oil wealth that could provide the basis for sound economic development, and it could become an engine for regional economic and political growth. If it can find a way to rise above ethnic and religious division, to overcome corruption, to absorb its burgeoning population, and to channel its oil wealth into building infrastructure and education, it could become Africa's first world power.

DISCUSSION QUESTIONS

1. Are Nigeria's ethnic and religious divisions insurmountable, or are there examples of divided societies in other parts of the world that could offer a recipe for overcoming them?
2. Is military government a thing of the past (in Nigeria and in other parts of sub-Saharan Africa)? If so, what has changed to make this possible?
3. How many of Nigeria's problems are the legacy of colonialism, and how many are self-created?
4. Given the many other options available, is the presidential executive model the best for Nigeria's circumstances?
5. Why is the military so much more politically influential in countries such as Nigeria than it is in countries such as Britain, the United States, and Japan?
6. To what extent do Achebe's concerns about a failure of leadership in Nigeria apply also to other countries with political problems?

CHAPTER CONCEPTS

- Biafra
- Boko Haram
- Caliphate of Sokoto
- Fourth Republic
- Hausa-Fulani
- Igbo
- National Assembly
- Nnamdi Azikiwe
- Second Republic
- Third Republic
- Yoruba

KEY TERMS

- Constitutional engineering
- Corruption
- Ethnicity
- Slave trade

NIGERIA ONLINE

Nigerian Government: www.nigeria.gov.ng
National Assembly: www.nassnig.org
Supreme Court of Nigeria: http://supremecourt.gov.ng
People's Democratic Party: http://peoplesdemocraticparty.com.ng
All Progressives Congress: www.allprogressivescongress.org
The Guardian: https://guardian.ng
Premium Times: www.premiumtimesng.com
This Day: www.thisdaylive.com
News Agency of Nigeria: www.nan.ng

FURTHER READING

Achebe, Chinua, *Things Fall Apart* (various publishers and years since 1958), and Chimamanda Ngozi Adichie (2007) *Half of a Yellow Sun* (Anchor Books). Two novels about life in Nigeria, the former a classic that looks into the heart of a family in a small village in Nigeria, and the latter which uses the Biafran war to comment on the Nigerian condition.

Adejumobi, Said (ed.) (2010) *State, Economy, and Society in Post-Military Nigeria* (Palgrave Macmillan). An edited collection of studies – by Nigerian scholars – of developments during the Fourth Republic.

Campbell, John (2013) *Nigeria: Dancing on the Brink*, updated edition (Rowman & Littlefield). A set of reflections on Nigeria by a former US ambassador to the country, focusing on how oil wealth, corruption, and elite competition compromise its prospects.

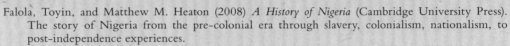

Falola, Toyin, and Matthew M. Heaton (2008) *A History of Nigeria* (Cambridge University Press). The story of Nigeria from the pre-colonial era through slavery, colonialism, nationalism, to post-independence experiences.

Kew, Darren (2016) *Civil Society, Conflict Resolution, and Democracy in Nigeria* (Syracuse University Press). An assessment of the role of civil society organizations in political change in Nigeria.

LeVan, A. Carl, and Patrick Ukata (eds) (2018) *The Oxford Handbook of Nigerian Politics* (Oxford University Press). An edited collection of chapters on different aspects of Nigerian politics, including institutions, civil society, and public policy.

Visit **www.macmillanihe.com/McCormick-Cases** to access additional materials to support teaching and learning.

TURKEY

PREVIEW

In few countries has government and politics offered such a mobile target as Turkey. Whether considering its transformation from an empire to a modern republic, its evolution from a parliamentary system to a presidential system, its ever-changing community of political parties, the competing influences of Islamism and secularism, or the opposing pull of nationalism and Westernization, Turkey has rarely sat still for long. It offers us a case study of a society that has found it difficult to build a stable democratic system, undermined as it has been by the influences of elitism, the periodic intervention of the military, and a heritage of nationalism. For now, at least, it remains a hybrid regime, but this seems unlikely to last; as a case, it offers a valuable example of a state whose halting efforts to build democracy have failed to prevent it from falling back into the grip of authoritarianism.

KEY ARGUMENTS

◆ Turkey is a hybrid regime that, after many decades of troubled efforts to build democracy, has recently trended towards authoritarianism.

◆ In less than a century, Turkey has been transformed from an empire to a multi-party presidential republic.

◆ Turkey has for most of its modern history been a parliamentary system, but it has recently been reformulated as a presidential system with authoritarian qualities.

◆ The military has long played a role in Turkish politics that has veered between the subtle and the obvious, and was most recently felt in an attempted coup in 2016.

◆ The political party landscape in Turkey has changed much in recent years, although the electoral system ensures that only two to four parties usually win seats in the national parliament.

◆ For now, at least, the ascendancy of Recep Tayyip Erdoğan and his conservative Islamist Justice and Development Party (AKP) seems clear.

OVERVIEW

As the chapters in this book progress, we move deeper into the world of hybrid and authoritarian systems. Turkey was for decades on a trajectory that many hoped would move it firmly into the community of democracies, and – at least superficially – it has many of the required features: regular elections, a multi-party system, an entrenched system of courts, and a division of executive and legislative powers. But every part of its political system must be conditioned with qualifiers: questions hang over the fairness of elections, the military has long played a role in politics, human rights and civil liberties have been under attack, and recent changes have placed more power in the hands of the executive. The effects are reflected in Turkey's political ranking: it has for many years been rated in the Democracy Index as a hybrid regime, but Freedom House in 2018 downgraded it from Partly Free to Not Free, warning that Turkey had seen the biggest ten-year democratic decline in the world (Freedom House, 2019).

In political terms, Turkey has undergone remarkable changes: in the space of barely a century, it has been transformed from an empire to a presidential republic, via many decades as a parliamentary system, with several interventions from the military. Little surprise, then, that it is not always easy to pin down the rules and personality of its political system. Superficially, it has been a presidential system since 2017, but one whose tendency has been towards authoritarianism, with a strong executive, a relatively weak legislature, and the lack of an independent judiciary or the kind of federal system that helps divide power in many other presidential systems. Politics is a changeable quality, as we have seen throughout this book, but in few places have the changes to the structure of government come as quickly – or with such uncertain long-term effects – as they have in Turkey. With so many recent and substantial changes to its political system, it is hard to predict where Turkey goes from here.

In economic terms, Turkey is usually classified as an **emerging economy**. China and India are regarded as the leading examples of the type, which also includes Brazil, Indonesia, Mexico, and South Africa. Turkey has the 17th largest economy in the world (ranking above those of Saudi Arabia and Argentina), but its GDP shrank by ten per cent between 2013 and 2017 thanks to high inflation, a high budget deficit, a large national debt, and market concerns about Turkey's growing authoritarianism. Members of the governing administration have even hinted darkly that Turkey's economic problems are part of a foreign conspiracy to undermine the country, a view supported (according to polls) by a large minority of Turks.

Emerging economy
One that is developing rapidly but does not yet have the features of a fully developed market.

In social terms, and despite the efforts made by the founder of modern Turkey – Mustafa Kemal Atatürk – to promote the idea of a Turkish state for the Turkish people (an idea since repeated by many of the country's leaders), questions remain about Turkish national identity. Turks make up about 75 per cent of the population of the country, but there is a large Kurdish minority living mainly in the south-east of the country, many of whom support efforts to set up an independent **Kurdistan**. The struggle has involved widespread violence and crackdowns by the military and by the Erdoğan administration. Questions also continue to be asked about the extent to which Turkey is a Muslim or a secular society, and – as Turkey continues, with declining enthusiasm, to gain entry to the European Union – about the extent to which the country is European or Middle Eastern.

POLITICAL DEVELOPMENT

Although Turks have a long history, the modern state of Turkey is both relatively new and quite different from its precursors. The story of the Turks as a definable people dates back at least 4,000 years, and runs through the rise and fall of multiple empires in central Asia, ranging from the Great Hun Empire (established in the 3rd century BCE) to the Great Seljuq Empire in 1040–1157. The peninsula of Anatolia (also sometimes known as Asia Minor) was home at various times to Hittites, Trojans, Romans, and Byzantines. Seljuq Turks from central Asia began to settle the region in the early 11th century, achieving complete control following their victory over the Byzantines at Malazgirt (in what is now eastern Turkey) in 1071.

The Anatolian Seljuq state subsequently became the dominating power in the area between Islam and Christianity, eventually making Konya its capital. Turmoil followed as the Byzantines tried to recover their territory and Crusaders occupied Constantinople. The region nonetheless began to be referred to as Turkey, or the land of the Turks, an identity that lasted until Mongol invasions that began in 1243. These brought an end to Seljuq control and left many smaller political units in their wake. One of these was the principality of another Turkish tribe, the Ottomans, in the north-western region of present-day Turkey. Followers of Islam, and named for their reputed founder, the ruler Osman I (or Othman in Arabic), the Ottomans began to expand their control over Anatolia during the 14th century.

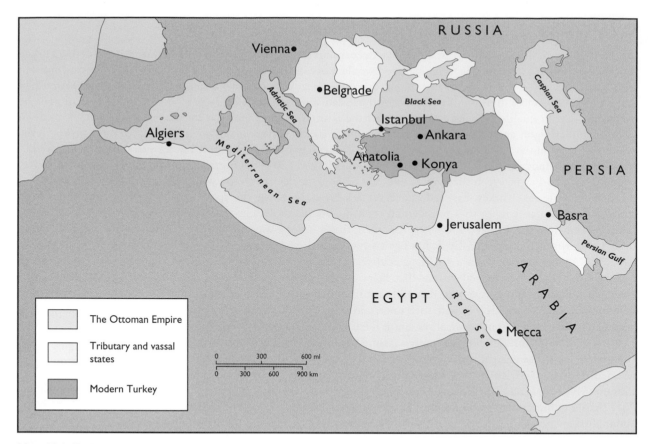

Map 11.1 Turkey and the Ottoman Empire

The era of the Ottomans, early 1300s–1922

The **Ottoman Empire** was to become one of the great empires of what we now think of as the Middle East, lasting more than 600 years and expanding north to Vienna, west to Algiers, and south to Mecca; see Map 11.1. The advance of the Ottomans began in 1326–37 with several major gains in western Anatolia and a crossing into Europe that allowed them to surround Constantinople and to advance into the Balkans. The Ottoman capture of Constantinople in 1453 marked the end of the Byzantine Empire, and even though the Ottoman Empire was already well established, the event marked its coming of age.

Constantinople became the major seat of the Ottomans, whose apogee was reached under the reign of Sultan Suleman the Magnificent (1520–66). However, the Ottomans faced much external resistance as well as opposition from rival Muslim forces, and the empire began its long decline in the late 16th century, as the economic and military reach of Europe and Russia began to expand. Its retreat from Europe began after the failed second siege of Vienna in 1683, the Russians captured Azov on the Black Sea in 1739, the Ottomans lost wars with Russia, and their growing weakness evolved into the **Eastern Question**: the concern that the major Western powers (Britain, France, Austria-Hungary, Russia, and later Germany) had over what might happen to the region as the Ottoman hold weakened, and each power tried to make sure that none of the others won an advantage. British and French concerns combined in the outbreak of the Crimean War of 1853–56, fought to discourage Russia from expanding its reach to the south.

As early as 1839, with the launch of a programme known as Tanzimat (from the Arabic for *organization*), efforts had been made by sultans to reform the Ottoman system. The rise of nationalism in the Balkans continued to whittle away at the northern territories of the empire, however, and Ottoman control continued to crumble in the face of expanded European interest in the Middle East. The first Ottoman constitution was adopted in 1876, but was suspended in 1878, then restored in 1908 following an uprising supported by the military. A group of exiles, students, bureaucrats, and military officers known as the **Young Turks** hoped to create a constitutional monarchy, but Turkey came to be ruled by the military with the sultan as a figurehead, and the Ottoman decline continued.

Ottoman weakness was reflected in the concerns of its rulers about the place of Christian Armenians in a Muslim Ottoman Empire and the instability of the border between Russia and Ottoman territory. This led in

April 1915 to the launch of systematic massacres of Armenians in Turkey, resulting in numerous deaths (estimates range between 600,000 and 1.5 million) and the forcible removal of many more by the time the massacres ended in the early 1920s. Turkey has refused to describe the events as constituting genocide, and even today the debate continues about how they should be understood and labelled.

The end came with World War I, in which the Ottomans took the side of the German-led Central Powers, and from which they emerged defeated in 1918. The Ottomans were compelled to submit to territorial occupation by Britain, France, Russia, and Greece. In response, a national resistance movement emerged led by **Mustafa Kemal** (1881–1938), an Ottoman military officer. He united disorganized groups into a structured army, which in 1919 launched a war of liberation. The Ottoman Empire came to a formal end on 1 November 1922 with the abolition of the sultanate. The new Turkish republic was proclaimed on 29 October 1923, the capital was moved to Ankara, a new constitution was written, and peace came with the Treaty of Lausanne. This came into force in August 1924, recognizing the existence and the borders of Turkey, and guaranteeing its independence. Kemal – known as such until 1934, when the Turkish parliament gave him the new surname Atatürk, or 'Father of the Turks' – was elected as first president of Turkey, and remained in office for the first 15 years of the new republic, helped by the creation in 1931 of his **Republican People's Party** (known as the CHP from its Turkish name).

Foundations of the Turkish republic, 1923–45

Under Atatürk's often authoritarian rule, Turkey was reorganized and reformed, with the end of traditional ideas about government and society, the creation of a new political and legal system based on the principle of parliamentary government, and the creation of a Turkish state out of the remains of the Ottoman Empire. Islam was no longer the state religion, Arabic script was replaced with Latin script, the Muslim calendar was replaced with the Western Gregorian calendar, women were given new rights, a new education system was developed, new legal codes were adopted from European models, Constantinople was formally renamed Istanbul, and Turkey pursued a policy of neutrality in international affairs.

TIMELINE

1453	Ottoman capture of Constantinople brings end to Byzantine empire
1683	Ottoman expansion into Europe ends at Battle of Vienna
1908	Uprising ushers in the Young Turks
1919–22	War of liberation
1923	Turkey declared a republic and Mustafa Kemal (Atatürk) becomes president
1924	New constitution comes into effect
1950	First free elections in Turkey
1960	Coup ushers in period of military rule and new constitution
1971	Second military coup
1974	Turkey invades northern Cyprus
1980	Third military coup and imposition of martial law
1982	Introduction of new constitution
1984	Beginning of armed struggle against Turkey by PKK
1987	Turkey applies for membership of the European Economic Community
2001	Foundation of AKP, which wins elections in 2002
2013	Gezi Park protests
2014	Recep Tayyip Erdoğan becomes Turkey's first popularly elected president
2016	Failed military coup; two-year state of emergency follows
2017	Constitutional referendum results in introduction of presidential system

So substantial were the changes that they earned their own label: **Kemalism** was a view of the needs of the new Turkey based on the principles of secularism, republicanism, nationalism, reformism, statism, and populism. It also resulted in unfortunate traditions of authoritarianism and elitism, the effects of which are still felt in Turkey today. Nonetheless, by the time of Atatürk's death in 1938, Turkey was well advanced on its transformation from a Middle Eastern empire to a state on the Western model.

Democracy, however, did not take root. Government centred on the legislature (the Grand National Assembly), a president elected by the Assembly for an unlimited number of four-year terms, and a system dominated by the CHP. The latter pursued Kemalist and social democratic policies, and while opposition parties could function, they were never able to take root, and the CHP's candidate İsmet İnönü became Turkey's second president in 1938. Turkey was neutral during World War II, and initially remained neutral in the emerging Cold War, but abandoned this policy in 1952 when it joined the North Atlantic Treaty Organization (NATO).

An evolving political identity, 1950s–90s

Turkey's first free elections were held in 1950, resulting in a landslide victory for the moderately conservative Democrat Party (DP) and its leader Adnan Menderes, who became prime minister. Although it also won the 1954 elections, economic conditions had begun to deteriorate, and the DP was showing signs of authoritarianism, suppressing the opposition and limiting freedom of the press. The military had mainly remained out of politics, but now became concerned about the trends in civilian politics, as well as the low status of the military in Turkish national life (Waldman and Caliskan, 2017). In May 1960, the country experienced its first military coup, followed by the purging of hundreds of military officers, judges, and university faculty, the banning of the DP, the trial and execution of Menderes, and the writing and adoption of a new constitution.

A second and less dramatic military intervention took place in 1971, prompted by concerns among military leaders about economic problems, social unrest, and political deadlock in the national parliament. Instead of sending tanks into the streets, the so-called 'coup by memorandum' took the form of written instructions given to Prime Minister Süleyman Demirel by the military chief of staff demanding the formation of a new government. Instead of governing directly, the military chose to manage from behind the scenes, appointing a new prime minister and imposing martial law in an effort to control an increasingly unstable country. Political unrest sparked a third coup in September 1980, resulting in the suspension of the constitution, the abolition of the legislature, and the declaration of martial law. Another new constitution was written under the supervision of the military, leaving it with an expanded role over civilian government.

On the foreign policy front, two key developments influenced the international standing of Turkey. The first involves Turkey's aspirations to join the European Union. It first applied to join the precursor to the EU, the European Economic Community, in 1959, and was given associate membership in 1963. It then applied for full membership in 1987, but had to wait 12 more years before it was recognized by the EU as a formal candidate for membership. Little progress has since been made (see section on political culture for more discussion), as a result of which Turkey today is no longer as enthusiastic as it once was about EU membership, and has instead focused on making itself a Middle Eastern power in its own right.

The second set of developments concerned neighbouring Cyprus. Following a coup there in July 1974, that was part of an effort by the military government in Greece to annex the island state (which, like Greece, had once been part of the Ottoman Empire), Turkey launched an invasion ostensibly to protect the interests of Turkish Cypriots. Although the Turkish Republic of Northern Cyprus was declared in 1983, the invasion and occupation were widely regarded as illegal, and continue today to be a problem in Turkish foreign relations.

At home, Turkey faced difficulties stemming from the struggle with Kurdish separatists in the east of the country. One of the effects of the post-Ottoman settlement of political borders in the Middle East was to leave Kurds divided territorially between Turkey, Iran, Iraq, and Syria. A Kurdish uprising in 1925 was used by Atatürk to tighten his grip on Turkey, but Kurdish nationalism never went away. In 1978, the Kurdistan Worker's Party (PKK) was founded, and in 1984 it began an armed insurgency against Turkey that has so far cost an estimated 40,000 lives. At least two ceasefires have been declared (in 1999 and in 2013), but both came to an end, and the long-term effect of the conflict has been substantial. For Waldman and Caliskan (2017), there have been virtually two states in Turkey since the 1980s: 'one that resembles any peacetime European state, albeit with its problems, and another that is governed by military law, curfews, violence, and disappearance, where killing is common and accountability and the rule of law virtually non-existent'. The prospects for a permanent peace, they conclude, are poor.

Meanwhile, the tensions between Islamism and secularism continue. The place of Islam as the formal state religion ended with a constitutional amendment in 1928, secularism lay at the heart of Kemalism, and freedom

of religion has long been a key principle of government. Much symbolism was attached to the decision by many Turkish female college students in the early 1980s to wear headscarves as confirmation of their commitment to Islam. A ban on headscarves was imposed in 1987, leading to protests and the final lifting of the ban in 2010. More politically telling has been the rise of Islamist political parties; the now-defunct Welfare Party won enough seats in the 1995 elections to form a government, and the more popular and politically adept **Justice and Development Party** (AKP) has dominated Turkish politics since forming its first government in 2002, and winning the presidency in 2007. Under the leadership of President Recep Tayyip Erdoğan (pronounced 'Eerdo-wan'), Turkey has both moved away from its secular traditions and towards increased authoritarianism.

Turkey today

Understanding Turkish politics today means appreciating the implications of two key developments. First, the AKP has strengthened its hold on government, forming every government between 2002 and the abolition of the office of prime minister in 2018, and winning the last three presidential elections. The advent of the AKP has been accompanied not just by increased authoritarianism and questionable political tactics, but also by a continued slide away from secularism. Public alarm about these trends was reflected in protests in 2013 that began as a local sit-in to oppose development plans for Taksim Gezi Park in Istanbul, and that quickly expanded to become nationwide protests against threats to civil liberties and the AKP's encroachments on secularism. There were estimates that as many as 3.6 million people (or about one in eight Turks) took part in nearly 5,000 separate demonstrations (Onbasi, 2016). Three years later, a failed military coup (see section on the military) was used as an excuse by the administration of President Erdoğan to declare a state of emergency and to launch a wide-ranging purge of thousands of positions held by people defined as enemies of the government.

Candles are burned to honour those killed in the Taksim Gezi Park demonstrations in 2013. What began as a local protest against cutting down trees in the park soon developed into anti-government demonstrations, reflecting concerns about the direction being taken in Turkish politics.
Source: iStock.com/EvrenKalinbacak.

The second and related theme has been Turkey's transition from a parliamentary system (characterized by sometimes frequent changes of government, a constantly evolving party system, predominantly secular politics, and a strong role for the military) to a presidential system that is more stable and yet more centralized and authoritarian, and in which the role of the military has been greatly curtailed. Erdoğan and his AKP government moved to centre-stage, won the first direct popular election for the presidency in 2014, and survived the attempted coup in 2016 in a way that strengthened rather than weakened their position. Under Erdoğan, the watchwords for government in Turkey have been conservatism, nationalism, security, and a crackdown on dissent, whether from his political opponents, the media, the military, or Kurdish separatists.

POLITICAL CULTURE

Understanding political culture in Turkey is a matter of understanding the relationship between several key pairs of competing influences. The first of these is history and modernity, which is addressed in more detail in Comparing Political Culture 11. The second is Kemalism and Islamism, whose contrasts reflect the ongoing tension between Turkey's Islamic roots and the heritage of Atatürk's efforts to secularize Turkey. Decades after the foundation of the Turkish republic, however, Turks still find themselves torn between these opposing pressures, which have been at the heart of the debate over the recent successes of Islamist parties. In this regard, Turkey can usefully be compared with Iran, where Islam has come to play a more central and observable role in politics and government – see Comparing Political Culture 14. Just because Islamism is less clearly part of political culture in Turkey, though, this does not mean that it is a less important political influence, just as we cannot assume that secularism is less important to Iranian political debates simply because it tends to be relegated to the background.

The third of these pairs of influences centres on the competing roles of civilians and the military in government, with the view held by groups of Turkish military officers that they can or should step in to take control when they believe that the civilians have lost control. This is a similar motivation to the thinking of the military in Nigeria (as we saw in Chapter 10), which has occasionally been alarmed by the declining capacity of civilians to maintain order, and has stepped in with a promise to restore order before handing power back to the civilians on the basis of a new constitution. Often, though, Nigerian military leaders have been reluctant to give up control, and have held on much longer than their Turkish peers.

The fourth theme is elitism and populism, which – as we saw in Chapter 2 – is one that has run through politics and government in many countries in recent years. The AKP in Turkey has argued the importance of moving power back to the people, in much the same way – if not necessarily for the same reasons, or on the same terms – as populist leaders and parties in several other cases in this book, including Britain, the United States, France, India, and Mexico. But just how far this is a reasonable claim, and just how far the argument is used by one elite to replace another, is a matter of debate. It can often seem that the outsiders who most resent the power of insiders, and take power on that basis, soon become insiders themselves. We have good reason to ask how far the AKP is genuinely a party of the people rather than a vehicle for new levels of elite control.

Finally, there are tensions in Turkey between nationalism and Westernization, found also in many other places (particularly, among the cases in this book, in Japan, India, Nigeria, China, and Iran). One of Atatürk's key goals was to reinvent Turkey as a modern republic, but – as we saw in the Japanese case – modern is not necessarily the same as Western, and the challenge in the Turkish case was to reinvent Turkey as a post-imperial society that would also be respected as an independent state by the major Western powers. This tension has more recently been reflected in Turkey's ambivalent views about membership of the European Union (returned, with a similar ambivalence, by most Europeans).

The EU wasted relatively little time in extending membership to former Soviet republics (Estonia, Latvia, and Lithuania) or to eastern European states such as Hungary and Poland, or even to Cyprus (which joined the EU in 2004 after just a few years of negotiations). By contrast, it has kept Turkey at a distance, concerned by a combination of its population size, its relatively underdeveloped economy, its record on democracy and human rights, questions about its European identity, concerns about its religion, and the Cyprus problem. (Albania has similar qualities to Turkey, but it is more clearly European and is also much smaller, and would therefore be easier for the EU to absorb.) Turkey introduced a package of political and social reforms in 2003 that were designed to strengthen its candidacy, including a reduced role for the military in government, reforms to the court system, and the abolition of capital punishment. Although negotiations began on the terms of Turkish membership of the EU in 2005, little progress has since been made.

COMPARING POLITICAL CULTURE 11
History and politics

We saw in earlier chapters that political culture is often shaped and influenced by factors such as national identity, patriotism, myths, and symbols. We have also seen in every case study in this book that history plays an important role in helping us understand contemporary politics and government. Successful states are more likely to have learned to understand and live with their past, while less successful states are more likely to have failed to learn from the past, or – at least – to have failed to integrate the past successfully into their modern approach to politics. The Spanish-American philosopher George Santayana (1863–1952) once famously argued that 'those who do not learn from history are doomed to repeat it'. It could be counter-argued, though, that those who live too much in the past are unlikely to be able effectively to address present needs or prepare for future challenges.

Turkey offers an example of a state where the past still plays an important role in the definition of national identity and political need. In a speech in early 2018, President Erdoğan criticized those who 'insistently try to start this country's history from 1923' and argued that while Turkey's borders and institutions of government had certainly changed, 'the Republic of Turkey, just like our previous states that are a continuation of one another, is also a continuation of the Ottomans' (Erdoğan, 2018). How far, though, should Turks define themselves by their history, and what role does the Ottoman heritage play in defining Turkish politics today? What does it tell us about the role of Islam in Turkey, the place of the Kurds, Turkey's split European/Middle Eastern identity, and even whether or not the massacre of Armenians should be defined as genocide or not? Perhaps predictably, Erdoğan has been described by at least one commentator (Cagaptay, 2017) as Turkey's 'new sultan', but is that a helpful description or is it too glib?

In many cases in this book and elsewhere, politics and identity is defined today by a reading of history that is either selective, or that has had its least desirable elements excised, or that tries to see the past as 'the good old days', viewing today's problems through the lens of a nostalgic but often inaccurate view of the past. In Britain, many who voted for their country to leave the European Union did so because of a nostalgic view that Britain had the capacity to go it alone, conveniently ignoring their country's long history of engagement with the rest of the world (not least through the construction of a global empire). In Germany, many have allowed concerns about the Nazi past of their country to drive contemporary decisions, whether or not this approach is appropriate. In Nigeria, many blame the problems of the country on its colonial past, which is only half true. As we will see in the chapter on Russia, many Russians regret the passing of the Soviet Union and believe that their future should be guided by efforts to rebuild Russia's status as a global power. The importance of using history to understand the present was emphasized in Chapter 2, but it must be done with care.

POLITICAL SYSTEM

After nearly a century as a parliamentary republic, Turkey in 2017 – following the approval in a national referendum of changes to the constitution – became a presidential republic. It now has a president elected directly by voters, in addition to its long-standing directly elected national parliament (with reduced powers), an independent system of courts, and numerous political parties. Where the president was once not much more than a figurehead (although opinion was long divided on the precise role of the office in government), power is today more clearly centralized in the office of the president. Turkey has, as a result, become an example of what is sometimes known as a **competitive authoritarian** system (see Levitsky and Way, 2002). How this new arrangement will evolve remains to be seen.

Competitive authoritarianism
A political system that has many of the features of democracy while being authoritarian in practice.

Name	Republic of Turkey (Türkiye Cumhuriyeti)
Capital	Ankara
Administration	Unitary republic, with 81 provinces and several hundred municipalities.
Constitution	State formed 1923. The 1982 constitution was the sixth since 1876, and it has been amended numerous times.
Executive	Unlimited presidential, in the process of transition from a parliamentary system. President directly elected for no more than two five-year terms, supported by a Council of Ministers. Office of prime minister abolished in 2017.
Legislature	Unicameral Grand National Assembly of Turkey (GNAT) with 600 members elected for renewable five-year terms.
Judiciary	Constitutional Court with 17 members serving non-renewable 12-year terms, with three elected by the GNAT and the rest appointed by the president based on nominations from different social sectors.
Electoral system	The legislature is elected using proportional representation with a (relatively high) ten per cent threshold. The president has been directly elected only since 2014. Candidates can be nominated by parties or clusters of parties that won at least five per cent of the vote at the previous legislative election, and compete against each other using a majority system.
Party system	Multi-party, dominated in recent years by the conservative Justice and Development Party (AKP) (founded in 2001) and the much older and social democratic Republican People's Party.

 Population 81m

 Gross Domestic Product $851 billion

 Per capita GDP $10,540

Democracy Index rating

- ✗ Full Democracy
- ✗ Flawed Democracy
- ✓ Hybrid Regime
- ✗ Authoritarian
- ✗ Not Rated

 Freedom House rating

- ✗ Free
- ✗ Partly Free
- ✓ Not Free
- ✗ Not Rated

 Human Development Index rating

- ✗ Very High
- ✓ High
- ✗ Medium
- ✗ Low
- ✗ Not Rated

The constitution

Turkey has had four modern constitutions (see Özbudun, 2011). The first – drawn up in haste in 1920 following the collapse of the Ottoman Empire – was short, served mainly as the legal basis for the war of independence, created a **Grand National Assembly of Turkey** (GNAT) with both legislative and executive powers, and was soon replaced following the end of the war. The second constitution lasted from 1924 to 1961, setting up a republic in which the president was elected by the legislature. When Turkey became a one-party system in 1925 under the Republican People's Party, the constitution quickly became an instrument of the party and a channel for authoritarianism, even when there was a change of government after the Democrat Party won the 1950 elections (Özbudun, 2008a).

Efforts by the DP to limit the political opposition fed into public unrest that led to the May 1960 coup, and the drawing up – under the direction of the military – of Turkey's third constitution. Although it expanded the protection of civil liberties, it left the elected offices of government with relatively few powers relative to the courts and the bureaucracy. Because the Democrat Party was banned after the coup and not allowed to participate in the design of the constitution, about half of the Turkish electorate was excluded from the process. The new constitution was adopted in 1961 following a national referendum, and remained in force until the 1980 coup. This was followed by the fourth and current constitution, once again written under the close eye of the military, and taking effect in November 1982 following another national referendum.

The Preamble opens by affirming 'the eternal existence of the Turkish Motherland and Nation and the indivisible unity of the Sublime Turkish State'. (Divided societies will often use constitutions to emphasize their indivisibility; the same point appears early in the Nigerian constitution, for example.) It goes on to point out that the constitution sits in line 'with the concept of nationalism introduced by the founder of the Republic of Turkey, Atatürk, the immortal leader and the unrivalled hero, and his reforms and principles'.

Article 2 notes that Turkey 'is a democratic, secular and social state governed by the rule of law, within the notions of public peace, national solidarity and justice, [while] respecting human rights'. Article 3 describes the national flag and the national anthem, while also confirming that the national language is Turkish. English is not the formal national language of either Britain or the United States, and in the case of the latter, suggestions that it should be declared as such have been controversial.

Although it might at first seem that the 1982 constitution has developed a healthy permanence, it has been amended so many times that it today looks quite different from its original form. More than half its 177 articles have been changed to some degree, and several recent rounds of amendments – each approved in a national referendum – have resulted in a new political system. The first such round came in 2007, and included the following:

◆ The president was to be elected directly rather than by parliament.
◆ The president could stand for a second term.
◆ Presidential terms were reduced from seven years to five years.
◆ Parliamentary terms were reduced from five years to four years.

Even more substantial changes followed in 2017 with a package of 18 amendments that brought the final switch from a parliamentary system of government to a presidential system. The post of prime minister was abolished, parliamentary terms went back to five years (with presidential and legislative elections to be held at the same time in future), the number of seats in the GNAT was raised from 550 to 600, and the number of potential rounds in presidential elections was reduced from three to two. The amendments were championed by a legislature and a parliamentary constitutional commission dominated by the ruling AKP, but were met with criticism by much of the Turkish opposition and by many European Union governments. *The Economist* (2017) warned that a Yes vote would leave Turkey with 'an elected dictator'.

Amendments to the constitution can be proposed by a group of at least one-third of the members of the GNAT, must then be debated twice in a plenary session of parliament, and need the support of at least three-fifths of the members of the GNAT (360 members) as well as the president of Turkey. Assuming they cross all these hurdles, they are then put to a national referendum, where they need to win only a majority of the valid votes cast in order to come into effect.

The executive: president

Turkey has a presidency along the lines of those in the United States, Mexico, and Nigeria, but this is a new development, dating from the changes made to the constitution in 2017. Prior to that, and except for two periods of military government, Turkey had both a president and a prime minister, but the extent to which this was a semi-presidential or a parliamentary system was contested. It is revealing, for example, that Özbudun (2008b) described the Turkish system of government as 'essentially parliamentary' while also likening it to the French semi-presidential system.

At first, the Turkish president was elected by the legislature for an unlimited number of four-year terms, an arrangement that meant stability in the office; during its first 37 years, Turkey had just three presidents, serving a total of 11 terms among them. One of the effects of the 1960 constitution was to limit presidents – still elected by the legislature – to a single seven-year term. Two of those presidents – Cemal Gürsel and Kenan Evren – came to power as a result of coups, and transformed themselves into civilian presidents without party affiliations. Two other presidents each saw out a full term under this arrangement, the second of whom – Fahri Korutürk – saw nine changes of prime minister during his term.

The 1982 constitution required that the presidency remain above politics, noting in Article 104 that the president (still elected by the legislature) was head of state and should represent 'the Turkish Republic and the unity of the Turkish nation'. At the same time, the office was given new powers that moved it away from its mainly symbolic position without becoming a full-fledged executive position. Presidents, could, for example, appoint prime ministers, appoint and remove ministers, appoint members of the Constitutional Court, preside over meetings of the Council of Ministers, call new elections to the GNAT, proclaim martial law or a state of emergency, and submit constitutional amendments to a national referendum. Özbudun (2008b) points out, though, that most of these powers could only be carried out on the recommendation of another body, while several required the participation of the prime minister or the Council of Ministers.

All changed in 2017, when Turkey adopted a full-fledged presidential system, making the Turkish executive an unlimited presidential system; Turkey's president today has almost complete control over the executive, including the power to appoint the Council of Ministers, to draw up the national budget, to issue decrees, to make all key appointments to the courts and the bureaucracy, and (with parliamentary approval) to call early elections to the legislature. Where once the executive powers of Turkish government were more clearly shared between the prime minister and the legislature, they today lie in the hands of the president, even more so given that Turkey is a unitary state.

The transition to the new system began during the administration of Turgut Özal, who became prime minister in 1983 when his new centre-right Motherland Party won the first elections held after Turkey's second military government. Özal opened a debate about a switch to a presidential system with a view to moving away from the instability created by the parliamentary system. The debate continued after he won the presidency in 1989, and during the term of his successor Süleyman Demirel (1993–2000) (Yilmaz, 2018).

A new element was added to the debate with the appointment of Recep Tayyip Erdoğan as prime minister in 2003. Even while wrestling with the standard political divisions of Turkey, and facing the ever-present possibility of a military coup, Erdoğan built on the successes of his new Justice and Development Party (AKP). He wielded growing power over the party, and became less tolerant of opposition, taking measures to limit freedom of expression. Proposals for a change to the powers of the presidency were introduced in 2011, and Erdoğan ran in – and won – Turkey's first popular presidential election in 2014. His party then reached agreement with the Nationalist Movement Party (the two combined had a majority of seats in the Turkish legislature) on the adoption of a bill on constitutional changes, which were approved in the 2017 national referendum. The changes included the following:

◆ The post of prime minister was abolished.
◆ The president is now both head of state and head of government.
◆ Presidents are limited to two five-year terms.
◆ The president has the power (previously restricted to the prime minister) to appoint and remove members of the Council of Ministers.
◆ The president can appoint one or more vice presidents.
◆ The president can issue executive decrees.
◆ Parliament can overturn a presidential veto with an absolute majority.
◆ Remarkably, the actions of the president had not previously been subject to judicial review; this was changed with the new amendments.
◆ If the president dies, retires, or otherwise leaves office, new presidential elections must be held within 45 days.

The powers of the Turkish president now look much like those of the presidents of the United States, Mexico, and Nigeria, at least on paper. There are fewer constitutional or political limitations on the actions of the president, though, creating the kind of competitive authoritarian system discussed earlier. This has also been described as a 'Turkish type of presidential system' (see Boyunsuz, 2016), and likened to the **hyper presidentialism** of countries such as Argentina and the Philippines (Rose-Ackerman et al., 2011). Even in democracies, presidents might be tempted to test the boundaries of their powers, according to their ambitions and the amount of resistance they find from other institutions and from public opinion. Donald Trump in the United States has often pushed the limits of his office, although whether from political ambition or a failure to understand those limits is debatable. As we will see in Chapter 12, Russian presidents are helped by the public preference for strong leaders. In the case of Turkey, meanwhile, presidents are helped by a long tradition of charismatic leaders dating back to Atatürk, whose mausoleum dominates a hill overlooking the centre of Ankara, and a visit to which has the feel of a religious pilgrimage. More recent leaders with charisma include Suleyman Demirel, Turgut Ozal, and Recep Tayyip Erdoğan (Waldman and Caliskan, 2017).

As in Argentina, the Philippines, Belarus, and Russia, but unlike France or the United States, the Turkish president has the power to declare a **state of emergency** and to rule by **decree**. The constitution contains a lengthy list of the circumstances under which an emergency can be declared, including war, uprisings against the state, 'widespread acts of violence of internal or external origin threatening the indivisibility of the country and the nation', acts of violence 'aimed at the destruction of the constitutional order', natural disasters, pandemic diseases, and severe economic crises. Clearly there is a degree of interpretation involved in the definition of emergency situations. Once declared, a state of emergency cannot last longer than six months, but it can be renewed for periods of four months at the request of the president. Following the 2016 attempted coup, the Erdoğan administration declared an emergency that was renewed multiple times and allowed to expire only in July 2018, even as its crackdown on alleged opponents continued.

The legislature: Grand National Assembly of Turkey (GNAT)

Just as the Turkish executive has undergone much change in recent years, so has the Turkish legislature, which has changed both in its structure and in its relationship with the executive. Kalayctoğlu (2008) describes a cycle of 'convocation, transition, suspension and reorganization' that has denied the legislature its role as an arena for conflict resolution, and in some ways has helped exacerbate political tensions in Turkey. Five phases can be identified in its development:

◆ From 1920 until 1946, Turkey had a unicameral Grand National Assembly of Turkey (GNAT), monopolized by the Republican People's Party (CHP).

◆ In 1946, a multi-party system emerged, and the first competitive elections were held in 1950, but CHP dominance was replaced by the control of the elitist and increasingly authoritarian Democrat Party.

◆ Following the military intervention of 1960, directed mainly at ousting the Democrats (who were banned), the new constitution restored the Ottoman model of a bicameral legislature with a Senate and a Chamber of Deputies.

◆ Following the 1980 military coup, the legislature was closed once again and the new constitution saw a return to a unicameral GNAT, at first with 450 members, with the number cut to 400 in 1983, then raised in increments to its current total.

◆ With Turkey's switch to a presidential system, the place of the assembly in government has changed. Until 2017, 'the government' was the prime minister and the Council of Ministers, and its membership was determined by the balance of party representation in the assembly. Today, 'the government' is the president and the Council of Ministers, and the assembly must try to forge a new place for itself in a system of checks and balances with a powerful executive.

Known more usually as 'the parliament' or 'the Assembly', the GNAT has 600 members who are elected for renewable five-year terms based on proportional representation. Because of the unusually high threshold of ten per cent (see later in this chapter), few of Turkey's many political parties win seats in the GNAT, giving it a degree of stability at the expense of its wider representative credentials.

Hyper presidentialism
A political system in which a strong president coexists with a relatively weak legislature and judiciary, perhaps helped by a large majority in the legislature.

State of emergency
A situation in which a government suspends the normal rules of administration and can take actions that are beyond its constitutional powers, usually in response to armed conflict, civil unrest, or natural disaster.

Decree
A formal and authoritative order, usually from an executive, that has the force of law but does not need to go through the formal legislative process.

Table 11.1 Modern presidents and prime ministers of Turkey

| President | | Prime minister | | |
Start of term	Name and party	Start of term	Name	Party
1946	İsmet İnönü, CHP	1946	Recep Peker	CHP
		1947, 1948	Hasan Saka	CHP
		1949	Semsettin Günaltay	CHP
1950, 1954, 1957	Celâl Bayar, Democrat	1950, 1951, 1954, 1955, 1957	Adnan Menderes	CHP
1960, 1961	Cemal Gürsel (military)	1960, 1961	Cemal Gürsel	Military
		1961	Fahrettin Özdilek	Military
		1961, 1962, 1963	İsmet İnönü	CHP
		1965	Suat Hayri Ürgüplü	Independent
1966	Cevdet Sunay, Independent	1965, 1969, 1970	Süleyman Demirel	Justice Party
		1971, 1971	Nihat Erim	Independent
		1972	Ferit Melen	Republican Resistance Party
1973	Fahri Korutürk, Independent	1973	Naim Talu	Independent
		1974	Bülent Ecevit	CHP
		1974	Sadi Irmak	Independent
		1975	Süleyman Demirel	Justice Party
		1977	Bülent Ecevit	CHP
		1977	Süleyman Demirel	Justice Party
		1978	Bülent Ecevit	CHP
		1979	Süleyman Demirel	Justice Party
		1980	Turhan Feyzioğlu	Republican Reliance Party
1980, 1982	Kenan Evren (military)	1980	Bülend Ulusu	Military
		1983, 1987	Turgut Özal	Motherland
		1989	Ali Bozer	Motherland
1989	Turgut Özal, Motherland	1989	Yıldırım Akbulut	Motherland
		1991	Mesut Yılmaz	Motherland
		1991	Süleyman Demirel	True Path Party
		1993	Erdal İnönü	Social Democratic Populist Party

President		Prime minister		
Start of term	Name and party	Start of term	Name	Party
1993	Süleyman Demirel, True Path	1993, 1995, 1995	Tansu Çiller	True Path
		1996	Mesut Yilmaz	Motherland
		1996	Necmettin Erbakan	Welfare Party
		1997	Mesut Yilmaz	Motherland
		1999, 1999	Bülent Ecevit	Democratic Left
2000	Ahmet Necdet Sezer, Independent	2002	Abdullah Gül	AKP
		2003	Recep Tayyip Erdoğan	AKP
2007	Abdullah Gül, AKP	2007, 2011	Recep Tayyip Erdoğan	AKP
2014	Recep Tayyip Erdoğan, AKP	2014, 2014, 2015, 2015	Ahmet Davutoğlu	AKP
		2016	Binali Yıldırım	AKP
2018	Recep Tayyip Erdoğan, AKP	2018	Position abolished	

Note: AKP = Justice and Development Party, CHP = Republican People's Party

The judiciary: Constitutional Court

Turkey has a shorter history of judicial politics than many other countries of its age, having established its Constitutional Court only with the 1961 constitution. Prior to that, parliament was the dominant legislative authority, but it lacked the power of judicial review (a principle which continues to be opposed by the Justice and Development Party). The court today has most of the powers typical of its peer institutions in other political systems, including the right to review laws, presidential decrees, and the rules of procedure of the GNAT. However, it functions against a background in which civil liberties and freedom of the press are often under attack (see Comparing Government 11), and has been less active than democratic courts in responding to such attacks.

The Court has 17 members elected for non-renewable terms of 12 years, with the requirement that they retire when they reach the age of 65. Fourteen are appointed by the president of Turkey from lower courts, academia, business, and private law, while the balance of members are elected by the GNAT from lists provided by lower courts and bar associations. The court elects its own president and two deputy presidents from among its members for renewable four-year terms, using an absolute majority system in a secret vote.

Sub-national government

As noted in Chapter 2, federal systems are most often found in states that either have large populations or are internally divided, the logic being that a division of vertical powers in such states improves the efficiency and accessibility of government. In population terms, Turkey ranks 19th in the world, and – as noted earlier – it has a large Kurdish minority. At first glance, then, it would seem to be a strong candidate for federalism, but Turkey – along with nine of the twenty biggest countries in the world by population (the others being China, Indonesia, Bangladesh, Japan, the Philippines, Egypt, Vietnam, Iran, and Thailand) – has opted for a unitary administration. The reason for this lies in a combination of the history of political divisions within the Ottoman Empire

COMPARING GOVERNMENT 11
Freedom of the press

One of the most telling measures of the efficiency and openness of government and politics is the degree to which freedom of the press (actually, the media in general) is respected and protected. Freedom of speech is critical to the health of democracy, and much of that freedom (or the limits to which it is subjected) is reflected in the extent to which traditional media and social media are allowed to debate the state of government and political issues of the day. A healthy democracy has a wide range of media outlets, owned and operated by a combination of public and private concerns, protected by the rule of law, and free to offer a range of opinions. In every respect, an authoritarian system has few or none of these features.

Turkey has a wide variety of media outlets, but they have not always been free or untouched by political control, and matters have worsened in recent years. In the 2017 Democracy Index (Economist Intelligence Unit, 2018), criticism was directed at the efforts of the Erdoğan administration to limit independent and critical media. Following the attempted coup of 2016, many media outlets were shut down, thousands of journalists and media workers lost their jobs, many more were prevented from leaving the country, controls were placed on the internet, and the government used criminal defamation laws to curb freedom of expression. By the end of 2017, Turkey was thought to have about 130 journalists in jail, or half the estimated global total of 262. The country had become, in the words of the Democracy Index, a 'vast prison' for journalists, jailed mainly or only because they were considered opponents of the president. Turkey was rewarded in the index with a media freedom score of 0/10 in 2017, placing it in a cluster of states that included China, Cuba, North Korea, and Saudi Arabia.

Turkey is not the only country that has faced new curbs on its press. In its *Freedom of the Press 2017* report, Freedom House (2017) noted that global press freedom had declined to its lowest point in more than a decade 'amid unprecedented threats to journalists and media outlets in major democracies and new moves by authoritarian states to control the media, including beyond their borders'. It calculated that only 13 per cent of the world's population enjoyed a free press, if this was defined as 'a media environment where coverage of political news is robust, the safety of journalists is guaranteed, state intrusion in media affairs is minimal, and the press is not subject to onerous legal or economic pressures'. Turkey, it argued, had suffered one of the largest declines, but Freedom House also ruefully noted that in all the time that it had been monitoring global press freedom, the United States had never figured so prominently in the public debate about that freedom.

The Freedom House ratings on press freedom for the countries in this book in 2017 were as follows:

Free	Partly Free	Not Free
Britain	India	China
France	Nigeria	Iran
Germany		Mexico
Japan		Russia
United States		Turkey

(Greeks and Armenians, among others, wanted to build their own states within the empire), of Atatürk's desire to eradicate secessionist forces, and of the concern that Kurdish separatism might be encouraged by a federal system in which Turkey's eastern states were dominated by Kurds. As if to assuage any doubt, the Turkish constitution is clear in its emphasis on the unity and indivisibility of Turkey, on the national integrity of the state, and in pointing out (in Article 6) that 'the exercise of sovereignty shall not be delegated by any means to any individual, group or class'.

Turkey is instead a unitary state divided into 81 provinces, each with its own governor appointed by the Council of Ministers with the approval of the president, offering another channel for centralized political control. The governors chair elected provincial assemblies which are elected for five-year terms, and provincial governments are responsible for local services and for overseeing the implementation of national policies at the local level. At the most local level, Turkey is divided into nearly 1,400 municipalities. This brief description does not capture the importance of sub-national politics in Turkey, driven as it is by differences in social class, culture, competing local demands, and the interplay of formal and informal expectations. In her study of Turkish municipal politics, Joppien (2018) describes the result as a 'personalization of institutional politics'.

The military

The military once played a key role in Turkish politics, staging several coups that resulted in the overthrow of the civilian government and – on two occasions – in the writing of two new constitutions. Although its role is now much diminished, it is important to remember how it intervened, and the effects of those interventions:

◆ In 1960, the military overthrew a government that it considered to be too authoritarian. A new constitution was drawn up and adopted and power was handed back to the civilians after elections in 1961. There were two failed coup attempts in 1962 and 1963.
◆ In 1971, a second coup – sometimes known as the 'coup of memorandum' – was launched against a government that the military considered unable to manage worsening political and social upheaval in the wake of economic recession. Power was handed back to the civilians in 1972.
◆ In 1980, a third coup was sparked by more concerns about political instability, and resulted in the writing and adoption of a new constitution that was designed to establish a more stable two-party system.
◆ In 1997, in what is sometimes described as a 'post-modern coup', the military arranged the ousting of Turkey's first Islamist-led government on the grounds that it posed a threat to the principles of Kemalism.

Following the 1960 coup, a National Security Council (NSC) was created through which military officers could influence civilian politics, and its mandate was steadily expanded by new laws and constitutional amendments; it went beyond security concerns, and oversaw government departments as well as allowing itself to veto government decisions and even to force the resignation of government ministers, and occasionally of prime ministers. For Sakallioğlu (1997), the result was the creation of a 'double-headed political system' in which the civilian Council of Ministers coexisted with the NSC, and the military system of justice operated independently of the civilian system. It was only after 2001, as Turkey began to make reforms in the wake of the requirements of potential membership of the European Union, that the membership of the NSC was changed to include more civilians. It is today less the military wing of government and more of a conventional committee dealing with security issues, and includes among its members the president of Turkey, key ministers, and the leadership of the different branches of the military.

An unexpected reminder of the political role of the military came with a failed coup on 15–16 July 2016, when a group of mid-level army officers supposedly opposed to the Erdoğan government tried to take power, but achieved little more than a brief occupation of the headquarters of TRT, the Turkish state broadcaster. A key element in the outcome of the coup attempt was its failure to draw popular, political, or media support (Esen and Gumuscu, 2017). There were shoot-outs between soldiers belonging to different military factions, parliament and the presidential palace were bombed, an attempt was made on the life of President Erdoğan, and there were estimates of several hundred deaths and more than 2,000 injuries. The Erdoğan government claimed that the coup had been organized by Fethullah Gülen, a businessman and cleric living in self-imposed exile in the United States, but he denied the charge, and counter-charged that the attempt had been staged by Erdoğan in order to give himself a stronger grip on power.

The Erdoğan government responded with a wide-ranging crackdown, declaring a state of emergency that allowed it to rule by decree and to make decisions that weakened the rule of law. By the end of the year, noted Freedom House (2018a), the following developments had taken place:

◆ Tens of thousands of people – the estimates on precise numbers vary – had either been suspended or dismissed from their jobs, or arrested. Among them were military officers, teachers, bureaucrats, university deans, judges, police officers, and soldiers. They were all accused of being members of a terrorist group known as the Gülen movement.
◆ More than 60,000 people had been arrested.
◆ Many elected local politicians had been removed from office on charges of 'terrorism' (often directed at Kurdish politicians and the Gulen movement) and replaced with government appointees.
◆ More than 1,500 civil society organizations had been closed.

◆ Wide use had been made of pre-trial detentions in which people were imprisoned for long periods without being tried.

◆ There was evidence of the torture and even the 'disappearance' of political detainees, and the arrest of human rights activists on charges of 'terrorism'.

Despite what might seem to be a perpetual presence for the military in Turkish politics, Waldman and Caliskan (2017) argue that it is now 'confined to barracks' and that 'the demise of the military as a political force is perhaps the most important development since the founding of the Turkish Republic in 1923'.

POLITICAL PROCESSES

Coming to grips with the Turkish political system has been complicated in recent years by two key factors. First, the party system has been anything but static, often presenting voters with a new array of options when they go to the polls. Second, questions are frequently raised about the fairness of elections, and about electoral manipulation. In its 2017 ranking, the Democracy Index (Economist Intelligence Unit, 2018) gave Turkey a score of 5.33 out of 10 on 'electoral process and pluralism', worse than any of the other cases in this book except Russia, China, and Iran. Since 1950, elections in Turkey have been overseen by a Supreme Electoral Council whose president, six members, and four alternatives are appointed by parliament. This injects an element of partisan control into the electoral process, one of the effects of which was felt with the way in which the 2017 referendum was managed – see later in this section.

The electoral system

We have seen how Britain, Japan, and France are unitary systems, as a result of which they have relatively few elective offices, and hence their electoral processes are relatively simple and quick in contrast to the processes found in federal systems such as Germany, the United States, and India. As another unitary system, Turkey also has a relatively simple electoral system; until 2014, the only national ballot was the general election for members of parliament, normally held every four years, using proportional representation. The electoral calendar has since expanded with the addition of direct elections for the president, normally scheduled to be held on the same day as parliamentary elections, using a majority system.

Executive elections

Turkish voters are not used to being able to choose their president directly. Until 2014, presidents were elected by members of the Grand National Assembly in a secret ballot using a majority system. Candidates came either from the GNAT itself, or else a group of at least one-fifth of the members of the Assembly could nominate a candidate from outside the Assembly. In order to win, a candidate needed the support of two-thirds of the members of the GNAT; if no one passed the two-thirds threshold in the first two ballots, a third ballot could be held requiring only an absolute majority. Failing that, a fourth ballot could be held involving just the two candidates who received the most votes in the third ballot. Party divisions in the Assembly ensured that the election routinely went to a third round, even in 2000 when none of the major parties had enough seats to ensure a victory for its candidate, so a compromise candidate was found in the chief justice of the Constitutional Court, Ahmet Necdet Sezer.

New complexities were added in 2007, when the first round was annulled by the Constitutional Court because a quorum of two-thirds was not met. Opposition parties had refused to participate because the leading candidate, Abdullah Gül, was a member of the Islamist AKP, and was running for an office traditionally seen as representative of the Turkish secular system. It took a second attempt – following a general election – and three rounds for him to win office.

The 2014 and 2018 elections were the first based on a direct popular mandate, and continued to use the majority method. Any party that wins at least five per cent of the vote in the previous parliamentary election – or any alliance of smaller parties that together win at least five per cent of the vote – can nominate a candidate, and independents can also run if they collect 100,000 signatures. If one candidate wins 50 per cent + 1 of the vote in the first round of the election, they are declared the winner. Failing that, the top two finishers run off in a second round (much like the system used in France and Russia). So far, Recep Tayyip Erdoğan has won enough votes in the first round to be declared the winner; see Table 11.2. The 2018 poll was a snap election held 17 months early at the insistence of the opposition Nationalist Movement Party, and the next election is scheduled for 2023.

Table 11.2 Results of recent presidential elections in Turkey

Year	Candidate	Party	Number of votes (millions)	% share
2014	Recep Tayyip Erdoğan	Justice and Development	21.0	51.8
	Ekmeleddin Mehmet İhsanoğlu	Independent	15.6	38.4
	Selahattin Demirtas	People's Democrat Party	4.0	9.8
2018	Recep Tayyip Erdoğan	Justice and Development	26.3	52.6
	Muharrem Ince	Republican People's Party	15.3	30.6
	Selahattin Demirtas	People's Democrat Party	4.2	8.4
	Three others	İyi Party	4.2	8.4

Legislative elections

Turkey uses party list proportional representation for elections to the GNAT, with contests held on a fixed five-year calendar. Its 600 members are elected from 87 multi-member electoral districts; these are the local administrative districts in every case except the larger cities, with Istanbul and Ankara each divided into three districts, while Izmir and Bursa each have two districts. Despite the fixed schedule, there is the potential for elections to be called

A campaign poster proclaims the achievements of Recep Tayyip Erdoğan and his AKP party. Erdoğan built on his record as mayor of Istanbul and then as prime minister of Turkey, finally becoming president in 2014 and quickly redefining the terms of the position.
Source: iStock.com/imranahmedsg.

earlier if circumstances demand a snap election. In 2015, for example, two sets of elections were held. The first, in June, brought an end to the period of one-party rule that had begun in 2002 with the victory of the AKP. It won a plurality of 41 per cent of the vote, with the balance shared between three other parties. Discussions were then opened to form a coalition government, but the failure to reach agreement led to a second general election in November, as a result of which the AKP won a majority.

One of the most notable features of the Turkish legislative electoral system is its threshold, which – at ten per cent – is the highest in the world. Most countries that use proportional representation set their thresholds at 4–5 per cent, which has the effect of making sure that most parties win seats while keeping out smaller parties and avoiding excessive fragmentation of the legislature. Greece, Italy, and Spain have opted for the lower number of three per cent, while Israel for many years had the almost meaningless threshold of one per cent. This low bar was part of the reason why so many smaller parties could win seats in the Israeli legislature (the Knesset), leaving most governments as unstable multi-party coalitions in which smaller and often more politically extreme parties could hold governments hostage and have strong influence over policy. The threshold was later raised in stages, reaching its current level of 3.25 per cent in 2003. However, 10–12 parties still win seats at Israeli general elections, and with a national legislature of just 120 members, the presence of multiple parties with less than half a dozen seats each can be disruptive.

With its high threshold, Turkey feels the opposite effect: few parties can cross the threshold (typically no more than four in recent elections), but while this creates the kind of stability that Turkey once lacked (nine parties won seats after the 1969 elections, although only two won seats in 2002), it also means that many smaller parties (and their supporters) are denied representation. Kurdish parties have particularly found it hard to win seats, and have had to run their candidates as independents or as members of other parties.

Local elections

Just as there have been changes in the structure of national government in recent years, so there have been changes at the local level. Local elections have long been held on a five-year schedule, and while that schedule persists, a reorganization of local government in 2013 significantly reduced the number of elected officials. Turks now elect members of provincial assemblies, metropolitan and district mayors, and members of local councils. Since the elections are not held at the same time as national elections, they are often – as in many other countries – seen at least in part as a measure of the performance of national government. This was certainly the case in 2014, when local elections were the first opportunity for voters to go to the polls following the 2013 Gezi Park protests. The elections themselves were surrounded by charges of electoral fraud and manipulation, including voter bribery, the destruction of ballots, and power cuts while votes were being counted. Protests led to elections in several areas being declared void, and new elections being held several weeks later.

Referendums

Turkey has made more use of national referendums than any other case in this book, with the result that such votes have become an important part of understanding the dynamics of politics in Turkey; see Comparing Politics 11. In the modern era, seven referendums have been held, all of them dealing with constitutional issues; see Table 11.3. The first two, in 1961 and 1982, were designed to engage voters in the adoption of new constitutions, leaving them with much to consider before making their choice. The outcomes were somewhat tainted by the role of the military; both came soon after military coups, and the military played a key role in drafting the new constitutions and in organizing the referendums. Turnout in both cases was high, however, and solid majorities accepted the new constitutions.

The most recent referendum, in April 2017, posed a set of complex questions while falling short of proposing a new constitution. Voters had to consider 18 amendments to the constitution that had the effect of replacing a parliamentary system with a presidential system. The vote was surrounded by allegations of voter suppression, and protests broke out when Turkey's Supreme Electoral Council allowed ballots that had not been officially stamped to be accepted. There was high turnout, but the margin in favour of accepting the changes was just under 2.4 per cent, which – combined with charges of voting irregularities – left a cloud hanging over the result. Freedom House described the vote as 'deeply flawed'.

Political parties

Even if Turkey's democratic credentials are becoming weaker, and even if the electoral process limits the number of such parties that can win seats in the Grand National Assembly, Turkish voters are still faced with a varied and variable selection of political parties. Perhaps, in some ways, the selection is too broad, since the formula for a stable and democratic political system lies somewhere in the middle of a continuum between (on the one hand) zero- and

Table 11.3 Referendums in Turkey

Date	Topic	Result	Turnout	Effect
1961	New constitution	62% in favour	81%	New constitution adopted
1982	New constitution	91% in favour	91%	New constitution adopted
1987	Limited constitutional amendment	50% in favour	93%	
1988	Holding local elections early	65% opposed	89%	Proposal failed
2007	Electoral reform	69% in favour	67%	Changes to elections and terms in office of president, and parliamentary terms
2010	Bringing constitution into compliance with EU standards	58% in favour	74%	Changes to judicial system, and to economic, social, and individual rights
2017	Constitutional change	51% in favour	85%	Replacement of parliamentary system with presidential system

Note: Percentages are rounded out.

COMPARING POLITICS 11
Referendums

Referendums are one of the few examples of direct democracy in practice. They offer voters the opportunity to express their opinions on a (usually) focused proposal for policy change, either at the national or at the local level. The United States has a long record of using them at the state and local level, while no country uses them at the national level as much as Switzerland, with its emphasis on local government; between 1940 and 2017 it held nearly 500 referendums (see Figure 11.1) on a wide range of questions, including nuclear power, military service, same-sex partnerships, immigration, and even the hours of business of local petrol stations.

> **Referendum**
> A vote of the electorate on a limited issue of public policy such as a constitutional amendment.

Elsewhere, as in Australia, Ireland, and Turkey, most referendums are called on questions of changes to the constitution. One of the more notable examples in Australia was the 1999 referendum on whether it should cut its last links with the British crown and become a republic; nearly 55 per cent of voters said No, but the issue has not gone away. In Britain, meanwhile, a 2014 referendum in Scotland turned down the prospect of independence from the rest of the UK, while a 2016 referendum came down in favour of Britain's departure from the European Union, bringing chaos and division in its wake.

Referendums have both advantages and disadvantages. On the positive side of the ledger, they are democratic in the sense that they bypass legislatures and allow voters to have a direct say on a policy question. They also encourage voter engagement and turnout, encourage voters to play closer attention to public issues (although this is not guaranteed), can help governments better understand the wishes of voters, and might engage voters as decision-makers in cases where governments are unable to reach agreement on an issue.

Referendums also come with many problems. They assume that voters both care about and are informed about the issues at stake, they can be expensive to organize, they can polarize the electorate (as revealed by the highly divisive Brexit vote in Britain), they can be undermined by confusion or ambiguity over the wording of the question posed, and the questions in referendums can sometimes be too complex to be reduced to a simple Yes/No option. Overall, Qvortrup (2012) argues that while referendums are being used with increased frequency, there is little evidence that they improve policy outcomes, although more studies need to be done. Comparison can be particularly valuable in this regard, giving us insights into the strengths and weaknesses of referendums by looking at the effects of timing, the importance of the questions being asked (some will be of much wider interest than others), turnout rates, the characteristics of those voters who participate and those who stay away, and the impact of referendums on the quality of government in different circumstances.

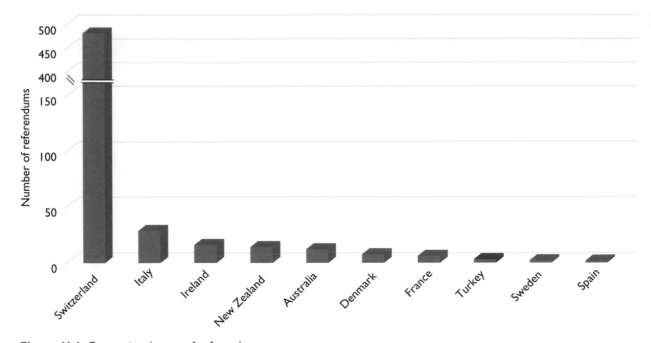

Figure 11.1 Comparing the use of referendums

Sources: Adapted from Morel (2007), table 1, containing data for the period 1940–2007. Updated to 2017 using information in public domain.

one-party systems of the kind found in Iran and China, and (on the other hand) systems in which many parties create confusion. It is interesting though, to compare Turkey with India and its numerous national and regional political parties.

The evolution of Turkish parties can be divided into three broad phases. In the first phase, in the early years of the Turkish republic, government was based on a one-party system: the Republican People's Party (CHP) was founded in 1919 in order to represent a united front in the war of independence, declared itself a formal political organization in 1923, and won the next seven general elections on a Kemalist and social democratic platform. Two opposition parties were created in 1924 at the behest of Atatürk in an effort to establish a multi-party system, but they were quickly banned for being too Islamist in their outlook.

After World War II, democratic elections were introduced for the first time, the CHP lost power after the 1950 elections, and Turkey entered a second phase of party activity when multiple parties became active, sitting broadly on a centre-right spectrum. The CHP initially competed mainly with the mildly conservative Democrat Party. With the banning of the latter by the military following the 1960 coup, the Justice Party (AP) took up where the Democrats had left off, and the CHP and the AP were to remain the main parties until the late 1970s, competing with an increasingly crowded field of smaller parties, nine of which won seats in the 1969 general election.

The military hoped after the 1980 coup that a new two-party party system would emerge, with one party on the centre-left and one on the centre-right. It banned the CHP and the AP was dissolved in 1981, but new parties emerged to inherit their ideological positions; Motherland and the True Path Party both now came to sit on the centre-right. They were to alternate in control of the office of prime minister until the party landscape was made more complex by the successes of the Welfare Party, an Islamist party. Although Islamist parties had been active since at least 1970, they remained on the margins until the Welfare Party (founded in 1983) was able to exploit divisions among Turkish voters to win a bare plurality of seats in 1995, giving it enough power to see its leader Necmettin Erbakan becoming prime minister at the head of Turkey's first Islamist government. He was forced out of office after just two years by the military in the so-called 'post-modern' coup, and the Welfare Party was banned in 1998 on charges of violating the constitutional separation of religion and state. It was succeeded by the Virtue Party, which was in turn banned for the same reasons in 2001.

The third and current phase in Turkish party politics, in which the old centre-right division has been replaced by a secular-religious division, dates from the 2002 general election. CHP was once again competitive after several years of internal problems, and a substantial new party had arrived in the form of the Justice and Development Party (AKP,

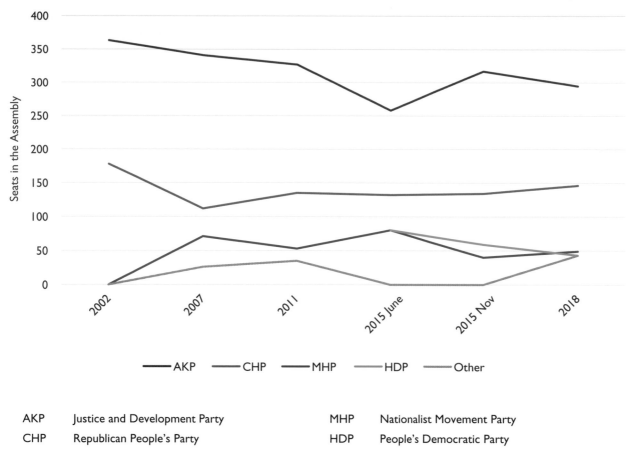

Figure 11.2 Legislative electoral trends in Turkey

AKP	Justice and Development Party	MHP	Nationalist Movement Party
CHP	Republican People's Party	HDP	People's Democratic Party

from its Turkish name *Adalet ve Kalkınma Partisi*). This had been formed in 2001 by several smaller conservative parties, and while initially claiming to be pro-Western, pro-American, pro-Turkish membership of the EU, and pro-free market, it had soon moved further to the right, with policies associated with populism and Islamism. So successful has been its record, argues Abbas (2017), that 'Islamism has replaced Kemalism as Turkey's dominant political hegemony'.

The AKP's first leader was Recep Tayyip Erdoğan (formerly a member of the Welfare Party and then of the Virtue Party), and the AKP went on to win the largest number of seats in every general election between 2007 and 2018, as well as providing the last three prime ministers of Turkey before the position was abolished, and – with Abdullah Gül and then Recep Tayyip Erdoğan – holding the office of president since 2007. Not only has the ideological balance changed, but Turkey since 2002 has been something of a one-party dominant system, although how long this will continue remains to be seen.

As matters currently stand, four parties are of note:

◆ *Justice and Development (AKP).* The AKP has become Turkey's strongest political party, with several qualities described by Esen and Gumuscu (2017) as being keys to it success: a membership of about 10 million (approximately one in eight Turks belong to the party), an efficient party machine that keeps its leaders present in the everyday lives of members and local party members engaged through weekly meetings, an ideology based around a compelling combination of Islamic sentiment and Turkish nationalism, and the leadership abilities of President Erdoğan.
◆ *Republican People's Party (CHP).* Now the oldest party in Turkey, the CHP has become the major opposition in the GNAT, and continues to promote social democratic ideas influenced by Kemalism, whose six principles (listed earlier in this chapter) are reflected in the six arrows in the CHP party logo.
◆ *Nationalist Movement Party (MHP).* Founded in 1969, the MHP is the most conservative of the parties that has recently won seats in the GNAT, taking strongly nationalist and Eurosceptic policy positions. It had its best election result in 1999, when it won 129 seats, since when it has settled to about 50–70 seats.

◆ *People's Democratic Party (HDP).* Founded in 2012, the HDP is a moderate socialist party that is anti-capitalist, supports minority rights, and has a close association with Turkey's Kurdish communities. It first ran in the 2014 local elections, its candidate placed a distant third in the 2014 and 2018 presidential elections, and it has won about 60–80 seats in legislative elections.

Although this is the current party arrangement in Turkey, history has shown that realignments are never out of the question. However, unlike previous periods of new party formation, Turkey today has a presidential executive, authoritarian government, a strong Islamist party in the form the AKP, and a marginalized military.

THE FUTURE OF TURKISH GOVERNMENT AND POLITICS

The political future of Turkey is grim. For many years, it seemed to be building a viable democratic system, even if it moved in fits and starts, with the military playing an unwelcome role in the background (and sometimes in the foreground). It never rose above the status of a hybrid regime in the Democracy Index, and languished with a ranking of Not Free in Freedom in the World. But many Turks long saw their country as having the potential to become a full-fledged member of the community of democracies, a view symbolized by their desire to achieve the credentials needed to join the European Union.

Unfortunately, a string of AKP governments – led by Recep Tayyip Erdoğan (first as prime minister and more recently as executive president) – have moved Turkey away from democracy and into the realms of authoritarian government and politics. The rules of the political system have been changed so as to set aside the doubts and confusions often created by too many political parties and regular changes in the office of the prime minister. Turkey now has a strong presidency, an initiative approved (barely) by Turkish voters in a 2017 referendum. To his supporters, Erdoğan has brought welcome growth and political stability, but to his opponents he has brought authoritarianism and an intolerance for opposition, more than reversing the democratic gains of recent decades.

Many Turks do not like what they see, and there is always the prospect of a reaction that could put Turkey back on its course to democracy. Opposition parties are still active and Turkey has a vibrant media establishment, even in the face of the new authoritarianism. Whichever direction the country takes, we can continue to expect Turkey to provide a compelling case study of political change.

DISCUSSION QUESTIONS

1. To what extent have Atatürk's principles of secularism, republicanism, nationalism, reformism, statism, and populism taken hold in Turkey?
2. How should multi-national states with significant separatist movements – such as Turkey, Britain, India, and Russia – address demands for self-government or independence?
3. The Western tradition supports a clear separation between religion and the state. To what extent can or should Western principles be expected to apply in Turkey?
4. Comparing Turkey with unitary and federal cases in this book, what are the arguments for and against the creation of a federal system in Turkey?
5. Has Turkey set its electoral threshold too high?
6. To what extent do the labels authoritarian, Islamist, populist, and nationalist apply to the Erdoğan administration?

CHAPTER CONCEPTS

- ◆ Eastern Question
- ◆ Grand National Assembly of Turkey
- ◆ Justice and Development Party
- ◆ Kemalism
- ◆ Kurdistan
- ◆ Mustafa Kemal (Atatürk)
- ◆ Ottoman Empire
- ◆ Republican People's Party
- ◆ Young Turks

KEY TERMS

- ◆ Competitive authoritarianism
- ◆ Decree
- ◆ Emerging economy
- ◆ Hyper presidentialism
- ◆ Referendum
- ◆ State of emergency

TURKEY ONLINE

Presidency of the Republic of Turkey: www.tccb.gov.tr/en
Grand National Assembly of Turkey: https://global.tbmm.gov.tr
Supreme Court: https://web.archive.org/web/20110712105707/http:/www.yargitay.gov.tr:80/eng/index.php
Justice and Development Party: www.akparti.org.tr/en
Republican People's Party: www.chp.org.tr (Turkish only)
Hurriyet Daily News: www.hurriyetdailynews.com
Daily Sabah: www.dailysabah.com
Turkish Radio and Television: www.trtworld.com

FURTHER READING

Abbas, Tahir (2017) *Contemporary Turkey in Conflict: Ethnicity, Islam and Politics* (Edinburgh University Press). An assessment of recent changes in Turkey and of the origins and possible long-term effects of Erdoğan's policies.

Baser, Bahar, and Ahmet Erdi Öztürk (eds) (2017) *Authoritarian Politics in Turkey: Elections, Resistance and the AKP* (I B Taurus). An edited collection focused on the transformation of Turkey from a weak democracy to an authoritarian system.

Cagaptay, Soner (2017) *The New Sultan: Erdoğan and the Crisis of Modern Turkey* (I B Taurus). A critical assessment of the political impact of President Erdoğan, looking at his background, methods, and potential long-term influence on Turkey.

Heper, Metin, and Sabri Sayari (eds) (2012) *The Routledge Handbook of Modern Turkey* (Routledge). An edited collection with chapters on the history, culture, politics, society, geography, and economy of Turkey.

Yesilada, Birol (2013) *EU-Turkey Relations in the 21st Century* (Routledge). One of the many studies of the troubled relationship between Turkey and the European Union.

Zurcher, Erik J. (2017) *Turkey: A Modern History*, 4th edn (I B Taurus). A history of Turkey, with an emphasis on the post–Ottoman era, taking the story up to the advent of Erdoğan.

 Visit **www.macmillanihe.com/McCormick-Cases** to access additional materials to support teaching and learning.

RUSSIA ▲ 12

CONTENTS

- Overview
- Political development
- Political culture
- Political system
- Political processes
- The future of Russian government and politics

PREVIEW

As a case, Russia offers valuable insights into the dynamics of an authoritarian system. Its political system has changed dramatically since the break-up of the Soviet Union in 1991, but initial hopes that it would become a democracy have been dashed as President Vladimir Putin has strengthened his grip. The Soviet heritage is still clear in Russian political culture, the rules of the political system have been changed, and understanding that system is often less a matter of appreciating constitutional formalities than it is of grasping the political psychology of Putin. Russia may have moved away from a one-party communist system to a multi-party capitalist system, but the office of the presidency is powerful, both the legislature and regional governments have been reduced to supporting institutions, and the Russian model of federalism is one that is dominated by the centre. More and significant changes are undoubtedly yet to come.

KEY ARGUMENTS

- Russia has undergone many changes, evolving from an empire to a communist state to an authoritarian system.

- Despite the many changes Russia has seen since the break-up of the Soviet Union, many of the political values of its imperial, Soviet, and Cold War past are still evident, not least its tradition of patrimonialism and collectivism.

- The preference among many Russians for strong leaders helps explain the dominating role and ongoing high public approval ratings of Vladimir Putin.

- Even though Russia is formally a semi-presidential system, most of the institutions of Russian government are subservient to its powerful presidency.

- Russian elections give the impression of being free and fair, but they have been manipulated to the benefit of Vladimir Putin and the United Russia party.

- Party politics in Russia has evolved from the monopoly of the communists to the multi-party variety of the 1990s to the current dominance of United Russia.

OVERVIEW

Russia has undergone such dramatic changes in recent decades that we have had to rethink our perceptions of the country, its government, and its national identity. Much as outsiders failed to understand it during the Cold War, we are still not always sure how to interpret the changes it is undergoing, raising concerns about where it is headed. For nearly 70 years, Russia was the dominant partner in the Union of Soviet Socialist Republics (USSR), a state that most Westerners feared, distrusted, and misunderstood. The USSR broke up in 1991, and Russia has since been an independent state, but the heritage of the state socialist political and economic system can still be felt and seen.

In political terms, the efforts to build a democracy in a state that has known only monarchy, one-party rule, totalitarianism, or oligarchy have stalled. At first the changes seemed to be making Russia more democratic, but its leaders have never lost sight of the Soviet tradition of strong and centralized executive authority. President Vladimir Putin has governed directly or indirectly since 1999, has exploited the powers of his office to retain control, has undermined the political opposition, has engineered rigged elections, and has even been implicated in efforts to interfere with elections in other parts of the world. Reflecting recent trends, Freedom House downgraded Russia from Partly Free to Not Free in 2004, while it was downgraded from a hybrid to an authoritarian regime in the 2011 Democracy Index.

In economic terms, Russia continues to wrestle with the challenge of making the transition from an economy that was centrally planned and geared toward the military and heavy industry to a free-market system geared toward the consumer. It has enormous potential, as the largest country in the world by area, stretching across 11 time zones and containing a wealth of natural resources, including land, minerals, oil, natural gas, timber, gold, coal, and iron. However, it lacks the capital and technology to fully exploit these resources, few of its corporations outside the energy sector are yet in the position to address foreign competition, and it suffers from widespread corruption and deep inequalities in the distribution of wealth. Russia's best hope lies in foreign investment, but this would demand more efficient government and more open markets.

Where Russians could once rely on the state to provide jobs and to subsidize food and basic services, many now face shortages, lost jobs, falling wages, and rising prices. Industrial output, agricultural output, and GDP have all grown, but they have not met their potential. Meanwhile, attempts to build economic stability have been undermined by corruption, organized crime, and the black market. Although these problems are serious, Russians have long been fatalistic, all too familiar with hard times and sacrifice. There have been regular predictions of social unrest, rebellion, and violence, but most Russians continue to survive, as they have done many times before.

In social terms, Russia still reflects its imperial past; the Russian empire that emerged between the mid-15th century and the 19th century incorporated many different ethnic groups, and even in today's Russia there are still as many as 90 national minorities, including Tatars, Ukrainians, Bashkirs, and nearly 1 million Germans; together they account for nearly 20 per cent of the population. Several of these groups, especially in the volatile Caucasus region, resent being under the control of Moscow and have agitated for independence. To further complicate matters, as many as 25 million Russians still live in neighbouring former republics of the USSR (notably Ukraine), posing a problem for relations between Russia and those countries.

POLITICAL DEVELOPMENT

For hundreds of years, Russia was a feudal empire that was mainly bypassed by political and economic developments in nearby Europe. In the last century, however, Russians have seen dramatic change. The revolutions of 1917 removed a centuries-old and autocratic monarchy that made way for several decades of brutal repression under the Stalin administration. Then came the tensions of the Cold War and the Gorbachev 'revolution' of the late 1980s, which ended decades of central planning and one-party government. Finally, the break-up of the Soviet Union created an independent Russia, which has once again had to redefine itself and its place in the world, mostly under the baleful eye of Vladimir Putin.

The Russian empire (15th century to 1917)

For most of its history, Russia was more an imperial power than a nation-state. From humble beginnings as Kievan Rus in the 9th century, it was liberated in the 15th century from more than 200 years of Mongol control by Ivan the Great (1440–1505), who set up his capital at Moscow. Under Ivan the Terrible (1533–84), Russia expanded into Kazan, Astrakhan, and Siberia. Under Peter the Great (1682–1725), Russia became a European power, the nobility adopted European culture and values, the army and bureaucracy were based on European models, and the new capital – St Petersburg – was overtly a European city. But Russia remained a feudal society in which most people were powerless peasants (or serfs), a small aristocracy controlled almost all national wealth, there were no free elections or free speech, land was often arbitrarily seized and redistributed, and the tsars violently suppressed opposition.

The serfs were emancipated in 1861, but unlike other more pragmatic European monarchs, Tsar Nicholas II (1894–1917) failed to respond to the pressures for change. Popular opposition was led by the Social Revolutionary Party and the smaller Russian Social Democratic Labour Party (RSDLP), a party founded in 1898 and based on the principles of **Marxism**. At its Second Congress in London in 1903, the RSDLP split into two factions: the Mensheviks (or 'minority'), who advocated a mass membership party, and the more elitist **Bolsheviks** (or 'majority'). Led by the activist Vladimir Ilyich Ulyanov, better known as **Lenin** (1870–1924), the Bolsheviks subscribed to his idea of a vanguard party and developed a tight and disciplined structure with Lenin's authority at the core. Russia came close to revolution in 1905, when it was defeated in a war with Japan, but the tsar survived with the help of the military. A new parliamentary assembly (the Duma) was convened in 1906, but Nicholas II was never able to fully accept the idea of limits on his power.

Marxism
The philosophy developed by Karl Marx, arguing that history is a tale of class antagonism, that social divisions are created by private property, and that revolution is inevitable.

Lenin and the 1917 revolutions

In 1917, Russia underwent two revolutions that grew out of three interconnected factors: the huge losses suffered by Russia in World War I; the theories of Karl Marx and the related ideas of Russian thinkers; and the leadership skills of Lenin and his fellow revolutionary Leon Trotsky (1879–1940), who were able to identify themselves with the popular issues of peace and the redistribution of land. Feeding off Russian losses in the war, worker demonstrations and food riots in March 1917 turned into a revolution against Tsar Nicholas, who abdicated and was replaced by a provisional government, which made the fatal error of continuing the war (see McMeekin, 2017). In April, Lenin returned from exile in Europe and in November, he and his followers staged a second 'revolution' (actually a coup rather than a popular uprising), took over the government, and established a one-party regime based on **state socialism**. He changed the name of his party to the Communist Party, created the Red Army, and in March 1918 negotiated a peace treaty with Germany at Brest-Litovsk, which he was able to repudiate when Germany was defeated. In July 1918, the tsar and his family were murdered on the orders of the Bolsheviks.

State socialism
An arrangement under which there is large-scale state intervention in the economy, centralization of political authority, government by a single political party, state ownership of property, and the elimination of the free market.

Russia was almost immediately split by a civil war between Lenin's Red Army and White Armies led by former tsarist generals. The Whites were defeated in 1922, but the newly declared **Union of Soviet Socialist Republics (USSR)** found itself the only socialist revolutionary state in the world, cut off by a Western economic blockade, and faced with falling industrial and agricultural output and public discontent. Lenin had decided in 1921 to compromise on his principles by launching a New Economic Policy, based partly on free enterprise policies designed to encourage peasants and small businessmen, but he died in 1924 before he could press forward these reforms. A succession struggle followed, and after a brief collective leadership, Joseph Vissarionovich Jugashvili (better known as **Stalin**, or 'man of steel') had by 1929 won uncontested control over both the party and the state, going on to create the political and economic system that was to persist until the late 1980s.

The Stalin era (1928–53)

Under Stalin, the USSR moved further away from Marxist principles and toward a totalitarian style of government that was distinctive enough to earn its own label: **Stalinism** was an absolutist, inflexible, and undemocratic version of communism that demanded unquestioning support for the state and a belief in the unchallenged authority of the party and its leaders (see McCauley, 2013). Abandoning Lenin's idea of promoting global revolution, Stalin chose to build 'socialism in one country' in hopes of making the USSR a political, industrial, agricultural, and military model for others. He used systematic oppression to enforce his reforms, in the process of which perhaps as many as 20 million people died from famine, execution, or war, and many millions more were purged, or

Stalinism
Stalin's political, economic, and social values, including centralized economic planning, a cult of personality, a police state, and mass terror.

Map 12.1 Russia in the Soviet Union

exiled to *gulags* (concentration camps) in Siberia. Stalinism also meant the elimination of human rights and the use of a **cult of personality** (later inspiring the character of Big Brother in George Orwell's novel *1984*).

Stalin also established a **command economy** in which state planners decided what should be produced, when it should be produced, where it should be delivered, and at what prices it should be sold. A series of **five-year plans** set targets with the goal of increasing industrial production by 100 per cent, and meanwhile the Soviet bureaucracy became bigger and more inefficient. Stalin forced millions of farmers into huge new collective farms, eliminating an entire social class (the *kulaks*, or wealthy peasants) and causing a famine that claimed several million lives. He also closed small shops, allowed the state to take over all services, and promoted one-party rule. The **Communist Party of the Soviet Union (CPSU)** infiltrated every part of Soviet life by ensuring that its members had positions of authority in every institution and community, creating a new class of privileged political leaders and dashing any real hope of achieving Marx's goal of a classless society. Finally, Stalin ruled through the use of terror, making sure that his opponents and rivals – including Leon Trotsky, Georgy Zinoviev, Lev Kamenev, and Nikolai Bukharin – were silenced, murdered, or sent to labour camps in Siberia.

> **Cult of personality**
> A political regime based on the idealized and heroic representation of the leader as the focus of the state.

> **Command economy**
> One in which production, investment, supply, and wages are set by a government rather than being left to the free market. Also known as a planned economy.

The rise and fall of the USSR (1945–91)

The Soviet Union took much of the brunt of fighting and the destruction during World War II, with the Nazis occupying the Baltic states, Belarus, and Ukraine, and advancing to within a few miles of Moscow. The Soviets fought back, pressing their advantage in 1943–44 to advance deep into Eastern Europe. With peace in 1945, they had established control over Poland, Romania, Hungary, Czechoslovakia, and Eastern Germany, leaving Europe divided into Western and Soviet spheres of interest that were to persist until the end of the Cold War.

Stalin died in 1953, and was succeeded as Soviet leader by Nikita Khrushchev, whose priority was to end the years of terror. In February 1956 he electrified the Twentieth Party Congress of the CPSU with a 'secret speech' denouncing the excesses of Stalin and extolling the virtues of collective leadership. To prove Soviet technological prowess, Khrushchev launched a space programme that sent the first satellite (*Sputnik*) into space in 1957 and the first human (Yuri Gagarin) in 1961, sparking a space race with the United States. The Khrushchev years also saw

⚙ TIMELINE

9th century	Founding of Kievan Rus
1147	Founding of Moscow
1812	Napoleon invades Russia, advancing as far as Moscow
1861	Emancipation of the serfs
1905–06	Russian defeat in war with Japan, and establishment of Duma
1917	Revolution ousts Tsar Nicholas II; Bolsheviks take power
1918–22	Russian civil war; establishment of USSR (December 1922)
1929	Stalin establishes a dictatorship
1941	Hitler attacks the USSR
1945	USSR emerges from the war with control over much of Eastern Europe
1953	Death of Stalin
1957	*Sputnik* becomes first satellite in space
1985–91	Gorbachev era
1991	USSR ceases to exist (December)
1993	New Russian constitution approved
1994–96	Civil war in Chechnya claims as many as 100,000 lives
2000	Vladimir Putin elected to first term as president
2014	Russia annexes Crimea
2015	Russia begins intervention in Syria
2018	Putin returned to office for fourth term

the perpetuation of the Cold War, reaching a peak in 1962 with the Cuban missile crisis, when – for a few weeks – the world stood on the brink of nuclear war.

Khrushchev was ousted by the CPSU in 1964 and replaced by the more conservative Leonid Brezhnev. There was a military build-up that led to near parity with the United States, and the Soviet Union helped several nationalist movements in Africa and Asia. The Brezhnev era culminated in the ultimately disastrous decision by the Soviets in 1979 to invade Afghanistan, which led to a costly and unpopular war. When Brezhnev died in November 1982, he was followed by two transitional leaders, Yuri Andropov and Konstantin Chernenko, both of whom were elderly and in poor health, and both died in office. The way was then cleared for the rise of Mikhail Gorbachev (born 1931), the man who, in his own words, set about launching the second Russian revolution (Taubman, 2017).

Gorbachev denounced the stagnation of the Brezhnev era and set out to make many of the reforms envisioned by Khrushchev and Andropov. There were two core planks to his programme: *perestroika* (the 'restructuring' of the Soviet economic and political system) and *glasnost*, or a greater 'openness' and willingness to encourage more public discussion of key issues and a greater frankness in admitting mistakes A third plank – *demokratizatsiia*, or democratization – had been added by 1988. Gorbachev's goal was to make state socialism more efficient and more democratic, and to reduce the role of central planning, but his position was undermined by several problems: he preached democratic accountability, but was never popularly elected to office and insisted on maintaining the CPSU monopoly; he found himself caught between liberals who thought his reforms were too timid and conservatives who thought they had gone too far; and his reforms brought into the open the underlying tensions among the Soviet republics, sparking nationalism and secessionism. Partly because of the entrenched power of the Soviet bureaucracy to sabotage and delay his changes and partly because of his own caution, Gorbachev lost control.

In August 1991, on the eve of the signing of a new union treaty that would have redefined the relationship among the Soviet republics, a group of communists staged an attempted coup in Moscow. Although it quickly failed, Gorbachev's credibility was fatally undermined, he resigned as president of the USSR on 25 December 1991, and the following day the Soviet Union ceased to exist. Where there had once been a superpower, there were now 15 independent states. The biggest and most influential was Russia, which just six months before had elected Boris Yeltsin as its president.

The new Russia (since 1991)

Yeltsin found himself plagued by the same problems as Gorbachev: balancing the demands of reformers and hard-liners, working to promote greater political and economic liberalism, and trying to negotiate a new federal treaty that would keep Russia from civil war. The changes were given urgency by attempts made during 1993 to unseat Yeltsin, peaking in September when he dissolved the Russian legislature, the Congress of People's Deputies. A small group of conservatives barricaded themselves inside the Congress building, a move to which Yeltsin responded by lining tanks up outside the Congress building and ordering them to fire. The plot failed, and several of the participants were briefly jailed.

Throughout 1992 and 1993, Russian politics was diverted by a conflict between conservatives and reformers anxious to stake their claims before the new political system was committed to paper with a new constitution. The constitution was approved in a hurried public referendum in December 1993, and a new legislature was elected. Despite threats from communists on the left and nationalists on the right, a civil war in the southern republic of **Chechnya** (see Chapter 3), and his own health problems, Yeltsin was elected to a second term as president in July 1996. Trust in government had fallen, however, the legislature failed to be an effective source of policy ideas or of opposition to the president, nationalist problems in the south boiled over into war and urban terrorism, wealth and power accumulated in the hands of a new elite, the value of the rouble fell, confidence in the banking system declined, and unemployment grew. In December 1999, Yeltsin suddenly resigned. He was replaced as acting president by his prime minister, Vladimir Putin (b. 1952), who was elected president in his own right in March 2000.

Russia today

Putin moved quickly to build on the power of the presidency, and to direct Russia away from any democratic tendencies that might have occurred under Yeltsin. He has worked to prevent the development of meaningful political competition, and to limit the rise of either a free media or competitive opposition political parties. Putin has been intolerant of criticism in the media, given increased powers to the security services, and expanded his powers over regional governments. With a two-term limit on the presidency, and not enough support in the Federal Assembly to change the constitution in order to give himself a third term, Putin was obliged to step down at the end of his second term in 2008, but manipulated the election to make sure that his favoured candidate Dmitry Medvedev won the presidency. It was clear that Medvedev was a seat-warmer for Putin, who bided his time (while pulling strings from behind the scenes) until allowed by the constitution to run again in the 2012 presidential election. He won handily, and was returned to office for a fourth term with a record share of the vote in 2018.

Economically, there has been growth under Putin, but there is little foreign investment and there is still much resistance to change, both among ordinary Russians and among old-style bureaucrats. Infrastructure is poor, although Russia ranks as Very High on the Human Development Index, in the same league as most advanced democracies. Its population is ageing and contracting, but the middle class has grown, and a few entrepreneurs have made great wealth out of the opening of the Russian market, creating a new class of **oligarchs** who – more so in the Yeltsin years than the Putin years – have played a key role in Russian politics.

On the global stage, Russia initially struggled to come to terms with its new status as a former superpower, a problem that Putin addressed by taking a more assertive position in international affairs. 'The collapse of the Soviet Union', he said in a 2005 address, 'was a major geopolitical disaster of the century'. When asked at a 2018 press conference what Russian historical event he would change if he could, he quickly responded 'the collapse of the Soviet Union'. His new approach was reflected in his violent crackdown on separatists in Chechnya, in the annexation of the Ukrainian province of Crimea in 2014, in his support for Russian separatists in Ukraine, and in his support for the al-Assad regime in Syria. It was also reflected in the creation of what Treisman (2018) describes as an 'informational autocracy': Putin has employed social media, fake news, hackers and trolls to interfere in elections at home as well as those abroad, notably the 2016 presidential election in the United States.

Pro-Russian protesters stage a rally in the Ukrainian city of Odessa in March 2014. While they may have supported Russia's occupation of the Crimean peninsula in Ukraine, it was in contravention of international law and confirmed the Putin government's desire to rebuild Russian power in the world.
Source: AFP/Getty Images.

POLITICAL CULTURE

In spite of all the political and economic changes that Russia has seen since the break-up of the Soviet Union, recent events suggest a strong continuity between public attitudes toward politics and government from the pre-Soviet era through to the present. Sakwa (2014) argues that 'it is impossible to understand contemporary Russia without some understanding of what went before'. Few adjustments have been harder to make than dealing with Russia's long history of authoritarian government. The tsars clung to autocracy long after most other European monarchs had given up their powers to popularly elected assemblies, and government during the tsarist era was centralized, bureaucratic, authoritarian, and intrusive. The Soviet experience after 1917 was little different because tsarist autocracy was replaced by Leninist elitism, which was followed by Stalinist totalitarianism. Russia since 1991 has seen more democracy than the country has ever had, but democracy has had trouble taking root, mainly because Russians have had little opportunity to learn how it works, while some regard it with doubt.

The authoritarian tradition is reflected in the Russian preference for strong leaders. Many Russians look back nostalgically on the authority (and unity) of the past, some even admiring Stalin as someone who provided a stable and tightly regulated social order and whose use of force is often excused as being 'necessary for the time'. Views such as these have been both a cause and an effect of a tradition of Russian political **patrimonialism**: a sense of leaders as father figures. The tradition helps explain the place of Stalin in the Soviet system and the emergence of something close to a cult of personality surrounding Vladimir Putin. Although strong leadership has its place (see Comparing Political Culture 12), no political system that relies on the fortunes and methods of one person or ruling elite can hope to develop long-term stability.

> **Patrimonialism**
> A political system based on a leader as a father figure who has limited accountability to his people but who claims to understand their interests and needs.

COMPARING POLITICAL CULTURE 12
Political leadership

There is little question that many Russians prefer 'strong' leadership, based on their definition of the particular needs of Russia. The definition of a strong leader, though, or of a good or efficient leader, is often a matter of opinion than of verifiable fact. This has become increasingly evident in recent years in the United States, for example, where opinion has been divided on the merits of Barack Obama and Donald Trump as leaders; in both cases, most of their supporters and detractors will define them as good or bad leaders regardless of objective measures.

In a comparative study of leadership over several decades, Brown (2014) challenges the perception that strong leaders are the most successful and admirable, and suggests that effective leaders are most likely to be those who are cooperative and collegial. He makes a distinction between 'redefining' leaders such as Roosevelt and Thatcher (who expanded the limits of what was possible during their time in office) and 'transformational' leaders such as de Gaulle, Gorbachev, and Mandela (who played a key role in bringing about decisive change). Vladimir Putin probably straddles the two types, because he has both expanded the reach of the Russian presidency and brought about much fundamental change in Russia.

What makes for a good leader? At a minimum, he or she should have a sense of direction, the ability to inspire, the skills to communicate their policies and the underlying logic of those policies, the ability to place the needs of the society they lead within their broader context, and the capacity to build the support needed to encourage people to follow the direction they have set. Such a combination rarely comes in a single package, and the number of truly great leaders in history is quite small. Often, strong leaders have simply been the right people in the right place at the right time. In contrast, there have been many leaders who have either started out on a wave of optimism but failed to live up to expectations (thanks either to their own failings or to difficult circumstances), or whose leadership proved to have caused more problems than it solved, or were simply incompetent (see analysis in Rhodes and Hart, 2014).

Brown (2014) warns of the particular dangers posed by a strong leader in countries making a transition from highly authoritarian rule either to democracy or an intermediate hybrid regime. He quotes a 2007 study in Russia and several Eastern European countries that found high levels of support for the idea that it would be worth supporting a leader who could solve the problems of a country even if it meant overthrowing democracy in the process. Vladimir Putin has been unable to address many of Russia's most persistent economic problems, and yet there is clearly a widely held view among Russians that a strong leader is preferable to a cooperative one.

The Russian tolerance for authoritarianism is reflected in Russian worries about the security of the state, and their fear of chaos. Western Russia is flat and difficult to defend from conventional attack, and it has not been forgotten how close Napoleon came to reaching Moscow in 1812, and how much blood was shed defending Russia against the Nazis in 1941–45, during what the Soviets labelled the Great Patriotic War. Russian nationalism is partly a reaction to these fears, and an explanation of why Russians continue to place so heavy a reliance on the state to maintain order and security. Given the extent of the changes the Russian people have experienced in the last few years, many believe that their country is headed towards what is sometimes popularly described as 'the abyss'. These traditions make it difficult to build democracy, given that democracy by definition involves a high degree of uncertainty.

Another example of the heritage of the past can be found in the Russian tradition of the **collective society**. While liberal democracies value individualism and self-determination, Russia is more group-oriented. Even after the emancipation of the serfs in 1861, they owned land not individually but collectively. During the Soviet era, opinion polls showed a high level of support for state planning and ownership of the economy, for state ownership of transport and communications, for collectivist public welfare in the fields of education and health care, and for living in a welfare state. While the Soviet era is gone, big government is still widely supported among Russians, who are mainly comfortable with the role of the state in ensuring prosperity, maintaining equality and security, and guaranteeing economic and political freedom (Remington, 2016).

Name	Russian Federation (Rossijskaja Federacija)
Capital	Moscow
Administration	Federal republic with 85 'subjects', including republics, provinces, and territories.
Constitution	Modern state formed 1991, and most recent constitution adopted 1993.
Executive	Semi-presidential. The president is directly elected, and limited to two consecutive six-year terms. The prime minister comes out of the State Duma, heads the Council of Ministers, and succeeds the president if needed (no vice president).
Legislature	Bicameral Federal Assembly: a 450-member State Duma elected for five-year terms, and a relatively weak 166-member Federation Council with two members appointed by the president from each federal unit.
Judiciary	Based on civil law and the constitution of 1993. Headed by a 19-member Constitutional Court (members nominated by the president and confirmed by the Federation Council) and, for civil and administrative cases, a Supreme Court.
Electoral system	Direct elections for the president, with the possibility of two rounds if no one wins a majority in the first ballot. Mixed single-member and party list proportional representation is used for the State Duma.
Party system	Multi-party, but parties are weak and unstable – reflecting, rather than shaping, power. The leading party, United Russia, provides a foundation for the authoritarian rule of Vladimir Putin.

RUSSIA

Arctic Ocean

St Petersburg · MOSCOW · UKRAINE · KAZAKHSTAN · MONGOLIA · CHINA

144m Population

$1,577 billion Gross Domestic Product

$10,740 Per capita GDP

- ✗ Full Democracy
- ✗ Flawed Democracy
- ✗ Hybrid Regime
- ✓ Authoritarian
- ✗ Not Rated

Democracy Index rating

- ✗ Free
- ✗ Partly Free
- ✓ Not Free
- ✗ Not Rated

Freedom House rating

- ✓ Very High
- ✗ High
- ✗ Medium
- ✗ Low
- ✗ Not Rated

Human Development Index rating

POLITICAL SYSTEM

The watchword in Russian government and politics in the 1990s was *reform*, but since 2000 it has been something more like *reversion* (to old authoritarian ways). Russians have had to rethink their old assumptions as a society once founded on one-party rule and central economic planning made its first tentative steps towards adopting an open, competitive political and economic system, then found the process slowed down and redirected. The Soviets claimed that their political system was democratic, but all real power was focused in the Communist Party of the Soviet Union (CPSU), which was run by an elite that made all policy, which was implemented in turn by a bureaucracy directed by the party. Gorbachev had barely warmed to the task of making the system more democratic and efficient before he lost control, leaving his successors with the challenge of building a new system while taking care not to leave Russia without direction or generating a backlash among disgruntled Russians.

Formally, Russia today is a federal republic with a semi-presidential executive. In reality, the Russian form of federalism is weak, with enormous power concentrated in Moscow, while the balance among the key governing institutions clearly favours the executive. Russia's legislature has been split among a changing array of political parties, and only in 2007 did one of them – United Russia – finally win a majority. The weakness of the legislature played into the hands of an already powerful presidency, and Vladimir Putin was able to exploit the growth of pro-Kremlin parties to extend his control. It remains to be seen how much long-term effect Putin's turn at the helm will have on Russian political development, and what will happen once he leaves office. The prognosis is not good, given that few authoritarian regimes have been able to make a smooth transition to a meaningful system of democracy.

The constitution

When the Soviet Union collapsed, Russia inherited the 1978 constitution of the Russian republic, which was amended so many times during 1990–91 that work was begun on drafting an entirely new document. The job was complicated by the fact that no previous Soviet or Russian constitution had clearly spelled out the relative powers of executive and legislature. Concern grew among legislators in the Russian legislature (the Congress of People's Deputies) that Boris Yeltsin was using the hiatus to consolidate presidential power before the relationship between executive and legislature was committed to paper. Their concerns sparked the resistance of September–October 1993.

In December 1993, elections were held to the reformed Russian legislature (by then renamed the Federal Assembly), and the new constitution was put to a public referendum. Voter turnout was just under 55 per cent, and just 58 per cent of those who voted expressed their approval. In other words, 68 per cent of eligible voters either voted against the constitution or did not vote at all. This was hardly a popular mandate, but the constitution went into force regardless. It created a federal republic in which power is shared between an elected and powerful executive president, a prime minister and Council of Ministers, a bicameral Federal Assembly, a complex court system, and 83 local units of government.

The legacy of the Soviet era encouraged the framers to open the constitution with a lengthy bill of rights (Articles 17–64) that not only established the personal freedoms normally associated with a democracy but went into more detail, including the right to a private life, nationality, artistic expression, ideological diversity, and even protection from being subjected to medical experiments without consent. Amendments to the constitution can be proposed by the president, by either chamber of the Federal Assembly, by the Russian government (the prime minister and Council of Ministers), by local legislatures, and even by a group of at least 20 per cent of the deputies of either chamber of the Assembly. There are complex rules on the confirmation of amendments, but in most cases they demand the support of both chambers of the Federal Assembly along with local legislatures. The first substantial amendments were introduced and passed in 2008, lengthening the terms of the State Duma and the president to five and six years respectively.

Russia today is a leading example of the argument made in Chapter 2 about distinguishing between constitutional claims and political realities. On paper, there are many checks and balances between the presidency and other institutions, and Russia would seem to enjoy important constitutional guarantees. In reality, Vladimir Putin has been able to manipulate the system such that each of the checks on his power has been neutralized. While it is true that most Russians like strong leaders, this is only part of Russia's modern political story, which – more than the stories of many other powerful countries – has been written by one man.

The executive: president, prime minister, and Council of Ministers

Executive power in the old Soviet system was theoretically vested in a prime minister and Council of Ministers. In reality, power lay with the Communist Party, and the *de facto* leader of the Soviet Union was the general secretary of the party, the post to which Mikhail Gorbachev was appointed by the party leadership in 1985. In March 1990, Gorbachev was hastily elected by the reformed Soviet legislature to a new post of executive president, in an attempt to shift authority from the party to the government and to make the executive more accountable to the people. It was too little and too late, however, and the office was eliminated with the collapse of the USSR in 1991. Boris Yeltsin – who had been elected president of Russia six months before – now became leader of an independent Russia. He struggled to establish the new office between 1991 and 1993, finally winning a legal base with the passage of the 1993 constitution, which set the new terms of the position.

With their headquarters in the Kremlin in central Moscow, presidents of Russia can serve an unlimited number of six-year terms, but no more than two consecutively. The president has the conventional roles of head of state, commander-in-chief, and overseer of foreign policy, but also has several particular powers that make the office more powerful than many other presidencies:

◆ *The power to issue decrees.* So long as they do not contravene the constitution or federal law, presidents can issue decrees that have the force of law unless and until the legislature passes laws that supersede them (see Remington, 2014a). Yeltsin used this power extensively, as when he privatized state-owned industries, reformed the banking system, and took on organized crime. Putin followed suit, issuing decrees that re-established mandatory training for military reservists, censored news from Chechnya, and in 2012 set an eight-year deadline for the creation of 25 million high productivity jobs. Since they often involve making changes over which the president has little direct control, decrees are of mixed value.

◆ *The power of appointment.* The Russian presidency comes with conventional powers of appointment and dismissal, but they go much further than is the case with most executives. Presidents can appoint and dismiss the prime minister and federal ministers, move ministers from one job to another, influence the appointment of senior ministerial staff, appoint the heads of all major government agencies (such as the Russian Central Bank), nominate justices to the Constitutional Court (who must win approval by the Federation Council), and appoint and dismiss military commanders and ambassadors.

The State Duma must approve all key appointments, but if it turns down the president's nominee for prime minister three times in a row, then new elections are called for the Duma. Because most members of the Duma want to see out their full term, they are unlikely to push a president that far; they would be more likely instead to pass a vote of no confidence in the government. In the event of such a vote, the president can either dismiss the prime minister or ignore the vote, but – if it was passed again within three months – he would be required either to replace the prime minister or dissolve the Duma and call a new election.

◆ *The power to call elections.* Presidents can dissolve the State Duma and call new elections any time they see fit. To prevent them from arbitrarily dissolving the Duma and holding repeated elections until they get a result they like, though, they cannot dissolve the house if it is considering impeaching the president, during a state of national emergency or martial law, or within a year of a vote of no confidence.

◆ *Martial law and a state of emergency.* If the president believes there is a threat of aggression against Russia, he can introduce martial law (under which he can use the military to control and govern using direct force) or declare a state of emergency (under which normal legislative and judicial powers are suspended). A president must have the approval of the Federation Council to do either.

Putin has combined the constitutional powers of the office with his personal views about leadership and about Russia's needs to create what Willerton (2014) describes as a 'paramount leader' holding a 'hegemonic executive'. True, the president cannot completely ignore public opinion, and he can also be impeached by the Federation Council for treason or a serious crime. But much like the 'high crimes and misdemeanours' clause in the US constitution, this is an ambiguous idea that is open to wide interpretation, and impeachment is difficult to actually achieve: it must be brought by one-third of the members of the Duma, its grounds must be confirmed by the Constitutional Court and the Supreme Court, and it must then be confirmed by a two-thirds majority in both chambers of the Federal Assembly.

Table 12.1 Post-Soviet leaders of Russia

Start of term	President	Prime minister
June 1991*	Boris Yeltsin	Boris Yeltsin
		1992 Viktor Chernomyrdin
December 1993		1998 (April) Sergei Kiriyenko
		1998 (September) Yevgeny Primakov
		1999 (May) Sergei Stepashin
		1999 (August) Vladimir Putin
December 1999	Vladimir Putin (acting)	
March 2000	Vladimir Putin	Mikhail Kasyanov
March 2004		Mikhail Fradkov
March 2008	Dmitry Medvedev	Vladimir Putin
March 2012	Vladimir Putin	Dmitry Medvedev
March 2018		

* Prior to break-up of Soviet Union

As with all executives, the presidency in Russia is much more than the individual who holds the office. The president has a supporting network of offices and institutions that play a key role in determining the character of an administration, including the State Council (a consultative forum created by Putin in 2000 and made up of Russia's 83 regional leaders), the Executive Office (with representatives from nearly 40 government agencies), and the Security Council (which gives advice on national security).

As a semi-presidential system, the president also governs in association with a prime minister and a Council of Ministers. The latter is the functional equivalent of a parliamentary-style cabinet and consists of the prime minister, several deputy prime ministers, and about two dozen federal ministers, the most influential of which are the five 'power ministers': foreign affairs, defence, internal affairs, justice, and emergency situations. The main jobs of the government are to draft the federal budget, oversee economic policy, and oversee the implementation of law and policy by the bureaucracy.

The prime minister (formally the Chairman of the Government of the Russian Federation) has a thankless task, occupying an office that is caught between the president and the legislature. Prime ministers do not need to come out of the Federal Assembly (contrast this with the rules in France – see Chapter 7), but they are nominated by the president and need the approval of the State Duma. Once in office, they follow the broad direction of government policy established by the president, and must work to guide the president's programme through the Duma. Prime ministers help select ministers, advise the president on policy, and – because there is no vice presidency – stand as next in line to become president if the incumbent dies, resigns, or becomes permanently incapable of governing. In such an event, the prime minister takes power as acting president, and new presidential elections must be held within three months. This has only happened once to date: when Yeltsin resigned in December 1999, he was replaced by Vladimir Putin and new elections were held in March 2000.

Russian prime ministers have mainly been little known at the time of their appointment, and – once in office – are expected to be loyal and unthreatening. For example, Yeltsin's prime minister from 1992 to 1998 was Viktor Chernomyrdin, a moderate liberal on economic issues and the former chairman of Russia's state-owned natural gas monopoly, Gazprom. He was both loyal and a good manager, with a style that was so understated as to be dull. After several years of stability in the office of prime minister, Yeltsin caused a stir during his second term by appointing and dismissing four prime ministers in less than 18 months (1998–99). Some saw this as a sign that he wanted to prevent any one prime minister from becoming too powerful or popular (Sakwa, 2008) while others saw it as a sign that he was out of control. Yet others suggested that the changes were designed to create contenders for the presidential election in 2000, and to make it more difficult for the communists to win the election. As it happens, his final prime minister – an all-but-unknown member of Yeltsin's staff named Vladimir Putin – was the man who went on to win the presidency.

Putin had two prime ministers during his first two terms: the technocrat and economist Mikhail Kasyanov (who confounded predictions that he would not last long, quickly becoming a close Putin confidante), and Mikhail Fradkov, a former Russian trade minister and ambassador to the European Union. Under the Medvedev presidency, all the previous assumptions about the prime ministership were abandoned: he appointed Vladimir Putin to the position, his hands tied by the fact that it had been Putin's support that had made Medvedev's victory possible, and by the large majority won in the State Duma by United Russia, the political party that had been created in 2003 as a platform for Putin. Rather than a powerful president and a functionary prime minister, the roles were now reversed. The roles were reversed again when the two men exchanged positions after the 2012 presidential election, continuing with what Willerton (2014) describes as a 'tandemocracy'.

The legislature: Federal Assembly

Russia has not had much of a history of legislative politics. During the Soviet era, the national legislature was the 1,500-member Supreme Soviet, whose lower chamber was elected from local districts and the upper chamber from the 15 Soviet republics. Meeting only twice each year for sessions of three to five days each, it did little more than rubber-stamp decisions of the CPSU, the real power being held at other times by a 39-member Presidium, whose members were appointed by the party leadership and which could take any action that was constitutional, provided that it was ratified by the Supreme Soviet. (A similar model is still found today in China – see Chapter 13.) In his attempts to turn the Soviet Union from a 'party-governed' state into a 'law-governed' state, Gorbachev created a tricameral Congress of People's Deputies and a smaller and more powerful Supreme Soviet, which sat for two sessions of four months each year.

When the USSR broke up, Russia's regional parliament became the legislative body of the newly independent state. This was virtually a mirror image of the Gorbachev model, with a Congress of People's Deputies elected for five-year terms, a smaller and more powerful bicameral Supreme Soviet, and a prime minister and Council of Ministers. Elements of this system worked their way into the 1993 constitution, but the powers of the executive grew at the expense of those of the legislature, with the result that today's Federal Assembly – consisting of an upper Federation Council and a lower State Duma – has become largely a rubber stamp for Putin's policy initiatives (Remington, 2014b).

Federation Council (*Sovet Federatsii*)

As with the upper chambers in most federal systems (see Comparing Government 12), the Federation Council in Russia is formally designed to represent the regions. It is not as powerful as the Duma, though, and – thanks to the lack of any explanation in the Russian constitution about how it should be formed – has gone through several changes of personality. It was created by Boris Yeltsin as a meeting place for regional representatives to discuss an early draft of the new Russian constitution, and was then made a permanent part of government. It initially consisted of two representatives elected from each of the 85 'subjects' of Russia (regions and republics), for a total membership of 170. They were replaced in 1995 by the appointed representatives of executives and legislatures of the subjects; in most cases, the chief executives and the chairs of the legislatures appointed themselves.

Another change was made by Putin soon after coming to office in 2000. In an attempt to limit the powers of the regional leaders, who he felt had accumulated too much influence over national politics, he steered a new law through the State Duma that stripped the local leaders of their rights to sit in the Federation Council, replacing them with full-time representatives appointed by local legislatures and their executives. In 2012, yet another change was made whereby one member from each subject would be elected by members of the local legislature, and a second chosen by local governors. In reality, all appointments are subject to Putin's approval.

The Council has jurisdiction over relations between the federal government and the subjects and can discuss all laws passed by the Duma. Its approval is needed only for laws involving economic or defence issues, although – even then – the State Duma can override a Council veto with a two-thirds majority. It confirms presidential nominations to the Constitutional Court and Supreme Court, must approve changes to the internal borders of Russian subjects, must approve decisions by the president to declare martial law or a state of emergency, schedules presidential elections, and has the sole power to initiate impeachment proceedings against the president.

State Duma (*Gosudárstvennaya Dúma*)

The State Duma is the lower chamber of the Federal Assembly, and Russia's major law-making body. It has 450 members elected for maximum five-year terms, using a mix of single-member plurality and proportional

COMPARING GOVERNMENT 12
Upper chambers of legislatures

As we saw in Chapter 2, only about 40 per cent of the world's legislatures have two chambers, and they are found mostly in countries that are either large or diverse, and where it is thought better to provide two different forms of representation. There would not be much point in having two chambers with the same structure and powers, so a system is usually set up in which the electoral pie is sliced differently, and the so-called upper chamber is often given unique powers, such as confirming executive appointments.

Federations are the most logical sites for bicameral legislatures, and it makes the most sense that lower chambers are divided on a per capita basis (each seat represents roughly the same number of voters) while upper chambers give representation to the states or provinces in the federation. The natural role for the Federation Council in Russia would be to represent the country's 83 'subjects', but while it is indeed made of representatives from local legislatures and executives, Putin has made sure to maintain control over appointments, reducing the Council's independence.

In other countries, the means by which members of the upper chamber of the legislatures are elected or appointed varies widely, leaving little in the way of a standard approach to organizing upper chambers. Consider these examples:

◆ In Britain, members are either hereditary aristocrats, peers appointed for life, or senior members of the Church of England.
◆ In Germany, members are appointed by state governments.
◆ In the United States, the Senate is elected by voters in the states, with two members from each state regardless of differences in population size.
◆ In India, most members are indirectly elected through state legislatures, with a small number appointed by the president of India.
◆ In Mexico, three-quarters of Senators are elected from the states, while the remainder are elected as at-large representatives for the entire country.

As a result of this variety, it is not always easy to make generalizations about the powers and the political significance of upper chambers, most of which have structures tied to history and local circumstances.

representation. The Duma is overseen by a chairman (equivalent to a Speaker) who is appointed by the Duma and so needs the support of the majority of representatives. The Russian law-making process has two notable qualities:

◆ The Federal Assembly can discuss and adopt both federal laws and constitutional laws (which change or clarify the constitution).
◆ Proposals for new laws can be submitted by the president, the government, either house of the Federal Assembly, legislatures of local units of government, or even the Constitutional Court and Supreme Court.

As well as its key role in the law-making process, the State Duma must confirm the president's choice for prime minister and must approve all government ministers except defence, foreign affairs, and internal affairs. It can also introduce motions of no confidence in the government. If one succeeds, the president can either ignore it or dismiss the prime minister, but if another follows within three months, the prime minister must be dismissed and replaced. An isolated near-miss occurred in March 2001 when the communists – accusing Putin of 'suicidal' policies and talking of a decade wasted on so-called 'democratic reforms' – called for a vote. They were initially supported by the Unity Party (precursor to today's United Russia), which backed the proposal because it hoped it could win more seats in the subsequent election. But when Unity withdrew, the motion was soundly defeated.

Once passed by the State Duma, federal laws must go within five days to the Federation Council, which has just two weeks to vote in favour or against. A rejection can be overruled by a two-thirds majority in the Duma, or else the law is sent to a conciliation committee to settle the differences. Once a law has been adopted by the Assembly, it must be submitted within five days to the president, who has two weeks to sign it or reject it. A presidential veto can be overruled by a two-thirds majority of both houses of the Assembly.

With no party winning a majority in the Duma in its early years, it offered little real opposition to the president. It was further handicapped by the president's powers to issue decrees, and by ongoing uncertainty about the balance of power between the executive and the legislature; Putin took advantage of the situation by manipulating the Assembly to his own ends. When pro-Kremlin parties won a stranglehold after the 2003 elections, Putin was given a strong foundation on which to pursue his legislative agenda. The 2007 elections gave a large majority to United Russia, the party with which both Putin and Medvedev were subsequently associated. The Duma today is dominated by United Russia (which won 76 per cent of seats in the chamber at the 2016 legislative elections), and is less a source of policy alternatives than of policy support.

The judiciary: Constitutional Court

Russia has a Constitutional Court, which – like most such courts – has the task of protecting and interpreting the constitution. It does this by resolving disputes over political jurisdiction (including disputes between federal government departments) and making sure that the legislative and executive branches abide by the constitution. Its work should not be confused with that of Russia's Supreme Court, which is the highest court of appeal for civil, criminal, and administrative cases and has the power of oversight over the activities of lower courts. Meanwhile, a Higher Arbitration Court deals with economic and business matters, and the constitution also provides for a single, centralized system of prosecution, headed by a prosecutor-general.

The Constitutional Court has 19 members nominated by the president and confirmed by the Federation Council, and it is headed by a Chairman. The terms of their appointment are indefinite, but – except for the Chairman – they cannot serve beyond the age of 70. Valery Zorkin (b. 1943) was appointed first Chairman in 1991, was forced to resign by Boris Yeltsin in 1993, and then was reappointed to the position by Vladimir Putin in 2003.

In its early days the Court had no constitution to defend or interpret (other than the discredited 1978 version), so its members were unable to define a place for themselves in the new Russian system or to act as neutral arbiters as Yeltsin and the legislature bickered. The passage of the 1993 constitution provided the legal foundation for the Court's powers, but its structure was only finally settled with the passage of a 1994 law. The Court has since faced four major challenges: building legitimacy for the constitution, giving more definition to the principles and objectives of the constitution, establishing a tradition of judicial review, and promoting public respect for the rule of law in a society in which both the law and the constitution were discredited by being manipulated to suit the ends of the CPSU.

Sub-national government

The USSR was legally a federation, but in practice it was governed more like a unitary state. It consisted of 15 republics, which varied in size and power from the vast and sprawling Russian Soviet Federated Socialist Republic, which covered 76 per cent of the land area of the USSR, to the three Baltic republics (Estonia, Latvia, and Lithuania), which together made up less than one per cent of the land area of the USSR. Local elections provided the same illusion of democracy as those at the federal level, while the heads of local government bodies were appointed by the general secretary of the CPSU and were accountable to no one but the higher levels of the party.

Russia today has 85 'subjects', or components: 22 republics, 46 oblasts (provinces), nine krais (territories), four autonomous okrugs (districts), three federal cities (Moscow, St Petersburg, and Sevastopol), and an autonomous Jewish oblast in the far east of Russia. (The latter was set up by Stalin in order to allow Jews to pursue Yiddish culture, but barely one per cent of the oblast's population today is Jewish.) All these subjects have their own government institutions and their own systems of law; they have constitutions, executives (collectively described as governors even if their formal titles are different), legislatures, and courts, although – much like other federal systems – the national power of each unit varies. Republics are the most powerful, in part because they are the biggest, while krais and oblasts are less significant because most exist on the political and/or geographical margins of Russia.

POLITICAL PROCESSES

Russians have had little sustained experience of multi-party democracy, and although they now take part in elections in healthy numbers, the choices laid before them were initially confusing, and have since become highly predictable. During the Soviet era, all significant policy decisions were made by the Communist Party of the Soviet

Union (CPSU). Voters were offered no choice at the polls, and the media were controlled and censored. Gorbachev began encouraging a more open society, but he neither lifted all controls on the media nor allowed the free expression of opposition sentiment, inside or outside government. In the new Russia, voters have been given multiple choices at the polls, and have cast their votes in several sets of presidential, legislative, and local elections. However, electoral manipulation has undermined the prospect of free elections before they had much time to take root.

The electoral system

The USSR was governed on the Leninist principle of **democratic centralism**, meaning that limited democracy existed within a single legal party, the CPSU. In theory, every level in the party delegated its authority to the next highest level through the electoral process. All decisions passed down by the higher levels were to be followed by the lower levels, but the higher levels were also supposedly accountable to the lower levels. In reality, rank-and-file party members had little impact on party policy, all electoral nominations were controlled by the CPSU, and because the CPSU claimed to represent the public interest, only one CPSU-approved candidate was slated for each seat. The CPSU decided the dates of elections, made all the arrangements, counted the ballots, and even organized light entertainment to keep voters amused. According to official statistics, turnout was never less than an implausible 99 per cent.

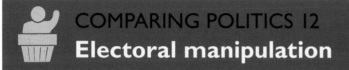

COMPARING POLITICS 12
Electoral manipulation

In an ideal world, elections would be free and fair in the sense that they allow all participating voters an equal role in deciding the outcome, and all participating candidates and parties an equal opportunity to win voter support. This ideal, though, is never reflected in reality. Even in the most democratic of states, there are mathematical problems with the design of elections, which is why – as we saw in Chapter 2 – so many different electoral systems have been designed and used, in a (failed) effort to find the perfect system.

The problem goes beyond arithmetic and is exacerbated by deliberate efforts to manipulate elections and electoral outcomes. This can be done through subtle means, such as complicating the process of registering to vote, or by making the act of voting more difficult through ploys such as the inconvenient placement of polling locations, opening them for reduced hours, misdirecting voters, or illegally turning them away. Manipulation can also be built in to the electoral system, as in the infamous habit in the United States known as gerrymandering – see Chapter 5.

The problem is most acute in authoritarian states such as Russia, where interference in elections is not unusual. Putin may have won nearly 80 per cent of the vote in the 2018 presidential election, but his administration became adept at using social media to shape news coverage. Videos and photos were published after the election showing people apparently voting more than once, or placing multiple ballots into voting boxes. Monitors had been sent to the election by the Organization for Security and Cooperation in Europe (OSCE), a Vienna-based body with 57 state members, whose interests include free and fair elections. It issued a statement saying that while the election was run efficiently, it took place in 'an overly controlled legal and political environment marked by continued pressure on critical voices', and that restrictions on freedom of assembly, association and expression, and on candidate registration, had resulted 'in a lack of genuine competition'.

Figure 12.1 shows the Democracy Index rankings of the countries in this book (and selected others) on the measure of electoral process and pluralism. This asks whether elections are free and fair, looking at the range of choices offered to voters, the conditions imposed on candidates, irregularities in the voting process, restrictions on voters, campaign laws, party financing, and the independence of parties. Seven countries (including Norway, New Zealand, Denmark, and Uruguay) head the list with perfect scores of 10, and most free and flawed democracies score 8 or better. Russia languishes towards the end of the scale with a score of 2.17, and while this is better than the zeroes scored by nearly twenty countries, it is weak, and says much about the comparative absence of freedom of elections in Russia.

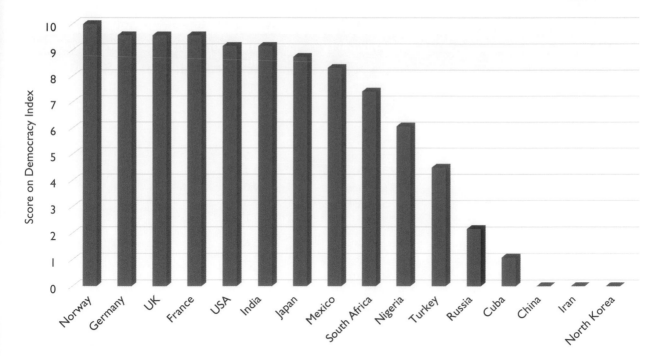

Figure 12.1 Comparing electoral records
Source: Economist Intelligence Unit (2019).
Note: Scores out of 10. China, Iran, and North Korea each score zero.

Against this background, it took some time for Russians to become used to the idea of competitive elections, and – at least at first – they were swamped with options; elections in the new Russia were far more open and competitive than they had ever been during the Soviet era. The new habits did not last long, however, and even in the Yeltsin era and the early years of the Putin era, there were signs of electoral fraud and manipulation, a problem that has only worsened with time – see Comparing Politics 12.

Presidential elections

Tsarist Russia lived under an absolute monarch, while the Soviet Union lived under a monopoly party in which the only position of power that mattered was that of general secretary of the party. Unsurprisingly, it took some time for the idea of competitive presidential elections to take hold in the new Russia. They had barely established even a tentative grip on the political imagination before Vladimir Putin stepped forward to manipulate presidential elections to his own ends.

Formally, Russia (like France) uses a majority system for presidential elections. Candidates qualify if they register and collect 1 million signatures in support of their candidacy. All qualified candidates compete in the opening round, and if one of them wins more than half the vote, they are declared the winner. If no one crosses the 50 per cent barrier, the top two finishers run off against each other in a second round held within 15 days. Only once to date, in 1996, has an election gone to a second round. In that year, Boris Yeltsin won a marginally bigger share of the vote in the first round (35.3 per cent) than his communist opponent Gennady Zyuganov (32 per cent), increasing his share to a not particularly convincing 54 per cent in the runoff. Significantly, nearly 4 million voters – about five per cent of those who turned out – made a political statement in the second round by voting for 'none of the above' (an option that was abolished by law in 2006, but that is used in India – see Chapter 8).

The March 2000 election was different both in its character and its outcome. A change of leadership was inevitable (because Yeltsin could not run again), and 11 candidates contested the election. The clear front-runner was former prime minister and incumbent acting president Vladimir Putin, whose lead in opinion polls was never seriously challenged. Putin won the first round with more than 52 per cent of the vote, ensuring that a runoff was

Table 12.2 Results of recent presidential elections in Russia

Year	Candidate	Ideology/party	Number of votes (millions)	% share of votes
2004	Vladimir Putin	Independent	49.6	71.2
	Nikolai Kharitonov	Communist	9.5	13.7
	Others		7.4	10.8
	None of the above		2.4	3.5
2008	Dmitry Medvedev	United Russia	52.5	70.3
	Gennady Zyuganov	Communist	13.2	17.7
	Vladimir Zhirinovsky	Liberal Democrat	7.0	9.4
	Andrei Bogdanov	Democratic Party	1.0	1.3
	Invalid votes		1.1	1.3
2012	Vladimir Putin	United Russia	45.6	63.6
	Gennady Zyuganov	Communist	12.3	17.2
	Mikhail Prokhorov	Self-nominated	5.7	8.0
	Vladimir Zhirinovsky	Liberal Democrat	4.5	6.2
	Sergey Mironov	A Just Russia	2.8	3.8
	Invalid votes		0.8	1.1
2018	Vladimir Putin	Independent	56.4	76.7
	Pavel Grudinin	Communist	8.7	11.8
	Vladimir Zhirinovsky	Liberal Democrat	4.1	5.7
	Five others		3.5	4.8
	Invalid votes		0.8	1.0

unnecessary. Gennady Zyuganov came in second with a slightly smaller share of the vote than he had won in 1996 (just under 30 per cent), and all the remaining candidates were in single figures. The March 2004 election produced few surprises (Putin won with a handy 71 per cent of the vote), and the outcomes of the 2008, 2012, and 2018 elections were so predictable that they attracted few news headlines, either abroad or even occasionally within Russia.

Legislative elections

As regards elections to the State Duma, Russia initially followed the lead of several European states in using a mixed member majoritarian (MMM) voting system, with half the 450 members elected using a single-member plurality system, and the remaining 225 seats filled using proportional representation (PR) based on party lists. In 2005, the law was changed at the urging of Vladimir Putin to switch exclusively to a PR system, using a seven per cent threshold, his argument being that it would strengthen the party system by reducing the number of parties and the number of independent candidates that could win seats. He was right: the number of parties represented in the Duma fell from 13 to four, and independents were eliminated. The fact that his own favoured party – United Russia – did so well in subsequent elections was hardly coincidental. Continuing with the theme of the constantly changing the rules of Russian politics, the law was changed in 2014 to return to the MMM system with effect from the 2016 State Duma elections.

The first three sets of elections in the 1990s were all regarded as relatively free and fair, and as a big improvement on the way elections were run during the Soviet era. But by 2003, there were concerns about manipulation. Observers from the OSCE charged that the elections were distorted by government bias, including the use of taxpayer money and state television to promote parties that supported the Putin administration, and described them as a 'regression in the democratization of Russia'. Unsurprisingly, Putin hailed the results as 'another step' in the democratization of Russia, and despite Western concerns about his strong-arm tactics, they seemed to show that he was well regarded by many Russians. The 2007 elections were criticized for the clear bias of the media towards Putin's party, and there were charges of ballot stuffing, bribery, and coercion, but also a general consensus among foreign observers that United Russia would have won anyway. The 2011 elections were the last held under the four-year rule, all subsequent terms for the State Duma growing to five years.

Local elections

Russians go to the polls to elect officials to local government, but these elections have not been held at the same time as the presidential elections, meaning that voters – as is the case in many local elections around the world – will be less inclined to turn out. A series of elections for governors held in the last four months of 1996 allowed voters to confirm or reject leaders previously appointed by Yeltsin, thereby extending democracy to local government. With Putin's efforts to rein in unruly and sometimes corrupt provincial leaders, local elections have since lost much of their significance, although governors have been elected since 2012.

Political parties

One of the most important transitions that Russians have had to make has been from Soviet-style party politics (only one legal political party, which was indistinguishable from government) to multi-party politics, with a multitude of parties to choose from, most of them independent from the state. During the Soviet era, the CPSU was an all-pervasive part of the political system, and membership – open only to the privileged few – was a basic condition of promotion to any position of leadership. Party organization was hierarchical, beginning with several thousand primary party organizations (PPOs), to which every party member belonged, and moving up through local, provincial, and republican levels to the national level, where the CPSU was dominated by a Party Congress (which met only once every four or five years) and a Central Committee (which ran the party between meetings of the Congress). At the top of the pyramid was a governing **Politburo**, whose members included the president, the prime minister, the foreign and defence ministers, the head of the KGB security agency, and senior military officers. It was chaired by the general secretary of the CPSU, who was the *de facto* leader of the USSR. This is still much the way that matters work in China – see Chapter 13.

Today's party system is quite different: Russians are faced with a wide range of competing political parties that offer different views about Russia's problems and priorities and different ideas about how the country should be governed. So many parties have come and gone, and their membership has been so unstable and changeable, that they were once jokingly called 'taxicab' parties because they seemed to go around in circles, stopping occasionally to let old members jump out and new members climb aboard. The prospects for a more orderly system – but also one in which the opposition could be more easily controlled – were improved in 2001 when the State Duma passed a law limiting the number of small political parties that could take part in elections; no party can now compete unless it has at least 50,000 members and branches in at least half of Russia's provinces. Consolidation was then further promoted by the switch in 2005–14 to an all-PR electoral system with a relatively high threshold, which made it more difficult for small parties to win seats in the State Duma.

The result has been a more restricted party system, which – for now at least – can be summarized as a one-party dominant arrangement: United Russia has emerged as the clear leader in almost every respect, while the communists and the nationalists have developed some long-term stability, even if they have rarely done well at elections.

United Russia

This is the party associated with Putin, and that dominates both the centre of Russian politics and the Russian party system more generally. Tracing its origins to the Party of Russian Unity and Women of Russia, its heritage can be traced through Our Home Is Russia, a coalition of parties led by Prime Minister Viktor Chernomyrdin that described itself as the 'party of the establishment'. It won the second biggest block of seats in the 1995 Duma elections, and – although Boris Yeltsin chose not to ally himself with any one party – tended to be most closely in tune with the president's policies. It then evolved during 1999 into the Unity bloc of parties, created just three months before the December 1999 State Duma elections and designed to be a platform for Vladimir Putin.

In preparation for the 2003 elections, the United Russia coalition was formed and won 222 seats, at that time the biggest block of seats won by any one party or party group in post-communist Russia, although still short of a majority. Putin – like Yeltsin before him – avoided a formal party affiliation, claimed to be non-ideological, and said that he wanted to look for solutions to problems from across the political spectrum (Wegren, 2016). But he made clear at the 2003 election his support for United Russia, and there were fears that the party might win the two-thirds majority needed to change the constitution and give Putin a third term in office, but in the event this did not happen. The dominance of United Russia was finally confirmed in 2007 – see Figure 12.2 – when it won 64 per cent of the popular vote and 70 per cent of the seats in the Duma, pushing all other parties into near irrelevance. It performed even better in 2016.

Delegates to the annual convention of the United Russia party in Moscow in 2018 wait to be addressed by Vladimir Putin. Under his guidance, the party has become a classic example of the single-party dominant model often found in authoritarian political systems.
Source: Kirill Kudryavtsev/AFP/Getty Images.

So dominant has United Russia become that Putin is even in the position to be able to encourage the creation of what have been called 'virtual parties' that are designed to give the impression of meaningful opposition and contested elections, taking votes away from actual opposition parties while not acting against the interests of the administration (Wilson, 2005). The most prominent of these today is A Just Russia, a social democratic party sitting to the left of United Russia, but which has not fared well, winning barely half as many seats as the Communists in the 2016 State Duma elections.

Communist Party

The dominant party on the left of Russian politics is the Communist Party of the Russian Federation. The communists are only indirectly related to the old CPSU, but it is natural to think of them as pursuing similar goals. They have worked hard to reassure foreign investors and Russian entrepreneurs that a communist government would not restore state ownership and a planned economy, but their long-time presidential candidate Gennady Zyuganov once caused nervousness by being an apologist for Stalin (blaming his worst excesses on Stalin's acolytes), speaking of his hopes for a voluntary future reunification of the former Soviet republics, expressing concerns about Jewish influence in the world, and blaming the West for the fall of the USSR.

The communists won only 14 per cent of State Duma seats in 1993, but then surprised many by winning nearly a quarter of the vote in 1995 and the biggest block of seats in the Duma (up from 65 to 157). Zyuganov used this as a launchpad for his presidential bid in 1996, and was briefly described as a possible winner until Yeltsin was able to snatch victory from the jaws of defeat as a result of media manipulation. The Communist Party has since fallen on hard times, never winning more than 20 per cent of votes in State Duma elections, and winning about 12–18 per cent of the vote in presidential elections. Despite these poor numbers, the party often places second after United Russia, and remains the only party in opposition with a large and independent following (Hale, 2014).

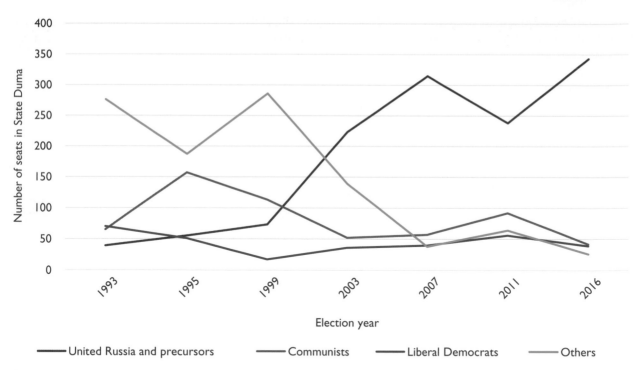

Figure 12.2 Legislative electoral trends in Russia

Liberal parties

This part of the party spectrum has been the most changeable of the four mainstream options and ultimately the least successful. At the 1993 State Duma elections, the main party in this group was Russia's Choice, which strongly supported Yeltsin's economic policies and won the biggest block of seats in the Duma. Another liberal party that rose and then fell was Yobloko (an acronym based on the last names of its three founders), which peaked in 2003 before falling by the wayside. By the time of the 2007 State Duma elections, the only serious contender for the title of a reformist party was Fair Russia, which claimed to be a challenger to United Russia but supported the policies of Vladimir Putin. Founded in 2006, the party considers itself to the left of United Russia, but not far enough for a proposal that it merge with the Communists to be taken seriously.

Nationalist parties

Once a potentially important part of the party spectrum, the nationalists – united mainly by their concerns about Russia's place in the world – have become less influential than they might have been. The most notorious among them is the Liberal Democratic Party, which – despite its name – is a neo-fascist party that surprised many in the West by doing well in the earliest State Duma elections. Many of its supporters resented Russia's loss of empire and the influence of the West, and believed that an alternative to capitalism could be developed. Its leading figure is Vladimir Zhirinovsky, whose popularity once attracted comparisons with the rise of Hitler in Germany in 1933. Zhirinovsky threatened to launch nuclear attacks on Japan and Germany, spoke of taking Alaska back from the United States, and promised to respond to Russian feminism by finding husbands for all unmarried women. His poor showing in the 1996 presidential election (he won just under six per cent) started a decline from which the party has never recovered; Zhirinovsky won less than six per cent of the vote at the 2018 presidential election.

THE FUTURE OF RUSSIAN GOVERNMENT AND POLITICS

'I cannot forecast to you the action of Russia', once quipped Winston Churchill. 'It is a riddle wrapped in a mystery inside an enigma.' He was speaking in 1939 about Russia's potential war aims, but the sentiment still applies today; Russia is not always easy to understand, and many of the Western interpretations of Russia have failed to come to grips with its peculiarities. It appears to defy logic, argues Monaghan (2016), and appears to be 'a country of incongruity', the actions and decisions of its leaders appearing to be irrational. It contains numerous contradictions, he continues, including 'strength and weakness, tradition and novelty, wealth and poverty, [and] freedom and restrictions'.

After the break-up of the Soviet Union, it underwent a transition on at least three fronts: from empire to nation-state, from one-party state socialism to democracy, and from a command economy to a free-market system. On all three fronts, though, it has fallen back on old ways; Putin and his supporters hark back to the 'good old days' of the Soviet Union, Russia's government has become more authoritarian (with centralized leadership and a one-party dominant system), and its market may be more free but the benefits of that freedom are not broadly felt. Russia has also become more assertive on the international foreign and military fronts, prompting questions about whether the Cold War – after a brief break – is back.

If Churchill were still alive, he would probably still be reflecting on the difficulties of forecasting Russia's future. For now, it is being steered by the assertive leadership of Vladimir Putin, but while he is admired by many Russians, he is also resisted. Whether his authoritarian attitudes will persist once he has left office remains to be seen.

DISCUSSION QUESTIONS

1. To what extent does Russia's state socialist past still affect and influence its political and economic system?
2. How does Russia compare with the other cases in this book regarding the influence of patrimonial ideas in government and politics?
3. How does the dynamic of the semi-presidential system in Russia compare with that in France, and what explains the differences?
4. How does the dynamic of federalism in Russia compare with that in other federal systems, such as the United States, Germany, India, Mexico, and Nigeria?
5. How, and to what extent, does Russia's manipulation of elections overseas pose a threat to global trends in democracy?
6. What do examples from other countries tell us about the best means by which smaller Russian political parties can respond to the growth of a dominant party such as United Russia?

CHAPTER CONCEPTS

◆ Bolsheviks
◆ Chechnya
◆ Collective society
◆ Communist Party of the Soviet Union (CPSU)
◆ Democratic centralism
◆ Federation Council
◆ Five-year plans
◆ *Glasnost*

◆ Lenin
◆ Oligarchs
◆ *Perestroika*
◆ Politburo
◆ Stalin
◆ State Duma
◆ Union of Soviet Socialist Republics (USSR)
◆ United Russia

KEY TERMS

◆ Command economy
◆ Cult of personality
◆ Marxism

◆ Patrimonialism
◆ Stalinism
◆ State socialism

RUSSIA ONLINE

Russian Government: http://government.ru/en
President of Russia: http://en.kremlin.ru
Federation Council: www.council.gov.ru/en
State Duma: www.duma.gov.ru/en
United Russia: https://er.ru ★
TASS Russian News Agency: http://tass.com
Pravda: www.pravdareport.com
RT: www.rt.com
The Russia Journal: www.therussiajournal.com

★ *Russian only*

FURTHER READING

Bacon, Edwin (2014) *Contemporary Russia*, 3rd edn (Red Globe Press). The Russian volume in the Red Globe Press series, offering an overview of history, society, culture, government, and the economy.
Remington, Thomas F. (2016) *Politics in Russia*, 7th edn (Routledge); Catherine J. Danks (2013) *Politics Russia* (Routledge). Two general surveys of politics and government in Russia.

Riasanovsky, Nicholas V., and Mark D. Steinberg (2018) *A History of Russia*, 9th edn (Oxford University Press). A popular history of Russia, in an edition revised to account for developments during the Putin era.

Sakwa, Richard, Henry E. Hale, and Stephen White (eds) (2019) *Developments in Russian Politics 9* (Red Globe Press). The Russian volume in the Red Globe Press series, with chapters on the presidency, parties, policies, and the non-Russian former Soviet republics.

Treisman, Daniel (ed.) (2018) *The New Autocracy: Information, Politics, and Policy in Putin's Russia* (Brookings Institution Press). An edited collection of assessments about Putin's Russia, arguing that many Western assumptions are either outdated or wrong.

Wegren, Stephen K. (ed.) (2018) *Putin's Russia: Past Imperfect, Future Uncertain*, 7th edn (Rowman & Littlefield). An edited collection of studies of the domestic and international problems faced by Russia.

Visit **www.macmillanihe.com/McCormick-Cases** to access additional materials to support teaching and learning.

CHINA

13

PREVIEW

China offers another case of a political system that has undergone enormous change, with the critical difference that those changes have global implications. As the biggest country in the world by population, and one that will soon have the world's biggest economy as well, China is an important case in comparative politics. It is clearly authoritarian, with a political system in which much of China's communist heritage persists: government revolves around the dominance of a single party – the Chinese Communist Party – and a complex network of government institutions. Since a revolution in 1949, China has undergone many changes, most recently based on efforts by new generations of leaders to change the direction of domestic and foreign policy. The free market continues to take a firmer hold in China, but political choice remains restricted, creating many political features that, while unique, offer important insights into the nature of authoritarianism.

KEY ARGUMENTS

◆ China has been in an almost constant state of change since 1949, making it difficult always to be sure about the path of its political trajectory.

◆ China took many wrong turns during the unpredictable leadership of Mao Zedong, and is still to some extent adjusting itself to the fallout from his decisions.

◆ Among the more consistent features of Chinese political culture have been a preference for collectivism and consensus.

◆ Several generations of leaders have emerged in China over the decades, each bringing their own preferences to Chinese politics and government.

◆ China has institutions with executive, legislative, and judicial responsibilities, but the line between the state and the Chinese Communist Party is blurred.

◆ The directions taken by China for the foreseeable future seem likely to be determined in large part by the preferences of one person: Xi Jinping.

OVERVIEW

Few countries are currently witnessing such historic change as China. Once one of the backbones of the communist world, China has for several years now been undergoing an economic transformation that has made it the world's second largest economy and – in the views of some – a new superpower (see, for example, Jacques, 2012, and Yueh, 2013). While it has been moving steadily towards a quasi-capitalist future, however, and there is no denying the growing reach of its economy, it is still both a relatively poor country and an authoritarian one, its military has regional rather than global reach (although this is changing), it lacks an important global currency, and Chinese corporations do not yet have the international presence of their American, European, Japanese, or South Korean competitors (although this is also changing).

In political terms, China underwent dramatic changes during the 20th century that pulled it in several different directions before opting for a path to state socialism that was shaped by the often idiosyncratic ideas of Mao Zedong, the towering figure in 20th-century Chinese history. China today continues to have many of the standard features of a state socialist political system, the most important of which is the dominance of a single political party – the **Chinese Communist Party (CCP)** – and a system of government that is centralized, hierarchical, and elitist. It has a poor record on human rights, and changes in its administration are determined more by decisions within the CCP than by the wishes of the citizens. How long China can continue to sustain this arrangement in the light of its economic development and demands for democratic change remains to be seen. Freedom House ranks China as Not Free, condemning it for its failure to encourage democratic choice, while it is listed as an authoritarian state in the Democracy Index.

On the economic front it has seen rapid growth and a steady freeing of the market, and has all but taken over the global market for cheap and disposable consumer products that was once dominated by Japan. Its economy is expanding, but China has much more to do to catch up with the world's wealthiest economies: some of its more successful entrepreneurs have amassed considerable new wealth, but many Chinese live in poverty, nearly half live in rural areas and make a living off the land, and per capita GDP is only one-seventh that of the United States (but more than four times that of India). China is the world's biggest coal producer and has rich deposits of iron ore, but it lacks enough iron to feed its expanding industries or oil to feed its growing energy needs. As a result, it has been busy reaching out to resource-rich states in Africa and Asia, exerting more influence through its voracious appetite for raw materials than through acting as a model of political and economic development.

In social terms, China is relatively homogeneous. The clear majority of its people are ethnic Han Chinese, and only about seven per cent belong to an ethnic minority (of which there are officially 55, but actually many more). But given the sheer size of China (it has a population of more than 1.3 billion), some of those minorities are big enough to make up the population of a medium-sized country: there are about 17 million Thais, 6 million Mongols, and 5 million Tibetans, for example. Many of these groups live in areas thought to have rich mineral resources, and others live on the borders of China, close enough to related groups in other countries to pose a potential threat to China's territorial integrity.

POLITICAL DEVELOPMENT

China has the longest recorded history of any country in the world, dating back more than 4,000 years. For most of that time, the Chinese lived under an imperial system of government, relatively untouched by the outside world. China sometimes called itself Zhongguo (Middle Kingdom), a term referring to the Central Plain (Zhongyuan) around the Yellow River that was the birthplace of Chinese civilization. It was during the Han dynasty (206 BCE– 220 CE) that a distinct culture first spread across what is now China (Roberts, 2011). That culture was rich and sophisticated, making great strides in the arts and the sciences and developing an intricate political system and social structure. However, the old imperial China is not today's modern state socialist China, which is mainly a product of events that have taken place in the last 100 years, including three revolutions (1911, 1927–28, and 1949), periods of near anarchy, and lengthy debates about the goals of political, economic, and social development.

The imperial era (2205 BCE–1911)

Imperial China was based on an agrarian economy and influenced heavily by the ideas of the philosopher Confucius (551–479 BCE) (see Gardner, 2014). **Confucianism** was a secular and ethical system of moral rules and principles (currently undergoing a revival in China), but although it was akin to a religion, it had no institutionalized church and was more tolerant towards other systems of thought than Christianity has been. Confucian theory taught the importance of obeying the authority of the emperor, but it also promoted 'government by goodness', arguing that the emperor had the right to govern only so long as he ruled with honour and virtue. Citizens also had to know their roles, so Confucianism provided a social code governing interpersonal relationships, emphasizing (like Japanese culture) conformity and self-discipline, while discouraging individualism. Emperors ruled through senior government officials, or mandarins, whose appointment was based largely on a test of their 'morality' and knowledge of Confucian ethics. The mandarins formed a small but powerful ruling elite, running a sprawling and hierarchical bureaucracy.

The decline and fall of the last of China's 24 imperial dynasties – the Manchus (1644–1911) – began in the early 19th century when the dynasty was unable to respond to the needs of a growing population for land and food. Imperial power was further weakened by the opium war with Britain in 1839–42, which resulted in China being forced to open its doors to traders and missionaries from the outside world and to cede harbours (such as Hong Kong and Shanghai) to European powers. Growing resentment sparked the Taiping Rebellion of 1850–64, in which an estimated 20–40 million people died before the rebellion was put down with Western help. Financially and politically drained, the Manchus suffered a final blow when China was ignominiously defeated by Japan in the war of 1894–95.

Nationalism and chaos (1911–49)

With pressures for revolutionary change mounting, an expatriate secret society was formed around **Sun Yat-sen** (1866–1925), a Chinese physician. Sun's followers launched attacks on the Manchu regime, finally succeeding (on their 11th attempt) in October 1911. However, Sun's government relied on the military for its authority, was undermined by continuing Western inroads into China, understood little about how Western democracy worked, and was unable to win the allegiance of the people; it soon lost control and China fell into chaos. Between 1916 and 1926, the country was torn apart by warlords fighting among themselves for power. In 1922, having failed to win help from the West, Sun signed an agreement with Soviet communists through which he received help to transform his Nationalist Party (the Kuomintang) and to provide arms and training for the Chinese army. In the interests of national reunification, he also entered a brief and acrimonious coalition with the new Chinese Communist Party (CCP), which had been founded in 1921.

When Sun died in 1925, he was replaced by his senior military commander, Chiang Kai-shek (1886–1975), who abhorred communism and set about defeating the warlords and uniting China. He set up his own right-wing nationalist government in Nanjing, which was widely recognized in the West as the legitimate government of China. While making many changes, however, he made the fatal mistake of doing little about land reform, leaving the peasants poor, unhappy, and more open to communist influence. The CCP was by now being directed by **Mao Zedong**, who – in the face of a Kuomintang campaign – decided in 1934 to uproot his 150,000 followers and move them west and then north on the 6,000-mile **Long March** (Fritz, 1988). The movement lasted a year, and the party lost almost 90 per cent of its number to disease, starvation, and nationalist attacks, but Mao was now beyond the reach of the nationalists and was able to strengthen his control over the CCP.

In 1936, Chiang was obliged to agree to a second alliance with the CCP to stave off the Japanese, who had invaded Manchuria in 1931 and begun moving southward. Mao's army expanded its membership; by 1945, when Japan surrendered and civil war broke out in China between the Kuomintang and Mao's forces, the latter were in a strong position. Attempts by the United States to mediate failed, and in 1949 Chiang fled with his followers to **Taiwan**, an island off the coast of mainland China. On 1 October 1949, the People's Republic of China (PRC) was proclaimed in Beijing.

China under Mao (1949–76)

The opening of the communist era saw enormous social upheaval, considerable violence, disruptive political change, and a vocal debate about how best to achieve the goals of socialism. Mao took some of the core ideas of Marx and Lenin, originally shaped for urban societies, and reshaped them for rural China; **Maoism** (or Mao Zedong Thought) stressed communalism, small-scale social and economic units, thought reform and indoctrination, and saw the state as the supreme educator. While Mao may have played a central role in the restoration of China's independence, and his goals of combating bureaucracy, improving health care and education, and encouraging popular participation and self-reliance were laudable, the methods he used were often self-defeating.

His priority was land redistribution, so 300 million landless peasants were given their own plots. It soon became obvious, however, that many of these plots were too small to support a family, so the government set up new and bigger cooperatives, on the lines of Stalinist collectivization. His second priority was to build industry, to which end he initially followed

Maoism
Mao's application of Marxist-Leninist ideas to rural societies such as China, rejecting elitism, and emphasizing communalism and social experimentation.

⚇ TIMELINE

1271–1368	Mongols conquer China; Beijing established as capital
1839–42	Opium wars with Britain; Britain gains Hong Kong
1850–64	Taiping rebellion
1911–12	Nationalist revolution; abdication of last emperor
1927–49	China under Kuomintang rule
1937–45	Sino-Japanese war
1945–49	Chinese civil war
1949	Proclamation of People's Republic of China and Republic of China (Taiwan)
1950	Chinese invasion of Tibet
1958–60	Great Leap Forward
1966–76	Great Proletarian Cultural Revolution
1976	Death of Mao
1979	Launch of open door policy to encourage foreign investment
1989	Tiananmen Square massacre
2001	China joins World Trade Organization
2003	Launch of China's first manned spacecraft
2008	Olympic Games held in Beijing
2011	China overtakes Japan to become the world's second largest economy
2013	Xi Jinping becomes president of China; launch of Belt and Road initiative
2018	Xi Jinping becomes lifetime president

the Stalinist model of long-term centralized planning based on five-year plans. These produced impressive growth rates, but they relied too heavily on professionals and bureaucrats, ignoring millions of peasants.

To defuse the growing criticism of his policies, Mao in 1957 allowed public discussion of China's problems. Alarmed at the extent to which his critics took up his invitation, he then decided to decentralize industry and agriculture and – by substituting capital (of which China had little) with manpower – encouraged the Chinese to use their own resources. Under the **Great Leap Forward** (1958–60), the peasant masses were mobilized, and the employed forced to work harder under almost military discipline.

Mao turned his attention to ideological reform in 1966 with a programme of mass criticism known as the **Great Proletarian Cultural Revolution**. Supposedly a debate on the nature of the revolution, it was actually a scheme to neutralize Mao's opponents by attacking bureaucrats, Confucianism, and those accused of wanting to follow the 'capitalist road' (see Dikötter, 2016). Radical students known as Red Guards ran criticism sessions, and tens of millions of leaders and 'intellectuals' (defined as anyone with at least a high school education) were sent to the rural areas to work on the land and to discuss Maoist thought. Public education and government came to a virtual standstill, and the period 1966–76 is now described by the CCP as the Ten Catastrophic Years.

China after Mao (1980s–2000s)

The early 1970s saw an ageing Mao withdraw from public life, and China came under the steadying influence of Premier Zhou Enlai. The deaths of both Zhou and Mao in 1976 intensified a power struggle that had been brewing within the CCP for several years. Despite holding no formal positions in government (see the later discussion about formal titles), Deng Xiaoping became the informal 'paramount leader', and implemented a policy of Four Modernizations: industry, agriculture, national defence, and science and technology. He also spoke of 'socialism with Chinese characteristics', and oversaw the drafting of a new constitution that established liberalizing tendencies, leading some to call democracy the Fifth Modernization.

Deng's economic reforms went well beyond anything envisaged in the USSR by Mikhail Gorbachev; Deng ran the economy on a mix of capitalism and socialism, allowing factories and farms to produce for market demand as long as they filled their basic state quotas and to buy raw materials through the market rather than depending on central allocation. He also allowed more prices to be set by supply and demand, and stressed the opening of China to the outside world. The result of Dengism (or Deng Xiaoping Theory) was rapid growth and a consumer boom that at times threatened to run out of control.

Deng was unable to replace conservatives at the head of the party and the government, and was thus unable to take complete control. This was confirmed in April 1989 when peaceful pro-democracy demonstrations broke out in several major towns and cities, and when more than a million students occupied **Tiananmen Square** in Beijing. They planned to stay there until the 20 June meeting of the Chinese legislature (the National People's Congress), but the army was sent in on 3–4 June to break them up. No one knows how many died in the events that followed, but the most generally accepted figures today are in the range of 1,000 to 1,500, a toll that included soldiers from the Beijing garrison, which apparently rebelled and took the side of the students. The West, which had begun to warm to China during the 1980s, was reminded of the repressive nature of Chinese government. (Today, the memories of Tiananmen have been almost entirely excised from China's national consciousness, prompting one journalist (Lim, 2015) to write a book titled *The People's Republic of Amnesia*.)

Deng's death in February 1997 led to a new power struggle, resolved when Jiang Zemin, Deng's hand-picked successor, was re-elected as general secretary of the CCP. China under Jiang continued to build links with its Asian neighbours and its major trading partners. In 2001, China's place in the global economic system was transformed when it joined the World Trade Organization (WTO). It was obliged to open up its markets more fully to foreign investors and importers, and to better coordinate its economic policies with those of other WTO members.

In 2002–03, China underwent its first orderly change of leadership in decades, beginning when Jiang Zemin was replaced as party leader by Hu Jintao, who also became China's president. Although the presidency was at that time a job with more symbolic power than real power, the change nonetheless ended Jiang's formal leadership role. The change in leadership was also emblematic of the transformation in the way in which China saw itself, and was increasingly seen by the rest of the world. Under the old leadership it had been introverted, and never regarded by the West in the same light as the former Soviet Union; now, it was becoming more extroverted and attracting new attention as an emerging economic power.

China overtook Japan in 2010 to become the world's second largest economy, and it is projected soon to overtake the United States for the top slot – see Figure 13.1. But while Chinese products have worked their way into consumer

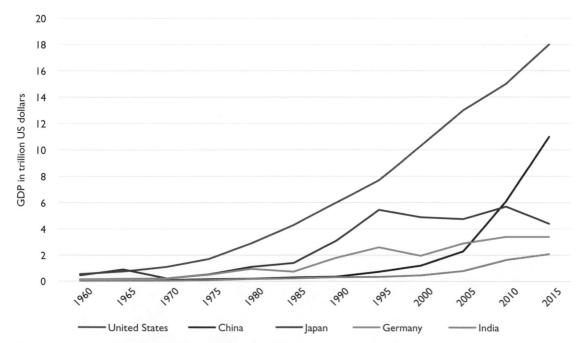

Figure 13.1 Comparing economic growth

Source: Based on data in World Bank (2019).

markets all over the world, there have been trade tensions between China and the industrialized world; concerns centre on the large Chinese trade surplus, its efforts to manipulate the value of its currency (the yuan) in order to keep imports cheap, and its role in stealing Western intellectual property. China must also deal with problems such as underdeveloped industrial infrastructure, expanding demand for energy, endemic corruption, and serious environmental problems.

China today

Although China is changing, and seems to be more open both to itself and to the outside world, it continues to have a poor democratic record. Opposition to the Chinese Communist Party is not tolerated, political dissenters are often sent to labour camps, torture is still widely used, access to the internet is restricted, and China has the highest rates of capital punishment in the world; see Chapter 14.

International interest in China reached a new peak with the August 2008 summer Olympic Games in Beijing, widely portrayed in the West as a coming-out party for China, and yet the CCP was careful to impose a clampdown on dissent so that pro-democracy activists could not use the event as an opportunity to publicize their cause. The absence of electoral democracy in China was once again emphasized as the term of president Hu Jintao began to draw to a close and speculation grew about his successor. The man who replaced him as general secretary of the CCP in 2012 and as president of China in 2013 was vice president **Xi Jinping** (b. 1952). The fact that he could win both posts as a result of decisions taken within the higher reaches of the CCP rather than in an open public and competitive vote was another reminder of the authoritarian nature of Chinese politics. This was confirmed yet again in 2018 when Xi was able to convince the party to allow him to remain president for life.

Questions are now being asked about the extent to which the norms of consensus politics and collective leadership will persist (Li, 2016a). Xi has become the most powerful Chinese leader since Mao Zedong, and has pursued policies based on clamping down on corruption, reforming the economy based on market principles, being more assertive on foreign policy, and rejecting Western ideas about democracy and the protection of human rights. It remains to be seen how far the views of one person can change the direction of the most populous country on earth. It has happened before, notably during the Mao era, but China today is a much different place than it once was.

The rapid growth of China's eastern port city of Shanghai – which has long had a reputation as a global city – symbolizes the new international economic role of China, fast on its way to becoming the world's largest economy.

Source: iStock.com/cuiphoto.

POLITICAL CULTURE

Several thousand years of political continuity gave imperial China a political culture that was both stable and sophisticated, bound together by Confucian ideals that emphasized morality and authoritarianism and by social and political values that were both elitist and hierarchical. The 1949 revolution had a disruptive effect on the picture, but it did not completely clean the slate: many elements of traditional political culture remain intact, even if new values and norms have emerged as China's political and economic identity has been transformed since the 1990s.

Like Japan (see Chapter 6), China has traditionally been a collective society marked by group orientation. Individual well-being, economic security, and the definition of political functions have long been based around kinship and the family unit. The head of the family has traditionally been held responsible for the behaviour of members of the group, who can bring collective honour or shame to the family. Recourse to the law or to the intervention of government officials is rare, because most disputes are settled locally and family heads are responsible for punishing wrongdoers.

Consensus has also long been at the heart of Chinese political culture – see Comparing Political Culture 13. It may sometimes seem as though China has lurched back and forth since 1949 between rule by conservatives and by reformers, but radical change has often been rejected, delayed, or watered down in the interests of reaching a

COMPARING POLITICAL CULTURE 13
Consensus politics

At the heart of the idea of democracy is free speech and an open marketplace of ideas. However, once competing views have been aired, decisions must be taken and policies carried out, and the course of action taken is usually based on a **consensus** reached among those involved in making decisions. This, at least, is the theory. In practice, achieving a consensus is often a matter of wearing down the opposition to an idea or a course of action, based on a combination of negotiating skills, superior numbers, or superior power. In many democracies, the winner in a disagreement is simply the political party (or coalition) that has the greatest number of votes in a legislature, or that is most closely tied to the key economic players.

> **Consensus**
> A general or widespread agreement on a course of action, with which all those involved can agree and no one disagrees, although there may not be unanimity.

China has had a recent reputation for often building a consensus among its ruling elites, meaning the highest levels of the Chinese Communist Party. What this has meant in practice has been a competition among ideas and approaches pursued by different leaders, one ultimately emerging at the head of a generation of leaders founded on a network of supporters. First it was Mao, then Deng, then Jiang, then Hu, and now Xi; see Political System for more details. The more authoritarian habits of Xi, his boldness in foreign affairs, and his suppression of dissent within the Party are a notable exception to the general rule.

In the United States, by contrast, it can often seem as though consensus decision-making has been abandoned in the interests of the dominant political party, or of large corporations, or of privileged social elites (mainly wealthy white men). It is hard to achieve a political consensus when there are only two political parties that hold seats in Congress (the Democrats and the Republicans), a reality that presents every decision as a binary choice. In his book *The Fractured Republic*, Levin (2016) argues that the institutions that once dominated American culture (particularly its governing institutions and mass media) have become smaller, more diverse, and personalized, and that individualism has come at the cost of dwindling solidarity. The public finds little evidence of real engagement with real problems in the resulting debates, he argues, and few attractive solutions.

In multi-party systems, consensus is much more usual, although in more extreme cases – such as Brazil, Israel, or Italy – the sheer number of political parties, combined with the capacity of many small parties to control governing coalitions and thereby become the tail that wags the dog, can sometimes mean that decision-making goes to the opposite extreme: decisions are often driven by small minorities who wield a degree of power out of all proportion to their size, undermining the possibilities of achieving a consensus.

PROFILE CHINA

Name	People's Republic of China (Zhonghua Renmin Gongheguo)
Capital	Beijing
Administration	Unitary communist republic, with multiple levels of government ranging from 34 provinces down through several hundred prefectures to 2,850 urban and rural counties and more than 47,000 townships.
Constitution	State formed 1949, and most recent constitution adopted 1982.
Executive	Unlimited presidential. The State Council, headed by the premier, is the top executive body, supervising the work of the ministries. A president serves as head of state, but ultimate power rests with the general secretary of the CCP.
Legislature	Unicameral National People's Congress of nearly 3,000 members, chosen indirectly through local and provincial congresses. Meets only for brief periods, its work carried out when in recess by a 150-member Standing Committee.
Judiciary	No constitutional court. Rule through law has strengthened but the judicial system remains underdeveloped.
Electoral system	There are no national elections. Voters take part in elections only at the local level, and all votes above that level are indirect, with each level of government electing the next highest.
Party system	Single-party, in practice. The Chinese Communist Party (CCP) remains the dominant political force, its leadership being a parallel government within which most real power is focused.

 1,386m **Population**

 $12,240 billion **Gross Domestic Product**

 **$8,830** **Per capita GDP**

- ✘ Full Democracy
- ✘ Flawed Democracy
- ✘ Hybrid Regime
- ✔ Authoritarian
- ✘ Not Rated

Democracy Index rating

- ✘ Free
- ✘ Partly Free
- ✔ Not Free
- ✘ Not Rated

Freedom House rating

- ✘ Very High
- ✔ High
- ✘ Medium
- ✘ Low
- ✘ Not Rated

Human Development Index rating

consensus. Allied to this has been a traditional preference for gradual and cautious change, even if – in practice – change has often been tumultuous. The emphasis on consensus and gradualism may also explain why China achieved many of the same reforms as those once proposed by Mikhail Gorbachev for the USSR, but over a longer period of time and without the same explosive consequences.

Although the legal system may impinge little upon the life of the average Chinese citizen, politics impinges upon their lives almost daily. Even the most minimal political activity means regular exposure to propaganda, attendance at meetings, and the regular expression of support for government policy. China has witnessed massive and pervasive political education and indoctrination and a system of government whose policy decisions have reached into the home, the school, the workplace, and every other sphere of human existence to a greater extent than in almost any other society (including Stalinist Russia). This has created a society that emphasizes the state, the party, and the idea of mass cooperation at the expense of individualism and competition. At the same time, however, Chinese political culture is not opposed to political liberalization, and one of the challenges that continues to face the CCP is correctly gauging the pressures for democratic change. Its grip on society has loosened in recent years, and with it the dominance of the state.

The argument that China could become the next superpower tends to focus on two measures: the size of its economy and its population. Being a superpower, though, is not just about size – it also involves wielding political influence, which requires credibility. For example, while not everyone in the world agrees with US foreign policy, the pronouncements of American presidents matter because the United States is a democracy (albeit a flawed one), has deeply invested interests in political events around the world, and has both the economic and the military power to back up its words. The same cannot be said for China, whose biggest handicap – in terms of positive global influence – is its poor record on human rights. It is widely criticized for executing dissidents, for using torture to achieve political ends, for stamping out dissent among ethnic minorities, for continuing to threaten neighbouring Taiwan with violence, and for continuing its occupation of Tibet, more than half a century after it invaded the country. It should also not be forgotten that the CCP has a monopoly on political power, and that Chinese voters are offered no choices at elections.

POLITICAL SYSTEM

The Chinese political system can be briefly described as a unitary republic controlled by the Chinese Communist Party, but there is more to the story than one short sentence can convey. Three points are worth making:

◆ All significant power is centralized in the national government. The sheer size of China suggests that a federal system might be more suitable, but this enormous country is still governed by a small group of people based at the apex of government in the capital city of Beijing.
◆ While China has an intricate governmental structure, with a cabinet, a legislature, and a network of supporting agencies, they do little more than legitimize the decisions already taken by the party leadership, and subscribe to the authority of that leadership (Saich, 2015).
◆ Identifying those who hold power in China is less a question of formal titles and offices than of understanding links across institutions, personal networks, and the standing of key figures in the political system.

Studies of Chinese leadership are peppered with words such as *fluid*, *ambiguous*, *shadowy*, and *flexible*. The marginal importance of formal positions was illustrated by the example of Deng Xiaoping, who was the 'paramount leader' of China from 1978, but the most senior posts he ever held were those of party vice chairman, vice premier, and chairman of the party's Military Commission (a powerful post from which he retired in 1989). By 1993, the only position of any kind that Deng held was the presidency of China's bridge association. Technically, Jiang Zemin was the leader of the Communist Party and thus of China, but Deng remained *de facto* leader of China by virtue of his personal power and influence until his death in 1997.

Much like Japan, power in China is based around factions, which are based less on ideological differences than on personal relationships (or *guanxi*). Power is also based on the leadership skills of perhaps no more than two or three people and on the abilities of these individuals to keep control, a process that long involved regular purges of rivals and opponents. For example, Mao held on to power for decades, but only because he regularly dismissed or shuffled his lieutenants. Around him he built what has been described as a 'first generation' (or echelon) of supporters, most of whom were veterans of the Long March. Among those shuffled during these changes was Deng Xiaoping, who was purged from the highest levels of the party no fewer than three times.

With Mao's death in 1976, at least two major factions emerged within the party leadership: Mao loyalists and a group of reformists led by Deng Xiaoping and including veteran party and military leaders. Beginning in 1978, Deng and his reform-minded supporters wrested power for themselves, forming a second generation of leaders. Realizing that many of them were old and ailing, Deng developed a third generation of leaders – both younger and more technocratic – who would build on the economic reforms he had begun. The most important of these was Jiang Zemin, but he never had the status or authority of Mao or Deng. Following his retirement in 2002, leadership passed to a fourth generation of leaders, headed by Hu Jintao, but the China they inherited was quite different from that ruled by the first generation, and significantly different even from the China of the third generation.

Xi Jinping today – at the head of a **fifth generation** of leaders that has emerged since 2012 (Li, 2011) – is a leader of a quite different kind. He holds the top three positions in Chinese politics (president of China, general secretary of the party, and chairman of the Military Commission) and he has continued the trend of making the presidency into more of a true executive (and more, now that it is a lifetime appointment). In other words, titles are today more what they seem, and informal networks are less important than they once were. Xi oversees an economy from which the state is steadily retreating, a political system in which the future of the CCP is questioned less than it was even a decade ago, and a society whose cracks have been papered over in large part with firm political responses. Not long ago, it seemed unlikely that old-style paramount leaders would ever be seen again in China. Today, that is not so certain.

The constitution

In liberal democracies, constitutions usually focus on the structure of government and the rights of individuals, and political parties play an independent and separate role in government. By contrast, the Chinese constitution not only describes the system of government but it also mentions the leading role of the CCP. The goals of the party are further elaborated in the constitution of the CCP itself, which in many ways is more politically significant than the state constitution, is more regularly revised, and offers important indicators of new policy directions being taken by China's government.

There have been four state constitutions since 1949. The first, published in 1954 after several years of debate, was replaced by new versions in 1975, 1978, and 1982. Together with their various amendments, each reflected the changed thinking of new leaders. For example, the 1954 constitution reflected Mao's ideas on government and society, and although these themes can be traced through the 1975 and 1978 versions, the 1982 constitution finally deleted lavish praise for Mao. Recent amendments have shown growing acceptance of the role of the non-state sector of the economy, which has moved from being 'a complement to the socialist public economy' to being 'an important component of the socialist market economy' (Saich, 2015).

The 1982 state constitution took two years to draft and was reportedly read and debated at several million meetings held across the country before being adopted by the National People's Congress in December 1982. With 138 articles, it is one of the longest constitutions in the world. It describes China as 'a socialist state under the people's democratic dictatorship led by the working class and based on the alliance of workers and peasants'. It emphasizes the importance of continuing 'socialist modernization' and argues that it is China's fundamental goal to follow the socialist road and 'step by step to turn China into a socialist country'. Although it vests all power in the people, it also emphasizes that China is led by the CCP, functioning as the vanguard of the people under the guidance of (1) Marxism-Leninism, (2) Mao Zedong Thought, (3) Deng Xiaoping Theory, and – since 2018 – (4) Xi Jinping Thought on Socialism with Chinese Characteristics for a New Era. The latter has been summarized (Buckley, 2018) in three points: a 'great rejuvenation' for China in the world (through its economic and military power), revitalized control of the party over every corner of society, and a central role for Xi in Chinese leadership.

Articles 33–65 contain an impressive list of the rights and duties of citizens, including freedom of speech, the press, assembly, association, demonstration, and religion and the right to criticize any state organ or functionary. However, Article 51 says that the exercise of personal rights may not infringe upon the interests of the state or society, or upon the freedoms and rights of other citizens, and Article 54 prohibits acts 'detrimental to the security, honour and interests' of China. These clauses clearly allow the party or the government to neutralize any dissent regarded as being against the national interest and to limit the civil rights and liberties listed in the constitution.

The executive: president and premier

China has a president (and a vice president), but the significance of the post has waxed and waned depending on the other positions held by the incumbent. Where the presidency was once usually held by a semi-retired former leader of China, it has been transformed since the 1990s when Jiang Zemin was both president of China and general secretary of the communist party. Xi Jinping holds both positions today, allowing him to carry out political and non-political jobs at the same time (see Brown, 2016). Xi was first elected to the post in March 2013, and re-elected to a second term in March 2018. He might have begun the process during his second term of arranging a transfer of power to a sixth generation of leaders, but chose not to, thereby sending worrying indications of a reversion back to more authoritarian rule. This was perhaps unsurprising, given that Xi had – in 2013 – identified 'seven subversive currents' running through Chinese society, including Western constitutional democracy, human rights, civil society, and media freedom, and 'nihilist' criticisms of the past of the communist party.

The office of president (described in China as the State Chairman) traces its roots back to the 1954 constitution, which provided for the election by the National People's Congress (NPC) of a chairman and vice chairman of the People's Republic. The chairman effectively became the head of state, with all the ceremonial duties this entailed, but the job also came with significant political powers, such as the ability to hire and fire the premier, vice premiers, and other members of the State Council. Mao was elected first chairman in 1954 but did not stand for re-election in 1959. After several years in which the offices were vacant, the powers of chairman (or president) and vice chairman (or vice president) were revived by the 1982 constitution.

The president and vice president were both nominated by the Standing Committee of the NPC, and then elected (or confirmed) by the NPC for a maximum of two five-year terms. The job of president was transformed in 2018 when it was converted into a lifetime position. Candidates must be Chinese citizens with the right to vote and stand for election, and must be at least 45 years of age. The president has the power to appoint (with NPC approval) all members of the State Council (including the premier and vice premier), departmental ministers, chairs of legislative committees, and China's foreign ambassadors. He also has authority over Chinese foreign affairs, and the power to declare a state of emergency and to declare war. These powers (except for the last two) would normally make the job similar to that of a semi-presidential executive, but the last three presidents have also been general secretaries of the CCP, giving the officeholder enormous power.

Behind the president of China and the leader of the CCP (two jobs typically held by the same person), another powerful office in China is that of the **premier**. The nearest equivalent to a prime minister in a semi-presidential executive, the premier is usually charged with heading the bureaucracy and with overseeing the implementation of China's economic policy. The personality of the office was shaped in large part by Zhou Enlai, premier from 1949 until his death in 1976. In 1982 a decision was made to limit premiers to two consecutive five-year terms. The job always comes with membership of the party Politburo (see coverage of the CCP later in this chapter).

Table 13.1 Modern leaders of China

Party Leader*	Premier	Chairman of Standing Committee of National People's Congress	President of People's Republic of China†
1949 Mao Zedong	1949 Zhou Enlai	1954 Liu Shaoqi 1959 Zhu De 1965 Zhu De	1949 Mao Zedong 1959 Liu Shaoqi 1968–82 vacant
1976 Hua Guofeng	1976 Hua Guofeng 1980 Zhao Ziyang	1976–78 vacant 1978 Ye Jianying	
1981 Hu Yaobang		1983 Peng Zhen	1982 Li Xiannian
1987 Zhao Ziyang	1988 Li Peng	1988 Wan Li	1988 Yang Shangkun
1989 Jiang Zemin	1998 Zhu Rongji	1993 Qiao Shi 1998 Li Peng	1993 Jiang Zemin
2002 Hu Jintao 2007 Hu Jintao	2003 Wen Jiabao 2008 Wen Jiabao	2003 Wu Bangguo 2008 Wu Bangguo	2003 Hu Jintao 2008 Hu Jintao
2012 Xi Jinping 2017 Xi Jinping	2013 Li Keqiang 2018 Li Keqiang	2013 Zhang Dejiang 2018 Li Zhanshu	2013 Xi Jinping 2018 Xi Jinping

* Chairman (1949–82), then general secretary.

† Chairman of Chinese People's Political Consultative Conference (1949–54), then Chairman of the PRC (1954–66), and president of China from 1982. The position became a lifetime appointment in 2018.

Note: In 1978–97, the 'paramount leader' of China was Deng Xiaoping, who held none of the positions listed above.

COMPARING GOVERNMENT 13
Cabinets and councils of ministers

Government everywhere, even in authoritarian political systems with strong leaders, is to some degree a collective affair. Leaders cannot do everything alone, or master the details of all the problems that need resolution, or keep an eye on all the threats to their position or opposition to their policies. As a result, they must rely on a supporting group of ministers or secretaries to oversee the work of the public bureaucracy, and to provide them with information. These are known in some countries as cabinets, and in others as councils of ministers.

The Chinese version of this group is the State Council, which – were it to function like a democratic council of ministers – would be at the heart of the collective Chinese government. In reality, the State Council is relatively weak: it is large, meets infrequently, and is elected by another weak institution, the National People's Congress. The real focus of group decision-making in China is with the Standing Committee of the State Council, and – even more so – the Standing Committee of the Politburo of the Chinese Communist Party (see Table 13.2).

In parliamentary executives, by contrast, cabinets have a more open and active political role. Ministers might take their lead from the prime minister (as in the cases of Britain and Germany), they might be a true committee of government in that ministers and the prime minister work closely together (as in the case of Finland), or they might have a high degree of freedom to operate without instructions from either the prime minister or other ministers (as in the case of Italy). In short, the question at the heart of the relationship between the parts and the whole is whether ministers should be considered leaders, team players, or followers (Andeweg, 2014).

In presidential executives, cabinets or councils of ministers typically have a two-way function, as advisors to the president and as transmitters of the policies of the administration. A change of president also usually means a change at the top of every major government department, with incoming secretaries inheriting a large body of career bureaucrats in the departments they are heading, and being given instructions by the president on the direction in which they would like to see each department headed. In parliamentary systems, ministers are usually also members of the legislature, emphasizing the fusion of the executive and the legislature; in presidential systems, they are usually not allowed to be members of the legislature, emphasizing the separation of powers.

China also has a **State Council**, the nearest functional equivalent to a cabinet. Normally meeting once per month, the Council is elected by the National People's Congress and has a membership of about 50, including the premier of China, four vice premiers, and the heads (and their deputies) of ministries and government departments. Until the late 1980s, the Council was little more than the executive arm of the CCP, responsible for making sure that party policies were implemented by government ministers. The Council has begun to reassert itself in recent years, however, particularly as military officers who once headed up ministries have been replaced by a new generation of civilian technocrats. Because meetings of the full Council are too large to function efficiently, the key decisions are made by a small Standing Committee consisting of the premier, the vice premiers, five state councillors, and the general secretary, who meet twice weekly as a group.

The legislature: National People's Congress

Theoretically the 'highest organ of state power', the unicameral **National People's Congress** (NPC) is the Chinese legislature, with members elected for five-year terms. On paper, it represents the people of China and has the power to make and enforce laws, to amend the constitution, to designate and remove the premier and the State Council, and to elect the president of China and the president of the Supreme People's Court. In reality, its powers are limited in several ways:

◆ Although it has the power to discuss, pass, and oversee the execution of laws, it is expected to do little more than discuss and endorse decisions already made by the party leadership. This is as would be expected in a one-party state, and is not too different from the arrangement in democracies with majority parties.

◆ It is huge and unwieldy. Its membership began at 1,226 members in 1954, peaked at a staggering 3,497 members in 1978, and was down to just under 3,000 in the Thirteenth NPC (2018–23).

◆ It meets only briefly, for one session of two to three weeks in March each year. Even then it rarely meets in full plenary session, spending most of its time in group sessions. During meetings, delegates can question senior government ministers, submit motions, make suggestions, and raise questions about government policy, but there is obviously a limit to what can be achieved in the time available.

◆ Delegates are only indirectly elected by the people. Voters elect local congresses, which elect county congresses, which elect provincial congresses, which finally elect the NPC. Membership is structured so that workers, peasants, intellectuals, and soldiers have occupational representation, and delegates tend to be appointed as a reward for exemplary work and public service rather than because they have particular administrative or political abilities.

In spite of its huge size, short sessions, and lack of much apparent power, the NPC has not always accepted the party line; it has been known occasionally to criticize the party leadership and has not always been unanimous on votes. In recent years it has become a forum for working out policy differences between different factions in the party and government, and although it rarely rejects government proposals, it has been known to refuse to vote on constitutional amendments proposed by the party, and its opposition has sometimes been enough to encourage the State Council to withdraw proposals for new bills.

When the NPC is in recess (which is most of the time), its work is carried out by a Standing Committee. Elected by the NPC, this meets twice per month and consists of about 150 members, including a chairman, several vice chairs, and senior members of Congress. The position of chair is considered the fourth most senior person in the Chinese political system. The Committee has the power to declare and enforce martial law, oversee NPC elections,

Delegates attend the closing meeting of the first session of the 13th National People's Congress at the Great Hall of the People in Beijing in March 2018. While meetings of the NPC are impressive in size, they are much less impressive in substance.

Source: Visual China Group/Getty Images.

Table 13.2 Party and political institutions in China

Function	Party	Government	Bureaucracy
Overall leader		**President**	
Senior position	**General Secretary**	**Chairman**	**Premier**
Peak managing committee	**Standing Committee** 6–10 members. Apex of the Chinese political system. Meets weekly.	**Standing Committee** About 150 members. Meets bimonthly.	**Standing Committee** About 12 members: premier, vice premiers, senior counsellors. Meets twice weekly.
	Politburo About two dozen party leaders. Meets monthly.		
General managing committee	**Central Committee** About 200 senior party members. Meets annually for varying periods.		**State Council** About 50 members: premier, vice premiers, heads of ministries and commissions. Meets monthly.
Plenary body	**National Congress** About 2,000 delegates; meets once every 5 years for 1–2 weeks to confirm party policy.	**National People's Congress** Unicameral, with 2,970 members elected by provincial congresses. Meets once per year for 2–3 weeks.	
Local bodies	**Local party groups** Provincial, county, and primary party organizations.	**Local, county and provincial congresses**	**Government ministries**

supervise the work of the State Council and Supreme People's Court, appoint and remove members of the State Council on the recommendation of the premier when the NPC is not in session, and serve as the interim NPC when Congress is not in session. Since the Communist Party controls the Standing Committee, it also controls the NPC.

The judiciary: Supreme People's Court

China's judiciary and law enforcement agencies exist less to protect individual rights than to enforce party and state policies and regulations. This is ensured through a dual judicial system:

◆ Justice is administered through a system of more than 3,000 people's courts at the district, county, municipal, and provincial levels. These all answer to the Supreme People's Court, which is accountable in turn to the National People's Congress. The Court has more than 200 members, overseen by a president who is elected by the NPC, while the other members are appointed by the NPC Standing Committee. Members of lower-level courts are elected or appointed by the corresponding state organ at each level.

◆ China also has a Supreme People's Procuratorate, whose origins lie in the Chinese imperial era and the Napoleonic civil code (see Chapter 7), which also influenced the Soviet legal system. A procurator is a monitor who reviews the work of government bodies, making sure that they observe the constitution and deciding whether cases should be brought to trial.

Chinese courts developed a reputation for independence during the 1950s, but suffered during the Cultural Revolution when the formal court system was regularly bypassed. The 1982 constitution restored their independence, although questions remain about the extent to which this is respected in practice. Law enforcement in China relies less on a formal legal system than on ideological control. While the rule of law dominates liberal democracies, party policy dominates in China. 'Class enemies' (however that concept is defined) were long treated as different from – and unequal to – class allies, especially during the Cultural Revolution, when the administration of law was taken out of the hands of the formal legal system and placed in the hands of mass groups, notably the Red Guards.

Sub-national government

Because it is a unitary state, all effective political power in China rests with the leadership of the party. Although China subscribes in theory to the principle of Leninist democratic centralism (see Chapter 12), local government has little if any real power or independence. The most important local government units are the provinces, or *sheng* (34 in all, including Chinese-Claimed Taiwan), four major municipalities (Beijing, Tianjin, Chongqing, and Shanghai), two Special Administrative Regions (Hong Kong and Macau), and five 'autonomous' regions for ethnic minorities (including Tibet and Inner Mongolia). Provincial government in China is roughly equivalent to state or provincial government in a federal system, except that all Chinese provincial leaders are appointed by central government. Another feature unique to Chinese local government is the military region, of which there are eleven. The significance of these regions is heightened by the political role of the military, which – as noted later – has been particularly important during times of civil unrest.

Below the provinces are more than 330 prefectures, just over 2,850 urban and rural counties, and just over 47,000 townships. The lowest level of government was once the commune, introduced in 1958 and consisting typically of about 10,000 people. The original intention was that communes would become the focus for almost all political, social, and economic activity and that the government could use them as the front line for the modernization of China. However, most were either too small or too large for the job, and they were finally closed during the early 1980s. The township has since largely replaced the commune, with powers over the administration of law, education, public health, and family planning. In the rural areas, local administration is overseen by nearly 1 million village committees.

China is a multinational state, although ethnic minorities make up only about seven per cent of the population. Among the minority groups are the Zhuangs, Tibetans, Mongols, Koreans, Hui, Manchu, and Uyghurs. Although small in number, they are spread out so thinly in the more physically hostile regions of China that they inhabit nearly 60 per cent of Chinese territory. More important, most of this territory is on China's borders, raising the constant danger of minority grievances spilling over into border disputes involving related ethnic groups in neighbouring countries. The problem that long attracted most international attention concerns the autonomous region of **Tibet**. Incorporated by China in 1950, Chinese troops were sent into Tibet in 1959 to put down a rebellion, and the Dalai Lama (born 1940), spiritual and political leader of the Tibetan theocracy, went into exile. He has since posed a constant embarrassment to the Chinese government, drawing attention to Chinese repression, agitating for the creation of an autonomous Tibet, and winning the Nobel Prize for peace for his efforts.

More recently, attention has focused on the plight of the Uyghurs (pronounced *Wee-gerrs*), a Muslim Turkic minority living mainly in the north-western Xinjiang Uygur Autonomous Region, concentrated on the Chinese border with Kyrgyzstan, Tajikistan, and Kashmir. China has imposed harsh controls on their religious, social, and cultural life, detaining tens of thousands of Uyghurs in 're-education camps' (essentially concentration camps) where brainwashing and indoctrination techniques have reportedly been used to change their religious beliefs and ethnic identity. The Chinese government has claimed that the camps are designed to address the threat of terrorism, but much of the evidence leaving the country suggests a darker set of goals (see Hillman and Tuttle, 2016).

The People's Liberation Army

China is one of the three cases in this book, along with Nigeria and Iran, where the military plays a significant political role. The **People's Liberation Army (PLA)** has in many ways been the third arm of the political structure, working as an extension of the party and the government. Tracing its roots back to 1927–28, it perfected its techniques during World War II, based on the strategic ideas that people were more important than weapons and that winning the hearts and minds of the people could overcome even the most sophisticated military hardware (a principle convincingly illustrated in the US struggles in Vietnam in the 1960s and 1970s). During the Cultural Revolution – when regular government effectively broke down and many government posts went unfilled – the PLA took over administrative duties, kept the Chinese economy functioning, and essentially held the country together. In any other country, it might have used the opportunity to stage a coup; instead, it helped neutralize Mao's Red Guards during the Cultural Revolution, and – on Mao's orders – helped restore the authority of the CCP.

Since then, the party leadership has tried to reduce the political influence of the army by delegating powers of internal security to other agencies, reducing the number of military officers in the Politburo, cutting the size of the PLA, and playing down the army's role as the guardian of socialist ideological purity. The party supervises the military through the Central Military Commission, but the Tiananmen Square demonstrations of 1989 showed just how much the party still relied on the PLA to control dissent and how nervous the party leadership had become about the possibility of an army revolt. That the army would back Deng was not certain; several military regions made it clear they had divided loyalties, and many soldiers were reportedly killed in fighting between rival units.

The PLA has been involved in few foreign military excursions (and none since a brief war in 1979 between China and Vietnam), and has been used instead as a means of extending and consolidating internal political control. Its political role is illustrated by the roles of the Central Military Commission of the CCP, and the Central Military Commission of the People's Republic of China. Although they have different names, they are in fact one body with the same membership, a peculiarity that emphasizes the intertwining of party and state. The chairman of the latter is appointed by the National People's Congress, and is considered the commander-in-chief of the PLA. However, the CMC reports to the leadership of the party, meaning that the military is under the control of the party, not of the government (Li, 2016b).

Control of the CMC has long been in the hands of China's leaders, from Mao through to Xi Jinping today. One of the key changes made by Xi has been a reorganization of the PLA, changing its internal structure so as to move away from an army-centric state while at the same time promoting his loyalists in a manner that allows him to extend his political control (Li, 2016a).

As noted earlier, Xi is also working to transform the Chinese military from a regional force to a global force. China's armed forces number about 2.3 million members, making them the world's largest. However, the military has not been structured to have a global reach, focusing instead on national defence and on fighting short regional wars if needed; new concerns have recently been raised about the military threat that China poses to Taiwan (whose separate status Xi has described as 'a wound to the Chinese nation left by history'. The PLA is also trained to help with economic reconstruction and emergency relief; it played a key role, for example, in cleaning up after a devastating earthquake in May 2008 in central China that left at least 69,000 people dead and about 375,000 injured.

POLITICAL PROCESSES

Voting is a small and relatively insignificant part of political life in China. Voters elect only the members of their local people's congresses, the schedule of elections is regularly changed, and the party system is dominated by the CCP. How this has affected turnout is difficult to say; official figures have not been released since the 1956 elections, when 86 per cent of voters were reported to have turned out. Because elections are so marginal to an understanding of the Chinese political process, most studies of Chinese politics refer to them only in passing, and more emphasis is placed on other channels through which citizens can take part in the political process, most of which have a more direct effect on party policies.

The electoral system

Chinese voters (the legal voting age is 18) participate directly in only one election, that of delegates to county and township congresses. Every other election above the local level is indirect; members of county or district congresses elect delegates to provincial congresses for five-year terms. These delegates in turn elect delegates to the NPC for five-year terms. Although the 1982 constitution fixed the terms of local congressional delegates at three years, elections in post-revolutionary China have been sporadic, with as few as two years and as many as 13 years between them. The 1982 constitution even stipulates that the term of the NPC can be extended if necessary.

The entire electoral process is overseen by the CCP, which controls the election committees that draw up the approved slates of candidates for every elective office. Until 1980, only one candidate was put forward for each office, so the party effectively determined the outcome of every election. In this sense, elections were little more than exercises in building consensus, with agreement on candidates being decided in advance by the party and the election itself functioning simply as a rubber stamp. Public and media debate in 1978–79 about the fairness of this system led to changes in electoral laws that allowed multiple candidates in elections, a more open nomination process, and the use of secret ballots.

One of the effects of the changes has been to make local politics in China more important and engaging than it is in many other parts of the world, even in leading democracies (where there tends to be more of a focus on the national level, which – for most Chinese – is far out of reach). The situation in China comes closest in the level of its significance to that of local government in India; see Chapter 8. Village democracy in China, argues He (2007) has greater variety and diversity than many sceptics have typically believed, while Schubert and Ahlers (2012) – after undertaking numerous interviews with villagers – concluded that direct village elections have helped reduce local corruption and increased the sense of empowerment in Chinese villages, even if they have not provided the broader sense of participation needed for a true sense of democratization. Although the party has been known to interfere in the outcome of elections by actively supporting its preferred candidates, unpopular local party officials have occasionally lost re-election.

Political parties

Political parties in liberal democracies exist to put forward different sets of policy options and leaders, allowing voters to choose the direction in which they want their country to move. Parties are (theoretically, at least) subservient to the state and can be removed or kept in office by voters casting ballots at regular elections. In China, by contrast, there is only one significant political party – the Chinese Communist Party – and it is the source and holder of all meaningful political power: it controls all other political organizations, plays a key role in directing the outcome of elections, and dominates both the state and the government. Policy changes come not through a change of party at an election or a substantial public debate, but rather through changes in the balance of power within the leadership of the party.

Strictly speaking, China is a multi-party system because there are eight officially sanctioned 'democratic parties and groups' with alternative policy platforms, including the Democratic League and the Democratic National Construction Association. These have representation in the National People's Congress under the umbrella of the United Front, which held about 28 per cent of the seats in the Thirteenth NPC in 2018–23. The Front, however, is organized by the CCP, and its members and leaders are mainly selected by the CCP, which has always been adept at identifying potential sources of competition for power and has usually moved quickly to ensure that they have never developed into a significant threat. For example, when the China Democracy Party was launched in 1998, posing a potential challenge to CCP rule, it was quickly closed by the government and its members arrested or harassed (Saich, 2015).

COMPARING POLITICS 13
The role of opposition parties

We looked in Chapter 2 at the differences in party systems. In the cases used in this book, we have looked in more detail at how they work, contrasting the no-party system of Iran to the one-party system of China, the one-party dominant systems of Japan and Russia, the two-party system of the United States, the two-party dominant system of Britain, and the multi-party systems found in most of the remaining cases. There is a temptation in all these cases to focus only on the political role of governing parties, for the obvious reason that they have the most influence and visibility. Democracy, however, is also defined by the choices among parties and by the role of the opposition in both checking the government and offering policy alternatives.

In China, the opposition is restricted to a limited and controlled cluster of alternative 'parties', offering little in the way of a meaningful opposition. Certainly, no political party other than the CCP has a realistic chance of taking control of the government. Much the same can be said for the opposition in unlimited presidential systems (including Russia), based as they are on an arrangement in which the place of the ruling elite is ensured by keeping the numbers of legislators from the governing party at a level that makes it impossible for the opposition to be more than token.

There are a few democracies that have single dominant parties, but the absence of change, combined with the methods sometimes used by these parties to remain in power, clearly erodes the quality of democracy in these states, and encourages corruption. Most of these countries – including Japan, Botswana, Malaysia, Singapore, and South Africa – are classified in the Democracy Index as flawed democracies. With its two-party dominant system, meanwhile, the United States is only removed by a small degree from the problems faced by some of these countries, and is also considered a flawed democracy.

A potentially more serious threat was posed in the 1990s by the **Falun Gong**, a movement variously described as a sect, cult, or religion (see Ownby, 2008). Its members practise a combination of breathing exercises (*qigong*), Buddhism, Taoism, martial arts, and faith healing. It claims to have its origins in prehistoric culture, but only began to attract wider interest after 1992 when its self-proclaimed leader Li Hongzhi set up a study centre in Beijing. It claimed a worldwide following of more than 100 million, of which 70 million lived in China, numbers which – if true – would have made it about as big as the CCP. It described itself as apolitical, but several thousand of its adherents staged a demonstration in April 1999 outside the compound in Beijing where China's senior leaders live. This not only frightened and embarrassed the leadership but indicated that the movement was well organized. It was immediately banned, and while it today attracts much less attention, it continues to function underground in China, and stands as an example of the kinds of fears that can be generated in the Chinese leadership by movements that would seem to challenge CCP dominance.

Parliamentary democracies offer an interesting contrast, because they often lack a majority party, meaning that government and opposition routinely mingle in the form of governing coalitions; see Chapter 4. Britain offers another model, because whichever party is in power, it routinely faces pressure from Her Majesty's Loyal Opposition: the Leader of the Opposition (the leader of the second biggest party in Parliament) and a shadow cabinet of members of Parliament whose job is to shadow their counterparts in the cabinet; see Chapter 3. At all times, voters can see who is in government, and can also see who might be in government were the opposition to take power at the next election. Being an official opposition also gives the second party the opportunity to constantly place its policies before the electorate, and to offer a set of alternatives to the government.

Chinese Communist Party (CCP)

The dominant role of the CCP is symbolized by the Chinese flag, which consists of one large gold star and four small stars on a red background; the four smaller stars were originally intended to represent the four major classes (peasants, workers, petty bourgeoisie, and owners of enterprises), and the large star to represent the party. (Xi's government now claims that the five stars represent the unity of the Chinese people under the leadership of the CCP.) In 2012 the party had a membership of 85 million (Li, 2016b), making it bigger than many large countries and the largest party political organization in history. Despite this, it remains elitist, since only about seven per cent of Chinese adults are members. Application for membership is a convoluted process, requiring careful screening, but the rewards for members include status, influence, and career opportunities.

Although party membership is growing, the balance of that membership is changing. With the expansion of the private economic sector and the resulting fall in the number of urban Chinese employed by state-owned businesses, there has also been a fall in the number of party branches that were once so much a part of their lives. At least in towns and cities, the party is increasingly associated with government departments and institutions, rather than with the economic sector. And where the Chinese would once accept and follow the dictates of the party (at least in public), it has come under criticism for China's crime problems, the persistence of corruption, the steady emergence of an economic class system that has led to the growth of an underclass, and economic changes that are causing social unrest and unemployment.

Organizationally, the CCP has four major bodies:

◆ *National Congress*. In theory at least, the National Congress of the Chinese Communist Party (not to be confused with China's legislature, the National People's Congress) is the most important body in the party hierarchy. It meets once every five years in Beijing for no more than two weeks, and is attended by more than 2,000 delegates. Given the size and the rarity of meetings, Congresses have time to do little more than rubber-stamp party policies and decisions. In theory, delegates are selected at lower party levels; in practice, allocations are engineered by the party leadership to ensure representation of the central party, often at the cost of seats for representatives from the provinces.

Normally, the National Congress does little more than hear reports from the party leadership, and – more significantly – 'elect' members to the Central Committee, although all it really does is confirm a list already drawn up by party leaders. Nonetheless, balloting and politicking have occasionally produced changes in the list and there are now more candidates than there are posts for party positions, so even influential figures have been known to fail to be voted into the Central Committee. Generally, however, the Congress has little significant power.

◆ *Central Committee*. As in the former Soviet system, the Central Committee is the key governing body of the party. Although it rarely initiates or introduces policies, it must approve the policies of the leadership. As with most Chinese political institutions, size is again a determining factor in the powers of the Committee; as membership of the CCP grew, and as appointment to the Central Committee was used increasingly as a means of rewarding service to the party, so Committee membership grew from just over 40 members in the mid-1950s to almost 350 members in 1982, settling down to just over 200 today. The Committee usually meets annually for varying periods, during which time it approves a slate of candidates for the Politburo and of the Standing Committee of the Politburo.

◆ *Politburo.* Ultimate party power in China (and therefore ultimate political power) lies in the **Politburo** of the CCP. With a membership of about 20 to 24 people, it meets about once a month to initiate and discuss party policy, taking collective responsibility for its decisions. Although the Central Committee technically appoints the members of the Politburo, its membership has been self-perpetuating, driven by the ambition of individuals to stay in the Politburo and by their ability to win and keep the support of their peers and of the general secretary. For decades there was little change in membership, most Politburo members came from the military, and the average age of members climbed to well over 70. Deaths and replacements brought the average age by the mid-1980s down to just over 60, and the military members were replaced by younger and more professional members. The membership stays relatively young today, and consists of a combination of key members of the State Council, selected local party chiefs, and senior members of the party.

◆ *Standing Committee of the Politburo.* When the Politburo is not in session, the party is run by a Standing Committee of between six and ten members, who constitute the most powerful and senior group of individuals in the Chinese political system. The senior member is the general secretary of the CCP, who is normally confirmed for a maximum of two five-year terms in the position. Formally approved by the Central Committee, its membership is in fact negotiated among the leaders of the CCP, and the core attributes of members are loyalty and usefulness to the general secretary, who is leader of the party and of China. In mid-2018, the committee had nine members, including Xi Jinping (general secretary), Li Keqiang (premier), and Li Zhanshu (chairman of the NPC Standing Committee). Little is known about its inner workings, other than it meets at least weekly, and that it mainly functions on the basis of consensus, but always has an odd number of members in order to ensure no hung votes.

Party strategy and policies constitute the '**party line**', a term describing the official position of the Chinese Communist Party, and implying the principal guide for government and citizens alike. Despite the official criticism of faction, party politics is ultimately driven by factionalism, clientelism, and the establishment of personal ties and networks (Saich, 2015). Leaders rise and fall according to their abilities to make (and keep) friends and allies in the right places and to identify and control, sideline, or eliminate their opponents. In that sense, at least, the CCP is not so different from a conventional liberal democratic political party.

The structure and role of the CCP follows almost exactly the hierarchical model of the old CPSU. At the lowest level are about 4 million **primary party organizations (PPOs)**, formed wherever there is a minimum of three full party members. They can be formed in the workplace or local neighbourhoods or within units of the People's Liberation Army, and each has a committee elected for three-year terms. PPOs are overseen in turn by provincial and county-level party organizations. These have committees elected for five-year terms, have considerable power over economic activities, and have responsibility for convening provincial and county party congresses. Despite this show of concern for the input of the people, however, real power is focused at the national level, and the party is ultimately a closed institution on which outsiders have no significant influence.

The CCP is clearly much more than the kind of independent political party that we find in most other cases in this book. It is not only organized differently, and voted upon differently, but it also has a different relationship with government. Finally, its reach is much greater than is the case with what we might define as conventional political parties. Two examples illustrate that reach: China's remarkable one-child policy and its equally remarkable plans for trade connections across Asia. The first had far-reaching domestic effects, the second promises to have far-reaching global effects, and both reflect the way in which China's government can impose policies that would be unthinkable in democratic and free-market societies.

The **one-child policy** was introduced in 1979, following a two-child policy that had been in place for a decade. Both were designed to address the problem of China's expanding population, which had grown by 45 per cent between 1950 and 1970. Apart from exceptions for ethnic minorities and for rural couples whose first child was a daughter, all families were formally limited to only one child, and contraception, sterilization, and even abortion (if necessary) were used to ensure that the policy was followed. The policy was finally abandoned in 2015, with a reversion to a two-child policy, and opinion is split on its consequences. The Chinese government claimed that 400

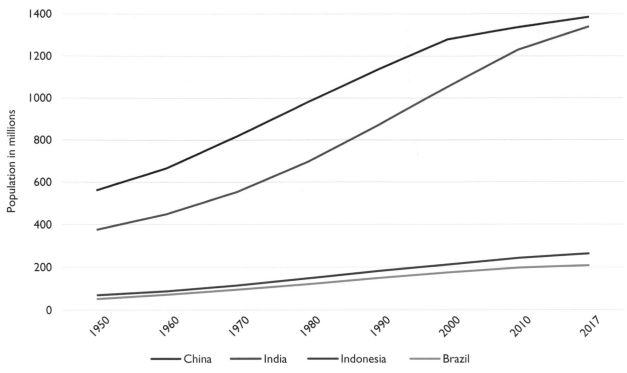

Figure 13.2 Comparing population growth
Based on data in World Bank (2019).

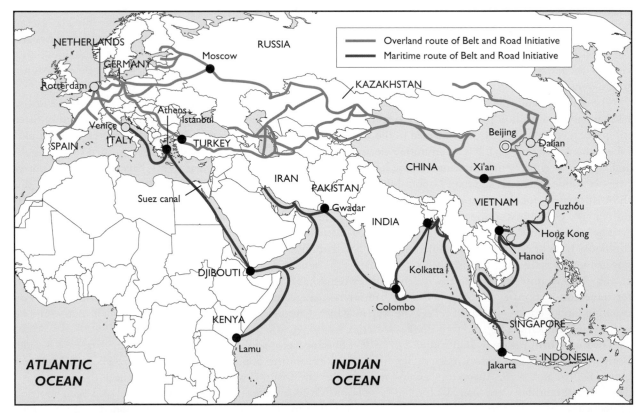

Map 13.1 China's Belt and Road initiative

million births had been prevented, but rates of population growth in other countries with similar levels of social and economic development were not that different from China's; see Figure 13.2.

On the international stage, China's growing economic reach has become increasingly obvious in recent decades as consumers all over the world buy consumer and electronic products labelled 'Made in China', and as Chinese investment and commercial interests find their way to Australia, other parts of Asia, and much of sub-Saharan Africa. Little exemplifies China's global plans quite as clearly as its **Belt and Road Initiative**, launched in 2013; see Map 13.1. It was inspired by the model of the Silk Road that famously connected China with the West, beginning in the 3rd century CE. The aim of this newer enterprise is to streamline China's trade interests in Asia, to ensure stable energy supplies, to promote the development of Asian infrastructure, and consolidate Chinese regional influence (McBride, 2015). The ultimate goal is a new trading network centred on China, and a shift of the focus of the global trading system away from the North Atlantic to Asia. With the power of the Chinese state behind it, the initiative goes far beyond the kind of project that could be considered by even the most powerful of free-market states.

THE FUTURE OF CHINESE GOVERNMENT AND POLITICS

Although this chapter has tried to outline the structure of the Chinese political system, and some of the forces that have helped shape it, this may – if James Palmer, Asia editor at the journal *Foreign Policy*, is to be believed – have been an exercise in futility.

> We don't know China. Nor, however, do the Chinese – not even the government. We don't know China because, in ways that have generally not been acknowledged, virtually every piece of information issued from or about the country is unreliable, partial, or distorted. The sheer scale of the country, mixed with a regime of ever-growing censorship and a pervasive paranoia about sharing information, has crippled our ability to know China (Palmer, 2018).

Although this is an interesting argument, containing a high degree of truth, we actually know a great deal in general about China; we just lack much certainty about the details of its politics, its economy, and its social structure. We can identify trends, and we know enough about the way government works and about the way many Chinese think to be able to recognize many of China's contradictions. We also know that there is a difference between the formal description of the Chinese system of government and the informal mechanisms that fuel that system.

We can also be sure that China is undergoing changes of a kind that promise to make it one of the major powers of the 21st century. It is also fair to conclude that the economic and political changes begun by Deng and developed by Jiang, Hu, and Xi remain incomplete, and it will be some time before we can really see the extent to which reform has taken root in Chinese society. Even as the CCP and its leadership works to maintain its control, the steady rise of the Chinese consumer and entrepreneur will continue to place growing pressure on the leadership for democratic change (Tang, 2017). It will be fascinating to watch as the changes continue to unfold and as we work to understand their implications for China, and for its place in the world.

DISCUSSION QUESTIONS

1. Who governs China?
2. How does leadership change in China, and how does the process compare with changes of leadership in liberal democracies?
3. Is it possible to have democracy within a single political party?
4. Is there an independent Chinese state structure outside the Chinese Communist Party?
5. What effect are the changes currently taking place in the United States, Russia, and China likely to have on the balance of power in the world?
6. What will China look like in 20 years?

CHAPTER CONCEPTS

◆ Belt and Road Initiative
◆ Chinese Communist Party
◆ Confucianism
◆ Falun Gong
◆ Fifth generation
◆ Great Leap Forward
◆ Great Proletarian Cultural Revolution
◆ Long March
◆ Mao Zedong
◆ National People's Congress
◆ One-child policy

◆ Party line
◆ People's Liberation Army
◆ Politburo
◆ Premier
◆ Primary party organizations
◆ State Council
◆ Sun Yat-sen
◆ Taiwan
◆ Tiananmen Square
◆ Tibet
◆ Xi Jinping

KEY TERMS

◆ Consensus

◆ Maoism

CHINA ONLINE

Government of China: www.gov.cn/english
State Council: http://english.gov.cn
National People's Congress: www.npc.gov.cn/englishnpc/news
ChinaSite: http://chinasite.com
China Today: www.chinatoday.com
South China Morning Post: www.scmp.com/frontpage/international
China Daily: www.chinadaily.com.cn

FURTHER READING

Brown, Kerry (2019) *Contemporary China*, 3rd edn (Red Globe Press). The Chinese volume in the Red Globe Press series, offering an overview of history, society, culture, government, and the economy.

Economy, Elizabeth C. (2018) *The Third Revolution: Xi Jinping and the New Chinese State* (Oxford University Press). A review of the political changes being made by Xi, and their implications for the rest of the world.

Jacka, Tamara, Andrew B. Kipnis, and Sally Sargeson (2013) *Contemporary China: Society and Social Change* (Cambridge University Press). An assessment of society and social change in China, looking at the heritage of history as well as the effects of current forces.

Joseph, William A. (ed.) (2014) *Politics in China: An Introduction*, 2nd edn (Oxford University Press); Tony Saich (2015) *Governance and Politics of China,* 4th edn (Red Globe Press); and Sebastian Heilman (ed.) (2016) *China's Political System* (Rowman & Littlefield). Three general surveys of government and politics in China.

Lam, Willy Wo-Lap (2015) *Chinese Politics in the Era of Xi Jinping: Renaissance, Reform, or Retrogression?* (Routledge), and Cheng Li (2016) *Chinese Politics in the Xi Jinping Era: Reassessing Collective Leadership* (Brookings Institution). Two assessments of the political changes instituted by Xi Jinping.

Roberts, J. A. G. (2011) *A History of China*, 3rd edn (Red Globe Press). A history of China from the prehistoric era to the beginning of the Xi administration.

Visit **www.macmillanihe.com/McCormick-Cases** to access additional materials to support teaching and learning.

IRAN

14

Source: iStock.com/fotokon

PREVIEW

Iran's main value as a case study lies in what it can tell us about the nature of politics and government in Islamic societies. It has long played a critical role in the Middle East, dating back to its origins at the heart of the Persian Empire, its vast oil reserves having more recently been of interest to external powers, notably during the Cold War. Hostility to foreign influence was one of the sparks behind the 1979 Iranian revolution that led to the creation of an Islamic republic in which power is shared by mainly elected political institutions and by non-elected Islamic clerics holding positions that allow them to wield considerable power and influence. Iran is an authoritarian state in which politics is highly factionalized, religion lies at the heart of government, oil wealth and political centralization breed corruption, political rights are limited, women are marginalized, and the future remains uncertain.

KEY ARGUMENTS

◆ Iran is formally an Islamic republic, although there is an ongoing debate about what this means in practice, and about the place of religion in politics.

◆ There have been many changes in Iranian government and politics since the 1979 revolution, and the country is still in search of a settled political model.

◆ Iran continues to be torn between the influences of its conservative clerics and of its pragmatist politicians, and between competing factions within each of these groups.

◆ While the executive and the legislature in Iran have many of the features of their counterparts in other countries, the roles of the Supreme Leader and the Guardian Council inject unique elements into the Iranian political system.

◆ The military has an unusually central role in Iranian politics, particularly through the influence of the Revolutionary Guards.

◆ Two of the most important features of politics in Iran are the marginalized position of women and the absence of a system of formalized political parties.

OVERVIEW

For outsiders, Iran is a controversial country. Its position in the global system is given heightened significance by its strategic position at the heart of the Middle Eastern oil industry, and by its efforts to build an **Islamic republic**. It is widely regarded as a destabilizing influence in the Middle East, with a poor record on human rights, and concerns about its association with militant Islamist organizations such as Hezbollah and its sometimes belligerent position on Israel. As a result, many in the West find it hard to look objectively at Iran.

In political terms, Iran compares poorly to electoral democracies, even if it has the trappings of a responsible political system, such as regular and competitive elections. There is an elected president and legislature, but power is controlled by an unelected supreme leader surrounded by a supporting clerical elite, candidates for public office are vetted and laws approved according to their fit with the goals of the revolution, elections are manipulated, political parties are proscribed, corruption is a persistent problem, and women are marginalized. As a result, it is ranked as Not Free by Freedom House, and by the Democracy Index as one of the most authoritarian states in the world.

Since the 1979 revolution, Iran has formally been an Islamic republic, but whether or not it is a full-blown theocracy (see section on political culture), or whether religious and secular politics truly coexist, is a debatable proposition. Not all Iranians agree on the place of religion in politics, and the struggle between Islamist conservatives and moderate religious reformists has been at the heart of recent Iranian politics. Conservatives have had the upper hand since 1979, but they have been challenged at legislative elections, two of the last three presidents have been reformists, and the possibility of a political opening that would improve both Iran's internal democratic record and its external relations has never entirely gone away.

In economic terms, Iran is a poor country, with a per capita GDP of about $5,500 (slightly above that of Iraq, but well below Saudi Arabia). This is despite its enormous energy wealth (accounting for about ten per cent of the world's reserves of oil and about 16 per cent of its natural gas), as well as mineral wealth in the form of chromium, copper, iron, and lead. Iran's oil has been a mixed blessing: while it has the potential to become the basis of an economic revolution in Iran, it dominates the economy, oil profits have been manipulated – both internally and externally – for political ends, and most ordinary Iranians have not seen the benefits of that wealth.

In social terms, Iran is ethnically diverse, with barely half the population being Persian, and the balance made up of nearly a dozen different minorities, including Azeris, Gilakis, Kurds, Arabs, and Lors. While minorities are not always treated equally before the law, and there are differences over political agendas, Iran does not suffer the degree of social division that affects many of the other states covered in this book, particularly India and Nigeria. One of the reasons for this is that Iranians do not suffer significantly from tensions over religious difference: almost all Iranians are Muslims, and nine out of every ten Iranian Muslims is Shi'a (see later in this chapter for an explanation). Even so, religious minorities do face discrimination, and Iran is divided by an ongoing debate over the interpretation of religious values and over the role of Islam in politics.

> **Islamic republic**
> A state that formally abides by the principles of Islam, with religious leaders playing a key role in government, and Islamic *sharia* law overriding civil law.

POLITICAL DEVELOPMENT

Iran sits at the heart of one of the world's most historically dynamic regions, where it has come under the control or influence of numerous different powers, ranging from the Greeks under Alexander the Great to the Arabs, the Turks, and the Mongols, before playing a key role in the great power competition of the 19th century between the British and the Russians. A revolution in the early 20th century brought the prospect of modernization, but first British and then American interest in Persia (renamed Iran in 1935) prevented the development of long-term stability. Its location at the heart of the Middle East coupled with its control of vast oil resources gave it enormous strategic significance, and made it a critical Western partner in the Cold War. But this entailed the propping up by the West of the authoritarian regime of the Shah of Iran (1941–79), feeding into resentment that led to the 1979 revolution that brought to power a militantly anti-Western Islamic clerical government. This long history of external influence continues unabated thanks to Iran's position at the heart of developments in Islamic and Middle Eastern politics.

The Persians and the arrival of Islam

Evidence has been found in modern Iran of human settlements and a sophisticated culture dating back to 4000 BCE; parts of modern Iran were in the Fertile Crescent, where humans first raised crops in an organized fashion.

Persia was first unified politically under the Medes in 625 BCE, and then in 550 BCE became part of the Achaemenid Empire, the first of several empires that would rule the region for the next millennium. It was ruled by monarchs known as **shahs** (derived from the Achaemenid term *shahanshah*, meaning 'king of kings'), their power underpinned by Zoroastrianism, a religion that dates back as far as the 10th century BCE. Under Cyrus the Great (559–531 BCE) and Darius the Great (522–486 BCE), the Persian Empire grew to cover most of what was then considered (at least by its residents) as the civilized world: the region between the Nile and Euphrates-Tigris valleys.

The Sassanid Empire was the last major pre-Islamic influence in the region, lasting for approximately 400 years until overwhelmed by the spread of Islam in the 7th century. A steady process of Islamization now began, leading to the decline of Zoroastrianism and the near-complete conversion of the region to Islam by the 10th century CE. Although there was a change of religion, Persians protected their language and culture, encouraged by the manner in which Arabs treated many non-Arab Muslims as second-class citizens.

Rather than being subjugated, then, Persia contributed to the growth of Islamic civilization and helped shape the new Islamic order while remaining distinctive within that order. Even today, this remains a key point in understanding Iran. It is also important to appreciate Iran's doctrinal distinction as a **Shi'a** state in a world dominated by **Sunni** Muslims. The Shi'a (from *Shiat-i-Ali*, or partisans of Ali) believe they are the true Muslims in the model of the Prophet Muhammad, that the supreme leader of a country should be a religious leader, and that the *sharia* should be the law of the state. The Sunni believe that the Prophet (*al-sunna*) was an ordinary human being, and while they support the *sharia*, most do not believe in religious leaders on earth. About 85 per cent of Muslims are Sunni, while the biggest concentrations of Shi'a are found in Iran and Iraq.

Political control over Persia changed as the power of successive empires waxed and waned: the Arabs were followed by the Seljuk Turks in the 11th century and by the Mongols under Genghis Khan, who destroyed much of Persian culture and reduced the population by an estimated 90 per cent. The Safavids were in control between 1501 and 1732, and although the Qajars (1795–1925) tried to revive Persian power, they lacked religious legitimacy and were challenged by external influences when the region became caught up in British and Russian competition for influence in Central Asia, known as the Great Game. Central government became increasingly weak and corrupt, the shahs relying on powerful regional aristocrats for both income and security, and signing concessions on trade with foreign powers, notably the British and the Russians. This led to demands from aristocrats, religious leaders, and the educated elite for more accountability and democracy.

Modernization and the Pahlavis (1891–1979)

In 1891–92, protests erupted against a decision to offer a British company a monopoly over Persia's tobacco trade, the ensuing debate about Persian democracy sparking demands for reform (Gheissari and Nasr, 2006). In 1905–06, more protests led to the signing of Iran's first constitution, creating the first elected **Majlis** (legislature), a constitutional monarchy, and a prime minister and cabinet. The **Persian Constitutional Revolution** (1905–11) was the first movement of its kind in the Middle East, and might have led to more long-term democratic changes were it not for the discovery of oil and developments at the international level. In 1901, the British businessman William Knox D'Arcy had been given a concession to search for oil in Persia, and when the first discoveries were made in 1908, British control tightened. In that same year, D'Arcy created the Anglo-Persian Oil Company, which in 1954 became British Petroleum, and as BP is now one of the world's biggest multinational corporations.

Persia hoped to remain neutral during World War I, but was occupied by British and Russian forces, and the 1919 Anglo-Persian Agreement was widely seen as an attempt by Britain to establish a protectorate over Persia. The Majlis refused to support it, and in 1921, a Cossack officer named Reza Khan seized power in a military coup. In 1925 the shah was deposed, ending the Qajar dynasty, and in 1926, Reza was crowned hereditary **Shah of Persia** at the head of the new Pahlavi dynasty. (Khan was his title, and he adopted the surname Pahlavi for himself.)

The new shah resisted British control, but nonetheless gave the Anglo-Persian Oil Company a 60-year concession. He also set out to modernize and secularize the newly renamed Iran, but his dictatorial tendencies and his desire to stay neutral in World War II – combined with Iran's strategic importance as a source of oil – led to simultaneous British and Soviet invasions in August 1941. The shah was forced to abdicate and was succeeded by his pro-British son, who became Mohammad Reza Shah Pahlavi. Following the war, it appeared that the new shah was in favour of a constitutional monarchy, but elections were marred by corruption, unstable governments were elected, and Iran remained a target of interest for Britain and increasingly for the United States.

🖧 TIMELINE

636	Arab invasion brings end of Sassanian dynasty and start of Islamic rule
1906	Signature of Iran's first constitution
1908	Discovery of oil in Persia
1921	Reza Khan seizes power; crowned Reza Shah Pahlavi in 1926
1936	Persia is renamed Iran
1941	Anglo-Russian invasion, and deposition of the shah in favour of his son Mohammad Reza Pahlavi
1953	Coup engineered by British and US intelligence services
1963	Launch of the White Revolution; opposition revolt led by Ayatollah Khomeini
1979	Iranian revolution unseats the shah and ushers in Islamic republic
1980	Outbreak of eight-year war with Iraq; exiled shah dies in Egypt
1981	End of 444-day US Embassy hostage crisis
1989	Death of Ayatollah Khomeini; constitutional amendment gives more power to the Iranian Supreme Leader and removes the position of prime minister
2000	Reformists win Majlis elections
2002	President George W. Bush includes Iran in 'axis of evil'
2007	International Atomic Energy Administration says Iran capable of developing nuclear weapons in 3–8 years
2015	Agreement between six world powers and Iran over its nuclear programme
2017–18	Iran witnesses its largest and most widespread protests since 1979

With the British government now earning a bigger share of Iranian oil royalties than the Iranian government, support grew for nationalizing the oil industry. A bloc of Majlis deputies led by Mohammad Mossadeq led the fight, winning enough political and public support to oblige the shah to appoint him prime minister in April 1951. Concern grew in the United States about Mossadeq's refusal to compromise, and about the support he received from communist deputies in the Majlis. In August 1953, with the collusion of the US Central Intelligence Agency (CIA) and the British intelligence service MI6, Mossadeq was removed from power in a coup. The shah was now encouraged – in return for US economic and military aid – to allow the Iranian oil industry to be run by an Anglo-American-French-Dutch consortium for 25 years, the profits being shared equally by the consortium and the government of Iran.

The pre-war programme of modernization continued with the launch in 1963 of the **White Revolution**, a series of economic and social reforms intended to regenerate Iran, focusing on land reform and privatization, giving the vote to women, allowing non-Muslims to hold public office, and launching a literacy campaign in schools. Although industrial production grew, economic conditions for most Iranians did not much improve, most wealth remained in the hands of a small number of people, and the reforms upset conservative religious groups already opposed to the shah's pro-Western policies and to the secularization of Iran.

In 1965 prime minister Hassan Ali-Mansur was assassinated and an attempt was made on the life of the shah, sparking a crackdown by the government and increased use of the notorious National Intelligence and Security Organization (SAVAK); it was to be responsible for the deaths of thousands of dissidents and the arrest and torture of thousands more. Islamists, leftists, and nationalists were at the heart of opposition to the regime, one of its most vocal critics being the Ayatollah Ruhollah Khomeini. A previously non-political cleric (an **ayatollah** is an Iranian cleric with the authority to make legal decisions in accordance with the *sharia*), he had led a revolt against the White Revolution in June 1963, and had been sent into exile in 1964.

Tensions with Iraq meanwhile led to a massive increase in Iranian military spending, and to growing US military influence in the country, feeding into domestic resentment at the extent to which the shah had allowed Iran to become part of US Cold War policy in the Middle East; for many Iranians he was seen as a puppet of the Americans, just as his father had been seen as a puppet of the British (Katouzian and Shahidi, 2008). New oil profits meant more power for the shah, but ordinary Iranians continued to see little improvement in the quality of their lives, and could not help but contrast their situations with the profligacy of the shah and his family.

In 1975 the shah created the Rastakhiz political party, antagonizing many Iranians by making membership mandatory for the voting-age population. In 1976 he upset religious Iranians by replacing the Islamic calendar (dating from 622, the year of Muhammed's *hijra* or exodus from Mecca to Medina) with a calendar based on the first year on the throne of Cyrus the Great. (Iran, like most Muslim countries, uses the Islamic calendar but based on the solar cycle; hence 2018 in the West was 1397 in Iran.) He further upset ordinary Iranians by imposing austerity measures to deal with inflation. Although he took some steps to improve Iran's human rights record, including the freeing of political prisoners and greater press freedom, the shah's popularity plummeted, and by the late 1970s he found himself faced with irresistible pressures for political change.

Revolution and war (1979–88)

In January 1978 a major public demonstration was held in Tehran against the shah, emboldening opponents of the regime – who came from almost every sector and class of Iranian society – to go public with their criticism. More demonstrations followed, along with strikes that nearly brought the country to a halt. Politically weakened and in increasing ill health, the shah went into exile in January 1979, ending nearly 2,500 years of monarchical rule in Iran. Two weeks later, the **Iranian revolution** concluded when the Ayatollah Khomeini returned to Iran from exile in France. On 1 April, Iran became an Islamic republic following overwhelming support in a public referendum.

Khomeini became supreme leader, new populist economic policies were launched, most of Iranian industry was nationalized, Western cultural and political influences were banned, the compulsory wearing of the *hejab* (or veil) was imposed, and the legal and educational systems were Islamicized. Khomeini's tenure was also marked by worsening relations with the United States (which he famously described in a November 1979 speech as the 'Great Satan'), by the ruthless suppression of opposition, and by economic decline leading to the emigration of many of Iran's professionals and entrepreneurs.

The shah, meanwhile, had been diagnosed with cancer and visited the United States for treatment. This was met with outrage in Iran, and demands were made that he be required to return to Iran and stand trial. (Instead, he moved to Egypt, where he died in July 1980.) In November, Iranian students invaded and seized the US Embassy in Tehran, holding 54 Americans hostage, and demanding the return of the shah in exchange for their freedom. The hostage crisis strengthened the political standing of Khomeini, but further undermined the troubled administration of US President Jimmy Carter, which broke diplomatic relations with Iran in April 1980 (they have never been renewed). An agreement on the hostages was eventually reached, and they were released in January 1981.

Meanwhile, in neighbouring Iraq, Saddam Hussein (a minority Sunni Muslim) was concerned about the possible impact of Iranian revolutionary fervour on Iraq's Shi'a majority. He also hoped to take advantage of the instability in Iran to build his strength in the Middle East and gain greater access to the Persian Gulf. On 22 September 1980, Iraq launched a surprise attack on the oil-rich western Iranian province of Khuzestan, and for the next eight years the two countries engaged in a bitter and costly war. With Iran now something of an international pariah, Iraq was backed by all the major Western powers, and by Russia, China, Egypt, and the states of the Persian Gulf. This was in spite of the fact that Saddam was reported as having used chemical weapons (including mustard gas) against Iran, and of systematically executing thousands of Iranian war prisoners. Against a background of increasing US support for Iraq, a collapsing economy, and declining enthusiasm for the war, Iran agreed to a UN ceasefire resolution, and the war ended in August 1988. While it had been expensive in both human and financial terms, it had helped further consolidate the Khomeini regime.

The Ayatollah Khomeini died in June 1989, and was succeeded as supreme leader by Ayatollah Ali Khamenei. Economic problems sparked demands for change, but the efforts of President Mohammad Khatami (1997–2005) to reform the system met with public demonstrations and a clampdown on dissent by conservatives. Tensions with the United States continued, President George W. Bush fanning the flames in 2002 by describing Iran, Iraq, and North Korea as an 'axis of evil' that provided support for international terrorism and sought to develop weapons of mass destruction. Iran has been criticized for its support of Hezbollah, a Shi'a political group that uses violence to work for its goals of an Islamic state in Lebanon, and there has also been criticism of Iran's human rights record, with charges that Iran routinely uses torture and solitary confinement against imprisoned political dissidents.

Iran today

The dominating matter in Iran's global position in recent years has been its nuclear power programme. Launched in the 1950s with US support and assistance, it was temporarily shelved after the 1979 revolution, and then revived. Rejecting efforts by the European Union to provide economic incentives in return for halting its uranium-enrichment and plutonium-processing programmes, Iran announced in 2006 a resumption of nuclear fuel research and an end to its voluntary cooperation with the International Atomic Energy Agency (IAEA). When the IAEA announced in 2007 that Iran could have nuclear weapons within three to eight years, international efforts to control the Iranian nuclear programme escalated, culminating in a 2015 agreement between Iran and major world powers by which international sanctions on the country were lifted in return for a promise that Iran would limit its nuclear activity. Doubts were cast on the future of the agreement in 2018 with the unilateral withdrawal of the Trump administration in the United States.

Domestically, Iran continues to go through the process of change that began with the 1979 revolution, but which Ehteshami (2017) believes has become bogged down. He argues that the changes wrought by the revolution came relatively suddenly, beginning a cycle of transition that has resulted in the creation of 'a complex but unique and non-transferrable system of government'. The past continues to be reflected in the present, he continues, so that Iran 'is a new republic in old clothes – the old clothes of Persian Empires and of Islamic traditions'. More perhaps than is the case in many other countries, the balance of political power continues to be contested not just by different institutions and competing political ideas, but also by a struggle between the demand for a secular regime and the religious one, and by factions within each of those groups. Despite these struggles, argues Axworthy (2013), the Iranian regime has successfully motivated waves of revolutionary Islam across the Middle East, from Afghanistan to Lebanon and Egypt.

POLITICAL CULTURE

Tying down patterns and consistencies in the political culture of a state such as Iran is difficult. Not only has it undergone numerous changes, but it has long been impacted by foreign interest in its internal affairs, it is ethnically diverse, it carries out almost no reliable public polling, and it not long ago went through a revolution whose effects are still being played out. The result is that Iran's political identity is still unclear, and it is not easy to sort out long-term political values from short-term trends.

Islam clearly has a central place in the constitution, in the structure of political institutions, and in its legal system, although most Iranians support a separation of religion and state; there are deep disagreements over how far culture, society, and the structure of government should be shaped by religion. There are also ongoing debates about just how far Iran has travelled down the road to achieving the goals of the 1979 revolution (assuming that agreement is even possible on what those goals were). For example, it has some of the features of a **theocracy**, but pragmatism and the political role of pragmatist leaders are both still important factors in understanding Iran, and Iranians themselves are divided over what the revolution has meant, and what the core features of a finished Islamic republic should be.

Theocracy
Literally, rule by religious leaders. Describes a political system in which all or most key leaders also hold religious office.

The place of women in Iranian society has been particularly troubled. The pre-revolutionary ideal (for men, certainly, but it was also supported by many women thanks to societal conditioning) was a society in which women's roles were confined to the home while men went out to work. The Pahlavi shahs tried to promote a change of attitude, but desegregation and gender equality were associated with the West, and the 'modernization' promoted by the shahs brought them into conflict with Shi'a clergy. Women – who had been allowed to vote only since 1963 – played an active role in the revolution, taking part in street demonstrations and even occasionally in the work of underground groups, and assumed that they would achieve the equality they sought after the revolution. But under Khomeini they saw a move back to traditional values, with the marriage age reduced from 18 to 9, and heated debate over the wearing of the *hejab* (Esfandiari, 2010).

Iranian women today are better off than their counterparts in several other Islamic states (notably Saudi Arabia, where women were allowed to vote for the first time only in 2015, and were not allowed to drive until 2017), and are given better educational and career opportunities, but they still play only a marginal role in politics; they hold few of the important positions in government (President Mahmoud Ahmadinejad's second cabinet in 2009 was the first since the 1979 revolution to contain women), and make up just six per cent of the membership of the Majlis; see Comparing Politics 14. One of the few women to have made a mark on modern Iran is Shirin Ebadi, a dissident lawyer who was Iran's first female judge before the revolution, and who in 2003 won the Nobel Peace Prize for her work in promoting human rights in Iran, particularly those of women and children. She was the first Iranian and the first Muslim woman ever to win the prize.

Iran's overall place in the Muslim world is distinctive, its sense of superiority toward other Islamic societies encouraged by five traits in its history and demography: it was never formally colonized by the Europeans, it is not an Arab country (unlike most of its Muslim neighbours to the west), it has a large population (it is more than twice as big as either Iraq or Saudi Arabia), its people take a deep pride in the history of their country, and it is one of only five countries in the world with a Shi'a majority (the others being Azerbaijan, Bahrain, Iraq, and Lebanon). At the same time, Iran also has something of an inferiority complex, as shown in its deep suspicion of the views and actions of others. Thanks to centuries of external threats and imperial domination, it has developed a worldview in which its problems are routinely blamed on the actions of foreign powers and influences, in which conspiracy theories abound, and in which the motives of both its near neighbours and of the West (notably the United States) are regarded with suspicion.

COMPARING POLITICAL CULTURE 14
Politics and religion

Politics and religion have long overlapped, even if there have been many who have argued over the centuries that they should not. For example, St. Augustine (354–430) wrote of the distinction between the 'earthly city' and the 'city of God', while the theologist Martin Luther (1483–1546) articulated a two kingdoms doctrine in which God ruled the worldly kingdom through a secular government and a spiritual kingdom through the gospel.

The distinction between the religious and the secular, though, has been most actively supported in the Western tradition (although even in the West it did not gain wider acceptance until the Enlightenment), and is less actively acknowledged in the Islamic world. There, religion plays an important role in politics, economics, and society, even if there are debates about just what that role should be, the discussions driven mainly by differences in interpretation. One school of thought sees Islam as an ideology, argues that it needs to become more political, and believes that religion should be tailored toward more radical political ends. Another argues that religion and state should be kept separate and that a dominant role for Islam runs the danger of creating a powerful group of religious leaders who would offset the authority of the secular government and make the people fatalistic and easy to dominate and manipulate.

In most Western states, including Catholic Europe and Latin America, a line is drawn between religion and politics, and few political leaders can hope to gain much by injecting religion or religious ideas into their platforms and statements. One exception might be the United States, where religion has often been an issue in the race for the presidency (John F. Kennedy's Catholicism was controversial, for example), the support of evangelical Christians is important to the Republican Party, and presidential candidates are careful either to boast of their faith, or – at least – to try to avoid being asked about it.

In most Islamic states, by contrast, Islamic law (the *sharia*) is central to the legal and political system, although it almost always coexists with Western law; Islamic states use the latter for serious crime and the former most often for family law. The *sharia* includes obligations as well as prohibitions; thus Muslims should *not* drink alcohol, gamble, steal, commit adultery, or commit suicide, but they *should* pray every day, give to charity, be polite to others, and dress inoffensively. *Sharia* law is both deep and sophisticated, with its own courts, legal experts, and judges and its own tradition of jurisprudence (see Ahmad, 2017, for a survey). To assume that religion plays a similar role in Islamic societies as in Western societies, is to run the risk of misunderstanding countries such as Iran. As we saw in Chapter 8, the same argument also applies to India and the important role of Hinduism in politics.

PROFILE IRAN

Name	Islamic Republic of Iran (Jomhūrī-ye Eslāmī-ye Īrān)
Capital	Tehran
Administration	Unitary Islamic republic, with 30 provinces, below which are counties, districts, and townships.
Constitution	Date of state formation debatable, and most recent constitution adopted 1979.
Executive	Presidential. President elected for maximum of two consecutive four-year terms, but shares power with a Supreme Leader appointed for life by an Assembly of Experts. The Leader must be an expert in Islamic law, and acts as head of state with considerable executive powers.
Legislature	Unicameral Majlis, with 290 members elected for renewable four-year terms.
Judiciary	Supreme Court with members appointed by the head of the judiciary for five-year terms. The Iranian legal system is based on a combination of Islamic law (*sharia*) and civil law.
Electoral system	Single-member plurality for the legislature, simple majority (with the possibility of two rounds) for the president.
Party system	No-party system. Only Islamist parties can operate legally, but organizations that look like parties operate regardless. They are not formal political parties as conventionally understood, however, and instead operate as loose coalitions representing mainly conservative or reformist positions.

81m Population

$440 billion Gross Domestic Product

$5,415 Per capita GDP

Democracy Index rating
- ✗ Full Democracy
- ✗ Flawed Democracy
- ✗ Hybrid Regime
- ✓ Authoritarian
- ✗ Not Rated

Freedom House rating
- ✗ Free
- ✗ Partly Free
- ✓ Not Free
- ✗ Not Rated

Human Development Index rating
- ✗ Very High
- ✓ High
- ✗ Medium
- ✗ Low
- ✗ Not Rated

POLITICAL SYSTEM

As an Islamic republic, Iran is a member of a small and exclusive club, along with Afghanistan, Mauritania, and Pakistan. In spite of their formal declarations, though, it is debatable just how far each of these states has actually gone in achieving the true qualities of an Islamic republic. Furthermore, several states that are not formally Islamic republics (such as Egypt, Libya, and Saudi Arabia) can claim just as strong a record as Iran on abiding by the principles of Islam. In many ways, the concept of an Islamic republic (like that of a democracy) is an ideal rather than a reality, particularly because its precise meaning is unclear. While in exile, the Ayatollah Khomeini developed the idea that government should be in the hands of Muslim clergy with appropriate training, a concept he described as *velayat-e faqih*, or the guardianship of the religious jurist. But he did not specify how this would translate into institutions and processes, a job that was left to the new revolutionary government.

The constitution

Iran has had two constitutions: the 1906 document that came out of the Persian Constitutional Revolution, and its 1979 replacement that came out of the Iranian revolution. The 1906 constitution – one of the first to be adopted by a country outside Europe and North America – is often considered to have brought Iran (or Persia, as it was then) into the modern era. However, while it was based on a constitutional monarchy with a representative legislature, and included the protection of key civil rights and liberties, it was not sufficiently rooted in society that it could protect against abuses of political power. It was later to be mainly ignored by the two Pahlavi shahs.

The 1979 constitution was quite different from its 1906 predecessor, having a theocratic character in contrast to the more secular and democratic character of the earlier document. It replaced the monarchy with a president, created an Islamic republic, and gave clerics a powerful role in government. In terms of the institutions of government, it borrowed heavily from the 1958 constitution of France, which as we saw in Chapter 7 – is based around a semi-presidential executive. This ended in 1989 when constitutional amendments abolished the post of prime minister.

In contrast to the Western democratic model, religion is front and centre in the 1979 constitution: Article 1 states that Iran is an Islamic republic, which Article 2 defines as a belief that there is no god except Allah, that understanding his divine nature is the key to law-making, and that god is just. Article 3 notes that the goal of an Islamic republic is to direct all resources to the following:

◆ The creation of a favourable environment for the growth of moral virtues based on faith and piety and the struggle against all forms of vice and corruption.
◆ Free education.
◆ The promotion of advanced scientific research.
◆ The elimination of imperialism and foreign influence.
◆ Universal military training as a means to strengthening the foundations of national defence and safeguarding the Islamic order of the country.
◆ A 'correct and just economic system in accordance with Islamic criteria' (defined as the creation of welfare, the elimination of poverty, and the abolition of all forms of deprivation).
◆ The expansion and strengthening of Islamic brotherhood and public cooperation.
◆ A foreign policy based on Islamic criteria, a fraternal commitment to all Muslims, and support to 'the freedom fighters of the world' (hence support for organizations such as Hezbollah).

In addition to the conventional institutions charged with executive, legislative, and judicial responsibilities, the constitution also created institutions with a unique role in government, and for which there is no equivalent in liberal democracies:

◆ *Assembly of Experts*. This is a group of 86 Islamic scholars (known as *mujtahid*) whose job is to appoint, monitor, and – if necessary – dismiss Iran's supreme leader. In this sense, it acts as something of an electoral college. The scholars are elected to eight-year terms in public elections from each of Iran's 30 provinces, with as many as five to eight from each of the larger provinces, and 16 from the capital city of Tehran. The Assembly rarely meets, and there is no evidence that it has called either of Iran's two supreme leaders to task on any policy issue or any of the decisions they have made. The only time the Assembly changed its mind on an appointment was in 1989, when Hossein Ali Montazeri – the designated successor to Ayatollah Khomeini – went public with his criticism of the government of Khomeini, likening his approach at one point to that of the shah and SAVAK (Bakhash, 1990). A furious Khomeini denounced Montazeri, who was dismissed by the Assembly of Experts. Following Khomeini's death, the incumbent president of Iran – Ayatollah Ali Khamenei – was appointed as supreme leader by the Assembly of Experts.

◆ *Guardian Council*. This is a group of 12 members, with six clerics chosen by the supreme leader and six jurists selected by the head of the judiciary with Majlis approval, each for six-year terms. It is charged with making sure that all candidates for public office fit with the ideals of the revolution, and with vetting all proposals for new laws (making it something akin to a second chamber of the legislature, motivated by the desire of clerics to have input into the legislative process). The Council has been criticized for taking a narrow view of the appropriate qualifications of candidates, particularly regarding their religious background and the requirement that they should be well-known political figures. There are also accusations that the Council has deliberately excluded women from the final shortlist of approved candidates, and concerns that it has perpetuated the grip of political conservatives over the political process. In the lead-up to the March 2008 Majlis elections, it was reported that the Council had disqualified nearly 2,000 of the 9,000 candidates who had planned to run, and that most of those disqualified were reformists. One of them – later reinstated – was a grandson of the Ayatollah Khomeini.

◆ *Expediency Council* (Council for the Discernment of Expediency). This is a group of about 30 politicians and clerics – appointed by the supreme leader for terms of five years – that exerts supervisory authority over the executive, judicial, and legislative branches, resolves differences of opinion between the Majlis and the Guardian Council on legislative matters, and advises the supreme leader on questions of national policy.

Amendments to the constitution are proposed by a Council for the Revision of the Constitution, which consists of five members of the Assembly of Experts, all 12 members of the Guardian Council, the heads of the three branches of government, ten members selected by the supreme leader, three university professors, and 16 representatives from the Majlis, the judiciary, and the Council of Ministers. The proposal then goes to the supreme leader, after which – if he approves – it is put to a national referendum. This has only happened once to date, with a 1989 vote that abolished the office of prime minister, increased the power of the supreme leader (who became an absolute ruler), and ended the requirement that a supreme leader should be a Grand Ayatollah; now, anyone who is a *faqih* (an expert in Islamic law) can be considered.

Head of state: Supreme Leader

Under the terms of the 1979 constitution, a new post of Leader of the Revolution, or **Supreme Leader**, was created, in some ways replacing the traditional position of the shah, but in other ways fulfilling a quite different role. Appointed for life by the Assembly of Experts, the supreme leader (generally known simply as the Leader, or *Rahbar*) is the head of state, but also plays critical roles in both politics and religion. The Leader has many of the figurehead and symbolic duties associated with a monarch or a non-executive president in a liberal democracy, but also has substantive executive powers, including the following:

◆ Control over Iran's foreign policy and command of the armed forces.
◆ The power to declare war and peace.
◆ The power to appoint and remove the six clerical members of the Guardian Council, and overseeing the work of the Expediency Council.
◆ The power to appoint leaders of the judiciary.
◆ Control over key appointments to the Council of Ministers.
◆ The power to appoint and dismiss the heads of Iran's state-run radio and television services.
◆ The power to dismiss the president if he has been impeached by the Majlis or found guilty by the Supreme Court of a violation of his constitutional duties.
◆ The power to initiate and supervise the process of amending the constitution.

The two men who have so far held the post offer contrasting positions and styles of leadership. The first Leader – the Ayatollah Khomeini (1902–89) – was also the hero of the Iranian revolution, and a man uncompromising in his approach to government, expanding the role of religion in public life, and ruthlessly suppressing political opposition (estimates of the number of political prisoners who were executed during his tenure run into the thousands). His role in Iranian politics and in the Islamic world more widely brought him considerable media

Iranian Supreme Leader Ayatollah Ali Khamenei casts his ballot for elections for the Majlis and the Assembly of Experts at a polling station in the capital city of Tehran in 2016.
Source: Anadolu Agency/Getty Images.

attention in the West, where his glowering personality was often regarded as the most public face of Islamic politics, while his presidents had a relatively low profile.

He was succeeded by the Ayatollah Khamenei (b. 1939), a conservative who was a close confidant of Khomeini, and served as Iran's Deputy Minister of Defence before being elected in 1981 as Iran's third president, and the first cleric to hold the office. During the election campaign he was giving a press conference when a tape recorder wired with a bomb exploded beside him, nearly killing him and leaving his right arm paralysed. Khameini is a conservative who has lacked the aura or charisma of his predecessor, making him more insecure, prone to being upstaged by Iran's presidents, and vulnerable to criticism from religious and political groups. Nonetheless, he has been an astute politician who has tried (not always successfully) to cultivate the image of someone who works above the political fray (Sadjadpour, 2010). Helped by changes to the constitution in 1989 that consolidated the power of the Leader, Khamenei has worked to undermine all possible challengers to his position and all challengers to his preferred conservative candidates (Takeyh, 2008).

The role and the powers of the Leader emphasize the manner in which Iran's political system has evolved into one that is neither a monarchy (or an old-style shah), nor a presidency along the lines of those found in the United States or Nigeria, nor a semi-presidential system such as those found in France and Russia. It instead combines a presidential executive and a religious leader with significant political powers, creating a unique political arrangement.

The executive: president

Executive power in Iran is held by a president, who can be elected for an unlimited number of four-year terms, the only stipulation being – as in France and Russia – that no more than two terms can be consecutive. Few presidents have made a bid for a third term, one exception being Akbar Hashemi Rafsanjani, who served two terms between 1989 and 1997, and made an unsuccessful bid for a third term in 2005. The president of Iran is the head of government, with most of the same formal powers and expectations as most other executive presidents, the notable

Table 14.1 Post-revolutionary leaders of Iran

| Supreme Leader: | | President: | | |
Start of term	Name	Start of term	Name	Political philosophy
1979	Grand Ayatollah Ruhollah Khomeini	1980	Abolhassan Bani-Sadr*	Liberal
		1981	Mohammad Ali Rajai†	Conservative
		1981 1985	Ali Khamenei	Conservative
1989	Grand Ayatollah Ali Khamenei	1989 1993	Akbar Hashemi Rafsanjani	Pragmatic conservative
		1997 2001	Mohammad Khatami	Reformist
		2005 2009	Mahmoud Ahmadinejad	Conservative
		2013 2017	Hassan Rouhani	Reformist

* Impeached and fired.

† Assassinated after 28 days in office.

exceptions being the lack of authority over foreign policy and over the Iranian military (the preserve of the Leader). According to the constitution, presidents must be Iranian, must be elected 'from among religious and political personalities' (in practice, only men), must have 'administrative capacity and resourcefulness', must be trustworthy and pious, and must believe in the fundamental principles of the Islamic republic and the official *madhhab* (the Islamic school of thought) of Iran. Also, all presidential candidates must be vetted and approved by the Guardian Council.

The president may not be as powerful as the Leader, whose approval is needed for all government actions, but the office of the presidency has become more powerful as recent officeholders have stamped their personalities on the job. One of the indicators of the power of a political office is the amount of support and public interest that it attracts, but another is the amount of opposition it generates; powerful presidents, notes Bakhash (2010), arouse powerful opposition, and Iranian presidents have had to deal increasingly with factionalism between their parties and the opposition, as well as tensions over authority between the president and the Leader.

During the Khomeini era, the post of president was mainly that of a figurehead, most real power lying with the Leader. The first post-revolutionary president was Abolhassan Bani-Sadr, a close ally of Khomeini who won a landslide victory in 1980 but then began working to reduce the power of clerics in the political system. He was impeached by the Majlis in June 1981, apparently at the instigation of Khomeini, and fled into exile. His successor was Mohammad Ali Rajai, Bani-Sadr's prime minister, who was assassinated less than a month into office by an organization seeking to overthrow the new Iranian regime. He was succeeded by Ali Khamenei, who was the first cleric elected to the position and lived very much under the shadow of the Ayatollah Khomeini. He was in office during an era in which the political opposition was violently suppressed in 1981–83, but steering Iran through the dominating issue of the decade – the war against Iraq – fell mainly to the prime minister of the time, Mir Hossein Mousavi (Bakhash, 2010).

Following Khomeini's death, the constitution was changed in order to give the supreme leader more power. Also, the office of prime minister was abolished and all its executive powers moved to the presidency. The more hands-on leadership style of the four post-Khomeini presidents has combined with the relative modesty of Leader Ali Khamenei to cause a further shift in powers. Conservatism may have continued to dominate the office of the Leader and some of the other key institutions in Iran, but the office of president has been won only once – in the case of Mahmoud Ahmadinejad – by someone with a clearly conservative agenda (see Naji, 2008). He drew new attention to his country with a series of bellicose statements and actions on international issues (such as his assertion that the Holocaust was a myth), and there were charges that his administration tried to influence developments in Iraq through its support of insurgents and through its links with Iraq's Shi'a majority. Ahmadinejad was elected to a second term in 2009, in a contest widely dismissed as fraudulent. When supporters of opposition candidates formed a protest **Green Movement** and took to the streets (prompting some sections of the Western media to talk of a Persian Spring), the government responded with force and as many as 100 people were killed and more than 1,000 arrested.

Ahmadinejad was succeeded as president in 2013 by the reformist Hassan Rouhani, who came to the job with a background in law, diplomacy, and as deputy speaker of the Majlis. He was the fourth of Iran's presidents to be a cleric, and his accession to the office marked a return to the reformist policies of the pre-Ahmadinejad era. In 2017 he won election to a second term as president with an increased majority.

The president governs in association with a Council of Ministers, consisting of eight vice presidents and 22 ministers, all of whom are nominated by the president and must be confirmed by the Majlis; the Leader also has some influence over appointments to the more important positions (defence, intelligence, foreign affairs, and the interior). In the event of the death, resignation, or removal of the president, or an illness or absence lasting more than two months, the First Vice President takes over as interim president (assuming approval by the Leader). Rather than seeing out the term of the former president, though, as is the case in the United States and Mexico, a presidential election must be held within 50 days and a new president elected. This has happened twice so far, in 1980 and 1981.

The legislature: Majlis

Iran has had a national legislature since 1906, when the new constitution created a bicameral National Consultative Assembly, with a 136-member chamber known as the **Majlis**, elected for two-year terms. Provision was also made for a 60-member Senate, half elected and half appointed, but this was not finally created until 1950. Significantly, women were not allowed to vote in legislative elections nor to stand for election until the 1963 reforms made as part of the White Revolution. Conservative religious leaders opposed the development, which led to national demonstrations and was instrumental in the decision of the Ayatollah Khomeini to go into exile. The change went ahead regardless, and the first women deputies took their place in the legislature in October 1963. Iran, however, still lags far behind most other countries in the role of women in legislative politics; see Comparing Politics 14, later in this chapter.

Following the 1979 revolution, the Senate was abolished and a new Islamic Consultative Assembly (*Majlis-e Shouraye Eslami*) was created, consisting of a single chamber, the Majlis. This has 290 members elected for four-year renewable terms on the basis of a multi-member plurality, with five members elected to represent Iran's Jews, Zoroastrians, and Christians. At least on the surface, the Majlis has most of the typical powers of a legislature, including the right to draft, discuss, and vote upon new legislation, to discuss and approve the national budget, to ratify international treaties, to force the dismissal of members of the Council of Ministers through votes of no confidence, and to impeach the president for misconduct. In reality, it is the weakest of the major government institutions in Iran, its powers limited in three key ways:

◆ The Guardian Council has a high degree of control over the work of the Majlis, thanks to its power to vet and approve all candidates running for election to the Majlis, and all legislation being considered by the Majlis.

◆ Most new legislation is proposed by the executive, and although deputies can introduce legislation and propose amendments to bills proposed by the executive, there is a clear limit to the extent to which the president can be opposed.

◆ With a high turnover of members, and lacking a conventional political party system, the Majlis is unable to build the kind of consistent positions it needs to be able to support or oppose the government. It can, though, force some accountability on the executive through its powers over the budget and its ability to confirm and impeach government ministers (Farhi, 2010).

The Majlis is overseen by a Speaker, who has most of the same functions as speakers in parliamentary systems, but also has the potential to become a leading political figure; one speaker (Akbar Hashemi Rafsanjani) and one deputy speaker (Hassan Rouhani) have gone on to be elected president of Iran. In 2008, the speakership went to Ali Larijani, former head of Iran's state broadcasting agency, and a conservative presidential candidate in 2005.

The judiciary: Supreme Court

There are two main elements to the Iranian judicial system:

◆ The Supreme Court is an appellate body responsible for ensuring that the laws and actions of government fit with the goals and principles of the constitution. It is headed by a Chief Justice, who must be an expert in Islamic jurisprudence, and is appointed by the Leader for a period of five years.

◆ The judiciary is responsible for implementing laws and overseeing the criminal justice system, which is based on the interpretations by Iranian clerics of the *sharia*. The constitution describes the judiciary as 'an independent power' in government, but in fact it is quite the opposite. The head of the judiciary is appointed for a five-year term by the Leader, and is in turn responsible for appointing half the members of the Guardian Council and all the members of the Supreme Court, for managing the court system, and for appointing, monitoring, promoting, disciplining, and dismissing judges. Judges in turn hold absolute power, acting not only as judges but also as prosecutor and jury.

No attempt has been made to divorce religion and politics in the judicial system: all its senior members must be *mujtahid*, and all judges must be trained in Shi'a jurisprudence. At the same time, the central control exerted over the system by the Leader is clear, and Iran is routinely criticized by the United Nations Commission on Human Rights and by international judicial watchdogs for the absence of judicial freedom and its poor record on human rights. Among the charges: women and religious minorities are not treated equally before the law, the prison system is overcrowded, investigations into the murder of dissidents has been slow, the right of the defence to call witnesses is often denied, suspects are sometimes tried in closed session without access to legal counsel, and judgements are issued without allowing adequate time for the preparation of a defence.

Criticism has also been directed at one of the most distinctive features of the Iranian legal system: the frequent use of capital punishment. Iran is consistently second only to China in the number of people it executes each year (see Figure 14.1), even if current numbers are much lower than they were during the 1980s, when courts routinely sentenced political prisoners to death. Many executions today are for drug-related offences, but Iran is also one of only ten countries in the world (all of them Islamic) that allows the death penalty for homosexual acts, and is also one of only a handful of states (a group that until 2005 included the United States) that still allows capital punishment for juveniles. According to Amnesty International (2018), death penalties might be imposed after 'confessions' extracted under torture, some executions are carried out in public, and Iran also allows capital punishment for robbery, rape, 'spreading corruption on earth', and has issued the death penalty for 'enmity against God' as well as 'insulting the Prophet'.

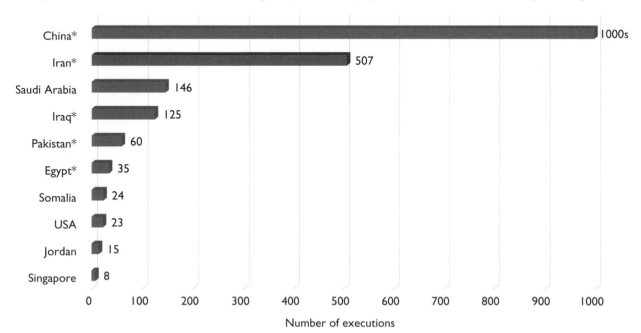

Figure 14.1 Comparing rates of capital punishment

Source: Amnesty International (2018).

* *indicates numbers that Amnesty International was able to confirm, while believing the actual number to be higher. The figure for China (classified as a state secret) runs into the thousands.*

Overall, Iran has a poor record on the protection of political rights and civil liberties. Freedom of expression is severely limited, with controls on radio and television broadcasting, a close watch being kept on journalists and on independent newspapers and magazines, limits and gag orders being placed on the reporting of key stories (such as the nuclear power issue), the censorship of internet content, and a vetting system for all books published in Iran or imported from outside. Religious and academic freedom are both limited, with dissenting clerics often harassed and sometimes tried before a Special Court for the Clergy, which is supposed to deal with criminal acts by members of the clergy but is often used to exert political pressure. Challenges to what are loosely defined as the core principles of Islam are used to prohibit public demonstrations, to control the establishment of political parties and interest groups, and to limit activism by workers; there is only one legal labour federation (Worker's House), and any other activity designed to draw attention to working conditions is likely to lead to harassment and prison sentences. For these and many other reasons, Iran is classified by Freedom House as Not Free, and is the subject of frequent reports and criticisms by groups such as Amnesty International and Human Rights Watch.

The Revolutionary Guards

Although the Iranian military has played nothing like the role in national politics that the Nigerian military plays, it is a critical part of the expression of power in Iran, and also has important links with political leaders and institutions. During the Pahlavi era, military leaders were close to the ruling elite, and the political influence of the United States in Iran was expressed in part through military aid and arms sales from the US, and Iran's membership in regional security agreements. Since the revolution, Iran's aspirations as a regional power have combined with Western concerns over Chinese and North Korean arms sales to Iran, and Iran's development of medium-range missiles capable of reaching Israel, to push defence matters to the top of the policy agenda. Most telling in a political sense, however, has been the role in Iranian national life of the Islamic **Revolutionary Guards Corps**, more properly known as the Army of the Guardians of the Islamic Revolution (*Sepah-e-Pasdaran-e Enqelab-e Eslami*, or simply the Sepah).

Created by Khomeini as a means of exerting control over the military and countering possible threats from officers still loyal to the shah, the Guards have evolved – argues Forozan (2015) – into 'one of the most powerful political, ideological, military and economic players in Iran'. They are separate from the regular Iranian military, so that while the latter is charged with national security, the Guards are charged with preserving the ideals of the revolution. They have their own army, navy, air force, and intelligence services, as well as their own government ministry and bureaucracy, and also control the volunteer *Basij* force that was created by Khomeini, and that is now thought to have as many as 11 million members. The *Basij* are responsible for activities as diverse as law enforcement, emergency management, the organization of public religious ceremonies, and for policing morals and suppressing dissent. They are most famous for their role in the 'human wave' attacks during the Iran–Iraq war, when formations of the *Basij* attacked Iraqi positions.

There is mandatory military service in Iran, and one of those who chose to serve his time in the Revolutionary Guard was Mahmoud Ahmadinejad. While he apparently spent most of his time as an engineer, and saw little active service during his two years with the Guard, he did make important political contacts, and was to make much of his 'war veteran' status when he campaigned for the presidency in 2005.

Sub-national government

Iran is a unitary system, with most political power focused in the capital city of Tehran. While the structure of national government was changed almost out of all recognition after the 1979 revolution, the structure of sub-national government remains more or less what it was during the time of the shahs. Iran is divided into 30 provinces (*ostans*), and further sub-divided into counties, districts, and townships. By population, Tehran is the biggest of the provinces, with a population of more than 15 million people (nearly 20 per cent of the Iranian total); most other provinces have populations of between half a million and three million.

Each province is overseen by a governor general, who is appointed by the Iranian Minister of the Interior with the approval of the cabinet. The Leader exerts influence over the process through his role in approving the appointment of the Minister of the Interior. Since the revolution, the powers of the governor general have declined at the expense of prayer leaders, or *imam jomeh*, who are the elected representatives of the Leader in the counties. As with almost all unitary systems, local units of government play only a minimal role in national politics; the fact that Mahmoud Ahmadinejad picked up his early political experience as a provincial governor general was the exception rather than the rule.

COMPARING GOVERNMENT 14
The political role of militaries

In much the same way as religion and politics have historically had a close relationship in many parts of the world, but have drifted apart in most countries, so militaries and government have also long had a close relationship, which has also mainly weakened with time. The emergence of the state system in medieval Europe was based on a close association between rulers and their armies, and by the need to raise money to support wars; political and military leaders were often the same person, and many political leaders led their armies into battle.

Militaries continued to play a strong role in politics in the second half of the 20th century in many parts of Latin America, sub-Saharan Africa, and Asia, often taking power from civilians through military coups. Today, military governments are both rare and short-lived, although there are still a few examples of countries (including Egypt and Nigeria) where former military leaders have transformed themselves into civilian leaders, or where the military plays a critical role behind the scenes.

In only three of the other cases in this book does the military remain a significant factor in national politics:

◆ Nigeria, as we saw, has spent a total of 27 years under military government since independence in 1960, but while it may remain an important actor in a country threatened by the insurgency of the Islamic militant Boko Haram, there is today less public tolerance for the idea of military government than ever before; see Chapter 10.
◆ In Turkey, the military has several times intervened in politics, three times taking control, and once arranging for a change of government. An effort by mid-level officers to take power in 2016 failed, showing that most Turks now oppose a political role for the military.
◆ In China, meanwhile, the People's Liberation Army (PLA) has been an important arm of the Chinese Communist Party, but it is now focused more on security than political matters as it undergoes a transformation from a regional force to a global force.

Considering these three, Iran perhaps comes closest to the example of the PLA as it once was, in the sense that the military – particularly the Revolutionary Guards – are a branch of the revolutionary structure, with ideological and religious goals as well as a security role.

POLITICAL PROCESSES

Iran has an incomplete system of political representation (at least in conventional liberal democratic terms), because although it has regular elections for its presidents and its legislature, supreme leaders are exempt from the process, political parties are controlled so closely as to be all but non-existent, and elections are manipulated by the Guardian Council and Iran's religious elite to reduce the prospects of religious moderates winning too much power. No secular or critical figures pass the filter of the Council.

The electoral system

Although Iran appears to have a set of elected institutions that provide its people with representation, the system is arranged to ensure that clerics exert close control over the decisions and directions taken by government. This is evident in the electoral system, over which the Guardian Council exerts a level of influence that goes far beyond the 'supervisory' role it is given in the constitution. It reviews the credentials of all candidates for office – including the presidency – as well as having a role in running elections, and even verifying the validity of ballots. Elections might be held every four years on a predictable schedule (or earlier for presidential elections, should an incumbent leave office early), but the kinds of uncertainties inherent in competitive elections are absent in Iran thanks to the close watch of the clerics.

Presidential elections

The president of Iran is elected every four years in a national election in which a simple majority is required. As in France, Russia, and Nigeria, if no candidate wins a majority, a second round of elections must be held the following week in which the two top-placed candidates in the first round run off against each other. There were 12 sets of presidential elections between 1980 and 2017, but only in one of those – the 2005 election – was a second round necessary. Seven candidates split the first-round vote, none winning more than a 21 per cent share, and Mahmoud Ahmadinejad convincingly beat Akbar Hashemi Rafsanjani in the second round. Turnout at recent presidential elections has been a reasonably healthy 60 per cent.

Candidate choice at the presidential election is carefully controlled. Although almost anyone can register to run, and there are often hundreds of hopeful candidates (including, sometimes, children), the Leader uses his powers to undermine candidates who might threaten the conservative agenda that has dominated Iranian politics since 1979, while the Guardian Council checks the credentials of all candidates in order to make sure that they support the ideals of the revolution. The result is an exclusionary system in which the constitution is specifically interpreted in order to approve only candidates associated with the ruling elite (known as *khodi*, or insiders), and to exclude *gheir-khodi*, or outsiders.

All candidates are required to proclaim their loyalty to the rule of the Leader and to the idea that religious clerics hold ultimate political power. But since this philosophy is supported only among Shi'a Muslims (but even then, not all Shi'a religious leaders agree with it), many potential candidates are almost automatically excluded. The Guardian Council has also interpreted the constitutional requirement that candidates should be 'religious or political personalities' to mean that all women be excluded. The effects of this exclusionary philosophy were seen clearly in 2017, when a record 1,636 candidates registered for the presidential election (including 137 women), but only four male candidates were approved (United States Institute of Peace, 2017).

Supporters of Iranian President Hassan Rouhani campaign ahead of the 2017 presidential election. Rouhani, a moderate, was seeking re-election in a vote that served in part as a referendum on his efforts to reach accommodation with the West on his country's nuclear programme.
Source: Majid Saeedi/Getty Images News.

Table 14.2 Results of recent presidential elections in Iran

Year	Candidate	Philosophy	Number of votes (millions)	% share
2009	Mahmoud Ahmadinejad	Conservative	24.5	62.6
	Mir-Hossein Mousavi	Reformist	13.2	33.8
	Mohsen Rezaee	Conservative	0.7	1.7
	Mehdi Karroubi	Reformist	0.3	0.9
	Blank or invalid votes		0.4	1.0
	Turnout: 85 per cent			
2013	Hassan Rouhani	Reformist	18.6	50.7
	Mohammad Bagher Ghalibaf	Conservative	6.0	16.6
	Saeed Jalili	Conservative	4.2	11.4
	Mohsen Rezaee	Conservative	3.9	10.6
	Ali Akbar Velayati	Conservative	2.3	6.2
	Mohammad Gharazi	Independent	0.4	1.2
	Turnout: 72.7 per cent			
2017	Hassan Rouhani	Reformist	23.6	57.1
	Ebrahim Raisi	Conservative	15.8	38.3
	Mostafa Mis-Salim	Conservative	0.5	1.2
	Mostafa Hashemitaba	Reformist	0.2	0.5
	Turnout: 73.3 per cent			

Legislative elections

Iranians are offered the chance to take part in elections to the Majlis every four years. Until just before the 2008 Majlis elections, when it was raised to 18, the voting age was 15, the lowest in the world. Unlike the single-member plurality system used in the United States and Britain, legislative elections in Iran are based around 28 multi-member districts, each of which is given a number of seats in the Majlis based on its population size. Voters are given ballots on which cells are printed into which they write the names of their preferred candidates. Any candidate who wins at least 25 per cent of the vote is declared elected; this usually applies to the majority of seats. For undecided seats, a runoff is held between the two candidates with the most support, with a simple majority needed to win. Out of the 290 Majlis seats contested in 2016, for example, 56 went to a second round, when voter turnout was much lower.

Majlis elections are less a genuine contest for power among competing political groups or candidates, and more a measure of which view – conservatism, pragmatism, or reformism – has the upper hand at the time. Voter choices are again limited by the control exerted over the list of approved candidates by the Guardian Council, and are compromised by the absence of political parties and by the wide array of positions offered by competing candidates. The selection process is not foolproof, however; at the 2008 elections, for example, nearly 7,500 candidates initially applied to register, and about 2,200 were disqualified. When it was revealed that one of the latter was Ali Eshragi, a grandson of the Ayatollah Khomeini, there was such an outcry (even President Khatami called the vetting process 'a catastrophe') that many candidates – including Eshragi – were reinstated. In the end, about 4,500 candidates ran.

Local elections

Local elections in Iran are held only for village and city councils, the former in turn nominating members from among their ranks to serve on district councils, who in turn nominate members to serve on county councils, a process that continues until the Supreme Council of the Provinces. City councils, meanwhile, elect mayors. The distribution of power is mainly top–down, but even though their powers are few, village and city councils offer a modest arena within which Iranians can express themselves, so long as they are not seen to pose a threat to the state. Lacking a party system, the dynamic of elections at the local level is the same as that at the national level.

COMPARING POLITICS 14
Women and politics

However much progress there has been around the world with democratization, it is clear that almost everywhere – including in liberal democracies – the political power of women has lagged behind that of men. Whether measured by the number of women in positions of political leadership, the number of women winning elective office, or the prominence of women's issues on public agendas, men still have a clear advantage. This spills over into the economic sphere as well, where women generally do not have the same career options as men, do not become business leaders in the same numbers as men, and are not paid the same as men for equal work.

Iran fares poorly in regard to the empowerment of women. None of the senior positions in politics since 1979 have been held by a woman, and the Majlis ranks at the lower end of global tables of the number of women legislators. While the numbers in many countries – particularly those in Scandinavia – have grown, only in Rwanda and Cuba have they reached parity with men, and in many countries (including liberal democracies) the numbers remain low – see Figure 14.2. Of the case studies in this book, Mexico does best with 43 per cent of its legislators in 2017 being women, while Iran and Nigeria do worst, with figures of just six per cent.

The numbers do not tell the whole story, however, which is also explained by history and culture. Europe and Japan, for example, both have a feudal past, but while most European countries have left that past behind, it is still reflected in Japan (and in Iran) by a tradition of **paternalism** that is reflected most obviously in the subsidiary position of women; in few other democracies is the gender gap so obvious or the feminist movement so weak as it is in Japan, where women earn just over half as much as men, women have made only limited inroads into the higher levels of the corporate world, and the number of women in Japanese politics has actually fallen since World War II.

We can compare the political role of women by looking at the number who have been elected to the highest political offices. The number of states that have elected women presidents or prime ministers, for example, has grown since 1960, when Sirimavo Bandaranaike became the first female elected leader of a modern state (Sri Lanka). Since then, women have been heads of government in more than three dozen countries, including Argentina, Australia, Bolivia, Brazil, Britain, Canada, France, Germany, India, Israel, Liberia, New Zealand, Nicaragua, Pakistan, the Philippines, and Portugal, and Iceland in 2009 became the first country with an openly lesbian prime minister, Johanna Sigurdardottir. Positive trends, to be sure, but what effect has this had – if any – on the broader place of women in politics?

> **Paternalism**
> An infringement on the rights and liberties of a person or class, supposedly with a beneficial intent but actually as a means of social control. Reflects the values of patriarchal societies in which men are seen as the head of families.

Political parties

The existence or non-existence of political parties in Iran is a matter of some debate. The constitution allows them, provided that they do not violate 'the principles of independence, freedom, national unity, the criteria of Islam, or the basis of the Islamic republic' (Article 26). This condition is so ambiguous, though, as to allow considerable room for different interpretations, with the result that while parties may not exist in Iran in the form that they are found in liberal democracies, many organizations exist that have most of the standard features of parties, but stop short of the final, formal step of being set up as such. In other words, Iran has *de facto* parties, even if it does not have *de jure* parties.

One of the many ironies of the Islamic republic – the design of which was meant to usher in a sharp break with the era of the shahs – is that this tradition of a quasi-party system was inherited from the pre-revolutionary era. During that time, interest groups or movements were formed to support or oppose policy without becoming full-fledged parties. One example was the National Front, an opposition group formed by Prime Minister Mohammad Mossadeq that formed the base of support for his programme of nationalization. It was outlawed following the 1953 coup, but then relaunched in 1960 in an attempt to return Mossadeq to power, and again in 1963 in an attempt to

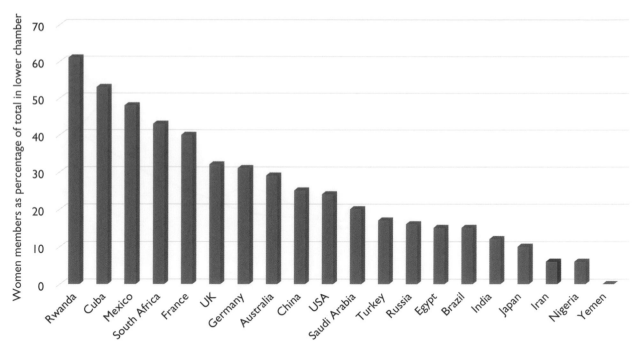

Figure 14.2 Comparing women's membership of legislatures
Source: Inter-Parliamentary Union (2019).

encourage the shah to agree to constitutional limits on his powers. Another example was the communist Tudeh Party, which was founded in 1941 and whose support for Mossadeq's policy of nationalization was used by the United States as part of the justification for his overthrow.

In 1975 the shah made an ill-advised attempt to create an official government political party, known as Rastakhiz (or Resurrection). Rather than providing any kind of firm foundation for his authority, the party instead caused so much resentment among apolitical Iranians that they were encouraged to become politically engaged in opposition to the shah, their biggest complaints being the compulsory membership of the party forced on them by the government, and what was widely seen as the party's unwarranted interference in the political and religious lives of Iranians.

The Iranian revolution saw the creation of new political parties supporting revolutionary ideas, but within months they had been closed down or proscribed, and only one – the Islamic Republican Party (IRP) – was allowed to flourish, and was identified closely with the programme of Ayatollah Khomeini. The only other parties that played much of a role in electoral politics were the Islamic Mojahedin and the liberal Iran Freedom Movement. When disagreement broke out within the IRP over economic policy, however, President Khamenei decided that it would be best if it was closed down, which it was in 1987.

Since then, there has not been a formal party system in Iran; instead, deputies have organized themselves into political groups that can be broadly defined as conservatives, pragmatists, and reformists. Their differences are in part ideological, but they are distinguished from one another mainly by their competing interpretations of the role of religion in people's life:

◆ *Conservatives* believe in an uncompromising interpretation of what Islam means for politics (they follow a stricter line on social and cultural issues, for example, and favour an anti-Western foreign policy), and promote the legacy of the Ayatollah Khomeini. They are also known as principlists (sic), based on their support of the first principles or fundamentals of the Iranian revolution. The United Front of Principlists contested the 2008 and 2012 Majlis elections, winning the biggest share of seats in 2012, and was associated with the two election victories of President Mahmoud Ahmadinejad, while the Principlists Grand Coalition came second in 2016.

◆ *Pragmatists* or reformists believe that the values of Islam can be followed and respected while at the same time supporting a more open economy, a higher degree of cultural freedom, greater respect for political rights, and

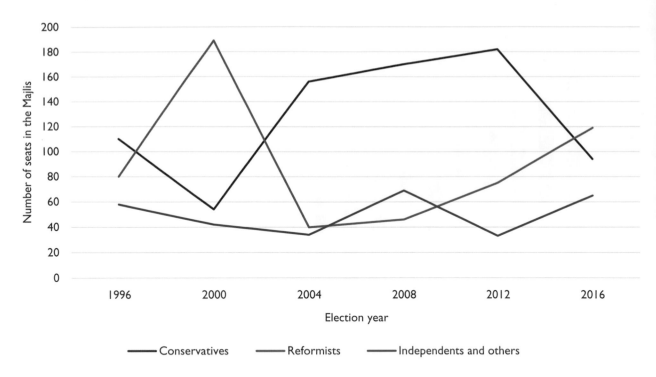

Figure 14.3 Legislative electoral trends in Iran

a more moderate line in foreign policy. They place a greater stress on political institutions, the public will, and elected government, favouring strong government but also worrying about political gridlock. They seek better management of the economy and social services, and improved prosperity for Iranians. The Pervasive Coalition of Reformists (otherwise known as the List of Hope) won the biggest share of seats in the 2016 Majlis elections.

◆ There are arguably third and fourth strands as well, consisting of political dissidents who hold a wide range of critical views of the regime, including so-called 'transformists' and 'overthrowers' who believe in political secularism, fundamental reforms and even regime change, but who are excluded from public debate.

Conservatives have had their most telling impact through their control of the position of Leader, but this has not prevented reformists from continuing to try to change the system from within. For example, reformists seemed to be about to wrest change following the election of President Khatami in 1997 and reformist gains at the Majlis elections in 2000. A coalition named the Second Khordad Front, which had been created in support of the 1997 Khatami reforms, brought together numerous pro-reform groups including the Islamic Iran Participation Front, the Solidarity Party, the Islamic Labour Party, and the Militant Clerics Society, and helped reformist candidates make gains. But in spite of widespread public dissatisfaction with conditions in Iran, conservatives were able to use their control of the key government institutions – notably the Guardian Council – to block reforms and to manipulate elections to their own ends.

The victories of President Ahmadinejad in 2005 and 2009 (the latter surrounded by considerable evidence of fraud) confirmed the lock on power of the conservatives, who also swept the 2008 legislative elections, but probably only because so many reformists (more than 1,700) were prevented from running. Questions continue to be asked, though, about the extent to which conservative politicians truly represent public opinion in Iran. Reformists made a comeback in 2013 with the election victory of president Hassan Rouhani and the success of the List of Hope in the 2016 Majlis election.

THE FUTURE OF IRANIAN GOVERNMENT AND POLITICS

The overwhelmingly negative image that Iran has in the West fails to recognize the complexity of this intriguing country, and its prospects for political change. President Bush's characterization of Iran as part of an 'axis of evil' is still often quoted, even if it was always too simplistic. True, successive Iranian governments since 1979 have not done much to win friends abroad, nor to strengthen the country's democratic credentials; witness the uncompromising imposition of conservative religious values, the poor record on human rights, the failure to free up the marketplace and to capitalize on oil profits, supporting and sponsoring destabilizing militia groups in the region as well as Syrian president Bashar al-Assad, and some of the more outrageous public statements of its leaders.

But Iranian politics is not the monolith that many of its critics would have us believe. In many ways it has two competing governments: a government of clerics dominated by the Leader, and a more pragmatist government headed by the president. At the same time, Iranians are divided among themselves about the correct balance between religion, politics, and society, and reformists recognize the need to break the power of religious elites, to take a more progressive position on the role of Islam in public life, and to pursue policy change both at home and abroad. The manner in which Iranian politics evolves depends upon the relative balance of power between these competing views, which depends in part on how demographic changes in Iran play out: the country's population is young, and the government's failure to keep up with the creation of new jobs is causing much restlessness. It also depends on how Iran's foreign relations evolve (and in this regard, the bellicose statements of Iran's foreign critics are not very helpful), and on the relative success or failure of conservatives and reformists to work the system to their advantage, or the rise of excluded strands, transformists, and overthrowers, who seek a secular democracy for the country.

DISCUSSION QUESTIONS

1. To what extent can Iran's failure to achieve the core principles of an Islamic republic be likened to the failure of liberal democracies to achieve the core principles of a democracy?
2. Looking at the examples of the American, French, Mexican, Russian, and Iranian revolutions, is it possible to conclude that they can ever truly achieve their objectives?
3. Why is political corruption so much of a problem in India, Nigeria, and Iran, but not in Britain, Germany, or France?
4. Why has the political position of women improved so much in countries such as the United States, Britain, and France, while it has continued to lag in Japan, Mexico, and Iran?
5. Do any other countries have a political office that can be likened to the position of the Supreme Leader in Iran?
6. Comparing Iran to democracies, what are the advantages and disadvantages of its lack of a formalized system of political parties?

CHAPTER CONCEPTS

- ◆ Assembly of Experts
- ◆ Ayatollah
- ◆ Expediency Council
- ◆ Green Movement
- ◆ Guardian Council
- ◆ Iranian revolution
- ◆ Majlis
- ◆ Persia

- ◆ Persian Constitutional Revolution
- ◆ Revolutionary Guards
- ◆ Shahs
- ◆ Shi'a
- ◆ Sunni
- ◆ Supreme Leader
- ◆ White Revolution

KEY TERMS

- ◆ Islamic republic
- ◆ Paternalism

- ◆ Theocracy

IRAN ONLINE

Office of the Supreme Leader: www.leader.ir/langs/en/index.php
Presidency: www.president.ir/en
Majlis: https://en.parliran.ir
Iranian Ministry of Foreign Affairs: http://en.mfa.ir
IranOnline: www.iranonline.com/Newsroom

FURTHER READING

Axworthy, Michael (2013) *Revolutionary Iran: A History of the Islamic Republic* (Oxford University Press). A history of the revolutionary era in Iran, showing how it has been inspired by religious rather than secular principles.

Brumberg, Daniel, and Farideh Farhi (eds) (2016) *Power and Change in Iran: Politics of Contention and Conciliation* (Indiana University Press). An edited collection on current Iranian politics, including chapters on key institutions, elections, and human rights.

Ehteshami, Anoushiravan (2017) *Iran: Stuck in Transition* (Routledge). An assessment of Iran's contemporary politics, government, and political economy, which argues that Iran's revolutionary transition has become stuck.

Misagh, Parsa (2016) *Democracy in Iran: Why It Failed and How It Might Succeed* (Harvard University Press), and Abbas Milani and Larry Diamond (eds) (2015) *Politics and Culture in Contemporary*

Iran: Challenging the Status Quo (Lynne Rienner). Two assessments of the prospects of democracy in Iran, and the ongoing barriers to change.

Tamadonfar, Mehran (2015) *Islamic Law and Governance in Contemporary Iran: Transcending Islam for Social, Economic, and Political Order* (Lexington Books). A study of Islamic law and its place in Iran, including chapters on the constitution and the judicial system.

Wright, Robin (ed.) (2010) *The Iran Primer: Power, Politics and US Policy* (Washington DC: United States Institute of Peace Press). A primer on Iranian government and politics, with multiple short chapters dealing with everything from politics to the economy and foreign relations.

Visit **www.macmillanihe.com/McCormick-Cases** to access additional materials to support teaching and learning.

CONCLUSIONS

If there is anything predictable about life, it is the persistence of change. People change, societies change, and circumstances change, driven by multiple pressures, some of them expected but many of them unexpected. To add to the uncertainties, the pace of change seems to grow from one year to the next. Advances in science, technology, and communications redefine our lives, habits, and expectations at a speed that is often hard to absorb; we are just becoming used to one new set of circumstances, it seems, when new influences force us to rethink old assumptions.

The same is true of politics and government. The core ideas about how modern societies might best govern themselves, and about how ordinary people can or should be involved, have been fairly persistent over an extended period: most of us agree that democracy is good and dictatorship is not. There has also been consistency in the structure of political systems: most of us agree that effective government needs equivalents of executives, legislatures, courts, and bureaucracies, supported by political parties, elections, interest groups, and free media. As we have seen in the preceding chapters, though, the structures of political systems come in many different forms, and revolutions have occasionally upset the steady flow of ideas and taken us off in new directions.

It seemed for many years as though we were headed in the direction of more open and responsive government, and comparative typologies – ranging from the Three Worlds system to the Democracy Index and Freedom in the World – suggested that we were making good progress. The number of democracies grew while the number of authoritarian systems declined. One observer – the American political scientist Francis Fukuyama – was so impressed by what he saw with the imminent collapse of the Soviet Union and the end of the Cold War in 1989 that he was moved to declare 'the end of history'. By this he meant 'the end point of mankind's ideological evolution and the universalization of Western liberal democracy as the final form of human government' (Fukuyama, 1989). In short, democracy had won.

Although it was a pleasing and attractive idea, Fukuyama spoke too soon, because the world was about to enter a phase of enormous political and economic change whose causes and effects are still not entirely understood:

◆ In 1997, the political commentator Fareed Zakaria was warning of the rise of what he called 'illiberal democracies', meaning countries that hold free and competitive elections but whose governments limit free speech and opposition. Russia and Turkey are often cited as examples.
◆ The global financial crisis that began in the United States in 2007 and soon spread to Europe shook many assumptions about the stability and promise of free markets, sparking austerity measures in many countries that fed into growing disappointment with government.
◆ In 2008, the political commentator Robert Kagan wrote of the 'return of history', arguing that the world had become 'normal again' in the sense that struggles for status and influence were back, along with the old competition between liberalism and autocracy.
◆ The Arab Spring – the wave of change that came to several North African and Middle Eastern countries in 2010–11 – briefly promised hope for democratic gains in a particularly troubled part of the world, but soon imploded on the back of reversals in Egypt and chaos in Syria and Libya.
◆ In 2015, Diamond worried about the 'democratic recession' brought by a halt to the expansion of freedom and democracy. There was increased talk among scholars and others of a democratic backsliding. Soon after, Diamond et al. (2016) argued that 'illiberal powers' such as China, Russia, and Saudi Arabia were building new confidence and influence in the world, creating an 'authoritarian surge' based on the development of new tools to contain the spread of democracy and to challenge the liberal international political order.
◆ By 2015–17, Freedom in the World was warning that after years of democratic progress, the number of countries considered Free was starting to decline, and the number of those considered Not Free was growing. Perhaps most famously, the Democracy Index downgraded the United States from a full to a flawed democracy in 2016.
◆ Along the way, a growing body of data suggested declining levels of faith and trust in government. This was even the case in those countries long regarded as leaders in the democratic crusade, such as the United States and most western European states.

◆ The rise of populism in many countries was often interpreted not just as a rejection of political elites and expression of concern by marginalized communities, but as a move away from democratic principles.

◆ There has been growing concern about the role of social media in shaping political opinions, about the spread of political misinformation, and about interference in elections by internet trolls, hackers, and the creators of fake social media accounts.

Clearly, we are in an era of enormous political change, whose causes are still being assessed and whose implications remain debatable and uncertain. We need all the tools we can muster to understand what is happening, and prime among those is comparative politics. It is only by comparing and contrasting the experiences of multiple states and communities that we can hope to identify common themes in this era of change, to develop meaningful theories of that change, and to reject weaker explanations.

As almost any scholar of comparative politics will readily admit, there are considerable holes in our understanding of political systems. We know the most about democracy and its major proponents in North America and Europe, mainly because most political scientists are based in these countries, as are most publishers of political science research. Search the shelves of libraries, or online catalogues, or the indices of academic journals, and you will be spoiled for choice on democracy and democracies. But as you move away from these countries, the list of publications becomes shorter. Considering just the twelve cases used in this book, sources of data and analysis fall off steadily as we transition from the chapters on democracies to the chapters on Nigeria, Turkey, and Iran. (The general rule does not apply so much to Russia and China, which have long attracted the interest of Western scholars.) At the same time, the relative volume of scholarship published in English by scholars from these countries falls off, although the balance has changed in recent years.

In short, the importance of comparative politics is clear, but the need for more research on a wider variety of cases is even more clear. We need the sub-field to better understand the critical changes taking place in the world today, and we also need more research to fill the holes in our knowledge and understanding. As we try to understand not just how political systems work, but the changes to which most of them are currently subject, it is worth considering six key principles.

1. **All societies are interrelated.** The only way that each of us as individuals can effectively relate to our social and political environment is to understand how we fit in and what drives others. The same is true of states. Domestic policy of every kind in every state is influenced by a combination of internal and external political, economic, and social forces, and we cannot develop effective policies without understanding those forces. The home front is obviously the most immediate, but all states are part of a global community linked by politics, trade, investment, and technology, and we overlook this at our peril.

2. **Political, economic, and social issues are intimately interlinked.** This may be a book about comparative politics, but no study of systems of government would be complete without an understanding of the links between government, markets, and people. We cannot understand government without looking at how it impacts – and is impacted by – the economic and social structure of states. And with time this is increasingly becoming a global reality as the networks that bind states continue to tighten.

3. **The performance of a system of government depends on its record in the delivery of political goods.** We have seen how political systems that fail to take root in society and respond to the changing needs of their people will ultimately collapse under the weight of their internal contradictions. We have seen that Britain, Germany, the United States, Japan, and France enjoy relatively high levels of legitimacy, even if their political systems face new challenges. Meanwhile, India, Mexico, Nigeria, and Turkey struggle to find a workable formula, while Russia, China, and Iran still have large gaps between the goals of government and the wishes of the people.

4. **No political system is perfect.** Americans often talk about the United States as the greatest country in the world and a shining beacon of liberty and democracy; Britons assume that their political system has endured because it was built on more solid foundations than those of their European neighbours; Westerners look on the problems of politics in countries such as Russia and China and wonder why liberal democracy does not take root in those societies. But the way things are done in liberal democracies is not necessarily the way they are done or even should be done in other political systems. The competitive multi-party democracy used by liberal democracies, for example, may not be the best option for societies that place a premium on consensus.

5. **Nothing is predictable about politics except its unpredictability.** Political scientists have tried for decades to understand human society and to draw up predictive rules about politics, but they have been constantly tripped up by the idiosyncrasies of human relationships. The environment in which politics takes place is always changing,

making it difficult to predict the outcome of political developments. Imagine, for example, political science professors in 1980 making forecasts about the world in 2020. How many would have foreseen the reunification of Germany, the break-up of the Soviet Union, the end of apartheid in South Africa, the rise of international terrorism, economic liberalization in China and India, the Arab Spring, or challenges to democracy in the United States?

6.   **Social divisions are a fact of life in virtually every political system.** Whether they are based on class, ethnicity, religion, gender, region, or wealth, these divisions play a central role in determining how well a political system meets the needs of its citizens. We have seen in this book how politics in countries such as India and Nigeria is driven in large part by the need to address social conflict, but even relatively stable democracies such as the United States and Britain are faced with resolving internal ethnic, religious, and economic divisions.

You have just finished reading a book designed to introduce you to the variety of political systems in the world, and – by comparing their political structures, values, and processes – to illustrate the differences and similarities among those systems with a view to shedding light on the changes the world is undergoing. There are more than 190 independent states in the world, and although we have looked at just twelve of them, the examples used in this book were chosen because they offer a representative sampling of the forms and shapes in which government and politics can be found.

Opinion is divided on what the future holds. Optimists believe that the democratic backsliding is nothing more than a political recession from which we will recover, and that we are still headed towards more and better democracy as one government after another improves its ability to respond to the needs of its citizens. They argue that in spite of current worries and doubts, peace has broken out in many states that have a tradition of instability and war and that economic prosperity and political stability are coming to other states that were once destabilized by colonialism.

Pessimists point at the regional and local wars that continue to disrupt life in many parts of the world; at the continued conflicts caused by nationalism; at questions about the transition to democracy in Russia and other parts of the world; at the social problems that trouble societies on every continent; at the widespread poverty in sub-Saharan Africa and Latin America; at global population growth and the universal threat of climate change; and at the repeated inability of political leaders to meet the needs of all their citizens. But wherever we are headed, comparative politics can give us insight into the paths we are taking and help us make decisions that will make the world a better, safer, and more fulfilling place in which to live.

GLOSSARY

Absolute monarch: One who typically has a large measure of control and power, standing in contrast to the kind of constitutional monarchies found in democracies.

Abstract review: Advice (not usually binding) given by a court on the constitutionality of a law or public policy. Sometimes known as the European model.

Cabinet: The group of heads of government departments and senior administrators who act collectively as the government or the administration. Also sometimes known as a council of ministers.

Case: An instance or example of a phenomenon that is used to illustrate a broader set of arguments or principles, or to narrow a broad field of research into more manageable quantities.

Caste: A system of social and economic divisions that pervades Indian society and politics.

Christian Democracy: A political philosophy associated mainly with continental Europe that applies Christian principles to public policy without being overtly religious. Christian Democratic parties are moderately conservative on social and moral issues, and progressive on economic issues.

Civil liberties: The rights that citizens have relative to government, and that should not – in democracies, at least – be restricted by government. They include freedom of expression and association.

Coalition government: An arrangement in which a government is formed through an alliance involving two or more political parties.

Cohabitation: An arrangement in which a president from one party is obliged – because of party numbers in the legislature – to appoint and work with a prime minister from another party.

Cold War: A 'war' of words, ideas, ideology, and proxy military conflicts between the United States and the Soviet Union between the late 1940s and 1989–90.

Collective responsibility: The idea that decisions taken by a group (as in parliamentary government) are taken collectively and that all members must stand or fall by those decisions.

Command economy: One in which production, investment, supply, and wages are set by a government rather than being left to the free market. Also known as a planned economy.

Comparative method: The process by which different cases are compared in order to better understand their qualities, and to develop hypotheses, theories, and concepts.

Comparative politics: The systematic study of the institutions, processes, personality, and performance of government and politics in different societies so as to better understand each of them.

Competitive authoritarianism: A political system that has many of the features of democracy while being authoritarian in practice.

Concrete review: Judgements made on the constitutional validity of law in the context of a specific case. Sometimes known as the American model.

Consensus: A general or widespread agreement on a course of action, with which all those involved can agree and no one disagrees, although there may not be unanimity.

Constitution: A document or set of documents that outlines the powers, institutions, and structure of government, the responsibilities of the government, and the rights of citizens.

Constitutional engineering: A deliberate attempt to change political and social behaviour through the rules and goals included in a constitution.

Constitutional monarchy: A hereditary monarchy whose powers (typically reduced from what they once were) are limited by the constitution.

Corporatism: An arrangement by which groups in society are incorporated into the system of government.

Corruption: The abuse of public office for private gain.

Corruption Perceptions Index: A ranking system maintained by Transparency International, based on perceptions of levels of corruption, and scoring states out of 100.

Cult of personality: A political regime based on the idealized and heroic representation of the leader as the focus of the state.

Decree: A formal and authoritative order, usually from an executive, that has the force of law but does not need to go through the formal legislative process.

Democracy Index: A political ranking system maintained by the Economist Intelligence Unit, dividing states into full democracies, flawed democracies, hybrid regimes, and authoritarian regimes.

Devolution: The transfer of powers from the centre to the parts, as in the case of powers being transferred from national government in London to regional governments. Differs from federalism in that such powers can be withdrawn by central government.

Divine right: The pre-modern idea that monarchs ruled with a direct mandate from God.

Economic nationalism: Attempts made by a country to protect its economy from foreign control by limiting access.

Electoral College: A body of electors brought together to decide the holder of a higher office.

Elitism: The belief or philosophy that a particular group of people in a society have positions or qualities that give them advantages and powers over others.

Emerging economy: One that is developing rapidly but does not yet have the features of a fully developed market.

Ethnicity: The identification of a group of people with one another, based on a shared language, history and culture, and encouraging adherence or loyalty to the group.

European Union: A regional integration association through which most European states have built closer economic and political ties, notably a single European market.

Euroscepticism: Opposition to the process of European integration, or to the direction being taken by that process.

Exceptionalism: The belief by its people and leaders that their country is a unique and exceptional society.

Executive: The part of government responsible for providing leadership and executing laws and policies, typically with a single leader at the head of a pyramid of government ministers and bureaucrats.

Factionalism: The division of society, government, or institutions into groups formed around a leader and competing with one another for authority and influence.

Federal system: One in which two or more levels of government coexist, each with independent powers and responsibilities.

First- and second-order elections: Elections ranked according to the stakes in the results, with first-order elections shaping national governments, while local elections are often considered second-order.

Freedom in the World: A political ranking system maintained by Freedom House, based on political rights and civil liberties.

Gini coefficient: A measure of income inequality, used to show the distribution of wealth in a given population.

Global city: A city that holds a key place within the global system via its financial, trade, communications, or manufacturing status. Examples include Dubai, London, Moscow, New York, Paris, Shanghai, and Tokyo.

Globalization: The process by which the political, economic, social, and cultural links between and among states become integrated through cooperation, trade, travel, communications, media, investment, market forces, and technology.

Government: The institutions and structures through which societies are governed.

Grand coalition: An arrangement in which the major political parties in a country form a coalition, rather than one major party forming a coalition with smaller parties.

Green politics: A political philosophy based on ecological wisdom, sustainability, social justice, grassroots democracy, and non-violence.

Gross domestic product: The total value of all goods and services produced by a state in a given year.

Head of government: The elected leader of a government, who comes to office because of the support of voters who identify with his/her party and platform.

Head of state: The figurehead leader of a state, who may be elected or appointed, or – in the case of monarchs – may inherit the position.

Historical method: An approach to research based on studying cases from the past, an approach that increases the number of possible cases and can help improve predictions.

Human Development Index: A social ranking system maintained by the UN Development Programme, dividing states into those with very high, high, medium, or low levels of development.

Hyper presidentialism: A political system in which a strong president coexists with a relatively weak legislature and judiciary, perhaps helped by a large majority in the legislature.

Industrial revolution: The era (roughly 1760–1860) during which Britain, followed by other countries, switched from an agricultural to an industrial economy.

Iron triangle: An arrangement by which political power in countries such as Japan is focused on a relationship between the governing party, bureaucrats, and business.

Islamic republic: A state that formally abides by the principles of Islam, with religious leaders playing a key role in government, and Islamic *sharia* law overriding civil law.

Isolationism: A line of policy that supports the avoidance of foreign involvement and alliances.

Judicial activism: The willingness of judges to venture beyond narrow legal reasoning so as to influence public policy.

Judicial restraint: The view that judges should apply the letter of the law, leaving politics to elected bodies.

Judicial review: The process by which a judiciary rules on the laws or actions of government on the basis of its interpretation of the constitution.

Judiciary: A collective term for the judges within the system of courts that interpret and apply the law in keeping with the constitution.

Lame duck: A term describing elected officials or institutions whose successors have already been elected or appointed, and who are seeing out the closing days of their term.

Legislative turnover: The rate of change in the membership of a legislature following an election.

Legislature: A multi-member representative body which debates public issues and considers and decides upon proposals for new laws and policies.

Maoism: Mao's application of Marxist-Leninist ideas to rural societies such as China, rejecting elitism, and emphasizing communalism and social experimentation.

Marxism: The philosophy developed by Karl Marx, arguing that history is a tale of class antagonism, that social divisions are created by private property, and that revolution is inevitable.

Monarchy: A political system in which the head of state is determined by heredity, and holds power for life or until voluntarily renouncing that power. The role of monarchs in democracies is constitutionally limited.

Nation: A mainly cultural and historical concept describing a group of people who identify with one another based on a shared history, culture, language, and myths.

National identity: Identification with a state or nation, as determined by a combination of language, place of birth, and citizenship.

Nationalism: The belief that a group of people with a common national identity has the right to form an independent state and to govern itself free of external intervention. Can also indicate a sense of exclusivity and superiority over others.

Natural rights: Those rights (such as to life, liberty, and property) supposedly given to humans by God or by nature, their existence taken to be independent of government.

Nazism: A form of extreme nationalism based on theories of racial superiority, hostility to welfare and communism, and hostility to democracy, with a single all-powerful leader.

Patron–client democracy: An informal relationship between governors and the governed, often involving the trading of favours in return for political support.

Partisan dealignment: The weakening of links between voters and parties, as voters identify less with parties, and membership of parties falls.

Paternalism: An infringement on the rights and liberties of a person or class, supposedly with a beneficial intent but actually as a means of social control. Reflects the values of patriarchal societies in which men are seen as the head of families.

Patrimonialism: A political system based on a leader as a father figure who has limited accountability to his people but who claims to understand their interests and needs.

Patriotism: Pride in country, identification with country, or devotion to country, as reflected in an association with the history, symbols, and myths of that country.

Personal rule: A phenomenon in which a leader accumulates so much power, and such a key role in the political system, that government is shaped and operated on the basis of a single person rather the office of the executive.

Personalism: Political allegiance to a person rather than to a political party or ideology.

Political class: A group of professional politicians with similar backgrounds, interests, and values.

Political cleavage: The tendency for voters to divide into like-minded voting groups based on political, economic, or social differences.

Political culture: The sum of a society's values, beliefs, customs, and norms regarding government and politics.

Political economy: A branch of the social sciences that studies the relationships between markets and the state.

Political goods: The commodities or services whose provision is widely considered the primary purpose of government.

Political party: A group identified by name and ideology that fields candidates at elections in order to win public office and control government.

Political system: The institutions, rules, and procedures that shape how people interact in their effort to make and implement collective decisions.

Politics: The process by which people decide – or have others decide for them – how to manage and share the resources of the society in which they live.

Populism: The belief or philosophy that ordinary people are at a disadvantage in political decisions, and that they have been marginalized at the expense of the growing wealth and authority of elites.

Power: The ability to act, or to exert authority and control over others.

Pragmatism: A practical view of politics, emphasizing what is possible over what is desirable.

Primary: An election in which voters choose the candidate that will run for their party in the general election.

Prime minister: The head of government in a parliamentary system, typically the person who heads the party or coalition with the most seats in the national legislature.

Proportional representation: An electoral system in which the number of seats won by each of the competing parties is proportional to the number of votes they each win.

Purchasing power parity: A method of calculating economic productivity by accounting for differences in the purchasing power of national currencies.

Qualitative method: An approach to research that seeks to understand underlying reasons, motivations, and trends, often using direct observation of a limited number of cases.

Quantitative method: An approach to research based on the generation and use of numerical data, with an emphasis on quantifying patterns and trends in behaviour, often using many cases.

Referendum: A vote of the electorate on a limited issue of public policy such as a constitutional amendment.

Regionalism: An ideology or philosophy favouring the interests of regions and localities within states over the interests of those states as a whole, including autonomy and in some cases independence.

Republic: A political system in which all members of the government are either elected or appointed by elected officials, and there are no hereditary positions, as there are in monarchies.

Rule of law: The idea that the distribution of power is determined and limited by a system of laws to which all citizens are equally subject.

Second-order elections: See *first-order elections*.

Semi-presidential system: One in which executive powers are shared between a president and a prime minister.

Separation of powers: An arrangement in which the executive, the legislature, and the judiciary are given distinct but complementary sets of powers, such that

neither can govern alone and that all should, ideally, govern together.

Single-member plurality: An electoral system based on districts that each have one representative, and in which the winner is the candidate with the most votes.

Slave trade: The organized shipment of slaves from West Africa to the Americas, beginning in the 15th century and ending with abolition in 1833.

Snap election: One called unexpectedly before the end of the full term of a legislature.

Social contract: An actual or philosophical agreement between the rulers and members of a community regarding their respective rights and duties.

Stalinism: Stalin's political, economic, and social values, including centralized economic planning, a cult of personality, a police state, and mass terror.

State: A legal and political entity based on the administration of a sovereign territory.

State of emergency: A situation in which a government suspends the normal rules of administration and can take actions that are beyond its constitutional powers, usually in response to armed conflict, civil unrest, or natural disaster.

State socialism: An arrangement under which there is large-scale state intervention in the economy, centralization of political authority, government by a single political party, state ownership of property, and the elimination of the free market.

Strong bicameralism: See *weak bicameralism*.

Structural violence: The intangible forms of oppression built into social and political systems.

Superpower: A state with the military, economic, and political resources to be active at a global level.

Term limits: The placing of limits on the number of terms that can be served by elected officials, either consecutively or in total.

Theocracy: Literally, rule by religious leaders. Describes a political system in which all or most key leaders also hold religious office.

Three Worlds system: The typology that prevailed during the Cold War, dividing states into three groups based on their place in the conflict.

Totalitarianism: An absolutist form of authoritarian rule, based either on a guiding ideology or the goal of major social change, with total control exercised by a leader, state, or party over all aspects of public and private life.

Typology: A system of classification based on groupings or types with common sets of attributes, often ranking them within each type.

Unitary system: One in which all significant power rests with the national government, and in which local units of government have little or no independent power.

Variable: A changeable feature, factor, quantity, or element.

Vote of confidence: A formal vote in Parliament on the performance of the government, which – if lost – would trigger the resignation of the prime minister.

Weak bicameralism: An arrangement in which one chamber of a bicameral legislature clearly has more power than the other, in contrast to the more balanced arrangement found in a system with **strong bicameralism**.

Welfare state: A state that provides through law for people in need, such as the poor, the elderly, the handicapped, or anyone otherwise economically or physically disadvantaged.

Westminster model: The system of government based on the British parliamentary model, with a prime minister, a cabinet, and a bicameral legislature.

BIBLIOGRAPHY

A

Abbas, Tahir (2017) *Contemporary Turkey in Conflict: Ethnicity, Islam and Politics* (Edinburgh: Edinburgh University Press).

Achebe, Chinua (1983) *The Trouble with Nigeria* (Oxford: Heinemann).

Achebe, Chinua (2013) *There Was a Country* (London: Penguin).

Adams, James Truslow (1931) *The Epic of America* (New York: Little, Brown).

Adediji, Ademola (2015) *The Politicization of Ethnicity as Source of Conflict: The Nigerian Situation* (Cologne: Springer).

Adejumobi, Said (2010) 'Democracy and Governance in Nigeria: Between Consolidation and Reversal', in Said Adejumobi (ed.) *State, Economy, and Society in Post-Military Nigeria* (London: Palgrave Macmillan).

Ahmad, Ahmad Atif (2017) *Islamic Law: Cases, Authorities and Worldview* (London: Bloomsbury).

Alcocer, V. Jorge (1995) 'Recent Electoral Reforms in Mexico: Prospects for a Real Multiparty Democracy', in Riordan Roett (ed.) *The Challenge of Institutional Reform in Mexico* (Boulder, CO: Lynne Rienner).

Allen, Peter (2018) *The Political Class: Why it Matters Who our Politicians Are* (Oxford: Oxford University Press).

Allmark, Liam (2012) 'More than Rubber-Stamps: The Consequences Produced by Legislatures in Non-Democratic States beyond Latent Legitimation', in *Journal of Legislative Studies* 18:2, pp. 198–202.

Almond, Gabriel A. (1966) 'Political Theory and Political Science', in *American Political Science Review* 60:4, December, pp. 869–79.

Almond, Gabriel, and G. Bingham Powell (1966) *Comparative Politics: A Developmental Approach* (Boston: Little, Brown).

Amnesty International (2018) *Death Sentences and Executions 2017* (London: Amnesty International).

Andeweg, Rudy B. (2014) 'Cabinet Ministers: Leaders, Team Players, Followers?' in R. A. W. Rhodes and Paul 't Hart (eds) (2014) *The Oxford Handbook of Political Leadership* (Oxford: Oxford University Press).

Arter, David (ed.) (2013) *Comparing and Classifying Legislatures* (Abingdon: Routledge).

Arudou, Debito (2015) *Embedded Racism: Japan's Visible Minorities and Racial Discrimination* (London: Lexington).

Avalos, Francisco A. (2013) *The Mexican Legal System: A Comprehensive Research Guide*, 3rd edn (New York: William S. Hein).

Axworthy, Michael (2013) *Revolutionary Iran: A History of the Islamic Republic* (Oxford: Oxford University Press).

B

Bagehot, Walter (2017) *The English Constitution* (Cambridge: Cambridge University Press).

Bakhash, Shaul (1990) *The Reign of the Ayatollahs: Iran and the Islamic Revolution* (New York: Basic Books).

Bakhash, Shaul (2010) 'The Six Presidents', in Robin Wright (ed.) *The Iran Primer: Power, Politics and US Policy* (Washington DC: United States Institute of Peace Press).

Baldwin, Kate (2015) *The Paradox of Traditional Chiefs in Democratic Africa* (Cambridge: Cambridge University Press).

Barnett, Anthony (2016) 'Why Britain Needs a Written Constitution', in *The Guardian*, 30 November.

Birch, Anthony H. (2007) *The Concepts and Theories of Modern Democracy*, 3rd edn (Abingdon: Routledge).

Bivar, Venus (2018) *Organic Resistance: The Struggle over Industrial Farming in Postwar France* (Chapel Hill: University of North Carolina Press).

Bourguinon, Francois (2015) *The Globalization of Inequality* (Princeton, NJ: Princeton University Press).

Bowen, Roger W., and Joel J. Kassiola (2016) *Japan's Dysfunctional Democracy: The Liberal Democratic Party and Structural Corruption* (Abingdon: Routledge).

Boyunsuz, Şule Özsoy (2016) 'The AKP'S Proposal for a "Turkish Type of Presidentialism" in Comparative Context' in *Turkish Studies* 17:1, pp. 68–90.

Brookings Institution (2017) 'Vital Statistics on Congress', at www.brookings.edu/multi-chapter-report/vital-statistics-on-congress. Retrieved April 2019.

Brown, Archie (2014) *The Myth of the Strong Leader: Political Leadership in the Modern Age* (London: Bodley Head).

Brown, Kerry (2016) *CEO, China: The Rise of Xi Jinping* (London: I B Taurus).

Buckley, Chris (2018) 'Xi Jinping Thought Explained: A New Ideology for a New Era' in *New York Times*, 26 February.

Burke, John P. (2016) *Presidential Power: Theories and Dilemmas* (Boulder, CO: Westview).

C

Cagaptay, Soner (2017) *The New Sultan: Erdoğan and the Crisis of Modern Turkey* (London: I B Taurus).

Camp, Roderic Ai (2013) *Politics in Mexico: Democratic Consolidation or Decline?* 6th edn (New York: Oxford University Press).

Caress, Stanley M., and Todd T. Kunioka (2012) *Term Limits and Their Consequences: The Aftermath of Legislative Reform* (Albany, NY: State University of New York Press).

Central Intelligence Agency (2019) The World Factbook, 'Distribution of Family Income: Gini Index', at www.cia.gov/library. Retrieved February 2019.

Centre for Responsive Politics (2019) 'Most Expensive Midterm Ever: Cost of 2018 Election Surpasses $5.7 billion', 6 February, at www.opensecrets.org/news/2019/02/cost-of-2018-election-5pnt7bil. Retrieved April 2019.

Chanda, Asok (1965) *Federalism in India* (London: George Allen & Unwin).

Clark, Alistair (2012) *Political Parties in the UK* (London: Red Globe Press).

Clinton, Bill (1996). Speech at George Washington University, 5 August.

Cohen, Marty, David Karol, Hans Noel, and John Zaller (2016) 'Party Versus Faction in the Reformed Presidential Nominating System', in *PS: Political Science and Politics* 49:4, October, pp. 701–8.

Cole, Alistair (2017) *French Politics and Society*, 3rd edn (Abingdon: Routledge).

Cole, Alistair, Sophie Meunier, and Vincent Tiberj (2013) 'From Sarkozy to Hollande: The New Normal?', in Alistair Cole, Sophie Meunier, and Vincent Tiberj (eds) *Developments in French Politics 5* (London: Red Globe Press).

Cole, Alistair, and Romain Pasquier (2013) 'Local and regional governance', in Alistair Cole, Sophie Meunier, and Vincent Tiberj (eds) *Developments in French Politics 5* (London: Red Globe Press).

Comparative Constitutions Project (2018), at http://comparativeconstitutionsproject.org. Retrieved March 2018.

Corbridge, Stuart, John Harriss, and Craig Jeffrey (2013) *India Today: Economy, Politics and Society* (Cambridge: Polity Press).

Coutinho, Luís Pereira, Massimo La Torre, and Steven D. Smith (eds) (2015) *Judicial Activism: An Interdisciplinary Approach to the American and European Experiences* (Heidelberg: Springer).

Cowley, Philip, and Dennis Kavanagh (2016) *The British General Election of 2015* (London: Palgrave Macmillan).

Crawford, James (2007) *The Creation of States in International Law* (Oxford: Oxford University Press).

Credit Suisse Research Institute (2018) *Global Wealth Report 2018* (Zurich: Credit Suisse).

Cullen, Jim (2017) *Democratic Empire: The United States Since 1945* (Chichester: Wiley Blackwell).

D

Dalton, Emma (2015) *Women and Politics in Contemporary Japan* (Abingdon: Routledge).

Dalton, Russell J. (2014) 'Partisan Dealignment and Voting Choice', in Stephen Padgett, William E. Paterson, and Reimut Zohlnhöfer (eds) *Developments in German Politics 4* (London: Red Globe Press).

Darnton, John (1993) 'London Journal; With a Mace, Madam Rules a Most Unruly House', in *New York Times*, 27 September.

Denver, David, and Mark Garnett (2014) *British General Elections since 1964: Diversity, Dealignment, and Disillusion* (Oxford: Oxford University Press).

Diamond, Larry (2008) 'The Rule of Law versus the Big Man', in *Journal of Democracy* 19:2, April, pp. 38–149.

Diamond, Larry (2015) 'Facing up to the Democratic Recession', in *Journal of Democracy* 26:1, January, pp. 141–55.

Diamond, Larry, Marc F. Plattner, and Christopher Walker (eds) (2016) *Authoritarianism Goes Global: The Challenge to Democracy* (Baltimore, MD: Johns Hopkins University Press).

Dikötter, Frank (2016) *The Cultural Revolution: A People's History 1962–1976* (New York: Bloomsbury).

Dogan, Mattei, and Dominique Pelassy (1990) *How to Compare Nations: Strategies in Comparative Politics*, 2nd edn (Chatham, NJ: Chatham House Publishers).

Dowding, Keith (2012) 'The Prime Ministerialisation of the British Prime Minister', in *Parliamentary Affairs* 66:3, 1 July, pp. 617–35.

Drèze, Jean, and Amartya Sen (2013) *An Uncertain Glory: India and its Contradictions* (Princeton, NJ: Princeton University Press).

E

Economist, The (2008) 'Comrades in Arms', 22 May.

Economist, The (2017) 'Turkey is Sliding into Dictatorship', 15 April.

Economist, The (2018) 'Why Being a Mayor in Mexico is so Dangerous', 5 May.

Economist Intelligence Unit (2018) *Democracy Index 2017: Free Speech Under Attack* (London: Economist Intelligence Unit).

Economist Intelligence Unit (2019) *Democracy Index 2018* (London: Economist Intelligence Unit).

Edelman (2018) *Edelman Trust Barometer 2018* at www.edelman.com/trust-barometer. Retrieved April 2019.

Edgerton, David (2018) *The Rise and Fall of the British Nation: A Twentieth Century History* (London: Allen Lane).

Edmonds-Poli, Emily, and David A. Shirk (2015) *Contemporary Mexican Politics*, 3rd edn (Lanham, MD: Rowman & Littlefield).

Ehteshami, Anoushiravan (2017) *Iran: Stuck in Transition* (Abingdon: Routledge).

Ekeh, Peter (1989) 'Nigeria's Emergent Political Culture', in Peter Ekeh et al. (eds), *Nigeria since Independence: The First Twenty-Five Years* (lbadan, Nigeria: Heinemann Educational Books).

Election Commission of India (2019) List of political parties and election symbols, at https://eci.gov.in/candidate-political-parties/list-of-political-parties. Retrieved April 2019.

Elgie, Robert (2011) *Semi-Presidentialism: Sub-Types and Democratic Performance* (Oxford: Oxford University Press).

Elgie, Robert, Emiliano Grossman, and Amy G. Mazur (2016) 'A Framework for a Comparative Politics of France' in Robert Elgie, Emiliano Grossman, and Amy G. Mazur (eds) *The Oxford Handbook of French Politics* (Oxford: Oxford University Press).

Ellis, Stephen (2016) *This Present Darkness: A History of Nigerian Organized Crime* (London: Hurst).

Erdoğan, Recep Tayyip (2018) Speech marking the centenary of the death of Ottoman Sultan Abdulhamid II, Reported in *Hurriyet Daily News*, 10 February.

Esen, Berk, and Sebnem Gumuscu (2017) 'Turkey: How the Coup Failed' in *Journal of Democracy* 28:1, January, pp. 59–73.

Esfandiari, Haleh (2010) 'The Women's Movement', in Robin Wright (ed.) *The Iran Primer: Power, Politics and US Policy* (Washington DC: United States Institute of Peace Press).

Evans, Jocelyn, and Gilles Ivaldi (2018) *The 2017 French Presidential Elections: A Political Reformation?* (London: Palgrave Macmillan).

Ezrow, Natasha M., and Erica Frantz (2011) *Dictatorships: Understanding Authoritarian Regimes and Their Leaders* (London: Continuum).

F

Falola, Toyin, and Matthew M. Heaton (2008) *A History of Nigeria* (Cambridge: Cambridge University Press).

Farhi, Farideh (2010) 'The Parliament', in Robin Wright (ed.) *The Iran Primer: Power, Politics and US Policy* (Washington DC: United States Institute of Peace Press).

Farrell, David M. (2011) *Electoral Systems: A Comparative Introduction*, 2nd edn (London: Red Globe Press).

Finer, S. E. (1997) *The History of Government, Volume I: Ancient Monarchies and Empires* (Oxford: Oxford University Press).

Fisher, Michael H. (2016) *A Short History of the Mughal Empire* (London: I B Taurus).

Forozan, Hesam (2015) *The Military in Post-Revolutionary Iran: The Evolution and Roles of the Revolutionary Guards* (Abingdon: Routledge).

Freedom House (2017) *Freedom of the Press 2017*, at https://freedomhouse.org/sites/default/files/FOTP_2017_booklet_FINAL_April28.pdf.

Freedom House (2018a) *Freedom in the World 2018*. Report on Turkey at https://freedomhouse.org/report/freedom-world/2018/turkey. Retrieved December 2018.

Freedom House (2018b) *Freedom in the World 2017* at https://freedomhouse.org/report/freedom-world/freedom-world-2018. Retrieved February 2019.

Freedom House (2019) *Freedom in the World 2018* at https://freedomhouse.org/report/freedom-world/freedom-world-2018. Retrieved February 2019.

Fritz, Jean (1988) *China's Long March: 6,000 Miles of Danger* (New York: Putnam).

Fukumoto, Kentaro (2011) 'Legislators', in Takashi Inoguchi and Purnendra Jain (eds) *Japanese Politics Today: From Karaoke to Kabuki Democracy* (New York: Palgrave Macmillan).

Fukuyama, Francis (1989) 'The End of History?' in *The National Interest*, Summer.

G

Gaddis, John Lewis (2006) *The Cold War: A New History* (New York: Penguin).

Gannon, Martin J., and Rajnandini Pillai (2016) *Understanding Global Cultures: Metaphorical Journeys through 34 Nations, Clusters of Nations, Continents, and Diversity*, 6th edn (Thousand Oaks, CA: Sage).

Gardner, Daniel K. (2014) *Confucianism: A Very Short Introduction* (Oxford: Oxford University Press).

Gaunder, Alisa (2011) 'The Institutional Landscape of Japanese Politics', in Alisa Gaunder (ed.) *The Routledge Handbook of Japanese Politics* (Abingdon: Routledge).

Geddes, Andrew (2013) *Britain and the European Union* (London: Red Globe Press).

Gheissari, Ali, and Vali Nasr (2006) *Democracy in Iran: History and the Quest for Liberty* (New York: Oxford University Press).

Ginsburg, Tom, and Alberto Simpser (eds) (2014) *Constitutions in Authoritarian Regimes* (Cambridge: Cambridge University Press).

Gordon, Andrew (2013) *A Modern History of Japan: From Tokugawa Times to the Present*, 3rd edn (Oxford: Oxford University Press).

Gouglas, Athanassios, Bart Maddens, and Marleen Brans (2018) 'Determinants of legislative turnover in Western Europe, 1945–2015', in *European Journal of Political Research* 57:3, August, pp. 637–61.

Gougou, Florent, and Simon Labouret (2103) 'Elections in France: Electoral Disorder in a Realignment Era', in Alistair Cole, Sophie Meunier, and Vincent Tiberj (eds) *Developments in French Politics 5* (London: Red Globe Press).

Gould, William (2016) 'Corruption and Anti-corruption in Modern India: History, Patronage and the Moral Politics of Anti-colonialism', in Knut A. Jacobsen (ed.) *Routledge Handbook of Contemporary India* (Abingdon: Routledge).

Graf, William D. (1988) *The Nigerian State: Political Economy, State Class and Political System in the Post-Colonial Era* (London: James Currey).

Green, Simon, and Ed Turner (eds) (2015) *Understanding the Transformation of Germany's CDU* (Abingdon: Routledge).

Greenstein, Fred I. (2009) *The Presidential Difference: Leadership Style From FDR to Barack Obama*, 3rd edn (Ithaca: Princeton University Press).

Grindle, Merilee S. (2009) *Going Local: Decentralization, Democratization, and the Promise of Good Governance* (Princeton: Princeton University Press).

Gwartney, James, Robert Lawson, and Joshua Hall (2017) Economic Freedom Dataset, published in *Economic Freedom of the World: 2017 Annual Report* (Toronto, ON: Fraser Institute).

H

Hackett, Conrad (2017) 'Five facts about the Muslim Population in Europe', in Pew Research Center at www.pewresearch.org/fact-tank/2017/11/29/5-facts-about-the-muslim-population-in-europe. Retrieved April 2019.

Haegel, Florence (2013) 'Political Parties: The UMP and the Right', in Alistair Cole, Sophie Meunier, and Vincent Tiberj (eds) *Developments in French Politics 5* (London: Red Globe Press).

Hale, Henry E. (2014) 'Russia's Political Parties and their Substitutes', in Stephen White, Richard Sakwa, and Henry E. Hale (eds) *Developments in Russian Politics 8* (London: Red Globe Press).

Hart, Vivien (1978) *Distrust and Democracy* (Cambridge: Cambridge University Press).

Hayes, Louis D. (2017) *Introduction to Japanese Politics*, 7th edn (Abingdon: Routledge).

He, Baogang (2007) *Rural Democracy in China: The Role of Village Elections* (London: Palgrave Macmillan).

Healy, Gene (2008) *The Cult of the Presidency: America's Dangerous Devotion to Presidential Power* (Washington, DC: Cato Institute).

Heffernan, Richard, and Paul Webb (2007) 'The British Prime Minister: More Than First among Equals' in Thomas Poguntke and Paul Webb (eds) *The Presidentialization of Politics: A Comparative Study of Modern Democracies* (Oxford: Oxford University Press).

Herron, Erik S., Robert J. Pekkanen, and Matthew S. Shugart (2018) *The Oxford Handbook of Electoral Systems* (Oxford: Oxford University Press).

Hillman, Ben, and Gray Tuttle (eds) (2016) *Ethnic Conflict and Protest in Tibet and Xinjiang: Unrest in China's West* (New York: Columbia University Press).

I

Ike, Nobutaka (1972) *Japan: Patron-Client Democracy* (New York: Kopf).

Inoguchi, Takashi, and Purnendra Jain (eds) (2011) *Japanese Politics Today: From Karaoke to Kabuki Democracy* (New York: Palgrave Macmillan).

Inter-Parliamentary Union (2019) *Parline Database on National Parliaments*, at www.ipu.org. Retrieved February 2019.

Itoh, Mayumi (2015) 'The New Komei Party: Japan's Buddhist Party and the LDP's Coalition Partner', in Ronald J. Hrebenar and Akira Nakamura (eds) *Party Politics in Japan: Political Chaos and Stalemate in the Twenty-first Century* (Abingdon: Routledge).

J

Jackson, Robert H. (1990) *Quasi-states: Sovereignty, International Relations and the Third World* (Cambridge and New York: Cambridge University Press).

Jacques, Martin (2012) *When China Rules the World: The End of the Western World and the Birth of a New Global Order*, 2nd edn (London: Penguin).

Jodkha, Surinder S. (2018) *Caste in Contemporary India*, 2nd edn (Abingdon: Routledge).

Joppien, Charlotte (2018) *Municipal Politics in Turkey: Local Government and Party Organization* (Abingdon: Routledge).

Judd, Denis (2005) *The Lion and the Tiger: The Rise and Fall of the British Raj* (Oxford: Oxford University Press).

K

Kabashima, Ikuo, and Gill Steel (2010) *Changing Politics in Japan* (Ithaca, NY: Cornell University Press).

Kagan, Robert (2008) *The Return of History and the End of Dreams* (New York: Knopf).

Kalayctoğlu, Ersin (2008) 'Cyclical Development, Redesign and Nascent Institutionalization of a Legislative System', in Ali Çarkoğlu and William Hale (eds) *The Politics of Modern Turkey: Critical Issues in Modern Politics, Vol II* (Abingdon: Routledge).

Katouzian, Homa, and Hossein Shahidi (2008), 'Introduction', in Homa Katouzian and Hossein Shahidi (eds) *Iran in the 21st Century: Politics, Economics and Conflict* (Abingdon: Routledge).

Khan, Yasmin (2017) *The Great Partition: The Making of India and Pakistan* (New Haven, CT: Yale University Press).

Kingston, Jeff (2011) *Contemporary Japan: History, Politics, and Social Change Since the 1980s* (Chichester: Wiley Blackwell).

Kingston, Jeff (2017) 'What Conspires to Make Japanese Seem so Unhappy?' in *Japan Times*, 1 April.

Kumar, C. Raj (2011) *Corruption and Human Rights in India* (New Delhi: Oxford University Press).

L

Lammy, David (2011) *Out of the Ashes: Britain after the Riots* (London: Guardian Books).

Landman, Todd, and Edzia Carvalho (2017) *Issues and Methods in Comparative Politics*, 4th edn (Abingdon: Routledge).

Langenbacher, Eric, and David P. Conradt (2017) *The German Polity*, 11th edn (Lanham, MD: Rowman & Littlefield).

Lasswell, Harold D. (1968) 'The Future of the Comparative Method', in *Comparative Politics* 1:1, October, pp. 3–18.

Leach, Robert, Bill Coxall, and Lynton Robins (2018) *British Politics*, 3rd edn (London: Red Globe Press).

Lee, H. P. (2011) *Judiciaries in Comparative Perspective* (Cambridge: Cambridge University Press).

Lees, Charles (2006) 'We are all Comparativists Now: Why and How Single-country Scholarship Must Adapt and Incorporate the Comparative Politics Approach', in *Comparative Political Studies* 39:9, November, pp. 1084–108.

Lemke, Christiane, and Helga A. Welsh (2018) *Germany Today: Politics and Policies in a Changing World* (Lanham, MD: Rowman & Littlefield).

Levin, Yuval (2016) *The Fractured Republic: Renewing America's Social Contract in the Age of Individualism* (New York: Basic Books).

Levitsky, Steven, and Lucian A. Way (2002) 'The Rise of Competitive Authoritarianism', in *Journal of Democracy* 13:2, April, pp. 51–65.

Li, Cheng (2011) 'The Fifth Generation of China's Leaders: Challenges of the Next Succession', in *Brookings* at www.brookings.edu. Retrieved April 2019.

Li, Cheng (2016a) *Chinese Politics in the Xi Jinping Era: Reassessing Collective Leadership* (Washington DC: Brookings Institution).

Li, Cheng (2016b) 'China's Communist Party-State: The Structure and Dynamics of Power', in William A. Joseph (ed.) (2014) *Politics in China: An Introduction*, 2nd edn (New York: Oxford University Press).

Lim, Louisa (2015) *The People's Republic of Amnesia: Tiananmen Revisited* (New York: Oxford University Press).

Loewenberg, Gerhard (2016) *On Legislatures: The Puzzle of Representation* (Abingdon: Routledge).

Lukes, Steven (2005) *Power: A Radical View*, 2nd edn (London: Red Globe Press).

M

Madsen, Deborah L. (1998) *American Exceptionalism* (Jackson: University Press of Mississippi).

Magleby, David B., Paul C. Light, and Christine L. Nemachek (2015) *Government by the People*, 25th edn (Boston: Pearson).

Mark, Monica (2012) 'Nigerian Police Recover Part of Sani Abacha's $4.3bn Hoard from Robbers', in *The Guardian*, 5 October.

Marr, Andrew (2017) *A History of Modern Britain* (London: Pan Macmillan).

Matland, Richard E., and Donley T. Studlar (2004) 'Determinants of Legislative Turnover: A Cross-National Analysis', in *British Journal of Political Science* 34:1, January, pp. 87–108.

McBride, James (2015) 'Building the New Silk Road', Backgrounder published by Council on Foreign Relations, 22 May, at www.cfr.org/backgrounder/building-new-silk-road. Retrieved November 2018.

McCargo, Duncan (2012) *Contemporary Japan*, 3rd edn (London: Red Globe Press).

McCauley, Martin (2013) *Stalin and Stalinism*, 3rd edn (Abingdon: Routledge).

McMeekin, Sean (2017) *The Russian Revolution: A New History* (New York: Basic Books).

Mezey, Michael L. (2013) *Presidentialism: Power in Comparative Perspective* (Boulder, CO: Lynne Rienner).

Mitchell, Maria D. (2012) *The Origins of Christian Democracy: Politics and Confession in Modern Germany* (Ann Arbor, MI: University of Michigan Press).

Monaghan, Andrew (2016) *The New Politics of Russia: Interpreting Change* (Manchester: Manchester University Press).

Moore, Barrington (1967) *Social Origins of Dictatorship and Democracy: Lord and Peasant in the Making of the Modern World* (Boston: Beacon).

Morel, Laurence (2007) 'The Rise of "Politically Obligatory" Referendums: The 2005 French Referendum in Comparative Perspective', in *West European Politics* 30:5, pp. 1041–67.

Mutch, Robert E. (2014) *Buying the Vote: A History of Campaign Finance Reform* (New York: Oxford University Press).

N

Naji, Kasra (2008) *Ahmadinejad: The Secret History of Iran's Radical Leader* (London: I B Taurus).

Norton, Philip (2014) 'The Crown', in Bill Jones and Philip Norton, *Politics UK*, 8th edn (Abingdon: Routledge).

Norton, Philip (2016) *The British Polity*, 5th edn (Abingdon: Routledge).

Ntomba, Reginald (2015) 'Why are Military Coups Going out of Fashion in Africa?' in *New African*, 11 November.

O

Odukoya, Adelaja (2013) 'Party System and Party Conflicts in Nigeria's Fourth Republic', in A. Sat Obiyan and Kunle Amuwo (eds) *Nigeria's Democratic Experience in the Fourth Republic Since 1999: Policies and Politics* (Lanham, MD: University Press of America).

Okoosi-Simbine, Antonia T. (2011) 'Corruption in Nigeria', in Said Adejumobi (ed.) *State, Economy, and Society in Post-Military Nigeria* (London: Palgrave Macmillan).

Onbaşi, Funda Gençoğlu (2016) 'Gezi Park Protests in Turkey: From "Enough is Enough" to Counter-hegemony?' in *Turkish Studies* 17:2, pp. 272–94.

Oppenheimer, Andres (1998) *Bordering on Chaos: Mexico's Roller-Coaster Journey Toward Prosperity* (New York: Little, Brown).

Organisation for Economic Co-operation and Development (2015) *Environment at a Glance 2015* (Paris: OECD).

Organisation for Economic Co-operation and Development (2017) *Better Life Index 2017* at www.oecdbetterlifeindex.org. Retrieved April 2019.

Organisation for Economic Co-operation and Development (OECD) (2018). Data for average annual hours worked at https://data.oecd.org/emp/hours-worked.htm. Retrieved September 2018.

Osborne, Roger (2013) *Iron, Steam and Money: The Making of the Industrial Revolution* (London: The Bodley Head).

Ownby, David (2008) *Falun Gong and the Future of China* (Oxford: Oxford University Press).

Őzbudun, Ergun (2008a) 'The Politics of Constitution Making', in Ali Çarkoğlu and William Hale (eds) *The Politics of Modern Turkey: Critical Issues in Modern Politics, Vol II* (Abingdon: Routledge).

Őzbudun, Ergun (2008b) 'The Status of the President of the Republic Under the Turkish Constitution of 1982', in Ali Çarkoğlu and William Hale (eds) *The Politics of Modern Turkey: Critical Issues in Modern Politics, Vol II* (Abingdon: Routledge).

Őzbudun, Ergun (2011) *The Constitutional System of Turkey* (London: Palgrave Macmillan).

P

Padgett, Stephen, William E. Paterson, and Reimut Zohlnhöfer (eds) 2014) *Developments in German Politics 4* (London: Red Globe Press).

Padmanabhan, Ananth (2016) 'Foundations for a Sustainable Growth: India's Constitution and its Supreme Court', in Knut A. Jacobsen (ed.) *Routledge Handbook of Contemporary India* (Abingdon: Routledge).

Palmer, James (2018) 'Nobody Knows Anything about China. Including the Chinese Government', in *Foreign Policy*, 21 March, at http://foreignpolicy.com. Retrieved April 2019.

Paz, Octavio (1979) 'Reflections: Mexico and the United States', in *New Yorker*, 17 September.

Pegg, Scott (1998) *International Society and the De Facto State* (Aldershot: Ashgate).

Pekkanen, Robert J., Steven R. Reed, Ethan Scheiner, and Daniel M. Smith (2018) 'Introduction: Abe on a Roll and the Polls', in Robert J. Pekkanen, Steven R. Reed, Ethan Scheiner, and Daniel M. Smith (eds) *Japan Decides 2017: The Japanese General Election* (New York: Palgrave Macmillan).

Pekkanen, Robert J., and Steven R. Reed (2018) 'The Opposition: From Third Party Back to Third Force', in Robert J. Pekkanen, Steven R. Reed, Ethan Scheiner, and Daniel M. Smith (eds) *Japan Decides 2017: The Japanese General Election* (New York: Palgrave Macmillan).

Pennock, J. Ronald (1966), 'Political Development, Political Systems, and Political Goods', in *World Politics* 18:3, April, pp. 415–434.

Peters, B. Guy (2018) *The Politics of Bureaucracy: An Introduction to Comparative Public Administration*, 7th edn (Abingdon: Routledge).

Pew Research Center (2015) 'Trust in Government: 1958–2015', 23 November at www.people-press.org/2015/11/23/1-trust-in-government-1958-2015. Retrieved April 2019.

Pitkin, Hanna Fenichel (1967) *The Concept of Representation* (Berkeley: University of California Press).

Preston, Julia, and Samuel Dillon (2004) *Opening Mexico: The Making of a Democracy* (New York: Farrar, Straus & Giroux).

Prestowitz, Clyde (2003) *Rogue Nation: American Unilateralism and the Failure of Good Intentions* (New York: Basic Books).

Q

Qvortrup, Matt (2014) *Referendums Around the World: The Continued Growth of Direct Democracy* (London: Palgrave Macmillan).

R

Reed, Steven R. (2011) 'The Liberal Democratic Party: An Explanation of its Successes and Failures', in Alisa Gaunder (ed.) *The Routledge Handbook of Japanese Politics* (Abingdon: Routledge).

Remington, Thomas F. (2014a) *Presidential Decrees in Russia: A Comparative Perspective* (Cambridge: Cambridge University Press).

Remington, Thomas F. (2014b) 'Parliamentary Politics in Russia', in Stephen White, Richard Sakwa, and Henry E. Hale (eds) *Developments in Russian Politics 8* (London: Red Globe Press).

Remington, Thomas F. (2016) *Politics in Russia*, 7th edn (Abingdon: Routledge).

Rhodes, R. A. W., and Paul 't Hart (eds) (2014) *The Oxford Handbook of Political Leadership* (Oxford: Oxford University Press).

Roberts, Geoffrey K. (2016) *German Politics Today*, 3rd edn (Manchester: Manchester University Press).

Roberts, J. A. G. (2011) *A History of China*, 3rd edn (London: Red Globe Press).

Rose-Ackerman, Susan, Diane A. Desierto, and Natalia Volosin (2011) 'Hyper-Presidentialism: Separation of Powers without Checks and Balances in Argentina and Philippines', in *Berkeley Journal of International Law* 29:1, pp. 246–333.

Rotberg, Robert I. (2004) 'The Failure and Collapse of Nation-States: Breakdown, Prevention and Repair', in Robert I. Rotberg (ed.) *When States Fail: Causes and Consequences* (Princeton, NJ: Princeton University Press).

S

Sadjadpour, Karim (2010) 'The Supreme Leader', in Robin Wright (ed.) *The Iran Primer: Power, Politics and US Policy* (Washington DC: United States Institute of Peace Press).

Safire, William (1978) *Safire's Political Dictionary: The New Language of Politics* (New York: Random House).

Saich, Tony (2015) *Governance and Politics of China*, 4th edn (London: Red Globe Press).

Sakallioğlu, Ümit Cizre (1997) 'The Anatomy of the Turkish Military's Political Autonomy', in *Comparative Politics* 29:2, January, pp. 151–66.

Sakwa, Richard (2008) *Russian Politics and Society*, 4th edn (Abingdon: Routledge).

Sakwa, Richard (2014) 'Politics in Russia', in Stephen White, Richard Sakwa, and Henry E. Hale (eds) *Developments in Russian Politics 8* (London: Red Globe Press).

Sawicki, Frédéric (2013) 'Political Parties: The Socialists and the Left', in Alistair Cole, Sophie Meunier, and Vincent Tiberj (eds) *Developments in French Politics 5* (London: Red Globe Press).

Schlesinger, Arthur M. (2004) *The Imperial Presidency* (New York: Mariner Books).

Schubert, Gunter, and Anna L. Ahlers (2012) *Participation and Empowerment at the Grassroots: Chinese Village Elections in Perspective* (Lanham, MD: Lexington Books).

Selee, Andrew (2018) *Vanishing Frontiers: The Forces Driving Mexico and the United States Together* (New York: Public Affairs).

Sharma, Jyotirmaya (2011) *Hindutva: Exploring the Idea of Hindu Nationalism* (New Delhi: Penguin).

Shugart, Matthew, and John Carey (1992) *Presidents and Assemblies. Constitutional Design and Electoral Dynamics* (Cambridge: Cambridge University Press).

Smith, Mike (2015) *Boko Haram: Inside Nigeria's Holy War* (London: I B Taurus).

Sowerwine, Charles (2018) *France since 1870: Culture, Politics and Society*, 3rd edn (London: Red Globe Press).

Soyinka, Wole (1996) *The Open Sore of a Continent: A Personal Narrative of the Nigerian Crisis* (Oxford: Oxford University Press).

Stockwin, Arthur, and Kweku Ampiah (2017) *Rethinking Japan: The Politics of Contested Nationalism* (Lanham, MD: Lexington Books).

Stockwin, J. A. A. (2008) *Governing Japan: Divided Politics in a Major Economy*, 4th edn (Oxford: Wiley Blackwell).

Sugimoto, Yoshio (2015) *An Introduction to Japanese Society*, 4th edn (Cambridge: Cambridge University Press).

T

Takeyh, Ray (2008) 'Iran's Orchestrated Elections', in *International Herald Tribune*, 13 March.

Tang, Liang (2017) *China's Authoritarian Path to Development: Is Democratization Possible?* (Abingdon: Routledge).

Taubman, William (2017) *Gorbachev: His Life and Times* (New York: W W Norton).

Taylor, Alan (2012) *Colonial America: A Very Short Introduction* (Oxford: Oxford University Press).

Taylor, Ros (2007) 'France gets Royal Assent for Sixth Republic', in *The Guardian*, 19 March.

Tetlock, Philip E. (2006) *Expert Political Judgment: How Good is it? How can we Know?* (Princeton: Princeton University Press).

Tetlock, Philip E., and Dan Gardner (2015) *Superforecasting: The Art and Science of Prediction* (New York: Broadway Books).

Thiruvengadam, Arun K. (2017) *The Constitution of India: A Contextual Analysis* (Oxford: Hart).

Transparency International (2017) Corruption Perceptions Index 2017, at www.transparency.org/news/feature/corruption_perceptions_index_2016. Retrieved August 2018.

Treisman, Daniel (ed.) (2018) *The New Autocracy: Information, Politics, and Policy in Putin's Russia* (Washington DC: Brookings Institution Press).

Tuckman, Jo (2012) *Mexico: Democracy Interrupted* (New Haven, CT: Yale University Press).

U

UN Development Programme (2018) Human Development Index 2017 in *Human Development Report 2017*, at http://hdr.undp.org. Retrieved August 2018, available under the Creative Commons IGO license: https://creativecommons.org/licenses/by/3.0/igo/legalcode

United Nations Statistics Division (2018) *United Nations Demographic Yearbook 2017* (New York: United Nations).

United States Institute of Peace (2017) 'The Iran Primer', 24 April, at http://iranprimer.usip.org/blog/2017/apr/24/latest-race-election-factoids. Retrieved April 2019.

V

Vanberg, Georg (2015) 'Constitutional Courts in Comparative Perspective: A Theoretical Assessment', in *Annual Review of Political Science* 18, May, pp. 167–85.

W

Waldman, Simon A., and Emre Caliskan (2017) *The 'New Turkey' and its Discontents* (Oxford: Oxford University Press).

Wallace, Paul (ed.) (2015) *India's 2014 Elections: A Modi-led BJP Sweep* (New Delhi: Sage).

Weber, Max (1947) *The Theory of Social and Economic Organizations* (Glencoe, IL: Free Press).

Wegren, Stephen K. (ed.) (2016) *Putin's Russia: Past Imperfect, Future Uncertain*, 6th edn (Lanham, MD: Rowman & Littlefield).

Weldon, Jeffrey (1997) 'Political Sources of *Presidencialismo* in Mexico', in Scott Mainwaring and Matthew Soberg Shugart (eds) *Presidentialism and Democracy in Latin America* (New York: Cambridge University Press).

Wheare, Kenneth (1951) *Federal Government* (New York: Oxford University Press).

Whiteley, Paul (2011) *Political Participation in Britain: The Decline and Revival of Civic Culture* (London: Red Globe Press).

Wiarda, Howard J., and Harvey F. Kline (eds.) (1990) *Latin American Politics and Development* (Boulder, CO: Westview Press).

Willerton, John P. (2014) 'The Hegemonic Executive', in Stephen White, Richard Sakwa, and Henry E. Hale (eds) *Developments in Russian Politics 8* (London: Red Globe Press).

Wilson, Andrew (2005) *Virtual Politics: Faking Democracy in the Post-Soviet World* (New Haven, CT: Yale University Press).

Wolf-Phillips, Leslie (1979) 'Why Third World?' in *Third World Quarterly* 1:1, February, pp. 105–14.

World Bank (2019) World Development Indicators database, at https://datacatalog.worldbank.org/dataset/world-development-indicators. Retrieved February 2019.

Wurman, Ilan (2017) *A Debt Against the Living: An Introduction to Originalism* (Cambridge: Cambridge University Press).

Y

Yilmaz, Battal (2018) *The Presidential System in Turkey: Opportunities and Obstacles* (London: Palgrave Macmillan).

Yueh, Linda (2013) *China's Growth: The Making of an Economic Superpower* (Oxford: Oxford University Press).

Z

Zakaria, Fareed (1997) 'The Rise of Illiberal Democracy' in *Foreign Affairs* 76:6, November/December, pp. 22–43.

INDEX

Key references (usually with definitions) indicated in **bold**.

Some terms and concepts – such as *government*, *politics* and *state* – appear throughout the book, so page references are restricted to their main occurrence.

A